NEURAL AND ADAPTIVE SYSTEMS:
Fundamentals through Simulations

JOSÉ C. PRINCIPE

NEIL R. EULIANO

W. CURT LEFEBVRE

JOHN WILEY & SONS, INC.

New York / Chichester / Weinheim / Brisbane / Singapore / Toronto

To our families

Acquisitions Editor   *Bill Zobrist*
Marketing Manager   *Katherine Hepburn*
Senior Production Editor   *Robin Factor*
Senior Designer   *Harry Nolan*
Cover Illustration   *Norm Christensen*

This book was set in New Times Roman by Publication Services and printed and bound by Malloy Lithographers. The cover was printed by Lehigh Press.

This book is printed on acid-free paper.

Library of Congress Cataloging-in-Publication Data:
Principe, J. C. (José C.)
Neural and Adaptive Systems: Fundamentals through Simulation /
Jose C. Principe, Neil R. Euliano, W. Curt Lefebvre.
p.   cm.
Includes bibliographical references and index.
1. Neural networks (Computer science) 2. Adaptive control systems.
I. Euliano, Neil R. II. Lefebvre, W. Curt. III. Title.
ISBN 0-471-35167-9 (paper)
QA76.87.P74   1999
006.3'2–dc21   99-27794
                                                                                                          CIP

Printed in the United States of America

10 9 8 7 6 5 4 3 2 1

PREFACE

This book presents neurocomputing from a different perspective. Throughout the discussion we blend the power of a software simulator with the theory of neurocomputing to constantly reinforce the synergism between the conceptual equations and their behavior in practical neural systems. In our presentation model, which we call an interactive electronic book (i-book) [Principe et al., 2000], the text co-exists with a functional simulator. This is much different from the two common methods of integrating a text and computer software. We do not simply add computer-based examples to the end of the text, we use computer simulations early and often in the presentation. In addition, the i-book is not simply a laboratory manual where exercises are wrapped with text. We have reorganized the theory of neurocomputing into fine-grain conceptual modules, each of which is illustrated with a simple simulation to enhance conceptual understanding throughout the text. At the end of every chapter there is at least one full simulation, which is incrementally built and explained throughout the chapter, that can be used for a project. The simulation thus becomes an essential piece of information delivery, deeply affecting the organization of the textbook, and allowing visualization and reader interaction with the material.

Our intent is to present the concepts at a level that can be understood by senior-level undergraduate students in science and engineering. The link between the hypertext and the simulator creates an interactive learning environment especially appropriate for self-guided study of neural networks and adaptive systems. Our more practical, simulation-driven approach will be particularly beneficial to professionals in the fields of science, engineering, and economics.

We strive to fully cover the major topics in neurocomputing, from theory to applications. Because adaptation is the key to neurocomputing, we give it special attention, covering both the supervised and unsupervised paradigms. We treat neural networks as a nonlinear extension of linear adaptive systems, thus discussing both linear and nonlinear adaptive topologies in detail. In fact, we start with the well-known regression problem to introduce the idea of data fitting and many of the concepts of adaptation. Time, so important for engineering applications, is covered from the perspective of digital signal processing and is integrated with neural topologies. Our hope is to show that adaptive filters and neural networks, normally taught in two different disciplines, can be integrated under the common theme of neural and adaptive systems. Each chapter contains extensive simulation examples (more than 200 simulations overall) to illustrate the concepts, and to provide for further exploration with instructor- or student-supplied data. We emphasize the design and use of neural and adaptive systems. Readers can use the electronic book in other disciplines, or for senior projects, master's theses, or even Ph.D. dissertations.

The textbook is presented in two formats: an electronic version on CD-ROM, consisting of a hypertext document linked with a software simulator, and the paper version duplicating the text material.

Electronic Version

The electronic version is a hypertext document in the Windows help format, so any PC with the Windows NT or Windows 95 (or higher) operating system will be able to install and run the interactive book. The hypertext is linked to NeuroSolutions, a neural network simulator developed by NeuroDimension that is included on the CD-ROM. The simulator is called from the hypertext by clicking on an icon. The simulation examples include fully functional neural networks with explanations of the network topology, and directions for the reader to use and study the relevant aspects of the simulation. A key point is that the simulator is open to experimentation: Students can change parameters and topologies, and open new probes to answer "what if" questions, which normally leads toward a much deeper understanding of the concepts. Once the simulations are complete, control passes to the point where the simulator was called. Hence a seamless integration of the text with the simulator is achieved.

Because of this organization, it is very important that the reader (as well as the instructor) learn how to interact with NeuroSolutions. We include a NeuroSolutions tutorial as Appendix B, and we strongly encourage everyone to consult and run the different examples in the tutorial in order to learn how to create, configure, probe, and adequately control the simulator.

The text is geared toward the presentation of the fundamental concepts of adaptive systems and how they can be applied in practice. Derivation of equations is encapsulated in hot links (which we call "know-more" boxes) that can be called from the main text but can be skipped in a first reading pass. Important definitions, equations, and references are accessible in pop-up windows.

The text can be navigated in several different ways. The beginning of each chapter contains hyperlinks to its section headings, and a hyperlink to the preface, as well as the next chapter. At the end of each section there is a hyperlink to the next section, providing a sequential, paper-book style of organization. Hot links to the appendix are called from the text (return to the text with the *Back* button in the control bar). At the end of each chapter we present hyperlinks to all the examples of the chapter, and a concept map with hot-links to all the chapter section headings and to conceptually related chapters.

Paper Version

The paper version is a carbon copy of the electronic hypertext and is composed of three fundamental elements: the text, the "know-more" boxes, and the NeuroSolutions examples. The know-more boxes are marked in the left margin with gray diamonds, and they contain further details about the topic (normally derivations). They correspond to the hot-links in the hypertext. They can be skipped in a first reading, but no thorough understanding of the material is possible without studying them. The NeuroSolutions examples are shaded boxes, and they contain the details to run the simulator.

We suggest that even when using the paper version of the textbook, the reader should execute the examples on the computer as soon as they appear in the text because they are intrinsically bound to the material, and enhance the understanding. For convenience, at the end of each chapter in the electronic version we provide a list of the examples with their corresponding hot-links as a quick reference for readers of the paper version. After executing the example, the reader can go back to the example listing by clicking on the *Back* button of the control bar.

Topics

The material is divided into 11 chapters, 3 appendices, and a glossary. Chapter 1 covers the concept of data fitting with the linear model, and at the same time, gradient-descent learning. We decided to start with the linear regression model because it is at least vaguely familiar to students in science, economics, and engineering. Linear regression exemplifies the central theme of the book, which is adapting parameters from data. The link between least squares and the search for the minimum of the mean square error is established in this chapter. Gradient-descent learning and the elegant LMS algorithm are also presented here. The style of computation and the properties of the iterated solution are covered for single and multiple regression. Newton's method is presented as well. At the end of the first chapter a project using data from the Internet is set up to help students apply what they learned to real-world data.

Chapter 2 presents the concepts of statistical pattern recognition. This chapter formulates classification as the placement of discriminant functions in pattern space to minimize the probability of the classification error. We stress the difference between data fitting and classification but show that the same basic methodology can be used to train both classifiers and regressors. The design of the Bayes' classifier is introduced. We also present the concept of using high dimensional spaces to simplify the placement of the discriminant function. The concept of linear and quadratic classifiers, and their links to likelihoods are also discussed.

Chapter 3 studies multilayer perceptrons (MLPs). We systematically treat the processing power of the topology and the adaptation of the parameters as two different aspects of the problem. We start very simply, with a single McCulloch-Pitts processing element in two-dimensional space to build up intuition. We define the perceptron and show how to adapt its parameters with gradient-descent learning by using the chain rule. We also present a large-margin learning rule (the Adatron algorithm) linked to the perceptron learning rule. We then introduce the need for more powerful topologies. The study of the one-hidden-layer MLP is first conducted with fixed parameters (in terms of discriminant functions), and then backpropagation is derived and applied. The two-hidden-layer MLP is also studied as a topology and adapted using backpropagation. The method of ordered derivatives, important for practical implementations, is covered, and its implications for constructing general-purpose simulators are explored. Since Neuro-Solutions uses a data-flow implementation, it very clearly illustrates the concepts of backpropagation and ordered derivatives. Training embedded adaptive subsystems in larger fixed parameters systems, so often forgotten but so relevant to solving practical problems, is also addressed with examples. The chapter finishes with the interpretation of an MLP as an a posteriori probability estimator.

Chapter 4 delves into the details of how to use MLPs in real-world applications. The practical aspects of initialization, alternative search methods, topology size, and stopping criterion are all addressed. We start by pointing out the stochastic nature of training and its implications. We cover only first-order search methods in detail (gradient descent, momentum, adaptive step sizes, and noise), but we present the full framework. Cross-validation is presented as the preferred method of stopping the training, but other methods are also covered. For good generalization we demonstrate the use of weight decay as a way to control the size of topologies. Norm selection is also addressed as an extra control of performance. We explain committees as a practical way of controlling the variance of the estimator. After covering all of these aspects, we present two practical applications of MLPs, and we set up a simulation again using the Internet.

Chapter 5 presents the unifying view that regression and classification are special cases of the more general problem of function approximation. Adaptive systems should ultimately be interpreted as parametric function approximators. This chapter is a bit more demanding in terms of mathematics, but the goal is to introduce the problem of function approximation and the use of MLPs, and radial basis functions (RBFs) as universal function approximators. The statistical view of nonlinear regression is provided, and RBFs are also used as classifiers. We finish the chapter by providing a very brief introduction to support vector machines. Two projects, one with financial data and the other with housing prices, are constructed in the simulator.

Chapter 6 covers the principles of Hebbian learning. The estimation of correlation with local rules is stressed and shown to be a universal principle in learning systems. We present principal component analysis (PCA) as a robust and efficient data reduction methodology. The extensions of Hebbian learning to forced- and anti-Hebbian learning are also covered. The linear associative memories and their applications both to hetero-association and autoassociation receive a special place in the presentation.

Chapter 7 is devoted to competition, the other major learning principle. We apply competitive networks to clustering, and develop the Kohonen self-organizing network from the point of view of a topology-preserving map. Modular networks are briefly reviewed, and applications are presented.

Chapter 8 covers the fundamentals of extracting (and quantifying) information in time. The relationship between time signals and vectors is stressed. We motivate filtering as projections in vector spaces. This chapter is a summary of the fundamental concepts of linear signal and systems analysis. The concepts of impulse response, convolution, frequency response, and transfer function as descriptors of system properties are emphasized. This chapter also covers Fourier transforms, and a simple filter design method.

The remaining chapters exploit combinations of previous topics. Chapter 9 brings together the concepts of regression and time processing in the form of adaptive filters. The idea of optimal filters is presented, and the LMS algorithm is utilized for adaptation. We present system identification from the point of view of function approximation. Hebbian learning extended to time produces eigenfilters and Karhunen-Loeve transforms. This chapter contains a showcase of examples to illustrate the exceptional appliability of the simple linear adaptive network. Over 20 practical examples are offered, including

- System identification
- Prediction
- Model-based spectral analysis
- Noise cancellation
- Interference cancellation
- Echo cancellation

- Inverse modeling
- Inverse adaptive controls
- Eigenfiltering
- PCA in time
- Subspace spectral analysis
- Blind source separation

Readers may modify all of these models to solve their own problems.

Chapter 10 brings together time and nonlinear processing elements to yield systems that can be interpreted either as extensions of the MLP to time processing, or as nonlinear extensions of adaptive filters. The topologies covered are called time-lagged-feedforward networks (TLFNs), and they are feedforward combinations of linear filters with nonlinear PEs. The adaptation can still be performed with static backpropagation. The design of short-term memories is covered in detail. Many problems can be solved using these intermediate topologies. We present examples of temporal pattern recognition, nonlinear system identification, and nonlinear prediction.

Chapter 11 teaches the training of recurrent topologies in time, and presents the general case of first-order distributed dynamic systems. We extend static backpropagation to the training of recurrent systems, for both static patterns (fixed point learning) and for trajectory learning. Real-time recurrent learning (RTRL) and backpropagation through time (BPTT) are presented and compared. We discuss applications to nonlinear system identification and control. This chapter covers the Hopfield model, and the concept of computational energy. The hierarchy of neural models is introduced with the Grossberg additive model. The last topic is an extension of first-order dynamics to systems that are locally stable, but globally chaotic, to illustrate some of the challenges ahead in the field of neurocomputing.

Appendix A provides a topical view of matrix computations and probabilities, and is a quick reference to the underlying concepts necessary to understand the text material. Appendix B is the NeuroSolutions tutorial and is a must for the student (and instructor) who is not familiar with the software package. It contains the basic concepts to construct networks, configure and probe components, and set up the simulations. A description of the data included on the CD-ROM is found in Appendix C. For quick reference, we also include a glossary section with definitions of the terms used in the text.

The extensive coverage of topics makes the book impossible to cover in one semester, but it permits different organizations of topics depending on the special goals of the instructor. Many topic sequences are possible. Chapters 1 through 5 form a short sequence that can be used as an introduction to neural networks covering regression, multi-layer perceptrons, and radial basis functions. A second course could cover Chapters 6, 7, 9, 10, and 11, which would include unsupervised learning rules, SOMs, and temporal neural networks. Chapters 1, 8, and 9 cover linear adaptive systems and filters and can be used separately or as an introduction to the nonlinear systems.

Classroom Experience and the Simulator

The i-book can be used in a normal classroom setting, improving the explanation of the material through the simulations with real data, and providing the students with a way to practice at home what has been demonstrated in class. However, the full potential of the i-book is achieved with some improvements to the conventional classroom format. We would like to share our experience of teaching an elective course for electrical engineering undergraduates at the University of Florida using this electronic book. For further information, please consult the paper [Principe et al., 2000]. The course is taught in a laboratory format where we use a computer projector and an electronic white board, and each student has access to a computer during every lecture. The white board allows the text to be interactive, and examples are executed by touching the board. We cover a concept for 15 minutes and then allow the students 15 minutes to run the simulator and explore the example. Then we conclude and move to the next topic. The text naturally provides conceptual boundaries, with each concept illustrated by an example. The function of the instructor in this environment is as a conductor: explaining the concepts, answering questions, and timing the experiments. Students are allowed two hours of self-study a day in the classroom. Office hours are conducted in the classroom. Projects involve searches for data on the Internet.

The simulator is one of the central tools of learning. We slowly cover the most important parts of the simulator in Chapters 1 and 3, at the same time the material in those chapters is covered. However, we recommend that the instructor be familiar with the simulator before the course begins. The simulator's user interface is iconic, which makes learning easy. Icons are organized into families: five neural component families (Synapse, Axon, search, and supervised and unsupervised criteria), and simulation and visualization functions such as Probes, Controllers, Inputs, Transmitters, and Schedulers. Each icon has a corresponding Inspector that changes the component parameters. The mechanics are intuitive, with drag-and-drop functionality. Configuration is a bit more detailed, but the user interface mimics the design steps. Therefore the choices are logical if the material is understood. Students can use other data supplied on the CD-ROM, and even modify the topologies given in the examples up to the limits imposed by the software developer.

The simulator is such an important part of the course presentation that we include a tutorial with the book. The instructor should master the simulator because it facilitates the answers to "what if" questions that make learning more interesting and productive. Students should also learn the simulator so that they can run the examples independently, make modifications for better learning, work out the problems at the end of the chapters, and apply newly acquired knowledge to projects.

References

Principe J., N. Euliano, C. Lefebvre, "Innovating Adaptive and Neural Systems Instruction with Interactive Electronic Books," *Proceedings of the IEEE,* special issue on engineering education, January 2000 (in press).

CONTENTS

CHAPTER 7   *COMPETITIVE AND KOHONEN NETWORKS*   **333**

CHAPTER 8   *PRINCIPLES OF DIGITAL SIGNAL PROCESSING*   **364**

DATA FITTING WITH LINEAR MODELS

The goal of this chapter is to introduce the following concepts:

- Data fitting and the derivation of the best linear (regression) model
- Iterative solution of the regression model
- Steepest descent methods
- The least mean square (LMS) estimator for the gradient
- The trade-off between speed of adaptation and solution accuracy
- Examples using NeuroSolutions

1.1   INTRODUCTION

The study of neural and adaptive systems is a unique and growing interdisciplinary field that considers adaptive, distributed, and mostly nonlinear systems—three of the ingredients found in biology. We believe that neural and adaptive systems should be considered another tool in the scientist's and engineer's toolbox. They will effectively complement present engineering design principles and help build the preprocessors to interface with the real world and ensure the optimality needed in complex systems. When applied correctly, a neural or adaptive system may considerably outperform other methods.

Neural and adaptive systems are used in many important engineering applications, such as signal enhancement, noise cancellation, classification of input patterns, system identification, prediction, and control. They are used in many commercial products, such as modems, image-processing and -recognition systems, speech recognition, front-end signal processors, and biomedical instrumentation. We expect that the list will grow exponentially in the near future.

The leading characteristic of neural and adaptive systems is their adaptivity, which brings a totally new system design style (Figure 1-1). Instead of being built a priori from specification, neural and adaptive systems use external data to automatically set their parameters. This means that neural systems are parametric. It also means that they are made "aware" of their output through a performance feedback loop that includes a cost function. The performance feedback is utilized directly to change the parameters through systematic procedures called learning or training rules, so that the system output improves with respect to the desired goal (i.e., the error decreases through training).

The system designer has to specify just a few crucial steps in the overall process: He or she has to decide the system topology, choose a performance criterion, and design the adaptive algorithms. In neural systems the parameters are often modified in a selected set of data called the training set and are fixed during operation. The designer thus has to know how to specify the input and desired response data and when to stop the training phase. In adaptive systems the system parameters are continuously

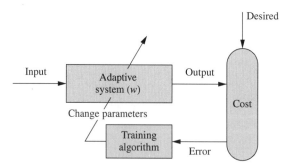

FIGURE 1-1   Adaptive system's design

adapted during operation with the current data. We are at a very exciting stage in neural and adaptive system development because

- We now know some powerful topologies that are able to create universal input-output mappings.
- We also know how to design general adaptive algorithms to extract information from data and adapt the parameters of the mappers.
- We are also starting to understand the prerequisites for generalization, that is, how to guarantee that the performance in the training set extends to the data found during system operation.

Therefore we are in a position to design effective adaptive solutions to moderately difficult real-world problems. Because of the practicality derived from these advances, we believe that the time is right to teach adaptive systems in undergraduate engineering and science curricula.

Throughout this textbook we explain the principles that are necessary to make judicious choices about the design options for neural and adaptive systems. The discussion is slanted toward engineering, both in terminology and in perspective. We are very much interested in the engineering model-based approach and in explaining the mathematical principles at work. We center the explanation on concepts from adaptive signal processing, which are rooted in statistics, pattern recognition, and digital signal processing. Moreover, our study is restricted to model building from data.

1.1.1 Engineering Design and Adaptive Systems

Engineering is a discipline that builds physical systems from human dreams, reinventing the physical world around us. In this respect it transcends physics, which has the passive role of explaining the world, and also mathematics, which stops at the edge of physical reality. Engineering design is like a gigantic Lego construction, where each piece is a subsystem grounded in its physical or mathematical principles. The role of the engineer is to develop the blueprint of the dream through specifications and then to look for the pieces that fit the blueprint. Obviously, the pieces cannot be put together at random, since each has its own principles, so it is mandatory that the scientist or the engineer learn the principles attached to each piece and specify the interface. Normally, this study is done using the scientific method. When the system is physical, we use the principles of physics, and when it is software, we use the principles of mathematics.

Development of the Phone System

A good example of engineering design is the telephone system. Long and meticulous research was conducted at Bell Laboratories on human perception of speech. This created the specification for the required bandwidth and noise level for speech intelligibility. Engineers perfected the microphone that would translate the pressure waves into electrical waves to meet the specification. Then these electrical waves were transmitted through copper wires over long distances to a similar device, still preserving the required specification. For increased functionality the freedom of reaching any other telephone was added to the system, so switching of calls had to be implemented. This created the phone system. Initially, the switching among lines was done by operators. Then a machine was invented that would automatically switch the calls. Operators were still used for special services such as directory assistance, but now that the fundamental engineering aspects are stable, we are asking machines to automatically recognize speech and directly assist callers.

The development of the phone system is an excellent example of engineering design. Once we have a vision, we try to understand the principles at work and create specifications and a system architecture. The fundamental principles at work are found by applying the scientific method. The phenomenon under analysis is first studied with physics or mathematics. The importance of models is that they translate general principles, and through *deduction* we can apply them to particular cases like the ones we are interested in. These disciplines create approximate models of the external world using the principle of divide and conquer. The problem is divided in manageable pieces, each is studied independently of the others, and protocols among the pieces are drawn such that the system can work as a whole, meeting the specifications drawn a priori. This is what engineering design is today.

The scientific method has been highly successful in engineering, but let us evaluate it in broad terms. First, engineering design requires the availability of a model for each subsystem. Second, when the number of pieces increases, the interactions among the subsystems increase exponentially. Fundamental research will continue to provide a steady flux of new physical and mathematical principles (provided the present trend of reduced federal funding for fundamental science is reversed), but the exponential growth of interactions required for larger and more sophisticated systems is harder to control. In fact, at this point in time, we simply do not have a clear vision of how to handle complexity in the long term. But there are two more factors that present major challenges: the autonomous interaction of systems with the environment and the optimality of the design. We will discuss these now.

Humans have traditionally mediated the interaction of engineering systems with the external world. After all, we use technology to reduce our physical constraints, so we have traditionally maintained control of the machines we build. Since the invention of the digital computer, there has been a trend to create machines that interact directly with the external world without a human in the loop. This brings the complexity of the external world directly into engineering design. We are not yet totally prepared for this, because our mathematical and physical theories about the external world are mere approximations—very good approximations in some cases, but rather poor in others.

This disturbs the order of engineering design and creates performance problems (the worst subsystem tends to limit the performance of the full system).

Mars Pathfinder Mission

When machines have to autonomously interact with the environment or operate near the optimal set point, we cannot specify all the functions a priori and in a deterministic way. Take, for instance, the Mars Pathfinder mission. It was totally impossible to specify all the possible conditions that the rover Sojourner would face, even if remotely controlled from Earth, so the problem could not be solved by a sequence of instructions determined a priori in JPL's laboratory. The vehicle was given high-level instructions (way points) and was equipped with cameras and laser sensors that would see the terrain. The information from the sensors was analyzed and catalogued in general classes. For each class a procedure was designed to accomplish the goal of moving from point A to point B. This is the type of engineering system we will build more and more of in the future.

The big difference between the initial machines and Sojourner is that the environment is intrinsically in the loop of the machine function. This brings a very different set of problems, because, as we said earlier, the environment is complex and unpredictable. If our physical model does not capture the essentials of the environment, errors accumulate over time, and the solution becomes impractical. We thus no longer have the luxury of dictating the rules of the game, as we did in the early machine-building era. It turns out that animals and humans do Sojourner-type tasks effortlessly.

System optimality is also a rising concern to save resources and augment the performance/price ratio. We might think that optimally designing each subsystem would bring global optimality, but this is not always true. Optimal design of complex systems is thus a difficult problem that must also take into consideration the particular type of system function, meaning that the complexity of the environment is once again present. We can conclude that the current challenges faced in engineering are the complexity of the systems, the need for optimal performance, and the autonomous interaction with the environment that will require some form of intelligence. These are the challenges for engineering in the 21st century and beyond.

Whenever there is a new challenge, we should consider new solutions. Quite often the difficulty of a task is also linked to the particular method we are using to find the solution. Is building machines by specification the only way to proceed?

Let us look at living creatures from an engineering systems perspective. The cell is the optimal factory, building directly from the environment at the fundamental molecular level what it needs to carry out its function. The animals we observe today interact efficiently with the environment (otherwise they would not have survived); they work very close to optimality in terms of resources (otherwise they would have been replaced in their niche by more efficient animals); and they certainly are complex. Biology has, in fact, already conquered some of the challenges we face in building engineering systems, so it is worthwhile to investigate the principles at work.

Biology has found a set of *inductive* principles that are particularly well tuned to the interaction with a complex and unpredictable environment. These principles are not known explicitly but are being intensively studied in biology, computational neurosciences, statistics, computer science, and engineering. They involve extraction of information from sensor data (feature extraction), efficient learning from data, creation of invariants and representations, and decision making under uncertainty. In a global sense, autonomous agents have to build and fit models to data through their daily experience; they have to store these models, choose which shall be applied in each circumstance, and assess the likelihood of success for a given task. An implicit optimization principle is at play, since the goal is to do the best with the available information and resources.

From a scientific perspective, biology uses *adaptation* to build optimal system functionality. The anatomical organization of the animal (the wetware) is specified in the long term by the environment (through evolution), and in the short term it is used as a constraint to extract in real time the information that the animal needs to survive. At the nervous-system level, it is well accepted that the interaction with the environment molds the wetware using a learning-from-examples metaphor.

1.1.2 Experimental Model Building

The problem of data fitting is one of the oldest in experimental science. The real world tends to be very complex and unpredictable, and the exact mechanisms that generate the data are often unknown. Moreover, when we collect physical variables, the sensors are not ideal (of finite precision, noisy, with constrained bandwidth, etc.), so the measurements do not represent the real phenomena exactly. One of the quests in science is to estimate the underlying data model.

The importance of inferring a model from the data is to apply mathematical reasoning to the problem. The major advantage of a mathematical model is the ability to understand, explain, predict, and control outcomes in the natural system [Casti, 1989]. Figure 1-2 illustrates the data-modeling process. The most important advantage of the

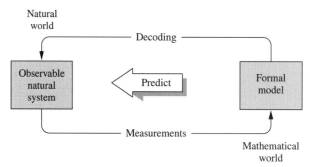

FIGURE 1-2 Natural systems and formal models

existence of a formal equivalent model is the ability to predict the natural system's behavior at a future time and to control its outputs by applying appropriate inputs.

In this chapter we address the issues of fitting data with linear models, which is called the *linear regression* problem [Dunteman, 1989]. Notice that we have not specified what the data is, because it is really immaterial. We are seeking relationships between the values of the external (observable) variables of the natural system in Figure 1-2. This methodology can therefore be applied to meteorological data, biological data, financial data, marketing data, engineering data, and so on.

1.1.3 Data Collection

The data-collection phase must be carefully planned to ensure that

- Data will be sufficient.
- Data will capture the fundamental principles at work.
- Data is as free as possible from observation noise.

Table 1-1 presents a data example with two variables (x, d) in tabular form. the measurement x is assumed error free, and d is contaminated by noise. From table 1-1 very little can be said about the data, except that there is a positive trend between the variables (i.e., when x increases d also increases). Our brain is somehow able to extract much more information from pictures than from numbers, so data should first be plotted before performing data analysis. Plotting the data allows verification, assures the researcher that the data was collected correctly, and provides a "feel" for the relationships that exist in the data (e.g., natural trends).

TABLE 1-1   Regression Data

x	d
1	1.72
2	1.90
3	1.57
4	1.83
5	2.13
6	1.66
7	2.05
8	2.23
9	2.89
10	3.04
11	2.72
12	3.18

1.2   LINEAR MODELS

From the simple observation of Figure 1-3, it is obvious that the relationship between the two variables x and d is complex, if we assume that no noise is present. However, there is an approximately linear trend in the data. The deviation from a straight line could be produced by noise, and underlying the apparent complexity could be a very simple (possibly linear) relationship between x and d, that is

$$d \approx wx + b \tag{1.1}$$

or more specifically,

$$d_i = wx_i + b + \varepsilon_i = y_i + \varepsilon_i \tag{1.2}$$

where ε_i is the instantaneous error that is added to y_i (the linearly fitted value), w is the line slope, and b is the d axis intercept (or bias). Assuming a linear relationship between x and d has the appeal of simplicity. The data-fitting problem can be solved by a linear system with only two free parameters, the slope w and the bias b.

    The system of Figure 1-4 is called the linear *processing element* (PE), or *Adaline* (for adaptive linear element), and it is very simple. It is built from two multipliers and one adder. The multiplier w *scales the input,* and the multiplier b *is a bias,* which can also be thought of as an extra input connected to the value $+1$. The parameters (b, w) have different functions in the solution. We will be particularly interested in studying the dependence of the solution on the parameter(s) that multiply the input x_i.

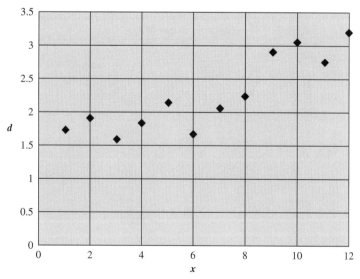

FIGURE 1-3   Plot of x versus d

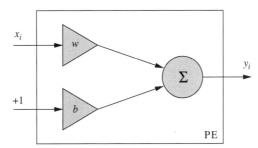

FIGURE 1-4 Linear regressor

NEUROSOLUTIONS EXAMPLE 1.1

The linear processing element in NeuroSolutions

The goal of this book is to demonstrate as many concepts as possible through demonstrations and simulations. NeuroSolutions is a very powerful neural network/adaptive system design and simulation package that we will use for the demonstrations. We highly recommend that you read through the NeuroSolutions Tutorial in Appendix B. NeuroSolutions constructs adaptive systems in a Lego style, that is, component by component. The components are chosen from palettes, selected with the mouse, and dropped into the large window called the Breadboard. This object-oriented methodology allows for the simple creation of adaptive systems by simply dragging and dropping components, connecting them, and then adjusting their parameters. Particularly in the early chapters we will automatically create the adaptive systems for you through a set of macros. This will shield you from the details of NeuroSolutions until you have a better grasp of the fundamentals of adaptive systems and the use of NeuroSolutions.

In this first example we introduce a few simple components. The first component required in any simulation is an input component, which belongs to the Axon family. Its function is to receive data from the computer file system or from signal generators within the package. In this case, we will add a file input component to the input Axon to read in the data from Table 1-1. The linear PE shown in Figure 1-4 can be constructed with a Synapse and a Bias Axon. The Synapse implements a sum of products and the Bias Axon adds the bias. The output of such a system is exactly Eq. (1.1). The Controller manages the system and controls the firing of data

Input Axon   Synapse   Bias Axon   File Input   Controller   Data Storage and Scatter Plot

through the system. Since Table 1-1 has 12 data points, the Controller is configured to send 12 points through the system.

The purpose of this example is to display the output of the linear PE, which is a line, and to modify its location in the space by entering different slope and bias values. To display the input and regression line, we use the Data Storage component (stores 12 samples) and the Scatter Plot component. The Scatter Plot component allows us to plot the input (x axis) versus the system response (y axis). We also add two Matrix Editor boxes to allow you to change the values of the two parameters: the weight (slope) and bias (y intercept). After changing these parameters, you use the Control Palette to run the network.

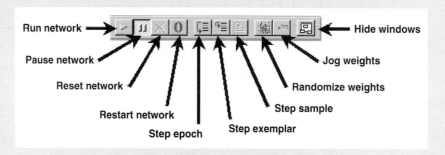

The *Run* button (a green triangle) tells the Controller to send the data through the network. The other buttons are not important now but will be used and explained later. Run the NeuroSolutions example by clicking on the yellow NeuroSolutions icon available in the CD-ROM version of the text. It will walk you through the creation of the Breadboard and allow you to see how the regression line changes as you change the weight (slope) and bias (y intercept).

1.3   LEAST SQUARES

We face a problem when trying to fit a straight line to the noisy observations of Table 1-1. A single line will fit any two observations (two points define a line), but it is unlikely that all points will fall on exactly the same line. Since no single line will fit every point, a global property of the points is needed to find the best fit. The problem of fitting a line to noisy data can be formulated as follows: What is the best choice of (w, b) such that the fitted line passes the closest to all the points?

Least squares solves the problem of fitting a line to data by finding the line for which the sum of the square deviations (or residuals) in the d direction (the noisy variable direction) are minimized. The fitted points in the line will be denoted by $\tilde{d}_i = b + wx_i$. The residuals are defined as $\varepsilon_i = d_i - \tilde{d}_i$. The fitted points $\tilde{d}_i$ can also be interpreted as approximated values of d_i estimated by a linear model when the input x_i is known:

$$d_i - (b + wx_i) = d_i - \tilde{d}_i = \varepsilon_i \tag{1.3}$$

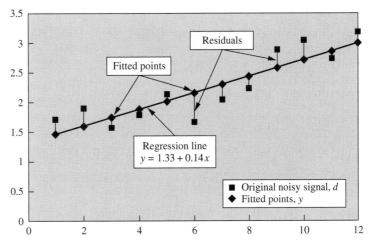

FIGURE 1-5   Regression line showing the deviations

This linear model will be called the *linear regressor.* Estimated quantities will be denoted by the tilde (˜) throughout the book. The outputs of the linear system of Figure 1-4 are the fitted points $\tilde{d}_i = y_i$ in Figure 1-5. To pick the line that best fits the data, we need a criterion to determine which linear estimator is the "best." The average sum of square errors J (also called the *mean square error,* MSE) is a widely utilized performance criterion given by

$$J = \frac{1}{2N} \sum_{i=1}^{N} \varepsilon_i^2 \qquad (1.4)$$

where N is the number of observations. To simplify the notation, we sometimes drop the top index in the sum.

NEUROSOLUTIONS EXAMPLE 1.2

Computing the MSE for the linear PE

To create a simulation that displays the MSE, we have to add a new component to the Breadboard, the L2 Criterion. The L2 Criterion implements the mean square error of Eq. 1.4. The L2 Criterion requires two inputs to compute the MSE: the system output and the desired response. We will attach the L2 Criterion to the output of the linear PE (system output) and attach a File Input component to the L2 Criterion to load in the value of the desired response from Table 1-1. To visualize the MSE, we will place a Matrix Viewer probe over the L2 Criterion (cost access point). This Matrix Viewer simply displays the data from the component that it resides over—in this case, the mean square error.

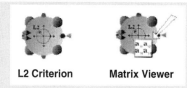

L2 Criterion   Matrix Viewer

Run the demonstration and try to set the slope and bias to minimize the mean square error. Compute the error by hand according to Eq. 1.4 and see whether it matches the value displayed.

Our goal is to minimize J analytically, which according to Gauss[1] can be done by taking its partial derivative with respect to the unknowns and equating the resulting equations to zero:

$$\frac{\partial J}{\partial b} = 0$$

$$\frac{\partial J}{\partial w} = 0$$

(1.5)

which yields, after some manipulation,

$$b = \frac{\sum_i x_i^2 \sum_i d_i - \sum_i x_i \sum_i x_i d_i}{N[\sum_i (x_i - \bar{x})^2]} \qquad w = \frac{\sum_i (x_i - \bar{x})(d_i - \bar{d})}{\sum_i (x_i - \bar{x})^2}$$

(1.6)

where an overbar represents the variable's mean value; for example, $\bar{x} = (1/N) \sum_{i=1}^{N} x_i$.

Least Squares Derivation

In Eq. 1.4 we substitute the value of the error given by Eq. 1.3 and take the derivative expressed by Eq. 1.5 to obtain

$$\begin{cases} \dfrac{\partial J}{\partial b} = \dfrac{1}{2N} \sum_i \dfrac{\partial (d_i - wx_i - b)^2}{\partial b} = -\sum_i \dfrac{1}{N}(d_i - wx_i - b) = 0 \\[4mm] \dfrac{\partial J}{\partial w} = \dfrac{1}{2N} \sum_i \dfrac{\partial (d_i - wx_i - b)^2}{\partial w} = \sum_i \dfrac{1}{N}(d_i - wx_i - b)x_i = 0 \end{cases}$$

(1B.1)

---

[1] Karl Friedrich Gauss (1777–1855) was a mathematical genius who proposed the use of least squares to solve sets of linear equations. He realized that a quadratic equation was obtained in optimization problems involving Gaussian distribution models (after taking the logarithm), which leads to an easy solution for the optimum.

Note that to simplify the notation, we omit the limits of the variable in the sum. We do this throughout the text when no confusion arises. Operating further, we get

$$\sum_{i=1}^{N} d_i = Nb + w \sum_{i=1}^{N} x_i$$

$$\sum_{i=1}^{N} x_i d_i = b \sum_{i=1}^{N} x_i + w \sum_{i=1}^{N} x_i^2$$

(1B.2)

The set of Eq. 1B.2 is called the normal equations. The solution of this set of equations is

$$b = \frac{\sum_i x_i^2 \sum_i d_i - \sum_i x_i \sum_i x_i d_i}{N \sum_i x_i^2 - (\sum_i x_i)^2} \qquad w = \frac{\sum_i x_i d_i - \dfrac{\sum_i x_i \sum_i d_i}{N}}{\sum_i x_i^2 - \dfrac{(\sum_i x_i)^2}{N}}$$

(1B.3)

which provides the coefficients for the *regression line of d on x*. The summations run over the input-output data pairs. Equation 1B.2 is solved by computing the value of b from the first equation and substituting it in the second equation to obtain w as a function of x and d. Then the value of w is substituted in the first equation to finally obtain b as a function of x and d (variable elimination). It is easy to prove that the regression line passes through the point

$$\left(\frac{\sum_i x_i}{N}, \frac{\sum_i d_i}{N} \right)$$

which is called the centroid of the observations. The denominator of the slope parameter of w and b is the corrected (for the mean) sum of squares of the input.

This procedure to determine the coefficients of the line is called the least square method. If we apply these equations to the data of Table 1-1, we get the regression equation (best line through the data):

$$y = 0.13951x + 1.33818$$

(1.7)

The least square computation for a large data set is time-consuming, even with a computer.

NEUROSOLUTIONS EXAMPLE 1.3

Finding the minimum error by trial and error

Enter these values for the slope and bias by typing them in the respective Edit boxes. Verify that with these values the error is the smallest. Change the values slightly (in either direction) and see that the MSE increases. Enter a negative slope and see how the error increases a lot. For the negative slope, what is the value of the bias that gives the smallest error? Note that when one of the coefficients is wrong, the value of the other for best performance is also wrong; that is, they are coupled.

It is important to explore the NeuroSolutions Breadboards. The best way to accomplish this is to open the Inspector associated with each icon. Select a component with the mouse. Then press the right mouse button, and select properties. The Inspector will appear in the screen. The Inspector has fields that allow us to configure the NeuroSolutions components and tell us what settings are being used. For instance, go to the input Axon and open the Inspector. You will see that it has one input, one output, and no weights (go to the Soma level to look at the weights). If you do the same in the Synapse, you will see that it also has a single input and output and one weight, which happens to be our slope parameter. The Bias Axon has a single input, a single output, and a single weight, which is the system's bias.

The large barrel on the input Axon is a probe that collects data. Since the barrel is placed on the Activity point, it is storing the 12 data samples that are injected into the network. This is exactly what gets displayed in the x axis of the Scatter Plot. The y axis values are sent from the L2 Criterion by the small barrel (a Data Transmitter), so the Scatter Plot is effectively displaying the pairs of points (x_i, d_i). Likewise, it is also displaying the output of the system in blue, that is the pairs of points (x_i, y_i).

If you want to know what the component is and what it does, just go to the NeuroSolutions control bar, select the arrow icon with the question mark, and click on the component that you want to know about (this is called context-sensitive help).

1.3.1 Correlation Coefficient

We have found a way to compute the regression equation, but we still do not have a measure of how successfully the regression line represents the relationship between x and d. The size of the mean square error (MSE) can be used to determine which line best fits the data, but it doesn't necessarily reflect whether a line fits the data tightly because the MSE depends on the magnitude of the data samples. For instance, by simply scaling the data, we can change the MSE without changing how well the data is fit by the regression line. The *correlation coefficient* (r) solves this problem. By definition, the correlation coefficient between two random variables x and d is

$$r = \frac{\dfrac{\sum_i (x_i - \bar{x})(d_i - \bar{d})}{N}}{\sqrt{\dfrac{\sum_i (d_i - \bar{d})^2}{N}} \sqrt{\dfrac{\sum_i (x_i - \bar{x})^2}{N}}} \tag{1.8}$$

The numerator is the *covariance* of the two variables (see Section 4.11), and the denominator is the product of the corresponding *standard deviation*.

Variance

Data collected from experiments is normally very complex and difficult to describe by few parameters. The mean and the variance are statistical descriptors of data clusters that are normally utilized in such cases.

The mean of N samples is defined as

$$\bar{x} = \frac{1}{N} \sum_{i=1}^{N} x_i$$

A physical interpretation for the mean is the center of mass of a body made up of samples of the same mass. It is the first moment of the probability density function (pdf).

We can have very different data distributions with the same mean, so the mean is not a powerful descriptor. Another descriptor very often used is the variance, which is defined as

$$\sigma^2 = \frac{1}{N} \sum_{i=1}^{N} (x_i - \bar{x})^2$$

The variance is the second moment around the mean, and it measures the dispersion of samples around the mean. The square root of the variance is called the standard deviation. Mean and variance are much better descriptors of data clusters. In fact, *they define* univocally Gaussian distributions, which are very good models for many real-world phenomena.

The correlation coefficient is confined to the range $[-1, 1]$. When $r = 1$, there is a perfect positive linear correlation between x and d; that is, they covary, which means that they vary by the same amount. When $r = -1$, there is a perfectly linear negative correlation between x and d; that is, they vary in opposite ways (when x increases, y decreases by the same amount). When $r = 0$, there is no correlation between x and d; that is, the variables are called *uncorrelated*. Intermediate values describe partial correlations. In our example $r = 0.88$, which means that the fit of the linear model to the data is reasonably good. Notice that the correlation coefficient is a property of the data, as we can see from Eq. 1.8 (it is independent of the model). However, the value r^2 also represents the amount of variance in the data captured by the optimal linear regression.

Correlation Coefficient and Linear Regression

Consider estimating a random variable d by a constant b according to the mean square estimation,

$$\min_{b} E[(d - b)^2] = E[d^2] - 2bE[d] + b^2$$

where $E[.]$ is the expected value operator (see Appendix A). The best b is obtained by taking the derivative with respect to b and setting the result to zero, yielding $b^* = E[d]$. If we substitute this value into the equation, we obtain the variance of d as the smallest error.

Now if we try to approximate d by $wx + b$ we obtain

$$\min_{w,b} E[(d - wx - b)^2]$$

and the best $b^* = E[d] - wE[x]$. Therefore the best w can be found solving the problem

$$\min_{w} E[((d - E[d]) - w(x - E[x]))^2]$$

It is easy to show by differentiation that the best w^* is

$$w^* = r\frac{\sigma_d}{\sigma_x} \qquad \text{(1B.4)}$$

Therefore the minimum mean square error linear estimator for d is

$$\hat{d} = w^*x + b^* = r\sigma_d\left(\frac{x - E[x]}{\sigma_x}\right) + E[d] \qquad \text{(1B.5)}$$

The term in parentheses is a zero-mean unit variance version of the input x, so the product with σ scales it by the variance of d. The term $E[d]$ just guarantees the correct mean. It is interesting to note that if d and x are uncorrelated, the best estimate of d is its mean. However, if x and d are exactly correlated ($r = \pm1$ in Eq. 1B.5), the best estimate is highly improved. The minimum mean square error is

$$\min_{w} E[((d - E[d]) - w^*(x - E[x]))^2] = \sigma_d^2(1 - r^2)$$

This equation shows that in fact r^2 can be interpreted as the amount of variance in the data that is captured by the linear model.

There is a very interesting interpretation of the mean square estimation solution. Note that

$$-E[(x - E[x])(d - E[d])] + 2w^*\sigma_x^2 = 0 = E[\{(d - E[d]) - w^*(x - E[x])\}(x - E[x])]$$

$$\text{(1B.6)}$$

which means that the error (the quantity inside the curly braces) is orthogonal to the input.

The method of least squares is very powerful. Estimation theory [Melsa and Cohn, 1978] says that the least square estimator is the best linear unbiased estimator (BLUE), since it has no bias and has minimal variance among all possible linear estimators. Least squares can be generalized to higher-order polynomial curves, such as quadratics, cubics, and so on (the *generalized least squares*). In this case, nonlinear regression models are obtained. More coefficients need to be computed, but the methodology still applies. Regression can also be extended to multiple variables, as we will do later in the chapter. The dependent variable d in multiple variable regression is a function of a vector $\mathbf{x} = [x_1, \ldots, x_D]^T$, where T means the transpose and D is the number of inputs. In this book, vectors are denoted by bold letters. In the multivariate case, the regression line becomes a *hyperplane* in the space $x_1, x_2, \ldots, x_D$.

1.4 ADAPTIVE LINEAR SYSTEMS

1.4.1 Least Squares as a Search for the Parameters of a Linear System

The purpose of least squares is to find parameters (b, w) that minimize the difference between the system output y_i and the desired response d_i. Regression is effectively computing the optimal parameters of an interpolating system (linear in this case) that predicts the value of d from the value of x.

Figure 1-6 shows graphically the operation of adapting the parameters of the linear system. The system output y is always a linear combination of the input x with the bias, so it has to lie on a straight line of equation $y = wx + b$. Changing b modifies the y intercept, while changing w modifies the slope. Therefore we conclude that the goal of linear regression is to adjust the position of the line to minimize the average square difference between the y values (on the line) and the cloud of points d_i (i.e., the criterion J).

The key point is to recognize that the error contains information that can be used to optimally place the line. Figure 1-6 shows this by including a subsystem that accepts the error as input and modifies the parameters of the system. Thus, the error ε_i is fed back to the system and indirectly affects the output through a change in the parameters (b, w). Effectively, the system is made "aware" of its performance through the error. With the incorporation of the mechanism that automatically modifies the system parameters, a very powerful linear system can be built that will constantly seek optimal parameters. Such systems are called neural and adaptive systems and are the focus of this book.

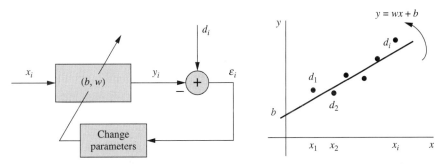

FIGURE 1-6 Regression as a linear system design problem

1.4.2 Neural and Adaptive Systems

Before pursuing the study of adaptive systems, it is important to reflect briefly on the implications of neural and adaptive systems in engineering design. System design usually begins with specifications. First, the problem domain is studied and modeled, specifications are established, and then a system is built to meet the specifications. The key point is that the system is built to meet the current specifications and will always use the designed set of parameters, even if the external conditions change.

Here we are proposing a very different system design approach based on adaptation, which has a biological flavor to it. In the beginning the system parameters may be way off, creating a large error. However, through the feedback from the error, the system can change its parameters to decrease the error as much as possible. The system's "experience" with the data designs the best set of parameters. An adaptive system is more complex because it has to not only accomplish the desired task but also be equipped with a subsystem that adapts its parameters. But notice that even if the data changes in the future, this design methodology will modify the system parameters so that the best possible performance is obtained. Additionally, the same system can be used for multiple problems.

There are basically two ways to adapt the system parameters: *supervised learning* and *unsupervised learning*. The method described until now belongs to supervised learning because there is a desired response. Later on in the book we will find other methods that also adapt the system parameters, but using only an internal rule. Since there is no desired response, these methods are called unsupervised. We will concentrate here on supervised learning methods.

The ingredients of supervised adaptive system design are

- A system (linear in this case) with adaptive parameters
- The existence of a desired or target response d
- An optimality criterion (the MSE in this case) to be minimized
- A method (subsystem) to compute the optimal parameters

The method of least squares finds the optimal parameters (b, w) analytically. Our goal is to find alternate ways of computing the same parameters using a search procedure.

1.4.3 Analysis of the Error in the Space of the Parameters: The Performance Surface

Let us analyze the mean square error (J) as we change the parameters of the system (w and b). Without loss of generality, we are going to assume that $b = 0$ (or equivalently, that the mean of x and d has been removed), so that J becomes a function of the single variable w:

$$J = \frac{1}{2N} \sum_i (d_i - wx_i)^2 = \frac{1}{2N} \sum_i (x_i^2 w^2 - 2d_i x_i w + d_i^2) \qquad \textbf{(1.9)}$$

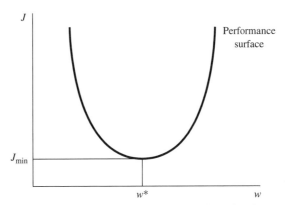

FIGURE 1-7 The performance surface for the regression problem

If w is treated as the variable and all other parameters are held constant, we can immediately see that J is quadratic on w with the coefficient of w^2 (i.e., x_i^2) being always positive. In the space of the possible w values, J is a parabola facing upward (J is always positive since it is a sum of squares). The function $J(w)$ is called the *performance surface* for the regression problem (Figure 1-7). The performance surface is an important tool that helps us visualize how the adaptation of the weights affects the mean square error.

NEUROSOLUTIONS EXAMPLE 1.4

Plotting the performance surface

The performance surface is just a plot of the error criterion (J) versus the value of the weights, so what we will do during the simulation is to vary the Synapse weight (which corresponds to the slope parameter of the linear regressor) between two appropriate values. We can imagine that the error will be minimum at an intermediate value of the weight and that it will increase for both lower and higher values.

To modify the Synapse weight incrementally, we attach a Linear Scheduler to the Synapse and place the Matrix Viewer on it so we can see how the weight is changing. To visualize the MSE, we bring another Scatter Plot to the L2 Criterion. This will allow us to plot the cost versus weight (performance surface).

**Linear Scheduler
on the Synapse**

Run the example and see how the slope parameter of the linear PE affects the mean square error of the linear regressor. As we are going to see, the input and desired signals tremendously affect the shape of the performance surface. But how can we change the shape of the performance curve without touching the data files? Let us substitute for the L2 Criterion with the Lp Criterion. Go to Palettes and open the Error Criteria menu. Click on the Lp Criterion and bring the pointer to the Breadboard. Notice that the pointer changed to a stamper. If you left-click on the L2 Criterion component, the L2 Criterion is replaced by the Lp component, which computes a cost given by the p norm:

$$J = \frac{1}{p} \sum_i \varepsilon_i^p$$

By default the norm is $p = 5$. Run the simulation again. What do you see? Does the location of the minimum change appreciably? What about the shape of the performance surface? Do you now better understand the function of the cost criterion?

Using the performance surface, we can develop a geometric method for finding the value of w, here denoted by w^*, which minimizes the performance criterion. Previously (Eq. 1.5), we computed w^* by setting to zero the derivative of J with respect to w.

The *gradient of the performance surface* is a vector (with the dimension of w) that always points toward the direction of maximum J change and with a magnitude equal to the slope of the tangent of the performance surface (Figure 1-8). If you visualize the performance surface as a hillside, each point on the hill will have a gradient arrow that points in the direction of steepest *ascent* at that point, with larger magnitudes for steeper slopes. A ball rolling down the hill will always attempt to roll in the direction opposite to the gradient arrow (the steepest descent). The slope at the bottom is zero, so the gradient is also zero (that is the reason the ball stops there).

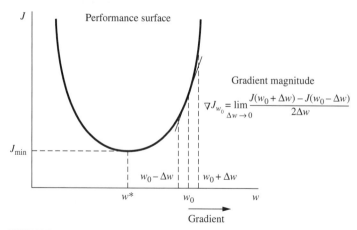

FIGURE 1-8 Performance surface and its gradient

Gradient Definition and Construction

The gradient is formally defined in terms of partial derivatives of a function $f(x, y)$. Let us consider a function $f(x, y)$ that has partial derivatives at x_0 and y_0. The gradient of f at x_0, y_0 is defined by

$$\text{grad } f(x_0, y_0) = \nabla f(x_0, y_0) = f_x(x_0, y_0)\mathbf{u}_x + f_y(x_0, y_0)\mathbf{u}_y$$

where $\mathbf{u}_x$ and $\mathbf{u}_y$ are the unit vectors along x and y, and f_x and f_y are the partial derivatives of f along the x and y directions, respectively, which are given by

$$f_x = \frac{\partial f(x, y)}{\partial x} \qquad f_y = \frac{\partial f(x, y)}{\partial y}$$

The gradient is associated with the concept of a directional derivative of a function. Let us assume we have a direction $\mathbf{u} = a\mathbf{u}_x + b\mathbf{u}_y$. The directional derivative of f at x_0, y_0 along $\mathbf{u}$ is

$$D_u f(x_0, y_0) = \lim_{h \to 0} \frac{f(x_0 + ha, y_0 + hb) - f(x_0, y_0)}{h}$$

The gradient can thus be defined as a function of the ordered derivatives:

$$D_u f(x_0, y_0) = (\text{grad } f(x_0, y_0)) \cdot \mathbf{u}$$

where the operation is the dot product of two vectors (for $\mathbf{v} = c\mathbf{u}_x + d\mathbf{u}_y, \mathbf{v} \cdot \mathbf{u} = ac + bd$).
    This expression means that the maximum value of the directional derivative as a function of the direction $\mathbf{u}$ is given by the size of the gradient, and it occurs exactly when the direction $\mathbf{u}$ coincides with the gradient direction.
    Moreover, we can also find this direction pretty easily. Let us consider the curve $C(x, y)$, defined as the line in the x, y plane where the function f has a constant value (this line is called the level curve or the contour of f). At a point x_0, y_0 in C the rate of change of f in the direction of the unit vector $\mathbf{u}$ tangent to C must be zero (see the preceding definition), that is,

$$D_u f(x_0, y_0) = (\text{grad } f(x_0, y_0)) \cdot \mathbf{u} = 0$$

But this implies that the gradient vector is perpendicular to the tangent vector $\mathbf{u}$ of the level curve at x_0, y_0. This explains the graphical construction outlined in the text.

    In our special case the gradient has just one component along the weight axis w, $\nabla J = \nabla_w J$ given by

$$\nabla_w J = \frac{\partial J}{\partial w} \tag{1.10}$$

A graphical way to construct $\nabla_w J$ at a point w_0 is to first find the level curve (curve of constant J value) that passes through the point (also called the contour plot). Then take the tangent to the level curve at w_0. The gradient component $\nabla_w J$ is always perpendicular to the contour curve at w_0, with a magnitude given by the partial derivative of J with respect to the weight w (Eq. 1.10). For one weight (one-dimensional problem), as in Figure 1-8, the construction is simplified, and we have to find only the direction of the gradient on the axis.

At the bottom of the bowl, the gradient is zero, because the parabola has slope zero at the vertex. Thus, for a parabolic performance surface, computing the gradient and equating it to zero finds the value of the coefficients that minimize the cost, just as we did in Eq. 1.6. The important observation is that the analytical solution found by the least squares coincides with the minimum of the performance surface. Substituting the value of w^* into Eq. 1.9, the minimum value of the error (J_{min}) can be computed.

More Properties of the Performance Surface

For a quadratic performance surface (Eq. 1.9), computing the gradient and equating it to zero finds the value of the coefficients that minimize the cost, that is,

$$\nabla J = \frac{\partial J}{\partial w} = 0 = \frac{1}{N}\left(-\sum_i d_i x_i + w \sum_i x_i^2\right) \tag{1B.7}$$

or

$$w^* = \frac{\sum_i x_i d_i}{\sum_i x_i^2} \tag{1B.8}$$

This solution is fundamentally the same as found in Eq. 1.6 ($b = 0$ is equivalent to assuming that the average values of x and d are zero). Substituting this value of w^* into Eq. 1.9, the minimum value of the error becomes

$$J_{min} = \frac{1}{2N}\left[\sum_i d_i^2 - \frac{\left(\sum_i d_i x_i\right)^2}{\sum_i x_i^2}\right] \tag{1B.9}$$

Equation 1.9 can be rewritten in the form

$$J = J_{min} + \frac{1}{2N}(w - w^*)\sum_i x_i^2(w - w^*) \tag{1B.10}$$

To verify this, solve Eq. 1B.10 substituting Eq. 1B.8 for w^* and Eq. 1B.9 for J_{min}. Notice the following observations:

- The minimum value of the error J_{min} (Eq. 1B.9) depends on both the input signal (x_i) and the desired signal (d_i).

- The location in coefficient space where the minimum w^* occurs (Eq. 1B.8) also depends on both x_i and d_i.
- The performance surface shape (Eq. 1B.10) depends only on the input signal (x_i).

NEUROSOLUTIONS EXAMPLE 1.5

Comparison of performance curves for different data sets

In this example we provide two sets of input files and two sets of output files. By changing the input data, we find that the minimum error, its location in the weight space (a simple line for this 1D example), and the shape of the performance surface change. On the other hand, if we change the desired signal, only the minimum value of the performance and its location change, but the overall shape remains the same.

1.4.4 Search of the Performance Surface with Steepest Descent

Since the performance surface is a paraboloid, which has a single minimum, an alternative procedure to find the best value of the coefficient w is to search the performance surface instead of computing the best coefficient analytically by Eq. 1.6. The search for the minimum of a function can be done efficiently using a broad class of methods based on gradient information. The gradient has two main advantages for the search:

- The gradient can be computed locally.
- The gradient always points in the direction of maximum change.

If the goal is to reach the minimum, the search must be in the direction opposite to the gradient. Thus the overall method of searching can be stated in the following way.

Start the search with an arbitrary initial weight $w(0)$, where the iteration number is denoted by the index in parentheses. Then compute the gradient of the performance surface at $w(0)$, and modify the initial weight proportionally to the negative of the gradient at $w(0)$. This changes the operating point to $w(1)$. Then compute the gradient at the new position $w(1)$, and apply the same procedure again; that is,

$$w(k + 1) = w(k) - \eta \nabla J(k) \tag{1.11}$$

where η is a small constant and $\nabla J(k)$ denotes the gradient of the performance surface at the kth iteration. The constant η is used to maintain stability in the search by ensuring that the operating point does not move too far along the performance surface. This search procedure is called the *steepest descent* method. Figure 1-9 illustrates the search procedure.

If we trace the path of the weights from iteration to iteration, intuitively we see that if the constant η is small, eventually the best value for the coefficient w^* will be found. Whenever $w > w^*$, we decrease w, and whenever $w < w^*$, we increase w.

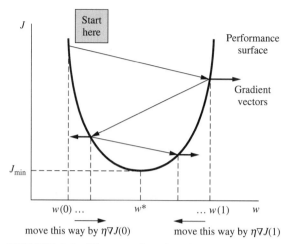

FIGURE 1-9 The search using the gradient information

1.5 ESTIMATION OF THE GRADIENT: THE LMS ALGORITHM

An adaptive system can use the gradient to optimize its parameters. The gradient, however, is usually not known explicitly and thus must be estimated. Traditionally, the difference operator is used to estimate the derivative, as outlined in Figure 1-8. A good estimate, however, requires many small perturbations to the operating point to obtain a robust estimation through averaging. The method is straightforward but not very practical.

In the late 1960s Widrow[2] proposed an extremely elegant algorithm to estimate the gradient that revolutionized the application of gradient descent procedures. His idea is very simple: Use the instantaneous value as the estimator for the true quantity. For our problem, this means to drop the summation in Eq. 1.9 and define the gradient estimate at step k as its instantaneous value. Substituting Eq. 1.4 into Eq. 1.10, removing the summation, and then taking the derivative with respect to w yields

$$\nabla J(k) = \frac{\partial}{\partial w(k)} J = \frac{\partial}{\partial w(k)} \frac{1}{2N} \sum_i \varepsilon_i^2 \approx \frac{1}{2} \frac{\partial}{\partial w(k)} (\varepsilon^2(k)) = -\varepsilon(k)x(k) \qquad \textbf{(1.12)}$$

What Eq. 1.12 tells us is that an instantaneous estimate of the gradient at iteration k is simply the product of the current input to the weight times the current error. The amazing thing is that the gradient can be estimated with one multiplication per weight. This is the gradient estimate that led to the famous *least mean square (LMS) algorithm* (or LMS rule). The estimate will be noisy, however, since the algorithm uses the error

[2]Bernard Widrow was one of the first researchers to explore engineering applications of adaptive systems. We are going to hear a lot about him in this book.

from a single sample instead of summing the error for each point in the data set (e.g., the MSE is estimated by the error for the current sample). But remember that the adaptation process does not find the minimum in one step. Normally, many iterations are required to find the minimum of the performance surface, and during this process the noise in the gradient is being averaged (or *filtered*) out.

If the estimator of Eq. 1.12 is substituted in Eq. 1.11, the steepest descent equation becomes

$$w(k + 1) = w(k) + \eta \varepsilon(k)x(k) \tag{1.13}$$

This equation is the *LMS algorithm.* With the LMS rule we do not need to worry about perturbation and averaging to properly estimate the gradient at each iteration; it is the iterative process that is improving the gradient estimator. The small constant η is called the *step size,* or the *learning rate.*

NEUROSOLUTIONS EXAMPLE 1.6

Adapting the linear PE with LMS

Several things have to be added to the previous Breadboard of the linear PE to make it learn automatically using the LMS algorithm. The methodology will be explained in more detail later. However, the technique used in NeuroSolutions is called backpropagation. In short, the algorithm passes the input data forward through the network and the error information (desired − output) backward through another network. The error is propagated through a second network, which can be obtained from the original network with minor and well-established modifications (more about this later). Thus at every component there is a local activity (x) and a local error (ε) such that the weights of the network can be modified by Eq. 1.13. NeuroSolutions implements this technique by adding two additional layers to the network: the backpropagation layer and the gradient-search layer. These two layers can be automatically added to the Breadboard. The backpropagation layer looks like a small version of the network that sits on top of the original network (in red instead of orange). The gradient-search layer sits on top of the backpropagation layer and uses one of the gradient-search methods to adjust the weights. In this case, the gradient-search layer is a simple "step" layer, which implements the gradient descent rule of Eq. 1.13. Notice that only the components that have adjustable weights [the Synapse (w) and Bias Axon (b)] have gradient-search components.

In addition to the two layers, we need an additional Controller to manage the back-propagation layer. The Backprop Controller sits above the yellow Controller and sets parameters such as whether we use batch or on-line learning. In this example we use batch learning; that is, the learning algorithm will compute all the weight updates for the training set, add them up, and at the end of the epoch (one presentation of all the training data) update the weights according to Eq. 1.13. The value of the step size will be set at 0.01 and the training will use 200 iterations.

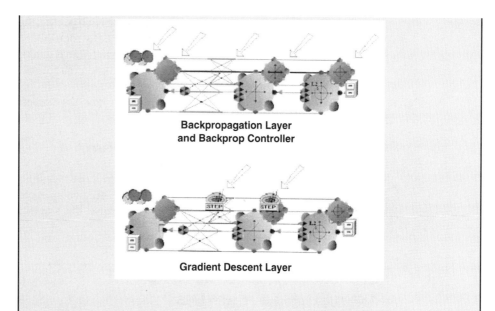

**Backpropagation Layer
and Backprop Controller**

Gradient Descent Layer

When you run the network, watch the regression line move toward the optimal value in the Scatter Plot. When the simulation stops, notice that the weight is approximately 0.139, the bias is approximately 1.33, and the error is approximately 0.033—all in excellent agreement with the optimal values we computed analytically.

You should explore this Breadboard by entering several values of the step size and opening the Inspector to see how each component is configured.

1.5.1 Batch and Sample-by-Sample Learning

The LMS algorithm was presented in a form in which the weight updates are computed for each input sample and the weights modified after each sample. This procedure is called sample-by-sample learning, or *on-line training.* As we have mentioned, the estimate of the gradient is going to be noisy; that is, the direction toward the minimum is going to zigzag around the gradient direction.

An alternative solution is to compute the weight update for each input sample and store these values (without changing the weights) during one pass through the training set, which is called an *epoch.* At the end of the epoch, all the weight updates are added together, and only then will the weights be updated with the composite value. This method adapts the weights with a cumulative weight update, so it will follow the gradient more closely. This method is called the *batch training mode,* or *batch learning.* Batch learning is also an implementation of the steepest-descent procedure. In fact, it provides an estimator for the gradient that is smoother than the LMS. We will see that the agreement between the analytical quantities that describe adaptation and the ones obtained experimentally is excellent with the batch update.

Batch versus On-line Learning

The on-line and batch modes are slightly different, although both will perform well for parabolic performance surfaces. One major difference is that the batch algorithm keeps the system weights constant while computing the error associated with each sample in the input. Since the on-line version is constantly updating its weights, its error calculation (and thus gradient estimation) uses different weights for each input sample. This means that the two algorithms visit different sets of points during adaptation. However, they both converge to the same minimum.

Note that the number of weight updates of the two methods for the same number of data presentations is very different. The on-line method (LMS) does an update each sample, while batch does an update each epoch, that is,

LMS updates $=$ (batch updates) $\times$ (# of samples in training set)

The batch algorithm is also slightly more efficient in terms of number of computations.

To visualize the differences between these two update methods, we will plot the value of the cost during adaptation (called the *learning curve*).

NEUROSOLUTIONS EXAMPLE 1.7

Batch versus on-line adaptation

It is important to visualize the differences in adaptation for on-line and batch learning. Up to now we have been using the batch mode. In this example we set the Backprop Controller to use on-line training. To display the learning curve, we have to introduce one new component: the MegaScope. The MegaScope is a probe, that acts just like an oscilloscope: It plots a continuous stream of inputs, using the iteration number as the *x* axis. The MegaScope sits on top of the Data Storage component.

MegaScope

The important controls of the MegaScope are the scales of the *x* and *y* axes. In the scope level of the Inspector, we can select the vertical scale (*y* axis) and the offset of each channel. Alternatively, we can use the autoscale feature. The horizontal scale is selected in the sweep level of the Inspector (number of samples per division). Remember that the number of samples displayed is defined by the Data Storage component.

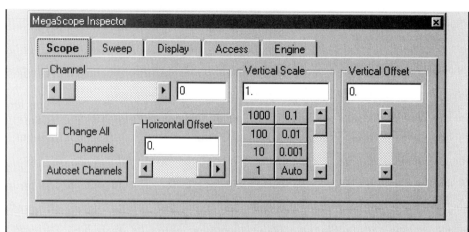

To create the learning curve, we simply place a Data Storage component over the L2 Criterion and then place a MegaScope on top of it. We will see that the learning curve is not smooth anymore because we are updating the weights after each example. Since the individual errors vary from sample to sample, our updates will make the learning curve noisy. The learning curve will have a periodic component superimposed on a decaying exponential. The exponential tells us that we are approaching a better overall solution. The periodic features show the error obtained for each input sample, while the envelope is related to the learning curve for the batch mode. Note that the weights never stabilize; the performance curve should otherwise be smooth and converge to a single final value. Since there is more noise in on-line learning, we must decrease the step size to get smoother adaptation. We recommend using a step size 10 times smaller than the step size for batch learning. But the price paid is a longer adaptation time; the system needs more iterations to get to a predefined final error. Experiment with the learning rates to observe this behavior.

1.5.2 Robustness and System Testing

One of the interesting aspects of the LMS solution is its robustness. From the explanation given (Figure 1-9), no matter what the initial condition for the weights, the solution always converges to basically the same value. We can even add some noise to the desired response and find out that the linear regressor parameters are basically unchanged. This robustness is rather important for real-world problems, where noise is omnipresent.

The group of input samples and desired responses (shown in Table 1-1) used to train the system are called collectively the training set for obvious reasons. It is with their information that the system parameters were adapted. But once the optimal parameters are found, the parameters should be fixed. When the system is utilized for new inputs never encountered before, it will produce for each input a response based on the parameters obtained during training. If the new data comes from the same experiment, the response should resemble the value of the desired response for that particular input value.

Thus we see that the system has the ability to extrapolate responses for new data. This is an important feature, since in general we wish the performance obtained in the training set to also apply (generalize) to the new data when the system is deployed. But due to the methodology utilized to derive the parameter values, we can never be exactly sure of how well the system will respond to new data.

For this reason it is a good methodology to use a test set to verify the system performance before deploying it in the real-world application. The test set consists of new data not used for training but for which we still know the desired response. It is like the final rehearsal before a play's inauguration. We should also compute the correlation coefficient in the test set. Normally, we will find a slight decrease in performance from the training set. If the performance in the test set is not acceptable, we have to go back to the drawing board. When this happens in regression, the most common problem is that the training data is inadequate—either in quantity or in exhaustive coverage of the experimental conditions. This point will be addressed in more depth in the following chapters.

NEUROSOLUTIONS EXAMPLE 1.8

Robustness of LMS to noise

The LMS algorithm is very robust. It works from any arbitrary location and even works well with noise added to the desired data. To demonstrate that the system works well even with noisy data, we add one additional component to the Breadboard from the previous example: the Noise component. The Noise component allows uniform, Gaussian, or "user-defined" noise to be added to the input or desired signals. We will add the Noise component to the desired signal and watch as the system moves close to the optimal location even with the noisy data.

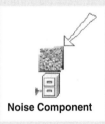

Noise Component

1.5.3 Computing the Correlation Coefficient in Adaptive Systems

The correlation coefficient, r, tells how much of the variance of d is captured by a linear regression on the independent variable x. As such, r is a very powerful quantifier of the modeling result. It has a great advantage with respect to the MSE because it is automatically normalized, while the MSE is not. However, the correlation coefficient is blind to differences in means because it is a ratio of variances (see Eq. 1.8); that is, as long as the desired data and input covary, r will be small, in spite of the fact that they may be far apart in actual value. Thus we need both quantities (r and MSE) when testing the results of regression.

Although the correlation coefficient can be computed directly from x and d (Eq. 1.8), we would like to estimate r at the output of the linear system to follow the adaptive systems' methodology. From Eq. 1B.4, we can write

$$\tilde{r} = \frac{\sqrt{\sum_i (y_i - \bar{d})^2}}{\sqrt{\sum_i (d_i - \bar{d})^2}} \tag{1.14}$$

Note, however, that y changes during adaptation, so we should wait until the system adapts to read the final correlation coefficient ($\tilde{r} \to r$ when $w \to w*$). During adaptation the numerator of Eq. 1.14 can be larger than the denominator, giving a value for r larger than 1, which is meaningless. We therefore propose to compute a new parameter $\tilde{r}$ that is a reasonable proxy for the correlation coefficient, even during adaptation. We subtract a term from the numerator of Eq. 1.14 that becomes zero at the optimal setting but limits $\tilde{r}$ so that its value is always between -1 and 1, even during adaptation. We can write

$$\tilde{r} = \frac{\sqrt{\sum_i (y_i - \bar{d})^2} - \dfrac{\sum_i \varepsilon_i (y_i - \bar{d})}{\sqrt{\sum_i (y_i - \bar{d})^2}}}{\sqrt{\sum_i (d_i - \bar{d})^2}} \tag{1.15}$$

Computation of the Correlation Coefficient

It is important to remember (Eq. 1B.6) that with the optimal coefficients the regression error ε_{min}, interpreted as a vector, is perpendicular to the Adaline output **y**. This condition is called the orthogonality condition. In fact, from the following figure it is easy to see that the smallest error is obtained when the projection of **d** on **y** is the orthogonal projection.

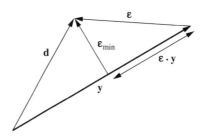

During adaptation the error will always be larger than ε_{min}, meaning that **y** can be larger than **d**, so Eq. 1.14 may be larger than 1, which is misleading since $|r| < 1$. Using the fact that the minimum error is perpendicular to **y**, we can compute the dot product of ε with

y and subtract it from the numerator of Eq. 1.14. We can prove that this new numerator is always smaller than **d** and that the dot product is zero at the optimal solution and so will not affect the final value of the correlation coefficient. This is exactly what is done in Eq. 1.14.

Note that all these quantities can be computed on-line with the information of the error, the output, and the desired response. Remember, however, that Eq. 1.15 measures the correlation coefficient only when the Adaline has been totally adapted to the data.

NEUROSOLUTIONS EXAMPLE 1.9

Estimating the correlation coefficient during learning

NeuroSolutions does not include a component to compute the correlation coefficient. It does, however, allow you to write your own components. These custom components are called DLLs. A custom component looks just like the component it takes the place of, except that its icon has "DLL" printed on it. In this example we include a custom component to compute the correlation coefficient. This component looks exactly like an L2 Criterion component, except it has "DLL" printed on it.

Plug in the values of the optimal weights and verify that the formula Eq. 1.15 gives the correct correlation coefficient. Slightly modify w to 0.120 and verify that the correlation coefficient decreases. If you plug in values for w and b that are very far away from the fitted regression, this estimation of r using Eq. 1.14 becomes less accurate, but is still bound by -1 and 1. The example also uses LMS to adapt the coefficients. Observe that the correlation coefficient is always between -1 and 1 during adaptation and that the final value corresponds to the computed one.

1.6 A METHODOLOGY FOR STABLE ADAPTATION

During adaptation the learning algorithm automatically changes the system parameters using Eq. 1.13. This adaptation algorithm has one free parameter (the step size) that must be user selected. To appropriately set the step size, the user should have a good understanding of what is happening inside the system. In this section we quantify the adaptation process and develop visualization tools that will help you understand how well the system is learning.

1.6.1 Learning Curve

As is readily apparent from Figure 1-9, when the weights approach the optimal value, the values of $J(k)$ (the MSE at iteration k) will also decrease, approaching its minimum value J_{min}. One of the best ways to monitor the convergence of the adaptation process is to plot the error at each iteration. The plot of the MSE across iterations is called the *learning curve* (Figure 1-10). The learning curve is as important for adaptive systems

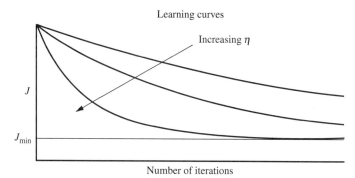

FIGURE 1-10   The learning curve

as the thermometer is to check your health. It is an external, scalar, easy-to-compute indication of how well the system is learning. But similar to body temperature, it is unspecific; that is, when the system is not learning, it does not tell us why.

Notice that the error approaches the minimum in a one-sided manner (i.e., always larger than $J_{\min}$). As you can expect, the rate of decrease of the error depends on the value of the step size η. Larger step sizes will take fewer iterations to reach the neighborhood of the minimum, provided that the adaptation converges. However, too large a step size creates a divergent iterative process, and the optimal solution is not obtained. We therefore must seek a way to find the largest possible step size that guarantees convergence.

NEUROSOLUTIONS EXAMPLE 1.10

The learning curve

The goal of this example is to display the learning curve and to show how the learning rate affects its shape. This example plots the mean square error during adaptation, which we called the learning curve, the thermometer of learning.

When you run the simulation, watch how the error moves toward zero as the regression line moves toward the optimal location. You can also change the learning rates and watch the regression line moving more quickly or slowly toward the optimal location, thus causing the learning curve to be steeper or shallower. The visualization of the regression line contains more information about what the system is doing but is very difficult to compute and display in higher dimensions. The learning curve, however, is an external, scalar quantity that can be easily measured with minimal overhead.

1.6.2 Weight Tracks

An adaptive system modifies its weights in an effort to find the best solution. The plot of the value of a weight over time is called the *weight track*. Weight tracks are an important

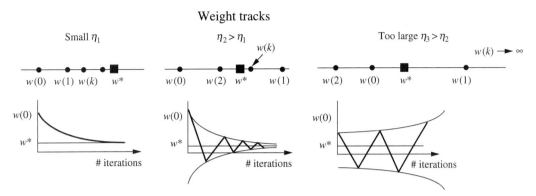

FIGURE 1-11   Weight tracks and plots of the weight values across an iteration for three values of η

and direct measure of the adaptation process. The problem is that normally our system has many weights, and we don't know what their optimal values are. Nevertheless, the dynamics of learning can be inferred and monitored from the weight tracks.

In the gradient-descent adaptation, adjustments to the weights are governed by two quantities (Eq. 1.11): the step size η and the value of the gradient at the point. Even for a constant step size, the weight adjustments become smaller and smaller as the adaptation approaches w^*, since the slope of the quadratic performance surface is decreasing near the bottom of the performance surface. Thus the weights approach their final values asymptotically (Figure 1-11).

Three cases are depicted in Figure 1-11. If the step size is small, the weight converges monotonically to w^*, and the number of iterations to reach the bottom of the bowl may be large. If the step size η is increased, the convergence will be faster but still monotonic. After η reaches a value called *critically damped,* the weight will approach w^* in an oscillatory fashion ($\eta_2 > \eta_1$); that is, it will overshoot and undershoot the final solution. The number of iterations necessary to reach the neighborhood of w^* will start increasing again. If the step size is too large ($\eta_3 > \eta_2$), the iterative process will diverge; that is, instead of getting closer to the minimum, the search will visit points of larger and larger MSE until there is a numeric overflow. We say that the learning diverged.

NEUROSOLUTIONS EXAMPLE 1.11

Weight tracks

It is very instructive to observe the linear PE parameters during learning and how they change as a function of the step size. Let us install a MegaScope over the Synapse to visualize the slope parameter of the regressor and over the Bias Axon to visualize the regressor bias. These are called weight tracks. Run the simulation and watch how changing the step sizes affects the way the system approaches its final weights.

> The weight tracks are a finer display of how adaptation is progressing, but the problem is that in systems with many weights it becomes impractical to observe all the weight tracks. Why do we say that weight tracks give us a better handle on the adaptation parameters? Enter 0.02 for the step size and see the weight tracks converge monotonically to their minimum value. Now enter 0.035. The weight tracks are oscillating toward the final value, which means that the system is already in the underdamped regime (but the learning curve is still monotonically decreasing toward the minimum at a faster rate). We can expect divergence if we increase the weights further. Try 0.038 and see it happen. Relate this behavior to Figure 1-11.

1.6.3 Largest Step Size for Convergence

As we have just discussed, we would like to choose the largest step size possible for fastest convergence without creating an unstable system. Since adjustment to the weights is a product of the step size and the local gradient of the performance surface, it is clear that the largest step size depends on the shape of the performance surface. We saw already (Eq. 1B.10) that the shape of the performance surface is controlled by the input data, so we can conclude that the maximum step size will be dictated by the input data. But how?

If we rewrite and manipulate the equations that produce the weight values in terms of the first weight $w(0)$, we get

$$w(k + 1) = w^* + (1 - \eta\lambda)^{k+1}(w(0) - w^*) \qquad (1.16)$$

where

$$\lambda = \frac{1}{N}\sum_i x_i^2$$

The term $(1 - \eta\lambda)^k$ must be less than or equal to 1 to guarantee weight convergence (and less than 1 to guarantee convergence to zero, giving the solution $w(k + 1) = w^*$). This implies that

$$|\rho| = |1 - \eta\lambda| < 1 \Rightarrow \eta < \eta_{\max} = \frac{2}{\lambda} \qquad (1.17)$$

where ρ is the geometric ratio of the iterative process. Hence the value of the step size η must always be smaller than $2/\lambda$. The fastest convergence is obtained with the critically damped step size of $1/\lambda$. The closer η is to $1/\lambda$, the faster is the convergence, but faster convergence also means that the iterative process is closer to instability. We can visualize this in Figure 1-11. When η is increased, a monotonic (overdamped) convergence to w^* is substituted by an alternating (underdamped) convergence that finally degenerates into divergence.

Derivation of the Largest Step Size

The best way to find the upper bound for η is to write the equation that produces the weight values. Let us rewrite the ideal performance surface (Eq. 1B.10) as

$$J = J_{min} + \frac{\lambda}{2}(w - w^*)^2 \qquad \textbf{(1B.11)}$$

where

$$\lambda = \frac{1}{N}\sum_i x_i^2 \qquad \textbf{(1B.12)}$$

By computing the gradient of J (Eq. 1B.11), we get

$$\nabla J = \lambda(w - w^*) \qquad \textbf{(1B.13)}$$

so the iteration that produces the weight updates (Eq. 1.11) can be written as

$$w(k + 1) = (1 - \eta\lambda)w(k) + \eta\lambda w^* \qquad \textbf{(1B.14)}$$

This is a first-order linear constant-coefficient difference equation, which can be solved by induction. First, let us subtract w^* from both sides to yield

$$w(k + 1) - w^* = (1 - \eta\lambda)(w(k) - w^*)$$

Start with a solution $w(0)$,

$$w(1) - w^* = (1 - \eta\lambda)(w(0) - w^*)$$
$$w(2) - w^* = (1 - \eta\lambda)^2(w(0) - w^*)$$
$$w(3) - w^* = (1 - \eta\lambda)^3(w(0) - w^*)$$

which provides by induction the equation

$$w(k) = w^* + (1 - \eta\lambda)^k(w(0) - w^*)$$

There is a slight practical problem that must be solved. During batch learning the weight updates are added together during an epoch to obtain the new weight. This effectively includes a factor of N in the LMS weight update formula, Eq. 1.13. To apply the analysis of the largest step size of Eq. 1.17, we have to use a normalized step size:

$$\eta_n = \frac{\eta}{N} \qquad \textbf{(1.18)}$$

With this modification, even if the number of samples in our experiment changes, the step sizes do not need to be modified. Note that for on-line learning ($N = 1$) we get the LMS rule again. We will always use normalized step sizes, but to make the notation simpler, we will drop the subscript n in the normalized step size. An added advantage of using normalized step sizes is that we can switch between on-line updates and batch updates without having to change the step size in the simulations.

The analysis of the largest step size of Eq. 1.17 also applies *in the mean* to the LMS algorithm. However, since LMS uses an instantaneous (noisy) estimate of the gradient, even when η obeys Eq. 1.17, instability may occur. When the iterative process diverges, the algorithm "forgets" its location in the performance surface; that is, the values of the weights change drastically. This means that all the iterations up to that point were wasted. Hence with LMS it is common to include a safety factor of 10 in the largest η ($\eta < 0.1\eta_{\max}$) or to use batch training which reduces the noise in the estimate of the gradient.

1.6.4 Time Constant of Adaptation

An alternative view of the adaptive process is to quantify the convergence of $w(k)$ to w^* in terms of an exponential decrease. We know that $w(k)$ converges to w^* as a geometric progression (Eq. 1.16). The envelope of the geometric progression of weight values can be approximated by an exponential decay $\exp(-t/\tau)$, where τ is the *time constant of weight adaptation*. A single iteration or epoch can be considered a unit of time. One may want to know approximately how many iterations are needed until the weights converge. The time constant of weight adaptation can be written as

$$\tau = \frac{1}{\eta\lambda} \tag{1.19}$$

which clearly shows that fast adaptation (small time constant τ) requires large step sizes. For all practical purposes the iterative process converges after four time constants.

Derivation of the Time Constant of Weight Adaptation

Writing $\exp(-1/\tau) = \rho$ and expanding the exponential in Taylor series,

$$\rho = \exp\left(-\frac{1}{\tau}\right) = 1 - \frac{1}{\tau} + \frac{1}{2!\tau^2} - \cdots$$

we get approximately $\rho \approx 1 - 1/\tau$. We saw that geometric ratio of the gradient descent is Eq. 1.17, so we get

$$\tau = \frac{1}{\eta\lambda}$$

The steps used to derive the time constant of weight adaptation can be applied also to come up with a closed-form solution to the decrease of the cost across iterations, which is called the *time constant of adaptation*. Equation 1.16 tells us how the weights converge to w^*. If the equation for the weight recursion is substituted in the equation for the cost (Eq. 1B.11) we get

$$J = J_{\min} + \lambda(1 - \eta\lambda)^{2k}(w(0) - w^*)^2$$

which means that J also approximates $J_{\min}$ in a geometric progression, with a ratio equal to ρ^2. Therefore the time constant of adaptation is

$$\tau_{\mathrm{mse}} = \frac{\tau}{2}$$

Since the geometric ratio is always positive, J approximates $J_{\min}$ monotonically (i.e., an exponential decrease). The time constant of adaptation describes the learning time (in number of iterations) needed to adapt the system in a practical way. Notice that these expressions assume that the adaptation follows the gradient. With the instantaneous estimate used in the LMS, J may oscillate during adaptation, since the estimate is noisy. But even in the LMS, J will approach $J_{\min}$ in a one-sided way (i.e., always greater than or equal to $J_{\min}$).

NEUROSOLUTIONS EXAMPLE 1.12

Linear regression without bias

The previous example solved the linear regression problem with one weight and one bias. To compare the equations previously given (which are a function of a single parameter) with the simulations, we have to make a modification in the data set or in the simulation. Shortly we will see how to extend the analysis for multiple weights, but for the time being let us work with the simpler case.

We replace the Bias Axon with an Axon, a component that simply adds its inputs, so the regression solution becomes $y = wx$, which has to pass through the origin. With this new Breadboard we can compare the numerical results of the simulations directly with all the equations derived in this section, since there is only one free parameter. Batch updates are used throughout.

The optimal value of the slope parameter is computed by Eq. 1.5, which gives $w = 0.30009$, with an average error of 0.23. This solution is different from the value obtained previously ($w = 0.139511$) for the bias regressor because the regression line is now constrained to pass through the origin. It turns out that this constrained solution is worse than before, as we can see by the error (0.23 versus 0.033). Observing the output (red points) and the input samples (blue) in the Scatter Plot shows clearly what we are describing.

Computing λ by Eq. 1.16 yields 54, so according to Eq. 1.17 the maximum step size is $\eta = 3.6 \times 10^{-2}$. The critically damped solution is obtained with a step size of 1.8×10^{-2}, and adaptation with a step size below this value is overdamped. When we run the simulator in the overdamped case, the weights approach the final value monotonically; for the critically damped case they stabilize quite rapidly, while for the underdamped case they oscillate around the final value, and the convergence takes more iterations. Notice also that the linear regressor "vibrates" around the final position, since the slope parameter is overshooting and undershooting the optimal value.

According to Eq. 1.19 the critically damped step size $\tau = 1$, so the solution should stabilize in four updates (epochs). This step size yields the fastest convergence. Go to the Controller Inspector and use the epoch button to verify the number of samples until convergence.

1.6.5 Rattling

Up to now our main focus was the speed of adaptation, that is, how fast the weights approximate w^* or, equivalently, how fast J approximates J_{min}. Unfortunately, this is only part of the story. For fast convergence we need large step sizes (η). But when the search is close to the minimum w^*, where the gradient is small but not zero, the iterative process continues to wander around a neighborhood of the minimum solution without ever stabilizing. This phenomenon is called *rattling* (Figure 1-12), and the rattling basin increases proportionally to the step size η. This means that when the adaptive process is stopped by an external command (such as the number of iterations through the data), the weights may not be exactly at w^*. We know they are in the neighborhood of the minimum point but not exactly at the optimum.

If we picture the performance surface (Figure 1-12) when the final weights are not at w^*, there will be a penalty in performance; that is, the final MSE will be higher than J_{min}. In the theory of adaptation the difference between the final MSE and the J_{min} (normalized by J_{min}) is called the *misadjustment M*.

$$M = \frac{J_{final} - J_{min}}{J_{min}} \tag{1.20}$$

This means that in search procedures that use gradient descent there is an intrinsic compromise between accuracy of the final solution (a small misadjustment) and speed

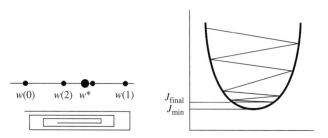

FIGURE 1-12 Rattling of the iteration procedure

of convergence. The parameter that controls this compromise is the step size η. High η means fast convergence but also large misadjustment, while small η means slow convergence but little misadjustment.

NEUROSOLUTIONS EXAMPLE 1.13

Rattling

We observed in Example 1.7 how noisy the learning curve became with the on-line update. This is an external indication that the weights were changing from sample to sample even after the system reached the neighborhood of the optimum. The implication of this random movement in the weights is a penalty in the final MSE. In this example we show and exactly quantify the rattling.

The rattling has important consequences for adaptation, since if we set the step size large for fast convergence, we pay a price of inaccurate coefficients, which are translated into an excess MSE. The rule of thumb for LMS is to use a step size that is 1/10 of the largest possible step size. For a step size close to the largest possible, the MSE for the epoch is effectively smaller than the theoretical minimum, which is impossible. This happens because the parameters are changing so much with each update that the slope is continuously varying. The problem is that when we stop the training, we do not know whether the final value of the weight is a good approximation to the theoretical regression line.

This shows that for adaptive systems the final MSE is only part of the story. We have to make sure that the system coefficients have stabilized. It is interesting to note that with batch updates there is no rattling, so in the linear case the batch solution is more appropriate. Observe this in the simulations by displaying the MSE for large and small step sizes. We are just paying the small price of storing the individual weight updates. For nonlinear systems the batch is unfortunately no longer always superior to the on-line update, as we will see.

This example shows that obtaining a small MSE is a necessary but not sufficient condition for stable adaptation. *Adaptation also requires that the weights of the model settle onto stable values.* This second condition is required because the system can endlessly change its parameters to fit the present sample. This will always give a small MSE, but from a modeling point of view it is a useless solution because *no single model is found to fit the data set.*

1.6.6 Scheduling the Step Sizes

As we saw in the latest examples, for fast convergence to the neighborhood of the minimum, a large step size is desired. However, the solution with a large step size suffers from rattling. One attractive solution is to use a large learning rate in the beginning of training to move quickly toward the location of the optimal weights, but then the learning rate should be decreased to obtain good accuracy on the final weight values. This is called *learning rate scheduling*. This simple idea can be implemented with a variable step size controlled by

$$\eta(k + 1) = \eta(k) - \beta \tag{1.21}$$

where $\eta(0) = \eta_0$ is the initial step size, and β is a small constant. Note that the step size is being linearly decreased at each iteration. If we have control of the number of iterations, we can start with a large step size and decrease it to practically zero toward the end of training. The value of β needs to be experimentally determined. Alternatively, we can decrease the step size slowly (in optimization this slow decrease is called annealing) using a linear, geometric, or logarithmic rule.

More on Scheduling Step Sizes

If the initial value of η_0 is set too high, the learning can diverge. The selection of β can be even trickier than the selection of η because it is highly dependent on the performance surface. If β is too large, the weights may not move quickly enough to the minimum and the adaptation may stall. If β is too small, the search may reach the global minimum quickly and must wait a long time before the learning rate decreases enough to minimize the rattling. There are other (more automatic) methods for adapting the learning rate that we discuss later in the book.

NEUROSOLUTIONS EXAMPLE 1.14

Scheduling of step sizes

In this demonstration we vary the step size using the scheduling component already introduced in Example 1.4. The scheduler is a component that takes an initial value from the component it is attached to, and changes the value according to a predetermined rule. Here we use the linear rule, and since we want to decrease the step size, the factor β is negative. We should set a maximum and a minimum value just to make sure that the parameters are always within the range we want. β should be set according to the number of iterations and the initial and final values ($\mu_{\text{Init}} - \beta N = \mu_{\text{Resid}}$).

Here the important parameter is the minimum (the residual step size is set at 0.001), because after scheduling we want to let the system fine-tune its parameters to find the best approximation of the minimum. However, notice that this implies that the parameter is already in its optimal neighborhood, and this depends on a lot of unknown factors. Thus if the scheduling is not right, the adaptation may stall in positions far from the minimum.

You should explore the Breadboard by entering other values for β and the final value and see their impact on the final weight value. You can also use the exponential and the logarithmic schedulers and see how they behave. Which one do you prefer for this case?

1.7 REGRESSION FOR MULTIPLE VARIABLES

Assume that d is now a function of several inputs $x_1, x_2, \ldots, x_D$ (independent variables), and the goal is to find the best linear regressor of d on all the inputs (Figure 1-13). For $D = 2$ this corresponds to fitting a plane through the N input samples or a hyperplane in the general case of D dimensions.

As an example, let us assume that we have two variables, x_1 (speed) and x_2 (feed rate), that affect the surface roughness (d) of a machined workpiece. In abstract units the values of x_1, x_2, and d for 15 workpieces are presented in Table 1-2. The goal is to

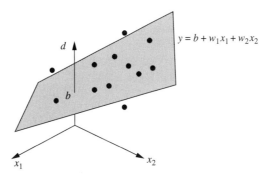

FIGURE 1-13 Fitting a regression plane to a set of samples in 2D space

TABLE 1-2 Multiple Regression Data

x_1	x_2	d
1	2	2
2	5	1
2	3	2
2	2	2
3	4	1
3	5	3
4	6	2
5	5	3
5	6	4
5	7	3
6	8	4
7	6	2
8	4	4
8	9	3
9	8	4

find how well one can explain the quality of machining by the two variables x_1 and x_2 and which is the most important parameter.

As before, we assume that the measurements **x** are noise free and that **d** is contaminated by a noise vector **ε** with these properties: Gaussian distributed with components that are zero mean, of equal variance σ^2, and uncorrelated with the inputs. The regression equation when $D = 2$ is now

$$\varepsilon_i = d_i - (b + w_1 x_{i1} + w_2 x_{i2}) \tag{1.22}$$

where x_{i1} is the ith value of x_1 (the ith workpiece in the training set). In the general case we write Eq. 1.22 as

$$\varepsilon_i = d_i - \left(b + \sum_{k=1}^{D} w_k x_{ik} \right) = d_i - \sum_{k=0}^{D} w_k x_{ik} \qquad i = 1 \ldots N \tag{1.23}$$

where we made $w_0 = b$ and $x_{i0} = 1$ (compare with Eq. 1.3). The goal of the regression problem is to find the coefficients $w_0, \ldots, w_D$. To simplify the notation we will put all these values into a vector $\mathbf{w} = [w_0, \ldots, w_D]^T$ that minimizes the MSE of ε_i over the N samples. Figure 1-14 shows that the linear PE now has D inputs and one bias.

The MSE becomes for this case

$$J = \frac{1}{2N} \sum_i \left(d_i - \sum_{k=0}^{D} w_k x_{ik} \right)^2 \tag{1.24}$$

The solution to the extreme (minimum) of this equation can be found in exactly the same way as before, that is, by taking the derivatives of J with respect to the unknowns (w_k) and equating the result to zero.

This yields a set of $D+1$ equations in $D+1$ unknowns called the *normal equation*

$$\sum_i x_{ij} d_i = \sum_{k=0}^{D} w_k \sum_i x_{ik} x_{ij} \qquad j = 0, 1, \ldots, D \tag{1.25}$$

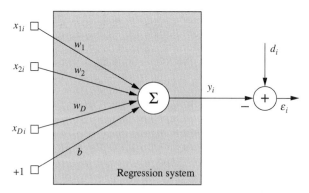

FIGURE 1-14 Regression system for multiple inputs

Derivation of Normal Equations

When the derivative of J with respect to the unknown quantities (the weights) is taken, we end up with a set of $D + 1$ equations in $D + 1$ unknowns:

$$\frac{\partial J}{\partial w_j} = -\frac{1}{N} \sum_i x_{ij} \left(d_i - \sum_{k=0}^{D} w_k x_{ik} \right) = 0 \qquad \text{for } j = 0, \dots, D \qquad \textbf{(1B.15)}$$

The solution is the famous normal matrix equation:

$$\sum_i x_{ij} d_i = \sum_{k=0}^{D} w_k \sum_i x_{ik} x_{ij} \qquad j = 0, 1, \dots, D \qquad \textbf{(1B.16)}$$

or expanding

$$\begin{cases} \sum_i x_{i0} d_i = \sum_k w_k \sum_i x_{ik} x_{i0} \\ \sum_i x_{i1} d_i = \sum_k w_k \sum_i x_{ik} x_{i1} \\ \qquad \vdots \\ \sum_i x_{iD} d_i = \sum_k w_k \sum_i x_{ik} x_{iD} \end{cases} \qquad \textbf{(1B.17)}$$

Notice that these equations are linear in the unknowns (the w_j), so they can be easily solved.

The normal equations can be written much more compactly with matrix notation (see Appendix A, Section 3). Let us define

$$R_{kj} = \frac{1}{N} \sum_i x_{ik} x_{ij} \qquad \textbf{(1.26)}$$

as the *autocorrelation* of the input samples for indices k and j. As you can see, the autocorrelation measures similarity across the samples of the training set. When $k = j$, **R** is just the sum of the squares of the input samples (the variance if the data is zero mean). When k differs from j, **R** measures the sum of the cross products for every possible combination of the indices. As we did for **w**, we will also put all these R_{kj} values into a matrix **R**, that is,

$$\mathbf{R} = \begin{bmatrix} R_{00} & \cdots & R_{0D} \\ \cdots & \cdots & \cdots \\ R_{D0} & \cdots & R_{DD} \end{bmatrix}$$

Thus we obtain pairwise information about the structure of the data set.

Let us call

$$P_j = \frac{1}{N} \sum_i x_{ij} d_i \tag{1.27}$$

the *cross-correlation* of the input x for index j and desired response d, which can also be put into a vector $\mathbf{p}$ of dimension $D+1$. P_j measures the similarity between the input x and the desired response d at shift j. Substituting these definitions in Eq. 1.25, the set of normal equations can be written simply

$$\mathbf{p} = \mathbf{R}\mathbf{w}^* \quad \text{or} \quad \mathbf{w}^* = \mathbf{R}^{-1}\mathbf{p} \tag{1.28}$$

where $\mathbf{w}$ is a vector with the $D+1$ weights w_i. $\mathbf{w}^*$ represents the value of the $D+1$ weights for the optimal (minimum) solution. $\mathbf{R}^{-1}$ denotes the inverse of the autocorrelation matrix (see Appendix A, Section 3.11). Equation 1.28 states that the solution of the multiple regression problem can be computed analytically as the product of the inverse of the autocorrelation matrix of the input samples and the cross-correlation vector between the input and the desired response. The least square solution for this problem yields

$$y = 1.353480 + 0.286191 x_1 - 0.004195 x_2$$

It is remarkable that we are able to write an equation that describes the relationship between the two variables when only measured data samples were given. This attests to the power of linear regression. But as for the single variable case, we still do not know how accurately the equation fits the data, that is, how much of the variance of the input is actually captured by the regression model. The multiple correlation coefficient r_m can also be defined in the multiple-dimensional case for a single output as

$$r_m = \sqrt{\frac{\mathbf{w}^{*T}\mathbf{U}_x\mathbf{d} - N\overline{d}^2}{\mathbf{d}^T\mathbf{d} - N\overline{d}^2}} \tag{1.29}$$

and measures the amount of variation explained by the linear regression, normalized by the variance of $\mathbf{d}$. In this expression $\mathbf{d}$ is the vector built from the desired responses d_i, and $\mathbf{U}$ is a matrix whose columns are the input data vectors. For this case $r_m = 0.68$, so there is a large portion of the variability that is not explained by the linear regression. (Either the process is nonlinear, or there are more variables involved.) We can still approximate the correlation coefficient for the multiple regression case by Eq. 1.15 after the system has adapted.

Multiple-Variable Correlation Coefficient

The idea of the correlation coefficient is the same for one or multiple dimensions. The equations get a little more complicated, since we are now working with an ensemble of input vectors, so the nice form of Eq. 1.8 has to be modified. An ensemble of vectors is better described as a matrix, so we are going to define a new matrix **U** as

$$\mathbf{U}_x = \begin{bmatrix} x_1^1 & \cdots & x_1^N \\ \cdots & \cdots & \cdots \\ x_D^1 & \cdots & x_D^N \end{bmatrix}$$

where each column is one of the input samples. We are likewise going to define a column vector **d** with all the desired responses (this is a vector for the single-output regression, otherwise it also becomes a matrix):

$$\mathbf{d} = \begin{bmatrix} d_1 \\ \cdots \\ d_N \end{bmatrix}$$

The total error variance can be written as

$$\boldsymbol{\varepsilon}^T \boldsymbol{\varepsilon} = \mathbf{d}^T \mathbf{d} - \mathbf{w}^{*T} \mathbf{U}_x \mathbf{d}$$

where **w*** is the set of optimal coefficients. This expression can be easily derived if the output of the regressor is substituted in the definition of the error [Dunteman, 1984]. The part of the error that is explained by the linear model is the second term. The variance of the output is expressed in the same way (just subtract the mean of the desired signal). Thus if we normalize this equation by the variance of the desired response, we get

$$r^2 = \frac{\mathbf{w}^{*T} \mathbf{U}_x \mathbf{d} - N\overline{d}^2}{\mathbf{d}^T \mathbf{d} - N\overline{d}^2}$$

which leads to the correlation coefficient for the multivariate case.

NEUROSOLUTIONS EXAMPLE 1.15

Multivariable regression

Moving to multi-dimensional inputs is very simple in NeuroSolutions. You simply change the input and desired files (for the new input data) and change the input Axon to accept two inputs. The rest is automatic. In this example we do all this for you using macros. Note that in the two-dimensional case the regression line is now a regression plane. In NeuroSolutions, there is not currently a good way of showing a plane in three dimensions, so we will not plot our regression plane. When we run the network, we will see that the learning curve (one of our only indications of whether the network is training correctly) decreases steadily and that the weights eventually approach the theoretical optimal weights.

The amazing thing about the adaptive system's methodology is that we changed the problem, but the technique to solve it did not change significantly. It is true that we have to dimension the system properly and choose new values for the step size, but the fundamental aspects of the methodology did not change at all.

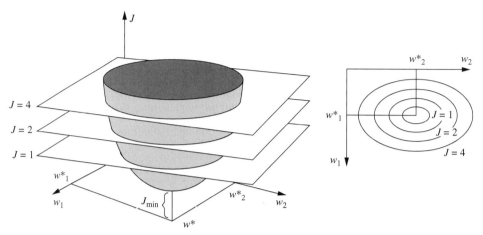

FIGURE 1-15 The performance surface for two dimensions and its contour plot

1.7.1 Setting the Problem as a Search Procedure

All the concepts previously mentioned for linear regression can be extended to the multiple regression case. The performance surface concept can be extended to multiple dimensions, making J a paraboloid in $D + 1$ dimensions, facing upward. (Figure 1-15 depicts the two weight-case.) J now involves matrix computations, but it remains a scalar quantity that is a quadratic function of the weights.

$$J = \left[0.5\mathbf{w}^T \mathbf{R} \mathbf{w} - \mathbf{p}^T \mathbf{w} + \sum_i \frac{d_i^2}{2N} \right] \tag{1.30}$$

where the superscript T means the transpose.

The coefficients that minimize the solution are

$$\nabla J = 0 = \mathbf{R}\mathbf{w}^* - \mathbf{p} \qquad \text{or} \qquad \mathbf{w}^* = \mathbf{R}^{-1}\mathbf{p} \tag{1.31}$$

which gives exactly the same solution as Eq. 1.28. In the space (w_1, w_2), J is a paraboloid facing upward.

Derivation of the Optimal Solution

Let us just take the derivative of J (Eq. 1.30) with respect to the weights, using matrix operations:

$$\frac{\partial J}{\partial \mathbf{w}} = 0.5\mathbf{R}\mathbf{w} + 0.5\mathbf{w}^T\mathbf{R} - \mathbf{p} = \mathbf{R}\mathbf{w} + \mathbf{R}^T\mathbf{w} - 2\mathbf{p} = 2\mathbf{R}\mathbf{w} - 2\mathbf{p}$$

since the transpose of **R** is equal to itself because of its Toeplitz structure. If we equate this to zero, we obtain the optimal weights:

$$\mathbf{w}^* = \mathbf{R}^{-1}\mathbf{p}$$

which is the equation in the text.

NEUROSOLUTIONS EXAMPLE 1.16

Checking the LMS solution with the optimal weights

Let us first consider a least square solution with only two weights, w_1 and w_2, since we can still compute it easily by hand. For the data set of Table 1-2, the autocorrelation matrix is (from Eq. 1.26)

$$\mathbf{R} = \frac{1}{15}\begin{bmatrix} 416 & 429 \\ 429 & 490 \end{bmatrix}$$

To determine the eigenvalues, we solve the equation

$$\det[\mathbf{R} - \lambda\mathbf{I}] = 0$$

which yields $\lambda_1 = 59$ and $\lambda_2 = 1.5$. From these results we can immediately see that the eigenvalue spread is roughly 40, so the performance surface paraboloid is very skewed (i.e., much narrower in one direction). The performance surface is shown in the following figure. Notice how it is very steep in one direction and very shallow

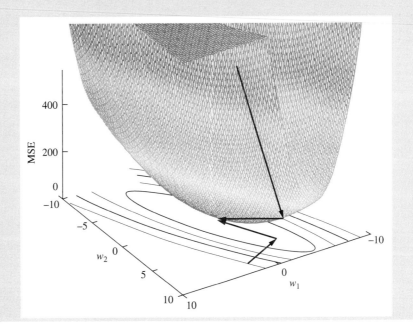

in the other. Thus, if we train the network with gradient descent, we would expect it to move very quickly down the steep slope at first and then to move slowly down the valley toward the optimum.

To compute the optimal solution, we first need to compute the cross-correlation vector (from Eq. 1.27):

$$\mathbf{p} = \frac{1}{15}\begin{bmatrix} 212 \\ 229 \end{bmatrix}$$

For the two-dimensional case it is still easy to solve for w_1 and w_2 by writing (from Eq. 1.28)

$$\begin{cases} 416w_1 + 429w_2 = 212 \\ 429w_1 + 490w_2 = 229 \end{cases}$$

which gives for optimal weights $w_1 = 0.2848$ and $w_2 = 0.2180$. The minimum J is 0.390. When we run the simulator with the Axon replacing the Bias Axon (no bias), the network weights approach these values.

Performance Surface Properties

The minimum value of the error can be obtained by substituting the optimal weight (Eq. 1.31) into the cost equation (Eq. 1.30), yielding

$$J_{\min} = \frac{1}{2}\left[\sum_i \frac{d_i^2}{N} - \mathbf{p}^T\mathbf{w}^*\right] \tag{1B.18}$$

We can rewrite the performance surface in terms of its minimum value and $\mathbf{w}^*$ as

$$J = J_{\min} + \frac{1}{2}(\mathbf{w} - \mathbf{w}^*)^T\mathbf{R}(\mathbf{w} - \mathbf{w}^*) \tag{1B.19}$$

For the one-dimensional case this equation is the same as Eq. 1B.10 (**R** becomes a scalar equal to the variance of the input). In the space (w_1, w_2) J is now a paraboloid facing upward. The shape of J is again solely dependent on the input data (through its autocorrelation function). One can show that

- The principal axes of the performance surface contours (surfaces of equal error) correspond to the *eigenvectors of the input correlation matrix* **R** *(see Appendix A)*.
- The eigenvalues of **R** give the rate of change of the gradient along the principal axis of the surface contours of J (Figure 1-16).

The eigenvectors and eigenvalues of the input autocorrelation matrix are all that matters to understand convergence of the gradient descent in multiple dimensions. The eigenvectors represent the natural (orthogonal) coordinate system to study the properties of **R**.

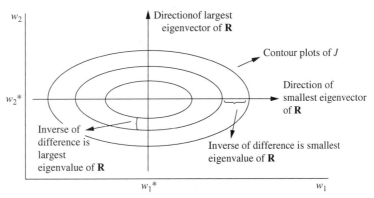

FIGURE 1-16 Contour plots of the performance surface with two weights

In fact, along these coordinates the convergence of the algorithm can be studied as a joint adaptation of several (one for each dimension of the space) unidimensional algorithms. Along each eigenvector direction (the axes of the ellipsoids) the algorithm behaves just like the one-variable case that we studied in the beginning of this chapter. The eigenvalue becomes the projection of the data onto that direction, just as λ in Eq. 1B.11 is the projection of the data on the weight direction. But in any other direction the adaptation is coupled.

The location of the performance surface in weight space depends on both the input and desired response (Eq. 1.31). The minimum error also depends on both (Eq. 1B.18). Multiple regression finds the location of the minimum of a paraboloid placed in an unknown position in weight space. The input distribution defines *the shape of the performance surface.* The input distribution and its relation with the desired response distribution define both the *value* of the minimum of the error and the *location in coefficient space* where that minimum occurs.

As in the one-dimensional case, the autocorrelation of the input ($\mathbf{R}$) completely specifies the shape of the performance surface (Eq. 1B.19). However, the location of the performance surface in the space of the weights (Eq. 1.31) and its minimum value (Eq. 1B.18) depend also on the desired response.

1.7.2 Steepest Descent for Multiple Weights

Gradient techniques can also be used to find the minimum of the performance surface, but now the gradient is a vector with $D + 1$ components

$$\nabla \mathbf{J} = \left[\frac{\partial J}{\partial w_0}, \ldots, \frac{\partial J}{\partial w_D} \right]^T \tag{1.32}$$

The extension of Eq. 1.11 is

$$\mathbf{w}(k + 1) = \mathbf{w}(k) - \eta \nabla \mathbf{J}(k) \tag{1.33}$$

where all quantities are vectors, that is, $\mathbf{w}(k) = [w_0(k), \ldots, w_D(k)]^T$. To calculate the largest step size η, we again rewrite the update equation in the form of (see the box "Derivation of Largest Step Size" and compare with Eq. 1B.14)

$$\mathbf{w}(k + 1) = (\mathbf{I} - \eta\mathbf{R})\mathbf{w}(k) + \eta\mathbf{R}\mathbf{w}^* \tag{1.34}$$

where $\mathbf{I}$ is the identity matrix, $\mathbf{R}$ is the input autocorrelation matrix, and $\mathbf{w}^*(k) = [w_0^*(k), \ldots, w_D^*(k)]^T$. The solution of this equation is *cross coupled;* that is, the way $\mathbf{w}$ converges to $\mathbf{w}^*$ depends on the behavior of the geometric progression in all the $D + 1$ directions. Therefore the simple picture of having $\mathbf{w}(k+1)$ converge to $\mathbf{w}^*$ with a single geometric ratio, as in the unidimensional case, has to be modified. One can show that the weights converge with different time constants, each related to an eigenvalue of $\mathbf{R}$.

Convergence for Multiple-Weights Case

One can show that the condition to guarantee convergence [Widrow and Stearns 1985] is

$$\lim_{k \to \infty} (\mathbf{I} - \eta\Lambda)^k = 0 \tag{1B.20}$$

where Λ is the eigenvalue matrix,

$$\Lambda = \begin{bmatrix} \lambda_0 & \cdots & 0 \\ \cdots & \cdots & \cdots \\ 0 & \cdots & \lambda_D \end{bmatrix} \tag{1B.21}$$

which means that in every principal direction of the performance surface (given by the eigenvectors of the input correlation matrix $\mathbf{R}$), we must have

$$0 < \eta < \frac{2}{\lambda_i} \tag{1B.22}$$

where λ_i is the corresponding eigenvalue. This equation also means that with a single η each weight $w_i(k)$ is approaching its optimal value w_i^* with a different time constant ("speed"), so the weight tracks bend, and the path is no longer a straight line toward the minimum.

This is the mathematical description of our earlier statement that the gradient descent algorithm behaves like many one-dimensional univariable algorithms along the eigenvector directions. Notice that Eq. 1B.21 is diagonal, so there is no cross coupling between time constants along the eigenvector directions.

In any other direction of the space there will be coupling. However, we can still decompose the overall weight tract as a combination of weight tracts along each eigendirection, as we did in Figure 1.16. Eq. 1B.22 shows that the step size along each direction obeys the same rule as the unidimensional case (Eq. 1.17).

1.7.3 Step Size Control

As we have seen, the set of values taken by the weight during adaptation is called the weight track. The weight moves in the opposite direction of the gradient at each point, so the weight track depicts the gradient direction at each point of the performance surface visited during adaptation. Therefore the gradient direction tells us about the performance surface shape. In particular, it is useful to construct the contour plot of J since the gradient has to be perpendicular to the lines that link points with the same J value. The contour plot provides a graphical construction for the gradient at each point of the performance surface.

Given a point in a contour, we take the tangent of the contour at that point. The gradient is perpendicular to the tangent, so the weights will move along the gradient line and point in the opposite direction. Likewise, if we run the adaptation algorithm with several initial conditions and we record the value of J at each point, we can determine the contour plots by taking ellipses that pass through the points of equal cost and are perpendicular to the weight tracks.

When the *eigenvalues* of **R** are the same (see Appendix A, Section 3.17), the contour plots are circular, and the gradient always points to the center, that is, to the minimum. In this case the gradient descent has only a single time constant as in the one-dimensional case. But this is an exceptional condition. In general, the eigenvalues of **R** will be different. When the eigenvalues are different, the weight track bends because it follows the direction of the gradient at each point, which is perpendicular to the contours (Figure 1-17). The gradient direction no longer points to the minimum, which means that the weight tracks will not be straight lines to the minimum. The adaptation will take longer for two reasons. First, a longer path to the minimum will be taken. Second, the step size must be decreased compared with the circular case. Let us address the step-size aspect further.

For guaranteed convergence the learning rate in each ith principal direction of the performance surface must be

$$0 < \eta < \frac{2}{\lambda_i} \tag{1.35}$$

where λ_i is the corresponding eigenvalue. The worst case condition to guarantee convergence to the optimal $\mathbf{w}^*$ in all directions is therefore

$$\eta < \frac{2}{\lambda_{\max}} \tag{1.36}$$

That is, the step size η must be smaller than the inverse of the largest eigenvalue of the autocorrelation matrix. Otherwise the iteration will diverge in one or more directions. Since the adaptation is coupled, divergence in one direction will cause the entire system to diverge.

In the early stages of adaptation the convergence is primarily along the direction of the largest eigenvalue, since the weight update along this direction will be bigger.

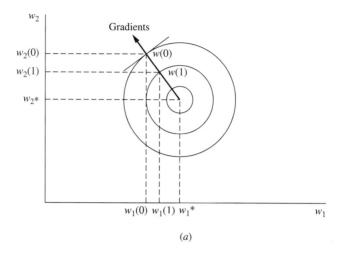

(a)

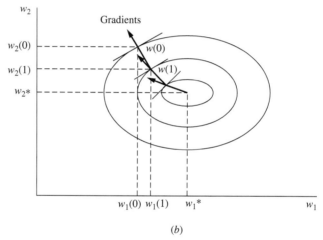

(b)

FIGURE 1-17 Weight track toward the minimum:
(a) equal eigenvalues; (b) unequal eigenvalues

On the other hand, toward the end of adaptation the algorithm will mainly adapt only the weight associated with the smallest eigenvalue (which corresponds to the smallest time constant). The time constant of adaptation is therefore

$$\tau = \frac{1}{\eta \lambda_{min}} \qquad (1.37)$$

An implication of this analysis is that when the *eigenvalue spread* of **R** is large, there will be very different time constants of adaptation in each direction. This reasoning gives a clear picture of the fundamental constraint of adapting the weights using gradient descent with a single step size η: The speed of adaptation is controlled by the smallest eigenvalue, while the largest step size is constrained by the inverse of the largest eigenvalue. This means that if the ratio between the largest and the smallest eigenvalues (the eigenvalue spread) is large, the convergence will be intrinsically slow. This problem cannot be avoided when only a single step size is used in the steepest descent.

The learning curve will approach $J_{\min}$ in a geometric progression as before. However, *there will be many different time constants of adaptation, one for each direction.* Initially, the learning curve will decrease at the rate of the largest eigenvalue, but toward the end of adaptation the rate of decrease of J is controlled by the time constant of the smallest eigenvalue.

Estimation of Eigenvalue Spread

The eigenvalue spread can be computed by an eigendecomposition of **R**, but this is a time-consuming operation and is hardly ever performed. An estimate of the eigenvalue spread for the multidimensional-data case is the ratio between the maximum and the minimum of the magnitude of the Fourier transform of the input data.

Alternatively, simple inspection of the correlation matrix of the input can provide an estimation of the time to find a solution. The best possible case is when **R** is diagonal, with equal values in the diagonal, because in this case the eigenvalue spread is 1 and the gradient descent travels in a straight line to the minimum. We cannot have a faster convergence than this, even when second-order methods (such as Newton's method, studied later) are used. When **R** is diagonal but with different values, the ratio of the largest number over the smallest is a good approximation to the eigenvalue spread. When **R** is fully populated, the analysis becomes much more difficult.

NEUROSOLUTIONS EXAMPLE 1.17

Visualizing the weight tracks and speed of adaptation

According to our previous calculations, the largest step size for convergence is (from Eq. 1.36) 3.3×10^{-2}. The critically damped mode along the largest eigenvector should be 1.6×10^{-2}. The time constant of adaptation for the largest step size is around 20 iterations (epochs for batch); that is, the convergence should take 80 epochs with this step size.

When we run the simulations, the algorithm converges first along the direction of the largest eigenvalue (largest eigenvector direction) and then along the direction of the smallest eigenvector. Since the eigenvalue spread is 40, the steps are much bigger along the largest eigenvector direction. If we look at the figure of Example 1.16, we can see that the weights converge perpendicular to the contour plots since this is the steepest descent path. As we will see, there are two distinct regions in the learning curve: In the beginning it is controlled by the geometric ratio along the largest eigenvector, while toward the end it is controlled by the geometric ratio of the smallest eigenvector.

> After running this example and observing the weight tracks, let us change the input data file to a data set with a smaller eigenvalue spread. Click the input file icon and bring up its Inspector by clicking the right mouse button. Remove the present input file, and add the file regression2a.asc from the *Data\ Chapters\ CH1* folder on the CD-ROM.
>
> The modification was made only in the variable x_2; all the rest is the same. Respond to the panel *associate* by clicking on the *close* button. In the *customize* panel, skip the desired signal, and click on *close*. You have just modified the input data to this example. This new file has a much smaller eigenvalue spread, so we can expect that the weight tracks are basically straight lines to the minimum. Compute the new eigenvalue spread, and adjust the learning rates so that the convergence is as fast as possible.

1.7.4 The LMS Algorithm for Multiple Weights

It is straightforward to extend the gradient estimation given by the LMS algorithm from one dimension to many dimensions. We just apply the instantaneous gradient estimate Eq. 1.12 to each element of Eq. 1.33. The LMS for multiple dimensions reads

$$\mathbf{w}(k + 1) = \mathbf{w}(k) + \eta \varepsilon(k)\mathbf{x}(k) \qquad \textbf{(1.38)}$$

An interesting feature is that the LMS *adaptation rule still uses local computations;* that is, for the ith weight we can write

$$w_i(k + 1) = w_i(k) + \eta \varepsilon(k)x_i(k) \qquad \textbf{(1.39)}$$

Note that although the analysis of the gradient descent techniques became complex, the LMS algorithm itself is still very simple. This is one reason why LMS is so widely used. But since LMS is a steepest-descent algorithm, the analysis and discussions concerning the largest step size for convergence and coupling of modes also apply to the LMS algorithm.

NEUROSOLUTIONS EXAMPLE 1.18

Visualizing weight tracks with on-line learning

In this example we configure the Backprop Controller to on-line learning to implement the LMS algorithm. Notice that the weight tracks follow basically the same path as before, but now the path is much more irregular due to the sample-by-sample update of the weights. When the eigenvalue spread is very large (the performance surface is very steep in one direction and shallow in others), the problem is difficult for LMS to solve. Any small perturbation in the smallest eigenvector direction gets amplified by the large eigenvalue spread.

1.7.5 Multiple Regression with Bias

Up to now we have implemented and solved analytically the multiple regression problem without bias. The reason for this is only for simplicity. With two weights we can still easily solve the multiple regression case by hand; however, if the bias is added, we must do the computations with three parameters. The simulations are transparent to these difficulties, since we just substitute the Axon by a Bias Axon. Note that the largest step size between the two cases differs since the input data is effectively changed if we interpret the bias as a weight connected to an extra constant input of one. Hence the autocorrelation function and its eigenvalue spread change.

We should state that the use of a bias is called the full least square solution, and it is the recommended way to apply least squares. The reason can be understood easily: When a bias is utilized in the PE, the regression line is not restricted to pass through the origin of the space, and smaller errors normally are achieved. There are two equivalent ways to solve the full least squares problem for D input variables:

- The input and desired responses need to be modified so that they become zero-mean variables. (This is called the deviation or z scores.) In this case a D weight regression will effectively solve the original problem. The bias b is computed indirectly by

$$b = \bar{d} - \sum_{i=1}^{N} w_i \bar{x}_i$$

where w_i are the optimal weights and the bars represent mean values.
- Alternatively, the input matrix has to be extended with an extra column of 1s (the first column). This transforms $\mathbf{R}$ into a $(D+1) \times (D+1)$ matrix, which introduces a $D + 1$ weight in the solution (the bias).

NEUROSOLUTIONS EXAMPLE 1.19

Linear regression without bias

We will now substitute a Bias Axon for the Axon in the previous Breadboard. This will effectively provide the regression solution without constraining the regression plane to pass through the origin. We see that the weight tracks are very similar in the beginning but that the error continues to drop, and the weights advance toward the $w_1 = 0$ line. This means that the optimal solution changed. We now have a better solution than before but with increased complexity of the performance surface (four dimensions instead of three) and an increased number of adjustable parameters in our system (two weights and a bias).

1.7.6 The LMS Algorithm in Practice

We can use some rules of thumb to choose the step size in the LMS algorithm. The step size should be normalized by the variance of the input data estimated by the trace of **R**.

$$\eta = \frac{\eta_0}{tr(\mathbf{R})} \tag{1.40}$$

where $\eta_0 = 0.1$ to 0.01. This normalization by the input variance was the original rule proposed by Widrow to adapt the Adaline. We can expect the algorithm to converge (settling time) in a number of iterations k given by four times the time constant of adaptation:

$$k \approx 4\tau_{\mathrm{mse}} = \frac{2}{\eta\lambda_{\min}} \tag{1.41}$$

The LMS algorithm has a misadjustment that is basically one half the trace of **R** times η:

$$M = \frac{\eta}{2}tr(\mathbf{R}) \tag{1.42}$$

When the eigenvalues are equal, the misadjustment can be approximated by

$$M \approx \frac{D+1}{4\tau_{\mathrm{mse}}}$$

which allows us to give the following rule of thumb: The misadjustment equals the number of weights divided by the settling time, or equivalently, selecting η so that it produces 10 percent misadjustment means a training duration in iterations of 10 times the number of inputs.

1.8 NEWTON'S METHOD

If you are familiar with numerical analysis, you may be asking why we aren't using Newton's method for the search. Newton's method is known to find the roots of quadratic equations in one iteration. The minimum of the performance surface can be equated to the root of the gradient equation Eq. 1.32, as outlined by Eq. 1.31. Hence Newton's method can also be used in the search. The adaptive weight equation using Newton's method is

$$\mathbf{w}(k+1) = \mathbf{w}(k) - \mathbf{R}^{-1}\nabla\mathbf{J}(k) \tag{1.43}$$

Compare this with Eq. 1.33 and note that the gradient information is weighted by the inverse of the correlation matrix of the input and that η is equal to 1. This means that Newton's method corrects the direction of the search so that it always points to

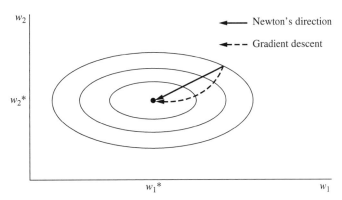

FIGURE 1-18 Directions of the steepest descent and Newton's method

the minimum, while the gradient descent points to the maximum direction of change. These two directions may or may not coincide (Figure 1-18).

They coincide when the contour plots are circles, that is, when the largest and the smallest eigenvalue of the correlation matrix are the same. When the ratio of the largest to the smallest eigenvalue (*the eigenvalue spread*) increases, the slope of the performance surface in the two directions differs more and more. Thus for large eigenvalue spreads the optimization path taken by gradient descent is normally much longer than the path taken by Newton's method. This implies that Newton's method will be faster than LMS when the input data correlation matrix has a large eigenvalue spread.

Newton's Derivation

The equation can be easily proved if we recall the gradient of the performance surface:

$$\nabla J = \mathbf{R}\mathbf{w} - \mathbf{p}$$

Left-multiply by $\mathbf{R}^{-1}$ to obtain

$$\mathbf{R}^{-1}\mathbf{p} = \mathbf{w} - \mathbf{R}^{-1}\nabla J$$

and then substitute in the optimal solution (Eq. 1.28) to obtain

$$\mathbf{w}^* = \mathbf{w} - \mathbf{R}^{-1}\nabla J$$

From this equation we can derive the incremental equation presented previously.

Another advantage of Newton's method versus the steepest descent method is in the time constant of adaptation. When the gradient is multiplied by $\mathbf{R}^{-1}$, not only is the direction of the gradient being changed, but also *the different eigenvalues in each direction are being equalized.* What this means is that Newton's method is automatically correcting the time constant of adaptation for each direction so that *all the weights converge at the same rate.* Hence Newton's method has a single time constant of adaptation, unlike the steepest descent method.

These advantages of Newton's method should not come as a surprise, because Newton's method uses much more information about the performance surface (the curvature). In fact, to implement Newton's method, you need to compute the inverse of the correlation matrix, which takes significantly longer than the single multiplication required by the LMS method and also requires global information. Newton's method is also brittle; that is, if the surface is not exactly quadratic, the method may diverge. This is the reason Newton's method is normally modified to also include a small step size η instead of using $\eta = 1$ as in Eq. 1.43.

$$\mathbf{w}(k + 1) = \mathbf{w}(k) + \eta \mathbf{R}^{-1} \varepsilon(k) \mathbf{x}(k) \qquad (1.44)$$

Note that $\mathbf{x}(k)$ is a vector and $\mathbf{R}^{-1}$ is a matrix, so the update for one weight influences all the other inputs in the system. This is the reason that the computations are no longer local to each weight. However, they are not difficult if one assumes that the inverse of $\mathbf{R}$ is known a priori. The algorithm of Eq. 1.44 is called the LMS/Newton algorithm. The case where $\mathbf{R}^{-1}$ has to be estimated on-line is much more involved and leads to the recursive least squares (RLS) algorithm.

Alternatively, to improve convergence speed with the LMS, we can implement an orthogonalizing transformation of the input correlation function followed by an equalization of the eigenvalues, which is called a whitening transformation (see Appendix A, Section 3.18). Since Newton's method coincides with the steepest descent for performance surfaces that are symmetric, this preprocessing will make the LMS perform as Newton's method.

NEUROSOLUTIONS EXAMPLE 1.20

Newton's method

In this example we implement Newton's method with a custom DLL. For this example we must compute $\mathbf{R}^{-1}$ and apply Eq. 1.44 to the simulator. The autocorrelation function for this example is

$$\mathbf{R} = \frac{1}{15} \begin{bmatrix} 416 & 429 \\ 429 & 490 \end{bmatrix}$$

so $\mathbf{R}^{-1}$ becomes (see Section A.3.11)

$$\mathbf{R}^{-1} = 15 \begin{bmatrix} 0.0247 & -0.0217 \\ -0.0217 & 0.0210 \end{bmatrix}$$

By applying Newton's method to the learning algorithm, we have essentially compensated for the eigenvalue spread. This means that Newton's method behaves as the steepest descent for a circular performance surface where the steepest descent direction always points directly to the optimal value. Thus, although the calculations are more complicated and more demanding (we need to know $\mathbf{R}^{-1}$), the convergence is much faster (in fact, the algorithm can converge in one epoch). When we run the simulator, notice that no matter where the algorithm starts, it always heads directly toward the optimum.

1.9 ANALYTIC VERSUS ITERATIVE SOLUTIONS

Selecting a search procedure to find the optimal weights is a drastic conceptual change from the analytic least square solution, albeit an equivalent procedure. In learning systems the iterative solution is the most common for several reasons.

When working with learning systems, the interest is very often in on-line solutions, that is, solutions that can be implemented sample-by-sample. The analytic solution requires data to be available beforehand to compute the autocorrelation matrix $\mathbf{R}$ and cross-correlation vector $\mathbf{p}$. Fast computers are required to crank out the solution (the inverse of $\mathbf{R}$ and the product with $\mathbf{p}$). The method produces a value that immediately gives the best possible performance. But several problems may surface when applying the analytic approach. If the matrix $\mathbf{R}$ is *ill conditioned,* the computation of $\mathbf{R}^{-1}$ may not be very accurate. Moreover, the analytic solution also requires a great deal of computation time. [Computation of a matrix inverse is proportional to the square of the number of columns D of the matrix. In the big O notation this means $O(D^2)$.]

The iterative solution is not free from shortcomings. We already saw that there is no guarantee that the solution is close to the optimal weight $\mathbf{w}^*$ when all the input samples are used by the algorithm. This depends on the data and on a judicious selection of the step size η. The accuracy of the iterative solution is not directly dependent on the condition number of $\mathbf{R}$, but matrices with large eigenvalue spread produce slow convergence because the gradient-descent adaptation is coupled. As we said previously, the slowest mode controls the speed of adaptation, while the largest step size is constrained by the largest eigenvalue.

The great appeal of the iterative approach to optimization is that *very efficient algorithms exist* to estimate the gradient (e.g., the LMS algorithm). Only two multiplications per weight are necessary, so the computation scales proportionally to the number of weights D [i.e., $O(D)$ time]. Moreover, *the method can be readily extended to nonlinear systems,* while the analytic approach for most cases of practical relevance cannot be computed.

1.10 THE LINEAR REGRESSION MODEL

We started this chapter by pointing out the advantages of building models from experimental data. In the previous sections we developed a set of techniques that adapt the parameters of a linear system (the Adaline) to fit the relationship between the input (x)

and the desired data (d) as well as possible. This is our first model, and it explains the relationship $f(x, d)$ as a hyperplane that minimizes the square distance of the residuals. We will have the opportunity to study other (nonlinear) models in later chapters.

It is instructive to stop and ask the question: How can we use the newly developed regression model? One interesting aspect of model building that we mentioned previously is the ability to *predict* the behavior of the experimental system. Basically, what this means is that once the Adaline is trained, we can forecast the value of d when x is available. We do this by computing the system output y and assume that the error ε is small (Eq. 1.3). You can now understand why we want to minimize the square of the error, since if the square of the error is small, d is going to be close to y in the training data. Figure 1-19 shows a productive way of looking at the input-output pairs that we used to train the Adaline.

We assume that the experimental system produces the desired response d for each input x according to a rule that we do not know. The purpose of building the model is to approximate as well as possible this hidden relationship.

We expect also that even for x values that the system did not use for training, y is going to be close to the corresponding unknown value d. Our intuition tells us that if

- the data used for training covered all the possible cases well,
- we had enough training data, and
- the correlation coefficient is close to 1,

then in fact y should be close to the unknown value d. However, this is an inductive principle, which has no guarantee of being true. The ability to extrapolate the good performance from the training set to the test set is called *generalization*. Generalization is a central issue in the adaptive systems approach since it is the only guarantee that the model will perform well with the future data that will be presented to the system while in operation.

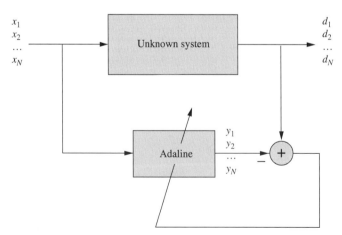

FIGURE 1-19 A view of the desired response as the output of an unknown model

Remember that in the test mode the system parameters must be kept constant; that is, the learning algorithm must be disabled. In the next section we familiarize ourselves with training and using the linear model.

1.10.1 Regression Project

Getting Real-World Data We end Chapter 1 by giving you a flavor of the power of linear regression to solve real-life problems. We will go to the World Wide Web and seek real data sets, import them into NeuroSolutions, and solve regression problems. We will use the Breadboard from Example 1.7.

The first thing is to decide on the data with which we will work. There are many interesting Web sites to visit in the search for data. We suggest the following sites:

climate data: http://ferret.wrc.noaa.gov/fbin/climate_server

http://seamonkey.ed.asu.edu/~behrens/teach/WWW_data.html

These sites have plenty of data (some duplicated). We assume that you know how to connect to the Web and how to download data. You should get the data in ASCII and store it in column format, with one of the variables (the independent variable) in the input file and the dependent variable in the output file. Alternatively, we have provided sample data on the CD-ROM under the Data directory. Read the *readme* file to choose the data sets that interest you.

NeuroSolutions Project The fundamental question is to find out how well a linear relation explains the dependence between the input data and the desired data. We will exemplify the project with a one-dimensional set of input data, but the multidimensional case is similar.

The first thing to do is to modify the NeuroSolutions breadboard so that it will be able to work with the data you downloaded. The data should be stored in an ASCII file and formatted in columns. Right-click on the input file icon and select *properties*. The Inspector will appear on the screen. Remove the present file (click the *remove* button), and click the *add* button. The Windows file inspector will appear; open the file that contains the input data, that is, the input to your linear model.

In NeuroSolutions, the *associate* panel appears, which you can close (we assume that the input file has ASCII data in column format). The next panel that pops open is the *customize* panel. Here you select the columns that you want to use (for those columns that you do not want, select the column label and click the *skip* button), and then click the *close* button. The input file is now open and ready to be used by NeuroSolutions. You should repeat the procedure for the desired data file. Make sure that the number of samples in the input and desired data files are the same.

Another thing that we should do is to normalize the data. Sometimes the input and desired variables have very different ranges, so we should always normalize both the desired and input data files between 0 (or -1) and 1. To do this, go to the *stream* page (click on the *stream* tab) of the Inspector to access the *normalization* panel. Click the *normalize* check box and set the normalization range.

We always recommend that you visually check the data—either with a plotting program or the Scatter Plot in NeuroSolutions—to ensure that there aren't any outliers present in the data. When outliers exist, they may distort any possible linear relationship that may exist.

Once the data sets are open, we can effectively start the adaptation of the linear regressor. The first important consideration is the largest step size that can be used for convergence. When the data is normalized, we can always guess an initial value of 0.1. By plotting the learning curve or the weight tracks (if the problem has few input channels), we can judge how appropriate this value might be. Alternatively, we can compute the eigenvalues and find the exact largest possible step size, but this is rarely done. The trial-and-error method is OK for small problems.

If the problem takes a long time to converge and increasing the step size creates instability, then the eigenvalue spread is large, and there is little we can do short of using Newton's method.

After the algorithm converges (the error stabilizes), we should use the correlation coefficient DLL to estimate the correlation coefficient. Note that it is always possible to pass a hyperplane through some data points, but the real issue is whether the hyperplane provides a good model. To answer this question, we need to estimate the correlation coefficient.

For the multiple-variable regression case, the relative weight magnitude tells us about the relative importance of each variable in the regression equation (for normalized inputs). It is therefore interesting to look at the values of the regression weights, including the bias. Remember that if the data is normalized, the displayed weight values must be "unnormalized" in order to compare them with the original data. You can find the values that NeuroSolutions used to normalize the data by going to the *dataset* page of the Inspector and opening the normalization file. NeuroSolutions multiplies the data set by the first value (range) in the normalization file and adds the second value (offset) in the normalization file. To reverse this process, you must subtract the second value and then divide by the first value.

Remember that the parameters of the regression equation can be used to predict the system output when only the input is known. We can do this by testing the system with another data file for which we do not have a desired response. To do this in Neuro-Solutions, you should go to the Controller Inspector (the yellow dial) and turn off the *learning* check box; this fixes the weights.

No problem is finalized without a critical assessment of the results obtained. You should start with a hypothesis about the data relationship and confirm your hypothesis with NeuroSolutions results. If there is a discrepancy between what you expect and the results, you must explain it. This is where the NeuroSolutions probes are very effective. You should verify that the data is being properly read, whether the input and output files are synchronized, whether the system (weight tracks, learning curve) is converging, and so on. Computers are great tools, but they are very susceptible to the "garbage in, garbage out" syndrome so it is the user's responsibility to check the input and the methodology of data analysis.

NEUROSOLUTIONS EXAMPLE 1.21

Linear regression project

We will illustrate the project with a regression between two time series: the sea temperature and atmospheric pressure downloaded from the NOAA site (climate database). We start with the Breadboard from Example 1.7. We replace the input with the file containing the sea temperature and replace the desired response data with the file containing the pressure data. NeuroSolutions automatically sets the number of inputs from the file (verify this in the File Inspector) and the number of exemplars in an epoch. (Verify this in the Controller Inspector). We also have to decide how many iterations we need. In the Controller Inspector enter 1,000 in the *epochs/run* field. This number may be too large, but when the weights and MSE stabilize, we can always interrupt the simulation. Experiment with everything we have learned in this chapter.

1.11 CONCLUSIONS

In this first chapter we introduced ideas that are very important for the rest of the book. Probably the most important was the concept of adaptive systems. Instead of designing the system through specifications, we let the system learn from the input data. To achieve this, the system has to be augmented with an external cost criterion that measures how well the model fits the data, and with an algorithm that will adapt the system parameters so that the minimum of the cost can be reached. We will use this concept throughout this book.

We covered much more in this chapter. We described an extremely simple and elegant algorithm that is able to minimize the external cost function by using local information available to the system parameters. The principle is to search the performance surface in the opposite direction of the gradient. The name of the algorithm is least mean squares (LMS), and in just two multiplications per weight and data sample it is able to move the system parameters towards the neighborhood of the optimal values. Gradient descent is a powerful concept that we will also use throughout this book.

When we apply the LMS to the linear network, we end up with a system called the linear regressor, or Adaline, that can fit hyperplanes to data. The solution is identical to least squares.

We quantified the properties of the LMS algorithm, and we showed the fundamental trade-off of adaptation: the compromise between speed of adaptation and precision in the final solution. We defined the learning curve, which we called the thermometer of learning, that we will also use over and over. Therefore this chapter covers the basic concepts for the intriguing adventure of designing systems that learn directly from data.

We have also provided a project to help you understand the power of adaptive systems. The applications of the Adaline are bounded by our imagination and the data we can find to train it. Thus, knowing how to get data from the Web and how to use it in NeuroSolutions is of great value.

1.12 EXERCISES

1.1 (a) Compute by hand the linear regressor for the following data:

$$X = \{-0.5, -0.2, -0.1, 0.3, 0.4, 0.5, 0.7\}$$
$$D = \{-1, 1, 2, 3.2, 3.5, 5, 6\}$$

(b) Compute the correlation coefficient.

(c) Estimate d for the values $x = 0$ and $x = 1$. Which d can you trust the most? Justify your answer.

(d) Use NeuroSolutions to confirm your results.

1.2 For the data of Problem 1.1, compute the performance surface and plot it. Estimate the gradient at the point $w = 2$.

1.3 (a) Compute the linear regression for the following data:

$$X_1 = \{-0.5, -0.2, -0.1, 0.3, 0.4, 0.5, 0.7\}$$
$$X_2 = \{3, 3, 2.5, 2, -1, -1, -4\}$$
$$D = \{-3, -1, 0, 1.2, 1.5, 3, 4\}$$

(b) Use NeuroSolutions to confirm your results.

1.4 Find the eigenvalues and eigenvectors of the following matrix:

$$\mathbf{R} = \begin{bmatrix} 3 & 1 \\ 1 & 3 \end{bmatrix}$$

1.5 Show that when you apply Eq. 1.5 to data that is Gaussian distributed, you effectively obtain a set of linear equations.

1.6 Rerun Example 1.8 with white noise that has a mean value of $m = 0.5$ and explain the results.

1.7 Show mathematically that Eq. 1.14 will always give a value of $|g| < 1$.

1.8 For the data set in Problem 1.3, estimate the largest step size, the critically damped step size, and the time constant of adaptation for each step size.

Run NeuroSolutions and verify your results by plotting the weight tracks. Also verify the time constant of adaptation. For which value does the system adapt the fastest?

1.9 If you know the eigenvalues of the input autocorrelation function, would you schedule the step size for fast adaptation? Justify your answer. Run NeuroSolutions to confirm your conclusion.

1.10 Verify in the data of Problem 1.3 the statement of Section 1.6.5 that when the step size is very large in on-line learning, the MSE in NeuroSolutions can decrease below the theoretical limit. Plot the weight tracks and comment on the validity of the model.

1.11 Compute the largest eigenvalue for the data of Problem 1.3, but now use a regressor with bias. Show all the work. What can you conclude about the largest step size for the bias?

1.12   Apply Newton's search to the data of Problem 1.3 and compare the speed of adaptation with LMS. You should use NeuroSolutions.

1.13   Go to the Data directory and open the folder Auto MPG. Read the instructions and determine the regression equation. Make sure the system is converging. What is the estimated misadjustment for the solution? How would you obtain a better linear fit? Compute also the correlation coefficient and discuss the applicability of your model.

1.14   Repeat Problem 1.13 with the data found in the folder Abalone.

1.15   Construct the NeuroSolutions Breadboard for Problem 1.13 from scratch, that is, one component at a time.

1.13   NEUROSOLUTIONS EXAMPLES

1.1   The linear processing element in NeuroSolutions

1.2   Computing the MSE for the linear PE

1.3   Finding the minimum error by trial and error

1.4   Plotting the performance surface

1.5   Comparison of performance curves for different data sets

1.6   Adapting the linear PE with LMS

1.7   Batch versus on-line adaptation

1.8   Robustness of LMS to noise

1.9   Estimating the correlation coefficient during learning

1.10   The learning curve

1.11   Weight tracks

1.12   Linear regression without bias

1.13   Rattling

1.14   Scheduling of step sizes

1.15   Multivariable regression

1.16   Checking the LMS solution with the optimal weights

1.17   Visualizing the weight tracks and speed of adaptation

1.18   Visualizing weight tracks with on-line learning

1.19   Linear regression without bias

1.20   Newton's method

1.21   Linear regression project

1.14 CONCEPT MAP FOR CHAPTER 1

REFERENCES

Casti, J. L., *Alternate Realities: Mathematical Models of Nature and Man,* Wiley, 1989.

Dunteman, G., *Introduction to Linear Models,* Sage Publications, 1984.

Haykin, *Adaptive Filter Theory,* Prentice Hall, 1996.

Melsa, J., and D. Cohn, *Decision and Estimation Theory,* McGraw-Hill, 1978.

Widrow, B., and S. Stearns, *Adaptive Signal Processing* (Chapter 4), Prentice Hall, 1985.

CHAPTER 2

PATTERN RECOGNITION

The goal of this chapter is to provide a basic understanding of the following concepts:

- Statistical pattern recognition
- Training of classifiers

2.1   THE PATTERN-RECOGNITION PROBLEM

The human ability to find patterns in the external world is ubiquitous. It is at the core of our ability to respond in a more systematic and reliable manner to external stimuli. Humans do it effortlessly, but the mathematics underlying the analysis and design of pattern-recognition machines are still in their infancy. In the 1930s R. A. Fisher[1] laid out the mathematical principles of statistical *pattern-recognition,* which is one of the most rigorous ways to formulate the problem.

[1]R. Fisher was a British statistician who in the late 1920s proposed the use of the maximum likelihood principle to solve the discriminant analysis problem (i.e., a rule to distinguish between sets of data).

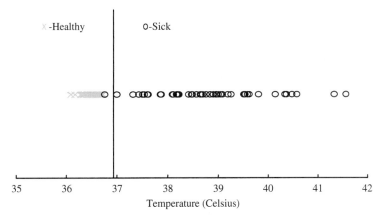

FIGURE 2-1   The sick–healthy problem in pattern space

A real-world example will elucidate the principles of statistical pattern-recognition at work: Assume that body temperature is used as an indicator of the health of a patient. Experience shows that in the healthy state the body regulates its temperature near 37°C (98.6°F; the low end of normality will not be considered for the sake of simplicity). With viral or bacterial infections the body temperature rises. Any measurement can be thought of as a point in a space called the *pattern space*, or the input space (one-dimensional in our example). If we plot the temperature of individuals on a line (Figure 2-1), we can verify that the region close to 37°C is assigned to healthy individuals and the higher-temperature region is assigned to sick individuals. This natural distribution of points leads to the definition of *classes*, or category regions, in pattern space. The goal of pattern-recognition is to build machines, called *classifiers*, that will automatically assign measurements to classes.

A natural way to make the class assignment is to define the boundary temperature between sick and healthy individuals. This boundary is called the *decision surface*. The decision surface is not trivially determined for many real-world problems. If we start measuring the temperature of healthy subjects with a thermometer, we will soon find out that individual temperatures vary from subject to subject and change for the same subject depending on the hour of the day, the subject's state (e.g., at rest or after exercise), and so on. The same variability occurs in sick individuals (aggravated by the seriousness and type of illness), and there may be overlap between the temperature of sick and healthy individuals. Thus we immediately see that the central problem in pattern-recognition is to define the shape and placement of the boundary so that the class-assignment errors are minimized.

2.1.1 Can Regression Be Used for Pattern-Recognition?

In Chapter 1 we presented a methodology that builds adaptive machines with the goal of fitting hyperplanes to data points. A legitimate question is to ask whether regression can be used to solve the problem of separating data into classes. The answer is no because the goals are very different.

- In regression both the input data and desired response are experimental variables (normally real numbers) created by a single, unknown, underlying mechanism.
- The goal in regression is to find the parameters of the best linear approximation to the input and the desired response pairs.

The regression problem is therefore one of representing the relationship between the input and the desired response.

In classification the issue is very different. We accept a priori that different input data may be generated by different mechanisms and that the goal is to separate the data as well as possible into classes. The desired response is a set of arbitrary labels (a different integer is normally assigned to each one of the classes), so every element of a class will share the same label. Class assignments are mutually exclusive, so a classifier needs a nonlinear mechanism such as an all-or-nothing switch. At a high level of abstraction, both the classification and the regression problems seek systems that transform inputs into desired responses, but the details of the mappings are rather different in the two cases.

We can nevertheless use the machinery utilized in linear regression, the Adaline and the LMS rule, as pieces to build pattern classifiers. Let us see how we can do this in NeuroSolutions and what the results are.

NEUROSOLUTIONS EXAMPLE 2.1
Comparing regression and classification

Suppose we are given the healthy and sick data, and we arbitrarily assign the value 1 as the desired system response to the healthy class and -1 as the desired response to the sick class. With these assignments we can train the Adaline of Chapter 1 to fit the input–desired response pairs.

The important question is to find out what the solution means. Notice that for equal numbers of sick and healthy cases, the regression line intersects the temperature line at the mean temperature of the overall data set (healthy and sick cases), which is the centroid of the observations. The regression line is not directly useful for classification. However, one can place a threshold function at the output of the Adaline such that when its output is positive, the response will be 1 (healthy), and when it is negative, the response is -1 (sick).

Now we have a classifier, but this does not change the fact that the placement of the regression line was dictated by the linear fit of the data and not by the requirement to separate the two classes as well as possible to minimize the classification errors. With the arrangement of an Adaline followed by a threshold, we have created our first classifier. But how can we improve its performance, estimate the optimal error rate, and extend it to multiple classes?

The Adaline can be applied for classification when the system topology is extended with a threshold as a decision device. However, there is no guarantee of good performance, because the coefficients are being adapted to fit (in the least square sense) the temperature data to the labels 1 and -1 and not to minimize the classification error. This is an especially simple example with only two classes. For the multiple-class case the results become even more fragile. The conclusion is that we need a new methodology to study and design accurate classifiers. The algorithms we developed in Chapter 1, however, will be the basis for much of our future work. All the concepts—learning curves, rattling, step sizes, and so on—will be applicable.

2.2 STATISTICAL FORMULATION OF CLASSIFIERS

2.2.1 Optimal Decision Boundary Based on Statistical Models of Data

The healthy–sick classification problem can be modeled in the following way: Assume that temperature is a random variable (i.e., a quantity governed by probabilistic laws) generated by two different phenomena, health and sickness, and further assume a *probability density function* (pdf) for each phenomenon (usually a Gaussian distribution). From the temperature measurements we can obtain the statistical parameters needed to fit the assumed pdf to the data (for Gaussians only the mean and variance need to be estimated; see Appendix A). Statistical decision theory proposes very general principles to construct the *optimal classifier*. Fisher showed that the optimal classifier chooses the class c_i that maximizes the *a posteriori probability* $P(c_i|x)$ that the given sample x belongs to the class; that is, x belongs to class c_i if

$$P(c_i|x) > P(c_j|x) \quad \text{for all } j \neq i \tag{2.1}$$

The problem is that the a posteriori probability cannot be measured directly. However, using Bayes' rule,

$$P(c_i|x) = \frac{p(x|c_i)P(c_i)}{P(x)} \tag{2.2}$$

one can compute the a posteriori probability from $P(c_i)$, the *prior probability* of the classes, multiplied by $p(x|c_i)$, the *likelihood* that the data x was produced by class c_i and normalized by the probability of $P(x)$. Both $P(c_i)$ and the likelihood can be estimated from the collected data and the assumption of the pdf. $P(x)$ is a normalizing factor that can be left out in most classification cases.

Understanding Bayes' Rule

There are two types of probabilities associated with an event: the a priori and the a posteriori probabilities. Suppose that the event is "x belongs to class c_1." The a priori probability is evaluated prior to any measurements. Without a value for x, the a priori probability is defined by the relative frequency of the classes, which is $P(c_1)$. However, we can also estimate the probability of the event after making some measurements. For a given x we can ask, What is the probability that x belongs to class c_1, denoted by $P(c_1|x)$. This is the a posteriori probability.

According to statistical pattern recognition, what matters for classification are the a posteriori probabilities $P(c_i|x)$, but they are generally unknown. Bayes' rule provides a way to estimate the a posteriori probabilities. In fact, Eq. 2.2 tells us that we can compute the a posteriori probability by multiplying the a priori probability for the class, $P(c_i)$, with the likelihood that the data was produced by class i. The likelihood $p(x|c_i)$ is the conditional of the data given the class; that is, if the class is c_i, what is the likelihood that the sample x is produced by the class? The likelihood can be estimated from the data by assuming a probability density function (pdf). Normally the pdf is the Gaussian distribution. Using Bayes' rule, we thus have a way to estimate a posteriori probabilities from data.

For our example $i = 1, 2$ (healthy, sick), and $P(c_i)$ can be estimated from the demographics, season, and so on. Figure 2-1 shows data from 100 cases. The likelihoods $p(x|c_i)$ can be estimated assuming a Gaussian distribution,

$$p(x) = \frac{1}{\sqrt{2\pi}\sigma} \exp\left(-\frac{1}{2}\left(\frac{(x-\mu)^2}{\sigma^2}\right)\right) \tag{2.3}$$

and estimating the means μ_i and standard deviations σ_i of the distributions for sick and healthy individuals from the data. Using the sample mean and variance (N is the number of measurements)

$$\mu = \frac{1}{N}\sum_{i=1}^{N} x_i \qquad \sigma^2 = \frac{1}{N}\sum_{i=1}^{N}(x_i - \mu)^2 \tag{2.4}$$

for this data set gives the results in Table 2-1.

The separation boundary, that is, the temperature $x = T$ for which the two a posteriori probabilities are identical, can be computed for the one-dimensional case with simple algebra. In this case the optimal threshold is $T = 37°C$ (Figure 2-2). It is rather easy to optimally classify healthy–sick cases using this methodology. Given a temperature x

TABLE 2-1   Statistical Measures for Figure 2-1 Data

Temperature	100 measurements	1,000 measurements
Healthy	Mean = 36.49 Standard deviation = 0.14	Mean = 36.50 Standard deviation = 0.15
Sick	Mean = 38.83 Standard deviation = 1.05	Mean = 39.00 Standard deviation = 1

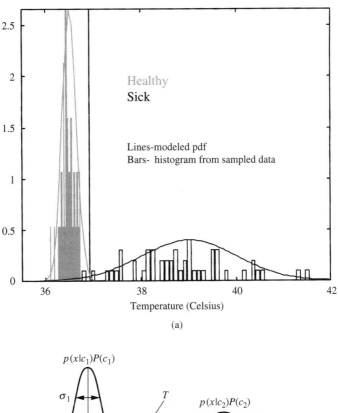

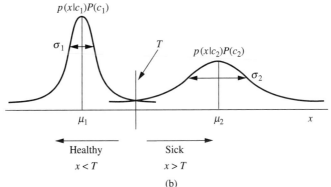

FIGURE 2-2 (a) Sampled data distributions, (b) Bayes threshold I

from an individual, we compute Eq. 2.2 for both classes and assign the label *healthy* or *sick* according to the one that produces the largest value (see Eq. 2.1). Alternatively, we can compare the measurement to T and decide immediately to use the label *healthy* if $x < T$ or *sick* if $x > T$. Notice that to the left of T the scaled likelihood of class *healthy* is larger than for the class *sick*, so measurements that fall in this area are more likely produced by healthy subjects and should be assigned to the healthy class. Similarly, the measurements that fall toward the right have a higher likelihood of being produced by sick cases.

Bayesian Threshold

The general methodology to compute the Bayesian Threshold is to substitute the likelihoods and find the value of x (temperature) which gives us equal a posteriori probabilities. For Gaussian distributions (Eq. 2.3) notice that x appears in the exponent, which complicates the mathematics a bit. Taking the natural logarithm of each side of the equation simplifies the problem without changing the solution (since the logarithim is a monotonically increasing function). Let us do this for the two-class case. We get

$$P(c_1)\sigma_2 \exp -\frac{1}{2}\left(\frac{x - \mu_1}{\sigma_1}\right)^2 = P(c_2)\sigma_1 \exp -\frac{1}{2}\left(\frac{x - \mu_2}{\sigma_2}\right)^2$$

Now taking the logarithm

$$\ln(P(c_1)) + \ln(\sigma_2) - \frac{1}{2}\left(\frac{x - \mu_1}{\sigma_1}\right)^2 = \ln(P(c_2)) + \ln(\sigma_1) - \frac{1}{2}\left(\frac{x - \mu_2}{\sigma_2}\right)^2$$

it is clear that the solution involves solving of a quadratic equation in x. With simple algebra the solution can be found, which corresponds to the threshold T,

$$\frac{x^2}{2}\left(\frac{1}{\sigma_2^2} - \frac{1}{\sigma_1^2}\right) + x\left(\frac{\mu_1}{\sigma_1^2} - \frac{\mu_2}{\sigma_2^2}\right) + \left[\ln\left(\frac{P(c_1)}{P(c_2)}\right) + \ln\left(\frac{\sigma_2}{\sigma_1}\right) - \frac{1}{2}\left(\frac{\mu_1^2}{\sigma_1^2} - \frac{\mu_2^2}{\sigma_2^2}\right)\right] = 0$$

The solution is rather easy to find when $\sigma_1 = \sigma_2$, since in this case the second-order term vanishes, and the result is

$$T = \frac{\mu_1 + \mu_2}{2} + k$$

where k depends on the ratio of a priori probabilities. This solution has a clear interpretation. When the variances are the same and the classes are equally probable, the threshold is placed halfway between the cluster means. If the two variances in our problem were the same, the value for $T = 37.75°C$.

The a priori probabilities shift the threshold left or right. If the a priori probability of class 2 is smaller than the a priori probability of class 1, the threshold should be shifted toward the class with smaller probability. This also makes sense because, if the a priori probability of one class is larger, we should increase the region that corresponds to this class to make fewer mistakes.

For the general case of σ_1 different from σ_2, we have to solve the quadratic equation. The distributions intersect at two points (two roots), but only one is the threshold we are looking for (it has to be between the means of our distributions). In our case for 1,000 measurements, the solutions are $x_1 = 34.35$ and $x_2 = 37.07$, so the threshold should be set at 37.07°C to optimally classify sick from healthy. Notice that this result was obtained with the assumptions of Gaussianity, the a priori probabilities chosen, and the given population (our measurements).

Note that the different variance of the classes effectively moved the threshold to the left, that is, in the direction of the smallest variance. This makes sense because a smaller variance means that the data is more concentrated around the mean, so the threshold should also be moved closer to the class mean. Therefore we conclude that the threshold selection depends on the variances of each cluster. We have discovered that for classification we need a new distance that is not only a function of the distance between cluster means, but also the variances of the clusters.

The class assignment is not error free. In fact, the tail of the *healthy* likelihood extends to the right of the intercept point, and the tail of the *sick* likelihood extends to the left of *T*. The error in the classification is given by the sum of the areas under these tails, so the smaller the overlap, the better the classification accuracy. The maximum a posteriori probability assignment (Eq. 2.1) minimizes this probability of error (minimum error rate) and is therefore optimal.

Minimum Error Rate

The probability of error is computed by adding the area under the likelihood of class 1 in the decision region of class 2 with the area under the likelihood of class 2 in the decision region of class 1. Since the decision region is a function of the threshold chosen, the errors depend on the threshold. As we can see from the figure, the error is associated with the tails of the distributions. To estimate this error, we need to integrate the likelihoods in prescribed areas of the input space, which becomes very difficult in high-dimensional space. The probability of error is

$$P(\text{error}) = \int_{R_2} p(\mathbf{x}|c_1)P(c_1)d\mathbf{x} + \int_{R_1} p(\mathbf{x}|c_2)P(c_2)d\mathbf{x}$$

where R_1 and R_2 are the regions assigned to class 1 and class 2, respectively, so it is a function of the threshold. One can show [Fukunaga, 1990] that the minimum error rate is achieved with Bayes' rule, that is, by selecting the threshold so that the a posteriori probability is maximized. This result also makes sense intuitively (see the following figure).

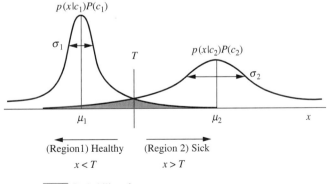

The classification error depends on the overlap of the classes. Intuitively, the larger the difference between the cluster centers (for a given variance), the smaller the overlap, so the smaller the overall classification error. Likewise, for the same difference between the cluster means, the error is smaller if the variance of each cluster distribution is smaller. We can thus conclude that what affects the error is a combination of cluster mean difference and cluster variance.

Metric for Classification There are important conclusions to be taken from the preceeding example. For a problem with given class variances, if we increase the distance between the class means, the overlap will decrease and the classification becomes more accurate. This is reminiscent of the distance in Euclidean space when we think of the class centers as two points in space. However, we cannot just look at the class means to estimate the classification error, since the error depends on the overlap between the class likelihoods. The tails of the Gaussians are controlled by the class variance, so we can have cases where the means are very far apart, but the variances are so large that the overlap between likelihoods is still high. Inversely, the class means can be close to each other, but if the class variances are very small, the classification can still be done with small error.

Hence, separability between Gaussian-distributed classes is a function of both the mean and the variance of each class. As we saw in the Bayesian threshold, the placement of the decision surface is determined by the class distance normalized by the class variances. We can encapsulate this idea by saying that the metric for classification is not Euclidean, but also involves the dispersion (variance) of each class. If we closely analyze the exponent for the Gaussian distribution (Eq. 2.3), we can immediately see that the value of the function depends not only on μ but also on σ. The value of $p(x)$ depends on the distance of x from the mean normalized by the variance. This distance is called the Mahalanobis distance.

Mahalanobis Distance

The Mahalanobis distance is the exponent of the multivariate Gaussian distribution, which is given by

$$p(x) = \frac{1}{(2\pi)^{D/2}|\Sigma|^{1/2}} \exp\left(-\frac{(x-\mu)^T \Sigma^{-1} (x-\mu)}{2}\right)$$

where T indicates the transpose, $|\Sigma|$ is the determinant of Σ, and Σ^{-1} the inverse of Σ. Note that in the equation μ is a vector containing the data means in each dimension, that is, the vector has dimension equal to D.

$$\mu = \begin{bmatrix} \mu_1 \\ \cdots \\ \mu_D \end{bmatrix}$$

Normally we estimate μ by the sample mean Eq. 2.4. The covariance is a matrix of dimension $D \times D$ where D is the dimension of the input space. The matrix Σ is

$$\Sigma = \begin{bmatrix} \sigma_{11} & \cdots & \sigma_{1D} \\ \cdots & \cdots & \cdots \\ \sigma_{D1} & \cdots & \sigma_{DD} \end{bmatrix}$$

and its elements are the product of dispersions among sample pairs in the ith and jth co-ordinates (N is the number of samples in the data set):

$$\sigma_{ij} = \frac{1}{N-1} \sum_{k=1}^{N} \sum_{m=1}^{N} \left(x_{i,k} - \mu_i\right)\left(x_{j,m} - \mu_j\right)$$

The covariance measures the variance among pairs of dimensions. Notice the difference in number of elements between the column vector μ (D components) and the matrix Σ (D^2 components).

The Mahalanobis distance formalizes what we have said for the 1-D classification example. Notice that this distance is a normalized distance from the cluster center. In fact, if we assume that $\Sigma = I$ (identity matrix), we have the Euclidean distance between the cluster centers, but for classification the dispersion of the samples around the cluster mean also affects the placement of thresholds for optimal classification. It is therefore reasonable to normalize the Euclidean distance by the sample dispersion around the mean, which is measured by the covariance matrix.

The covariance matrix for each class is formed by the sample variance along pairs of directions in the input space. The covariance matrix measures the density of samples of the data cluster in the radial direction from the cluster center in each dimension of the input space, *so it quantifies the shape of the data cluster*.

The covariance matrix is always symmetric and positive semidefinite. We assume that it is positive definite, that is, that the determinant is always greater than zero. The diagonal elements are the variance of the input data along each dimension. The off-diagonal terms are the covariance along pairs of dimensions. If the data in each dimension are statistically independent, the off-diagonal terms of Σ are all zero, and the matrix becomes a diagonal matrix.

The structure of the covariance matrix is critical for the placement and shape of the discriminant functions in pattern space. Since the distance metric for classification is normalized by the covariance, if the class means stay the same but the covariance changes, the placement and shape of the discriminant function will change.

Following this simple principle of estimating a posteriori probabilities, an optimal classifier can be built that is able to use temperature to discriminate between healthy and sick subjects. Once again, optimal does not mean that the process will be error free, only that the system will minimize the number of mistakes when the variable temperature is utilized.

2.2.2 Discriminant Functions

Assume we have N measurements $\mathbf{x}_1$, $\mathbf{x}_2$, $\mathbf{x}_N$, where each measurement $\mathbf{x}_k$ is a vector with D components,

$$\mathbf{x}_k = [x_{k1}, x_{k2}, \ldots, x_{kD}] \tag{2.5}$$

and can be visualized as a point in the D-dimensional *pattern space*. Following Eq. 2.1, the class assignment by Bayes' rule is based on a comparison of likelihoods scaled by the corresponding a priori probability. Alternatively, the measurement $\mathbf{x}_k$ will be assigned to class i if

$$g_i(\mathbf{x}_k) > g_j(\mathbf{x}_k) \quad \text{for all } j \neq i \tag{2.6}$$

Each scaled likelihood can be thought of as a *discriminant function* $g(\mathbf{x})$, that is, a function that assigns a "score" to every point in the input space. Each class has its individual scoring function, yielding higher values for the points that belong to the class. Discriminant functions intersect in the input space defining a *decision surface*, where the scores are equal (Figure 2-3). Thus decision surfaces partition the input space into regions where one of the discriminants is larger than the others. Each region is then assigned to the class associated with the largest discriminant.

In this view the optimal classifier just compares discriminant functions (one per class) and chooses the class according to the discriminant $g_i(\mathbf{x})$ that provides the largest

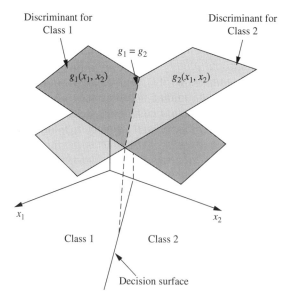

FIGURE 2-3 Discriminant functions and the decision surface

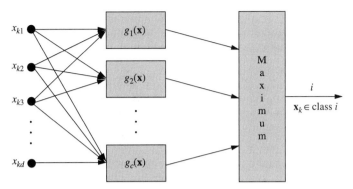

FIGURE 2-4   General parametric classifier for *c* classes

value for the measurement $\mathbf{x}_k$ (Eq. 2.6). A block diagram for the general case of c classes is presented in Figure 2-4.

The blocks labeled $g_i(\mathbf{x})$ compute the discriminants from the input data, and the block labeled *maximum* selects the largest value according to Eq. 2.1 or Eq. 2.6. Studying how the optimal classifier works, we arrive at the conclusion that the classifier system creates decision regions bounded by the intersection of discriminant functions. After this brief introduction, we realize that machines that implement discriminant functions can be used as pattern classifiers.

Parametric and Nonparametric Classifiers

The classifier we just discussed is called a *parametric classifier* because the discriminant functions have a well-defined mathematical functional form (Gaussian) that depends on a set of parameters (mean and variance). For completeness we should mention *nonparametric classifiers*, where there is no assumed functional form for the discriminants. Nonparametric classification is solely driven by the data (as in *K* nearest neighbors; see Fukunaga [1990]). These methods require a great deal of data for acceptable performance, but they are free from assumptions about the shape of discriminant functions (or data distributions) that may be erroneous.

2.2.3 A Two-Dimensional Pattern-Recognition Example

The temperature example is too simple (the input is one-dimensional) to illustrate the full method of deriving decision boundaries based on statistical models of the data, the variety of separation surfaces, and the details and difficulty of the design. We will treat here the two-dimensional case, because we can still use pictures to help guide our reasoning. The method, of course, can be generalized to any number of dimensions.

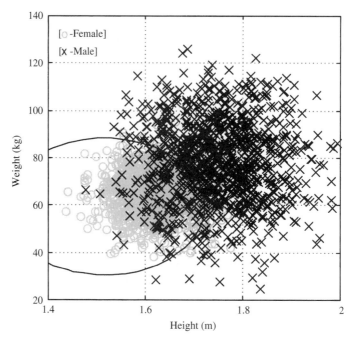

FIGURE 2-5   Scatter plot of the weight and height data with the optimal decision surface

Let us consider the following problem: Suppose that we wish to classify males and females in a population by using measurements of their height and weight. Since we selected two variables, this is a two-dimensional problem. We are going to assume for simplicity that the distributions of height and weight are multivariate Gaussians and that the probability of occurrence of each sex is $\frac{1}{2}$. Figure 2-5 shows the scatter plot of measurements for the two classes.

The goal is to determine the placement of the decision surface for optimal classification. According to our previous discussion of the one-dimensional case (see the sidebar on the Bayesian threshold), this is achieved by estimating the means and standard deviations of the likelihoods from measurements performed in the population. Then the decision boundary is found by solving for $g_i(\mathbf{x}) = g_j(\mathbf{x})$, where i and j are the classes *male* and *female*. The difference from our previous example is that here we have a two-dimensional input space.

One can show [Duda and Hart 1973] that for our two-dimensional, two-class case (normally distributed) with equal a priori probabilities, the classification will be a function of a normalized distance between the class centers, called the Mahalanobis distance:

$$d^2 = (\mathbf{x} - \boldsymbol{\mu})^T \boldsymbol{\Sigma}^{-1} (\mathbf{x} - \boldsymbol{\mu}) \qquad (2.7)$$

where $\boldsymbol{\mu}$ is the class center vector and $\boldsymbol{\Sigma}$ is the *covariance* matrix of the input data in two-dimensional space. Notice that instead of the class variances, in the multidimensional case we have to compute the covariance matrix that is built from the class variances along each input space dimension. For this case the discriminant function is given by

$$g_i(\mathbf{x}) = -\frac{1}{2}(\mathbf{x} - \boldsymbol{\mu}_i)^T \boldsymbol{\Sigma}_i^{-1}(\mathbf{x} - \boldsymbol{\mu}_i) - \frac{D}{2}\log(2\pi) - \frac{1}{2}\log|\boldsymbol{\Sigma}_i| + \log P(c_i) \qquad \textbf{(2.8)}$$

Our example is a two-dimensional problem ($D = 2$) with two classes ($i = 1, 2$). Since the classes are equiprobable, the last term in Eq. 2.8 will be the same for each discriminant and can be dropped (likewise for the term $D/2 \log(2\pi)$). When the discriminants for each class are equated to find the decision surface, we see that, in fact, its placement is going to be a function of the Mahalanobis distance and class covariances. As in the one-dimensional case, for classification, *what matters is the distance among the cluster means normalized by the respective covariance. This is the metric for classification, and it is beautifully encapsulated in the Mahalanobis distance.*

Derivation of Quadratic Discriminant

We saw that Bayes' rule chooses classes based on a posteriori probabilities. We can consider $P(c_i|\mathbf{x})$ a discriminant,

$$g_i(\mathbf{x}) = P(c_i|\mathbf{x}) = p(\mathbf{x}|c_i)P(c_i)$$

where $p(\mathbf{x}|c_i)$ is the likelihood associated with the class c_i. In this expression we omitted $P(\mathbf{x})$ (see Eq. 2.2.) because it is a common factor on all discriminants and will not affect the overall shape nor placement of the boundary. It can therefore be dropped for the definition of the discriminant function.

Now let us take the natural logarithm of this equation and obtain

$$g_i(\mathbf{x}) = \ln p(\mathbf{x}|c_i) + \ln P(c_i)$$

This is the general form for the discriminant, which depends on the functional form of the likelihood. If the density $p(\mathbf{x}|c_i)$ is a multivariate normal distribution, we get Eq. 2.8.

Estimating all the elements of the $\boldsymbol{\Sigma}$ matrix in high-dimensional spaces with adequate precision becomes a nontrivial problem. Very often the matrix becomes ill conditioned due to lack of data, resulting in discriminants that have the wrong shape and suboptimal performance.

Table 2-2 shows the estimates for the class covariances and means considering 100 and 1,000 samples per class. We will solve the problem with 1,000 samples first by computing the discriminants for each class.

TABLE 2-2 Data Statistics

	100 measurements	1,000 measurements
Women	Weight mean = 63.7385 Height mean = 1.6084 $Cov = \begin{bmatrix} 77.1877 & 0.0139 \\ 0.0139 & 0.0047 \end{bmatrix}$	Weight mean = 64.86 Height mean = 1.62 $Cov = \begin{bmatrix} 90.4401 & 0 \\ 0 & 0.0036 \end{bmatrix}$
Men	Weight mean = 82.5278 Height mean = 1.7647 $Cov = \begin{bmatrix} 366.3206 & 0.4877 \\ 0.4877 & 0.0084 \end{bmatrix}$	Weight mean = 78.02 Height mean = 1.75 $Cov = \begin{bmatrix} 310.1121 & 0 \\ 0 & 0.0081 \end{bmatrix}$

In this case the decision surface is given by the Bayes' classifier as

$$77.16x_2^2 - 233.95x_2 + 0.0039x_1^2 - 0.4656x_1 + 129.40 = 0$$

which is an equation for a quadratic curve in the input space (Figure 2-5).

Bayes' Classifier

The optimal classifier (also called Bayes' classifier) is obtained in the same form as for the 1-D case. We substitute the means and covariances estimated from the data for each class in Eq. 2.8. The inverse of the covariance for the class women is

$$\Sigma^{-1} = \begin{bmatrix} 0.00111 & 0 \\ 0 & 277.78 \end{bmatrix}$$

and the determinant of Σ is 0.3256, yielding

$$g_w(x) = -0.5[x_1 - 64.86 \quad x_2 - 1.62] \begin{bmatrix} 0.00111 & 0 \\ 0 & 277.78 \end{bmatrix} \begin{bmatrix} x_1 - 64.86 \\ x_2 - 1.62 \end{bmatrix} - \log(2\pi) - 0.5\log(0.3256)$$

For the class men the discriminant is

$$g_m(x) = -0.5[x_1 - 78.02 \quad x_2 - 1.75] \begin{bmatrix} 0.00032 & 0 \\ 0 & 123.46 \end{bmatrix} \begin{bmatrix} x_1 - 78.02 \\ x_2 - 1.75 \end{bmatrix} - \log(2\pi) - 0.5\log(2.512)$$

The separation surface is obtained by equating $g_w(x) = g_m(x)$, which yields

$$77.16x_2^2 - 233.95x_2 + 0.0039x_1^2 - 0.4656x_1 + 129.40 = 0$$

This is a quadratic in 2-D space as shown in Figure 2-5. This surface yields the smallest classification error for this problem, but just by inspection of the figure we can see that many errors are going to be made. Thus we have to get used to the idea that *optimal* does not necessarily mean *good* performance. It simply means the best possible performance with the data we have.

2.2.4 Decision Surfaces of Optimal Classifiers

It can be shown [Fukunaga, 1990] that the optimal classifier for Gaussian-distributed classes is always a quadratic. There are three cases of interest:

- Covariance matrices are diagonal and equal.
- Covariance matrices for each class are equal.
- The general case.

For the two first cases, both the optimal discriminants and the decision surface are linear (Figure 2-6). These plots tell us how the density of samples decreases away from the

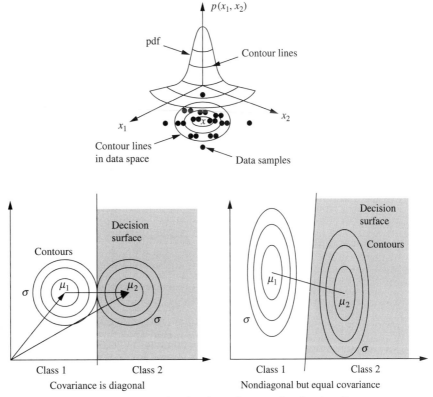

FIGURE 2-6 Contour plots for the data clusters that lead to linear discriminant functions

center of the cluster (the mean of the Gaussian). The optimal discriminant function depends on each cluster shape, and it is in principle a quadratic. When the cluster shapes are circularly symmetric with the same variance, there is no difference in the radial direction for optimal classification, so the discriminant defaults to a linear function (a hyperplane). The decision surface is also linear and is perpendicular to the line that joins the two cluster centers. For the same a priori probability the decision surface is the perpendicular bisector of the line joining the class means.

Even when the shapes of the clusters are skewed equally (the contour plots of each cluster are ellipses with equal axes), there is no information to be explored in the radial direction, so the optimal discriminants are still linear. But now the decision surface is a line that is slanted with respect to the line joining the two cluster means.

Figure 2-7 shows the contours of each data cluster and the discriminant for the case of arbitrary covariance matrices. Notice the large repertoire of decision surfaces for the two-class case when we assume Gaussian distributions. The important point is that the shape of the discriminants is highly dependent on the covariance matrix of each class. Knowing the shape of one data cluster is not enough to predict the shape of the optimal discriminant. We need knowledge about *both* data clusters to find the optimal discriminant.

Eq. 2.8 shows that the optimal discriminant for Gaussian-distributed classes is a quadratic function. This points out that the relationship between cluster distributions

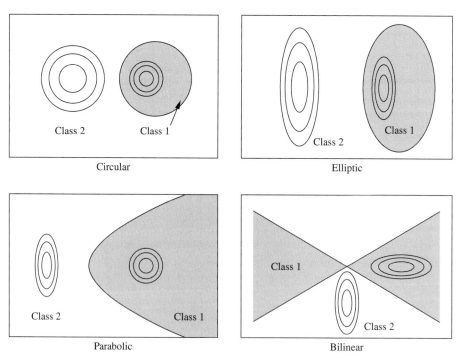

FIGURE 2-7 The general case of arbitrary covariance matrices

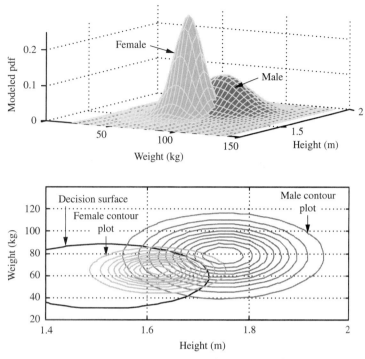

FIGURE 2-8 Modeled distribution of Figure 2-5 data

and discriminants for optimal classification is not unique; that is, there are many possible functional forms for the optimal discriminant (Gaussians, quadratics, and hyperplanes for this case). Observe that the parameters of the discriminant functions are a direct function of the parameters of the class likelihoods, so once the parameters of Eq. 2.8 are estimated, we can immediately determine the optimal classifier. For the female-male example Figure 2-8 shows the modeled distribution of the two classes.

Shapes of 2-D Discriminants

Diagonal Covariance Matrix If the two variables are uncorrelated and of the same variance, then the covariance matrix is diagonal:

$$\Sigma = \sigma^2 I$$

In this case the Mahalanobis distance defaults to the Euclidean distance:

$$\|x - \mu_i\|^2 = (x - \mu_i)^T (x - \mu_i)$$

and the classifier is called a *minimum distance classifier*. The interesting thing is that the discriminant function for this case defaults to a linear function:

$$g_i(x) = \mathbf{w}_i^T \mathbf{x} + b$$

where $\mathbf{w}_i = (1/\sigma^2)\boldsymbol{\mu}_i$ and $b_i = -(1/2\sigma^2)\boldsymbol{\mu}_i^T \boldsymbol{\mu}_i$, since the quadratic term is common to both classes and does not affect the shape of the discriminant. For this case the samples define circular clusters (hyperspherical in multidimensions).

Equal Covariance Matrix The case of equal covariance matrices for each class ($\boldsymbol{\Sigma}_i = \boldsymbol{\Sigma}$) is still fairly simple. In fact, the discriminant is still linear, but now the weights and bias of $g_i(\mathbf{x})$ in the previous equation are given by $\mathbf{w}_i = \boldsymbol{\Sigma}^{-1}\boldsymbol{\mu}_i$ and $b = -\frac{1}{2}\boldsymbol{\mu}_i^T \boldsymbol{\Sigma}^{-1}\boldsymbol{\mu}_i$, which means that each class is an ellipsoidal cluster of equal size and shape. Figure 2-6 shows both cases. Notice that the decision surfaces are both linear functions.

Arbitrary Covariances This is the most general case, and the general form of the discriminant function of Eq. 2.8 must be used. We can see that this discriminant function is quadratic in x:

$$g_i(x) = \mathbf{x}^T \mathbf{W}_i x + \mathbf{w}_i^T \mathbf{x} + b_i$$

where $\mathbf{W} = -\frac{1}{2}\boldsymbol{\Sigma}_i^{-1}$, $\mathbf{w}_i = \boldsymbol{\Sigma}^{-1}\boldsymbol{\mu}_i$ and $b_i = -\frac{1}{2}\boldsymbol{\mu}_i^T \boldsymbol{\Sigma}^{-1}\boldsymbol{\mu}_i - \frac{1}{2}\log|\boldsymbol{\Sigma}_i|$. The decision region is either a line, circle, ellipse, or parabola, depending on the shape of the individual clusters and their relative position (Figure 2-7).

These three cases illustrate our previous statement that the covariance matrix is exceptionally important in the definition of the shape (and placement) of the discriminant function. Note that the discriminant function changes from a hyperplane to a quadratic surface, depending on the covariance matrix of each class.

A classifier built from linear discriminant functions (called a linear classifier) exploits only differences in means among different classes, while the quadratic classifier exploits not only the mean difference but also the difference in "shape" of the data clusters. Hence, if we have two classes with the same mean, the linear classifier will always give very poor results. However, a quadratic classifier may perform better, as long as the shapes of the two data clusters are different. In fact, notice that for Gaussian-distributed classes the optimal classifier is a quadratic classifier given by Eq. 2.8. There is thus no need to find more sophisticated (higher-order) discriminant functions.

The improvement in performance between the linear and the quadratic discriminants comes at a computational cost. In fact, the number of parameters estimated for the case of an arbitrary covariance matrix in 2-D is seven per class for the quadratic (and increases as the square of the dimension due to $\mathbf{W}$), while it is simply three for the linear case. Quadratic discriminants require more data samples for the reliable estimation of their parameters.

Discriminant Sensitivity to the Size of the Data   We have developed a strategy that is able to construct optimal decision surfaces from the data under the assumptions that the pdf of each class is Gaussian. This is a powerful procedure, but it is based on assumptions about the pdf of the input and also requires enough data to estimate the parameters of the discriminant functions with little error. The ultimate quality of the results will depend upon how valid these assumptions are for our problem. We illustrate here the effect of the training data size on the estimation of the discriminant function parameters.

Let us assume that we had only 100 samples for the height–weight example (50 males and 50 females). We extracted these samples randomly from the larger data file and computed the means and covariances for each class, as shown in Table 2-2. Just by inspection you can see that the parameters changed quite a bit. For instance, the covariances are no longer diagonal matrices, and the elements also have different values. Note also that the mean estimates are more precise than the covariance estimates. When we build the optimal discriminant function from these parameters (Eq. 2.8), the shape and position in the input space is going to be different from the "ideal" case of 1,000 samples.

Figure 2-9 shows the differences in shape and placement of the optimal decision surface for the two data sets. In this case the differences are significant, producing

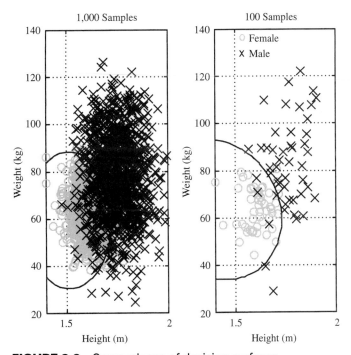

FIGURE 2-9   Comparisons of decision surfaces

different classification accuracy, but the decision surfaces still have the same overall shape. But remember that this is a simple problem in two-dimensions (seven parameters to be estimated with 50 samples per class). In higher-dimensional spaces the number of parameters to be estimated may be of the same order of magnitude of the data samples, and in this case catastrophic differences may occur. So what can we do to design classifiers that are less sensitive to the a priori assumptions and the estimation of parameters?

The answer is not clear-cut, but it is related to the simplicity of the functional form of the discriminant. We should use discriminant functions that have fewer parameters and that can be robustly estimated from the amount of data that we have for training. These simpler discriminants may be suboptimal for the problem, but experience shows that many times they perform better than the optimal discriminant. This seems a paradox, but the reason can be found in the brittleness of the parameter estimation. Even if we use the quadratic discriminant (which is optimal for Gaussian-distributed classes), the classifier may perform poorly if its discriminant functions are not shaped and positioned accurately in the input space.

2.3 LINEAR AND NONLINEAR CLASSIFIER MACHINES

2.3.1 The Linear Machines

Thus far we have encountered three types of discriminant functions: the linear, the quadratic, and the Gaussian. Let us compare them in terms of the number of free parameters for D-dimensional data. The linear discriminant function given by

$$g(\mathbf{x}) = w_1 x_1 + w_2 x_2 + \ldots + w_D x_D + b = \sum_{i=1}^{D} w_i x_i + b \qquad (2.9)$$

has a number of parameters that increases linearly with the dimension D of the space. The discriminant function with the next higher degree polynomial, the quadratic, has a square dependence on the dimensionality of the space (i.e., it has approximately D^2 parameters) as we can see in Eq. 2.8. The Gaussian gave rise to a quadratic discriminant by taking the logarithm. Although quadratics are the optimal discriminants for Gaussian-distributed clusters, it may not be feasible to properly estimate all these parameters in large-dimensional spaces unless we have a tremendous amount of data.

Notice that Eq. 2.9 is a parametric equation for a hyperplane in D dimensions, which we already encountered in linear regression (although there it had the function of modeling the input-output relationship). The hyperplane can be rotated and translated (an *affine* transformation) by changing the values of the free parameters w_i and b, respectively. The system that implements the discriminant of Eq. 2.9 is depicted in Figure 2-10 and is called a *linear machine*. Notice that the pattern-recognizer block

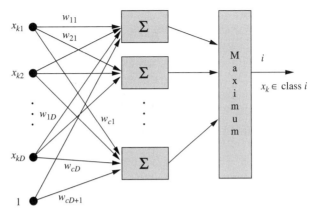

FIGURE 2-10   Linear classifier for *c* classes

is simpler (compared with Figure 2-4) because the unspecified functions $g(\mathbf{x})$ become simply a sum of products. We have seen that the linear machine is even optimal for Gaussian-distributed classes with equal variances, which is a case of practical relevance (for example data transmission in stationary, noisy channels).

It is ironic that in our classifier design methodology we are again considering linear functions for discrimination. It seems that we are back at the point where we started this chapter, the construction of a classifier based on the linear regressor followed by a threshold. But notice that now we have a much better idea of what we are seeking. The pattern-recognition theory tells us that we may use linear discriminants, but we use *one per class*, not a regression line linking all the input data with the class labels. We also now know that the linear discriminant may not be optimal but may be the best we can do because of the practical limitation of insufficient data to properly estimate the parameters of the optimal discriminant functions. The pattern-recognition theory thus gave us the insight to seek better solutions.

It is important to stress that the linear discriminant is less powerful than the quadratic discriminant. A linear discriminant primarily utilizes differences in means for classification. If two classes have the same mean, the linear classifier will always produce poor results. Examine Figure 2-11. A linear separation surface will always misclassify approximately half of the other class. However, the quadratic discriminant does a much better job because it can utilize the differences in the covariances.

2.3.2 Kernel-Based Machines

A more sophisticated learning machine architecture is obtained by implementing a non-linear mapping from the input to another space, followed by a linear discriminant function (Figure 2-12). See Nilsson [1990]. The rationale of this architecture is motivated by Cover's theorem. Cover basically states that any pattern-recognition problem is linearly separable in a sufficiently high dimensionality space, so the goal is to map the

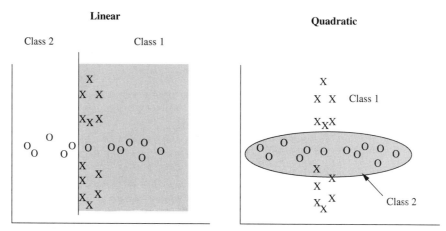

FIGURE 2-11 Comparison of the discriminant power of the linear and quadratic classifiers

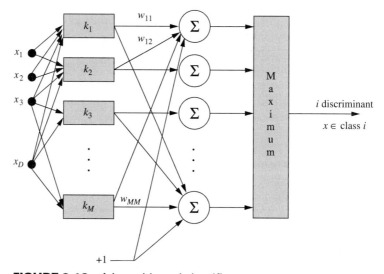

FIGURE 2-12 A kernel-based classifier

input space to another space, called the feature space Φ, using nonlinear transformations.

Cover's Theorem

Cover's theorem draws from a very interesting (and nonintuitive) result. Let us assume that we have a kernel-based machine with $M + 1$ weights. We want to classify N patterns.

There are 2^N possible divisions of these patterns into two categories (called dichotomies). The question is, What is the probability that a given dichotomy chosen at random is implementable by our kernel-based machine?

Cover showed that the probability is

$$P_{N,M} = \begin{cases} 2^{1-N} \sum_{i=0}^{M} \binom{N-1}{i} & N > M \\ 1 & N \leq M \end{cases}$$

This means that for spaces of size M larger than the number of samples N the probability is essentially 1; that is, we can always divide any data into two classes with probability 1. This probability has a sharp knee (the probability approaches 1 rapidly) at $N = 2(M + 1)$, and this value is normally defined as the capacity C of the learning machine. Thus if we set the number of free parameters (weights) of our learning machine above its capacity, we are almost certain to classify the input patterns correctly. For a linear classifier in D space the capacity is $C = 2D + 1$. However, kernel-based classifiers allow us to go to a higher-dimensional space and set their capacity independently of the input space dimension. This decoupling between the input space dimension and the machine capacity is the great advantage of the kernel-based machine.

Let us assume that the mapping from the input space $\mathbf{x} = [x_1, \ldots, x_D]$ to the higher dimensional Φ space is a one-to-one mapping operated by a kernel function family,

$$K(\mathbf{x}) = \{ k_1(\mathbf{x}), \ldots, k_M(\mathbf{x}) \}$$

applied to the input. For instance, we can construct a quadratic mapping in this way by equating the first D components of K to x_i^2, the next $D(D-1)/2$ components to all pairs $x_i x_j$ ($i \neq j$), and the last D components to x_i. The feature space Φ in this case is of size $M = [D(D + 3)]/2$.

There is great flexibility in choosing the family of functions $K(\mathbf{x})$. They need to be nonlinear, such as Gaussians, polynomials, trigonometric polynomials, and so on. Then in Φ space we can construct a linear discriminant function as

$$g(\mathbf{x}) = w_1 k_1(\mathbf{x}) + \ldots + w_M k_M(\mathbf{x}) + b$$

As before, the problem is to select the set of weight vector $\mathbf{w}$ in Φ space that classifies the problem with minimum error. The general architecture for the kernel classifier is to build a kernel processor (which computes $K(\mathbf{x})$) followed by a linear machine. In the previous example given, we actually constructed a quadratic discriminator. The major advantage of the kernel-based machine is that it decouples the capacity of the machine (the number of free parameters) from the size of the input space. Recently Vapnik [1995] has shown that if $K(\mathbf{x})$ are symmetric functions that obey the Mercer condition (i.e., $K(\mathbf{x})$ represents an inner product in the feature space), the solution for the discriminant function problem is greatly simplified. The Mercer condition basically states that the weights can be computed without ever solving the problem in the higher-dimensional space Φ, which gives rise to a new classifier called the support vector machine (SVM). We will study the SVM later.

Size of Feature Space

The conventional way of thinking about features in pattern recognition has been as a method of reducing the dimensionality of the input. A feature is a characteristic of the input data that preserves discriminability, for instance, color or edges in an image. Features are traditionally obtained with projections onto a subspace; that is, features have smaller dimensionality than the input. For 50 years the quest in pattern recognition has been to find small-dimensional projections that preserve the most information about the input. We realize that a projection onto a subspace reduces the discriminability somewhat, but experience has shown that for many problems a handful of small-dimensional projections produce workable classifiers.

The motivation for performing subspace projections is related to the "curse of dimensionality" we already mentioned. If we want to build the optimal Bayes' classifier in a high-dimensional space, we have to estimate too many parameters with the available data. One way to conquer this difficulty is to project the data to a smaller-dimensional space (feature extraction) and there develop the optimal classifier. The difficulty has been in choosing the features and their number. Moreover, if the data is hard to classify in the original space, very likely it will also be difficult to classify in the smaller-dimensional feature space. Nevertheless, this has been the traditional way to think about feature spaces.

The view we expressed using Cover's theorem to go to a higher-dimensional feature space has been only a curiosity in pattern-recognition until the recent work of Vapnik with support vector machines. High-dimensional spaces produce sparse data clusters; that is, no matter how many data samples we might have, if the size of the space is sufficiently large, there will always be lots of room among the data clusters. This means that the classification problem is potentially linearly separable, so a very simple classifier can do the job. The interesting thing is that good performance in the test set can still be controlled by placing discriminants half way between the boundary samples. We will discuss this in more detail later.

2.3.3 Classifiers for the Two-Class Case

The general classifier can be simplified for the two-class case since only two discriminant functions are necessary. It is sufficient to subtract the two discriminant functions and assign the classes based on the sign of a single, new discriminant function. For instance, for the sick–healthy classification

$$g_{new}(\mathbf{x}) = g_{healthy}(\mathbf{x}) - g_{sick}(\mathbf{x}) \tag{2.10}$$

which leads to the block diagram in Figure 2-13.

Note that $g_{new}(\mathbf{x})$ divides the space into two regions that are assigned to each class. For this reason, this surface obeys the definition of a decision surface, and its dimension

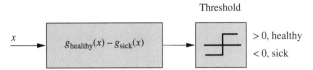

FIGURE 2-13 Classifier for a two-class problem

is one less than the original data space dimension. For the 1-D case it is a threshold (a point) at 37°C but a line (1-D surface) in 2-D space, and so on.

It is important at this point to go back to our NeuroSolutions Example 2.1, where we built a classifier from an Adaline followed by a threshold function, and compare that solution with Figure 2-13. We can conclude that the Adaline is effectively implementing the discriminant function $g_{new}(\mathbf{x})$. Due to the particular way that we defined the labels $(1, -1)$, the regression line will be positive in the region of the temperatures for healthy individuals and negative toward the temperatures of sick individuals. The sign of the regression thus effectively implements $g_{new}(\mathbf{x})$. There are several problems with this solution:

- First, there is no rigorous way to choose the values of the desired response, and they tremendously affect the placement of the regression line (try 0.9 and -0.1 instead of ± 1 and see how the threshold changes).

- Second, it is not easy to generalize the scheme for multiple classes (the sign information can be used only for the two-class case). As we saw, classification requires a discriminant function per class.

- Third, the way that the Adaline was adapted has little to do with minimizing the classification error. The error for training comes from the difference between the Adaline output (before the threshold) and the class labels (Figure 2-14). We are using a nonlinear system, but the information to adapt it is still derived from the linear part.

Only under very restricted conditions will this scheme yield the optimal classifier. In the following chapter we will learn to implement a classifier in which the classification

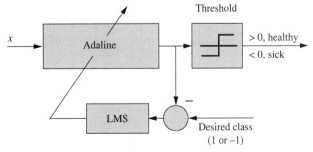

FIGURE 2-14 Schematic training of the Adaline with threshold

error (the error after the threshold) is used to train the network. The Adaline followed by a threshold as shown in Example 2.1 was applied in the 1960s by Widrow and Hoff [1960] for classification purposes.

2.4 METHODS OF TRAINING PARAMETRIC CLASSIFIERS

The methods that we present in this book assume that there is little information available to help us make principled decisions regarding the parameter values of the discriminant functions. Therefore, the parameters must be estimated from the available data. One must first collect sufficient data that covers all the possible cases of interest, then use this data to select the parameters that produce the smallest possible error. This is called *training the classifier*, and we found a very similar methodology in Chapter 1.

The accuracy of a classifier is dictated by the location and shape of the decision boundary in pattern space. Since the decision boundary is obtained by the intersection of discriminant functions, there are two fundamental issues in designing accurate parametric classifiers (i.e., classifiers that accept a functional form for their discriminant functions):

- The *placement* of the discriminant function in pattern space
- The *functional form* of the discriminant function

There are two different ways to use the data for training parametric classifiers (Figure 2-15): parametric and nonparametric training (do not confuse parametric classifiers with parametric training).

In *parametric training* each pattern category is described by some known functional form for which its parameters are unknown. The decision surface can then be analytically defined as a function of these unknown parameters. The method of designing classifiers based on statistical models of the data belongs to parametric training. We describe the data clusters by class likelihoods, and the discriminants and decision surfaces can be determined when these parameters are estimated from the data. For instance, for Gaussian-distributed pattern categories, we need to estimate the mean vector, the covariance (normally using the sample mean and the sample covariance), and the class probabilities to apply Eq. 2.1. Unfortunately, due to the analytic way in which discriminants are related to the likelihoods, only a handful of distributions have been studied, and the Gaussian is almost always utilized.

In nonparametric training the free parameters of the classifier's discriminant functions are directly estimated from the input data. Assumptions about the data distribution are never needed in nonparametric training. Very frequently, nonparametric training utilizes iterative algorithms to find the best position of the discriminant functions. However, the designer still has to directly address the two fundamental issues of parametric classifier design, that is, the functional form of discriminant functions and their placement in pattern space.

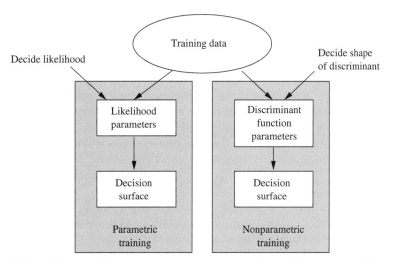

FIGURE 2-15 Parametric and nonparametric training of a classifier

2.4.1 Parametric versus Nonparametric Training

Let us raise an important issue. Is there any advantage in using nonparametric training? The *optimal discriminant function* depends on the distribution of the data in pattern space. When the boundary is defined by statistical data modeling (parametric training), optimal classification is achieved by the choice of good data models and appropriate estimation of their parameters. This looks like a perfectly fine methodology to design classifiers. Therefore, in principle, there seems to be no advantage in nonparametric training, which starts the classifier design process by selecting the discriminant functional form "out of the blue." In reality, there are some problems with parametric training for the following reasons:

- Poor choice of likelihood models. When we select a data model (e.g., the Gaussian distribution), we may be mistaken, so the classifier may not be the optimal classifier after all. Conversely, estimating the form of the pdf from finite training sets is an *ill-posed problem*, so this selection is always problematic.

- Too many parameters for the optimal discriminant. We saw earlier that the performance of the quadratic classifier depends on the quality of the parameter estimation. When we have few data points, we may not get a sufficiently good estimation of the parameters, and classification accuracy suffers. As a rule of thumb we should have 10 data samples for each free parameter in the classifier. If this is not the case, we should avoid using the quadratic discriminator. We can say that most real-world problems are data bound; that is, for the number of free parameters in the optimal classifier, there is not enough data to properly estimate its discriminant function parameters. Very often we are forced to trade optimality for robustness in the estimation of parameters. In spite of the fact that the quadratic classifier is optimal, sometimes the data can be classified with enough accuracy by simpler discriminants (such as the linear), as we showed in the shapes of 2-D discriminants. These discriminants have fewer parameters and are less sensitive to estimation errors (take a look at Table 2-2 and compare the estimations for the means and variances), so they should be used instead of the quadratic discriminants when there is not enough data to estimate the parameters accurately.

This raises the question of using the data to directly estimate the parameters of the discriminant functions, that is, choosing a nonparametric training approach. What we gain is classifiers that are insensitive to the assumption on the pdf of the data clusters. We can also control in a more direct way the number of free parameters of the classifier.

2.4.2 Issues in Nonparametric Training

The difficulties that are brought about by nonparametric training are twofold:

- Deciding the shape of the discriminant function for each class
- Finding ways to adapt the parameters of the classifier

Shape of Discriminant Functions   The central problem in nonparametric training of parametric classifiers can be restated as the selection of an appropriate functional form for the discriminant function that meets these two criteria:

- It produces small classification error.
- It has as few parameters as possible to enable robust estimation from the available data.

The linear-machine decision boundaries are always *convex* because they are built from the superposition of linear discriminant functions. This is very restrictive and solving realistic problems may thus require more versatile machines. The kernel-based classifiers are one option. They form convex boundaries in the high dimensional ϕ space, but not necessarily in the input space. Another class of more versatile machines is called *semiparametric classifiers* because they still work with parametric discriminant functions but are able to implement a larger class of discriminant shapes (eventually any shape, which makes them universal approximators). Semiparametric classifiers are very promising because they are an excellent compromise between versatility and the number of trainable parameters. Artificial neural networks are one of the most exciting types of semiparametric classifiers and will be the main subject of our study.

Adaptation of Classifier Parameters   We can use the ideas of iterated training algorithms to adapt the classifier parameters. In Chapter 1 we trained the Adaline parameters directly from the data, so the linear regressor was effectively nonparametrically trained. We can also foresee the use of the gradient descent method explained in Chapter 1 to adjust the parameters of the discriminant functions so that a measure of the misclassifications (output error) is minimized. Gradient descent will be extended in the next chapter for classifiers.

2.5 CONCLUSIONS

In this short chapter we covered the fundamental principles of pattern recognition. We started by briefly reviewing the problem of pattern recognition from a statistical perspective. We provided the concepts and definitions to understand the role of a pattern recognizer. We covered Bayes' classifier and showed that the optimal classifier is quadratic. Sometimes suboptimal classifiers perform better when the data is scarce and the input space is large, in particular, when the input is projected into a large feature space, as done in kernel classifiers.

The linear classifier was also reviewed, and a possible implementation was provided. These concepts are going to be very important when we discuss artificial neural networks in the next chapter.

2.6 EXERCISES

2.1 Modify the desired response to (1, 0) in NeuroSolutions Example 2.1 (use the *"Normalization"* function on the *"Stream"* page of the *"File"* inspector). Notice how the threshold changes. Elaborate on the dependence of linear machines in the actual values of the desired response. Is this good or bad?

2.2 In the CH2 folder of the data directory (CD-ROM), we provide data that can be used for classification (prob. 2.2 train and test). The last column is the class label. This data exists in a 2-D space such that we can still visualize the discriminant functions. It is also a two-class problem for simplicity. In this problem you will design a linear classifier, assuming first that each class can be modeled by a Gaussian distribution. You should first find the parameters for each Gaussian and then design the classifier. Plot the separation surface over the data.

2.3 For the data in Problem 2, design the optimal Bayes' classifier and compare performance with the linear classifier by determining the percent of correct classifications. Plot also the separation surface and compare it with Problem 2. Do you think that for this data set the Bayes' classifier is optimal?

2.4 If you want to use a linear classifier but train it nonparametrically, can you do it? What is missing? Why is it that LMS cannot be used?

2.5 Compare the performance of the Bayes' classifier developed in Problem 3 when you use only the first 10 percent of the data for training.

2.6 Estimate the probability of error of the Bayes' classifier developed in Problem 3.

2.7 State in your own words the reason why the metric of classification is not Euclidean.

2.8 In the Chapter 2 folder of the data directory (CD-ROM), we provide another data set ready to be used for classification (prob. 2.8 train and test). The last column is the class label. In this case, the problem is a bit more difficult, with three classes in five-dimensional space. Develop a linear classifier and test the results. Is it appropriate to develop a Bayes' classifier to improve performance?

2.7   NEUROSOLUTIONS EXAMPLE

2.1 Comparing regression and classification

2.8   CONCEPT MAP FOR CHAPTER 2

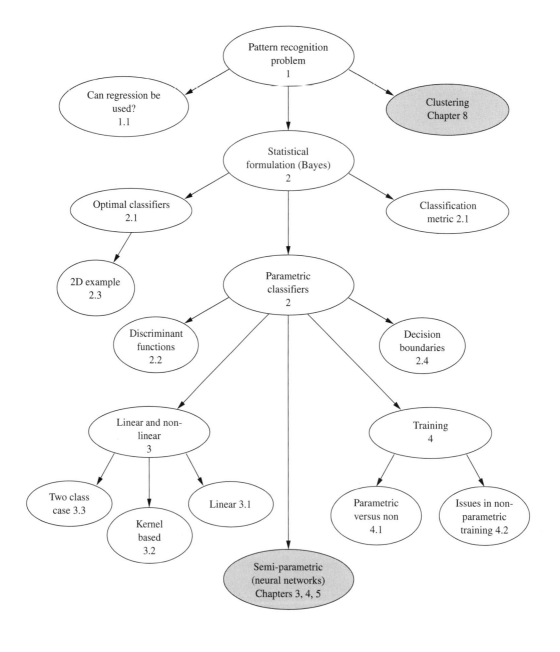

REFERENCES

Duda, R., and Hart, P., *Pattern Classification and Scene Analysis,* Wiley, New York, 1973.

Fukunaga, K., *Statistical Pattern Recognition,* Academic Press, Boston, 1990.

Nilsson, N. *Mathematical Foundation of Learning Machines,* Morgan Kaufmann, San Mateo, CA, 1990.

Vapnik, V. *The Nature of Statistical Learning Theory,* Springer Verlag, New York, 1995.

Widrow, B., and Hoff, M., Adaptive switching circuits, *IRE WESCON Convention Record*, 96–104, 1960.

MULTILAYER PERCEPTRONS

The goal of this chapter is to provide the basic understanding of the following concepts:

- Definition of neural networks
- McCulloch-Pitts PE
- Perceptron and its separation surfaces
- Training the perceptron
- Multilayer perceptron and its separation surfaces
- Backpropagation
- Ordered derivatives and computational complexity
- Data-flow implementation of backpropagation

3.1 ARTIFICIAL NEURAL NETWORKS

There are many definitions of artificial neural networks (ANNs). We will use a pragmatic definition that emphasizes the key features of the technology. ANNs are distributed, adaptive, generally nonlinear learning machines built from many different processing elements (PEs). Each PE receives connections from other PEs and/or itself. The interconnectivity defines the *topology* of the ANN. The signals flowing on the connections are scaled by adjustable parameters called weights, w_{ij}. The PEs sum all these contributions and produce an output that is a nonlinear (static) function of the sum. The PEs' outputs become either system outputs or are sent to the same or other PEs. Figure 3-1 shows an example of an ANN. Note that a weight is associated with every connection.

The ANN builds discriminant functions from its PEs. The ANN topology determines the number and shape of the discriminant functions. The shapes of the discriminant functions change with the topology, so ANNs are considered semiparametric classifiers. One of the central advantages of ANNs is that they are sufficiently powerful to create arbitrary discriminant functions, so ANNs can achieve optimal classification.

The placement of the discriminant functions is controlled by the network weights. Following the ideas of nonparametric training, the weights are adjusted directly from the training data without any assumptions about the data's statistical distribution. Hence one of the central issues in neural network design is to utilize systematic procedures (a training algorithm) to modify the weights so that as accurate a classification as possible is achieved. The accuracy is quantified by an error criterion.

There is a *style* in training an ANN (Figure 3-2). First, data is presented, and an output is computed. An error is obtained by comparing the output with a desired response, and it is used to modify the weights with a training algorithm. This procedure is repeated using all the data in the training set until a convergence criterion is met. Thus in ANNs (and in adaptive systems in general) the designer does not have to specify the parameters of the system. They are automatically extracted from the input data and desired response by means of the training algorithm.

The two central issues in neural network design (semiparametric classifiers) are the selection of the shape and number of the discriminant functions and their placement in pattern space such that the classification error is minimized. We will address all these

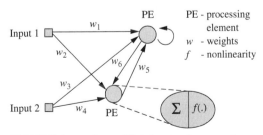

FIGURE 3-1   An artificial neural network

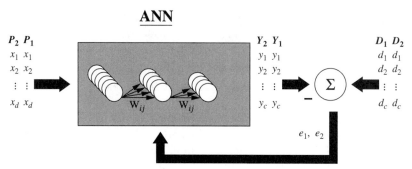

FIGURE 3-2 General principles of adaptive system's training

issues in this chapter in a systematic manner. The function of the PE is explained, both in terms of discriminant function capability and learning. Once this is understood, we will start putting PEs together in feedforward neural topologies with many layers. We will discuss both the mapping capabilities and training algorithms for each of the network configurations.

3.2 PATTERN-RECOGNITION ABILITY OF THE MCCULLOCH-PITTS PE

The McCulloch-Pitts[1] (M-P) processing element is simply a sum of products followed by a threshold nonlinearity (Figure 3-3). Its input-output equation is

$$y = f(net) = f\left(\sum_{i=1}^{D} w_i x_i + b\right) \tag{3.1}$$

where D is the number of inputs, x_i are the inputs to the PE, w_i are the weights, and b is a bias term. The activation function f is a threshold function defined by

$$f(net) = \begin{cases} 1 & \text{for } net \geq 0 \\ -1 & \text{for } net < 0 \end{cases} \tag{3.2}$$

which is commonly called the *signum function.* Note that the M-P PE is composed of the adaptive linear element (Adaline) studied in Chapter 1 followed by a nonlinearity.

We will now study the pattern-recognition ability of the M-P PE. The study will use the interpretation of a single discriminant function as given by Eq. 2.10. Note that

[1]McCulloch and Pitts were a very influential duo of researchers (Warren McCulloch was a neurobiologist and Walter Pitts a computer scientist) who in the 1940s proposed a model of the neuron as a system for logic computation. See *Brain Theory,* Vol. 1, Shaw and Palm, Eds., World Scientific, 1988.

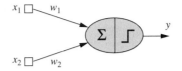

FIGURE 3-3 Two-input, one-output (2-1) McCulloch-Pitts PE

such a system is able to separate only two classes (one class associated with the $+1$ and the other with the -1 response). Figure 3-3 represents the network we are going to build in NeuroSolutions.

NEUROSOLUTIONS EXAMPLE 3.1

McCulloch-Pitts PE for classification

The McCulloch-Pitts PE is created by the concatenation of a Synapse and an Axon. The Synapse contains the weights w_i and performs the sum of products. The Synapse Inspector shows that the element has two inputs and one output. The number of inputs x_i is set by the Input Axon. The soma level of the Inspector shows that the element has two weights. The number of outputs is set by the component to its right (the Threshold Axon) and is one in this case.

The Threshold Axon adds its own bias b to the sum of products and computes a static nonlinearity. The shape of the nonlinearity is drawn on the icon of the Axon, which is a step for the Threshold Axon. So this M-P PE maps 2-D patterns to the values $\{-1, 1\}$. Basically, the M-P PE is like the Adaline we built in Chapter 1, but now the Bias Axon (which is linear) is enhanced with a nonlinearity. This network is very simple, but we can call upon our geometric intuition to understand the input-output map of the M-P PE.

In this example we use two new components, the Threshold Axon and the Function Generator. The Function Generator is a component that is typically used for input and can create common signals such as sine waves, ramps, impulse trains, and so on.

**Function Generator
on an Input Axon**

Threshold Axon

The question that we want to raise now is, What is the discriminant function created by this neural network? Using Eq. 3.2 the output of the processing unit is

$$
y = \begin{cases} -1 & \text{if } \sum_{j=1,2} w_j x_j + b < 0 \\ 1 & \text{if } \sum_{j=1,2} w_j x_j + b \geq 0 \end{cases} \tag{3.3}
$$

We can recognize that the output is controlled by the value of $w_1 x_1 + w_2 x_2 + b$, which is the equation of a plane in two dimensions. This is the *discriminant function* $g(x_1, x_2)$ used by the M-P PE, and we see that it is the output of the Adaline. When the threshold operates on this output, it divides the space into two half planes, one with a positive value $(+1)$ and another with a negative value (-1). This is exactly what we need to implement a classifier for the two-class case (see Section 2.3.3). The equation for the decision surface reads

$$
g(x_1, x_2) = w_1 x_1 + w_2 x_2 + b = 0 \rightarrow x_2 = -\frac{w_1}{w_2} x_1 - \frac{b}{w_2} \tag{3.4}
$$

which can be readily recognized as a line with slope

$$
m = \frac{-w_1}{w_2} \tag{3.5}
$$

passing through the point $(0, -b/w_2)$ of the plane (x_2 intercept), or alternatively, at a distance $-b/|w|$ from the origin, where $|w| = \sqrt{w_1^2 + w_2^2}$. For this reason b is called a *bias*.

Can we visualize the response of this system to inputs? If the system was linear, linear system theory could be applied to arrive at a closed-form solution for the input-output map (the transfer function). But for nonlinear systems the concept of a transfer function does not apply. Equation 3.3 provides the answer for the M-P PE, but this is a very simple case where the output has just two values $(-1, 1)$. In general, the output is difficult to obtain analytically, so we will resort to an exhaustive calculation of the input-output map; that is, values from every location of the input space are injected into the network, and the corresponding output is computed. Let us restrict our attention to a square region of the input space between $-1, 1$ ($x_1, x_2 \in [-1, 1]$) for now.

NeuroSolutions has a probe component that will compute and display the input-output map of Eq. 3.3. It is called the *discriminant probe*. Its function is to scan the input field (sequentially generating x_1, x_2 values), compute the corresponding output, and display it as a gray-scale image. Negative values are displayed as black, positive values as white. The discriminant function is a plane, and its intersection with the x_1, x_2 plane is a line (the decision surface) that is given by Eq. 3.4. This is the line we see in the discriminant probe between the white and the black regions, and it represents the decision surface.

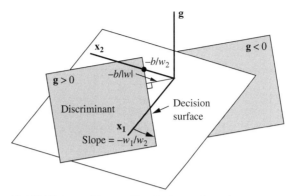

FIGURE 3-4 Linear discriminant function in two dimensions for the two-class case

Before actually starting the simulation, let us raise the question: What do you expect to see? Equation 3.4 dictates the position of the dividing line between the 1 and −1 responses. Using the values of NeuroSolutions Example 3.2, the decision surface is a line described by the equation

$$g(x_1, x_2) = x_1 + x_2 + 0.277 = 0 \qquad (3.6)$$

with slope $m = -1$ and passing through the point $x_2 = 0.277$. The dividing line (i.e., the decision surface for the two-class case) passes through the point $x_2 = -0.277$, and the slope is -1, corresponding to the angle 135° (second quadrant). The position of the decision surface allows us to imagine the location of the discriminant function (Figure 3-4).

Vector Interpretation of the Decision Surface

A vector interpretation of Eq. 3.4 is very useful. We are going to show that the weights, when interpreted as the coordinates of a vector, are perpendicular to the separation surface. Assume that $b = 0$ for simplicity. Note that $w_1 x_1 + w_2 x_2$ can be thought of as the dot product of two vectors of coordinates (w_1, w_2) and (x_1, x_2), respectively.

Let us consider the weights (1, 2) as the end point of a vector **v** drawn from the origin. The points of coordinates (x_1, x_2) in Eq. 3.4 can be interpreted as the end points of another vector **g** (drawn from the origin) that exists on a line. To satisfy $\mathbf{g}(x_1, x_2) = 0$, v and g are perpendicular because their dot product is zero. Hence, the linear decision surface $\mathbf{g}(x_1, x_2)$ has to be perpendicular to the weight vector **v**.

Remember that the PE weights are the coefficients of the discriminant function. Therefore the weights of the PE indicate the normal direction to the separation surface in the input space.

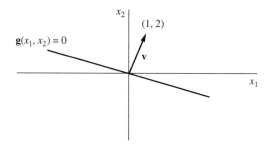

Let us now observe the simulation.

NEUROSOLUTIONS EXAMPLE 3.2

Discriminant probe to visualize the decision surface

This example brings the Discriminant Probe to the Breadboard. The Discriminant Probe is a pair of DLLs that force data through the network and display the system response, giving us an image of the input-output map of the system. In this case we use it to show the discriminant line (separation surface) created by the M-P PE as given by Eq. 3.4. One component of the Discriminant Probe is placed on the Input Axon to send the input coordinates through the network, and the other component is placed on the Output Axon to display the system response.

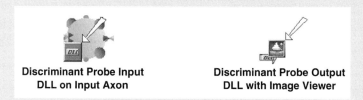

Discriminant Probe Input
DLL on Input Axon

Discriminant Probe Output
DLL with Image Viewer

You are free to experiment with the M-P PE. We suggest that you modify the Synapse weight values and the Threshold Axon bias by placing the cursor in the Matrix Editor field with the mouse and typing in the new values. For every combination you should first guess the solution by computing the slope and y intercept according to Eq. 3.4 and then finding out whether you are correct by running the example. To run the example you need to press the Start button on the Toolbar Controller.

3.2.1 Sigmoidal Nonlinearities

This simple example shows that the decision surface between the 1 and -1 responses created by the M-P PE is a line in 2-D space (a function that is linear in the parameters). The same conceptual picture works for higher-dimensional spaces, where the straight

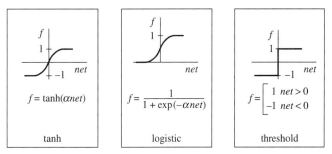

FIGURE 3-5 Common nonlinearities in neurocomputing

line becomes a hyperplane in a space of dimension one less than the input space dimension (but unfortunately we lose our visual intuition).

Notice also how crisp the decision surface is, since a hard threshold acts on the output of the discriminant function. However, other nonlinearities can be utilized in conjunction with the M-P PE. Let us now smooth out the threshold, yielding a *sigmoid* shape for the nonlinearity. The most common nonlinearities are the logistic and the hyperbolic tangent (tanh) functions of Figure 3-5.

hyperbolic tangent $\quad\quad\quad\quad f(net) = \tanh(\alpha net)$

logistic $\quad\quad\quad\quad\quad\quad f(net) = \dfrac{1}{1 + \exp(-\alpha net)}$

α is a slope parameter and normally is set to 1. The major difference between the two sigmoidal nonlinearities is the range of their output values. The logistic function produces values between $[0, 1]$, while the hyperbolic tangent produces values between $[-1, 1]$. An alternative interpretation of this PE substitution is to think that the discriminant function has been generalized to

$$g(x) = f\left(\sum_i w_i x_i + b\right) \tag{3.7}$$

which is sometimes called a ridge function. The ridge function is no longer a hyperplane, since it saturates at 0 (or -1) and $+1$. However, the intersection of ridge functions can still be approximated in most of the input space by the intersections of their arguments. In fact, the argument of the ridge function is still linear in the input variables, and as long as the function f is steep, the decision surface is still approximately linear. Thus the previous interpretation for threshold PEs still holds approximately for sigmoid PEs.

Decision Surfaces of the Sigmoid PEs

Thinking of the separation surfaces built by ANNs made of sigmoidal PEs as an intersection of hyperplanes is sometimes a crude approximation. Sigmoidal PEs create ridge functions that are functions limited between 0 and 1 (or −1 and 1). The weights and the bias still control the location and orientation of the ridge. Near the ridge region, the function is approximately linear, but it deviates from linearity outside this region. The intersection of ridge functions will produce very complex curves. Since the network can control the separation surface by the size of the weights, ANNs can build curved separation surfaces instead of piecewise linear ones, for those problems that require them.

The other big advantage of the Tanh Axon (and also of the Sigmoid Axon) is that the nonlinearity is smooth, which means that the derivative of the map exists. This point is going to be very important later for adaptation. We conclude that either the Tanh Axon or the Sigmoid Axon can be substituted for the Threshold Axon with some practical advantages.

We refer to the combination of the Synapse and the Tanh Axon (or the Sigmoid Axon) as the *modified McCulloch-Pitts PE* because they all respond to the full input space in basically the same functional form (a sum of products followed by a global nonlinearity).

NEUROSOLUTIONS EXAMPLE 3.3

Behavior of the sigmoid PEs

This Breadboard substitutes the Threshold Axon with a Tanh Axon and then a Sigmoid Axon. The difference between the Threshold Axon and the Tanh Axon is that there is a smooth transition between the values of −1 and 1. We can visualize the PE nonlinearity in the component's corresponding Inspector.

Tanh Axon   Sigmoid Axon

The net effect of this modification in the PE input-output function is that the crisp separation between the two regions [positive and negative values of $g(.)$] is substituted by a smooth transition region between the values of −1 and +1. Hence the name *ridge function*. However, the orientation of the separation surface is still defined by the ratio of w_1 and w_2, and its vertical placement is still controlled by the bias of the Axon. A new feature of this nonlinearity is that the absolute values of the weights control the width of the gray region. By increasing the values of the weights while leaving the ratio of the weights constant, we can make the separation surface become crisper—eventually approximating the one of the Threshold Axon.

> The logistic nonlinearity is similar to the tanh; however, the range is between 0 and 1. The tanh is an antisymmetric function (y intercept is zero), while the logistic is not (y intercept is 0.5). The Tanh Axon and Logistic Axon are normally interchangeable, with the final selection determined by the desired range of the output (either $[-1, 1]$ or $[0, 1]$).

The output of the logistic function varies from 0 to 1. It is interesting to note that under some conditions, the logistic function allows a very powerful interpretation of the output of the PE as a posteriori probabilities for Gaussian-distributed input classes. The tanh is closely related to the logistic function by a linear transformation in the input and output spaces, so neural networks that use either of these can be made equivalent by changing weights and biases.

Probabilistic Interpretation of Sigmoid Outputs

According to Bayes' rule, the a posteriori probability can be written as

$$P(c_i \mid \mathbf{x}) = \frac{p(\mathbf{x} \mid c_i)P(c_i)}{P(\mathbf{x})}$$

Note that for the two class case the denominator can be written as $P(\mathbf{x}) = p(\mathbf{x} \mid C_1)P(C_1) + p(\mathbf{x} \mid C_2)P(C_2)$, where C_1 and C_2 are the two classes. Now if the likelihoods are Gaussians of equal variance, it is not difficult to show that

$$P(C_1 \mid \mathbf{x}) = \frac{1}{1 + exp(-a)}$$

where

$$a = \ln \frac{p(\mathbf{x} \mid C_1)P(C_1)}{p(\mathbf{x} \mid C_2)P(C_2)}$$

Note that this is exactly the definition of the activation function of the logistic PE, so we can interpret the output of this PE as the a posteriori probability of the class given the data.

3.2.2 Classification Implies the Control of the Discriminant Function Location

Remember that the ratio of the weights controls the slope (orientation) of the separation surface, and the PE bias controls the x_2 intercept (Figure 3-4). So how can the M-P PE system be used to distinguish two classes of patterns?

The discriminant function placement should be controlled so that the system outputs the value 1 for one of the classes and -1 (or 0) for the other; that is, the discriminant function must be moved around in the input space to yield the minimum number of errors. As external observers, we can do this easily by looking at the data clusters in two dimensions and placing the separation line between them. But in higher-dimensional spaces we cannot visualize the data clusters, so we need to follow some type of step-by-step procedure.

NEUROSOLUTIONS EXAMPLE 3.4

Classification as the control of the decision surface

The input file placed on the Input Axon links NeuroSolutions to the computer file system. We created a file with eight points according to the following table. The third column represents the class membership. Since our network is built with a logistic function that ranges from 0 to 1, these values can also be interpreted as the desired network response.

X_1	X_2	Class
-0.50	0.35	0
-0.75	0.85	0
-0.60	0.65	0
-0.50	0.75	0
0.50	0.00	1
-0.30	-0.20	1
0.20	0.10	1
0.10	-0.10	1

We attached the L2 Criterion (mean square error) at the output of the Logistic Axon. This PE computes the square difference between the system output and the desired response for each input pattern. The output file works as the desired response, and in this case contains the values used in the "class" column of the table. Note that we have a Matrix Viewer on top of the L_2 Criterion to provide a numerical indication of the power of the error (MSE), that is, the difference between the machine output and the output file value. All the eight input samples are sent through the network to display the average error over the entire data set.

One other component deserves to be mentioned. The Scatter Plot probe is placed at the output of the Input Axon and will show the x, y locations of the input data. Since we are interested in displaying all the training patterns, the data buffer size is set to 8. The purpose of this example is to relate the position of the decision surface and the MSE, so experiment with several weights to obtain perfect classification of all the patterns.

As you adjust the network weights, note that the sign of the response may be correct, but the error is still not zero. This is the problem of using a saturating nonlinearity. We have to use very large weights to obtain a response close to 1 and 0. This example shows that acceptable solutions for classification do not require the error to be exactly zero.

Let us now experiment with a different set of data. On the book's CD-ROM, in the "InteractiveBook\ examples\ McPitts3" subdirectory, there is another file called mcpitts_data1.asc. Go to the Input File component and, with the Inspector open, select the "File List" page. Click the *Remove* button to deselect the present file and click the *Add* button. This will put you in the Win95 Open File panel. Select the file, and NeuroSolutions will ask if it is an ASCII column training file (click the *Close* button to finalize the selection). Another panel pops up, allowing you to select which columns are used in the experiment. Since the file has three columns—two for inputs and one for the desired response—and we are selecting the input data, we have to skip the third column. Select the third row, click the *Skip* button, and close the panel. We just completed the selection of the new file. You have to do the same thing for the desired signal file, but now you should skip the first two columns.

The procedure we outlined in the example can be automated by the machine itself, without any outside help, by *providing feedback to the machine* on how it is doing. As in regression, the feedback comes in the form of an error (ε_p) between the desired response (d_p) and the actual output (y_p). Note that when the error is zero, the machine output is equal to the desired response. Once the error is defined, the obvious thing to do is to minimize either the error directly or a function of the error that is normally called the cost function or the criterion.

There are many possible definitions of the error (we will treat error criterion in Chapter 4), but in neurocomputing one commonly uses the mean square error (or power), that is, the sum of the square difference between the desired response and the actual output. We already used this criterion in Chapter 1. For ease of explanation we copy it here,

$$J = \frac{1}{2N} \sum_p \varepsilon_p^2 = \frac{1}{2N} \sum_p (d_p - y_p)^2 \tag{3.8}$$

where p is the pattern index. The goal of the classifier is to minimize this cost function by changing its free parameters. This search for the weights to meet a desired response or *internal constraint* is the essence of any *connectionist* computation. The central problem to be solved on the road to machine-based classifiers is how to automate the process of minimizing the error so that the machine can independently make these weight changes, without need for hidden agents or external observers.

3.2.3 The First Learning Algorithm for a Nonlinear Machine

As a historical note, Rosenblatt [1958] proposed the following procedure to directly minimize the error by changing the weights of the M-P PE: Get an example from class 1 and examine the output. If the output is correct, do nothing. If the response is incorrect, tweak the weights and bias until the response becomes correct. Get the next example and repeat the procedure, until all the patterns are correctly classified. This procedure is basically the perceptron learning algorithm, which can be put into the following equation:

$$w(n + 1) = w(n) + \eta(d(n) - y(n))x(n) \tag{3.9}$$

where η is the step size, y is the M-P PE output, and d is the desired response.

Perceptron Learning Algorithm

Let us study in more detail the perceptron learning algorithm. Notice that Eq. 3.9 corrects the weights only under the condition that y is different from d. There are two cases to consider: either $d = 1$ (class 1) and $y = -1$, in which case

$$w(n + 1) = w(n) + 2\eta x(n)$$

or $d = -1$ (class 2) and $y = 1$, in which case

$$w(n + 1) = w(n) - 2\eta x(n)$$

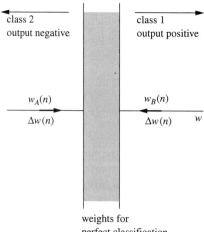

weights for
perfect classification

Now let us see how these cases arise in practice. Let us consider the 1-D case, with one weight, as in the figure. In the first case (case A) $x_A(n)$ belongs to class 1 but the output is -1, so the present weight $w_A(n)$ must be in the left part of the figure (otherwise the output would be positive and there would be no correction). In this case the update adds a value to the weight, moving it in the correct direction.

In the second case (case B), the input pattern $x_B(n)$ belongs to class 2, so if the perceptron is outputting a positive value, it is because the weight $w_B(n)$ is in the right part of the figure. In this case the weight is decreased according to the equation. In both cases we see that the weight is moved to the shaded region that produces the correct classification. One can show mathematically that for linearly separable patterns this algorithm converges in a finite number of steps [Haykin 1994].

It is important at this stage to compare Eq. 3.9 with the LMS algorithm we used to train the Adaline in the first example of Chapter 2. Note that the functional form is the same, that is, the old weights are incrementally modified proportionally to the product of the error and the input, but there is a significant difference. We cannot say that this corresponds to gradient descent since the system has a discontinuous nonlinearity. In the perceptron learning algorithm, $y(n)$ is the output of the nonlinear system. The algorithm is directly minimizing the difference between the response of the M-P PE and the desired response, instead of minimizing the difference between the Adaline output and the desired response.

This subtle modification has tremendous impact on the performance of the system. For one thing, the M-P PE learns only when its output is wrong. In fact, when $y(n) = d(n)$, the weights remain the same. The net effect is that the final values of the weights are no longer equal to the linear regression result, because the nonlinearity is brought into the weight update rule.

Another way of phrasing this is to say that the weight update became much more selective, effectively gated by the system performance. Notice that the LMS update is also a function of the error to a certain degree. Larger errors have more effect on the weight update than small errors, but all patterns affect the final weights, implementing a "smooth gate." In the perceptron the net effect is that the placement of the discriminant function is no longer controlled smoothly by all the input samples as in the Adaline, only by the ones that are important for placing the discriminant function in a way that explicitly minimizes the output error.

NEUROSOLUTIONS EXAMPLE 3.5

Perceptron learning rule

In this example we use the perceptron learning algorithm to classify the two previous data sets: the two-class problem from the previous example and the healthy–sick patient data. With the perceptron learning algorithm the system will learn automatically from the data without the need for us to select weights as we did in this chapter up to now.

This example uses two data sets that produce different results because one (the two-class problem with eight patterns) is linearly separable, while the other is not. The perceptron learning algorithm trains only when the system response is incorrect; therefore the weights will converge if all the inputs are classified correctly. Another side effect of training only on the errors is that if the problem is not linearly separable, the training will never stop. This can cause abrupt changes in the weights of the system near the end of the training, which may affect the classification performance. Since the perceptron learning algorithm does not search for the best answer, only a satisfactory answer, the network may not perform well on data that was not included in its training set. Note that there are many final weight values that produce an error of zero; that is, they exactly solve the linearly separable problem.

The network is now learning by itself, so we will again have to add the back-propagation and gradient descent planes that we used at the end of Chapter 1. At the end of this chapter we will finally explain the details of these two additional planes. We also have to control the learning rate or step size to make sure that the system will converge to the optimum. You should experiment with other learning rates and observe the learning curve as our thermometer for learning.

Let us assume that the patterns are linearly separable, that is, that there is a linear discriminant function that produces zero classification error. The solution of the perceptron learning rule is a weight vector $\mathbf{w}^*$ such that

$$\begin{cases} \sum_i x_i(n)w_i^* > 0 & \text{for } d(n) = 1 \\ \sum_i x_i(n)w_i^* < 0 & \text{for } d(n) = -1 \end{cases} \quad \textbf{(3.10)}$$

where n is an index that runs over the training set data. This equation can be written in simpler form as $d_i(\sum_i w_i^* x_i(n)) > 0$. Knowledge of the M-P PE tells us that for each input pattern (each n) there is a weight vector that produces the partitioning given by the desired response. The optimal weight vector is the vector that simultaneously meets all of these desired partitions. The solution in two dimensions is a line of equation $\mathbf{x}^T\mathbf{w}^* = 0$ (i.e., the optimal weight vector $\mathbf{w}^*$ has to be orthogonal to every data vector $\mathbf{x}$). The weight update equation moves the weights directly toward this solution when it corrects $\mathbf{w}(n)$ by $\pm\eta\mathbf{x}(n)$ depending on the sign of the error. This learning rule takes a finite number of steps to reach the optimal solution for *linearly separable patterns*. There are two major problems with this solution. First, as soon as the last sample is correctly classified, the discriminant function stalls, producing many different final decision surface placements that may not perform well in the test set. Second, this learning rule converges only if the classes are linearly separable. Otherwise the solution will oscillate.

3.2.4 The Delta Rule

We presented in Chapter 1 a systematic step-by-step procedure based on gradient descent (the LMS rule) that was able to modify the weights of the Adaline so that the minimum of the performance surface was reached. The algorithm (which you should have memorized by now) is beautifully simple. It adds to the present weight a quantity proportional to the product of the error and the activation available at the PE (just two multiplications per weight), that is,

$$w(n + 1) = w(n) + \eta \varepsilon_p(n) x_p(n) \tag{3.11}$$

We are going to reexamine the LMS algorithm using a different concept that is central to learning in neural networks. This concept is an old result from calculus that is called the *chain rule*. Basically, the chain rule tells how to compute the partial derivative of a variable with respect to another when a functional form links the two. Let us assume that $y = f(x)$, and the goal is to compute $\partial y / \partial x$, the *sensitivity* of y with respect to x. As long as f is differentiable, then

$$\frac{\partial y}{\partial x} = \frac{\partial y}{\partial f} \frac{\partial f}{\partial x} \tag{3.12}$$

Note that the value of Eq. 3.12 computes how much a change in x is reflected in y, that is, how sensitive y is to a change in x. When we work with sensitivities the calculations progress from the dependent variable to the independent variable. Keep this in mind.

One can show that the LMS rule is equivalent to the chain rule in the computation of the sensitivity of the cost function J with respect to the unknowns.

Derivation of LMS with the Chain Rule

Let us rederive the LMS algorithm for a linear PE using the chain rule. We want to compute the partial derivative of the cost J with respect to w and equate it to zero to find the minimum. Now, J is a function of the weights through the network output y_p, that is,

$$J = \frac{1}{2} \sum_p (d_p - y_p)^2 = \sum_p J_p$$

where J_p is the cost for the pth sample and

$$y_p = wx_p$$

so using the chain rule (Eq. 3.12) we get

$$\frac{\partial J_p}{\partial w} = \frac{\partial J}{\partial y_p} \frac{\partial y_p}{\partial w} = -(d_p - y_p)x_p = -\varepsilon_p x_p$$

Using the gradient-descent idea to update the weights as we did before,

$$\Delta w_p = -\eta \frac{\partial J}{\partial w} = \eta \varepsilon_P x_P$$

which is exactly the same result as obtained in the LMS algorithm.

Interpreting this equation with respect to the sensitivity concept, we see that the gradient measures the sensitivity. LMS is therefore updating the weights proportionally to how much they affect the performance, that is, proportionally to their sensitivity. This makes perfect sense, since if the goal is to decrease the error, the weights that impact the error the most should get the largest modifications.

Our goal is to extend the LMS concept to the M-P PE, which is a nonlinear system. How can we compute the *sensitivity* through a nonlinearity?

First, let us examine the problem. Figure 3-6 details the modified M-P PE, where we show multiple weights connected to its input. Note that the output of the modified M-P PE is a nonlinear function of the weights (Eq. 3.1). But we can still compute the partial derivative of the output PE with respect to its weights using the chain rule of Eq. 3.12. First compute the partial derivative of the output with respect to the intermediate signal *net,* and then compute the partial derivative of *net* with respect to the weight w_i, that is,

$$\frac{\partial y}{\partial w_i} = \frac{\partial y}{\partial net} \frac{\partial}{\partial w_i} net = f'(net)x_i \tag{3.13}$$

where $f'(.)$ is the partial derivative of the static nonlinearity.

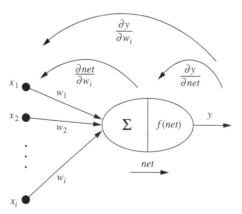

FIGURE 3-6 Illustration of the sensitivity computation through a nonlinear PE

Derivation of Sensitivity through Nonlinearity

Let us write

$$\frac{\partial y}{\partial w_i} = \frac{\partial y}{\partial net} \frac{\partial net}{\partial w_i}$$

and note that from Eq. 3.1

$$\frac{\partial y}{\partial net} = f'(net)$$

and

$$\frac{\partial net}{\partial w_i} = \frac{\partial}{\partial w_i}\left(\sum_k w_k x_k\right) = 0 + \cdots + \frac{\partial w_i x_i}{\partial w_i} + 0 + \cdots = x_i$$

so finally we have the result in the text, Eq. 3.13.

This is another application of the famous chain rule, but now the chain rule is applied to *the topology*. As long as the PE nonlinearity is smooth (differentiable), we can compute how much a change in the weight δw_i affects the output y or, from the point of view of the sensitivity, how sensitive the output y is to a change in a particular weight δw_i. Note that we compute this output sensitivity by a product of partial derivatives through intermediate points in the topology. For the nonlinear PE there is only one intermediate point, *net*, but we really do not care how many of these intermediate points there are. The chain rule can be applied as many times as necessary.

In practice, we have an error at the output (the difference between the desired response and the actual output), and we want to adjust all the PE weights so that the error is minimized in a statistical sense. The obvious idea is to distribute the adjustments according to the sensitivity of the output to each weight. Why is this obvious? If we want to minimize the output error, we should make larger changes in the weights that most affect the output value, which is measured by the sensitivity. This is what the gradient descent does, hence the LMS rule.

To modify the weight, we actually propagate back the output error to intermediate points in the topology and scale it along the way as prescribed by Eq. 3.13 according to the elemental transfer functions that we find, as shown in Figure 3-6. This methodology is very powerful, because we do not need to know explicitly the error at intermediate places, such as *net*. The chain rule automatically derives the error contribution for us. This observation is going to be crucial for adapting more complicated topologies and will result in the backpropagation algorithm.

Let us now complete the formulas to adapt the modified M-P PE weights. Note that now we have two indices—the index i for the weight and the index p for the pattern—

and n for the iteration number. The mean square error is rewritten

$$J = \frac{1}{2N} \sum_{p=1}^{N} (d_p - y_p)^2$$

$$y_p = f\left(\sum_i w_i x_{ip}\right)$$

(3.14)

By applying the chain rule twice, once for the output and again for the variable *net,* we get

$$\frac{\partial J}{\partial w_i} = \frac{\partial J}{\partial y_p}\frac{\partial y_p}{\partial net_p}\frac{\partial}{\partial w_i}net_p = -(d_p - y_p)f'(net_p)x_{ip} = -\varepsilon_p f'(net_p)x_{ip} \quad \text{(3.15)}$$

The application of the gradient descent gives (compare with Eq. 3.11)

$$w_i(n+1) = w_i(n) + \eta\varepsilon_p(n)x_{ip}(n)f'(net_p(n)) \quad \text{(3.16)}$$

This rule is called the *delta rule* and is a direct extension of the LMS rule to nonlinear systems with smooth nonlinearities. Note that the derivative of the nonlinearity is computed at the operating point $net_p(n)$ for the corresponding input pattern. Note also that the delta rule is local to the pattern and to the weight, that is, it only requires knowledge of that specific pattern, the PE error, and its input.

Optimizing Linear and Nonlinear Systems

You may know that our mathematical knowledge is very limited in computing solutions for nonlinear differential equations, so it may seem hopeless to attack the problem of optimizing a nonlinear system. Although it is true that we lose the ability to analytically solve for the minimum, we can still use iterative procedures to find it. This is one of the advantages of optimization techniques.

For the linear problem treated in Chapter 1, the analytical solution can be applied and always produces the best possible results. However, the analytic method cannot be used for the M-P PE. Iterative optimization (in the form of the gradient-descent procedure) can be applied to problems that are beyond analytical solutions. As we are going to see, we can apply gradient descent as long as the function is smooth, which can include many nonlinearities.

Since the smooth nonlinearities discussed so far exponentially approach the values of -1 (or 0) and 1, the multiplication by the derivative reduces appreciably the error in most of the operating range since the derivative is bell shaped around $net_P = 0$. The derivatives of the logistic function and the tanh are, respectively,

$$f'_{\text{logistic}}(net_i) = x_i(1 - x_i)$$

$$f'_{\text{tanh}}(net_i) = 0.5(1 - x_i^2)$$

(3.17)

Error attenuation

Let us look at the figure to understand how the error is attenuated. The top part of the figure shows the tanh nonlinearity and the bottom part its derivative. When the input variable *net* is in the linear region (region A), the derivative is close to 1, so the sensitivity (Eq. 3.13) is close to x_i, the equivalent sensitivity of the linear PE. However, when the operating point of the nonlinearity is close to saturation (case B or C), the derivative of the tanh is close to zero. This effectively corresponds to an attenuation of the sensitivity when compared with the linear PE. What this means is that y became much less sensitive to a change in x_i when the operating point is in region B or C.

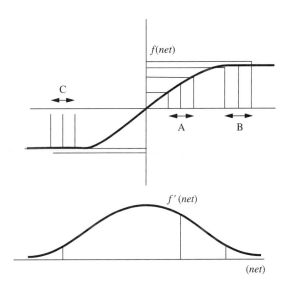

We thus see that nonlinear PEs have a dual role of saturating the activations for large values of the input and attenuating the corresponding sensitivities. These two factors bring stability to the learning process, because learning becomes much less dependent on out-liers. Moreover, the nonlinearity allows each PE in the network to specialize in a portion of the input space (the weights associated with a given PE learn more when that PE is in the linear region).

Our goal is to visualize the movement of the discriminant function during the adjustment of the PE weights using the delta rule. Let us go back to NeuroSolutions and automate the placement and display of the discriminant surface for this simple example.

NEUROSOLUTIONS EXAMPLE 3.6

Delta rule to adapt the M-P PE

We now use the delta rule to train the Breadboard from Example 3.5. We will use the same two-class data set with eight points. When we run the network, observe the discriminant function move. The output mean square error (MSE) decreases close to zero when the discriminant function is placed between the two classes of points. The output of the network toward the end of learning mimics the desired response. Notice that at the beginning of the run the discriminant line changes its orientation quickly, and then at the end there is a period of fine tuning. These are the two basic phases of learning; the discovery phase (what is the direction of the minimum?) and the convergence phase (fine-tune to get to the minimum). In our case the convergence phase corresponds to increasing both the weights and bias (while keeping the ratio constant) in order to get a sharper cutoff between the two classes.

A small exercise to test your knowledge is to guess the network weights upon visualization of the discriminant function. You should at least be able to correctly guess the signs of the weights and their approximate ratio. Note that the final MSE is much smaller than the value obtained when we entered the parameters for the M-P PE by hand. Also note that there is no analytic solution for the optimal weights as we had in the linear case (the least squares method). Iterative solutions are therefore very appealing and practical when dealing with nonlinear systems.

It is instructive to change the learning rates and see how the solution behaves. You should be able to do this by now, even if the Breadboard is not prepared for it (go to the Step icon, right-click the mouse button to open the Inspector, and then enter other values for the step size). Try very large step sizes (300) for both parameters and see what happens. In this case the data is linearly separable, and it is very difficult to make the system weights diverge. The nonlinearity is always keeping the output between 0 and 1, no matter what the values of the weights are, so divergence of a single PE nonlinear system is not apparent from the value of the output.

An interesting challenge is to find a set of learning rates that will prevent the system from finding the correct discriminant line.

3.2.5 Implications of the PE Nonlinearity

Several key aspects changed in the performance surface with the introduction of the nonlinearity. The nice, parabolic performance surface of the least squares problem is lost. Why is that? Note that the performance surface describes how the cost changes with the weights. But the performance depends on the topology of the network through the output error, so when nonlinear processing elements are used to solve a given prob-

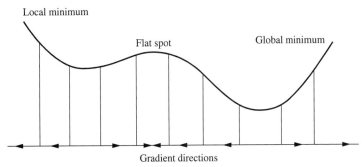

FIGURE 3-7   Nonconvex performance surface with gradients depicted

lem, the performance–weights relationship becomes nonlinear, and there is no guarantee of a single minimum. The performance surface may have several minima. The minimum that produces the smallest error in the search space is called the *global minimum*. The others are called *local minima*. Alternatively, we say that the performance surface is *nonconvex*. This affects the search scheme because gradient descent uses local information to search the performance surface. In the immediate neighborhood, local minima are indistinguishable from the global minimum, so the gradient search algorithm may be caught in these suboptimal performance points "thinking" it has reached the global minimum (Figure 3-7).

Other conditions where the gradient is basically zero are called *saddle points* (or flat spots). Since the weight update is ultimately produced by the gradient, when the gradient becomes very small, the weights do not change much and the adaptation may stall. Suboptimal performance may then result, since the designer may think that the best performance has been reached.

Fortunately, the noisy estimate produced by the LMS rule, which we called a nuisance before (rattling, see Chapter 1), becomes an advantage. In fact, the noisy gradient increases the chance of escaping both local minima and flat spots. It is obvious that the control of the adaptation algorithm becomes much more delicate in nonconvex performance surfaces. If the gradient search becomes less robust, a fair question is: Why nonlinear PEs?

Why Nonlinear PEs?

The answer to this question is related to better performance and new computing power. Nonlinear systems may provide, for instance, a better fit to data than linear regression. In terms of the performance surface, this means that the global minimum achieved by the nonlinear network is lower than the minimum of the linear network. More important, nonlinear PEs may affect new types of computation such as classification, which cannot be done well with linear systems. There is a real need for nonlinear processing, in spite of the added difficulty of working with nonlinear structures.

It is instructive to use the last example and train a linear system and a nonlinear system with the same data to understand the difference between them. The M-P PE separates the two data clusters. What do you think is going to happen if we use a linear system to provide a desired response of 1s and 0s?

Let us think in terms of least squares. If a set of points in 2-D space is given and a desired response of 1s and 0s is provided, the linear system will do regression between the input and the desired response. It will provide the best regression plane (this is a 2-D input) between the 0 and 1 responses, given the values of the input samples.

Let us go to NeuroSolutions to verify this behavior.

NEUROSOLUTIONS EXAMPLE 3.7

Comparing a linear and nonlinear PE for classification

Let us use the same problem as in the previous example, and simply change the PE from a Logistic Axon to a Bias Axon, which simply adds the contributions of the weights plus a bias. Running the simulations, we see that the discrimination probe shows a separation line passing between the classes of points, as in the nonlinear case. The minimum error is 0.011276 and cannot be decreased further, since the output must be a linear combination of the inputs, that is, all the possible outputs must exist in a plane. This should be compared with the nonlinear solution that is able to decrease the error further by operating nonlinearly on the inputs (a zero error is possible). This effectively corresponds to "bending" the regression plane to better fit the 0 and 1 responses in the two half planes.

It is also interesting to verify that the linear system is much more sensitive to the learning rates than its nonlinear counterpart. Explore the Breadboard by changing the learning rates, and observe the different speeds at which the regression plane moves to its final position.

3.3 THE PERCEPTRON

Rosenblatt's *perceptron* is a pattern-recognition machine that was invented in the 1950s for optical character recognition. The perceptron has multiple inputs fully connected to an output layer with multiple McCulloch-Pitts PEs (Figure 3-8). Each input x_j is multiplied by an adjustable constant w_{ij} (the weight) before being fed to the ith processing element in the output layer, yielding

$$y_i = f(net_i) = f\left(\sum_j w_{ij}x_j + b_i\right) \tag{3.18}$$

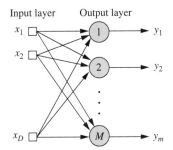

FIGURE 3-8 The perceptron with D inputs and M outputs (D-M)

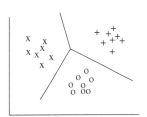

FIGURE 3-9 Decision surface for a three-output perceptron

where b_i is the bias for each PE. The number of outputs is normally determined by the number of classes in the data. These PEs add the individual scaled contributions and respond to the entire input space.

After studying the function of each M-P PE, we are ready to understand the pattern-recognition power of the perceptron. The M-P PE is restricted to classifying only two classes. The more general problem is to classify the input as one of M classes (Figure 3-9). The topology has to be modified to include a layer of M M-P PEs so that each one is able to create its own linear discriminant function in a D-dimensional space. The advantage of having multiple PEs versus the single M-P PE is the ability to tune each PE to respond maximally to a region in the input space. Each PE is essentially deciding if the input is in class i or not in class i (e.g., all other classes).

One of Rosenblatt's theoretical achievements was the demonstration that the perceptron could be trained with Eq. 3.9 to recognize linearly separable patterns in a finite number of steps. This showed not only that these adaptive devices produce useful pattern classification by tweaking parameters, but that there are systematic algorithms to change the weights that converge in a finite number of steps. These algorithms are called learning rules. The perceptron also had a remarkable property: It was able to *generalize*. Hence we can say that the perceptron started the field of learning theory. The recent interest in large margin classifiers shows that the perceptron and its algorithm are still at the center stage in designing practical classifiers.

3.3.1 Decision Surfaces of the Perceptron

An M-output perceptron can divide the pattern space into M distinct regions. Suppose that the ith and jth regions share a common boundary. The decision surface is a segment of a linear surface of equation $g_i(x) - g_j(x) = 0$. There are $M(M-1)/2$ such equations, so the decision surfaces of a perceptron are segments of at most the same number of hyperplanes. The hyperplanes that contribute to the definition of the decision boundary must be contiguous. (The others are called redundant.) The decision regions of the perceptron are always *convex* regions, because during training we require that one and only one of the outputs be positive. When a PE responds maximally to an input pattern, it means that the input is inside the region represented by the PE. Hence each PE identifies patterns that belong to a class. The perceptron is therefore a physical implementation of the linear pattern-recognition machine presented in Figure 2-12.

NEUROSOLUTIONS EXAMPLE 3.8
Decision boundaries of the perceptron

This example shows the discriminant function and the decision boundary created by the perceptron for a three-class problem in 2-D space. The data that created the example is shown in Figure 3-9. What we want to stress is the convex shape of each decision region. This is a characteristic of a single-layer network. Notice that there are areas in the space that have no class assigned to them.

3.3.2 Delta Rule Applied to the Perceptron

What changes in the delta rule when we go from a single PE to the perceptron? Not much, except that now there are several (M) outputs, so the cost of Eq. 3.8 must be computed not only as a sum over the training set but also as a summation of each output PE. Thus J becomes

$$J = \frac{1}{2N} \sum_{p=1}^{N} \sum_{i=1}^{M} \varepsilon_{pi}^2 \qquad (3.19)$$

where p is the index over the patterns and i over the output PEs. We can rewrite Eq. 3.15 to adapt the j weight of the ith PE as

$$\frac{\partial J}{\partial w_{ij}} = \frac{\partial J}{\partial y_{ip}} \frac{\partial y_{ip}}{\partial net_{ip}} \frac{\partial}{\partial w_{ij}} net_{ip} = -(d_{ip} - y_{ip})f'(net_{ip})x_{jp} = -\varepsilon_{ip}f'(net_{ip})x_{jp} \qquad (3.20)$$

and the update rule for the weights would be the same as Eq. 3.16. Note that the gradient of the cost with respect to the weight w_{ij} is computed by multiplying the partial derivative of the cost with respect to the PE state ($\partial J/\partial y_{ip}$) scaled by the derivative of the nonlinearity of the PE and the input activation. Let us define the *local error* δ_i for the ith PE as

$$\delta_{ip} = \frac{\partial J}{\partial y_{ip}} f'(net_{ip}) \qquad (3.21)$$

We can then conclude that the weight update using the delta rule is

$$w_{ij}(n+1) = w_{ij}(n) - \eta \frac{\partial J}{\partial w_{ij}} = w_{ij}(n) + \eta \delta_{ip} x_{jp} \qquad (3.22)$$

which are local quantities available at the weight, that is, the activation x_{jp} that reaches the weight w_{ij} from the input, and the local error δ_{ip} propagated from the cost. The amazing thing about this algorithm is that it is *local to the weight*. Only the local error δ_i and the local activation x_j are needed to update a particular weight. This means that it is immaterial how many PEs the net has and how complex their interconnection is. The training algorithm can concentrate on each PE individually and work only with the local error and local activation.

NEUROSOLUTIONS EXAMPLE 3.9

The perceptron for character recognition

This NeuroSolutions Breadboard implements Rosenblatt's perceptron with two minor modifications: Instead of using threshold PEs, it implements the classifier with tanh nonlinearities. This allows us to use the delta rule to train the machine instead of the perceptron learning algorithm developed by Rosenblatt.

The task is character recognition. We created 8-pixel-by-8-pixel black-and-white images of the 10 digits (0–9). We have placed an Image Viewer on the Input Axon so you can view the images. The output layer is made up of 10 PEs, one for each of the digits. Since we are going to use the delta rule, we placed an L_2 Criterion at the output and included an output file with the desired response, which is a value of 1 for the corresponding digit and 0 for the others. We will place a Bar Graph probe over the output file to show the net response for each input pattern.

Image Viewer

Training will be done using on-line learning; that is, the weights are modified after the presentation of each pattern. Learning rates are appropriately set for the task (more about this later). We will place a MegaScope at the cost access of the L_2 Criterion to display the change of the MSE versus the iteration number, producing our learning curve.

What do you expect to see? In the beginning the weights are random, so any combination of outputs can appear, which produces a large error. But after a few iterations the weights are modified to track the desired response. In the Bar Chart, the largest response scrolls from top to bottom, meaning that only one large output is present and that it matches the digits (presented in sequence 0–9). When the network is trained, the output follows the desired response.

It is remarkable that 640 weights (the Synapse Inspector displays the number of weights) are trained so quickly. In practice, however, the problem of digit recognition is much more difficult because the characters differ from person to person; they can appear concatenated and misaligned.

It is interesting to find out how robust the obtained solution is. This can be measured by altering the input with the weights fixed and finding the network response. We implement this modification by placing a noise generator over the input file. The network does not classify noisy inputs very well. The inputs are very different from the clean, noiseless images used for training. An interesting question is, Can we improve the robustness of the classification if we include noise during the training? This can be easily checked with the setup. The initial condition is the weights obtained without noise. We will continue to train the network with the new, noisy data and see whether it can improve its performance.

We see that the error decreases further, albeit in an erratic way. This means that the network has learned to cope with small amounts of noise. The outputs look cleaner, and we can even increase the noise variance and still obtain reasonable results. This experiment shows that adding a small amount of noise to clean data sets may improve the performance when noise is present. However, the method requires tight control of the experimentation to produce good results.

We ask you to single-step through the training to watch the input and output of the system for each data point. This is done by clicking the step exemplar button on the NeuroSolutions Control Palette. At the end of a run the network may not allow you to single-step through the network, since you have completed the experiment. You can fix this situation by either clicking on the Zero Counter button or by increasing the number of training epochs in the Controller Inspector panel.

Remember that this is a live Breadboard, so you can experiment with the Breadboard at will. We recommend that you change the learning rates, change the noise source variance, use other probes such as the Hinton probe to display the weight values, and so on.

3.3.3 Large-Margin Perceptrons

We have seen that the perceptron learning rule is very efficient but not very effective, because the movement of the discriminant function stalls as soon as the last sample is classified without error. This normally leaves the separation surface very close to the last sample properly classified. Obviously, this solves the problem in the training set, but we also feel that it may not produce the best possible classification for data in the test set. This is the reason we would like to modify the perceptron training so that the location of the decision surface is placed in the valley between classes and at equal distances from the class boundaries. For this we have to introduce and define the concept of *margin*. Suppose we have a set of data and labels $S = \{(x_1, d_1), \ldots, (x_n, d_N)\}$ with $d = \{-1, +1\}$, and we have a linear discriminant function defined by $(\mathbf{w}, b)$. We

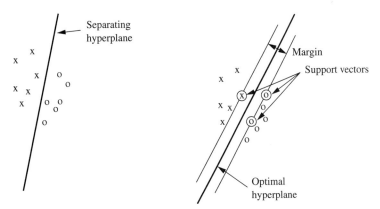

FIGURE 3-10 Hyperplane with largest margin

define the margin of the hyperplane to the sample set S as

$$\gamma = \min_{x \in S} |\langle \mathbf{x}, \mathbf{w} \rangle + b| > 0 \qquad (3.23)$$

where $\langle . \rangle$ means the inner product of $\mathbf{x}$ and $\mathbf{w}$. The margin is finding the output of the network that is closest to zero. A network output close to zero indicates uncertainty, so large margins are desirable. We can show that the margin is related to the inverse of the L_2 norm of the hyperplane's weight vector $\mathbf{w}$, that is, $\gamma = 2/\|\mathbf{w}\|^2$ [Vapnik 1995].

We define the *optimal hyperplane* as the hyperplane that maximizes the margin between the two classes (Figure 3-10). As shown in this figure, from all the possible hyperplanes that separate the data, the optimal one is halfway between the samples that are closest to the boundary between the classes.

Vapnik showed that the optimal hyperplane provides the smallest bound on the Vapnik-Chervonenkis (V-C) dimension, which is one of the best things we can do to guarantee a low error rate in the test set. The issue is how to find this optimal hyperplane. We see from Figure 3-10 that we first have to find the points that are closest to the boundary (called the *support vectors*) and then place the discriminant function midway.

3.3.4 The Adatron Algorithm

Here we give a very simple algorithm known as the *Adatron* algorithm [Aulauf and Biehl, 1989] to find the parameters of the discriminant function that possesses the largest margin. This algorithm is sequential and is guaranteed to find the optimal solution with an exponentially fast rate of convergence.

To explain the procedure, we have to write the discriminant function of the M-P PE in terms of the *data-dependent representation*,

$$f(x) = \text{sgn}(g(x)) \qquad \text{where } g(x) = \langle x, w \rangle + b = \sum_{i=0}^{N} \alpha_i \langle x, x_i \rangle + b \qquad (3.24)$$

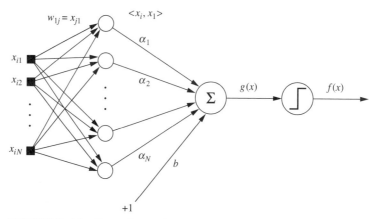

FIGURE 3-11 Data-dependent representation for the perceptron

where $\langle . \rangle$ is the inner product, N is the number of samples, and α_i are a set of multipliers, one for each sample. We consider the input space augmented by one dimension with a constant value of 1 to provide the bias. Let us see how to construct a topology that creates this data-dependent representation (Figure 3-11). Notice that we can implement the inner product by creating a linear network with N linear PEs where the input-layer weights are the values of the training-set samples, that is, $w_{ij} = x_{ji}$ where x_{ji} means the ith coordinate of the jth sample. The α_i are then weights connecting the ith first-layer PEs to the output. This system creates an output that is the same as the M-P PE. Note that once the training data is given, the first-layer weights are immediately fixed.

In this representation the perceptron learning algorithm of Eq. 3.9 would update α_i instead of the weights when there is an error (i.e., when $\text{sgn}(g(x_i)) \neq d_i$) and it becomes

$$\alpha_i(n + 1) = \alpha_i(n) + \eta x_i$$
$$b(n + 1) = b(n) + \eta x_i$$

where x_i is the input of the perceptron at iteration n and η is the step size. The Adatron algorithm, however, chooses the alphas so that the following quadratic form is optimized:

$$J(\alpha) = \sum_{i=1}^{N} \alpha_i - \frac{1}{2} \sum_{i=1}^{N} \sum_{j=1}^{N} \alpha_i \alpha_j d_i d_j \langle x_i, x_j \rangle$$

$$\text{subject to } \sum_{i=1}^{N} \alpha_i d_i = 0 \qquad \alpha_i \geq 0, \ \forall i \in \{1, \dots, N\}$$

(3.25)

This in general is a difficult optimization problem that nevertheless has a simple solution, provided that all the inner products among the input data are calculated beforehand (as specified by the Adatron algorithm). The algorithm is as follows: Define $g(x_i) = d_i(\sum_{j=1}^{N} d_j \alpha_j \langle x_i, x_j \rangle + b)$ and $M = \min_i g(x_i)$ and choose a common starting multiplier (e.g., $\alpha_i = 0.1$), learning rate η, and a small threshold (e.g., $t = 0.01$). Note that we can compute $g(x_i)$ locally at each PE if d_j is available at the input layer (from the data file) or, equivalently, if the weights to the hidden layer are stored after multiplication by the corresponding desired response. Then, while $M > t$, choose a pattern x_i, and calculate an update $\Delta\alpha_i = \eta[1 - g(x_i)]$ and perform the update

$$\begin{cases} \alpha_i(n+1) = \alpha_i(n) + \Delta\alpha_i(n), & b(n+1) = b(n) + d_i\Delta\alpha_i(n) & \text{if } \alpha_i(n) + \Delta\alpha_i(n) > 0 \\ \alpha_i(n+1) = \alpha_i(n), & b(n+1) = b(n) & \text{if } \alpha_i(n) + \Delta\alpha_i(n) \le 0 \end{cases}$$

Notice that for each input and corresponding desired response we can compute $\Delta\alpha_i$ locally, so the Adatron algorithm adheres with the local implementation constraint common in neurocomputation.

The Adatron algorithm is applied to a M-P PE; that is, it is able to discriminate only between two classes. If the problem has multiple classes, it must be solved as a sequence of two-class decisions. The algorithm resembles the perceptron learning algorithm given earlier, except in the form of the updates.

It is very useful to compare the Adatron algorithm with the delta rule previously described to contrast their differences. In the delta rule the positioning of the boundary is primarily controlled by the samples that produce outputs that differ from the desired values of 1 or -1. These samples tend to exist in the boundary between the classes (Figure 3-12), so the MSE is largely determined by the samples that are close to the boundary between classes. However, due to the fact that J (Eq. 3.19) is a continuous function of the error, all the samples contribute somewhat to J. Therefore the MSE is a function of the full data distribution, and the location of the boundary will be affected by the shape of the data clusters.

In the Adatron algorithm a very different behavior happens. During the adaptation, most of the αs go to zero, and the location of the boundary is solely determined from a few samples close to the boundary, which are called the support vectors. The adaptation algorithm thus is insensitive to the overall shape of the data clusters and concentrates on the local neighborhood of the boundary to set the location of the hyperplane. Depending on the data distributions, this may provide different boundaries. In particular, Vapnik [1995] has shown that the large-margin classifier controls generalization, while the delta rule does not.

Let us see how the Adatron works for the problem we solved in Section 3.2.3.

NEUROSOLUTIONS EXAMPLE 3.10

The Adatron algorithm

We are going to implement the Adatron algorithm in NeuroSolutions and compare it with both the perceptron learning rule of Eq. 3.9 and the delta rule of Eq. 3.22 to solve the same classification problem. Notice that the Adatron outperforms the perceptron learning rule, always providing a decision surface midway between the classes. In that respect, its behavior is similar to the delta rule. We will see later that the Adatron learning rule has some advantages with respect to MSE learning (such as the delta rule).

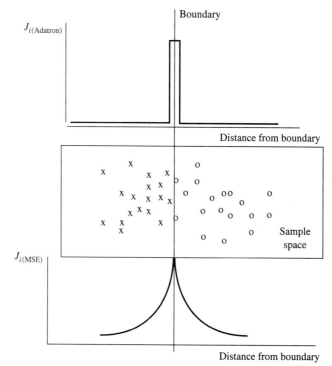

FIGURE 3-12 Differences in the distribution across samples in the Adatron and delta rule

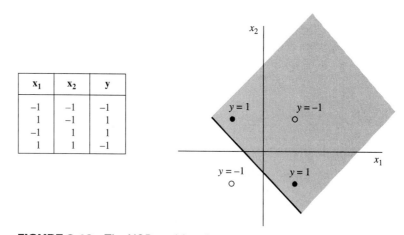

x_1	x_2	y
-1	-1	-1
1	-1	1
-1	1	1
1	1	-1

FIGURE 3-13 The XOR problem in pattern space

3.3.5 Limitations of the Perceptron

As with the M-P PE, the perceptron can only solve linearly separable problems. The prototype problem that is not linearly separable and thus cannot be solved by perceptrons is the exclusive-or function (XOR). The exclusive-or truth table is presented in Figure 3-13.

No matter where we place the half plane that includes the 1 responses, it will always include one of the −1 responses, so this is an example of *nonlinearly separable patterns*. The parity function extends the XOR to higher dimensions. NeuroSolutions can be used to demonstrate the XOR problem.

NEUROSOLUTIONS EXAMPLE 3.11

Perceptron and the XOR problem

This example shows what happens when the perceptron tries to solve the XOR problem. We start with a modified M-P PE, built with the tanh nonlinearity. The network has two inputs and one output. Training is done with the delta rule in batch mode. The Discriminant probe shows the separation surface; the MegaScope displays the learning curve to observe how learning progresses. There are two important points about the XOR problem. First, there is no way for the M-P PE to solve the problem. The XOR is not linearly separable. Second, there are many different local minima in the performance surface, the least interesting of which is the one where all the weights quickly approach zero and the network output is thus always zero. This will produce a discriminant plot that is all gray. The other more interesting minima are when the discriminant line separates one of the four points from the other three; this is the best the network can do. Notice that both of these minima produce the same mean squared error. Why is this so, when one network correctly classifies three of four points and the other produces no output at all?

With batch-mode training the weights are updated after an entire epoch. This produces a smoother weight track, but in this example the smooth weight track very often tends to lead directly to the all-zeros (uninteresting) solution. If we change the training to on-line, the network will find other solutions. Why? Because the on-line training is much noisier than the batch-mode training, thus it has a tendency to bounce out of local minima. Imagine doing gradient descent on the performance surface in Figure 3-7; a smooth track will lead to a single minimum, whereas a noisy track will bounce around and end up in various locations.

This example clearly shows that this problem has multiple minima, and depending on the update rule, some of the solutions are preferred. But none is able to correctly classify all the patterns. Notice that the inclusion of nonlinearity, even in a one-layer network, produced a performance surface that is nonconvex.

Minsky[2] showed that the perceptron was not a general-purpose processing device, because the possible decision regions that the machine can create are convex, formed through the intersection of hyperplanes (an extension of a plane to more than two dimensions).

3.4 ONE-HIDDEN-LAYER MULTILAYER PERCEPTRONS

Multilayer perceptrons (MLPs) extend the perceptron with hidden layers, that is, layers of processing elements that are not connected directly to the external world. Figure 3-14 shows a one-hidden-layer MLP with D inputs, K hidden PEs, and M outputs [MLP(D-K-M)]. Normally the PEs in MLPs are nonlinear sigmoid PEs. Let us analyze in terms of discriminant functions the extra processing power of a hidden layer of nonlinear PEs.

We extend the perceptron given in Figure 3-8 by cascading one extra layer of processing elements. The hidden layer has two processing elements, as shown in Figure 3-15. We start our study of the MLP with threshold processing elements. (To facilitate the explanation, we assume that the outputs are between 0 and 1.) The goal here is to find the discriminant functions produced by one-hidden-layer MLPs.

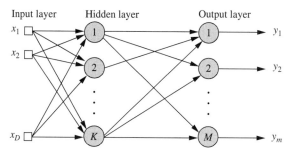

FIGURE 3-14 A multilayer perceptron with one hidden layer (D-K-M)

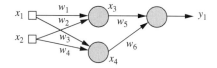

FIGURE 3-15 A one-hidden-layer (2-2-1) perceptron

[2]Marvin Minsky is one of the fathers of artificial intelligence who is credited with the downfall of neural networks in the late 1960s. This may be an exaggeration. In a very influential book (written with S. Papert) called *Perceptrons,* MIT Press, 1969, he posed the theory of perceptrons for predicate calculus and showed their limitation versus the Turing machine.

Conceptually, the one-hidden-layer MLP is a cascade of perceptrons. It is straightforward to see from this interpretation that the two PEs in the hidden layer create two linear discriminant functions in the (x_1, x_2) space. Let us label the output of each hidden processing element as x_3 and x_4. Each of these variables will be positive "above" their discriminant line with a slope given by the ratio of the respective local weights.

In the space (x_3, x_4) the output PE is also a perceptron. It will also construct a linear discriminant function; that is, it will have a positive response above a straight line with slope given by $-w_6/w_5$. The problem is that we are interested in finding the overall positive response in the input space (x_1, x_2). This is a straightforward (but messy) problem in the composition of functions, since we know the (nonlinear) parametric relation between x_3 and (x_1, x_2) and between x_4 and (x_1, x_2). It is instructive to write the overall input-output map as

$$
\begin{aligned}
y = f(w_5 x_3 + w_6 x_4 + b_3) &= f\{w_5[f(w_1 x_1 + w_2 x_2 + b_1)] \\
&+ w_6[f(w_3 x_1 + w_4 x_2 + b_2)] + b_3\} = f\{g_1 + g_2 + b_3\}
\end{aligned}
\tag{3.26}
$$

3.4.1 Discriminant Functions of the MLP

The multilayer perceptron constructs input-output mappings that are a nested composition of nonlinearities, that is, they are of the form

$$
y = f\left(\sum f\left(\sum (\bullet)\right)\right)
\tag{3.27}
$$

where the number of function compositions is given by the number of network layers. The resulting map is very flexible and powerful, but it is also hard to analyze. Our goal now is to find out what type of discriminant function can be created with the mapping of Eq. 3.27.

Let us assume that the output layer weights are $w_5 = w_6 = 1$. Each expression inside the brackets creates one linear discriminant function, yielding a function with a positive value across a half plane (a step function). The location of the transition in the input space is controlled by the discriminant function, so the expression inside the brackets is the addition of two step functions, g_1 and g_2, with a bias term b_3. In the region of the input space where both functions g_1 and g_2 are positive, the value of y will be the largest. The output y will have an intermediate value in a subspace where either one of the g functions is positive (but not both); finally, there is an area in the input space where y is equal to the bias b_3 because each one of the functions g_1 and g_2 is zero.

The shapes of these areas are controlled by the placement of the original discriminant functions (which in turn are controlled by the values of w_1, w_2, w_3, and w_4 of Eq. 3.26). Notice also that the bias value b_3 is added to the result of the hidden-layer partition. Its value will dictate whether only the peak value of y is positive, whether the peak and one of the plateaus are positive, whether all are positive, or whether all are zero. Hence the role of the bias at the output layer is substantially different from the simple control of the y intercept as in the hidden layer PEs. The bias reveals different details of the composition of functions, effectively changing the overall assignment of values to the partition created by the hidden layer. The output weights w_5 and w_6 enhance the flexibility (can give different weights to the output of each hidden PE) and further change the mixture of the hidden PE activations.

The interplay among all these parameters becomes quite involved, but we have the feeling that the discriminant function of the one-hidden-layer perceptron is much more flexible than that of the perceptron. Let us go to NeuroSolutions and create a Breadboard to help us get familiar with the discriminant function of the one-hidden-layer MLP. Remember that the discriminant probe provides a way to visualize the shape of the overall discriminant function by gray-coding the input space with the value of the output.

NEUROSOLUTIONS EXAMPLE 3.12

One-hidden-layer MLP in 2-D space

This Breadboard implements the one-hidden-layer perceptron shown in Figure 3-15 with two Threshold Axons in the hidden layer but a Tanh Axon at the output. We have the Discriminant probe attached to the output of the network; thus it will show the combination of the discriminant lines created by the hidden-layer PEs. We will see how the MLP separates the input space into multiple areas with different values (depending on the values of the weights); this is often called a *tessellation*. Notice that since the tessellation is made up additively, a change in sign of one of the weights changes all the regions, not only the ones that belong to the PE whose weights were modified. This tight coupling between the PEs is what makes the MLP so powerful, because to obtain a given tessellation, all the PEs have to contribute to it. In other words, the training procedure for the MLP is not *greedy*. Another interesting aspect of the MLP is that different weight combinations can lead to the same tessellation.

Figure 3-16 shows the tessellation obtained with the one-hidden-layer MLP for the parameters of the example. The conclusion is that by adding an extra layer to the

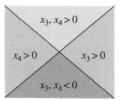

FIGURE 3-16 Tessellation of a one-hidden-layer MLP (2-1) in 2-D space

perceptron, we have *qualitatively* changed the shape of its discriminant function. The decision regions are no longer restricted to be *convex,* because the network has a more powerful composition mechanism.

There are several important conclusions to be drawn from this example.

- First, the maximum number of distinct regions of the input space is controlled by the number of hidden PEs (2^K for $K \gg D$). An alternative statement is that each hidden PE creates a linear discriminant function.

- Second, the PEs in the output layer have the ability to combine some of the regions created by the hidden PEs, by either a multiplicative or an additive effect. This creates decision regions that are no longer convex.

- Third, there is more than one weight combination that achieves a particular arrangement of decision regions.

Can we solve the XOR problem with the MLP (2-2-1)? The answer is yes, if the discriminant functions are modified according to the goal of creating a slanted (by 45 degrees) "bright" strip that passes through the origin (see Figure 3-13). Let us do this by hand in NeuroSolutions.

NEUROSOLUTIONS EXAMPLE 3.13

Solving the XOR problem by hand with the one-hidden-layer MLP

The input–desired response table for the XOR function is presented in Figure 3-13. Note that to solve this problem we have to define a "bright" region that includes two of the outputs only. This can be accomplished if we place two discriminant functions at 45 degrees that are parallel to each other and positive toward the center. We therefore need only two discriminant functions, that is, two hidden PEs. When you have finished the demonstration, try to find two other solutions to the XOR problem. Remember that the assignment of 1 or -1 to a given class is arbitrary, so reversing the assignments gives one more solution. The other solution is obtained with lines at 135 degrees. The important aspect of this problem is to observe how the single-layer MLP globally constructs the solution. Changing a single weight changes the overall decision surface.

We conclude that classification with the MLP is still accomplished by adequately controlling the position of the discriminant functions according to the input data and the desired response. This is the same principle used for linear regression and for the perceptron. What we gain with the MLP is much more freedom in the possible shapes of discriminant functions. We will soon discuss an algorithm that will allow the machine to automatically discover the position of the discriminant that correctly classifies the training data.

3.4.2 Mapping Capabilities of the One-Hidden-Layer MLP

An important consequence of the mapping capabilities of the one-hidden-layer MLP is that it can construct a *bump* in the input space, that is, a single, limited-extent region of large values surrounded by a region of low values. Notice that the discriminant function of the low values is no longer convex, so the bump cannot be implemented by a perceptron. The simplest bump is triangular, and it is obtained with three hidden PEs.

NEUROSOLUTIONS EXAMPLE 3.14

Creating a bump with the one-hidden-layer MLP

In this example we create a bump in a two-dimensional space using a one-hidden-layer perceptron. The goal is to create a bright triangular region around the origin of the input space. In this Breadboard we need three tanh PEs in the hidden layer, since a triangular region requires the combination of three linear discriminant functions. When you have successfully solved the problem, experiment with the Breadboard; for instance, resize the bump and make the boundaries crisper. This experience will be useful in the future.

This example shows that the one-hidden-layer perceptron is able to create a limited-extent (local) bump in the input space. This feature is going to be very important for function approximation in general and for classification in particular. But one-hidden-layer MLPs can also create other types of nonconvex regions and even disjoint regions.

Mapping Capabilities of the One-Hidden-Layer MLP

The one-hidden-layer MLP with sigmoid PEs is a universal mapper; that is, it can approximate arbitrarily well any continuous decision region, provided the number of hidden-layer PEs is large enough.

There have been proofs of this statement by Cybenko [1989], Gallant and White [1992], Hornik et al. [1989], many of them based on the Stone Weierstrass theorem. These proofs are difficult to follow and are omitted here. They discuss only the mapping capabilities (existence proofs); they do not describe how to create an MLP with the specified characteristics (constructive proofs), so they are only useful to describe the power of the technology.

An interesting thing is that the activation function does not seem to be that important for the mapping capabilities, since the proofs use several of them (even discontinuous nonlinearities). The key aspect is the form of the approximation function, which is an *embedding of functions;* that is, the result of one function becomes the argument for the next:

$$y = f(f(.))$$

Another important conclusion is that if the user knows the placement of the discriminant functions, then it is possible to synthesize the solution directly. The geometric picture that we developed also applies to higher-dimensional spaces, but we lose the ability to visualize the solutions.

3.4.3 Training the One-Hidden-Layer MLP

The perceptron and the multilayer perceptron are trained with *error-correction learning,* which means that the desired response for the system must be known. In pattern recognition this is normally the case, since we have part of our input data labeled, that is, we know which data belong to which class. We already know how to train the perceptron (Eq. 3.22). If we want to utilize the delta rule, we must know how to compute the error at each PE, which requires the availability of a desired response for each network PE. An explicit error is not available in the hidden-layer PEs of the MLP. This is known as the *credit assignment problem* and represented the stumbling block that ended the first connectionist era around 1970.

The resurgence of interest in neural networks can be traced to the discovery of a method to train MLPs that is best known as *backpropagation,* or *the generalized delta rule.* The method was reinvented many times,[3] and it was known in control theory since the late 1960s, but the connectionist version is much more efficient and can be considered a contribution of connectionism to the theory of gradient-descent learning.

We already covered one of the fundamental concepts required to extend the delta rule to MLPs when we discussed and applied the chain rule to the M-P PE. Remember that we showed that the chain rule is a systematic procedure to propagate sensitivities across an undetermined number of internal (hidden) points of a topology. As long as we have an analytic expression that relates the variables along the forward path, we can compute sensitivities to the same intermediate points in the path. If we accept that the output error should be scaled by the network weights as dictated by gradient descent, then we can propagate the output error to any point along the path and update the weights with the scaled error. In other words, we are effectively substituting the availability of the desired signal at the intermediate points in the path by the propagated and scaled output error. This worked for the M-P PE and works in general. How can this help us train the MLP?

Let us examine Figure 3-17, which depicts a piece of a one-hidden-layer MLP. The goal is to adapt the weights that are connected to the hidden *i*th PE. Notice that we do not have a desired response at this point, since the PE is not connected to the external world (i.e., it is hidden). To adapt its weights, we are going to apply the following methodology:

- Instead of using an explicit desired response to compute the error at the *i*th PE, we use an error derived from the outer layer.

[3]Many researchers worked in the computation of sensitivity across a network. Werbos, with the ordered derivative, was probably the first. In the connectionist arena the key paper that popularized backpropagation was written by Rumelhart, Hinton, and Williams. LeCun in France presented a method based on Lagrange multipliers at basically the same time.

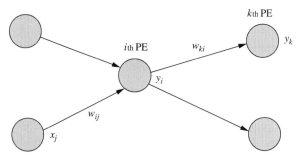

FIGURE 3-17   Detail of a hidden-layer network

- This error is the propagated and scaled output error.
- The sensitivity is automatically computed by the chain rule.

The weight update using backpropagation is

$$w_{ij}(n+1) = w_{ij}(n) + \eta f'(net_i(n))\left(\sum_k e_k(n)f'(net_k(n))w_{ki}(n)\right)y_j(n) \qquad (3.28)$$

Backpropagation Derivation

In this derivation we drop the dependence on the pattern for clarity. First assume that the kth PE is the only output PE in the net. With the machinery of the chain rule, let us write the gradient of the cost with respect to the weight as the product of the output error propagated to the PE (the gradient with respect to the PE state) times the sensitivity of the PE output with respect to the weight:

$$\frac{\partial J}{\partial w_{ij}} = \frac{\partial J}{\partial y_i}\frac{\partial y_i}{\partial net_i}\frac{\partial}{\partial w_{ij}}net_i = -\delta_i y_j \qquad (3B.1)$$

where we substituted the definition of the local error given by Eq. 3.21. Notice that the sensitivity of the cost with respect to the weights is decomposed into the sensitivity of the cost with respect to the state y_i times the sensitivity of the state with respect to the local weights. The state sensitivity $\partial J/\partial y$ can be computed by the chain rule, which yields from the figure

$$\frac{\partial J}{\partial y_i} = \frac{\partial J}{\partial y_k}\frac{\partial y_k}{\partial y_i} = \frac{\partial J}{\partial y_k}\frac{\partial y_k}{\partial net_k}\frac{\partial net_k}{\partial y_i} \qquad (3B.2)$$

Remember that the index k denotes a single PE in the layer to the right (i.e., in the layer closer to the output) of the ith PE. Now let us substitute these partial derivatives with network quantities and plug them into Equation 3B.1 to yield

$$\frac{\partial J}{\partial w_{ij}} = -e_k f'(net_k)w_{ki}f'(net_i)y_j \qquad (3B.3)$$

This expression computes the gradient of the cost with respect to the weight w_{ij}. We assumed a single output PE in this derivation. For completeness the case of multiple output PEs is treated next.

The idea is basically the same; the only difference is that now there are many output PEs (denoted by k) connected to the ith PE, each contributing additively to the gradient of the cost with respect to the PE state, that is,

$$\frac{\partial J}{\partial y_i} = \left(\sum_k \frac{\partial J}{\partial y_k} \frac{\partial y_k}{\partial net_k} \frac{\partial}{\partial y_i} net_k \right) = \sum_k e_k f'(net_k) w_{ki} \tag{3B.4}$$

Substituting Eq. 3B.4 back in the original equation Eq. 3B.1, we finally get

$$\frac{\partial J}{\partial w_{ij}} = \left[\sum_k e_k f'(net_k) w_{ki} \right] f'(net_i)(-y_j) \tag{3B.5}$$

According to the rules of gradient descent learning, we just change the weights proportionally to the negative of Eq. 3B.5:

$$w_{ij}(n+1) = w_{ij}(n) + \eta f'(net_i(n)) \left(\sum_k e_k(n) f'(net_k(n)) w_{ki}(n) \right) y_j(n) \tag{3B.6}$$

The algorithm just presented is the *backpropagation algorithm*. The expression that we arrived at seems pretty daunting, with a summation and lots of indices, but in fact can be easily interpreted.

Computer Algorithm Let us assume a sample-by-sample presentation of data, that is, $\{x(n), d(n)\}$.

Step 1: Present an input–desired response pair $\{x_1, d_1\}$.

Step 2: Compute the outputs of every PE starting from the input layer ($l = 1$) up to the output layer ($l = L$). We can formally write this step as

$$y_i^l(n) = f(net_i^l(n))$$

and

$$net_i^l(n) = \sum_{j=1}^p w_{ij}^l y_j^{l-1}(n)$$

where $f(.)$ is the nonlinearity, the superscript means layer $l = 1, \ldots, L$, n is the iteration number, and w_{ij} is the weight that links the ith PE to the jth PE. In the first layer $y_j^0 = x_j$. If the PEs have biases, $y_0^l = +1$. If the PE is in the output layer, make $y_j^L = y_j$.

Step 3: Compute the injected error as $e_i(n) = d_i(n) - y_i(n)$.

Step 4: Compute the local errors starting from the output layer and continuing until the first layer. In the output layer the error is (delta rule)

$$\delta_i^L(n) = e_i(n)f'(net_i^L(n))$$

In all the other layers

$$\delta_i^l(n) = f'(net_i^l(n))\sum_k \delta_k^{l+1}(n)w_{ki}^{l+1}(n)$$

Once we have these local errors and the activations of step 2, every weight in the network can be updated according to Eq. 3B.6. Note also that the weights to compute the errors and the activations are the "old weights."

Step 5: Repeat this procedure for every input pattern and for the number of iterations required for convergence. For best results the patterns should be randomized from presentation to presentation.

This summarizes the computer algorithm to implement backpropagation.

Let us reinterpret Eq. 3.28 using the definition of the local error (Eq. 3.21). The summation in Eq. 3.28 is a sum of local errors δ_k at each network output PE, scaled by the weights connecting the output PEs to the ith PE. Thus the term in parenthesis in Eq. 3.28 effectively computes the total error reaching the ith PE from the output layer (which can be thought of as the ith PE's contribution to the output error). When we pass it through the ith PE nonlinearity, we have its local error, which can be written as

$$\delta_i(n) = f'(net_i(n))\sum_k \delta_k w_{ki}(n)$$

Thus there is a unifying link in all the gradient-descent algorithms presented so far. *All* the weights in gradient descent learning are updated by multiplying the *local error* ($\delta_i(n)$) by the *local activation* ($y_j(n)$) according to Widrow's estimation of the instantaneous gradient first shown in the LMS rule:

$$\Delta w_{ij}(n) = \eta\delta_i(n)y_j(n) \tag{3.29}$$

What differs is the *calculation* of the local error, depending on whether the PE is linear or nonlinear and whether the weight is attached to an output PE or a hidden-layer PE.

Case 1: If the PE is linear and it is at the output layer,

$$\delta_i(n) = -\varepsilon_i(n)$$

since $f'(.)$ has a constant value of 1. This is the case found in the LMS rule (Eq. 3.11).

Case 2: If the PE is nonlinear and it is at the output, the delta rule (Eq. 3.21) used to train the perceptron is exactly Eq. 3.29 with δ_i substituted by

$$\delta_i(n) = -\varepsilon_i(n)f'(net_i(n)) \tag{3.30}$$

where ε_i is the error associated with the ith output. We can update the output weights of the MLP with the delta rule since we know the desired response at the output.

Case 3: If the PE is nonlinear and hidden, the local error is computed by summing all the contributions of the local errors in the output layer, scaled by the corresponding weights, which yields

$$\delta_i(n) = f'(net_i(n)) \sum_k \delta_k w_{ki}(n) \tag{3.31}$$

Structurally, the weight update equations do not change, since learning is still using gradient descent. Everyone should remember Eqs. 3.30 and 3.31 to apply gradient-descent learning to MLPs. Let us apply the backpropagation algorithm to train the one-hidden-layer MLP to solve the XOR problem.

Multilayer Linear Networks

Why did we not discuss multilayer networks with linear PEs? It turns out that from the point of view of input-output mappings, a multilayer network with linear PEs is normally equivalent to a no-hidden-layer network (Adaline), so there is little interest in studying such networks. However, if we want to train one with gradient descent, we will need to use the backpropagation algorithm.

NEUROSOLUTIONS EXAMPLE 3.15
Solving the XOR with backpropagation

In this example we use the same Breadboard from the previous example, set the number of hidden PEs to 2, and add the learning planes so that we can implement the backpropagation algorithm to train the network to solve the XOR problem. When you finish the demonstration, try changing the step size (learning rate) by selecting the Gradient Descent component, opening the Inspector, and typing new values. Notice how this changes the dynamics of learning, exemplified by the learning curve. Another thing that you might notice is that the learning curve sometimes has plateaus where the error remains basically the same. This corresponds to almost flat regions where the gradient is very small. We can imagine that the performance surface is no longer the simple "bowl" we found in linear regression. Sometimes instead of flat regions one gets local minima, and the search gets stuck there because a local minimum and the global minimum are indistinguishable with the local gradient. This is one of the added difficulties of working with nonlinear systems.

One other thing to observe is that although the classification is successful, that is, the MSE is very small, the weights of the system have very different values from run to run. This is due to the fact that the system starts with random initial conditions and there are many possible solutions to solve the XOR problem. During adaptation the search takes the system's state along different paths, and one of the solutions (we do not know which) is reached. But for classification any one of them is OK.

Notice that there are many different solutions to the XOR problem. When the network weights are seeded randomly, different solutions can be found. However, the most important conclusion is that the network can automatically find the placement of the discriminant functions that are so difficult for us to create by hand.

The other example that we will run at this point is the bump. The goal is to show that backpropagation is able to train a one-hidden-layer MLP to discover a triangularly shaped decision region. To train such an MLP, we need to construct a training set that will tell the network where its response must be 1 and where it should be 0. Here we selected 20 points in the plane. Ten points are organized in a triangle, and the desired response for these samples is 1. The remaining 10 samples are placed around the first cluster, and the desired network response is 0.

NEUROSOLUTIONS EXAMPLE 3.16
Solving the bump with backpropagation

In this example we use the same MLP that we used previously to construct the bump by hand (three hidden PEs) and add the learning dynamics. We have placed a Scatter Plot at the net input to help you visualize the correspondence between the samples and the discriminant function found through training. In particular, pay attention to the relationship between the discriminant function being created and the evolution of the learning curve. Depending on the initial conditions, the bright area can appear in the center, or more frequently, it appears in one corner and finds its way toward the center, until it finally creates a central bright spot. Notice that the learning curves are different for each case. Sometimes you will find an initial decrease in the error followed by a long period where the error basically is constant until the final solution appears. You should link the learning curve behavior to the positioning of the discriminant function.

At other times the discriminant functions form a wedge and stay there forever. This is a local minimum. It is important to figure out why this behavior occurs. It is obvious that this solution misclassifies one sample (see the Scatter Plot), and it is also obvious that there is one extra discriminant function that does not appear in the plot. The reason is that it has parameters very close to one of the other discriminants (i.e., they are superimposed on each other). This happens when the initial conditions or the gradient-descent path produce weight updates that create hidden-layer weights that are very similar. In such cases the error produced by misclassifying a single sample is not enough to pull the hidden weights apart, and the system rests in this solution. When this happens, open the Matrix Viewers and observe the weight values.

3.4.4 The Effect of the Number of Hidden PEs

One of the central issues in neurocomputing is to appropriately set the number of hidden PEs. There are two extreme cases: Either the network has too many hidden PEs to do the job, or it has too few. Understanding each case is important because correctly setting the number of PEs is still a difficult task at our present state of knowledge. Let us start with an overdimensioned hidden layer.

NEUROSOLUTIONS EXAMPLE 3.17

Effect of the number of hidden PEs

In this example we experiment with the number of hidden-layer PEs and how it affects the output and learning dynamics of the network. It is obvious that if the problem can be solved with three hidden PEs, it can also be solved with six. What happens to the positioning of the other three PEs' discriminant functions? The chances of getting the correct classification in the training set increase, and the system normally requires fewer iterations to reach the solution. However, the computational burden is increased, which slows down the training. But the big problem is that the redundant PEs may have detrimental effects on the test-set performance (data that the system has not seen before), because the MLP may memorize the training data. This may create spurious areas that produce in-class responses in regions of the input space that do not contain any training data (and therefore are "don't care" regions given the training data). Putting it another way, the machine may not perform very well on data with which it was not trained. This does not happen in this case because of the symmetry of the training data, but it can happen in practice.

You should use a Matrix Viewer to observe the values of the weights from the output layer to the input. You will find that some of the output weights are small, so they are not important for the mapping. This is a benign case. The problem occurs when some of the weights are large and make the system respond to regions of the input space void of training samples. This is when the system makes mistakes in the test data. The input-layer weights also appear duplicated (i.e., several superimposed discriminant surfaces). This is computationally inefficient but does not significantly affect the performance in the test set.

The other important condition to study is when the network does not have enough hidden PEs to solve the problem correctly. We saw a similar situation when we tried to solve the XOR problem with the perceptron (which effectively has zero hidden PEs). The machine does not know whether the problem is solvable or not, so it will try to do its best, classifying most of the samples correctly.

In general, the learning algorithm first finds the correct shape and placement for the discriminant functions to correctly classify the *majority* of the samples, and then slowly moves them to classify the areas with fewer samples. The reason for this behavior is rooted in the form of the cost function (a sum of the errors over all the training patterns) that is guiding the automatic placement of the discriminant function. If the learning machine does not have enough degrees of freedom, the error will stabilize at a high value, since the system cannot solve the problem. Sometimes oscillations can occur when the learning rates are large. The oscillations correspond to sudden changes in weights between two suboptimal solutions.

NEUROSOLUTIONS EXAMPLE 3.18

Fewer hidden PEs than required

Let us now train the MLP to create a bump, but in this case let us reduce the number of hidden PEs to 2. This MLP cannot solve the problem exactly, since at least three PEs are required. So what will the training do? The machine does not know whether it has enough degrees of freedom or not. It blindly changes the weights to decrease the MSE, so the solutions found will tend to correctly classify the majority of samples.

For some initial conditions we may observe an oscillation, where the error abruptly goes up and then down. During these periods the weights change rapidly, and the discriminant function oscillates between two positions. This means that the weights are driven to values that make the discriminant suddenly increase the number of errors, so the weights have to move back. One nice way to observe this effect is to place a MegaScope on top of the weights and see the weights change with each iteration.

3.5 MLPs WITH TWO HIDDEN LAYERS

3.5.1 Discriminant Functions of the Two-Hidden-Layer MLP

What are the discriminant functions of two-hidden-layer perceptrons? Such a network has three levels of function composition:

$$y = f\left(\sum f\left(\sum f\left(\sum(\bullet)\right)\right)\right)$$

We can once again study the problem by finding the decision regions created by the one-hidden-layer MLP (as in the previous section) and their composition created by the added output perceptron. This becomes more complex, but it is important to understand the basic capabilities of the overall discriminant functions.

From the previous discussion we know that the one-hidden-layer MLP can create local bumps in the input space. Another layer with several PEs can be thought of as combining bumps in disjoint regions of the space. This is a very important property, because in the theory of function approximation (we touch on this subject in Chapter 5) there are well-established theorems that state that a linear combination of localized bumps can approximate any reasonable function. Therefore an MLP with two hidden layers is also a *universal approximator;* that is, it can realize any input-output map, just as the one-hidden-layer MLP can.

A word of caution is in order at this point. These theorems are existence theorems (the number of PEs is unconstrained), so they do not address the engineering question, "How many PEs and layers does the MLP need to solve my problem?" This is still an open question for which experimentation is necessary. But it is extremely important to know that theoretically an MLP is a universal approximator and that one or two hidden layers are all it takes to reach this arbitrary mapping capability.

One should associate the number of PEs in the first hidden layer with the number of linear discriminant functions in the input space. One will need in general $2D$ hidden PEs in the first hidden layer (D is the number of dimensions in the input space) and a modified M-P PE in the second hidden layer to form a single bump. The number of PEs in the second hidden layer creates the number of bumps in the input space that are needed for the approximation. The output layer simply combines these bumps to produce the desired input-output map. This constructive reasoning shows that two-hidden-layer MLPs can approximate any function.

This view is valuable to understand the function of MLPs for classification and to appreciate the difficulty of selecting an appropriate topology. If we have some a priori knowledge of our data clusters, we can judiciously set the size of the network as in the following example.

NEUROSOLUTIONS EXAMPLE 3.19

Creating a Halloween mask by hand with a two-hidden-layer MLP

In this example we set the weights of a two-hidden-layer MLP by hand to create a Halloween mask in the input space as illustrated in Figure 3-18. This mask is a simple example of a general input-output function. It can be thought of as a classification problem where one of the classes is scattered (multimodal) in the input space (the location of the bright regions) and the other class is in the dark region.

We design the MLP by hand, since we know the placement of the discriminants. Observe that we have four distinct regions in the input space. Therefore we need four PEs in the second hidden layer, one to build each feature in the input

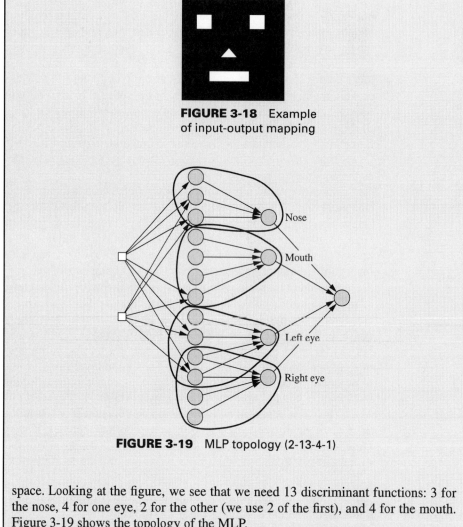

FIGURE 3-18 Example of input-output mapping

FIGURE 3-19 MLP topology (2-13-4-1)

space. Looking at the figure, we see that we need 13 discriminant functions: 3 for the nose, 4 for one eye, 2 for the other (we use 2 of the first), and 4 for the mouth. Figure 3-19 shows the topology of the MLP.

This is a long example, but you should get a good feel for how each layer's weights and bias affect the final discriminant function or tessellation. After creating the mask, change the weights and see whether you can predict how they will affect the output.

This example illustrates that when we know the decision regions, we can design the discriminant functions directly. Unfortunately, this is very rarely the case for two main reasons: The structure of our data sets may be unknown, but even if they are known, we are not able to visualize them in higher-dimensional spaces so that we can specify the placements of the discriminant functions. We therefore need to resort to training for the adjustment of the weights.

3.5.2 Training Two-Hidden-Layer MLPs with Backpropagation

The beauty of training using the backpropagation algorithm is that it is a systematic, step-by-step procedure that can be applied independent of the topology of the network and the input dimensionality. Larger, more complex networks may require more training time, but backpropagation is still fully capable of training them.

We can expect very similar behavior between the training of the one-hidden-layer and two-hidden-layer MLPs; that is, there are some solutions that take a long time to reach, if they are reached at all, due to the existence of local minima and saddle points.

NEUROSOLUTIONS EXAMPLE 3.20

Comparison of the perceptron and MLPs

In this example we summarize the network topologies that we have discussed so far by trying to solve the male–female classification problem using a single perceptron, one-hidden-layer MLP, and two-hidden-layer MLP. The male–female classification problem was discussed in Chapter 2 and involves trying to determine whether a subject is male or female based on height and weight. Please refer to Figures 2-5 and 2-8. As you can tell, there is no way to correctly classify all the data points. Remember that the optimal discriminant is quadratic. How will this affect the best choice of network topologies?

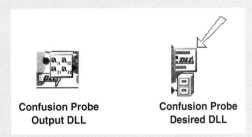

Confusion Probe
Output DLL

Confusion Probe
Desired DLL

We have added a new probe in this example, the Confusion probe. The Confusion probe generates a confusion matrix, which is a simple methodology to display the classification results of a network. The confusion matrix is defined by labeling the desired classification on the rows and the predicted classifications on the columns (or vice versa). For each exemplar, a 1 is added to the cell entry defined by (desired classification, predicted classification). Since we want the predicted classification to be the same as the desired classification, the ideal situation is to have all the exemplars end up on the diagonal cells of the matrix. Two confusion matrices follow:

Desired classification	Predicted classification		
		Male	Female
	Male	50	0
	Female	0	50

Desired classification	Predicted classification		
		Male	Female
	Male	45	5
	Female	9	41

In example 1 we have perfect classification. Every male subject was classified by the network as male, and every female subject was classified as female. There were no males classified as females or vice versa. In example 2 we have imperfect classification. We have nine females classified incorrectly by the network as males and five males classified as females.

One of the interesting things about this example is that the error sometimes increases during adaptation. This clearly shows that the weight tracks are not moving exactly along the gradient-descent direction. This may happen because we are using a local estimate of the gradient that may be noisy. The second thing to note is the relationship between the number of classification errors and the MSE. They are related in a coarse manner; that is, in the beginning of training, both are high and they decrease. However, the MSE may be decreasing, but the number of misclassifications can be stable or even increase. This is due to the fact that the MSE is sensitive to the differences between the desired responses and the actual output, while the number of mistakes is a digital quantity that looks only at the largest output (here the largest output is assigned to the class).

In the previous example the one-hidden-layer MLP and the two-hidden-layer MLP performed at the same level of accuracy. But sometimes there are problems for which the two-hidden-layer MLP has an advantage. The fact is that the two-hidden-layer machines can form all of the discriminant functions of the one-hidden-layer MLP and many others, so they are more versatile, although we know that asymptotically a very large one-hidden-layer MLP would approximate the same performance.

As a rule of thumb, we should always start our experiments with the simpler topology, since the two-hidden-layer MLP normally trains more slowly than the one-hidden-layer MLP due to the attenuation of errors through the nonlinearities.

NEUROSOLUTIONS EXAMPLE 3.21

Solving the bow tie with MLPs

This example solves a problem that a one-hidden-layer MLP can only approximate but that a two-hidden-layer machine can solve exactly. The class distribution in 2-D space looks like a bow tie, so we will call it the bow tie problem. We created the two-class problem with the distribution shown in the following figure.

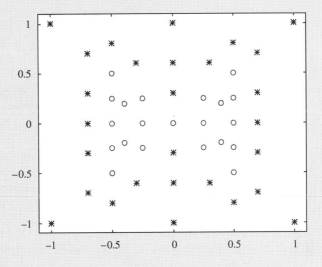

Let us experiment with the three topologies for this case (the perceptron and the one-hidden-layer and two-hidden-layer perceptrons). Modify the number of hidden-layer PEs and watch the confusion matrix. You will see that the two-hidden-layer MLP gives a lower error for this problem, but if you increase the number of hidden-layer PEs, the one-hidden-layer MLP's performance differential disappears.

3.6 TRAINING STATIC NETWORKS WITH THE BACKPROPAGATION PROCEDURE

We saw that a two-hidden-layer MLP can be trained with the backpropagation algorithm derived initially for the one-hidden-layer MLP. The backpropagation algorithm can be

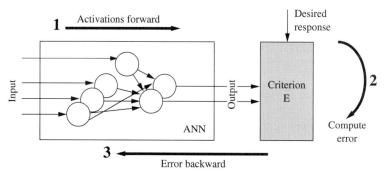

FIGURE 3-20 Chaining of operations in the backpropagation algorithm

applied without any modification to the two-hidden-layer MLP, or for that matter to *any* feedforward topology. This is because Eq. 3.31 applies locally to each hidden PE, no matter where it is placed in the topology.

The only fact to remember is that we have to start computing the local errors from the output of the network toward the input; that is, there is an intrinsic flow in the backpropagation algorithm. First, one data sample is sent through the network to find an output and compute an error (Figure 3-20). Then we calculate the injected error at the output layer and reflect it to the input of the output PE (the δ_k in Eq. 3.29). Then the errors in the previous layer can be computed by Eq. 3.31, and so on, until we reach the input layer. During the backpropagation of errors the old weights are used. Once all the local errors are found, Eq. 3.16 is used to compute the output weight updates, and Eq. 3.28 is used to compute the hidden-layer weight updates.

Although these general rules for computing the gradients seem pretty reasonable from our presentation, we have mostly focused on the local computations of the gradients, and we do not have a clear idea of the possible limitations of the technique, if any. To answer this question, a more rigorous approach to studying gradient calculations in distributed architectures seems necessary.

3.6.1 Gradient Computation and Ordered Networks

We will briefly study the gradient computations in ordered networks. An ordered network is a network where the *state variables* can be computed one at a time in a specified order. An MLP is such a network. Normally, each PE (and weight) is numbered, starting from the input (left) to the output (right) as in Figure 3-21.

For simplicity, assume the PEs are linear and that we want to compute the total partial derivative of $\partial y_3 / \partial y_1$. In ordered networks there are two contributions to this derivative: an *explicit* or direct dependence and an *implicit* or indirect dependence through the network. This total partial derivative is called an ordered derivative. The direct dependence is denoted with a superscript d. In the network of Figure 3-21, we

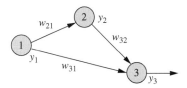

FIGURE 3-21 Simple three-PE ordered network

have

$$\text{Explicit } \frac{\partial^d y_3}{\partial y_1} = w_{31} \qquad \text{Implicit } \frac{\partial y_3}{\partial y_1} = w_{32}\frac{\partial y_2}{\partial y_1} = w_{32}w_{21} \tag{3.32}$$

$$\text{Ordered derivative} = w_{31} + w_{32}w_{21}$$

The output of a high-numbered PE (ith) in an ordered network with N PEs requires the computation of the output of *all* lower-numbered PEs (jth), that is,

$$y_i = f\left(\sum_{j<i} w_{ij}y_j\right) + x_i \tag{3.33}$$

where $f(.)$ is the static nonlinearity, and x_i is the PE input (if the PE is an input PE). Note that the summation index enforces $i > j$, which implies a feedforward topology. This is exactly what happens in the MLP. The intrinsic dependence in the computations can be captured in an *ordered list* L:

$$L = [\{w_{ij}\}, y_1, \dots, y_N] \tag{3.34}$$

where w_{ij} are the weights and y_i the PE activations (the state variables). What this means is that variable y_i depends only on the variables y_j that are located to its left in the ordered list, that is, $i > j$. Since the activations y are a function of the weights, these have to appear first in the list.

Let us define the performance function $J(y_1, \dots, y_N)$ for this network as Eq. 3.19. Werbos [1974] proved that in ordered networks the ordered partial derivatives of J with respect to the states y can be computed by

$$\frac{\partial J}{\partial y_i} = \frac{\partial^d J}{\partial y_i} + \sum_{j>i} \frac{\partial J}{\partial y_j}\frac{\partial^d y_j}{\partial y_i} \tag{3.35}$$

This expression states that the ordered derivatives can be composed from the explicit influence (first term) and the implicit effect through the topology (the sum). Note that the gradient computation must be ordered from high indices to low indices, that is, in the reverse order of the ordered list. This is a clean mathematical proof that the computation of the gradients must be done in the way we described, that is, from the output layers to the input. Hence the name *backpropagation* for the procedure.

Since the weights are first in the list, the sensitivity with respect to the weights is computed across all the network states

$$\frac{\partial J}{\partial w_{ij}} = \frac{\partial^d J}{\partial w_{ij}} + \sum_k \frac{\partial J}{\partial y_k} \frac{\partial^d y_k}{\partial w_{ij}} \tag{3.36}$$

Note the similarity with backpropagation: Eq. 3.35 is computing the backpropagated error, while Eq. 3.36 composes it with the local sensitivity of the state with respect to the weight and yields the local contribution for the gradient. What we have gained with this analysis is insight on the requirements to apply backpropagation and on the characteristics of the method. We will address two aspects: the computational complexity of the method and efficient implementations.

Rederivation of Backpropagation with Ordered Derivatives

With this theory we can rederive the backpropagation procedure for any ordered topology very quickly. We assume a network (with smooth nonlinearities) given by Eq. 3.33. Dependence on the iteration is not included for simplicity. The direct effect in Eq. 3.33 is computed as

$$\frac{\partial^d y_j}{\partial y_i} = f'(net_i) w_{ji} \qquad \frac{\partial^d J}{\partial y_i} = -\varepsilon_i \tag{3B.7}$$

where ε_i is the external injected error. We can rewrite Eq. 3.35 as

$$\frac{\partial J}{\partial y_i} = -\varepsilon_i + \sum_{j>i} \frac{\partial J}{\partial y_j} f'(net_j) w_{ji} \tag{3B.8}$$

Note that the partial derivative of J with respect to the state is equal to the injected error ε_i for an output PE and zero for the other cases. With the assignment that we used before,

$$\delta_i = \frac{\partial J}{\partial net_i} = e_i f'(net_i) \tag{3B.9}$$

we can write

$$e_i = -\varepsilon_i + \sum_{j>i} e_j f'(net_j) w_{ji} = -\varepsilon_i + \sum_{j>i} \delta_j w_{ji} \tag{3B.10}$$

To compute the gradients with respect to the weights, we use Eq. 3.36 to get

$$\frac{\partial J}{\partial w_{ij}} = \frac{\partial^d J}{\partial w_{ij}} + \sum_k \frac{\partial J}{\partial y_k} \frac{\partial^d y_k}{\partial w_{ij}} = 0 + \frac{\partial J}{\partial y_i} f'(net_i) y_j \tag{3B.11}$$

Note that the sum extended to all PEs reduces to one term, $k = i$, because we are computing the local contribution to the weight w_{ij}. The sensitivity of the cost can finally be written

$$\frac{\partial J}{\partial w_{ij}} = \delta_i y_j \qquad \text{(3B.12)}$$

We can recognize Eqs. 3B.12 and 3B.10 as the equations necessary to implement the backpropagation procedure (respectively, Eqs. 3.29 and 3.31) that we derived PE by PE in the text. But here they were derived in a much more compact form. The weight update using the gradient descent procedure is

$$w_{ij}(n + 1) = w_{ij}(n) - \eta \frac{\partial J(n)}{\partial w_{ij}(n)}$$

3.6.2 Computational Complexity

The backpropagation algorithm derived for neural networks is a very powerful and unique method that can also be applied to the larger field of gradient descent learning. To fully appreciate this point, we have to ask the question, How were gradients computed traditionally? The fields of control theory and digital signal processing addressed the same problem long ago.

They used what is called the direct differentiation method to compute gradients. The equations are simple to derive for the MLP. Suppose that we want to minimize the cost given by Eq. 3.19 with the forward structure of Eq. 3.33 with N PEs. Applying the chain rule to Eq. 3.19, we get

$$\frac{\partial J}{\partial w_{ij}} = - \sum_k \varepsilon_k \frac{\partial y_k}{\partial w_{ij}} \qquad \text{(3.37)}$$

Let us define the gradient variable

$$\alpha_{ij}^k = \frac{\partial y_k}{\partial w_{ij}} \qquad i, j, k = 1, \ldots, N \qquad \text{(3.38)}$$

where the superscript k refers to the kth state variable. The gradient variable can be computed by differentiating the state equation Eq. 3.33 to yield

$$\alpha_{ij}^k = \frac{\partial}{\partial net_k} f(net_k) \frac{\partial}{\partial w_{ij}} net_k = f'(net_k)[\Delta_{ik} y_j] \qquad \text{(3.39)}$$

where f' denotes the derivative and Δ_{ik} is the Kronecker delta that is equal to 1 only when $k = i$ and 0 otherwise. This expression applies to feedforward topologies such as the MLP.

This method is straightforward to implement, but it is computationally demanding. It basically says that one needs to compute the sensitivity α of every state to every weight (Eq. 3.38). Since in an N-PE fully connected MLP we have MN weights, this gives MN quantities. Equation 3.39 also shows that for each gradient variable we need a constant number of multiplications, so the end result is a computational complexity proportional to MN that we will denote by O(MN). The storage required for the algorithm is dominated by the storage of the gradient variables, which is O(MN).

Now let us analyze the backpropagation procedure. The backpropagation procedure is O(N^2), since for an N-PE net we have to compute N errors δ, and each needs N multiplications (Eq. 3.31). This is the same complexity of the forward path (Eq. 3.33), so the asymptotic complexity of the backpropagation algorithm is O(N^2). This should be compared with O(MN) for the direct method. Whenever the network has more weights than PEs (which is normally the case with MLPs), the direct procedure is more expensive computationally. In terms of storage the backpropagation algorithm is also more efficient than the direct computation.

The savings come from the use of the topology to compute the weight updates. However, this also brings a shortcoming that connectionism has not fully coped with, namely, the need to rederive the learning equations for each new topology. We will show later how to implement a topology-independent learning algorithm in the simulations if the principles embodied in the ordered derivatives are fully exploited.

3.6.3 Interconnection Algorithm for Backpropagation

The local nature of the backpropagation algorithm has very deep and important implications for simulation in digital computers. Unfortunately, it is not widely used in neurocomputing, so we discuss here a local implementation of backpropagation that requires knowledge only of the topology and of the PE input-output map. We call this implementation the *interconnection algorithm* because it uses the PE interconnection to specify the flow of the calculations.

For convenience, let us rewrite the activation equation and the error equations:

Forward equation
$$y_i = f\left(\sum_{j<i} w_{ij} y_j\right) + x_i$$

Backward equation
$$e_i = -\varepsilon_i + \sum_{j>i} w_{ji} \delta_j$$

Analyzing these equations closely, we can conclude that the expression that computes the local error in the internal PEs is tightly coupled with the original network topology. In the forward pass the network works with the input data x and produces activations y. The backward equation works with the injected error ε and produces errors e. Furthermore, note that the equations become essentially the same if w_{ij} is substituted by w_{ji}. This indicates that once the topology is known, both the forward and backward equations can be automatically computed. Figure 3-22 presents this similarity in more detail. In the top part we show the original neural network around the ith PE, while in

Original ANN

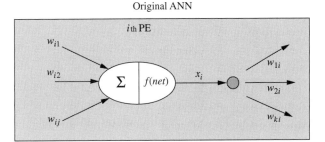

(a)

Dual ANN

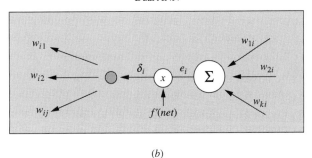

(b)

FIGURE 3-22 (a) Original and (b) dual networks

the bottom part of the figure we are implementing a network that realizes the backward equation. The network of Figure 3-22(b) is called the *dual* (or *transpose*) of the network of Figure 3-22(a), and is constructed with the following rules.

At the ith PE the flow of activations (x_i) in the original neural topology is from left to right, while in the topology that computes the error (δ_i) it is from right to left; that is, inputs become outputs and outputs become inputs. Note also that the summing junctions in Figure 3-22(a) become splitting nodes in Figure 3-22(b), and splitting nodes become summing junctions. The weights keep the same values. The incoming error in the dual network is multiplied by $f'(net_i)$ to produce δ_i.

The conclusion of this observation is that we can imagine that the injected error ε_i created by the difference between the network output and the desired response flows into the dual topology. Collecting the local error at each PE in the dual network is equivalent to deriving and computing the messy Eq. 3.31. Note also that in the dual topology the value of $f'(.)$ is computed at net_i, the activation level of the corresponding PE; that is, it corresponds to a linearization of the forward network at the operating point. This leads to the following alternative description of backpropagation (Figure 3-23).

The procedure starts by inputting data to the neural network and obtaining the local activation at every PE (step 1). Then the network output is computed and compared with the desired response to obtain the output error, using the appropriate error criterion

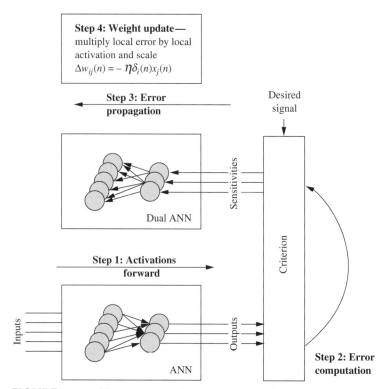

FIGURE 3-23 The algorithm for backpropagation with the dual network

(step 2). This error is injected through the dual network, and a local error is obtained at each PE (step 3). Note that the error in the dual network is scaled at each node by the derivative of the nonlinearity at the operating point (given by the activation in the original ANN). Now that we have the local error and the local activation, we can again apply Eq. 3.29 to compute all weight updates (step 4).

The beauty of this arrangement that we call the interconnection algorithm for backpropagation is twofold. First, the data flow has been separated from the local computations, which brings flexibility for the simulations. Later chapters demonstrate that this gradient-descent methodology is also valid for training recurrent networks and networks through time; that is, the interconnection algorithm is a general implementation of gradient-descent learning.

Second, the local error is available as a signal at the PEs of the dual topology, which means that we do not need to write equations to compute the local error, the biggest problem when simulating arbitrary neural networks with backpropagation. Only the topology of the network needs to be specified by the user. The flow of errors through the dual network topology is doing the backpropagation computations for us effortlessly. Implementing the backpropagation algorithm with the dual network is much more versatile than directly coding the previous equations, since the dual network can be programmed very simply from the user's specified topology. NeuroSolutions uses the interconnection algorithm presented in Figure 3-23. Next, we specify the operations required locally to implement the interconnection algorithm.

3.6.4 Specification of the Local Operations

The interconnection algorithm can be programmed in a data-flow fashion that is called a data-flow machine. Analyzing Figure 3-23, we can also see that the type of PE enters only in the choice of the local computation ($f(.)$ and its derivative in the dual network). What this means in practice is that the flow of signals through the network (i.e., the activations and the errors) can be *decoupled* from the operations of the PEs. This provides a very powerful way to simulate neural networks, because different PEs can be interchanged at will in the topology simply by specifying new local operations that each building block must execute. We therefore do not need to derive learning equations for each topology. Only two items need to be specified:

- The network topology (preferably in graphical form) by numbering PEs in a left-to-right manner. A computer program can easily produce an ordered list of interconnections.
- The PE and the dual PE input-output relations, which we call the *local maps*.

To be part of the data-flow machine, the ith PE must be programmed to do basically two things when it is activated (fired) by the interconnection algorithm:

- Propagate an activation forward (forward equation)

$$x_i = f\left(\sum_j w_{ij} x_j\right)$$ (3.40)

- Propagate an error backward (backward equation)

$$\delta_i = f'(net_i) \sum_k w_{ki} \delta_k$$ (3.41)

Both Eqs. 3.40 and 3.41 are required because the ith PE is part of a larger network. Thus the PE needs (x_i, δ_i) not only to update its weights (with the gradient-descent rule), but also to pass x_i forward to continue the chain and to pass δ_i backward so that the dual PEs in the preceding layer can perform adaptation of their own parameters. Figure 3-24 shows the mechanics of the method.

Finally, the weight updates are computed from (x_i, δ_i) with the gradient search method of choice. Until now we discussed only the straight gradient-descent algorithm, so this simply means $\Delta w_{ij} = x_j \delta_i$. But in general for first-order search methods the

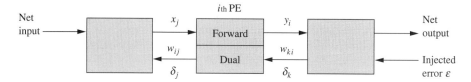

FIGURE 3-24 Communications among PEs in the topology

update is a function $h(.)$ of the activation and error

$$\Delta w_{ij} = h(x_j, \delta_i) \tag{3.42}$$

as we will discuss in Chapter 4. Different PE types (logistic, tanh, linear, quasi-linear, etc.) simply require different local maps for the PE and its dual. This means that PEs can be effectively organized into families of components using an object-oriented programming approach, as exploited in NeuroSolutions. Moreover, each PE can be associated with an icon that leads to a very effective graphical user interface to construct neural networks. Remember that the forward PE and its dual share the same weight values w_{ij}.

NEUROSOLUTIONS EXAMPLE 3.22

Data-flow implementation of backpropagation

This explanation needs to be compared with the iconic representation of the breadboard that implements the MLP. Note that the breadboard has three planes: the large-bubbles (the forward network, also called the forward plane) that is computing the forward activation (Eq. 3.40), the smaller-bubbles (the dual network, also called the back plane) that is computing local errors (Eq. 3.41), and the gradient-descent components (the search plane) that use the local activations and local sensitivities to compute the weight updates (Eq. 3.42).

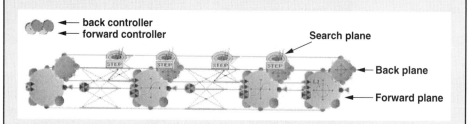

The data flow is implemented by the Controllers that normally sit at the top left of the network. To implement backpropagation, there are two controllers: the Forward Static Controller (which sends input data forward through the network)

and the Back Static Controller (which sends sensitivities through the dual network). The alternation between these Controllers implements the data flow necessary to update the weights using backpropagation. These controllers are crucial to deciding what type of backpropagation is implemented (static, fixed-point learning, or backpropagation through time), as we will see later.

The data flow still needs to be further specified (remember that backpropagation implicitly imposes a data flow). You can send one sample at a time through the network, compute the corresponding local error, and perform the adaptation. This is called the *on-line* or *pattern-mode learning*. An alternative is to fire all the samples of the training set. Store all the PE activations locally. Compute the network outputs for every input. Compare and compute the errors at the network output for each input–desired response pair, and send all the output errors in sequence through the dual network. Now you can compute the weight update for every sample, sum them up, and only then change the weights. This is called the *batch-learning mode,* where the weights are always updated with the information contained in the full training set.

To demonstrate how easy it is to construct the dual network, the Back Controller has a switch to automatically construct the backpropagation plane. If the *Remove* button is pressed, the backpropagation plane is deleted. The network now has only the forward dynamics, so it cannot learn. This is the way the network should be used for testing. Freeing the back plane is preferable to setting the learning rates to zero because it is more efficient (no sensitivities are ever calculated).

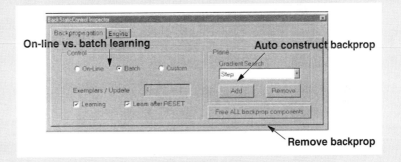

Now if the *Allocate* button is pressed, the back plane and the gradient plane are automatically constructed. The network will be able to learn again. Notice that with the arrangement of the simulations in planes, the user only has to worry about the construction of the forward plane, that is, the network topology. Once this is done, NeuroSolutions has the information to automatically construct the learning dynamics. The biggest advantage of this arrangement is the ability to create user-defined topologies, free of the conventional constraints. NeuroSolutions is always able to compute the dual network and train the weights with backpropagation. No learning equations are ever explicitly written.

3.7 TRAINING EMBEDDED ADAPTIVE SYSTEMS

Backpropagation is able to compute gradients in ordered networks with smooth non-linearities. The algorithm, however, can be applied to any system built from modules that are differentiable (not necessarily adaptive) and that can be ordered. This is indeed a very large class of systems that includes macroeconomical, life science, and engineering models. The beauty of the procedure is that we can propagate sensitivities up and down the modules with the goal of finding optimal coefficients that meet a given external criterion.

This is to say that we can mix adaptive and fixed-parameter subsystems and with backpropagation seek an *overall optimal* operating point. This is particularly important when we have a priori knowledge about the problem and we want to design subsystems that include that knowledge but have other subsystems that are adaptive. Even if only some of the modules are adaptive, we can propagate sensitivities through the ones with fixed parameters to optimally train the overall system. We use this property later in control applications.

Here we would like to treat the case of Figure 3-25, where an adaptive submodule of a system needs to be adapted, given a desired external response. Notice that the adaptive module is internal; that is, it is not in direct contact with either the input or the desired signal. Can we optimally set the parameters of this system? The answer is "yes," provided that submodule 2 is differentiable and the overall network is ordered.

Using our known tools of the chain rule and ordered derivatives, we can see that this adaptation problem can be easily solved, taking into consideration that

$$\frac{\partial J}{\partial w_{ij}} = \underbrace{\frac{\partial J}{\partial y_{\text{mod 2}}} \frac{\partial y_{\text{mod 2}}}{\partial y_{\text{MLP}}}}_{\varepsilon} \underbrace{\frac{\partial y_{\text{MLP}}}{\partial w_{ij}}}_{BP} \tag{3.43}$$

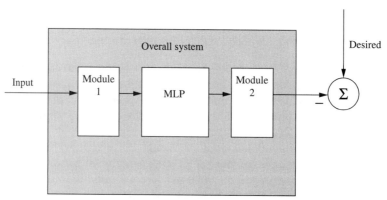

FIGURE 3-25 Adapting an embedded adaptive system

The first term is the injected error, while the last is the term that backpropagation computes for us. If we know the functional form of the input-output relation for module 2, we can calculate the effect of passing the injected error through module 2. We still have a small problem in computing the weight update using gradient descent, since we have to know the input to the MLP, but this is straightforward if we know the input-output relation of module 1. Of course, if the modules are themselves nonlinear, they may complicate the training because they attenuate errors and activations, but this does not affect the applicability of the method.

This analysis shows that we can adapt the parameters of an embedded adaptive system in larger systems built from fixed coefficients and differentiable input-output relationships. We can design the subsystem to optimize the overall system performance. This is a very important aspect of backpropagation that today is still largely unexplored.

NEUROSOLUTIONS EXAMPLE 3.23

Training embedded neural networks with backpropagation

In this example we adapt an embedded adaptive system (MLP) in a larger system built from a front-end fuzzy module with an output that goes through a nonlinear subsystem before it is compared with the desired response.

The goal of this example is to create an intelligent "bell-ringer" machine at a fair. The contestant uses a sledgehammer to hit a lever that projects an object up a column in the hope of ringing the bell at the top. Our goal is to make the device more fair by adjusting the height of the bell based on the size and weight of the contestant. But since we do not have a scale or a measuring device, we would like to use the quantifiers light, medium, and heavy for the weight, and short, medium, and tall for the height. We want to train an MLP to move the bell based on the "fuzzy" inputs to a position where the average person of that height and weight can ring it. The difficulty is that the pneumatic machinery used to move the bell has a discontinuous and nonlinear transfer function. The height of the bell is proportional to the cube of the control input (MLP output). In addition, if the control input is above 0.3, the machinery is warped out of calibration and the bell height must also be adjusted by adding 0.16 plus the square root of the already cubed input. These operations are shown in Figure 3-26. Given a set of heights, weights, and the distance the object has traveled up the "bell-ringer" column, can we still train the MLP?

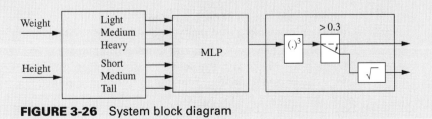

FIGURE 3-26 System block diagram

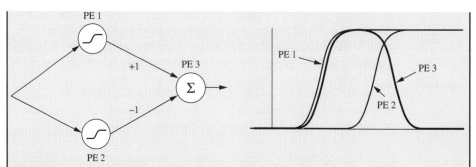

FIGURE 3-27 Creation of a fuzzy layer with sigmoids

We create the linguistic variables *light, medium,* and so on from the height and weight using fuzzifiers. The fuzzy module is built from sigmoid nonlinearities. The advantage of a fuzzy layer is that it includes in a very effective way the a priori knowledge that we may have about the task. Fuzzy sets are described by a membership function (MF), so the first problem is to devise a way to create membership functions in NeuroSolutions. This is not difficult because we can very easily create an MF by a cascade of one sigmoid layer with a linear layer with preset parameters (which may later be fine-tuned through adaptation). As an example, see Figure 3-27.

Pairs of sigmoids combined with +1 and −1 will create a Gaussian-like membership function (Figure 3-27). The maximum is located at the average value of the bias. Several of these paired PEs with different biases span the input space with the linguistic variables. The knowledge from the tasks sets the bias and the slope of each sigmoid such that the required membership functions are constructed. Notice that there are no adaptable parameters in this layer. Open the Matrix Editors in the breadboard to see how we have created this layer. As usual, you are free to modify any parameter.

The next submodule is the one-hidden-layer MLP, which is followed by a second module that adjusts the height of the bell-shaped curve. In this example, module 2 implements the function

$$y = \begin{cases} z^3 & z < 0.3 \\ \sqrt[2]{z^3} + 0.16 & z \geq 0.3 \end{cases}$$

where z is the output of the MLP. This function is coded in the DLL at the output of the MLP. Notice that the Dual component has to implement the dual of the function. NeuroSolutions with its data-flow implementation of backpropagation is capable of training the MLP, with the activations and sensitivities being passed through the fuzzy layer and the output function. Run the system and verify that the MLP can still optimize the overall system.

Feedforward neural networks are an example of ordered networks. But notice that the list of dependencies in Eq. 3.34 is static in the sense that it does not depend on time. When time dependencies are brought into the picture, as will be done in later chapters, the ordered list of dependencies must be revisited to apply backpropagation. Another requirement to apply this methodology is to choose smooth nonlinearities for the PEs, as was mentioned previously on several occasions. One aspect that should be stressed again is that backpropagation is computationally more efficient than direct differentiation to compute gradients in feedforward networks.

3.8   MLPs AS OPTIMAL CLASSIFIERS

Before concluding this chapter, let us go back to the framework of statistical pattern recognition and ask the question: Can MLPs in fact implement *optimal classifiers?* An optimal classifier must have the potential to create arbitrary discriminant functions that separate data clusters according to the a posteriori probability. Since we know that the MLP has known universal mapping capabilities, we suspect that the MLP meets this requirement. An optimal classifier using the Bayes' framework should produce outputs that are the a posteriori probability of the class given the data.

Does the MLP produce outputs that can be interpreted as probabilities? The answer to this question is yes if the training is done under certain conditions [Bishop 1995]. Moreover, we can also show that the MLP is directly producing estimates of a posteriori probabilities, unlike any of the classical methods of pattern recognition. Remember that in statistical pattern recognition we needed to use Bayes' theorem to evaluate the a posteriori probabilities. With the MLP we obtain their estimates directly as outputs, provided that the training and the topology are appropriately specified. This is a departure from the well-established statistical reasoning that applies Bayes' rule to estimate a posteriori probabilities. Let us briefly cover the basic concepts of this theory.

Assume the learning machine is being trained to minimize the MSE (Figure 3-28). We have to assume that the MLP has a sufficient number of PEs to produce the required map from input space to targets. We also have to assume that the training data is sufficient and that the training does indeed take the learning system to the global minimum. The final requirement is that the outputs are between 0 and 1 and that they all sum to 1 for every input pattern (so that each output can represent the probability that the input is in the specified class). To guarantee that the outputs sum to 1, we cannot utilize the logistic function PE. We must utilize a new output axon with the *softmax*

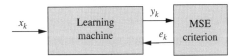

FIGURE 3-28 A learning machine whose outputs are estimates of a posteriori probabilities

activation function:

$$y_k = \frac{\exp(net_k)}{\sum_j \exp(net_j)} \tag{3.44}$$

where the denominator sums over all network outputs. The softmax function is similar to the tanh and logistic functions, except that the outputs are scaled by the total activation at the output layer (so that the sum of the outputs is 1). For the two-class case the single output PE can be a logistic function, since the probability requirements are still met. The probability of class 1 is the value of the output PE, and the probability of class 2 is 1 minus the value of the output PE.

Notice that we did not specify that the learning machine must be an MLP. The MLP is just an example of a viable and efficient implementation that produces this result since it is a universal mapper. The important aspect for this behavior is the minimization of the MSE.

The output y_k of such an MLP can be shown to be an estimator for the average conditional probability of the target data, given the inputs, that is,

$$y_k(x, w^*) = \sum_i t_{i,k} p(t_{i,k} \mid x) \tag{3.45}$$

where w^* is the optimal weight value and we are using t for the desired response. For a classification problem where the desired response is 1 and 0 and we assume c outputs (one output per class), it is easy to show that we have

$$y_k(x) = P(c_k \mid x) \tag{3.46}$$

What this equation says is that the output of the MLP is providing the a posteriori probability of the class given the data. Recall from the pattern-recognition chapter that the a posteriori probabilities minimize the classification error and are therefore the best one can hope for in building optimal classifiers. We can thus conclude that if the learning machine is powerful enough and has been trained appropriately, its outputs (with the restrictions previously mentioned) can be interpreted as a posteriori probabilities of the classes given the data. We now have a methodology to estimate a posteriori probabilities directly from the data, unlike when we use statistical pattern recognition, where Bayes' rule is conventionally applied.

Derivation of the Conditional Average

This result can be demonstrated (see Bishop [1995] for a full treatment) if we write the MSE for the case with a large number of patterns as an integral:

$$J = \frac{1}{2} \sum_k \int \int [y_k(x, w) - t_k]^2 p(t_k, x) \, dt_k \, dx$$

For clarity we denote the desired response by t. Note that the index k sums over the targets, and the sum over the data exemplars was transformed into the integral, which has to be written as a function of the joint probability of the desired response and the input. This joint probability can be factored in the product of the input pdf $p(x)$ and the conditional of the target data given the input $p(t_k \mid x)$.

The square can be written

$$(y_k(x, w) - t_k)^2 = (y_k(x, w) - \langle\langle t_k \mid x \rangle\rangle + \langle\langle t_k \mid x \rangle\rangle - t_k)^2$$

where $\langle\langle t_k \mid x \rangle\rangle$ is the conditional average given by $\langle\langle t \mid x \rangle\rangle = \int t_k p(t_k \mid x)\, dt_k$. We can write further

$$\begin{aligned}(y_k(x, w) - t_k)^2 =& (y_k(x, w) - \langle\langle t_k \mid x \rangle\rangle)^2 \\ &+ 2(y_k(x, w) - \langle\langle t_k \mid x \rangle\rangle)(\langle\langle t_k \mid x \rangle\rangle - t_k) + (\langle\langle t_k \mid x \rangle\rangle - t_k)^2\end{aligned}$$

Now if we substitute back into the MSE equation and simplify, we obtain

$$J = \tfrac{1}{2} \sum_k \int (y_k(x, w) - \langle\langle t_k \mid x \rangle\rangle)^2 p(x)\, dx + \tfrac{1}{2} \sum_k \int (\langle\langle t_k^2 \mid x \rangle\rangle - \langle\langle t_k \mid x \rangle\rangle^2) p(x)\, dx$$

The second term of this expression is independent of the network so will not change during training. The minimum of the first term is obtained when the weights produce

$$y_k(x, w^*) = \langle\langle t_k \mid x \rangle\rangle$$

since the integrand is always positive. This is the result presented in the text.

This is a very important result because it allows us to work with the numerical outputs of the network as a posteriori probabilities for a variety of applications in both pattern recognition and signal processing. Here are some of these applications:

- Applying rejection thresholds for decision making
- Implementing minimum risk decisions in detection and diagnostics
- Estimating observation probabilities in a variety of applications (hidden Markov models, statistical signal processing)

We address these aspects further in later chapters.

NEUROSOLUTIONS EXAMPLE 3.24

Softmax and a posteriori probabilities

This example uses the preceding probability considerations to show how an MLP can be used to estimate the a posteriori probabilities for the healthy–sick example discussed previously. We will train a one-hidden-layer MLP with two Softmax PEs.

The Softmax PEs are similar to Sigmoid PEs except they are normalized so that the sum of the outputs is always 1. The Softmax function allows the outputs of the MLP to be considered as a posteriori estimates of the probability that the input exemplar belongs to each class. For example, if the output from PE 1 is 0.90 and the output from PE 2 is 0.10, then the probability that the subject is healthy is 90 percent and the probability that the subject is sick is 10 percent.

Softmax Axon

To check how well this really works, we need quantitative data regarding the class distributions, so we created a two-class problem where each class is composed by two sets of Gaussian distributed data. The a posteriori probability is shown in the following figure.

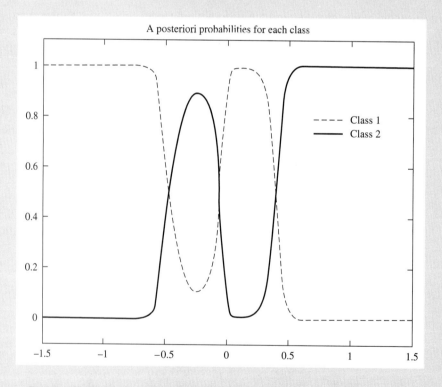

Red (represented by the dashed line) is the a posteriori probability of class 1, while black is the a posteriori probability of class 2. Run the network and observe how similar the discriminant functions of the MLP are to this plot. This is a more specific example of the important optimality property of MLPs. Change the number of PEs to test what the net does when it does not have enough degrees of freedom. Let it train for a long time and compare the final separation surface with the preceding picture. Overtraining makes the separation surface go to ± 1 and destroys the statistical interpretation.

3.9 CONCLUSIONS

In this chapter we covered one of the most important applications of neural networks: pattern recognition. ANNs are semiparametric classifiers, since the discriminant functions are functions that belong to a given class. But we do not know a priori the actual discriminants that will be employed by the ANN.

In this chapter we studied multilayer perceptrons (MLPs), which are feedforward topologies. The topology is what defines the functions that can be used for discriminants. The perceptron can construct only linear discriminants, but the two-hidden-layer MLP is a universal approximator; that is, it can construct arbitrarily complex input-output mappings. MLPs are very efficient approximators in high-dimensional spaces.

MLPs are trained with a gradient-descent procedure called backpropagation. Backpropagation is a very powerful and computationally efficient algorithm. It is, in fact, a contribution of the field of neural networks to optimization theory. We have shown how the algorithm is derived using the chain rule, and we also covered the ordered derivative method, which is more rigorous. In fact, it tells us a great deal about the types of topologies that can be trained with backpropagation. It also led us to the interconnection implementation, which is the best possible way to implement backpropagation with a computer algorithm. Its great advantage is that it can be applied to arbitrary topologies, as long as the computer can construct the dual (or transpose) network. This is trivial to do in ordered networks. Much of the power of NeuroSolutions is based on this innovation, which was first coded in 1991 [Lefebvre 1991].

This chapter concentrated on MLP principles, but little was said about how to apply them to real-world data. This is the purpose of the next chapter.

3.10 NEUROSOLUTIONS EXAMPLES

3.1 McCulloch-Pitts PE for classification

3.2 Discriminant probe to visualize the decision surface

3.3 Behavior of the sigmoid PEs

3.4 Classification as the control of the decision surface

3.5 Perceptron learning rule

3.6 Delta rule to adapt the M-P PE

3.11 EXERCISES

3.1 Create by hand the weights of a perceptron that will work as an AND function. Test the solution in NeuroSolutions. If you take out the bias of the PEs, can you still solve the AND problem? Confirm with NeuroSolutions.

3.2 For the data shown in the figure (dark circles are one class, white circles the other) solve the classification problem with an M-P PE by hand; that is, find the appropriate weights. Give the equation for the separation surface. If the perceptron weights are $(2, -2)$ and the bias $b = 1$, is the problem solved?

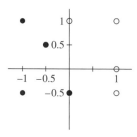

3.3 Explain why the classification regions created by a perceptron are always convex.

3.4 Specify the weights of a single-layer MLP that will create discriminants as in the figure (the shaded area should provide a response of zero). Confirm your solution with NeuroSolutions. Then create a data file with two classes that will provide the same basic discriminant function. Train an MLP to show that you are correct.

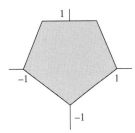

3.5 Construct by hand the MLP weights that will be able to create the following figure (shaded is 0, white is 1).

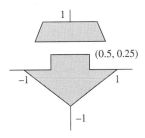

3.6 Specify the dual network of the softmax PE.

3.7 Suppose that you use the following activation function for a new PE:

$$\begin{cases} -1 & net < -0.5 \\ \sin(\pi net) & -0.5 \le net \le 0.5 \\ 1 & net > -0.5 \end{cases}$$

(a) Derive the learning equations.
(b) Create the dual network.
(c) Implement in NeuroSolutions a DLL that will implement your PE.

3.8 For the sigmoid nonlinearities of Section 2.1, derive the equations that will adapt the scalar α. What do you gain by adapting α? Can you achieve a similar result by adapting other learning parameters?

3.9 Compare experimentally a perceptron network trained with the perceptron learning rule, the delta rule, and the Adatron in the data set prob 3.9 train (and test) in the folder Chapter 3 contained in the data directory (CD-ROM). Use the confusion matrix to rank the different solutions.

3.10 Is the following network an ordered network? Determine the ordered list if your answer is affirmative.

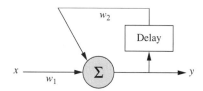

3.12 CONCEPT MAP FOR CHAPTER 3

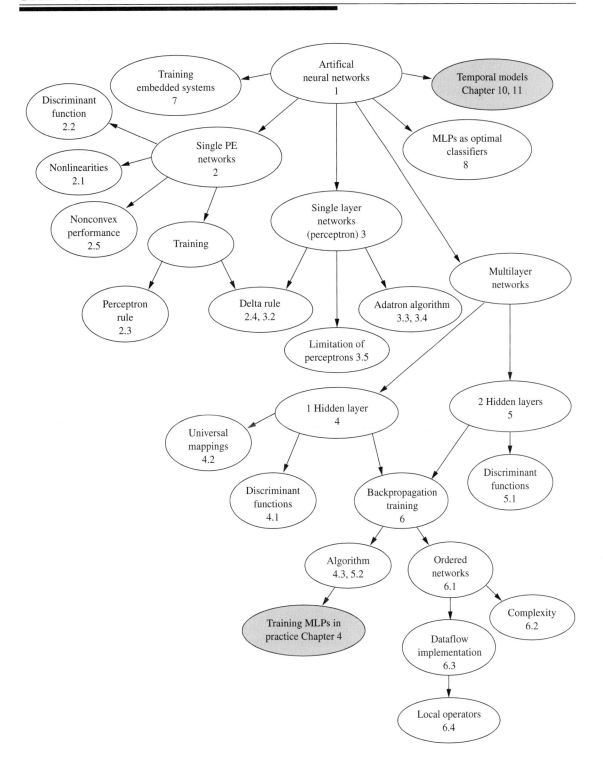

REFERENCES

Anlauf, J., and Biehl, M., The Adatron: An adaptive perceptron algorithm, *Europhysics Letters,* 10(7):687–692, 1989.

Bishop, C., *Neural Networks for Pattern Recognition,* Oxford Press, Oxford, 1995.

Cybenko, G., Approximation by superposition of a sigmoid function, *Mathematics for Control, Signals, and Systems,* 2(4):303–314, 1989.

Haykin, S., *Neural Networks: A Comprehensive Foundation,* MacMillan, New York, 1994.

Hornik, K., Stinchcombe, M., and White, H., MLPs are universal approximators, *Neural Networks,* 2:359–366, 1989.

LeCun, Y., Une procédure d'apprentissage pour réseau à seuil asymmétrique, *Cognitiva* 85:599–604, 1985.

Lefebvre, C., *An Object Oriented Approach for the Analysis of Neural Networks,* master's thesis, University of Florida, 1991.

Rosenblatt, F., The Perceptron: A probabilistic model for information storage and organization in the brain, *Psychological Review,* 65:386–408, 1958.

Rumelhart, D., Hinton, G., and Williams, R., Learning representations by backpropagation errors, *Nature,* 323:533–536, 1986.

Vapnik, V., *The Nature of Statistical Learning Theory,* Springer Verlag, New York, 1995.

Werbos, P. *Beyond Regression: New Tools for Prediction and Analysis in the Behavioral Sciences,* Ph.D. dissertation, Harvard, 1974.

DESIGNING AND TRAINING MLPs

In this chapter we address the more practical aspects of using MLPs, which include

- Search strategies to find the minimum
- Alternative cost functions
- Control of generalization (topologies)

After presenting these aspects from a practical point of view, real-world problems will be solved with the MLP topology.

4.1 INTRODUCTION

In the previous chapter, we presented the multilayer perceptron (MLP) topology and its learning algorithm, but we used very simple data sets to illustrate its performance. In this chapter we will address the most important design choices required to build and train neural network classifiers. We focus on MLPs, but many of the topics transcend feedforward multilayer networks and apply to adaptive systems in general. The fundamental issues that we cover in this chapter are

- Efficiency and control of learning
- Choice of error criterion
- Choice of network topology

A well-designed network that is poorly trained produces inadequate results. Thus, controlling and speeding up the learning process is an extremely important part of any successful neural network application. We therefore cover in detail issues regarding learning rates, more efficient search criteria, and how/when to stop the training for maximum performance.

The goal of presenting several error criteria is to provide added flexibility to the user. Although the MSE is the most widely used criterion, many other criteria exist that may be preferable in some circumstances. We cover the error norms and the information-theoretic criterion of cross entropy

The last issue we discuss is the problem of selecting an appropriate network topology to achieve good generalization. This is a crucial step in MLPs because MLPs do not control their generalization ability when trained with MSE. We thus learn how to prune MLPs and improve generalization.

With these issues covered, the user is ready to solve meaningful classification problems with MLPs. This chapter includes a number of interesting real-life classification problems, including the rock crab data, the iris data, and a computer-aided diagnostic example for breast cancer. Although these data are provided in files, we encourage students to browse the Internet and find new data.

4.2 CONTROLLING LEARNING IN PRACTICE

Learning (or adaptation) is a crucial step in neural network technology. Learning is the procedure that extracts the required information from the input data (with the help of the desired response in the supervised case). If learning is incomplete, the weight values will not be near their optimal values, and performance will suffer. As we have seen in Chapters 1 and 3, the good news is that there are systematic procedures to search the performance surface. The bad news is that the search has to be controlled heuristically.

The user directly affects the search through

- The selection of the initial weights
- The learning rates

- The search algorithms
- The stop criterion

We have to understand the issues affecting each one of these topics to effectively train neural networks. We should also remember that the ultimate performance also depends on the amount and quality of the data set used to train the system.

A large portion of this chapter is devoted to extending the basic gradient-descent learning developed in Chapter 3, so we will concentrate on the aspects that can be improved. But it is good to remember up front that straight gradient-descent learning and its different implementations (LMS, delta rule, backpropagation) are among the most widely utilized methods to train adaptive systems because they are an excellent balance of simplicity, efficiency, and power. So while the tone of the chapter may seem negative towards gradient-descent learning, this is just a consequence of the exposition goal. The reader should balance the impression with the amazing power of the technique already displayed in Chapters 1 and 3.

Algorithm Locality and Distributed Systems

One of the appealing issues of gradient-descent learning is the locality of the computation. Recall that any of the LMS, delta rule, and back-propagation algorithms use only local quantities available at the weight to perform their adaptation. This is crucial for the efficiency of the algorithms, in particular for distributed system implementations. If the algorithm was not local, the necessary variables would have to be fetched from intermediate storage or across the neural network. This means that there would be a great deal of overhead for algorithm implementation and, more important, that centralized control was necessary. Adaptation would lose the biological appeal that locality provides.

Complexity imposes stringent constraints on the system design. One of the luxuries that the designer must give up is centralized control, because otherwise most of the system resources will be eaten up by the control rather than used to perform the required function. This is the beauty of distributed systems with local rules of interactions: They do not require centralized control. They may potentially be the only way to break the barrier of system complexity, as exemplified by our own brains.

Going back to the learning rules, let's appreciate for a minute the formidable task of moving a distributed system with thousands of parameters towards its optimal parameter set. There is no one orchestrating the change in weights. Each weight receives an error and an activation and, independently of all the other weights, changes its own value using only two multiplications. Overall the system approaches the optimal operating point, but centralized control is not necessary. This is a great model to construct complex systems.

Before we develop a methodology to appropriately set the learning parameters, let's see how we can visualize what is happening inside the neural network during training and describe some of the features of learning.

4.2.1 Visualizing Learning in a Neural Network

An important point to remember is that learning is much richer than can be imaged from the learning curve (the thermometer of learning, as we call it in Chapter 1). All the internal parameters of the network are being changed simultaneously according to the *activation* flowing in the network, the *errors* flowing in the *dual* network, and the particular search algorithm used to update the weights.

Since the setup of the learning parameters is problem dependent, the user has to make decisions that are particular to the problem being solved. The only way to make appropriate judgments when a theory is lacking is to understand, through experimentation, the principles at work. Hence it is very instructive to visualize the behavior of the network parameters during learning, and we can do so effortlessly with NeuroSolutions.

NEUROSOLUTIONS EXAMPLE 4.1

Visualization of learning

In this example we use the XOR network from Chapter 2 and place scopes on the weights and backpropagated errors. By viewing the errors, weights, decision surface, and learning curve, we will get a much better feel for what is going on in the network. Compare the evolution of the weights with the back-propagated errors. Also compare the location of the decision surface with the actual value of the weights. Finally, compare all of this activity with the learning curve, the external variable that we normally observe. Do this several times. Try to understand the relationships among the different pieces. Ultimately, everything depends on the input data and the errors.

Notice that the time evolution of the weights differs every time we run the network, but the final MSE is almost the same from run to run. Every run also produces a different set of weights. Learning in a neural network is a very rich process, and the learning curve can only give a glimpse of these activities. Nonetheless it is a valuable tool for gauging the progress of learning.

4.2.2 Network Weights and Minimum MSE

It is important to understand why the adaptation of the same topology with the same training data produces so many different sets of final weights. There are three basic reasons for this fact.

- First, there are many symmetries in the input-output mapping created by the MLP. Thus, two networks that produce the exact same results may have different weights. For instance, as we discussed in Chapter 3, the position of the discriminant function is determined by the ratio of the weights, not their values. Also, changing the sign of the output weight of a PE compensates for input weights with a reversed sign.

- Second, there is no guarantee in general that the problem has a single solution. In particular, when nonminimal topologies are utilized, the redundancies may create many possible solutions. Remember that the minimization of the output error is an external constraint. Nothing is said about the uniqueness of the weight values to provide a given output error. In fact, from the point of view of the problem formulation, as long as the output error is minimized, any solution is as good as any other.

- Third, the final weights are obtained in an iterated fashion from a random initial condition. Even when we stop the adaptation at a fixed iteration number in two different training runs over the same data, the random initial weights create different weight tracks during adaptation. Therefore the final weight values will most likely be different.

The size of the topology often magnifies these differences and produces very different final weights from run to run. Additionally, if the topology is not minimal, there will be redundant discriminant functions, and thus there are many possible solutions for mapping the training data. Each one, however, may perform quite differently on data that the network has not seen yet (test set). This aspect will be addressed later.

This analysis points out one important methodological issue. *Learning is a stochastic process* that depends not only on the learning parameters, but also on the initial conditions. Thus, if we want to compare network convergence times (i.e., how much faster one update rule is with respect to another) or final values of the MSE after a number of iterations, it is pointless to run the network only once. We need to run each network several times with random initial conditions and pick the best (or use some other strategy such as committees).

When the goal is to compare different training algorithms, it is common practice to average the results, that is, to present the "mean" learning curve across the different trials. This means that learning curves should also be presented with error bars or at least with a percentage of the number of times the minimum was reached.

NEUROSOLUTIONS EXAMPLE 4.2

Learning as a Stochastic Process (XOR)

Remember that adaptation is a stochastic process: Depending on the initial conditions and other factors, the path that the network will take down the performance surface will be very different. There are many possible end points (local minimum, global minimum, saddle points, etc.) to the adaptation process and even more trajectories to get there. It is important to remember that if we are to compare one learning algorithm with another, we must average the comparison criteria over multiple runs. For example, the learning curve should always be presented as an average of the individual learning curves over many runs. In this example, we show the many possible trajectories and end points for the XOR problem. We use a custom DLL to compute the average learning curve.

System Identification versus Modeling

Not all the problems of interest can be formulated in terms of an external, input-output constraint, but the class of these problems is very large indeed, ranging from system identification, prediction, classification, and so on. For instance, when we are predicting the stock market, we are not interested in preserving the individual components of the economy in our network; we are simply interested in a small prediction error.

On the other hand, there are problems that require more than an accurate input-output relation, such as modeling. In modeling we are interested not only in small input-output errors, but also in preserving some (or all) of the underlying features of the phenomenon in which we are interested. Examples of modeling appear in the physical and biological sciences and in some engineering areas.

4.2.3 Control of the Step Size during Learning

We have already encountered the problem of step-size selection when we studied the linear regression and the MLP adaptation. In the linear case we can summarize the discussion by saying that the learning rate is a trade-off between speed of adaptation and accuracy in the final weight values.

It is important to realize that for quadratic performance surfaces there are ways of optimally selecting the step size at each iteration through a line search. Normally, however, we use a trial-and-error approach due to the computational complexity of determining the best step size at each iteration. For MLPs the line search algorithm cannot be computed analytically, so it is rarely used.

Line Search Methods

A principled approach to finding the optimal step size at each iteration is to minimize $J(w_k + \mu_k s_k)$ with respect to μ, where s_k represents the direction of the search at sample k. For quadratic surfaces there is an analytic solution given by

$$\mu_k = \frac{-\nabla J_k^T s_k}{s_k^T H_k s_k} \tag{4B.1}$$

where H is the Hessian and ∇J is the gradient vector. Since the Hessian for quadratic surfaces is independent of the point, it needs to be computed just once. We can prove that the algorithm zigzags to the minimum (in orthogonal directions) with this choice of the step size (see Figure 4-3). Note that at each iteration we need to perform vector computations, which makes the adaptation computationally more complex.

In general, the optimal value of μ must be solved by line search since the performance surfaces are not quadratic. This gives rise to the conjugate gradient algorithms.

In a nonlinear network (e.g., an MLP), the step-size selection is even more important. The new situation is the existence of local minima and saddle points that may stall learning. We discuss ways to manage this problem with more powerful search procedures later in the chapter.

A common technique for the step-size selection is to use a large learning rate in the beginning of training to decrease the time spent in the search phase of learning and then to decrease the learning rate to obtain good accuracy for the final weight values in the tuning phase. This is sometimes called learning rate scheduling or *annealing*. In addition to the step-size scheduling from Chapter 1, we can use another method where the step size is controlled by

$$\eta(n) = \frac{\eta_0}{1 + \dfrac{n}{n_0}} \tag{4.1}$$

where η_0 is the initial step-size, and n_0 is an iteration count. Note that for $n \ll n_0$, the step size is practically equal to η_0, while when $n \gg n_0$, it approaches zero geometrically.

The values of η_0 and n_0 need to be found experimentally. If the initial value of η_0 is set too high, learning may diverge. The selection of n_0 is tricky because it is highly dependent on the performance surface. If n_0 is too small, the search phase may be too short, and learning can stall. If n_0 is too large, then we spend too much time in the search phase, rattling around near the global minimum, before we fine-tune our solution with lower learning rates.

In nonconvex surfaces, the annealing schedule has the added advantage of enabling the search to escape from local minima when they are encountered early in the search. With a large learning rate, the search will bounce out of local minima, and when the learning rate decreases, the global minimum can be reached with accuracy. The problem is that we do not know *a priori* the best schedule rate, so selection of the learning constants in Eq. 4.1 is problem dependent. The following example illustrates how the learning rate affects performance and how to schedule learning rates during adaptation.

NEUROSOLUTIONS EXAMPLE 4.3

Learning rate scheduling

In this example we show how to anneal the learning rate (change the step-size over time during the simulation). We start with the XOR problem and add scheduling components to the gradient-descent layer. There are three available scheduling components in NeuroSolutions: the Linear, Exponential, and Logarithmic Schedulers. Each one varies the parameter over time in a slightly different manner.

Make sure you use the *randomize* button and play with the simulation. It is important that you change the learning parameters to make the network learn as fast as it can. You should also notice that from time to time the learning will get stuck at

Linear Scheduler

an MSE of 0.5 and will take a long time to get out of this mode. The weights remain practically constant, and the error does not decrease. This may be due to either a region of very low gradient (flat spot) or a local minimum.

4.2.4 Setting the Learning Rates across the Network PEs

The neurocomputing literature [Haykin 1995] suggests that the goal for robust and fast convergence is to have all the adaptive network parameters learn at the same rate. This is possible in linear networks (with the information of the Hessian), but it is not so easy for MLPs, since in nonlinear systems the error is attenuated by the derivative of the PE non-linearity evaluated at the operating point (see the Error Attenuation box of Chapter 3, Section 3.2.4). It is therefore essential to understand how the error flows inside the net-work to properly set the learning rates. The rule of thumb is to increase the learning rate from the output layer to the input layer by a factor of 2 to 5 from layer to layer. In the fol-lowing example we observe the squelching effect of the nonlinearity from layer to layer.

NEUROSOLUTIONS EXAMPLE 4.4

Flow of errors across MLP layers

In this example we again delve into the inner workings of the neural network. The problem to be solved is the star problem, a two-class problem with a set of four samples per class, which are placed on the vertices of two stars, one smaller than the other, rotated by 45 degrees.

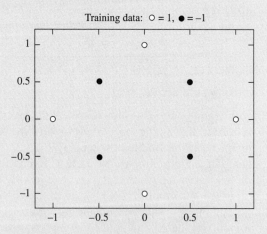

Training data: ○ = 1, ● = −1

We will place Matrix Viewers at nearly every access point in the MLP and single-step through the training. By doing this we gain many insights. We can watch the data flow through the network and understand exactly how each component of NeuroSolutions fits into the big picture. It is OK to gloss over the details of exactly

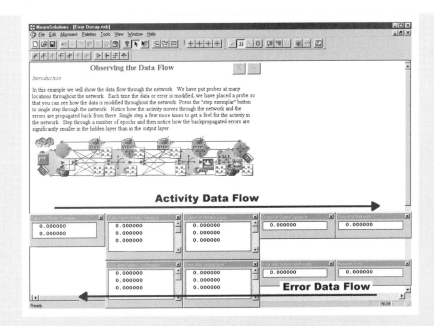

how the network operates for a while, but eventually it is important to understand the details. Notice that the data flows forward through the network, and then the error flows backward from the criterion back to the input layer. You should study these outputs in relation to the equations we derived for the MLP in Chapter 3. The figure above shows how the data flows through the arrangement of viewers in this example.

An important insight is that the average magnitude of the errors flowing back through the network shrinks through each layer. This is due to the multiplication by the derivative of the saturating nonlinearity that is a bell-shaped curve around zero. This means that large-magnitude (negative or positive) errors are multiplied by values close to zero. If we set the learning rates constant across the net, the network learns faster in the layers closer to the output than in those deeper in the net (closer to the input). Hence to equalize training in each layer, we should increase the learning rates of the components closer to the input. If we run the network with equal and with unequal learning rates (double the step size of the gradient search over the first synapse), there will be a marked difference.

4.2.5 Nonlinear PEs as a Source of Internal Competition

The MLP's ability to learn to discriminate patterns in the input space is linked to the attenuation of the error through the nonlinearity coupled with the saturation of the PE. The PE nonlinearity works as an internal competition mechanism, which allows different PEs to specialize in different areas of the input space. In fact, recall that the weight update is a product of the local activity, the error, and the derivative of the nonlinearity

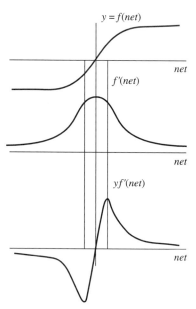

FIGURE 4-1 The derivative of
the nonlinearity and its effect on
the stabilization of learning

$f'(.)$, which is a bell-shaped curve for sigmoid nonlinearities (Figure 4-1). Thus the
question is this: Given several PEs in the hidden layer with different operating points
(different values of *net*), are they updated equally by the presentation of a given pattern?

For a particular input the weights connected to PEs that are operating just above
or below net = 0 will be adjusted the most (assuming that they receive a constant error
from the top layer). Effectively, these are the operating points with the highest product
of the activation and $f'_{\max}(net)$ (Figure 4-1). Thus, during learning, different PEs will
train more effectively on different areas of the input space. A ballpark analysis shows
that sigmoid PEs are most sensitive to samples that make *net* approximately ± 0.707.
For normalized inputs these values correspond to approximately 45 degrees from their
weight vectors. The overall effect is to stabilize the weight vector in the middle of the
cluster.

If one of the PEs is saturated (*net* is very large in absolute value), the weights
connected to it will be multiplied by a very small value of $f'(net)$, so the weights will
not change much. On the other hand, if the PE is operating near net = 0, its output
will also be small, so the weights leaving the PE will likewise have a small increment.
This diverse rate of updating the different weights is a source of *internal competition*
that tends to assign some PEs to one pattern cluster and other PEs to a different pattern
cluster. Since the PEs in an MLP create the discriminant functions, this is the source
of the power of nonlinear systems for classification and what differentiates them from
linear systems. If the PEs were linear (or nonlinear but nonsaturating), there would not
be any internal competition, and the weights associated with each PE would tend to

have the same value (remember what happens in the Adaline). PEs would never specialize, and the network would not be able to respond sharply with high values for some patterns and low values for other patterns.

4.2.6 Weight Initialization

The attenuation of the error across a layer also imposes some constraints on the learning process. Two such constraints involve the weight initialization and the choice of the number of hidden layers.

For the sake of training efficiency we should not create topologies with many layers, since the layers closer to the input will train very slowly, if at all. One should always start to solve a problem with shallow networks (i.e., a perceptron) for quicker training. If the perceptron does not provide a reasonable error, then try the one-hidden-layer MLP, and finally two-hidden-layer MLPs should be tested. Since two-hidden-layer MLPs are universal mappers, more than two nonlinear hidden layers are rarely recommended.

Another variable that the user can set before starting a training run is the initial weight values. The initial weights affect the learning performance of the network, because an initialization far away from the final weights increases the training time, but also because we would like for all the PEs in the network to learn at the same speed.

Good Initial Weight Values

Very little research has been conducted in finding good initial weight values for training, since the problem is very difficult to formulate. Intuitively we can see that if the initial weights can be chosen close to the optimum, then searching for the minimum will be fast and reliable. Unfortunately, we do not know where the optimal weights are in pattern space (this is why we are adapting the system). Some authors have proposed the linear solution for the initial weight values, but this does not always work. In many cases the linear solution is exactly the point that the search should avoid because it is a strong local minimum.

To break possible symmetries that could stall learning (i.e., the degenerate solution where all weights are zero in the XOR problem) or saturate the PEs, it is common practice to start the network weights with random initial conditions. The random initial condition is implemented with a random-number generator that provides a random value.

As we discussed earlier, a PE that is in its linear region learns faster than one that is in the saturated region. For better training performance the goal is to have each PE learn at approximately the same rate. If we set the variance of the random initial conditions based on the *fan-in* of the PE (i.e., the number of inputs it receives), each PE will be near its linear region, so all will learn at approximately the same rate. For the tanh nonlinearity, a rule of thumb is to set the variance of the random initial weights at

$$\left(\frac{-2.4}{I}, \frac{2.4}{I} \right) \tag{4.2}$$

where I is the fan-in of the PE.

NEUROSOLUTIONS EXAMPLE 4.5

Effect of initial conditions on adaptation

In this example we show how the initial conditions dramatically affect the adaptation of the weights in the XOR problem. When we set the initial conditions to the values previously discussed, we get significantly better performance and better learning curves.

4.3 OTHER SEARCH PROCEDURES

The popularity of gradient descent is based more on its *simplicity* (it can be computed locally with two multiplications and one addition per weight) than on its search power. There are many other search procedures more powerful than backpropagation. In Chapter 1 we discussed Newton's method, which is a second-order method because it uses the information on the curvature to adapt the weights. However, Newton's method is computationally much more costly to implement and requires information not available at the PE, so it has been used little in neurocomputing. Although more powerful, Newton's method is still a local search method and so may be caught in local minima or diverge due to the difficult neural network performance landscapes. Other techniques such as *simulated annealing* and *genetic algorithms (GA)* are global search procedures; that is, they can avoid local minima. The issue is that they are more costly to implement in a distributed system like a neural network, either because they are inherently slow or because they require nonlocal quantities. Global optimization is beyond the scope of this book, and the interested reader is directed to Horst, Pardalos, and Thoai [1995].

Here we cover improvements to the basic gradient-descent learning,

$$\Delta w_{ij}(n) = -\eta \nabla J(w_{ij})$$

which is generally called a *first-order search method*. Recall that the LMS algorithm, delta rule, and backpropagation use weight updates that are all implementations of this basic concept. They use a sample (noisy) estimate of the gradient that essentially multiplies the local error by the local activation

$$\Delta w_{ij}(n) = \eta \delta_i(n) x_j(n) \tag{4.3}$$

We will improve Eq. 4.3 to cope with the added difficulty of searching nonconvex performance surfaces or surfaces that may have flat regions. It is obvious that a gradient-based algorithm can be trapped in local minima, since the search is based on local gradient information only (see Chapter 3). In terms of local curvature, a local minimum and the global minimum are identical, so the gradient descent will be trapped in any local concavity of the performance surface. The gradient-descent method will move very slowly, if at all (called *stalling*), when the search traverses a flat region of the performance surface because the weights are modified proportionally to the gradient. If the gradient is small, the weight updates will be small (for a constant step size), so many iterations are needed to move through the flat spot. This situation is easily confused with the end of adaptation, when the search reaches the global minimum of the performance surface.

The preceding arguments indicate a need for an appropriate control of the step sizes or learning rates and for improved search methodologies. In this section we introduce a few methods that help alleviate the problems of gradient-descent search of nonconvex performance surfaces (local minima and saddle points).

4.3.1 Momentum Learning

Momentum learning is an improvement to the straight gradient-descent search in the sense that a memory term (the past increment to the weight) is used to *speed up and stabilize convergence*. In momentum learning the equation to update the weights becomes

$$w_{ij}(n + 1) = w_{ij}(n) + \eta \delta_i(n) x_j(n) + \alpha \big(w_{ij}(n) - w_{ij}(n - 1) \big) \tag{4.4}$$

where α is the momentum constant. Normally α should be set between 0.5 and 0.9. This is called momentum learning due to the form of the last term, which resembles the momentum in mechanics. Note that the weights are changed proportionally to how much they were updated in the last iteration. Thus if the search is going down the hill and finds a flat region, the weights are still changed, not because of the gradient (which is practically zero in a flat spot), but because of the rate of change in the weights. Likewise, in a narrow valley, where the gradient tends to bounce back and forth between hillsides, the momentum stabilizes the search because it tends to make the weights follow a smoother path. Figure 4-2 summarizes the advantage of momentum learning. Imagine a ball (weight vector position) rolling down a hill (performance surface). If the ball reaches a small flat part of the hill, it will continue past this local minimum because of its momentum. A ball without momentum, however, will get stuck in this valley. Momentum learning is a robust method to speed up learning, and we recommend it as the default search rule for networks with nonlinearities.

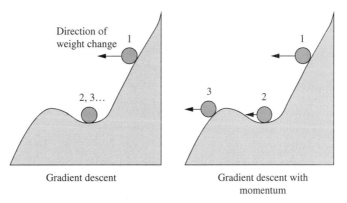

FIGURE 4-2 Why momentum learning helps

NEUROSOLUTIONS EXAMPLE 4.6

Momentum learning

This example compares the adaptation speed of the straight gradient-search procedure with momentum learning. There are many local minima in this problem; momentum learning works much better since it helps us "roll" through the flat parts of the performance surface. The problem is our well-known Star problem. Notice that with momentum learning the speed of adaptation is much higher for the same learning rate.

Momentum component

4.3.2 Adaptive Step Sizes

Simplicity is the only reason to use the same step size for each weight during the entire training phase. In fact, we know from Chapter 1 that the step size should be determined according to the eigenvalue for that particular direction. The problem is that eigenvalues are not normally known, so it is impractical to set them by hand. However, we have the feeling that observing the behavior of the error, weight tracks, or both should allow better control of the training. In fact, when the learning curve is flat, the step size should be increased to speed up learning. On the other hand, when the learning curve oscillates up and down, the step size should be decreased. In the extreme the error can go steadily up, showing that the learning is unstable. At this point the network should be reset. We can automate this reasoning in an algorithm by adapting the step sizes independently for each weight through the training phase.

The idea is very simple: Instead of looking at the learning curve, we use the weight tracks. When consecutive weight updates produce the same error sign, the learning rate is too slow. Conversely, when the error sign is toggling from iteration to iteration, the step size is too large. These simple principles can be put into a rule called the *adaptive step size method* that adapts each step size continuously during training. For the method to work correctly, you must use an independent step size for each weight; otherwise there will not be a significant improvement in the performance. Let us denote the learning rate for the weight w_{ij} as η_{ij}. The update to each step size is

$$\Delta\eta_{ij}(n+1) = \begin{cases} k & \text{if} \quad S_{ij}(n-1)D_{ij}(n) > 0 \\ -b\eta_{ij}(n) & \text{if} \quad S_{ij}(n-1)D_{ij}(n) < 0 \\ 0 & \text{otherwise} \end{cases} \qquad \textbf{(4.5)}$$

where S_{ij} measures the average of previous gradients and D_{ij} is the current gradient. When S_{ij} and D_{ij} have the same sign, their product will be greater than zero. The first case refers to slow convergence, so the step size is arithmetically increased at each iteration (by a constant, which is a slow process). The second case refers to the situation when the weight is oscillating, so the algorithm decreases the step size proportionally to its current value, which is a geometric decrease (very fast). The slow increase and fast decrease of the step size is designed to avoid divergence at any cost. If the algorithm diverges, it quickly loses all the information it has learned and must start over.

Now let us carefully analyze the conditions to increase or decrease the step size. $D_{ij}(n)$ is the partial derivative of the cost with respect to weight w_{ij} (i.e., the current gradient), and $S_{ij}(n)$ is a running average of the current and past partial derivatives given by

$$S_{ij}(n) = (1 - \gamma)D_{ij}(n) + \gamma S_{ij}(n - 1) \tag{4.6}$$

where γ is a number between 0 and 1 (the exponential time constant). The product of S_{ij} and D_{ij} is checking whether the present gradient has the same sign as the average of the previous gradients (reflected in the value of S_{ij}). This algorithm is called the delta-bar-delta algorithm.

NEUROSOLUTIONS EXAMPLE 4.7

Adaptive step sizes

Let us now solve the star problem with the adaptive step-size (delta-bar-delta) search to see the speedup achieved. The adaptive step-size algorithm gives us the flexibility to have high learning rates when we are in flat parts of the performance surface and low learning rates when the adaptation begins to rattle or become unstable. The NeuroSolutions version of the delta-bar-delta algorithm includes momentum, so this algorithm should work better than any of the methods we have discussed so far.

Delta-Bar-Delta component

There are many other alternative algorithms to adapt the step size, such as Fahlman's [1988] quickprop and Almeida's adaptive step [Silva and Almeida 1990]. You should experiment with them in NeuroSolutions since they are implemented there. The problem is that all these algorithms increase the number of free parameters that the user has to set heuristically, so they require fine-tuning for each application.

Almeida's Adaptive Step Size

The idea is very similar to the adaptive step size algorithm previously described, but it is more stable due to the inclusion of nonlinearity. As before, there will be a different step size for each weight. The reasoning of the algorithm is as follows:

1. If the gradient component has the same size in two consecutive iterations, the step size should be increased.

2. If the gradient alternates sign, the step size should be decreased.

The weight update is

$$w_{kj}(n) = w_{kj}(n-1) + \eta_{kj}(n)\nabla_{kj}C(n)$$

where $\nabla_{kj}C(n)$ is each gradient component, and at each iteration

$$\eta_{kj}(n) = \begin{cases} u\eta_{kj}(n-1) & \text{if} \quad \nabla_{kj}C(n)\nabla_{kj}C(n-1) > 0 \\ d\eta_{kj}(n-1) & \text{if} \quad \nabla_{kj}C(n)\nabla_{kj}C(n-1) < 0 \end{cases} \qquad \textbf{(4B.2)}$$

where u and d are positive constants with values slightly above and below unity, respectively. The authors suggest $d \simeq 1/u$. The initial value of each step size is set equal for all weights. Note that unlike the delta bar delta, here the update of the step size is geometric in both directions (decreasing or increasing).

There are four heuristics to help control the growth of the step size:

1. The error obtained at each iteration should be compared with the previous error. If the new error does not exceed the old error by more than 2.5 percent, then the new weight vector is accepted.

2. If the new error is higher than the previous by more than this margin, compute a new step size as in Eq. 4B.2, but do not change the weights.

3. If step 2 does not decrease the error in two to three iterations, then reduce all the step sizes by a constant factor α, until the error starts to decrease again.

4. At this point, restart with the normal adaptation of step sizes.

This method works well when the gradient is known with high precision, as in batch learning. The method can be also applied to on-line adaptation, but we cannot utilize the instantaneous estimates of the gradient since they are too noisy. Instead we maintain a running estimate of the gradient at each epoch (P is the number of training set exemplars):

$$\nabla_{kj}C(n) = \sum_{p=1}^{P} \frac{\partial J(e_p)}{\partial w_{kj}}$$

to be used in the adaptive step size computation.

4.3.3 Random Perturbation During Learning

Another alternative is to inject random noise at either the weights, or desired response. The motivation is to "shake" the weights during adaptation in order to minimize the probability of having the search caught in local minima. This idea is reminiscent of the operating principle of simulated annealing, which uses a scheduling of noise to reach the global minimum of the performance surface. The process is also very simple to implement when noise is added to the desired response. In fact, if we add zero-mean white Gaussian noise to the desired response, we obtain

$$d_w(n) = d(n) + n_w(n)$$

which is then transmitted to the injected error $e(n)$ and then to the weight update through backpropagation. The advantage of applying the noise to the desired response is that we have a single noise source, and since the dual network is linear, as we saw in Chapter 3, it is still an additive zero-mean perturbation to the weight update. But remember that the noise variance should be scheduled to zero so the optimal solution is obtained. Unfortunately, there is no rigorous approach to set the noise variance or to schedule it. The injection of noise at the input is not a linear contribution to the weight update, but it has been shown to produce better generalization (Bishop [1995]), which is highly desirable.

NEUROSOLUTIONS EXAMPLE 4.8

Adaptation with noise in the desired signal

This example adds the noise component to the desired signal to show how it can improve the performance. The noise helps the algorithm to bounce out of local minima. We also anneal the noise variance so that we have a large amount of noise at the beginning of training to help us move out of local minima quickly but little noise at the end of training to reduce the rattling and increase precision.

Noise component

Notice that until now all the modifications to the gradient-descent rule of Eq. 4.3 utilize the same basic information, namely, the activation of the PE and the error to its dual network, which characterize first-order search methods. In NeuroSolutions the data-flow architecture for backpropagation and the layered nature of its implementation provide a straightforward selection of any of these methods. In fact, only the weight-update rule (the search component) needs to be modified, which can be accomplished by simply changing the search component icon on the breadboard. This further enhances the value of the data-flow concept for simulation of neural networks.

4.3.4 Advanced Search Methods

Numeric optimization techniques are a vast and mature field. We provide here only a synopsis of the classes of search methods that are important for neural network researchers. The interested reader is referred to Luenberger [1984] and Fletcher [1987] for a full coverage of the topic.

The problem of search with local information can be formulated as an approximation to the functional form of the cost function $J(\mathbf{w})$ at the operating point $\mathbf{w}_0$. This immediately points to the Taylor series expansion of J around $\mathbf{w}_0$:

$$J(\mathbf{w} - \mathbf{w}_0) = J_0 + (\mathbf{w} - \mathbf{w}_0)\nabla \mathbf{J}_0 + \frac{1}{2}(\mathbf{w} - \mathbf{w}_0)\mathbf{H}_0(\mathbf{w} - \mathbf{w}_0) + \ldots$$

where ∇J is our already familiar gradient and $\mathbf{H}$ is the Hessian matrix, that is, the matrix of second derivatives with entries

$$H_{ij}(\mathbf{w}_0) = \left. \frac{\partial^2 J(w)}{\partial w_i \partial w_j} \right|_{w = w_0}$$

evaluated at the operating point. We can immediately see that the Hessian *cannot* be computed with the information available at a given PE, since it uses information from two different weights. If we differentiate J with respect to the weights, we get

$$\nabla J(\mathbf{w}) = \nabla J_0 + \mathbf{H}_0(\mathbf{w} - \mathbf{w}_0) + \ldots \tag{4.7}$$

so we can see that to compute the full gradient at $\mathbf{w}$ we need all the higher terms of the derivatives of J. This is impossible. Since the performance surface tends to be bowl shaped (quadratic) near the minimum, we normally are interested only in the first and second terms of the expansion.

If the expansion of Eq. 4.7 is restricted to the first term we obtain the gradient-search methods (hence they are called first-order methods), where the gradient is estimated with its value at $\mathbf{w}_0$.

If we expand to use the second-order term, we obtain Newton's method (hence the name second-order method). It is interesting to note that if we equate the truncated Eq. 4.7 to 0, we immediately get

$$\mathbf{w} = \mathbf{w}_0 - \mathbf{H}_0^{-1}\nabla J_0 \tag{4.8}$$

which is exactly the equation for the Newton's method presented in Chapter 1. Newton's method has the nice property of quadratic termination (it is guaranteed to find the exact minimum in a finite number of steps for quadratic performance surfaces). For most quadratic performance surfaces it can converge in one iteration.

The real difficulty is the memory and the computational cost (and precision) to estimate the Hessian. Neural networks can have thousands of weights, which means that the Hessian will have millions of entries. This is why methods of approximating the Hessian have been extensively researched. There are two basic classes of approximations:

- Line search methods
- Pseudo-Newton methods

The information in the first type is restricted to the gradient, together with line searches along certain directions, while the second seeks approximations to the Hessian matrix.

Line Search Methods The basic idea of line search is to start with the gradient-descent direction and search for the minimum along the line, that is,

$$\mathbf{w}(n + 1) = \mathbf{w}(n) + \lambda(n)\mathbf{s}(n) \quad \text{where} \quad \lambda(n) = \min_{\lambda} \mathbf{J}(\mathbf{w}(n) + \lambda s(n))$$

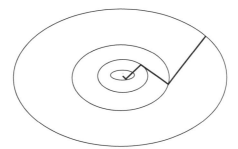

FIGURE 4-3 Path to the minimum with line search methods

The problem with the gradient direction is that it is sensitive to the eccentricity of the performance surface (caused by the eigenvalue spread), so following the gradient is not the quickest path to the minimum. We analyzed this aspect in Chapter 1. Alternatively, we can compute the optimal step size at each point, which corresponds to a line search, as we saw earlier. We can prove that successive directions have to be perpendicular to each other (see Figure 4-3); that is, the path to the minimum is intrinsically a zigzag path [Luenberger 1986].

We can improve this procedure if we weight the previous direction to the minimum with the new direction, that is, cutting across the zigzag. The formulation becomes

$$s^{new} = -\nabla J^{new} + \alpha s^{old}$$

where α is a dynamically computed parameter that compromises between the two directions. This is called the *conjugate gradient method*. For quadratic performance surfaces the conjugate gradient algorithm preserves quadratic termination and can reach the minimum in D steps, where D is the dimension of the weight space. As we will see later, the interesting thing is that we do not need to compute second derivatives (Hessian), and, in fact, the algorithm is compatible with backpropagation.

Notice that momentum learning is similar to the conjugate gradient method, since we can view the difference between the present and the previous weights as the estimate of the old direction. In momentum learning, however, α is fixed throughout instead of being estimated at each step, and there is no search for the best step size.

Conjugate Gradient Method

A set of vectors $\{\mathbf{s}_j\}$ is conjugate with respect to a positive definite matrix (e.g., the Hessian) if $\mathbf{s}_j^T \mathbf{H} \mathbf{s}_i = 0$ where $j \neq i$. What this expression says is that the rotation by $\mathbf{H}$ of the vector $\mathbf{s}_j$ must by orthogonal to $\mathbf{s}_i$. In the n-dimensional Euclidean space R^n there are an infinite number of conjugate vector sets. It is easy to show that the eigenvectors of the Hessian form a conjugate set and can then be used to search the performance surface. The problem is that we need to know the Hessian, which is not a practical assumption. However, there is a way to find a conjugate set of vectors that does not require knowledge of the Hessian. The idea is to express the conditions for a conjugate vector set as a function of differences in consecutive gradient directions as

$$(\nabla \mathbf{J}(i) - \nabla \mathbf{J}(i-1))^T \mathbf{s}(j) = 0 \qquad i \neq j$$

For this expression to be true, the minimum of the gradient of $J(i)$ in the direction $\mathbf{s}(j)$ is needed, so the algorithm works as follows.

Start with the gradient-descent direction, $\mathbf{s}(0) = -\nabla \mathbf{J}(0)$. Search the minimum along this direction. Then construct a vector $\mathbf{s}(j)$ that is orthogonal to the set of vectors $\{\nabla \mathbf{J}(0), \nabla \mathbf{J}(1), \ldots, \nabla \mathbf{J}(j-1)\}$, which can be accomplished by

$$\mathbf{s}(j) = -\nabla \mathbf{J}(j) + \alpha \mathbf{s}(j-1)$$

There are basically three well-known ways to find α, namely, the Fletcher-Reeves, the Polak-Ribiere, or the Hestenes-Steifel formulas, which are equivalent for quadratic performance surfaces and are given respectively by

$$\alpha_j = \frac{\nabla \mathbf{J}^T(j)\nabla \mathbf{J}(j)}{\nabla \mathbf{J}^T(j-1)\nabla \mathbf{J}(j-1)} \qquad \alpha_j = \frac{[\nabla \mathbf{J}(j) - \nabla \mathbf{J}(j-1)]^T \nabla \mathbf{J}(j)}{\nabla \mathbf{J}^T(j-1)\nabla \mathbf{J}(j-1)}$$

$$\alpha_j = \frac{[\nabla \mathbf{J}(j) - \nabla \mathbf{J}(j-1)]^T \nabla \mathbf{J}(j)}{\nabla \mathbf{J}^T(j-1)s(j-1)}$$

In quadratic performance surfaces, you will find the minimum in n iterations, where n is the size of the search space. The minimization along the line can be accomplished for quadratic performance surfaces as Eq. 4B.1. The problem is that, for nonquadratic performance surfaces such as the ones found in neurocomputing, quadratic termination is not guaranteed and the line search does not have an analytic solution.

The lack of quadratic termination can be overcome by executing the algorithm for n iterations and then resetting it to the current gradient direction. The problem of the line search is more difficult to solve. There are two basic approaches: direct search or the scaled conjugate method [Shepherd 1997]. The first involves multiple cost-function evaluations and estimations to find the minimum, which complicates the mechanics of the algorithm. The scaled conjugate is more appropriate for neural network implementations. It uses Eq. 4B.1 and avoids the problem of nonquadratic surfaces by massaging the Hessian so as to guarantee positive definiteness, which is accomplished by $\mathbf{H} + \lambda \mathbf{I}$, where $\mathbf{I}$ is the identity matrix. Equation 4B.1 becomes

$$\mu_j = \frac{-\nabla \mathbf{J}_j^T \mathbf{s}_j}{\mathbf{s}_j^T \mathbf{H}_j \mathbf{s}_j + \lambda \| s_j \|^2} \tag{4.B.3}$$

At first, we may think that this method is more computationally expensive than search, because of the Hessian matrix. But in fact, this is not the case, since there are fast methods to estimate the product of a vector by the Hessian (the product has only n components). We can use the perturbation method to estimate the product [LeCun, Simard, and Pearlmutter 1993]:

$$\mathbf{s}^T \nabla(\nabla \mathbf{J}) = \frac{\nabla \mathbf{J}(w + \varepsilon s) - \nabla \mathbf{J}(w)}{\varepsilon} + O(\varepsilon)$$

or use an analytic approach due to Pearlmutter [1994]. Both methods are compatible with backpropagation.

We still need to address how to set λ, which is not difficult but involves trial and error. The idea is as follows: If the error increases from one step to the next, it is because we are in an area of J that is far from quadratic, so the Hessian is not positive definite. In such cases we should increase λ until the error decreases. Notice that for large λ the denominator becomes approximately $\lambda \parallel s \parallel^2$. In this case we are essentially using gradient descent, which is known to be convergent to the minimum (albeit slowly). When the error decreases, then λ should again be decreased to fully exploit the potential of the local quadratic information of the performance surface.

Pseudo-Newton Methods   In pseudo-Newton methods the idea is to come up with computationally simple and reasonable approximations to the Hessian. The simplest is just to forget about the cross terms in the Hessian matrix and use only the diagonal terms. This is equivalent to performing Newton's algorithm separately for each weight, which transforms Eq. 4.8 into

$$\Delta w_i(n) = \frac{-\nabla J(n)}{\dfrac{\partial^2 J(n)}{\partial w_i^2}}$$

Normally we replace this rule by

$$\Delta w_i(n) = \frac{-\nabla J(n)}{\left| \dfrac{\partial^2 J(n)}{\partial w_i^2} \right| + \beta} \tag{4.9}$$

where β is a small constant that avoids the problem of negative curvature and a zero denominator. Notice that Eq. 4.9 is in fact very similar to the normalized LMS we presented in Chapter 1, since for the linear network we can estimate the diagonal entries of the Hessian by the power (or the trace) of the input.

This is a very crude approximation of the Hessian. More accurate approximations that are still less computationally expensive than the full procedure (which is $O(N^3)$, with N being the number of weights) are the Levenberg-Marquardt (LM), the Davidson-Fletcher-Powell (DFP), and the Broyden-Fletcher-Goldfarb-Shanno (BFGS). See Luenberger [1986]. LM is the most interesting for neural networks, since it is formulated as a sum of quadratic terms just like the cost functions in neural networks.

Levenberg-Marquardt Quasi-Newton Method

The Levenberg-Marquardt algorithm uses the Gauss-Newton method to approximate the Hessian. Let us assume that the performance function is a sum of individual components

$$J(w) = \sum_{i=1}^{N} e_i^2(w) = \mathbf{e}^T(w)\mathbf{e}(w)$$

where N is the number of samples in the training set, and $\mathbf{e}_i$ are the instantaneous errors. Then it is easy to show that the gradient is

$$\nabla \mathbf{J}(w) = 2\mathcal{J}^T(w)\mathbf{e}(w) \tag{4B.4}$$

where $\mathcal{J}$ is the Jacobian matrix given by

$$\mathcal{J}(w) = \begin{bmatrix} \dfrac{\partial e_1(w)}{\partial w_1} & \cdots & \dfrac{\partial e_1(w)}{\partial w_n} \\ \cdots & \cdots & \cdots \\ \dfrac{\partial e_N(w)}{\partial w_1} & \cdots & \dfrac{\partial e_N(w)}{\partial w_n} \end{bmatrix}$$

The Hessian is easily obtained from Eq. 4B.4 as

$$\nabla^2 \mathbf{J}(w) = 2\mathcal{J}^T(w)\mathcal{J}(w) + 2S(w) \qquad \text{where} \qquad S(w) = \sum_{i=1}^{N} e(w)\nabla^2 e_i(w)$$

Assuming that $S(w)$ is small, the Hessian can be approximated by

$$\nabla^2 \mathbf{J}(w) \cong 2\mathcal{J}^T(w)\mathcal{J}(w)$$

Thus Eq. 4.8 can be written

$$w(n+1) = w(n) - [\mathcal{J}^T(w(n))\mathcal{J}(w(n))]^{-1}\mathcal{J}^T(w(n))\mathbf{e}(w(n))$$

This weight update does not require second-order derivatives. The approximation that was introduced may result in difficulties in inverting **H**, but as we saw earlier for the conjugate gradient, we can add a small value (λ) to the diagonal of $\mathcal{J}$ to make sure that the matrix is full rank. This provides the Levenberg-Marquardt algorithm

$$\Delta w(n) = -[\mathcal{J}^T(w(n))\mathcal{J}(w(n)) + \lambda(n)\mathbf{I}]^{-1}\mathcal{J}^T(w(n))\mathbf{e}(w(n)) \tag{4B.5}$$

This is a very interesting formula: Notice that if λ is increased so that the first term of the inverse is negligible, the weight update is basically gradient descent with a step size $[1/\lambda(n)]$. On the other hand, if λ is zero, the information about the curvature is fully utilized in the search.

We mention this fact because we have to set λ during the adaptation. The goal is to have λ as small as possible while still guaranteeing inversion, but this depends on the data. We should therefore start with a small value of λ ($\lambda = 0.01$) and see whether the next weight vector produces a smaller error. If it does, continue. If the error for this new position is higher than before, we have to return to the old weight vector, increase λ, and try again. At each trial λ should be increased by a nominal amount (a factor of 5 to 10 is normally recommended). Notice that if we continue doing this, we will default to gradient descent, which is known to be convergent with small step sizes. When the error for the new evaluation of the weights produces a smaller error, then start decreasing λ by the same factor.

This algorithm is particularly well suited for training neural networks with the MSE. Moreover, it interfaces well with the backpropagation formalism. Note, however, that here we need to keep all the errors separated since we need to use the Jacobian matrix. In conventional backpropagation the errors from all the outputs get added together at each PE, and in batch learning we even add all these errors across the training set. However, here each partial derivative of the error must remain accessible during training of a batch, which causes huge storage requirements. Nevertheless, the backpropagation algorithm can still propagate sensitivities from the output to each node to evaluate each entry in the Jacobian. As a rule, backpropagation must be applied repeatedly and independently to each output to avoid the addition of errors; that is, the injected error vector for a P output system becomes

$$
e^1 = \begin{bmatrix} e_1 \\ 0 \\ \ldots \\ 0 \end{bmatrix} \longrightarrow e^2 = \begin{bmatrix} 0 \\ e_2 \\ \ldots \\ 0 \end{bmatrix} \longrightarrow e^P = \begin{bmatrix} 0 \\ 0 \\ \ldots \\ e_P \end{bmatrix}
$$

Each input–desired response pair creates P errors. Each of these backpropagation sweeps for a given sample creates a row of the Jacobian (the number of columns is given by the number of weights in the network). Each new sample will repeat the process. Thus we can see that the Jacobian matrix gets very large very quickly. The other difficulty is that the algorithm is no longer local to the weight. Nevertheless, the Levenberg-Marquardt algorithm has been shown to be much faster than backpropagation in a variety of applications. As a side note, the conjugate gradient of Eq. 4.10 also requires the use of the Jacobian matrix, so it uses the same basic procedure.

4.4 STOP CRITERIA

We have addressed many aspects of gradient-descent learning, but we have not yet discussed how and when to stop the training of the neural network. Obviously, training should be stopped when the learning machine has learned the task. The problem, however, is that there are no direct indicators that measure this condition.

4.4.1 Stopping Based on Training-Set Error

One of the simplest ways to stop the training phase is to limit the number of iterations to a predetermined value, as we have done so far, but the only appeal of this criterion is simplicity. It does not use any information or feedback from the system before or during training. When the number of iterations is capped at a predefined value, there is no guarantee that the learning machine has found coefficients that are close to the optimal values.

This suggests an analysis of the output MSE to stop the training. We can choose an acceptable error level for the problem and apply a threshold to the MSE. Choosing the MSE threshold value, however, is tricky because the MSE is just an indirect variable in classification. Moreover, we have no guarantee that the learning system will achieve the preselected MSE value, so the training may never end.

Another alternative is to let the system train until the decrease of the MSE from one iteration to the next is below a given value (applying a threshold to the incremental change in MSE). The idea is to let the system train until the point of diminishing returns, that is, until it basically cannot extract more information from the training data. Unfortunately, this method has the problem of prematurely stopping the training in flat regions of the performance surface.

NEUROSOLUTIONS EXAMPLE 4.9

Stopping based on MSE value

In this example we use a new component, the Transmitter, to stop training. There are two types of Transmitters, the Threshold Transmitter and the Delta Transmitter. The Threshold Transmitter transmits a message (in this case to the Controller to stop training) when the value of the error gets below a certain point. The Delta Transmitter stops training when the difference between two successive errors is below a certain value. When you look at the properties of the Delta Transmitter, you notice that there is a smoothing algorithm applied to the error—this can help reduce the probability of stopping because of outliers. Notice that both of these stop criteria have their problems. We discuss better methods in the next section.

Threshold Transmitter

Delta Transmitter

4.4.2 Stop Criterion Based on Generalization

The previous stop criteria did not address the problem of *generalization*, that is, how well the learning system performs with data that does not belong to the training set. Traditional knowledge from data modeling and recent developments in learning theory [Vapnik 1995] clearly indicate that after a critical point an MLP trained with backpropagation will continue to do better in the training set, but the test set performance will begin to deteriorate. This phenomenon is called *overtraining*.

One method to solve this problem is to stop the training at the point of maximum generalization (given the present data and topology). This method is called early

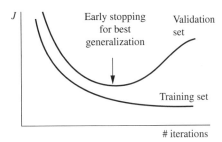

FIGURE 4-4 Cross-validation or early stopping

stopping, or stopping with cross-validation. It has been experimentally verified that the training error always decreases when the number of iterations is increased (for a sufficiently large net). If we plot the error in a set of data with which the network was not trained (the *validation set*), we find that the error initially decreases with the number of iterations but eventually starts to increase again (Figure 4-4). Training therefore should be stopped at the point of the smallest error in the validation set.

To implement this method, the training set should be divided into two sets: the *training* and the *cross-validation* sets. The cross-validation set is normally taken as 10 percent of the total training samples. Every so often (i.e., 5 to 10 iterations), the learning machine performance with the present weights is tested against the cross-validation set. Training should be stopped when the error in the cross-validation set starts to increase. This point is the point of maximum generalization.

The problem with this methodology is that cross-validation decreases the size of the training set. Since neurocomputing tends to suffer from a lack of data to begin with, cross-validation makes this situation even worse. In this case, however, the benefits (accurate stopping point) typically outweigh the costs (less data). This method is the recommended stop criterion for real-world applications. NeuroSolutions implements this method, as we exemplify next.

NEUROSOLUTIONS EXAMPLE 4.10
Stopping with Cross-Validation

We again solve the star problem, but this time using cross-validation as the stop criterion. We have created an additional set of points, which we use as our cross-validation (or test) set. The following figure shows the training and cross-validation sets. To implement cross-validation in NeuroSolutions, we will use two input/desired file pairs. In the File component we specify that one pair will be the training files, while the other will be the cross-validation files. Likewise, in the Controller we have to specify that we are using cross-validation.

This example clearly shows that overtraining can greatly reduce the generalization ability of the network. You will also see how important it is to have a

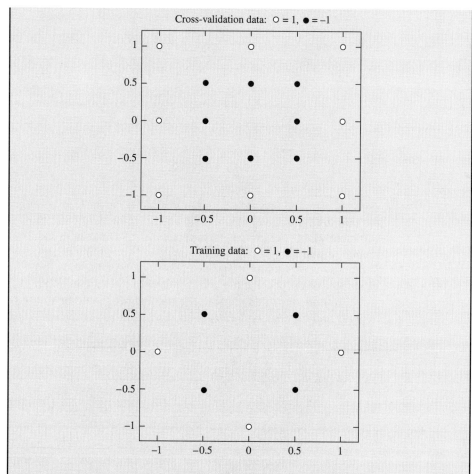

sufficient amount of training data to adequately cover the input space. Any points in the input space that are not in the training set are considered to be "don't cares" by the network. This can result in oddly shaped discriminant plots that have a very good mean square error in the training set but poor performance with new data.

4.5 HOW GOOD ARE MLPs AS LEARNING MACHINES?

4.5.1 Training Set Size

The size of the training set directly influences the performance of any classifier trained nonparametrically (e.g., as neural networks). This class of learning machines requires a lot of data for appropriate training, because there are no a priori assumptions about the data. It is important to know how the requirement on the size of the training set scales as a function of the size of the network for a given precision in the mapping.

The number of training patterns (N) required to classify test examples with an error of δ is approximately given by

$$N > \frac{W}{\delta} \qquad\qquad (4.10)$$

where W is the number of weights in the network [Haykin 1995]. This equation shows that the number of required training patterns increases linearly with the number of free parameters of the MLP, which is excellent compared with other classification methods. A rule of thumb states that $N \approx 10W$, that is, the training set size should be 10 times larger than the number of network weights to accurately classify test data with 90 percent accuracy.

In this rule of thumb it is assumed that the training data is representative of all the conditions encountered in the test set. The main focus when creating the training set should be to collect data that covers the full known operating conditions of the problem we want to model. If the training set does not contain data from some areas of pattern space, the machine classification in those areas will be based on extrapolation. This may or may not correspond to the true classification boundary (your desired output), so you should always choose samples for the training set that cover as much of the input space as possible.

We should remark that in Eq. 4.10 the practical limiting quantity is the number of training patterns; most of the time we need to compromise the size of the network to achieve appropriate training for the learning machine. A reasonable approach to reduce the number of weights in the network is to sparsely connect the input layer to the first hidden layer (which normally contains the largest number of weights). This will help achieve the requirement of Eq. 4.10. Another possibility is to use feature extraction (i.e., a preprocessor) that decreases the input space dimensionality, thus reducing the number of weights in your network.

NEUROSOLUTIONS EXAMPLE 4.11

Sparse connectivity in the input layer

Here we show that, with the Arbitrary Synapse, generalization can be improved with respect to the fully connected case. We will use the Star data set with four hidden

Arbitrary Synapse

> PEs. But instead of eight weights in the first synapse, now we restrict the number to four, randomly connected. Run the network and show that the solutions found are normally more reasonable than the ones using eight weights. One way to show this is to use the cross-validation data, as you did before.

4.5.2 Scalability

Another important point for learning machines is to address how well their properties scale when the size of the problem increases. The literature is full of examples of systems that perform very well in small problems but are unable to extend the same performance to larger problems. One important proof, advanced by Barron [1993] through the analysis of the MSE for several size problems, states that for large training sets the (one-hidden-layer) *MLP error is independent of the size of the input space and scales as the inverse of the number of hidden PEs* ($0(1/N)$). This is much better than polynomial approximators, where the error decreases geometrically with the dimension of the input space ($0(1/\sqrt[D]{N^2})$). Hence, MLPs are particularly well suited to deal with large-input-dimensional problems. This explains the excellent performance of MLPs in large classification problems.

4.5.3 Trainability

The training time of an MLP using back-propagation was experimentally determined to increase exponentially with the size of the problem; that is, although the required number of patterns increases only linearly with the number of weights, the training time of larger networks seems to scale exponentially to their size. This indicates that there are problems that cannot be solved practically with MLPs trained with back-propagation. However, to counteract this behavior, we can use modular network architectures or sparse connections as well as advanced training rules. In practice this exponential scaling of training times with network size provides another argument to start first with small networks and increase their size if the results are not satisfactory. Moreover, this property emphasizes the importance of training methods that extract information more efficiently from the data than gradient descent. Now you may understand better the importance of the discussion of the conjugate gradient and the quasi-Newton methods presented in Section 4.3.4.

4.5.4 Did the Network Learn the Task?

In the application of neural networks to real-world problems, it is very important to have a criterion for accepting the solution. Only then can we successfully act to overcome any potential difficulties.

The learning curve is a valuable indicator for observing the progression of learning, but the MSE in the training or test sets is only an indirect measure of classification performance. The MSE depends on the normalization and characteristics of the input data and desired response. We should normalize the total error by the variance of the

TABLE 4-1   Confusion Matrix

Machine true	Class 1	Class 2	Total true
Class 1	# correct class 1	# incorrect class 1	# class 1
Class 2	# incorrect class 2	# correct class 2	# class 2
Total machine	# classified as class 1	# classified as class 2	total samples

desired response to have an idea of how much of the desired variance was captured by the neural model. This is reminiscent of the correlation coefficient for linear regression, but there is no precise relationship between classification accuracy and MSE.

The performance of a classifier is measured in terms of *classification error*, as we saw in Chapter 2. The accuracy of the classifier is 1 minus the classification error. Therefore a much better approach is to construct the *confusion matrix* to count the number of misclassifications exactly. The confusion matrix is a table where the true classification is compared with the output of the classifier (see Table 4-1). Let us assume that the true classification is the row and the classifier is the output column. The classification of each sample (specified by a column) is added to the row of the true classification. A perfect classification provides a confusion matrix that has only the diagonal populated. All the other entries are zero. The classification error is the sum of off-diagonal entries divided by the total number of samples.

The confusion matrix also enables easy visualization of where the classifier has difficulties. In general, some of the classes will be more separable than others, so the confusion matrix immediately pinpoints which classes produce misclassifications (off-diagonal entries that have large values). In summary, the confusion matrix is an excellent way of quantifying the accuracy of a classifier. As we discussed in Chapter 2, the test of the classifier should be performed in the test set, so the confusion matrix should be constructed in the test set.

NEUROSOLUTIONS EXAMPLE 4.12

Confusion matrix for classification performance

In this example we show how the confusion matrix gives us a much better picture of the performance of the network for classification than the mean square error. The confusion matrix tells us exactly how well the network is classifying the data. The mean square error tells us only the average difference between the network output and the desired output. Since classification is an "all or nothing" type of problem, it doesn't always matter how close you are to the desired ± 1, as long as you are beyond the classification threshold.

Once we find that learning is not successful (a large classification error assessed by the confusion matrix), the next step is to find out why the network did not learn correctly. Poor performance may have many different explanations:

- The network may not have the discrimination power (number of layers) to correctly classify the data (remember the perceptron and the XOR).
- The network may not have enough PEs (remember the case of the bump with two hidden PEs).
- Learning may be stuck in a local minimum or flat spot.
- We may have overtrained the network.
- We may not have collected enough data to represent the problem well.
- The problem may be intrinsically difficult with the features (measurements) that we are using, so we may need to transform or filter the inputs or add new inputs to simplify the classification problem.

Unfortunately there is no general rule to test any of these issues, so the designer of classifiers must use insight and knowledge of the problem to improve the machine classification. The designer should also manually supervise the learning instead of setting the learning parameters and dimming the monitor until the next morning. NeuroSolutions probes are particularly useful for monitoring the learning process.

4.6   ERROR CRITERION

4.6.1 L_p Norms

In supervised learning the difference between the desired response and the actual learning system output is used to modify the system so that the minimum error of the performance surface is achieved. The issue is how to define the performance, also called the *error criterion* or the *cost*. In normal operation the learning machine provides an output for each input pattern, so the total cost J is computed as a sum of individual costs, $J_{n,k}$, obtained from each input pattern presentation,

$$J = \sum_k \sum_n J_{nk} \tag{4.11}$$

where k is an index over the system outputs and n is an index over the input patterns. J_{nk} is the individual cost, defined as $J_{nk} = f(d_{nk} - y_{nk}) = f(\varepsilon_{nk})$. The only issue is then how to compute the individual cost as a function of ε_{nk}, which is called the *instantaneous error*.

The mean square error (MSE) criterion defines the individual cost as the square of the instantaneous error between the desired response and the system output, that is, $J_{nk} = (d_{nk} - y_{nk})^2$. The error power (MSE) has a meaning in itself and has three other

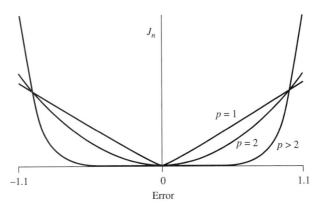

J_n

$p = 1$

$p = 2$ $p > 2$

−1.1 0 1.1

Error

FIGURE 4-5 Error norms

major appeals:

- In linear feedforward networks the MSE leads to a linear optimization problem that has an analytical solution.
- It provides a probabilistic interpretation for the output of the learning machine, as we discussed in Chapter 2.
- The criterion is easy to implement, since it is the instantaneous error that is injected into the dual system (no additional computations are needed).

Is there a need for other error criteria? Let's look at Figure 4-5 and understand what the MSE criterion does.

In Figure 4-5 we present several cost functions derived from different powers p of the instantaneous error. With the MSE the instantaneous cost is the square of the magnitude of the instantaneous error ($p = 2$). This means that when the learning machine minimizes the error power, it weights the large errors more (quadratically). If you recall the weight update performed by gradient descent, $\Delta w_{ij} = \eta \delta_j x_i$, you will realize that the weight values are updated proportionally to the size of the error, so the weights are more sensitive to the larger errors. This is reasonable if the data is clean without many large deviations, but in practice the data sets may have *outliers*. Outliers thus may have an inordinate effect on the optimal parameter values of the learning machine. Learning machines with saturating nonlinearities control this aspect better than linear PE machines, but they still are more sensitive to large errors than small errors. Since the values of the weights set the orientation and position of the discriminant function, we can deduce that outliers will "bias" the position of the discriminant function.

This argument shows that if we want to modify how the instantaneous error influences the weights, we can define the instantaneous cost more generally as

$$J_{nk} = \left| d_{nk} - y_{nk} \right|^p$$

(4.12)

where p is an integer, which is normally called the p norm of the instantaneous error ε_{nk}. When $p = 2$, we obtain the L_2 norm that leads to the MSE criterion. When $p = 1$ we obtain the L_1 norm, which is also called the Manhattan metric. Notice that the L_1 norm weights the differences proportionally to their magnitude, so it is far less sensitive to outliers than the L_2 norm. For this reason it is called a more *robust norm*. In general the L_p norm for $p > 2$ weights large deviations even more. Different norms provide different solutions to a learning problem, because the weights are modified with information that depends on the choice of the norm, so the positioning of the discriminant functions is affected by the norm (for the same training data set).

NEUROSOLUTIONS EXAMPLE 4.13
Regression performance as a function of the norm

In this example we use the linear regressor and the data from Chapter 1 to show how the choice of error criterion affects the performance of the linear regression. We have modified the data set so that one point is an outlier; it is much higher than the others. As you can see in the example, the norms that weight large errors more heavily skew their regression line much more closely to the outlier (giving a less accurate estimate of the rest of the data). Remember not to try to compare the errors as displayed in NeuroSolutions; the values of the error reported depend on the error criterion and thus can't be compared.

L1 Criterion

Lp Criterion

For positive finite integers p, the derivative of the norm can be computed quite easily as

$$\frac{\partial J_{nk}}{\partial y_{nk}} = \left| d_{nk} - y_{nk} \right|^{p-1} \mathrm{sgn}(d_{nk} - y_{nk}) \tag{4.13}$$

but L_p norms do not cover all the cases of interest. For errors larger than 1, the instantaneous cost J_{nk} for the L_p norms always increases at the same rate or faster than the instantaneous error, which may not be our goal. There are cases of practical relevance that do not have an analytic solution, such as the L_∞ norm (all errors are zero except the largest). Another possible criterion is to simply use the sign of the deviation ($p = 0$).

Minskowski Measures

An alternative interpretation of the error norms is provided in the statistical literature as the *Minskowski measures* (see Bishop [1995]). In this perspective the L_2 norm appears as the maximum likelihood solution when the instantaneous errors are Gaussian distributed. When the data set is such that they produce error pdf's that deviate from the Gaussian distribution, the L_2 norm does not provide the maximum likelihood solution. If we have a priori information about the error distributions, the appropriate Minskowski measure can thus be used to establish the best performance.

In classification problems the most reasonable distribution seems to be the *Bernoulli distribution*, which points to the use of the Kullback-Leibler criterion.

NEUROSOLUTIONS EXAMPLE 4.14

Classification performance as a function of the norm

In this example we show how the choice of error criterion affects the location of the discriminant function. We seek to classify male and female subjects based on their height and weight, but using different norms. You will see that the discriminant function ends up in different places, depending on the norms, since each norm weights the errors differently.

4.6.2 Constructing the Error Directly

In backpropagation learning, the partial derivative of the cost with respect to the weight is given by

$$\frac{\partial J}{\partial w_{ij}} = \frac{\partial J}{\partial y_k} \frac{\partial y_k}{\partial w_{ij}} \qquad (4.14)$$

The first partial derivative is the instantaneous error that is injected in the dual network. Given a cost function, we can differentiate it to compute the instantaneous error of Eq. 4.14 and then use backpropagation to compute the sensitivity with respect to the individual weights w_{ij} (the second term in Eq. 4.14).

An alternative practical approach is to separate the propagation of the instantaneous error (done with the backpropagation algorithm) from its generation. Instead of thinking of an error produced by the derivative of a cost function (which requires differentiable cost functions), a function of the error, $g(\varepsilon_{k,n})$, can be directly injected in the dual system:

$$\frac{\partial J}{\partial w_{ij}} = g(\varepsilon_k) \frac{\partial y_k}{\partial w_{ij}} \qquad (4.15)$$

The function $g(.)$ is derived to meet our needs. For instance $arctanh(\varepsilon_{k,n})$ implements a reasonable approximation of the L_∞ norm, since it weights large errors exponentially. Another example is simply to take the sign of the instantaneous error and inject ± 1, but many more examples with unexplored properties exist.

4.6.3 Information Theoretical Error Measures

In information theory we can measure the divergence (a relaxed definition of distance) between two probability mass functions $q(x)$ and $p(x)$ by the *Kullback-Leibler (K-L) information criterion* or *cross entropy*:

$$D(p \parallel q) = \sum_x p(x) \log\left(\frac{p(x)}{q(x)}\right) \tag{4.16}$$

Cross-Entropy Criterion

To understand cross entropy, we have to give a short definition of information and the related concept of entropy. Information theory was invented by Shannon in the late 1940s to explain the content of messages and how they are corrupted through communication channels. The key concept in information theory is that of information [Cover and Thomas 1991]. Information is a measure of randomness of a message. If the message is totally predictable, it contains no information. On the other hand, something very unexpected has a high information content, so the information is inversely associated with the probability of an event. We can define the amount of information in a random event x_k with probability $p(x_k)$ as

$$I(x_k) = \log\left(\frac{1}{p(x_k)}\right)$$

Entropy then becomes the mean value of $I(x)$ over the complete range of discrete messages $(2K + 1)$ with probabilities $p_k = p(x_k)$ as

$$H(x) = \sum_{k=-K}^{K} p_k I(x_k)$$

Entropy is a measure of the average amount of information contained in the event.

Now assume that we have two probability mass functions $\{p_k\}$ and $\{q_k\}$. The relative entropy of the probability distribution P (function of some event r) with respect to the second distribution Q is given by

$$D(p \parallel q) = \sum_x p(x) \log\left(\frac{p(x)}{q(x)}\right)$$

This concept is called *relative entropy* and was introduced by Kullback. It is commonly called the Kullback-Leibler distance [Cover and Thomas 1991].

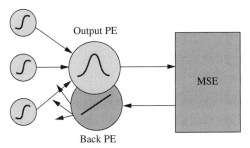

FIGURE 4-6 Implementation of the cross-entropy criterion

Since the learning system output is approximating the desired response in a statistical sense, it is reasonable to utilize the K-L criterion as our cost. In this case $p(x)$ becomes the target density constructed by $+1$ and -1, and $q(x)$, the learning system output density. This is particularly appropriate for classification problems where the L_2 assumption is weak because the distribution of the targets is far from Gaussian. For c classes the K-L information criterion becomes

$$J = \sum_n \sum_k d_{n,k} \log \left(\frac{y_{nk}}{d_{nk}} \right) \tag{4.17}$$

where n is the index over the input patterns and k over the classes. Since this criterion works on probabilities, the output PEs should be softmax PEs. It can be shown [Hertz, Krogh, and Palmer 1991] that the instantaneous error backpropagated through the network (the partial derivative of J with respect to y) with the softmax is

$$\frac{\partial J}{\partial net_k} = y_k - d_k \tag{4.18}$$

This is an interesting result, since it says that the cross-entropy criterion can be implemented by the MSE criterion (which also specifies the injection of the error as in Eq. 4.18). However, the network uses output PEs that implement the softmax function. This can be easily accommodated if we associate the softmax PE with a linear PE in the back plane as its dual (Figure 4-6).

In the two-class problem (single output PE) the softmax becomes a logistic output PE. By not subjecting the error to the attenuation produced by the derivative of the output PE nonlinearity, the network converges faster. It is also possible to show that the cross entropy is similar to the L_1 norm, which means that this criterion weights small errors more heavily than the L_2 norm.

The other important aspect of training the MLP with cross-entropy is that the interpretation of the output as the a posteriori probability of the class given the data also holds in this case [Bishop 1995].

> **NEUROSOLUTIONS EXAMPLE 4.15**
>
> *Cross-entropy training*
>
> In this example we show you how easy it is to implement the cross-entropy criterion for the two-class case in NeuroSolutions. All we need to do is change the Back PE of the logistic nonlinearity at the network output to a linear Back PE. This changes the backpropagated error so that the network will learn using entropy. Notice that the learning is faster, as we would expect, since the error is not attenuated by the derivative of the nonlinearity.

4.7 NETWORK SIZE AND GENERALIZATION

The coupling between the number of required discriminant functions to solve a problem and the number of PEs was heuristically established in Chapter 3, and the relation between the number of weights and training patterns was discussed in Section 4.5.1. From these facts we could think that the larger the learning machine, the better its performance (provided we have enough data to train it). The point about scalability shows, however, that larger machines may not learn well, but this is not the most pressing issue. All these arguments pertain to the training data. The fundamental question in any practical application is: How does the learning machine perform on the test-set data? This is the problem of *generalization.*

As we discussed earlier, MLPs trained with backpropagation do not control their generalization ability, which can be considered a shortcoming of the technology. Using a cross-validation set to stop the training allows us to maximize generalization for a given network size. However, it does not provide a mechanism for establishing the best network topology for generalization. The issue is the following: Do larger networks maintain the generalization of smaller ones?

If we reflect on how the network performs its function, we immediately see that the size of the machine (sometimes called the model complexity) is related to performance: Too few degrees of freedom (weights) affect the network's ability to achieve a good fit to the target function. If the network is too large, however, it will not generalize well, because the fit is too specific to the training-set data (memorization). An intermediate network size is our best choice. Therefore, for good performance, methods of controlling the network complexity become indispensable in the MLP design methodology.

The problem of network size can be stated in a simplified manner using Occam's razor[1] argument as follows: *Any learning machine should be sufficiently large to solve the problem, but not larger.* The issue is to know what is large enough. Structural learning theory (V-C dimension) gives a theoretical answer to generalization, but it is

---

[1]William of Occam was a monk who lived in the 14th century in England and enunciated a principle that has echoed across scientific circles for centuries. He said that a scientific model should favor simplicity, hence the name for the principle: Occam's razor (shave off the fat in the model).

difficult to apply to the MLP. Alternative theories give partial answers that elucidate the principles at work and are covered in Chapter 5.

Early Stopping and Model Complexity

We saw in Section 4.4.2 that early stopping provides a criterion to stop training at the point of smallest error in the validation set, that is, the point of best generalization for that particular combination of topology and training set. From the point of view of model complexity, early stopping effectively controls the complexity of the model, which may seem strange since the number of free parameters is constant. It turns out that in nonlinear systems the model complexity depends not only on the number of parameters (as in linear systems), but also on the actual value of the free parameters, so it may change during training.

Early stopping does not address the size of the learning machine, which is also a determining factor for controlling the model complexity. In linear machines, model size is the only way to control model complexity, so parsimonious architectures should be a design goal. The full discussion of this topic is rather theoretical and is left to Chapter 5. Here we will use a heuristic approach.

There are two basic approaches that deal with the learning machine size [Hertz, Krogh, Palmer, 1991]. Either we start with a small machine and increase its size (growing method), or we start with a large machine and decrease its size by pruning unimportant components (pruning method). Pruning is the only method we will address here.

Pruning reduces the size of the learning machine by eliminating either weights or PEs. The basic issue of pruning is to find a good criterion to determine which parameters should be removed without significantly affecting the overall performance of the network. We describe two basic methods: eliminating weights based on their values, and computing the importance of the weight in the mapping.

4.7.1 Weight Elimination

The idea in weight elimination is to create a driving force that will attempt to decrease all the weights to zero during adaptation. If the input-output map requires some large weights, learning will keep bumping up the important weights, but the ones that are not important will be driven to zero. This idea is called weight decay. Weight decay can be implemented very simply by adding an extra term into the weight adaptation, as shown here for the gradient descent rule:

$$w_{ij}(n+1) = w_{ij}(n)(1 - \lambda) + \eta \delta_i x_j \qquad (4.19)$$

where δ is the local error, x the local activation, η the learning rate, and λ the weight decay constant. Weights that are smaller than a certain value can be eliminated, reducing the overall number of degrees of freedom of the network. Weight decay should not be applied to the biases of the network, just to the weights.

Alternatively we can use only the sign of the weight to change its value:

$$w_{ij}(n + 1) = w_{ij}(n) + \eta \delta_i x_j + \lambda \text{sgn}(w_{ij}) \qquad \textbf{(4.20)}$$

where sgn(.) is the signum function. The problem with Eq. 4.20 is that it favors many small weights instead of a large one, normally producing model bias [Bishop 1995]. One way to counteract this problem is to create a weight-decay term that is smaller for larger weights:

$$w_{ij}(n + 1) = w_{ij}(n)\left(1 - \frac{\lambda}{(1 + w_{ij}^2)^2}\right) + \eta \delta_i x_j \qquad \textbf{(4.21)}$$

The weight-elimination method is very easy to implement because the weights are being updated and decayed during adaptation. The issue is how to select a good weight-decay constant λ such that convergence is achieved and unnecessary weights go to zero.

The weight-decay equations can also be applied in lieu of early stopping as a method to constrain the complexity of the model. It has been shown that for quadratic performance surfaces, weight decay is equivalent to early stopping. This will be further described in Chapter 5.

NEUROSOLUTIONS EXAMPLE 4.16

Weight decay

In this example we use the weight-decay algorithm from Equation 4.19. In general, we do not know how many PEs will be required to solve a given problem. However, based on generalization considerations, we know that we want as small a network as possible. If we have too many PEs, we can obtain low errors during training, but the network generalization will be poor due to overtraining; that is, a solution too specific to the training data will be obtained. Weight-decay subtracts a small portion from each weight during each update. Since the weights that are important to the solution will be constantly updated, while the others are not, the important weights will move to the correct value, and the other weights will approach zero. This effectively limits the number of PEs to only those that are required, which is the desired result.

4.7.2 Optimal Brain Damage

The previous method is based solely on weight magnitude, which is a crude measure of the importance of the weight in the input-output map. A better measure to compute weight *saliency* is to find the effect on the cost of setting a weight to zero [LeCun, Denker, and Solla 1993]. It has been shown that the Hessian **H** with elements

$$H_{ij} = \frac{\delta J}{\partial w_i \partial w_j} \qquad (4.22)$$

contains the required information. The problem with this computation is that it is non-local (requires information from pairs of weights). A local approximation (sometimes poor) to the Hessian can be computed by taking into consideration only the diagonal terms, which leads to the following calculation of the *saliency* s_i for each weight w_i:

$$s_i = H_{ii} w_i^2 / 2 \qquad (4.23)$$

To apply this method, a large network should be trained in the normal way, and saliencies computed for each weight. Then the weights are ordered in terms of their saliency, and a percentage with smaller saliencies discarded. The network needs to be retrained using the previous values of the weights as the initial condition. The process can then be repeated.

4.7.3 Committee of Networks

We saw that learning was a stochastic process, which means we should run the same network several times to make sure we get good and stable training. We just saw that the topology of a neural network is a difficult decision, because we have to take into consideration the generalization ability of the machine, which depends on its size.

A way of improving the performance of neural network classifiers is to use several networks of different sizes and characteristics to solve the same problem. Suppose we train C different networks with the same data. One temptation is to use the network that produced the best possible error in the training set. This strategy is not very good, first, because it wastes the training of all the other runs and, second, because the best performer in the training set does not necessarily extrapolate to the test set. A much better strategy is to use all the trained networks, that is, make decisions with a committee of networks. Let us analyze what happens if we simply add their outputs:

$$y_{\text{com}} = \frac{1}{C} \sum_{i=1}^{C} y_i \qquad (4.24)$$

If we assume that the errors from each network are zero mean and uncorrelated with each other, we can show [Perrone 1994] that the error of the committee is

$$J_{\text{com}} = \frac{1}{C} \overline{J} \qquad (4.25)$$

where $\overline{J}$ is the mean error of each network working individually. So the error of the committee is C times smaller, which is a large reduction. This is optimistic in general, since the errors among networks are not uncorrelated. The major advantage comes from a reduction in the variance of the error due to the averaging of each individual output. The size of a network in a committee should normally be larger than when used independently. The reason for this, which will be explained in Chapter 5, has to do with the bias-variance dilemma. Practically, each network should have an accuracy above 50%.

Weight factors (terms proportional to the performance of each network) can be used instead of fixed weighting for even better results. This is easy to do using the backpropagation formalism. The goal is to train just the weights from each network to the output adder (or softmax). We now demonstrate committees in NeuroSolutions.

NEUROSOLUTIONS EXAMPLE 4.17

Committees

The committee is an interesting way to avoid the approach of putting "all the eggs in one basket," that is, designing a single neural network that we tweak for optimal performance. We can in principle use very different topologies (the more distinct, the better, since their performances will tend to be less correlated) in a more or less ad hoc fashion to improve classification results. Of course, the price paid is a large increase in the computational cost of the simulation. But these days, with the increasing power of PCs and workstations, this is a small price to pay for increased performance. When taken to the limit, this method of design avoids some of the difficulties we found in selecting the optimal topology and setting the number of PEs, the stopping criterion, and the training parameters. Committees rely on statistics to improve individual suboptimal solutions and achieve performance comparable to the best possible solution. This is possible only because the main difficulty in neural network performance is the variance of the estimation.

Here we use on-line training for each of the individual networks. But notice that each network has its own criterion to guarantee that each network is trained independently. We use two MLPs (one-hidden-layer and two-hidden-layer) and an RBF network (another class of networks—more on this in Chapter 5) to solve the male–female classification problem. If you recall, we had about five errors when we solved this problem with the MLP in Chapter 3, so this is the number to beat.

We start by fixing the vote of each network to 1/3. Notice that the performance is basically the same as a single network. Then we also train the vote of each network. The performance improves dramatically, since the number of mistakes decreases to two misclassifications. As you can see, this is a powerful way to "throw technology at the problem."

You should create a test set to validate the improvement of the committee over a single network. Notice also that this method lends itself very nicely to parallelization, since each network can be run in a separate machine and the results combined.

Another option is to simply train all the networks concurrently with a single error criterion, as if they were a larger modular network made up of MLPs and the like. This is effectively similar to training a much larger network and setting some of its weights to zero, that is, adding some a priori structure. Normally, each will specialize in a given portion of the pattern space. The advantage comes when the networks have different discriminant functions. But notice that this training is collaborative, not competitive (as we will exemplify in Chapter 7), so it is not a committee. Modular networks can be implemented in NeuroSolutions, so you can modify the previous breadboard to create a modular network and compare the results.

4.8 PROJECT: APPLICATION OF THE MLP TO REAL-WORLD DATA

In this section we are going to use MLPs to solve several real-world classification problems. There are several Internet sites that store nice data for classification purposes. Please see the web sites in Chapter 1 and also the following:

http://markov.stats.ox.ac.uk/pub/PRNN

http://128.2.209.79/afs/cs/project/ai-repository/ai/areas/neural/bench/0.html

http://www.scs.unr.edu/~cbmr/research/data.html

http://neural-server.aston.ac.uk/NN/databases.html

4.8.1 Classifications

We start with the crab data, taken from an article by Campbell and Mahon [1974]. The goal is to classify rock crabs from two species as male or female using anatomic measurements of front lip, rear width, length, width, and depth. The data set is composed of 200 specimens, 50 males and 50 females from the two species.

We then move to a more demanding data set—the Iris data set [Fisher 1936]—to show the importance of classifier topology in the performance. The goal is to classify three types of Iris plants (Setosa, Versicolour, and Virginica) based on measurements of sepal length, sepal width, petal length, and petal width (all in centimeters). There are 50 samples of each class for a total of 150 samples. As you can see, this problem formulation is very similar to the previous one; however, the distribution of the data clusters in the input space is more complex. The difficulty of the task is not known a priori, so a step-by-step approach to define the optimal classifier is normally required.

NEUROSOLUTIONS EXAMPLE 4.18

Crab data classification

The first thing to do is to examine the data sets. The data is composed of five parameters per crab and one tag for the species, for a total of six inputs. The desired result is a classification of male or female, so we can either use one or two outputs. In the first case we would code male as 1 and female as 0 (or vice versa). In the second case each gender will have its own output. The desired response file is composed of two columns with pairs of values (0, 1) depending on the class membership.

The next step is to normalize and divide the data. Normalization of the data allows us to get experience with step sizes and use systematic weight initializations. Since the data is all positive, we will normalize it between [0, 1]. We divide the data into training, test, and validation sets. The training set is used to arrive at optimal weight, the test data is used to gauge the performance of the classifier, and the validation set is used to help us stop the training at the point of best generalization.

The next important definition is the topology. The idea is always to start small, so we should start with a perceptron to see whether the machine can separate the data. Since the data is normalized between [0, 1], we will use the logistic function as the nonlinearity.

The next important decision is how to stop the training. Here we can first use the number of iterations ($I = 200$) to get a feel for how difficult the problem is and then switch to cross-validation when the topology is finally chosen.

We still have to decide on the search method and the criterion. The search will be momentum and the criterion L2.

We are ready to run the network on the crab data. Do it several times and watch the learning curve. If the network converges to the same small error in basically the same number of epochs, then the training is successful and we can worry about how to stop the training with cross-validation. If the network does not converge, we should select a different learning rate or search procedure, modify the topology, or both.

The error is around 0.1, which means that almost all the data was classified correctly in the training set. We also see that the training is repeatable, since the learning curves are very similar to each other. Let us go to the test set to see the performance. As we mentioned earlier, the best way to test the classifier is not by MSE but with the confusion matrix. We see that we get three errors in the test set, which is reasonable. But can we improve the performance?

To answer this question, we have to change the topology and try a one-hidden-layer network with five hidden PEs. Let us train the network and check the performance. As you can see, the error is much smaller. Let us test the system. The confusion matrix shows that the classification is perfect. Since the MLP performed moderately better than the perceptron, we could conclude that the data is not linearly separable, but we do not have enough data to be sure. The errors could be due to imprecise measurements (noise in the data).

We can now fine-tune the system. We can first train it with cross-validation and see how far we should train. The cross-validation for this problem and topology does not help, since there is no observable increase in the learning curve.

An alternative to cross-validation is to use weight decay on the weights. We start with the same network, but we use the idea of driving all the weights to zero. Training the network, we can see that the network size was slightly reduced but that our initial guess was pretty good.

NEUROSOLUTIONS EXAMPLE 4.19

Iris data classification

To see how data-dependent the performance of a classifier is, let us change to the iris data. The inputs to the network are sepal length, sepal width, petal length, and petal width (i.e., four inputs), and the three classes of Iris plants (which are used as the desired outputs) are Setosa, Versicolour, and Virginica. There are 50 samples of each class for a total of 150 samples. The 150 samples have been prerandomized. Furthermore, 100 samples will be used for training and 50 samples for testing.

Starting with the perceptron, we see that the result is not satisfactory. There is significant confusion between the classes of Virginica and Versicolour, so we need to change to a one-hidden-layer MLP. The issue is how to choose the number of hidden PEs.

Let us run the MLP first with one PE in the hidden layer for several runs and record the minimum MSE value, then increase this number to 2, 4, and 6 and run the network several times for each. Finally, we should plot the mean MSE as a function of the number of PEs. The MSE error curve stabilizes after two PEs, so we will put two PEs in the hidden layer.

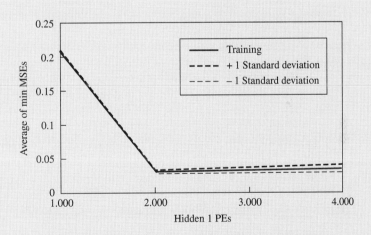

The classification performance for this network is much improved (only 3 mistakes instead of 19). We can thus conclude that the data set is not linearly separable, since the perceptron cannot solve it, but the one-hidden-layer MLP succeeded.

4.8.2 Neural Networks for Decision Making

The next problem we will discuss is very important, especially in decision making and medical diagnostics. Assume that we want to create a computer-aided diagnostic tool for breast cancer using a neural network. Ten features (radius, texture, perimeter, area, smoothness, compactness, concavity, concave points, symmetry, and fractal dimension) have been computed from a digitized image of a fine-needle aspirate of a breast mass. The inputs to the neural network model consist of the mean, standard error, and "worst" (mean of the three largest values) for each of these 10 features, resulting in 30 total inputs for each image. We have data from only 150 images. A two-hidden-layer MLP configured with 10 inputs and 2 outputs will be used as the neural network model.

The difficulty in this application is that we want to estimate a decision (sick or healthy) based on the outcome of the neural network; that is, we have to estimate the "probability" of a decision. How can a neural network do that? We saw that the MLP can be trained to give us the a posteriori probability of a class, given the input data example. The a posteriori probability interpretation means that a net output for class 1 of 0.9 can be interpreted as saying that the a posteriori probability of that example belonging to class 1 is 0.9. This is an important step, but many other things must be taken into consideration before we make a diagnostic decision.

First, we used 50 percent of sick and 50 percent healthy cases to train the system, but the ratio of sick to healthy in the population is (fortunately) very different, so we have to compensate for the a priori probabilities when we interpret the results. Recall from Chapter 2 (Figure 2-2) that when the a priori probabilities for each class are the same, the decision that minimizes the probability of misclassification is given directly by the likelihoods probability. In general, when the a priori probabilities are different, the corresponding likelihoods should be multiplied by the a priori probabilities, so the decision boundary is moved.

The advantage of ANNs is that we do not need to retrain the network. We can still interpret the outputs as likelihoods and, to obtain the a posteriori probability, simply multiply the outputs by the priors (Bayes' theorem). This assumes that the training set is constructed with an equal number of exemplars from each class. For example, suppose that the net output for the class *sick* was 0.9, we know that the probability of being sick in the population is 0.2, and equal numbers of cases were used in the training set. The probability that the subject has the disease is therefore 0.18. If the training set does not contain an equal number of the two classes, we should also divide the outputs by the relative frequency of training exemplars in the respective class.

The other difficulty is that there is a risk in making a decision, and the two types of errors (the subject is healthy and the network says sick, called a *false positive*, or the subject is sick and the network says healthy, called a *false negative*) have different costs. It is preferable to initially tell a healthy patient that she needs to have further exams than to simply state that she is healthy when in fact she has breast cancer, since the implications are vastly different.

This means that minimizing the probability of misclassification may not be the best strategy. We should weight the a posteriori probabilities by the risk of making the decisions. To do this a matrix of penalties L_{ij} of making the wrong decisions must first be constructed. Normally in medicine this is rather subjective, but the idea is as follows. We would like to penalize the false negatives (calling a sick subject healthy) much more than the false positives (calling a healthy patient sick). The penalties are numbers between 0 and 1, where the penalty for being correct is 0, while the penalty for being wrong is 1. Let us call *sick* hypothesis 1 and *healthy* hypothesis 2. Here let us say that the penalty of the false negative is $L_{12} = 0.3$ and the penalty of the false positive is $L_{21} = 0.5$. The matrix of penalties is therefore

$$\mathbf{L} = \begin{bmatrix} 0 & 0.3 \\ 0.5 & 0 \end{bmatrix}$$

We compute the average penalty by

$$R_i = \sum_{j=1}^{c} L_{ij} p(x_j | C_i)$$

where c is the number of classes and x is the random variable. We call *risk* the expected value of the penalties, that is,

$$R = \sum_{i=1}^{c} R_i P(C_i)$$

where $P(C_i)$ are the a priori probabilities. Thus the best decision should be done by minimizing the risk (instead of minimizing the probability of misclassification, as we did when we applied Bayes' rule), as

$$\sum_{i=1}^{c} L_{ik} p(x|C_i) P(C_i) < \sum_{i=1}^{c} L_{ij} p(x|C_i) P(C_i) \qquad \text{for all } k \neq j$$

Notice that when the network provides $p(x | C_i)$, it is trivial to make the decision based on risks.

NEUROSOLUTIONS EXAMPLE 4.20

Risk decision in the cancer data

To solve this problem we start with an MLP and make sure that the network is well configured (try several numbers of hidden PEs, as we did earlier) and well trained. We should use cross-validation to stop at the point of maximum generalization. We should also try different initial conditions to make sure that we are really converging to the absolute minimum.

Then the next step is to create a DLL that will compute the risk based on the preceding formulas. The computer-aided diagnosis is then made, based on the class that produces the smallest risk.

4.9   CONCLUSION

In this chapter we covered the most fundamental practical aspects of applying MLPs to real-world problems. We learned about new search procedures, how to control the initialization, the stopping criterion, and how to decide effectively whether a reasonable solution was obtained (the confusion matrix).

We also discussed ways to build more flexibility into the solution in the form of different norms. One of the fundamental problems of MLPs (and other learning machines) is that they cannot control their generalization ability. This is crucial for good results, so we presented a method (weight decay) to prune unnecessary weights to provide better generalization. Cross-validation was also presented as the method of choice to stop network training, because it ensures the best possible generalization for the chosen topology. We also introduced the idea of committees of networks as a way to decrease the variance of performance in the test set. We ended the chapter with the application of MLPs to several interesting real-world problems.

We now present a summary of heuristics that will help decrease the training times and produce better performance in general. For more information see [Orr and Muller, 1998]

- Normalize your data to the range of the network activations.
- Use the tanh nonlinearity instead of the logistic function.
- Use a softmax PE at the output layer.
- Normalize the desired signal to be just below the output nonlinearity "rail" values (i.e., if you use the tanh, use desired signals of ± 0.9 instead of ± 1).
- Add a constant value of 0.05 in the derivative of the nonlinearity (errors will always flow through the dual network).
- Set the step size higher in the layers closer to the input.
- Shuffle the training set from epoch to epoch in on-line learning.
- Initialize the network weights in the linear region of the nonlinearity (choose the standard deviation of the random noise source, as in Eq. 4.2).
- Use more sophisticated learning methods (delta bar delta, added noise, conjugate gradients).
- Always have more training patterns than weights. You can expect the test-set performance of your MLP to be limited by the relation $N > W/\varepsilon$, where N is the number of training patterns, W the number of weights, and ε the performance error. You should train until the mean square error is less than $\varepsilon/2$.
- Use cross-validation to stop training.
- Always run the network several times to gauge performance.
- Use a committee of networks to improve classification.

4.10   LIST OF NEUROSOLUTIONS EXAMPLES

4.1 Visualization of learning

4.2 Learning as a stochastic process (XOR)

4.3 Learning rate scheduling

4.4 Flow of errors across MLP layers

4.5 Effect of initial conditions on adaptation

4.6 Momentum learning

4.7 Adaptive step sizes

4.8 Adaptation with noise in the desired signal

4.9 Stopping based on MSE value

4.10 Stopping with cross-validation

4.11 Sparse connectivity in the input layer

4.12 Confusion matrix for classification performance

4.13 Regression performance as a function of the norm

4.14 Classification performance as a function of the norm

4.15 Cross-entropy training

4.16 Weight decay

4.17 Committees

4.18 Crab data classification

4.19 Iris data classification

4.20 Risk decision in the cancer data

4.11   EXERCISES

4.1 Explain why consecutive steps are orthogonal to each other in line-search methods.

4.2 Experimentally analyze the convergence of the MLP as a function of the step size using the Breadboard of NeuroSolutions Example 4.2. Use the basketball players data set contained in the data directory (CD-ROM). You should plot the learning curve every iteration and log the number of iterations required to reach a fixed MSE. Then do this for a range of step sizes. The end result may amaze you, but you should try to explain it.

4.3 Repeat Problem 2 using momentum learning.

4.4 Repeat Problem 2 for the delta-bar-delta search and compare performances.

4.5 Repeat Problem 2 with noise in the desired response and compare performances.

4.6 Repeat Problem 2 varying the α slope parameter of the PEs, but keep the step size constant. Compare performances.

4.7 For the female–male height–weight data set, compare the generalization obtained with cross-validation versus the one based on training-set error. Use the confusion matrix to evaluate the test-set performance.

4.8 Study the effect of the size of the cross-validation set on generalization. Use the data set in folder chapter 3 contained in the data directory (CD-ROM). You should construct cross-validation sets of different sizes (30, 60, 90 samples), taking data from the training set and plot the corresponding test-set accuracy.

4.9 Study the effect of different norms on classification. Choose the male–female data set. First study the convergence time of different norms, then study the test-set accuracy, and draw conclusions. Can you extrapolate these results to other data sets?

4.10 Right or wrong: One should compare the performance of different networks using cross-validation instead of imposing a threshold in the MSE? Carefully explain your reasoning.

4.11 Construct the sign error norm for a two-class problem,

$$\text{if} \begin{cases} \varepsilon(n) > 0 & \text{inject } 1 \\ \varepsilon(n) \leq 0 & \text{inject } -1 \end{cases}$$

and apply Eq. 4.12 to train the network. Experimentally verify its performance on the data set of your choice. Explain this error in terms of L_p norms.

4.12 Construct an asymmetric error using the concepts of Eq. 4.11 in the following way: Errors for class 1 should be weighted by I_{-8}, while errors for class 2 should have an L_1 norm. Explain what this does in terms of placement of decision surfaces (use the L_2 norm as a comparison). Apply the mixed norm to the breast-cancer data and compare performance with the risk analysis.

4.13 Experimentally compare the performance of the K-L criterion (Eq. 4.20) with the L_2 for a data set of your choice.

4.14 Experimentally compare the performance of the MLP (use the confusion matrix) with and without weight-decay in a data set of your choice. Work with large topologies to evaluate the differences.

4.15 Use the following two strategies to train an MLP for one of the data sets:

I. Use the minimum of the cross-validation error to find the best network architecture. This means you have to run different-sized networks over the data and choose the one that gives the smallest cross-validation error.

II. Use weight-decay to find the best network architecture.

Compare the performance of these strategies and also the number of weights different from zero. You should find the two very similar.

4.16 Experimentally verify the performance improvement of committees in one of the data sets. Start with two very different topologies (1- and 2-hidden-layer MLPs). All should be large networks. Train each separately and test the classification performance. Then combine all of them according to Eq. 4.21. Compare the testing results. Then train the combination weights and test the performance again.

4.12   CONCEPT MAP FOR CHAPTER 4

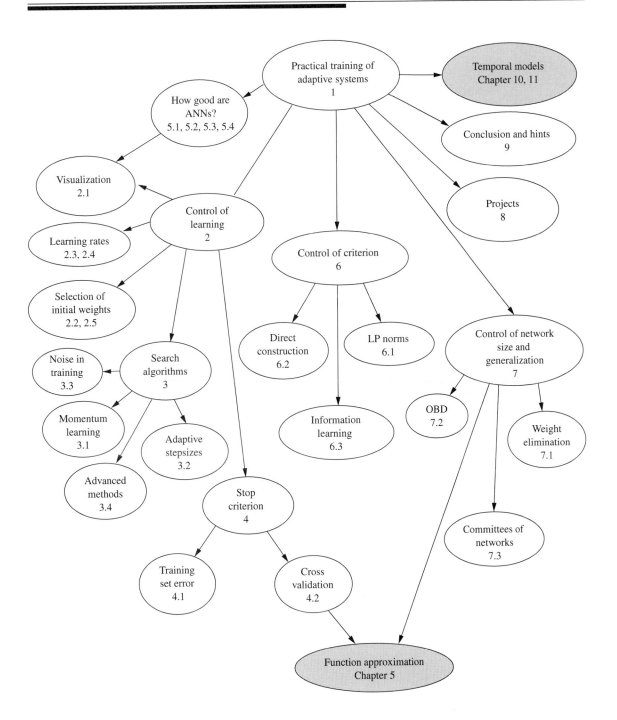

REFERENCES

Barron, A., Universal approximation bounds for superpositions of sigmoid functions, *IEEE Trans. Information Theory,* 39(3):930–945, 1993.

Bishop, C., *Neural Networks for Pattern Recognition,* Oxford, 1995.

Campbell, N., and Mahon, R., A multivariate study of variation in two species of rock crabs of genus *Leptograpsus, Australian Journal of Zoology,* 22: 417–425, 1974.

Cover, T., and Thomas, J., *Elements of Information Theory,* Wiley, New York, 1991.

Fahlman, S., Fast learning variations of back-propagation: An empirical study, in *Proceedings of the 1988 Connectionist Models Summer School,* 38–51, Morgan Kaufmann, 1998.

Fisher, R. A., The use of multiple measurements in taxonomic problems, *Annals of Eugenics,* 7(2):179–188, 1936.

Fletcher, R., *Practical Methods of Optimization,* Wiley, New York, 1987.

Haykin, S., *Artificial Neural Networks: A Comprehensive Foundation,* IEEE Press, New York, 1995.

Hertz, J., Krogh, A., and Palmer, R., *Introduction to the Theory of Neural Computation,* Addison-Wesley, Reading, MA, 1991.

Horst, R., Pardalos, P., and Thoai, N. *Introduction to Global Optimization,* Kluwer, 1995.

LeCun, Y., Denker, J., and Solla, S., Optimal brain damage, in *Advances in Neural Information Processing Systems,* vol. 2: 598–605, Morgan Kaufmann 1993.

LeCun, Y., Simard, P., and Pearlmutter, B., Automatic learning rate maximization by on-line estimation of the Hessian eigenvectors, in *Advances of Neural Information Processing Systems,* vol. 5, 156–163, Morgan Kaufmann, 1993.

Luenberger, D., *Linear and Nonlinear Programming,* Addison-Wesley, Reading, MA, 1984.

Orr, G., and Muller, K., Neural Networks: Tricks of the Trade, *Lecture Notes in Computer Science*, vol. 1524, Springer Verlag, New York, 1998.

Pearlmutter, B., Fast exact multiplications by the Hessian, *Neural Computation,* 6(1):147–160, 1994.

Perrone, M., General averaging results for convex optimization, in Mozer et al. (Eds.), *Proc. 1993 Connectionist Models Summer School,* 364–371, Lawrence Erlbaum, Hillside, NJ, 1994.

Shepherd, A., *Second-Order Methods for Neural Networks,* Springer, New York, 1997.

Silva, F., and Almeida, L., Acceleration techniques for the back-propagation algorithm, in Almeida and Wellekens (Eds.), *Neural Networks, Lecture Notes in Computer Science*, 110–119, Springer, 1990.

Vapnik, V., *The Nature of Statistical Learning Theory,* Springer Verlag, New York, 1995.

CHAPTER 5

FUNCTION APPROXIMATION WITH MLPs, RADIAL BASIS FUNCTIONS, AND SUPPORT VECTOR MACHINES

The goal of this chapter is to introduce the following concepts:

- Function approximation as a unifying perspective of adaptive systems
- Radial basis function (RBF) networks and applications
- Understanding the issues linking network size and generalization
- Support vector machines (SVMs)

5.1 INTRODUCTION

In Chapters 1 and 3 we presented two of the most common applications of adaptive systems, which are respectively linear regression using a linear adaptive system (the Adaline) and classification using the multilayer perceptron (MLP). We saw that the nature of the applications is different, since in regression the problem is one of representing the relationship between the input and the output data, while in classification the input data is assumed to be multiclass, and the purpose is to separate it into classes as accurately as possible. We also verified that the machinery developed for regression, namely gradient descent on a cost function, could be applied to classification. When properly extended, the gradient-descent procedure gave rise to the back-propagation algorithm developed to train the MLP.

The purpose of this chapter is to more formally unify the two applications of regression and classification. We will be demonstrating that both problems are in fact aspects of the more general problem of *function approximation.*[1] Linear regression is function approximation with linear topologies, and classification is function approximation with special functions called *indicator functions.* What we gain is a very broad and unifying perspective of adaptive systems that can be applied to many practical applications beyond classification. These applications range from system identification to data modeling and motivate the study of the MLP as a nonlinear regressor. This new perspective also raises the question of alternative topologies such as the radial basis function (RBF) network, which is another universal approximator that can also be used for classification. Later in the chapter we present different methodologies to study the problem of generalization, and we conclude with a brief introduction to support vector machines. To achieve this unifying view, we will present the basic concepts of function approximation.

---

[1]Function approximation became a field of study in the 19th century with the formal definition of a limit by Cauchy and Weierstrass. It culminated a long road of discoveries by mathematical giants such as Euler, Legendre, and Gauss, motivated by astronomical observations. The goal was to approximate difficult mathematical functions by ensembles of simpler functions. Approximation requires the definition of an error, which implies a metric space to define the distance between the true function and the approximation. Moreover, the availability of a set of simpler functions is postulated.

5.1.1 The Discovery of the Input-Output Map as Function Approximation

We demonstrated in Chapters 1 and 3 that a neural network combines a set of inputs to obtain an output that mimics the desired response. Given a set of input vectors $\mathbf{x}$ and a set of desired responses d, the learning system must find the parameters that meet these specifications. This problem can be framed as function approximation, if we assume that the desired response d is an unknown but fixed function of the input $d = f(\mathbf{x})$ (Figure 5-1).

The goal of the learning system is to discover the function $f(.)$ given a finite number (hopefully small) of input-output pairs $(\mathbf{x}, d)$. The learning machine output $y = \hat{f}(\mathbf{x}, \mathbf{w})$ depends on a set of parameters $\mathbf{w}$, which can be modified to minimize the discrepancy between the system output y and the desired response d. When the network approximates d with y, it is effectively approximating the unknown function $f(\mathbf{x})$ with its input-output map $\hat{f}(\mathbf{x}, \mathbf{w})$.

The nature of $f(.)$ and the error criterion define the learning problem. As studied in Chapter 1, *linear regression* is obtained when the error criterion is the mean square error (MSE) and $f(.)$ is linear. Classification, studied in Chapter 2, specifies functions $f(.)$ that produce 1, -1 (or 0), which are called *indicator functions*.

The problem of generalization, briefly discussed in Chapter 4, can also be treated mathematically with this view of function approximation. This means that the ideas embodied in Figure 5-1 are rather relevant for the design of learning machines, specifically neural networks. Neural networks are in fact nonlinear parametric function approximators, so we should not think of them simply as classifiers.

ANNs are useful for function approximation because

- They are universal approximators
- They are efficient approximators
- They can be implemented as learning machines

We already alluded to the universal approximation property of the MLP in Chapter 3. It basically says that any continuous function can be approximated by the MLP topology, provided that enough PEs are available in the hidden layer. Here we will present these concepts more precisely.

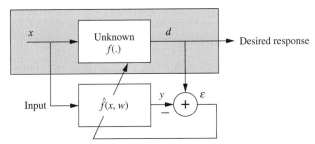

FIGURE 5-1 Supervised training as function approximation

With neural networks the coefficients of the function decomposition are automatically obtained from the input-output data pairs and the specified topology using systematic procedures called the learning rules, so there is no need for tedious calculations to obtain the parameters of the approximation analytically. Once trained, the neural network becomes not only a parametric description of the function but also its implementation. Neural networks can be implemented in computers or analog hardware and trained on-line. This means that engineers and scientists now have a means to solve function approximation problems involving real-world data. The impact of this advance is to take function approximation out of the mathematician's notebook and bring it to industrial applications.

We would like to argue that neural networks and learning are bringing focus to a very important problem in the *scientific method* called induction. Induction, along with deduction, are the only known systematic procedures to build scientific knowledge. Deduction applies general principles to specific situations. Deduction is fairly well understood and has had enormous impact on the entire fabric of mathematics, engineering, computer science, and science in general. For instance, deductive reasoning is the core of artificial intelligence. On the other hand, induction is poorly understood and less frequently applied. Induction is the principle of abstracting general rules from specific cases. As we all know from real life, this principle is much harder to apply with validity than deduction. Sometimes true statements in a small set of cases do not generalize. Mathematically, induction is also much less formalized.

It turns out that a neural network uses an inductive principle when it learns from examples. Examples are specific instances of a general rule (the function that created the examples), and the goal of neural network learning is to seek the general principle that created the examples. Theoretically, these issues are studied in *learning theory*. The difficulties we face in appropriately training a neural network are related to the difficulties of inducing general principles from examples. In practice, the ANN is not always able to capture the rule, and the prerequisites (neural network architecture, training data, stopping criterion) to extrapolate from examples need to be carefully checked, as we saw in Chapter 4.

5.2 FUNCTION APPROXIMATION

Function approximation seeks to describe the behavior of very complicated functions by ensembles of simpler functions. Very important results have been established in this branch of mathematics. Here we discuss only a few that bear a direct relation on our goal of understanding neural networks better. Legendre (and Gauss) used polynomials to approximate functions. Chebyshev developed the concept of best uniform approximation. Weierstrass[2] proved that *polynomials* can approximate any continuous real function in

---

[2] Augustin Cauchy (1789–1857) and Karl Weierstrass (1815–1897) were the fathers of calculus. They captured the idea of the limit in a precise mathematical way and opened up new horizons in approximation theory.

an interval arbitrarily well. *Series* expansions (i.e., Taylor series) have been utilized for many years to approximately compute the value of a function in a neighborhood of the operating point. The core advantage is that only multiplications and additions are necessary to implement a series approximation. Trigonometric polynomials are also widely used as function approximators, but their computation is a bit more involved. Before we apply any of this theory, we will formalize the concept of function approximation.

Let $f(\mathbf{x})$ be a real function of a real-valued vector $\mathbf{x} = [x_1 \ x_2 \ \ldots \ x_d]^T$ that *is square integrable* (over the real numbers). Most real-world data can be modeled by such conditions. We are also going to restrict this study to the *linear projection theorem*. The goal of function approximation using the projection theorem is to describe the behavior of $f(\mathbf{x})$, in a compact area S of the input space, by a combination of simpler functions $\varphi_i(\mathbf{x})$:

$$\hat{f}(\mathbf{x}, \mathbf{w}) = \sum_{i=1}^{N} w_i \varphi_i(\mathbf{x}) \tag{5.1}$$

where w_i are real-valued entries of the coefficient vector $\mathbf{w} = [w_1, w_2, \ldots, w_N]$ such that

$$\left| f(\mathbf{x}) - \hat{f}(\mathbf{x}, \mathbf{w}) \right| < \varepsilon \tag{5.2}$$

and where ε can be made arbitrarily small. The function $\hat{f}(\mathbf{x}, \mathbf{w})$ is called an *approximant* to $f(\mathbf{x})$. The block diagram of Figure 5-2 describes this formulation.

Let us examine Eqs. 5.1 and 5.2. A real function is a map from the input domain to the real numbers. This expression states that we can obtain the value of the function when $\mathbf{x}$ is in S by using an intermediate set of simpler functions, $\{\varphi_i(\mathbf{x})\}$, called the *elementary functions*, and then linearly combining them (Figure 5-2).

When one can find coefficients w_i that make ε arbitrarily small for any function $f(.)$ over the domain of interest, we say that the elementary function set $\{\varphi_i(.)\}$ has the property of universal approximation over the class of functions $f(.)$, or that the set of

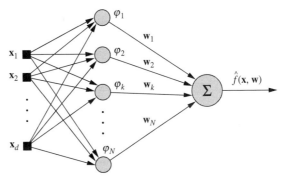

FIGURE 5-2 Implementation of the projection theorem

elementary functions $\varphi_i(\mathbf{x})$ is *complete*. From Eq. 5.1 we see that there are three basic decisions in function approximation:

- The choice of elementary functions $\varphi_i(.)$
- How to compute the weights w_i
- How to select the number of elementary functions N

The first problem is very rich because there are many possible elementary functions that can be used. We will illustrate this later, and we will show that the hidden PEs of a single-hidden-layer MLP implement one possible choice for the elementary functions $\varphi_i(.)$. The second problem is how to compute the coefficients w_i, which depends on how the difference or discrepancy between $f(\mathbf{x})$ and $\hat{f}(\mathbf{x}, \mathbf{w})$ is measured. In Chapter 1 we have already presented one possible methodology to solve this problem for the case of the minimization of the power of the error between $\hat{f}(\mathbf{x}, \mathbf{w})$ and $f(\mathbf{x})$. Least squares can also be used to analytically compute the values for w_i. If the number of input vectors $\mathbf{x}_i$ is made equal to the number of elementary functions $\varphi_i(.)$, the normal equations can be written as

$$\begin{bmatrix} \varphi_1(x_1) & \varphi_2(x_1) & \varphi_N(x_1) \\ \varphi_1(x_N) & \varphi_2(x_N) & \varphi_N(x_N) \end{bmatrix} \begin{bmatrix} w_1 \\ w_N \end{bmatrix} = \begin{bmatrix} f(x_1) \\ f(x_N) \end{bmatrix} \tag{5.3}$$

and the solution becomes

$$\mathbf{w} = \mathbf{\Phi}^{-1}\mathbf{f} \tag{5.4}$$

where $\mathbf{w}$ is a vector with the coefficients, $\mathbf{f}$ is a vector composed of the values of the function at the N points, and $\mathbf{\Phi}$ a matrix with entries given by the values of the elementary functions at each of the N points in the domain. An important condition that must be placed on the elementary functions is that the inverse of $\mathbf{\Phi}$ must exist.

In general, there are many sets $\{\varphi_i(.)\}$ with the property of universal approximation for a class of functions. We would prefer a set $\{\varphi_i(.)\}$ over another $\{\gamma_i(.)\}$ if $\{\varphi_i(.)\}$ provides a smaller error ε for a preset value of N. This means that the speed of convergence of the approximation (i.e., how fast the approximation error ε decreases with N) is also an important factor in the selection of the basis. Other considerations may be imposed by the computer implementation such as computational efficiency.

5.2.1 Geometric Interpretation of the Projection Theorem

Let us provide a geometric interpretation for this decomposition, because it exemplifies what is going on and what we are trying to accomplish. As long as the function $f(.)$ is square integrable and D is finite, this geometric representation is accurate. Consider $\mathbf{x}$ as a given point in a D-dimensional space. Its transformation by $f(.)$ is also assumed to be another point in the same D-dimensional space. We can alternatively think of $\mathbf{x}$ and $f(\mathbf{x})$ as vectors with end points 0 and $\mathbf{x}$. For illustration purposes let us make $D = 3$ and assume that we have only two elementary functions.

Equations 5.1 and 5.2 describe the projection of the vector $f(\mathbf{x})$ into a set of *basis functions* $\varphi_i(\mathbf{x})$. These basis functions can also be considered vectors, and they define a manifold (i.e., a projection space) in $M(M \leq D)$ dimensions, which is linear in our formulation. $\hat{f}(\mathbf{x}, \mathbf{w})$ is the *image* or projection of $f(\mathbf{x})$ in this manifold. In this example the projection manifold is a plane ($M = 2$) depicted as the horizontal plane, and $\hat{f}(\mathbf{x}, \mathbf{w})$ is a vector that exists in the horizontal plane. We can interpret w_i as the magnitude of (or proportional to) $\hat{f}(\mathbf{x}, \mathbf{w})$ along each one of the axes of the manifold.

If $f(\mathbf{x})$ belongs to the manifold, then there is always a set of constants w_i that will make $\hat{f}(\mathbf{x}, \mathbf{w})$ exactly equal to $f(\mathbf{x})$. Figure 5-3 represents this in case A. If $f(\mathbf{x})$ does not belong to the manifold created by the basis $\{\varphi_i(\mathbf{x})\}$, then there will always be an error between $\hat{f}(\mathbf{x}, \mathbf{w})$ and $f(\mathbf{x})$ (case B). The best solution (least possible error) found in Eq. 5.4 is the *orthogonal projection* of $f(\mathbf{x})$ onto the manifold. As we saw in Chapter 1, this is exactly the solution that the least squares provide, since the error becomes orthogonal to all the bases $\{\varphi_i(\mathbf{x})\}$.

When $f(\mathbf{x})$ is external to the projection manifold, decreasing the error means making $\hat{f}(\mathbf{x}, \mathbf{w})$ closer to $f(\mathbf{x})$. This can be accomplished by increasing the number of elementary functions (i.e., the dimension M of the manifold) because the manifold will fill more and more of the available signal space. This view is correct, provided that the basis set is complete, that is, that in the limit of large M the projection manifold will fill all the available signal space.

Let us now study in more detail each one of the steps in function approximation. We will see throughout this study that we obtain a very different view of what the MLP is, and we will tie this topology with other very well known basis functions.

5.3 CHOICES FOR THE ELEMENTARY FUNCTIONS

One decisive step in function approximation is the choice of the elementary functions $\varphi_i(.)$ because they affect how close $\hat{f}(\mathbf{x}, \mathbf{w})$ can be made to $f(\mathbf{x})$ for a given N. If the choice is not appropriate, there will be a nonvanishing error between $\hat{f}(\mathbf{x}, \mathbf{w})$ and $f(\mathbf{x})$,

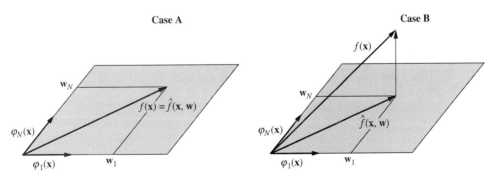

FIGURE 5-3 Approximation as a projection: (A) Vector is in the manifold; (B) Vector is outside the manifold

no matter how big N is. The search for sets of elementary functions $\{\varphi_i(.)\}$ that are universal approximators of a class of functions $f(.)$ is therefore very important. Moreover, we would like the elementary functions $\varphi_i(.)$ to have nice mathematical properties and to be easy to work with.

One requirement for the usefulness of elementary functions is that $\mathbf{\Phi}^{-1}(\mathbf{x})$ must exist (Eq. 5.4). This condition is met if the elementary functions constitute a *basis*, that is, if they are *linearly independent* or

$$w_1\varphi_1(\mathbf{x}) + \cdots + w_N\varphi_N(\mathbf{x}) = 0 \quad \text{iff} \quad (w_1, \ldots, w_N) = 0 \tag{5.5}$$

A simplifying assumption that is often imposed on the elementary functions is that the basis be *orthonormal*, that is,

$$\int_S \varphi_i(\mathbf{x})\varphi_j(\mathbf{x})d\mathbf{x} = \delta_{ij}(\mathbf{x}) \tag{5.6}$$

where $\delta(x)$ is the Dirac *delta function* and the integral is the continuous version of the dot product. This means that in orthogonal decompositions the projection of a basis in any other basis is always zero. An orthonormal basis is very appealing because we can evaluate the projection on each basis independently of the projection on the other bases, and they provide a unique set of w_i for the projection of $f(\mathbf{x})$. Many elementary functions obey the orthogonality conditions, and different sets provide different properties.

With complete orthonormal basis functions the weights of the decomposition become very simple to compute. It can be shown that

$$w_i = \langle f(\mathbf{x}), \varphi_i(\mathbf{x}) \rangle \tag{5.7}$$

where $\langle . \rangle$ is the inner product of $f(\mathbf{x})$ with the bases, given by

$$\langle f(\mathbf{x}), \varphi(\mathbf{x}) \rangle = \int_D f(\mathbf{x})\varphi(\mathbf{x})d\mathbf{x} \tag{5.8}$$

and D is the domain where $f(\mathbf{x})$ is defined.

Calculation of the Weights in Orthonormal Bases

Let us assume that the bases $\varphi(x)$ are orthonormal in D. Let $f(x)$ be any square integrable function. The goal is to find the coefficients w_i such that

$$f(x) = \sum_{i=1}^N w_i\varphi_i(x)$$

Taking the inner product of $f(x)$ with $\varphi_1(x)$

$$\langle f(x), \varphi_1 \rangle = \sum_{i=1}^N w_i\langle \varphi_i, \varphi_1 \rangle = w_1\langle \varphi_1, \varphi_1 \rangle$$

since the vectors are orthogonal. Moreover, since they are of unit length (orthonormal), we get

$$w_1 = \langle f(x), \varphi_1 \rangle$$

which corroborates the interpretation that the weight can be thought of as the projection in each elementary function. In general we get the pair of relations

$$
\begin{cases}
f(x) = \displaystyle\sum_i w_i \varphi_i(x) \\[2ex]
w_i = \displaystyle\int_D f(x)\varphi_i(x)dx
\end{cases}
$$

(Note: If the signals are complex, then the coefficients are given by

$$w_i = \int_D f(x)\varphi_i^*(x)dx$$

where * means complex conjugate.) On the other hand, if we are working with discrete spaces, this pair of equations becomes

$$
\begin{cases}
f(k) = \displaystyle\sum_{i=1}^N w_i \varphi_i(k) \\[2ex]
w_i = \displaystyle\sum_{k=1}^N f(k)\varphi_i(k)
\end{cases}
$$

where once again in the second equation the basis has to be the complex conjugate if the signals are complex. This pair is what we need to apply the projection theorem for orthonormal basis and provides the relationships for the Fourier transforms and Fourier series, for example.

5.3.1 Examples of Elementary Functions

Many important function approximation theories and decompositions are commonly applied in engineering. One example is digital signal processing that relies heavily on the sampling theorem. The sampling theorem shows that we can approximate any real, smooth signal (i.e., a function with finite slope) in an interval (infinitely many points) by knowing the functional values only at a finite set of equally spaced points in the interval (called the samples). The value of the signal at any other point in the interval can be exactly reconstructed by using sums of *sinc* functions. In this case the bases are the sinc functions, and the weights are the values of the signal at the sampling points, as shown in Figure 5-4.

This result opened up the use of sampled representations to reproduce sound (digital music on CDs) and to reproduce images (the forthcoming digital TV) and is the basis for the very important field of digital signal processing.

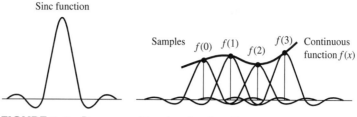

FIGURE 5-4   Decomposition by sinc functions

Sinc Decomposition

The formulas previously derived can be used to find the decomposition obtained when the bases are sinc functions. We would like to write

$$f(x) = \sum_i w_i \varphi_i(x)$$

The bases are

$$\varphi_i(x) = \text{sinc}(x - x_i) = \frac{\sin(x - x_i)}{x - x_i}$$

Now applying Eq. 5.7 the weights become

$$w_i = \int_D f(x)\text{sinc}(x - x_i)dx = f(x_i)$$

which means that the weights become the value of the function at the point (i.e., the sample value). This explains Figure 5-4.

NEUROSOLUTIONS EXAMPLE 5.1

Sinc interpolation

Here we use NeuroSolutions to interpolate an input waveform to a higher frequency using the sinc function. This example is not as dramatic as the one that produces a continuous representation from a digital sequence, but it is based on the same principles. We start with a digital waveform representing a ramp and introduce two zero samples between each two consecutive points, as shown in the input Megascope. As we can expect, the ramp becomes distorted. The idea is to recreate the ramp by filling in the missing values. We do this by designing an interpolator that implements a close approximation of the sinc function. We use a new component, the Delay Line, and enter in the Synapse the values that correspond to a sampling of the sinc function.

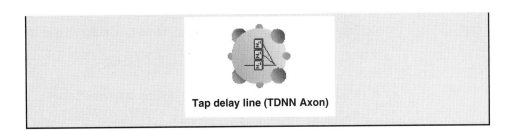

Tap delay line (TDNN Axon)

Another example of the power of function approximation is the *Fourier series*. Fourier series are an example of expansions with trigonometric polynomials. Everybody in engineering has heard of frequency representations (also called the spectrum) because of the following amazing property: Any periodic function (even with discontinuities) can be approximated by sums of sinusoids, as shown in Figure 5-5. Moreover, there are simple formulas that allow us to compute the components in the frequency domain from any time signal.

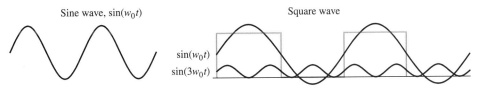

Sine wave, $\sin(w_0 t)$

Square wave

$\sin(w_0 t)$

$\sin(3w_0 t)$

FIGURE 5-5 Decomposition by sine waves

Fourier Formulas

Applying again the pair of formulas of Eq 5.7 and Eq. 5.8, we present the Fourier transform pair. Remember that the Fourier transform uses as bases the complex exponentials, that is,

$$\varphi_i(t) = e^{-j(2\pi/T)it}$$

where T is related to the interval where the function $f(t)$ is defined and $j = \sqrt{-1}$. The complex exponentials are a set of orthonormal bases. This means that we are going to expand the function $f(t)$ as

$$f(t) = \sum_{i=-\infty}^{\infty} w_i e^{-j(2\pi/T)it}$$

In the interval $D = [0, T]$ we can compute the weights as (Eq. 5.7)

$$w_i = \frac{1}{T} \int_0^T f(t) e^{j(2\pi/T)it} dt$$

This means that we have formulas to compute the weights, so we do not need to use adaptation. Note that the complex exponential can be expressed as (Euler relation)

$$e^{jwt} = \cos(wt) + j\sin(wt)$$

so in fact we are decomposing the signals in sums of (pairs of) sinusoids.

NEUROSOLUTIONS EXAMPLE 5.2

Fourier decomposition

This example is a demonstration of how an addition of sinusoids does in fact produce a waveform that resembles a square wave. To compute the coefficients, we have to perform a Fourier series decomposition of the square wave, which is not difficult but is cumbersome and requires an infinite number of sinusoids. By including more and more terms of the Fourier series, we make the composite waveform closer and closer to the square.

Wavelets are yet another example of elementary functions used for function approximation. One of the problems with Fourier decomposition is that the sine waves have infinite extent in time, that is, they exist for all time. In many practical problems we would like to decompose signals that have a finite extent (transients), in which case the Fourier analysis is not very efficient. Wavelets provide such a decomposition for transients. The idea is to choose a wave shape that is appropriate to represent the signal of interest (the mother wavelet) and create many translated and scaled versions of the wavelet so that we can reconstruct the desired signal.

The wavelet expansion uses a two-parameter decomposition:

$$\hat{f}(x, w) = \sum_i \sum_j w_{ij}\varphi_{ij}(x) \tag{5.9}$$

where the $\varphi_{ij}(x)$ are the wavelet bases. The bases are obtained from a single function [the mother wavelet $\varphi(x)$] by the operations of scaling and translation,

$$\varphi_{ij}(x) = 2^{j/2}\varphi(2^j x - i) \tag{5.10}$$

hence the two indices. Figure 5-6 shows the scaling and translation operations.

All the preceding methods construct arbitrary functions by weighting the contributions of predetermined elementary functions (sine waves of different frequencies, translation of sincs, or the dilation-translation of the mother wavelet). When decomposing the same function using different bases, only the weights of the decomposition vary. Normally, there are closed-form solutions to compute the weights from the signal. In neurocomputing the problem is more complicated for two reasons: First, we want to

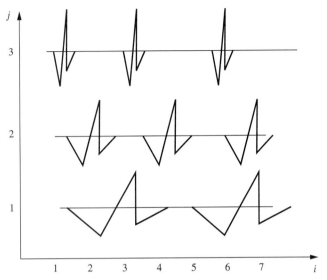

FIGURE 5-6 Translation and scaling for a wavelet

find the coefficients through adaptation instead of through analytic formulas as in the Fourier case; second, the bases themselves are dependent on the data and the coefficients (adaptive bases).

In some situations the basis can be chosen naturally from the type of problem being investigated, as in *linear systems theory*.

5.3.2 Bases for Linear Function Approximation

When the unknown function $f(x)$ in Figure 5-1 is linear, the linear regression concepts explained in Chapter 1 can be applied to construct an approximation.

NEUROSOLUTIONS EXAMPLE 5.3

Linear regression

Here we show that through adaptation we can find the coefficients of a very simple linear transformation between x and d of Figure 5-1. The transformation is simply

$$d = 2x + 3$$

For this case a linear system constructed from a synapse and a bias axon can solve the problem very easily. This is simply linear regression, which we studied in Chapter 1. We create the transformation by applying one of the function generators to the input of the system and using another function generator at the output, producing the same wave shape but with twice the amplitude and with a bias of 3. Then we let

> the system adapt using the LMS rule. We can see that the system very quickly finds the relationship, the synaptic weight becomes 2, and the bias becomes 3.

Most linear functions are much more complicated than the previous example. For linear systems with constant coefficients, there is actually a preferred choice for the elementary functions. Linear system theory shows that the natural bases are the complex exponentials e^{sx} because they are complete for square integrable functions and they are the *eigenfunctions* of linear *shift-invariant* operators.

Eigendecomposition

In engineering we use systems to modify time signals according to user specifications. A system is a piece of equipment that modifies input signals $x(t)$ to produce another signal $y(t)$ (see the figure).

Mathematically we can describe a system by a function H operating on the real (or complex) numbers

$$H : x \rightarrow Hx$$

and we will call H an operator. The output y of the system H when x is applied at the input is

$$y = Hx$$

The response of the system at time t is written $y(t) = [Hx](t)$.

A linear system is a system described by an operator H obeying the following properties:

$$H\alpha x = \alpha Hx$$
$$H[x + y] = Hx + Hy$$

where α is a scalar. We are normally interested in linear systems that are shift invariant, that is, where the response does not depend on the particular time of application. Let us define another operator T that delays x by τ seconds:

$$x(t - \tau) = [Tx](t)$$

In shift-invariant systems, H and T commute, that is, $THx = HTx$. Let's ask the following question: Which are the signals $x(t)$ that, when applied to a linear time-invariant system H, produce a response that has the same form as the input, apart from a multiplicative factor (gain factor)?

Mathematically this can be written

$$Hx = \lambda x$$

This is the same problem that gives rise to the eigenvector problem of matrices, and this is why the input x that obeys this condition is called an eigenfunction of H.

Linear shift-invariant systems have the special property that they commute with the derivative operator D, that is,

$$\text{If } y = Hx \text{ and } x' = Dx, \text{ then } y' = Hx'$$

or in words, if we know the response of the system to an input and we want to know the response to the derivative of the input, then it is enough to take the derivative of the output.

This is what we need to answer the original question. The derivative property shows that the question is equivalent to finding a signal x(t) that is proportional to its derivative:

$$\frac{dx(t)}{dt} = sx(t)$$

which we know accepts the solution $x(t) = \alpha e^{st}$, that is, a complex exponential. This means that a linear shift-invariant operator H, when applied to a complex exponential e^{sx}, will only change its magnitude and phase:

$$y = He^{sx} = \alpha e^{sx} \tag{5B.1}$$

where α is a *complex number*. Thus if an arbitrary function $u(x)$ is decomposed into exponentials,

$$u(x) = \sum_i e^{s_i x} \tag{5B.2}$$

then the response of H to $u(x)$ can always be evaluated as a sum of weighted responses to exponentials,

$$Hu(x) = H\left[\sum_i w_i e^{s_i x}\right] = \sum_i w_i H[e^{s_i x}] = \sum_i w_i \alpha_i e^{s_i x} \tag{5B.3}$$

where the α_i do not depend on $u(x)$. The importance of this equation has to be noted, since it tells us that no matter how complicated the input might be, we can always compute its output by adding the responses to individual exponential components. It also tells us that all we need to know to describe the linear system are the complex numbers α_i. Fourier analysis is a special case of this decomposition in which the complex exponentials have zero real parts, $s = jw$, yielding

$$e^{jw_i x} = \cos(w_i x) + j \sin(w_i x)$$

Now we understand why complex exponentials are so important when studying linear systems.

The implication of this fact is thoroughly explored in linear systems, which are networks that implement signal decomposition using complex exponentials. We use eigendecompositions in Chapter 9 when we study adaptive filters. Here we just remark that eigendecompositions are the most efficient, since we are constructing a function from its "elementary pieces," so the reconstruction error can be made equal to zero with a small number of bases. Sometimes other considerations, such as ease of implementation, may overshadow the use of complex exponentials.

5.3.3 Bases for Nonlinear System Approximation: The MLP Network

When the function $f(x)$ in Figure 5-1 is nonlinear, there is in general no natural choice of basis functions. Many have been attempted, such as the *Volterra expansions*, the *splines*, and the polynomials [Haykin, 1994]. Weierstrass proved that polynomials are universal approximators. The problem is that either many terms are necessary or the approximations are not very well behaved. One of our requirements is that the bases have to be powerful and easy to work with.

Weierstrass Theorem

Weierstrass proved the following important theorem: Let $S[a, b]$ be the space of continuous, real-valued functions defined in the real segment $[a, b]$. If $f \in S[a, b]$, then there exists a polynomial $P(x) = \sum_{i=0}^{N} \alpha_i x^i$ with real coefficients α for which $|f(x) - P(x)| < \varepsilon$ for $\varepsilon > 0$ and $x \in [a, b]$.

In words, this says that any function can be approximated arbitrarily well (i.e., with an error as small as we want) by a sufficiently large-order polynomial. The Weierstrass theorem is the starting point for most proofs of the universal mapping properties of the MLP.

In neurocomputing there are two basic choices for the elementary functions that build the approximant $\hat{f}(\mathbf{x}, \mathbf{w})$: *local* and *global* elementary functions. An elementary function is global when it responds to the full input space, while local elementary functions respond primarily to a limited area of the input space. It is easy to link the operation of function approximation (Figure 5-2) to a neural topology such as a one-hidden-layer perceptron with a linear output, where $\varphi_i(\mathbf{x})$ is

$$\varphi_i(x) = \sigma\left(\sum_k a_{ik} x_k + b_i\right) \tag{5.11}$$

and σ is one of the sigmoid nonlinearities (logistic or tanh). The system output is given by $y = \sum_i w_i \varphi_i$. Note that the first-layer weights are denoted by a_{ik} and they change the position and size of $\varphi_i(\mathbf{x})$. The one-hidden-layer MLP with a linear output PE can thus be thought of as an implementation of a system for function approximation

(Eq. 5.1), where the bases are exactly the outputs of the hidden PEs. Note that the sigmoid PE responds to the full input space x with a nonzero value [1, -1 (or 0), or intermediate values], so the MLP implements an approximation with global elementary functions.

The interpretation is that the MLP is performing function approximation with a set of *adaptive bases* that are determined from the input-output data. This means that the bases are not predefined as in the sinc, wavelet, or Fourier analysis but depend on the first-layer weights and the input. In this respect the MLP is much closer to the function approximation implemented by adaptive linear systems. Function approximation with adaptive bases is thus different from the picture we previously presented in Figure 5-3. First, the bases change with the data, which means that the projection manifold is data dependent, and second, the weights in the network layers perform different functions. The input-layer weights change the bases by orienting the manifold, while the output-layer weights find the best projection within the manifold. Training will find the set of weights (a_{ij}) that best orient the manifold (first-layer weights) and that determine the best projection (w_{ij}). Therefore the training is more difficult because not only the projection but also the basis is changing. However, we can obtain much more compact representations.

This view should be compared with the description of MLPs for classification in Chapter 3. Each PE in the hidden layer creates a discriminant function with a shape defined by the PE nonlinearity with an orientation and position defined by the first layer weights. Therefore the views agree, but in function approximation the PEs are less prone to saturate. Due to the highly connected topology and the global nature of the elementary functions, good fitting is obtained with reasonably few bases (i.e., few PEs). However, the training is difficult because the basis functions are far from orthogonal.

Multiple-Hidden-Layer MLPs

The multilayer perceptron architecture is not in the general form of the projection theorem previously discussed. As seen in Chapter 3, the MLP implements an embedding of functions, so its approximation properties cannot be directly studied with the projection theorem, except for the case of the one-hidden-layer MLP with linear output PE, as mentioned earlier. For this case we recognize that the output of each hidden PE is producing the elementary functions. When the output PE is a logistic (or tanh) function, these values are nonlinearly combined, so the projection space is no longer a hyperplane in the input space.

Remember also the properties discussed in Chapter 3 that the MLP with two hidden layers is a universal approximator and, even with a single hidden layer, can approximate any continuous function on a compact set. There are many theorems that provide proofs of this property irrespective of the choice of nonlinearity. We can therefore conclude that the essence of the power of the approximation is in the topology, not in the specifics of the nonlinearity. As remarked before, these are existence theorems, so the designer still needs to select the topology to actually create the universal approximation properties for the class of functions of interest.

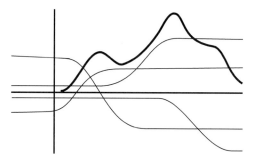

FIGURE 5-7 Function approximation with logistic functions

In terms of function approximation the one-hidden-layer MLP decides the orientation, placement, and relative amplitude of a set of multidimensional sigmoid functions (one per PE). This function decomposition is shown in Figure 5-7 and resembles the approximation obtained with step functions well known in linear systems.

NEUROSOLUTIONS EXAMPLE 5.4

Function approximation with the MLP

From this point on, many of the examples study the function approximation abilities of various networks. We have chosen a fourth-order polynomial as our target function. The polynomial was chosen to give an interesting shape over the input range of 0 to 1 and has the equation $27x^4 - 60x^3 + 39x^2 - 6x$. The graph of the polynomial from 0 to 1 is shown in the figure.

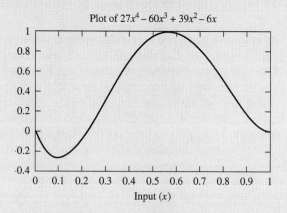

We will use an MLP with a linear output to approximate the preceding function. In this case the MLP approximates the function with tanh bases (the hidden-

> layer PEs are tanh). These elementary functions are stretched and moved over the range and then summed together to approximate the polynomial.

MLPs are universal approximators, as we stated in Chapter 3. The proof is based on an extension of the Weierstrass theorem. But as we stated earlier, another important characteristic to study is how the error decreases with the order or dimension of the problem or both. The importance of MLPs for function approximation was recently reinforced by the work of Barron [1993]. He showed that the asymptotic accuracy of the approximation with MLPs is approximately independent of the dimension of the input space. This is unlike approximation with polynomials, where the error convergence rate is exponentially related to the number of dimensions of the input (the error decreases exponentially with the dimension of the input space). This means that MLPs become much more efficient than polynomials for approximating functions in high-dimensional spaces. The better approximation properties of MLPs explain why MLPs are more efficient than other methodologies for classification and why they are key tools in identification of nonlinear systems, as we will see in Chapters 10 and 11.

Universal Approximation of MLPs

We outline here the proof for the universal mapping characteristics of the MLP. We start by extending the Weierstrass theorem to metric spaces (the Stone-Weierstrass theorem). Polynomials can be extended to metric spaces by defining the concept of an algebra. A family of functions F that map the metric space V to the real line is an algebra if their elements have the properties

$$f_1, f_2 \in F \Rightarrow \alpha f_1 + \beta f_2 \in F \quad \text{and} \quad f_1, f_2 \in F$$

where α and β are real numbers.

The Stone-Weierstrass theorem can be enunciated in the following way. Let V be a metric space and F an algebra that maps V into the reals. If there is a function $f \in F$ for which $f(v_1) \neq f(v_2)$ for $v_1 \neq v_2$ and $f(v) \neq 0$ in V, then F is dense in the mapping of V into the reals. The idea of *dense* is the same as *arbitrarily close approximation*, as stated in the Weierstrass theorem.

This theorem has been used to show the universal mapping capabilities of the MLP. In fact, the function $f(v)$ can be expanded in a special type of "Fourier series" with squashing cosine functions, that is,

$$f(v) = \sum_{i=1}^{N} \alpha_i \cos_t(\beta_i v + b_i)$$

where

$$\cos_t(v) = \begin{cases} 1 & v \geq \pi/2 \\ 0.5[1 + \cos(v + 3\pi/2) & -\pi/2 < v < \pi/2 \\ 0 & v \leq -\pi/2 \end{cases}$$

The nonlinearity of the MLP belongs to this family of squashing functions. Notice that $f(v)$ is exactly the output of the one-hidden-layer MLP with a cosine nonlinearity.

What are the differences between using an MLP for function approximation and for classification? The obvious answer is that for function approximation the output PE is linear, while for classification the output PE must be nonlinear. In fact, we can also use a nonlinear PE for function approximation if we carefully set the dynamic range of the output, so the difference is not solely in the output PE, but also in the nature of the problem. In function approximation the operating point of the hidden PEs is normally far away from saturation, since the mappings tend to be smooth. In classification, where the outputs are 1 and 0, the operating point of the hidden PEs is normally driven to saturation. This is easily observed when we use a square wave as the desired signal, because this choice implements an indicator function.

NEUROSOLUTIONS EXAMPLE 5.5

MLP to approximate a square wave (classification)

In this example we use an MLP with a tanh output to approximate a square wave. Notice that, since a square wave is either on or off, this function approximation problem is identical to a classification problem. Thus classification is a subset of function approximation with the desired signal having on/off characteristics. The important point to show here is that when doing classification, the PEs become saturated and the weights increase greatly. This allows the tanh or logistic function to approximate the on/off characteristics of the desired signal. Thus, for classification, the MLP tends to operate in the saturated regions of the hidden PEs (on/off), while for general function approximation the hidden PEs tend to operate closer to the linear region.

5.3.4 Alternative Basis for Nonlinear Systems: The RBF Network

In neurocomputing, the other popular choice for elementary functions is the *radial basis functions* (RBFs), where $\varphi_i(\mathbf{x})$ becomes

$$\varphi_i(\mathbf{x}) = \gamma(|\mathbf{x} - \mathbf{x}_i|) \tag{5.12}$$

where $\gamma(.)$ is normally a Gaussian function

$$G(x) = \exp\left(-\frac{x^2}{2\sigma^2}\right) \qquad \text{one-dimensional} \qquad (5.13)$$

$$G(x) = \exp\left(-\frac{\mathbf{x}^T\mathbf{\Sigma}^{-1}\mathbf{x}}{2}\right) \qquad \text{multidimensional}$$

with variance σ^2 or covariance $\mathbf{\Sigma} = \sigma^2\mathbf{I}$. Notice that the Gaussian is centered at $\mathbf{x}_i$ with variance σ^2, so its maximum response is concentrated in the neighborhood of the input $\mathbf{x}_i$, falling off exponentially with the square of the distance. The Gaussians are thus an example of local elementary functions. If we plug Eq. 5.13 in Eq. 5.1, we obtain the following implementation for the approximant to the function $f(\mathbf{x})$:

$$\hat{f}(\mathbf{x}, \mathbf{w}) = \sum_i w_i G(|\mathbf{x} - \mathbf{x}_i|) \qquad (5.14)$$

which implements the input-output map of the RBF network.

Let us think of an arbitrary function and a set of localized bell-shaped functions (of the Gaussian shape). Function approximation in a limited area of the input space (see Figure 5-8) requires

- The placement of the localized Gaussians to cover the space
- The control of the width of each Gaussian
- The setting of the amplitude of each Gaussian

If we can accomplish these three tasks, we can approximate arbitrary continuous functions with an RBF network.

The RBF and the MLP achieve the property of universal approximation with different characteristics, since the basis functions are very different. In the RBF the bases are local, so each can be changed without disturbing the approximation of the network in other areas of the space. But we need exponentially more RBFs to cover high-dimensional spaces (the curse of dimensionality). In the MLP this is not the case, as we mentioned in the result by Barron [1993]. As we saw in Chapter 3, changing one MLP weight has the potential to produce drastic changes in the overall input-output

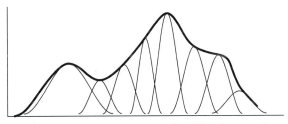

FIGURE 5-8 Approximation by RBFs in one dimension

map. This has advantages in some aspects, such as more efficient use of PEs, but also disadvantages, since the training becomes slower and the adaptation can be caught in local minima.

RBFs train very efficiently once the centers are determined, since the error is linear in the weights. This fact also guarantees the convergence for the global minimum (if the centers are optimally set). This makes RBFs very useful for system identification.

From the theoretical point of view of function approximation, RBFs possess the property of *best approximation* as defined by Chebyshev, unlike the MLP (i.e., there is always an RBF that provides the minimum error for a given function to be approximated).

Approximation Properties of RBF

The formulation of function approximation using the projection theorem (Eq. 5.1) can be directly applied to study the approximation properties of the RBF network. Park and Sandberg [1989] showed that the RBF network is, in fact, a general function approximator. This is an existence theorem, so it is up to the designer to choose the number, localize, and set the variance and the weighting of Gaussians to achieve an error as small as required.

Again using the Stone-Weierstrass theorem, they showed that the RBFs were dense in the mapping from a metric space V to the real number line. This is not difficult because the RBFs create an algebra, and they do not vanish in V.

NEUROSOLUTIONS EXAMPLE 5.6

Function approximation with RBFs

Now we solve the same polynomial approximation problem with a radial basis function network. We can vary the number of RBFs and see how this affects the power of the network to approximate the given polynomial.

Gaussian Axon

5.4 PROBABILISTIC INTERPRETATION OF THE MAPPINGS: NONLINEAR REGRESSION

So far we have assumed a deterministic framework to study the input-output mapping. It enhances our understanding to look now at the mappings discovered by MLPs and

RBFs from a statistical perspective. The result presented next is valid as long as the mean square error (MSE) criterion is utilized in the training.

We assume that the input data is a random variable x, and the desired response t is also a random variable, not necessarily Gaussian distributed. The topology is an MLP or an RBF with a linear output PE, as we have been discussing. The important result is the following: A network with weights obtained by minimizing the MSE has an output that approximates the conditional average of the desired response data t_k, that is, the regression of t conditioned on x:

$$y_k(x, w^*) = \langle\langle t_k | x \rangle\rangle \tag{5.15}$$

where w^* means the optimal weights, and $\langle\langle . \rangle\rangle$ refers to the conditional average defined by

$$\langle\langle t_k | x \rangle\rangle = \int t_k p(t_k | x) dt_k \tag{5.16}$$

This result was demonstrated in Section 3.8. The MLP and RBF networks are thus nonlinear regressors, extending the Adaline for cases where the input-output map is nonlinear. They will be able to "discover" any deterministic input-output relationship corrupted by additive zero-mean noise, since the network output will approximate the average of the desired response. The only requirements are that the network has converged to the global minimum, that the number of degrees of freedom in the network topology is large enough, and that there is enough data to train the system. These are nontrivial issues, but we have learned ways to cope with them in Chapters 3 and 4.

NEUROSOLUTIONS EXAMPLE 5.7

Nonlinear regressors

We illustrate this important point by creating a nonlinear mapping problem corrupted by additive noise. We again use the polynomial approximation case and add noise to the desired signal. Since the network output can be thought of as the average of d with respect to the distribution $p(d | x_i)$ at a given point x_i of the domain, the network should clean the noise and produce the polynomial. This clearly shows that the MLP is doing regression but now with nonlinear mappings. You can also use the RBF to produce the same result, since this behavior is derived from the use of the MSE criterion and is independent of the topology.

5.5 TRAINING NEURAL NETWORKS FOR FUNCTION APPROXIMATION

5.5.1 Training MLPs for Function Approximation

An important problem that needs to be solved in applying neural networks for function approximation is a procedure to automatically find the coefficients from the data. Notice that the backpropagation algorithm studied in Chapter 3 solves this problem. In fact, straight backpropagation minimizes the error power between the desired response and the system output (the L_2 norm). The backpropagation algorithm is independent of the fact that in function approximation the network has a linear output and the formulation uses the absolute value of the error instead of the error power. In fact, we saw how to integrate backpropagation with arbitrary norms in Chapter 4, so we can also solve Eq. 5.2.

L_1 versus L_2

There are minor differences between the two norms that have been used in function approximation. Equation 5.2 uses the absolute value of the error, which is commonly called *uniform approximation*. Strictly speaking, the L_1 norm should be used for function approximation. However, the L_2 norm, which minimizes the error power, not the absolute value of the error, is much easier to apply (in linear systems) and also produces an important interpretation of the results (nonlinear regression), as we saw in the probabilistic interpretation of the mappings. In practical situations either norm can be used.

NEUROSOLUTIONS EXAMPLE 5.8
MLPs for function approximation with L_1 norm

We again show the MLP network approximating the function of Example 5.4, except that this time the L_1 criterion is used. In theory, this should produce a better fit (uniform approximation) to the data but may train more slowly.

5.5.2 Adapting the Centers and Variances of Gaussians in RBFs

Backpropagation can be applied to arbitrary topologies made up of smooth nonlinearities, so it can also train the newly introduced RBFs. However, there are other procedures to adapt RBF networks that are worth describing. One simple (but sometimes wasteful) approach to assigning the Gaussians is simply to uniformly distribute their centers in the input space. This was the method used in Example 5.3. Although this may be a reasonable idea for approximation of complicated functions that cover the full input space, it is not recommended in cases where the data is clustered in certain areas of the input space. There are basically two ways to select the positioning and width of the Gaussians in RBFs: the supervised method and self-organization.

The supervised method is a simple extension of the backpropagation idea for the RBF network. In fact, the Gaussian is a differentiable function, so errors can be back-propagated through it to adapt μ and σ in the same way as done for tanh or sigmoid nonlinearities. The backpropagation algorithm can theoretically be used to *simultaneously* adapt the centers, the variance, and the weights of RBF networks. The problem is that the method may provide suboptimal solutions due to local minima (the optimization is nonlinear for the centers and variances).

Local Minima for Gaussian Adaptation

After Chapters 3 and 4 we should be able to understand the difficulty of using backpropagation to adapt the centers and variances of the Gaussians. With this method the centers (and variances) are moved in the input space by virtue of the gradient. However, with the RBF, both the local activity and the local error are attenuated by the shape of the Gaussian kernel, while in the MLP only the error was attenuated by the derivative of the sigmoid. The net effect is that training becomes very slow, and the chances of getting stuck in local minima are large. Another problem is that during adaptation the variances of the Gaussians can become very broad and the RBF loses its local nature.

The self-organizing idea is very different. It divides the training phase into the independent adaptation of the first layer weights (i.e., the location and width of the Gaussians), followed by a second step that only adapts the output weights in a supervised mode, keeping the first layer frozen. The idea is appealing because it treats the adaptation of the centers and variances as a resource-allocation step that does not require external labels. This means that only the input data is required in this step. Since training the hidden layer with gradient methods is time-consuming, the self-organizing method is more efficient.

The clusters of the data samples in the input space should work as attractors for the Gaussian centers. If there is data in an area of the space, the system needs to allocate resources to represent the data cluster. The variances can also be estimated to cover the input data distribution, given the number of Gaussians available. This reasoning means that there is no need for supervised learning at this stage. The shortcoming is that a good coverage of the input data distribution does not necessarily imply good results.

Once the centers and variances are determined, the simple LMS algorithm presented in Chapter 1 (or the analytic method of the least squares) can be used to adapt the output weights, since the adaptation problem is linear in the weights. Let us describe the algorithms that adapt the centers of the Gaussians and their variances.

Gaussian Centers   The goal is to center the Gaussians on data clusters. There are many well-known algorithms to accomplish this task (see Haykin [1994]). Here we address only the K-means and their on-line implementation, the competitive learning algorithm. In K-means the goal is to divide the N input samples into K clusters, minimizing the final variance. The clusters are defined by their centers c_i. First a random data assignment is made, and then the goal is to partition the data in sets S_i to minimize the Euclidean distance between the data partition N_i and the cluster centers c_i:

$$J = \sum_{i=1}^{K} \sum_{n \in S_i} |x_n - c_i| \tag{5.17}$$

where the data centers c_i are defined by

$$c_i = \frac{1}{N_i} \sum_{n \in S_i} x_n \tag{5.18}$$

K-means clustering requires a batch operation where the samples are moved from cluster to cluster to minimize Eq. 5.17. An on-line version of this algorithm starts by asking which center is closest to the current pattern x_n. The center that is closest, denoted by c_j^*, wins the competition, and it is simply moved incrementally toward the present pattern x_n:

$$\Delta c_j^* = \eta(x_n - c_j^*) \tag{5.19}$$

where η is a step size parameter. We recommend that an annealing schedule be incorporated in the step size. The c^* are the weights of the layer preceding the RBFs. This method is fully described in Chapter 7.

Variance Computation   To set the variance, the distances to the neighboring centers have to be estimated. The idea is to set the variance of the Gaussian to be a fraction (for example, approximately $\frac{1}{4}$) of the distance among clusters. This ensures adequate coverage of the input space between the clusters. The simplest procedure is to estimate the distance to the closest cluster,

$$\sigma_i^2 = \| w_{ij} - w_{kj} \|^2 \tag{5.20}$$

where the w_{kj} represent the weights of the kth PE that is closest to the ith PE. In general, the distances to more neighbors (P) provides a more reliable estimate in high-dimensional spaces, so the expression becomes

$$\sigma_i^2 = \frac{1}{P} \sum_{k=1}^{P} \| w_{ij} - w_{kj} \|^2 \tag{5.21}$$

where the P nearest neighbors to the ith PE are chosen.

NEUROSOLUTIONS EXAMPLE 5.9

Training RBFs for classification

In this example we train an RBF network using the competitive learning approach. We use a new Synapse called the Competitive Synapse, which clusters the centers of the RBFs where most of the data resides. Notice that the Gaussian Axon will appear "cracked," meaning that the data flow is interrupted. This is implemented in the simulator because there is no point in adapting the top-layer weights until the centers are properly placed over the input data.

Competitive (Conscience Full) Synapse

5.6 HOW TO SELECT THE NUMBER OF BASES

The selection of the number of bases is rather important. If too few bases are used, the approximation suffers throughout the domain. At first you might think that for better approximation more and more bases are needed, but in fact this is not so. In particular, if the bases are orthogonal, more bases mean that the network has the potential to represent a larger and larger space. If the data does not fill the input space but is corrupted by white noise (white noise always fills the available space), the network starts to represent the noise also, which is wasteful and provides suboptimal results. Let us illustrate this with NeuroSolutions.

NEUROSOLUTIONS EXAMPLE 5.10

Overfitting

This example demonstrates that when the data is noisy, too many bases distort the underlying noiseless input-output relationship. We use an RBF to approximate the polynomial, but instead of doing it without noise as before, we are going to add random noise to the desired signal. We then change the number of bases and the width of the Gaussians. We see that for larger networks, the noise begins to contaminate the discovered function. We also see that if the network doesn't have enough degrees of freedom, the approximation is inadequate and oversimplified.

Experience shows that the problem is not just one of the pure size of the network, but the values of the coefficients are also very important. Learning therefore complicates the matter of selecting the number of bases. Effectively, this is the same problem that was encountered in selecting the size of the MLP for classification. Here we revisit the problem, presenting a statistical view and then offering two approaches to deal with it: penalizing the training error and using regularization. Although this problem was briefly treated in Chapter 4, here we provide a more precise view of the problem and relate the findings to the previous techniques.

5.6.1 The Bias–Variance Dilemma

The optimal size of a learning machine can be framed as a compromise between the bias and variance of a model. We will address this view fully in the next section, so here we will motivate the arguments with a simple analogy. Let us use polynomial curve fitting to exemplify the problem faced by the learning machine. A polynomial of order N can exactly pass through $N + 1$ points, so when a polynomial fits a set of points (*fiducial points*) two things can happen. If the polynomial degree is smaller than the number of points, the fitting may have errors (*model bias*) because there are not enough degrees of freedom to pass the polynomial through every point (left panel of Figure 5-9). For example, the linear regressor, which is a first-order polynomial, produces errors at nearly every point of a quadratic curve (second-order polynomial). At the other extreme, if the order of the polynomial is higher than the number of fiducial points, the polynomial can pass exactly through every point. The problem is that for the other points in the domain the polynomial was not constrained, and thus its values can oscillate widely between the fiducial points (*model variance*), as illustrated in the right panel of Figure 5-9. The best solution is to find an intermediate polynomial order that will provide low bias and low variance across the domain.

This simple example provides a conceptual framework for the problem of generalization encountered in learning machines.

- The fiducial points are the training samples.
- The full domain represents all the possible test data that the learning machine will encounter.
- The polynomial becomes the input-output functional map created by the learning machine.
- The learning machine weights are equivalent to the coefficients of the polynomial.
- The size of the polynomial is the number of weights.

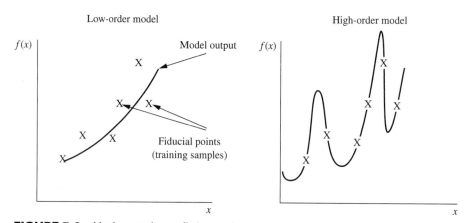

FIGURE 5-9 Under- and overfitting polynomials to a set of points

Therefore we can see that for a good fit over the entire domain, both the size of the network and the amount of training data are relevant.

The model bias is the error across the full data set, which can be approximated by the error in the training set. Given a set of training samples, the learning machine will try to approximate them to minimize the training-set classification error. If the complexity of the machine is low (few parameters), the error in the training set is high, and performance in the test set will also suffer, meaning that the separation surfaces have not been properly placed (Figure 5-9, left). If the machine complexity is increased, the training-set error will decrease, showing a smaller model bias.

Too large a model produces an exact fit to the training set samples (*memorization* of the training samples) but may also produce large errors in the test set. The source of this test-set error for larger machines (Figure 5-9, right) differs from the small-machine case. It is produced by the model variance, that is, using parameters fine-tuned for a specific subset of samples (training samples) that do not generalize to a different set of samples. This is the reason that the committees, which basically reduce the variance through weighted averaging, improve the test-set performance.

The difference in performance between the training and the test set is a practical measure of the model variance. We can always expect that the error in the test set will be larger than in the training set. However, a large performance difference between the training and test sets should be a red flag indicating that learning or model selection, or both, was not successful.

This argument means that the goal of learning should not be a zero error in the training set. It also clearly indicates that information from both the training and test sets must be used to set a compromise between model bias and variance appropriately. This is why we presented cross-validation in Chapter 4 as the best way to stop the training of a learning machine, since cross-validation brings the information from the unseen samples to stop training at the point where the best generalization occurs.

5.6.2 The Bias–Variance Dilemma Treated Mathematically

The problem of generalization can be studied using a statistical framework by interpreting the network as a regressor and decomposing the output error into its bias and variance.

A measure of how close the output is to the desired response is given by

$$(y - d)^2 \tag{5.22}$$

But note that this error depends on the data set utilized. To remove this dependence, we average over the training set to yield

$$E_{TS}[(y - d)^2] \tag{5.23}$$

where E_{TS} indicates the expected value (mean) over the training set. Now rewrite the expression inside the square brackets of Eq. 5.23 as

$$(y - d)^2 = [y - E_{TS}(y) + E_{TS}(y) - d]^2 \tag{5.24}$$

When we compute the expected value we obtain

$$E_{TS}[(y - d)^2] = \underbrace{E_{TS}[E_{TS}(y) - d]^2}_{\text{bias}^2} + \underbrace{E_{TS}\{[y - E_{TS}(y)]^2\}}_{\text{variance}} \tag{5.25}$$

The first term is the square of the bias of the model because it measures how much, on average, the output differs from the desired response. The second term is the variance because it measures how much each particular output y differs from its mean across the training sets.

Now let us assume that we add noise to the desired response, that is,

$$d = f + \varepsilon \tag{5.26}$$

where f is the true input-output map and ε is the noise. One extreme is the case where the model is so small that the output is not dependent at all on the variability of the data (no free parameters, just an a priori chosen function g). The model bias may therefore be large (if the function g we picked is not the true function f), but the model variance is zero, since y is the same across all training sets.

The other extreme is a model with so many parameters that it passes by every training data point exactly. In this case, the first term of Eq. 5.25, which measures the model bias, is zero, but the second term, which measures the model variance, is the power of the noise ε. A good-sized model is one where both the model bias and variance are small. This view, however, does not tell us how to select the size of the model, but it illustrates the issues.

5.6.3 Penalizing the Training Error

The problem is to find a general criterion to determine the model order for the problem under consideration. Generalization can also be formulated in this way. Many theories have addressed this issue. One that we would like to mention is Rissanen's [1989] minimum description length (MDL) criterion, because it is central to extracting models from data (or composing complex functions from simpler ones).

The previous explanation shows that we cannot look only at the fitting error as the criterion of optimality. We have to counterbalance it with the number of degrees of freedom of the model. Rissanen presented this idea very intuitively in terms of code lengths.

Our data can be thought of as having an intrinsic code length in the following way: We may try to describe the data using a *code* we define. The data set thus requires a certain number of bits to be described (Figure 5-10). If the data is random noise, every sample needs to be used to describe the data, and the code length is the same as the data length. But the data may have been created by a linear system, for which two numbers (slope and bias) are sufficient to describe all the samples.

When we model the data, we are effectively describing it in a different way: by the topology and parameters of our model and also by the fitting error. If we add the

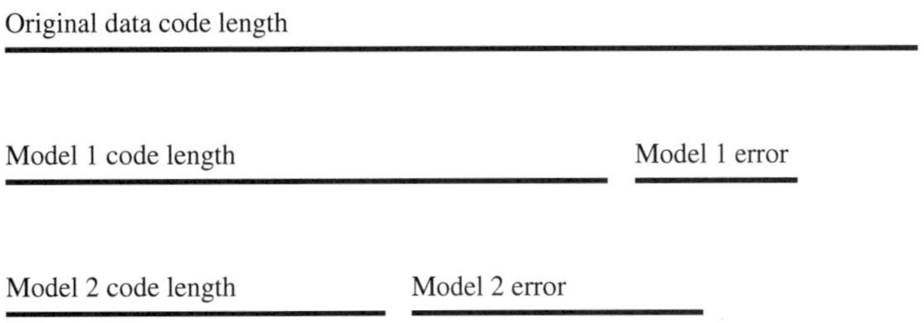

Original data code length

Model 1 code length   Model 1 error

Model 2 code length   Model 2 error

FIGURE 5-10   Code lengths of data and several models

error length to the model code length, we again describe the original data exactly. Consider that we have to assign bits to codify the error, $C(E_i)$, and also to represent the parameters of our model, $C(M_i)$. Thus the description of the data using a particular model i is

$$C(M_i, E_i) = C(M_i) + C(E_i)$$

The most efficient description of the data set is the one that minimizes the overall code length, that is, the total number of bits to represent both the error and the model parameters (Figure 5-10),

$$\min_i C(M_i, E_i)$$

Notice that this is a very interesting idea because it couples the complexity (size) of the machine with the size of the fitting error. If we use a small number of parameters, the error will be larger, and we use many bits to represent the error. On the other hand, if we use too large a machine, we use too many bits to describe the machine, although only a few are needed to represent the error. The best compromise in terms of code length lies in the middle of smaller machines and manageable errors.

MDL and Bayesian Theory

There are some technical details in implementing this idea of measuring models and errors by code lengths, but they have been worked out in information theory. See Rissanen [1989]. Another interesting concept is to look at model selection from the point of view of Bayes' theory. The probability of a model M given the data D can be computed using Bayes' rule:

$$P(M_i \mid D) = \frac{P(D \mid M_i)P(M_i)}{P(D)}$$

We can ignore $P(D)$, since it is common to all the models, so the most probable model maximizes the numerator. We know that the maximization is not affected if we take the log (since the log is a monotonic function), that is,

$$\max_i[\log(P(D \mid M_i)) + \log(P(M_i))]$$

This expression is very similar to the result obtained using Rissanen's MDL principle. In fact, we can interpret Rissanen's description length as the sum of the error and the complexity of the model. The minimum amount of information required to transmit a message x is given by $-\ln p(x)$. If $p(x)$ is the correct distribution for the message x (our model), it will correspond to the smallest message length for a given error. The error in turn can be interpreted as the conditional probability of the data given the model. We can therefore say that the description length can be expressed as

$$MDL = -\log(p(D \mid M)) - \log(p(M))$$

Since maximization is equivalent to the minimization of the negative functional, we get the minimal code lengths for the data and the model. See Zemel [1993] for a complete treatment.

Possibly the simplest implementation of this idea is to penalize the mean square error obtained in the training by including a term that increases with the size of the model, as was first proposed by Akaike [1974]. Akaike's information criterion (AIC) reads

$$\min_k AIC(k) = N \ln J(k) + 2k \qquad (5.27)$$

where $J(k)$ is the MSE in the training set, k is the number of free parameters of the model, and N is the number of data samples. AIC has been used extensively in model-based spectral analysis [Kay 1988]. This expression shows that even if the error decreases with the size of the model k, there is a linear penalty with k, so the minimum value is obtained at some intermediate value of model order k (Figure 5-11).

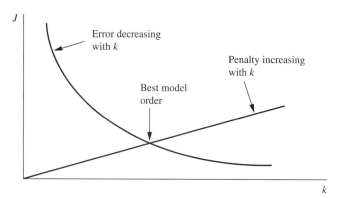

FIGURE 5-11 Best model order according to Akaike's criterion

Notice that in Akaike's criterion the penalty is independent of the number of samples of the training data. According to Rissanen's MDL criterion, a larger penalty for larger data sets can be obtained by substituting $2k$ with $k/2 \ln(N)$, yielding

$$\min_k \text{MDL}(k) = N \ln J(k) + \frac{k}{2} \ln(N) \qquad (5.28)$$

The appeal of these equations is that they allow us to use all the available data for training (unlike cross-validation) and can be easily computed for practical applications since they require only the mean square error in the training set for a collection of models of different sizes k. Akaike's method works well for one-layer systems (particularly linear ones). However, it becomes less accurate for multilayer networks, since the size of the model is not uniquely related to the number of weights.

It is also important to relate this method to the early stopping criterion that we established in Chapter 4 using cross-validation. Remember that we stopped training based on the performance in the validation set. The early stopping criterion directly measures some type of distance between the model and the data. We can choose the best model by utilizing different model sizes k and picking the one that provides the minimum error in the cross-validation set, that is

$$\min_k J_{val}(k) \qquad (5.29)$$

It has been shown that this use of cross-validation is *asymptotically equivalent* to Akaike's criterion. In neural networks these equations have to be interpreted in an approximate sense, particularly for multilayer architectures. In fact, the role of the PEs and their weights is very different, so it is not enough to naively count the number of free parameters. The principle of structural risk minimization and the V-C dimension is a more rigorous way to select the best-sized model. We will address it shortly.

NEUROSOLUTIONS EXAMPLE 5.11

Akaike's criterion for RBFs

This example demonstrates Akaike's criterion for selecting the number of PEs in the RBF network. We have added a few DLLs to the breadboard, one of which computes Akaike's criterion. The others change the widths and centers of the RBFs to automatically span the input range [0, 1] based on the number of hidden PEs. Thus you can change the number of RBFs and run the network to see what the final Akaike's criterion value will be. Akaike's criterion normally provides a good estimate of the "best" number of centers in RBF networks.

5.6.4 Regularization

Regularization theory was proposed by Tikhonov and Arsenin [1977] to deal with *ill-posed problems*. As an example, the equation $\mathbf{xA} = \mathbf{y}$ is said to be ill conditioned when a slight modification $\Delta \mathbf{y}$ due to noise in the dependent variable $\mathbf{y}$ produces an enormous change in the solution for $\mathbf{x}$. One way to solve this type of problem is to minimize the residue:

$$R(\mathbf{x}) = \left| \mathbf{A}\mathbf{x} - (\mathbf{y} + \Delta \mathbf{y}) \right|^2 \tag{5.30}$$

Tikhonov proposed to stabilize the solutions to such problems by adding a regularizing function $\Gamma(\mathbf{x})$ to the solution:

$$R(\mathbf{x}) = \left| \mathbf{A}\mathbf{x} - (\mathbf{y} + \Delta \mathbf{y}) \right|^2 + \lambda \Gamma(\mathbf{x}) \tag{5.31}$$

and was able to show that when $\Delta \mathbf{y}$ approaches zero, the solution approaches the true value $\mathbf{A}^{-1}\mathbf{y}$. λ is a small constant called the *regularization constant*, and the regularizing function is a nonnegative function that includes a priori information to help the solution. Normally these regularizers impose smooth constraints; that is, they impose limits on the variability of the solution.

When we deal with the determination of the complexity of a learning machine with information restricted to the training set, the problem is ill posed because we do not have access to the performance in the test set. The basic idea of regularization theory is to add an extra term to the cost function so that the optimization problem becomes more constrained, that is,

$$J_{\text{new}} = J_c + \lambda J_r \tag{5.32}$$

where J_c is the cost function, J_r is the regularizer, and λ is a parameter that weights the influence of the regularizer versus the cost. Tikhonov regularizers penalize the curvature of the original solution; that is, they seek smoother solutions to the optimization problem. If we recall the training algorithms, we should choose regularizers for which derivatives with respect to the weights are efficiently computed. One such regularizer is

$$J_r = \sum_n \left(\frac{\partial^2 y_n}{\partial x_n^2} \right)^2 \tag{5.33}$$

which penalizes large values of the second derivative of the input-output mapping. There is evidence that even a first-order penalty works in practice. The value of λ must be experimentally selected.

Regularization is closely related to optimal brain damage (which uses the Hessian to compute saliencies) and to the weight-decay ideas to eliminate weights. In fact, weight decay (Eq. 4.16) is equivalent to a regularization term that is a function of the L_2 norm of the weights (Gaussian prior), that is,

$$J_{\text{new}} = J_c + \lambda \sum_i w_i^2 \tag{5.34}$$

The square in Eq. 5.34 can be substituted by the absolute value to obtain an L_1 norm of the weight, yielding Eq. 4.19 (Laplacian prior).

It is interesting to compare Eq. 5.34 with Eq. 5.27. Both effectively create a new cost function that penalizes large models. However, the principles used to derive both expressions are very different. This analogy suggests that the determination of the regularization constant λ is critical to find the best possible model order. Too large a value for λ will choose networks that are smaller than the optimum, while too small a λ will yield networks that are too large. Moreover, we can relate these choices to the bias and variance of the model. We can expect that a large λ will produce smooth models (too large a bias), while a small λ will produce models with large variance. The best value of the regularization constant can be computed from statistical arguments [Wahba 1990]. Let us experimentally verify these statements.

NEUROSOLUTIONS EXAMPLE 5.12

Weight decay to prune RBFs

The weight-decay DLL that we introduced in Chapter 4 can be used to implement the regularization discussed above. We use the same RBF breadboard and set the number of hidden PEs to 20. Then, using weight decay on the output synapse, we can dynamically "turn off" unnecessary PEs by driving their output weights to zero. By adjusting the decay parameter of the weight-decay algorithm, we can produce smoother or more exact outputs from the network.

5.7 APPLICATIONS OF RADIAL BASIS FUNCTIONS

5.7.1 Radial Basis Functions for Classification

Let us interpret Eqs. 5.1 and 5.2, for a classification problem. In classification $f(\mathbf{x})$ becomes the indicator function $\{-1 \text{ (or 0), } 1\}$. What these equations say is that one can construct an arbitrary discriminant function in the input space by constructing linear discriminant functions in an auxiliary space (the space of the elementary functions) of large dimension that is nonlinearly related [by $\varphi(\mathbf{x})$] to the input space x. This is a counterintuitive result that was first proved by Cover (Cover theorem) and is associated with the fact that in sufficiently high-dimensional spaces, data is always sparse. If the data clusters are always far apart, it is always possible to use hyperplanes to separate them. The problem is that we need to determine many parameters.

Radial-basis-function networks implement this idea directly by using Gaussian functions to project the input space to an intermediary space where the classification is done with a hyperplane implemented as the weighted sum of the Gaussian PE outputs. This result can be understood if we focus on the output of each Gaussian. No matter how intertwined the classes are, if the centers of the Gaussians and their radius (the variance) are properly controlled, each Gaussian can always be made to respond to a single class. The obvious limit is to assign a Gaussian to each sample, but generally this is not necessary.

We can assign a Gaussian to each subcluster of the classes. The classification is then made by linearly combining the responses of each of the Gaussians so that it is +1 for one class and −1 (or 0) for the other. From this discussion, you see that there are two fundamental steps in designing RBFs for classification: The first is the placement and the radius selection for each Gaussian, and the second is the weighting of the individual Gaussian responses to obtain the desired classification. It would also be convenient to have Gaussians with a different radius in each direction. This extends the contours of the Gaussians from circles to ellipses.

NEUROSOLUTIONS EXAMPLE 5.13

MLPs and RBFs for classification

This example uses RBFs to do classification. We repeat the problem from Chapter 1 of classifying various people as male or female based on their height and weight data. Remember that we cannot achieve perfect classification. For reference, we have included a link to the MLP example that solves this problem.

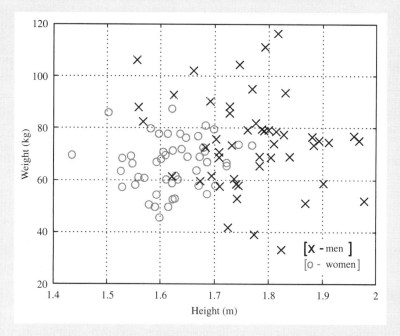

Run the RBF network and see that the classifier performs at the same level but the discriminant functions are different (here they are more curved). You should change the number of RBF PEs and see how the discriminant plot and confusion matrix are affected.

5.7.2 Radial Basis Functions as Regularizers

Radial basis functions can be derived mathematically from the theory of Tikhonov regularizers [Poggio and Girosi 1990]. Interestingly, when the solution of Eq. 5.32 is carried out using the calculus of variations, radial basis functions appear as the natural solution for regularization (for rotationally and translation-invariant kernels). This means that instead of using the data collected from the outside world directly, there are advantages in first fitting one radial basis function to each data point and working with their outputs. In a sense, the RBFs are interpolating the collected data, but the method is too cumbersome for large data sets (and the variances must be experimentally determined).

5.7.3 Radial Basis Functions as Regressors: The Probabilistic Neural Network

We can also utilize radial basis functions to estimate a regression function from noisy data following the ideas of kernel regression. In kernel regression we seek to estimate the probability density function $p(x, d)$ of the input–desired pairs (x_i, d_i) using the Parzen [1962] window method (which is a nonparametric method). It can be shown that the regression of the target data yields

$$y(x) = \frac{\sum_i d_i \exp\{-\|x - x_i\|^2 / (2\sigma^2)\}}{\sum_i \exp\{-\|x - x_i\|^2 / (2\sigma^2)\}} \tag{5.35}$$

where σ is the width of the Gaussian and has to be experimentally determined. Basically, the method places a Gaussian at each sample multiplied by the desired response d_i and normalized by the response in the input space. This network is called the *probabilistic neural network* and can be easily implemented using RBF networks.

Parzen Window Method

The Parzen window method is a nonparametric density-estimation method widely used in statistics. It is related to learning because it provides a way to estimate the pdf of the data, and it can be applied to a wide range of functions.

In the Parzen window method we start by choosing a symmetric, normalized area and unimodal kernel function

$$K(x, x_i, \beta) = \frac{1}{\beta^n} K\left(\frac{x - x_i}{\beta}\right)$$

and construct the pdf estimator

$$p(x) = \frac{1}{M} \sum_{i=1}^{M} K(x, x_i, \beta)$$

Commonly used kernels are the Gaussian, the rectangular, and the spectral windows (Tukey, Hanning, Hamming). The Parzen estimator is consistent, and its asymptotic rate of convergence is optimal for smooth densities, but it requires a large number of samples to provide good results.

RBF as Kernel Regression

For RBF kernel regression the windows are symmetric multidimensional Gaussian functions (as utilized in RBF networks) that quantify the joint data distribution in the input–desired signal space, given by

$$p(x, t) = \frac{1}{N} \sum_{i=1}^{N} \frac{1}{(2\pi\sigma^2)^{t+c/2}} \exp\left(-\frac{\|x - x_i\|}{2\sigma^2} - \frac{\|t - t_i\|}{2\sigma^2}\right)$$

As we discussed in Section 5.3.4, regression can be thought of as estimating the conditional average of the target data t_i conditional to the input x_i, $\langle\langle t_i | x_i \rangle\rangle$. When the MSE is used, the output of the network approaches this value. The conditional average can be written as a function of the pdf

$$y(x) = \langle\langle t | x \rangle\rangle = \frac{\int t p(x, t) dt}{\int p(x, t) dt}$$

This yields Eq. 5.35 in the text. In general, we can use fewer Gaussians, as done in the RBF network, yielding

$$y(x) = \frac{\sum_i P(i)\theta_i \exp\left(-\frac{\|x - \mu_i\|^2}{2\sigma^2}\right)}{\sum_i P(i) \exp\left(-\frac{\|x - \mu_i\|^2}{2\sigma^2}\right)}$$

where θ are the centers of the Gaussians in the desired signal space.

NEUROSOLUTIONS EXAMPLE 5.14

Density estimation with RBFs

In this example we train a normalized radial-basis-function network according to Eq. 5.35 to show how the network handles probability density function approximation. We have a few samples in the input space that belong to two classes, and we train a probabilistic neural network to solve the problem. We select the number of RBFs to equal the number of samples. During training, notice that the RBF centers converge to the input data and that the output of the net provides the conditional average of the target data conditioned on each input. Change the variance of the RBFs to see how they affect the estimates for the targets as given by the output weights.

5.8   SUPPORT VECTOR MACHINES

Support vector machines (SVMs) are a radically different type of classifier that have attracted a great deal of attention lately due to the novelty of the concepts that they bring to pattern recognition, their strong mathematical foundation, and their excellent results in practical problems. In Chapters 2 and 3 we covered two of the motivating concepts behind SVMs, namely, the idea that transforming the data into a high-dimensional space makes linear discriminant functions practical and the idea of large margin classifiers to train the perceptron. Here we will couple these two concepts and create the support vector machine. We refer to Vapnik's books [1995,1998] for a full treatment.

Let us go back to the concept of kernel machines. We saw in Chapter 2 that the advantage of a kernel machine is that its capacity (number of degrees of freedom) is decoupled from the size of the input space. By mapping the input to a sufficiently large feature space, patterns become linearly separable, so a simple perceptron in feature space can do the classification. In this chapter we have discussed the RBF network, which can be considered a kernel classifier. In fact, the RBF places Gaussian kernels over the data and linearly weights their outputs to create the system output. It conforms exactly with the notion of the kernel machine presented in Chapter 2, Figure 2-12. When used as an SVM, the RBF network places a Gaussian at each data sample such that the feature space becomes as large as the number of samples.

But an SVM is much more than an RBF. To train an RBF network as an SVM, we will use the idea of large margin classifiers discussed in Chapter 3. There we presented the Adatron algorithm, which works only with perceptrons. Training an RBF for large margins will decouple the capacity of the classifier from the input space and at the same time provide good generalization. We cannot get better than this on our road to powerful classifiers. We extend the Adatron algorithm here in two ways: We apply it to kernel-based classifiers such as RBFs, and we modify the training for nonlinearly separable patterns.

5.8.1 Extension of the Adatron to Kernel Machines

Recall that the Adatron algorithm was able to adapt the perceptron to maximize its margin. The idea was to work with data-dependent representations, which lead to a very simple on-line algorithm to adapt the multipliers.

We will write the discriminant function of the RBF in terms of the data-dependent representation:

$$g(x) = \sum_{k=1}^{L} w_k G_k(x, \sigma^2) + b = \left\langle \sum_{i=0}^{N} \alpha_i G(x, \sigma^2) \cdot G(x_i, \sigma^2) \right\rangle + b = \sum_{i=0}^{N} \alpha_i G(x - x_i, 2\sigma^2) + b$$

$$(5.36)$$

where $G(x, \sigma^2)$ represents a Gaussian function, L is the number of PEs in the RBF, w_k are the weights, N is the number of samples, α_i are a set of multipliers (one for each sample), and we consider the input space augmented by one dimension with a constant value of 1 to provide the bias. Notice that for the special case of a Gaussian kernel the inner product of Gaussians is still a Gaussian. The kernel function (the Gaussian) first projects the inputs (x, x_i) onto a high-dimensional space and then computes an inner product there. The amazing thing is that the Gaussian kernel avoids the explicit computation of the pattern projections into the high-dimensional space, as shown in Eq. 5.36 (the inner product of Gaussians is still a Gaussian). Any other symmetric function that obeys the Mercer condition has the same properties. This topology is depicted in Figure 5-12, where we can easily see that it is an RBF, but where each Gaussian is centered at each sample and the weights are the multipliers α_i.

The Adatron algorithm can be easily extended to the RBF network by substituting the inner product of patterns in the input space by the kernel function, leading to the following quadratic optimization problem:

$$J(\alpha) = \sum_{i=1}^{N} \alpha_i - \frac{1}{2} \sum_{i=1}^{N} \sum_{j=1}^{N} \alpha_i \alpha_j d_i d_j G(x_i - x_j, 2\sigma^2)$$

$$\text{subject to } \sum_{i=1}^{N} d_i \alpha_i = 0 \qquad \alpha_i \geq 0, \forall i \in \{1, \ldots, N\}$$

(5.37)

Following the same procedure as in Chapter 3, we define

$$g(x_i) = d_i \left[\sum_{j=1}^{N} d_j \alpha_j G(x_i - x_j, 2\sigma^2) + b \right] \qquad \text{and} \qquad M = \min_i g(x_i)$$

and choose a common starting multiplier (e.g., $\alpha_i = 0.1$), learning rate η, and small threshold (e.g., $t = 0.01$). Then, while $M > t$, we choose a pattern x_i and calculate an update $\Delta\alpha_i = \eta[1 - g(x_i)]$ and perform the update

$$\begin{cases} \alpha_i(n+1) = \alpha_i(n) + \Delta\alpha_i, & b(n+1) = b(n) + d_i\Delta\alpha_i & \text{if } \alpha_i(n) + \Delta\alpha_i > 0 \\ \alpha_i(n+1) = \alpha_i(n), & b(n+1) = b(n) & \text{if } \alpha_i(n) + \Delta\alpha_i \leq 0 \end{cases}$$

After adaptation only some of the α_i are different from zero (called the support vectors). They correspond to the samples that are closest to the boundary between classes. This algorithm is called the *kernel Adatron* and can adapt an RBF to have an optimal margin. This algorithm can be considered the "on-line" version of the quadratic optimization approach utilized for SVMs, and it can find the same solutions as Vapnik's original algorithm for SVMs [Freiss 1998]. Notice that it is easy to implement the kernel Adatron algorithm since $g(x_i)$ can be computed locally to each multiplier, provided that the desired response is available in the input file. In fact, the expression for $g(x_i)$ resembles the multiplication of an error with an activation, so it can be included in the framework of neural network learning. The Adatron algorithm essentially prunes the RBF network of Figure 5-12 so that its output for testing is given by

$$f(x) = \text{sgn}\left(\sum_{i \in \text{support vectors}} d_i \alpha_i G(x - x_i, 2\sigma^2) - b \right)$$

Center at x_1

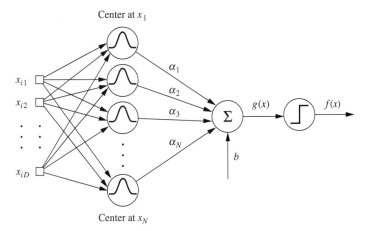

FIGURE 5-12 Topology of the SVM machine with RBF kernels

NEUROSOLUTIONS EXAMPLE 5.15

The kernel Adatron and the spiral problem

In this example we compare the performance of the kernel Adatron to the MLP on the spiral problem. The goal of the spiral problem is to separate the two-dimensional input into two classes, when the inputs correspond to points in the space that spiral inward toward the center as shown below.

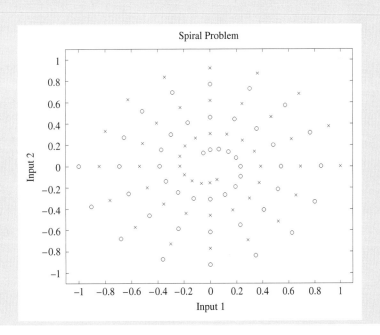

Since the two classes are intertwined, this is a very difficult problem. Imagine trying to correctly place the discriminant lines of an MLP to create the correct decision surface. The MLP does very poorly on this task, although there are special training rules in the literature that perform much better than gradient descent on this particular problem. The kernel Adatron, however, can easily solve this problem. The only difference between the Adatron from Chapter 3 and the kernel Adatron is that the dot product is replaced with RBF PEs (Gaussians), thus providing a kernel projection instead of a linear projection.

5.8.2 The Adatron with a Soft Margin

What happens if the patterns in feature space are not exactly linearly separable? The idea is to introduce a soft margin using a slack variable $\zeta_i \geq 0$ and a function $F(\zeta) = \sum_{i=1}^{N} \zeta_i$, which will penalize the cost function. We still minimize the function F, but now subject to the constraints $d_i(w \cdot x_i + b) \geq 1 - \zeta_i$, $i = 1, \ldots, N$, and $w \cdot w \leq c_n$. The new cost function becomes

$$J(\alpha, C) = \sum_{i=1}^{N} \alpha_i - \frac{1}{2C} \sum_{i=1}^{N} \sum_{j=1}^{N} \alpha_i \alpha_j (d_i d_j G(x_i - x_j, 2\sigma^2)) - \frac{c_n C}{2}$$

$$\text{subject to } \sum_{i=1}^{N} d_i \alpha_i = 0 \qquad 1 \geq \alpha_i \geq 0, \forall i \in \{1, \ldots, N\} \qquad C \geq 0$$

Normally, instead of computing the optimal C, we choose a value a priori. C can be regarded as a regularizer. This means that the matrix of kernel inner products is augmented in the diagonal by the factor $1/C$, that is,

$$\text{if } i = j \text{ then } \Omega(x_i, x_j) = G(x_i, x_j) + 1/C \quad \text{else} \quad \Omega(x_i, x_j) = G(x_i, x_j)$$

The only difference in the algorithm for this case is the calculation of $g(x_i)$, which becomes

$$g(x_i) = d_i \left[\sum_{j=1}^{N} d_j \alpha_j \Omega(x_i, x_j) + b \right]$$

As we can see, these calculations can be easily implemented as an iterative algorithm, but notice that large data sets produce very large RBF networks (one Gaussian per data sample). Since the input layer has no free parameters, the mapping can effectively be computed once and saved in memory.

SVMs have been applied to numerous problems with excellent results. Their performance is consistently on par with the best reported results, which have taken many years of fine-tuning. One of the weaknesses of the method is that it does not directly specify the number of support vectors to solve the problem. In principle, SVMs should be sensitive to outliers, even when using a soft margin.

5.8.3 Summary of the SVM Theory

We would like to present in a more rigorous manner the beautiful theory that gave rise to the SVMs and show its equivalence to the preceding algorithms. However, this theory is beyond the scope of an introductory textbook such as this one, so we will only highlight the most important concepts that gave rise to this design methodology. We will see how the ad hoc observations made in Chapters 2 and 3 have been formulated mathematically by Vapnik.

Learning theory can be framed as a function approximation problem in spaces with a probability measure. The goal is to approximate a function $d = f(\mathbf{x})$ where $f(.)$ is a fixed but unknown conditional distribution function $F(d|\mathbf{x})$. The approximant is a learning machine that implements a set of functions $\hat{f}(\mathbf{x}, \mathbf{w})$ where the parameters $\mathbf{w}$ are to be determined through learning. The inputs $\mathbf{x}$ are random vectors with a fixed but unknown probability distribution function $F(\mathbf{x})$. The selection of the parameters $\mathbf{w}$ is done through a finite number M of input-output observations $(\mathbf{x}_i, d_i)$, which are independent and identically distributed (i.i.d.).

You should be able to see how similar this is to the block diagram of Figure 5-1. We are saying that what links the desired response to the input is a conditional distribution function, which is unknown but fixed. The machine should discover this function by the repeated presentation of a finite set of exemplars that are assumed i.i.d. In learning theory the best parameters $\mathbf{w}^*$ are chosen to minimize the *risk functional*,

$$R(\mathbf{w}) = \int L(d, f(\mathbf{x}, \mathbf{w}))dF(\mathbf{x}, d) \qquad (5.38)$$

where $L(d, f(\mathbf{x}, \mathbf{w}))$, the *loss function*, measures the discrepancy between the desired response d and the learning machine output. However, we cannot compute this integral because we do not know the joint distribution $F(\mathbf{x}, d)$. Since we have the finite number of observation pairs $(\mathbf{x}_i, d_i)$, we will substitute Eq. 5-38 by

$$R_{\text{emp}}(\mathbf{w}) = \frac{1}{N} \sum_{i=1}^{N} L(d, f(x_i, \mathbf{w})) \qquad (5.39)$$

which is called the *empirical risk*, and we will minimize this quantity instead. This method of solving the risk problem is called the *empirical risk minimization (ERM) principle*. Notice that ERM is a principle based on induction. We may think that this substitution of the risk functional by the empirical risk would constrain the possible cases that could be solved. It turns out that Glivenko and Cantelli proved that the empiric distribution function (Eq. 5.39) converges to the actual distribution (Eq. 5.38). Kolmogorov even proved that the empirical distribution function has an asymptotic exponential rate of convergence. These are the basis for statistical inference.

The two problems treated so far in Chapters 1 and 3, respectively—the regression problem and the classification problem—are special cases of this formulation. In fact, it is enough to define the loss function as

$$L(d, f(\mathbf{x}, \mathbf{w})) = [d - \hat{f}(\mathbf{x}, \mathbf{w})]^2 \qquad (5.40)$$

to obtain the formulation of the regression, provided that the output y is a real value and we assume that the class of functions $\hat{f}(\mathbf{x}, \mathbf{w})$ includes the regression function that we are seeking.

If the output y takes the integer values $d = \{0, 1\}$, if the function $\hat{f}(\mathbf{x}, \mathbf{w})$ is the set of indicator functions (i.e., functions that take only two values—0 and 1), and if the loss function is defined as

$$L(d, \hat{f}(\mathbf{x}, \mathbf{w})) = \begin{cases} 0 & \text{iff } d = f(\mathbf{x}, \mathbf{w}) \\ 1 & \text{iff } d \neq f(\mathbf{x}, \mathbf{w}) \end{cases} \tag{5.41}$$

then the risk functional computes the probability of an error in the classification. We could even show that this same formalism can provide density estimation over the class of functions $p(\mathbf{x}, \mathbf{w})$ if as a special case

$$L(p(\mathbf{x}, \mathbf{w})) = -\log p(\mathbf{x}, \mathbf{w}) \tag{5.42}$$

Learning theory provides the most general way to think about training adaptive systems. The theory mathematically addresses the problem of generalization that is vital to neurocomputing. Vapnik [1998] establishes four fundamental questions for learning machines:

- What are the necessary and sufficient conditions for consistency of a learning process?
- How fast is the rate of convergence to the solution?
- How can we control the generalization ability of the learning machine?
- How can we construct algorithms that implement these prerequisites?

We will restrict ourselves to the special case of pattern recognition (where the function is an indicator function). To study SVMs, we need to address the last two questions, but first we provide the definition of VC (Vapnik-Chervonenkis) dimension. One of the fundamental problems in pattern recognition has always been the estimation of the Bayes' error. There is no known procedure to directly minimize the Bayes' error, because it involves integration over the tails of the pdf's, which are unknown (and the multidimensional integral is not trivial either). Our procedure of designing classifiers by minimizing the training error (which in this theory corresponds to the empiric risk) is not appropriate, as we discussed in Chapter 4 and also in this chapter. All the methods we discussed to control the generalization error are, in fact, indirect (and sometimes ad hoc), so researchers have tried to find methods that minimize an upper bound of the Bayes' error. It is in this framework that Vapnik's contributions should be placed. Vapnik argues that the necessary and sufficient conditions of consistency (generalization) of the ERM principle depend on the capacity of the set of functions implemented by the learning machine. He has shown that the VC dimension provides a way to estimate an upper bound for the Bayes' error.

The VC dimension h of a set of functions is defined as the maximum number of vectors that can be separated into two classes in all 2^h possible ways, using functions of the set. For the case of linear functions in n-dimensional space, the VC dimension is $h = n + 1$. So the VC dimension is a more rigorous way to measure the capacity of a learning machine, which we discussed in Chapter 2. For general topologies the VC dimension is not easy to determine, but the trend is that larger topologies will correspond to larger VC dimensions.

The VC dimension of a learning machine appears as a fundamental parameter to determine its generalization ability. In fact, Vapnik proved that the generalization ability (the risk R) of a learning machine $Q(x, \alpha)$ of size k parameterized by α is bounded by

$$R(\alpha) \leq R_{\text{emp}}(\alpha) + \Phi\left(\frac{N}{h}\right) \tag{5.43}$$

where $R_{\text{emp}}(\alpha)$ is the empirical risk (the error measured in the training set) and the second term is a confidence interval. The generalization ability depends on the training error, the number of observations, and the VC dimension of the learning machine. There are basically two ways to handle the design.

The first is to design a learning machine with a given topology, which will have a given VC dimension (which needs to be estimated). This is the conventional neural network design. Once this is done, Eq. 5.43 tells us everything. We train the ANN, and this gives us an estimate of the empirical risk, but also a confidence interval. Equation 5.43 describes the bias–variance dilemma very precisely. To decrease the training-set error, we may have to go to large ANNs, which will provide a large confidence interval; that is, the test error may be much larger than the training error. We say that the machine memorized the training data, so the problem becomes one of trading off training-set error and small VC dimension, which is handled heuristically by the size of the learning machine. This compromise was thought intrinsic in inductive inference, encapsulated by the famous Occam's razor principle (the simplest explanation is the best).

The second approach is called the structural risk minimization (SRM) principle and gives rise to the SVMs. The principle specifies keeping the empirical risk fixed (at zero, if possible) and minimizing the confidence interval. Since the confidence interval depends inversely on the VC dimension, this principle is equivalent to searching for the machine that has the smallest VC dimension. Notice that there is no compromise in the SRM principle. It states that the best strategy is to use a machine with the smallest VC dimension. Another point to make is that the VC dimension and number of free parameters appear as two distinct quantities, unlike the indications from Akaike's [1974] and Rissanen's [1989] work. We now know that we can apply very large machines to small data sets and still be able to generalize due to capacity control, so this SRM approach has profound implications in the design and use of classifiers. Let us now see how we can implement SRM in practice.

Here the concepts of hyperplanes and margin become critical. Although the VC dimension of the set of hyperplanes in n dimensions is $n + 1$, it can be less for a subset. In fact, Vapnik proved that the optimal hyperplane (the smallest norm) provides the smallest confidence interval, so the problem in SRM is one of designing a large margin classifier. Let us briefly describe Vapnik's formulation here to allow a comparison with our previous approaches.

Assume we have a set of data samples

$$S = \{(\mathbf{x}, d_1), \ldots, (\mathbf{x}_N, d_N)\} \qquad d_i \in \{-1, 1\}$$

What we want is to find the hyperplane $y = \mathbf{w} \cdot \mathbf{x} + b$ with the smallest norm of coefficients $\|\mathbf{w}\|^2$ (largest margin). To find this hyperplane we can solve the following quadratic programming problem: minimize the functional

$$\Phi(\mathbf{w}) = \frac{1}{2}(\mathbf{w} \cdot \mathbf{w})$$

under the constraint of inequality

$$d_i[(\mathbf{x}_i \cdot \mathbf{w}) + b] \geq 1 \qquad i = 1, 2, \ldots, N$$

where the operation is an inner product. The solution to this optimization is given by the saddle points of the Lagrangian:

$$L(\mathbf{w}, b, \alpha) = \frac{1}{2}(\mathbf{w} \cdot \mathbf{w}) - \sum_{i-1}^{N} \alpha\{[(\mathbf{x} \cdot \mathbf{w}) + b]d_i - 1\} \qquad \textbf{(5.44)}$$

By using the dual formulation, we can rewrite Eq. 5.44 as

$$J(\alpha) = \sum_{i=1}^{N} \alpha_i - \frac{1}{2}\sum_{i=1}^{N}\sum_{j=1}^{N} \alpha_i \alpha_j d_i d_j(\mathbf{x}_i \cdot \mathbf{x}_j) \qquad \text{subject to } \alpha_i \geq 0, \forall i \in \{1, \ldots, N\}$$

under the constraint $\sum_{i=1}^{N} \alpha_i y_i = 0$. The solution is a set of α^*. We can show that only some of the samples will correspond to Lagrangian multipliers different from zero and will be called the support vectors. They are the ones that control the positioning of the optimal hyperplane. The large margin classifier thus is specified by

$$f(\mathbf{x}) = \text{sgn}\left(\sum_{\substack{\text{support} \\ \text{vectors}}} d_i \alpha_i^*(\mathbf{x}_i \cdot \mathbf{x}) - b^*\right) \qquad \textbf{(5.45)}$$

One of the characteristics of the SVM is that the user has no control over the number of support vectors (i.e., the size of the final machine). During training, all the RBFs are used, but once the SVM is trained, the RBF should be trimmed, discarding the RBFs that are not support vectors. The number of support vectors depends on the data, which makes sense but is not always useful since we never know the size of the model. The expressions we arrived at are exactly the same as the one for the Adatron algorithm discussed in this chapter, except that Vapnik suggests a quadratic programming solution, while the Adatron is an "on-line" solution, easily implemented in neural network software. Like any on-line algorithm, the Adatron requires control of learning rate and suffers from the problem of misadjustment and stopping criterion. We can expect that training SVMs with large data sets demands a lot from computer resources (memory or computation).

Now we have a better understanding of why optimal margins are good for classification. SVMs can also be used for regression and density estimation.

5.9 PROJECT: APPLICATIONS OF NEURAL NETWORKS AS FUNCTION APPROXIMATORS

In Chapter 4 we saw how neural networks can be applied to classification. Here we would like to show how the same topologies can be applied as function approximators (nonlinear regressors) in a wealth of practical applications. We selected one application in the financial industry and another in real estate. The goal is to discover nonlinear mappings between input variables and important outcomes. In the financial arena the outcome is to predict the value of the S&P 500 using several financial indicators, while in the real estate application the problem is to estimate the price of a house based on several indicators. We will see that neural networks provide a very powerful analysis tool.

5.9.1 Prediction of S&P 500

This example develops a very simple model for predicting the S&P 500 one week in advance. You can use this demonstration as a starting point for developing your own more complex financial models. The inputs to the model consist of the one-year treasury bill yield, the earnings per share and dividend per share for the S&P 500, and the current week's S&P 500. The desired output is the next week's S&P 500. There are 507 weeks worth of data, which is approximately 10 years.

The data has been presampled so that the first 254 exemplars contain the data for weeks $1, 3, 5, \ldots, 505, 507$ and the last 253 exemplars contain the data for weeks $2, 4, 6, \ldots, 504, 506$. The first 254 exemplars will be used for training, and the last 253 exemplars are used for evaluating the trained network's performance.

NEUROSOLUTIONS EXAMPLE 5.16

Prediction of S&P 500

We use a simple, one-hidden-layer MLP to model this data. The network has four inputs, and the desired response is the next week's value of the S&P 500. The topology has to be carefully developed, as we exemplified in Chapter 4. We recommend that weight decay be used to avoid overfitting. Alternatively, Akaike's criterion could be used to find the best model order, as we did in Example 5.11. Let us train the network until the error stabilizes.

The next step is to verify the performance of the network on the unseen data. In the figure we show the performance of the network that we trained. The solid line is the actual value, while the network output is dashed. As we can see, the network fits the actual value of the S&P 500 rather well with the four inputs selected. We can compute the correlation coefficient between the actual and predicted curves to have a normalized (but linear) measure of performance.

We suggest that you try RBFs for the same problem and compare performances. This can be the embryo of a financial model, but remember that predicting the value of the stock market is just one of many factors needed to come up with an investment strategy.

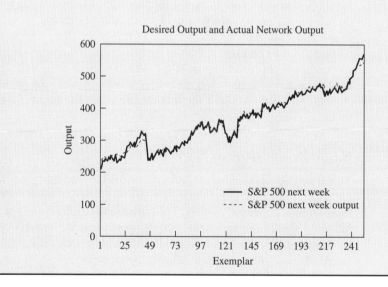

5.9.2 Estimating the Price of a House

The final example that we address in this chapter is how to decide which inputs are more significant in our application. This is an important issue because in many practical problems we have many different indicators or sensors, which may require very large input layers (hence many network weights), and very few exemplars to train the networks. One possibility is to prune the number of inputs without affecting performance. We have to understand that this is a compromise. The more variables we have for a problem, the better is the theoretical performance, assuming that we have infinite, noise-free data. You might think that each variable is a dimension to represent our problem, so the higher the number of dimensions, the better the representation. But notice that for each extra input the representation problem is posed in a larger-dimensionality space, so training the regressor (or the classifier) appropriately requires many more data samples. This is where the compromise comes in. Since we always have finite, noisy data, the fundamental issue is to find the best "projection" to represent our data well.

One approach is to use all the available data to train a neural network and then ask which are the most important inputs for our model. It is obvious that this requires the calculation of the relative importance of each input for the overall result, that is, the sensitivity of the outcome with respect to each input.

In this example we develop a model for real estate appraisal in the Boston area. We use 13 indicators as inputs to this model. These indicators are per capita crime rate by town (CRIM), proportion of residential land zoned for lots over 25,000 square feet (ZN), proportion of non–retail business acres per town (INDUS), bounds Charles River (CHAS), nitric oxides concentration (NOX), average number of rooms per dwelling (RM), proportion of owner-occupied units built prior to 1940 (AGE), weighted distances to five Boston employment centers (DIS), index of accessibility to radial highways (RAD), full-value property tax rate per \$10,000 (TAX), pupil–teacher ratio by town (PTRATIO), racial mix [$1000(\text{Bk} -0.63)^2$, where Bk is the proportion of blacks by town] (B), percentage of the lower-status population (LSTAT).

The desired output for this model is the median value of owner-occupied homes (in \$1000s). Hence this is a mapping problem, which we solve with an MLP (nonlinear regression). There are 400 total samples. Three hundred of them are used as training data, and the other 100 as testing data.

The way we can perform input-sensitivity analysis is to train the network as we normally do and then fix the weights. The next step is to randomly perturb, one at a time, each channel of the input vector around its mean value, while keeping the other inputs at their mean values, and then measure the change in the output. The change in the input is normally done by adding a random value of a known variance to each sample and computing the output. The sensitivity for input k is expressed as

$$S_k = \frac{\sum_{p=1}^{P} \sum_{i=1}^{o} (y_{ip} - \bar{y}_{ip})^2}{\sigma_k^2}$$

where $\bar{y}_{ip}$ is the ith output obtained with the fixed weights for the pth pattern, o is the number of network outputs, P is the number of patterns, and σ_k^2 is the variance of the input perturbation. This is very easy to compute in the trained network and effectively measures how much a change in a given input affects the output across the training data set. Inputs that have large sensitivities have more importance in the mapping and therefore are the ones we should keep. The inputs with small sensitivities can be discarded.

This helps the training (because it decreases the size of the network), decreases the cost of data collection, and—when done right—has negligible impact on performance.

NEUROSOLUTIONS EXAMPLE 5.17

Estimating prices in the Boston housing data

Let us initially train a one-hidden-layer MLP with 14 inputs and one output. The choice of the number of hidden PEs should be done as before, that is, by starting small and plotting the output MSE for several different runs as a function of the number of PEs. Train the network and run it on the test set to observe the performance in the test set. The network produces a very good fit in most cases, indicating a successful model.

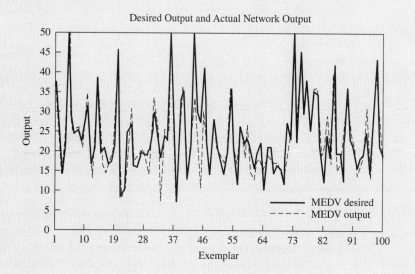

The next step is to run the sensitivity analysis, which estimates the importance of each input to the overall performance. NeuroSolutions has a built-in feature to do this. Let us work with the trained network and turn learning off (fix the weights). We have to specify the amount of random noise that we want to add to each individual input (which is done automatically, one input at a time), while keeping the other inputs at their mean values. NeuroSolutions computes the sensitivity at the output. Let us place a Matrix Viewer at the L_2 Criterion in the sensitivity access point and write down the values. We should use different values for dithering to obtain a reasonable linear approximation to the operating point of the regressor. We can then plot the different values of the sensitivity for each input variable, as shown in the following figure.

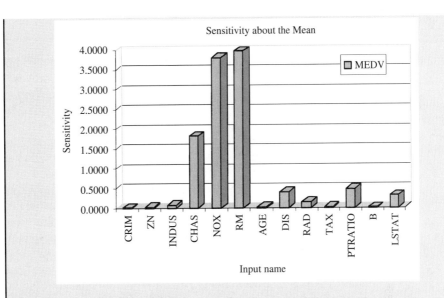

From the figure we see that there are five inputs that display a very low sensitivity, so they can be omitted without appreciably affecting the quality of the mapping. Hence a reduced network with the inputs INDUS, CHAS, NOX, RM, DIS, RAD, PTRATIO, LSTAT will be trained again. As you can see in the following figure, the performance is basically the same, but now we have a smaller network that will generalize better, and we can reduce the cost of collecting data for this problem.

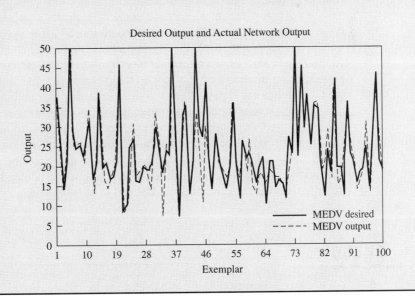

5.10   CONCLUSION

In this chapter we provided a view of neural networks as function approximators. This is the more general view of this family of systems and improves our understanding about their capabilities, establishes new links to alternative methods, and provides a better understanding of the problems faced in training and using adaptive systems.

One of the interesting things about neurocomputing is that it lies at the intersection of many diverse and complementary theories, so it is a very rich field. The price paid is that the reader is bombarded with many different concepts, and since our goal is to keep the text at an introductory level, the presentation addressed only the key concepts. Our hope is that the reader was motivated enough to pursue some of these topics.

MLPs are very important for function approximation because they are universal approximators, and their approximation properties have remarkably nice properties (the approximation error decays independently of the size of the input space). This may explain why MLPs have been shown to outperform other statistical approaches in classification.

In this chapter we also introduced another class of neural networks, called the radial-basis-function networks (RBFs). RBFs can be used in the same way as MLPs since they are also universal approximators; that is, they can be classifiers, regressors, or density estimators.

We also presented the basic concepts of the structural risk minimization principle and support vector machines (SVMs). This is a difficult theory, so we merely highlighted the many important implications, from the paradigm shift from the conventional compromise between generalization and network size, to the strict recipe of using the smallest-capacity machine for best generalization. The innovative ideas contained in the SVM principle will tremendously affect the evolution of the whole field of learning from examples and inductive inference.

SVMs are practical learning machines that minimize an upper bound to the Bayes' error, so they are very useful in pattern recognition. SVMs are very easy to apply to practical problems, provided that the user has large computers. For small data sets the kernel Adatron algorithm allows a simple, "neural"-like implementation of the quadratic programming required to find the support vectors and conquers one of the difficulties of the method (having access to easy-to-use quadratic programming software).

For the reader with a background in engineering this chapter provided a view of MLPs and RBFs as function approximation implementations with a new set of bases (the sigmoids, which are global, or the Gaussians, which are local). For the reader with a statistical background, the chapter provided a new view of generalization. Neural networks belong to the exciting class of nonparametric, nonlinear models, which learn directly from the data and thus can be used in experimental science.

5.11   EXERCISES

5.1   **(a)** Compare the approximation capabilities of the linear regressor and the MLP for the following mapping: input ramp to output sine function. Use the Breadboard from Example 5.4, and change the input–desired response files with the signal generators in NeuroSolutions. Choose the number of hidden PEs of the network, and correlate with the MSE. Observe the values of the weights, and conclude how the network is doing the mapping.

(b) Repeat 1(a) using for input the triangular function. What did you observe? Explain the differences.

(c) Now go to the Inspector of the input component and include a 90-degree phase shift. Explain the results.

(d) Now with this experience, predict what will happen when you use a square wave at the input. Run NeuroSolutions to see if you are right.

5.2 Repeat Problem 1(a) for the RBF network. Run the network. Can you explain what you see? You have to modify the setting of the centers, since they are chosen by hand in this example. Enter values between -1 and 1, and run the network again. Are you satisfied with the performance? You have also to control the width of the Gaussian. Go to the Inspector and change the width to 10. Repeat the simulation and compare the performances.

5.3 Add a bias to the noise term of the Breadboard in Example 5.7 and explain the results.

5.4 Let us analyze in more detail the Breadboard in Example 5.8. First, add an impulse of magnitude 0.5 to the desired response (by placing the function generator in the staked access). For visualization purposes, enter -45 in the phase. Now retrain the system. You have to control learning a little better by decreasing the step size. Notice how the impulse changed the fit only marginally. Now repeat with the L_2 norm and compare the fits.

5.5 Experiment with the number of neighbors for the adaptation of the RBFs in Example 5.9. Try 1 and 5. Place the matrix viewer on the width access point to see the center values. What do you conclude?

5.6 For Example 5.13 the MLP provides fairly good performance. Now try to achieve a similar result with an RBF network. Modify the number of PEs and the training (both centers and variances), as well as the number of training iterations for the unsupervised part. Observe the end results on the scatter plot.

5.7 Solve the classification of Problem 6 with an SVM.

5.8 Use the sonar data to compare the performance of the SVM, RBF, and MLPs. You should train the RBF and MLPs with cross-validation before you do the comparisons.

5.12 NEUROSOLUTIONS EXAMPLES

5.1 Sinc interpolation

5.2 Fourier decomposition

5.3 Linear regression

5.4 Function approximation with the MLP

5.5 MLP to approximate a square wave (classification)

5.6 Function approximation with RBFs

5.7 Nonlinear regressors

5.8 MLPs for function approximation with L_1 norm

5.13   CONCEPT MAP FOR CHAPTER 5

REFERENCES

Akaike, H., A new look at the statistical model identification, *IEEE Trans. Auto. Control,* AC-19:716–723, 1974.

Barron, A., Approximation and estimation bounds for ANNs, *IEEE Trans. Information Theory,* 39(3):930–945, 1993.

Freiss, T., *Support Vector Neural Networks: The Kernel Adatron with Bias and Soft Margin,* University of Sheffield Technical Report, 1998.

Haykin, S., *Neural Networks: A Comprehensive Foundation,* McMillan, New York, 1994.

Kay, S., *Modern Spectral Estimation,* Prentice Hall, Englewood Cliffs, NJ, 1988.

Park, J., and Sandberg, I., Universal approximation using radial basis function networks, *Neural Computation,* 3:303–314, 1989.

Parzen, E., On estimation of a probability density function and mode, *Annals of Mathematical Statistics,* 33:1065–1076, 1962.

Poggio, T., and Girosi, F., Networks for approximation and learning, *Proc. IEEE,* 78, 1990.

Rissanen, J., *Stochastic Complexity in Statistical Inquiry,* World Scientific, Singapore, 1989.

Tikhonov, A., and Arsenin, V., *Solution of Ill-Posed Problems,* Winston, Washington, DC, 1977.

Vapnik, V., *The Nature of Statistical Learning Theory,* Springer Verlag, New York, 1995.

Vapnik, V., *Statistical Learning Theory,* Wiley, New York, 1998.

Whaba, G., *Splines Models for Observational Data,* SIAM, 1990.

CHAPTER 6

HEBBIAN LEARNING AND PRINCIPAL COMPONENT ANALYSIS

The goal of this chapter is to introduce the following concepts:

- Correlation learning
- Hebbian rule and its modifications
- Principal component analysis (PCA)
- PCA networks
- Associative memories

6.1 INTRODUCTION

In the 1940s the neurophysiologist Donald Hebb [1949] enunciated a principle that became very influential in neurocomputing. By studying the communication between neurons, Hebb verified that once a neuron repeatedly excited another neuron, the threshold of excitation of the latter decreased; that is, the communication between them was facilitated by repeated excitation. This means that repeated excitation lowered the threshold or, equivalently that the excitation effect of the first neuron was amplified (Figure 6-1).

We can extend this idea to artificial systems very easily. In artificial neural systems, neurons are equivalent to PEs, and PEs are connected through weights. Hence Hebb's principle will increase the common weight w_{ij} when there is activity flowing from the jth PE to the ith PE. If we denote the output of the ith PE by y_i and the activation of the jth PE by x_j, then

$$\Delta w_{ij} = \eta x_j y_i \tag{6.1}$$

where η is our already known step size, which controls the percentage of the product that is used to change the weight. There are many more ways to translate Hebb's principle in equations, but Eq. 6.1 is the most commonly used and is called *Hebb's rule*.

Unlike all the learning rules studied so far (LMS and backpropagation), there is no desired signal required in Hebbian learning. To apply Hebb's rule, only the input sig-

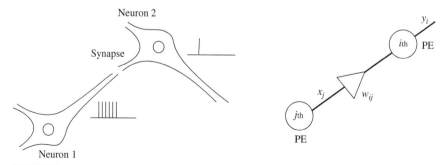

FIGURE 6-1 Biological and modeled artificial system

nal needs to flow through the neural network. Learning rules that use only information from the input to update the weights are called *unsupervised*. Note that in unsupervised learning the learning machine changes the weights according to some internal rule specified a priori (here the Hebb rule). Note also that the Hebb rule is local to the weight.

6.2 EFFECT OF THE HEBBIAN UPDATE

Let us see the net effect of updating a single weight w in a linear PE with the Hebbian rule. Hebbian learning updates the weights according to

$$w(n + 1) = w(n) + \eta x(n)y(n) \tag{6.2}$$

where n is the iteration number and η a step size. For a linear PE, $y = wx$, so

$$w(n + 1) = w(n)[1 + \eta x^2(n)] \tag{6.3}$$

If the initial value of the weight is a small positive constant ($w(0) \approx 0$), the update will always be positive. Hence the weight value will increase with the number of iterations without bounds, irrespective of the value of η. This is unlike the behavior we observed for the LMS or backpropagation, where the weights would stabilize for a range of step sizes. Hence Hebbian learning is intrinsically unstable, producing very large positive or negative weights. In biology this is not a problem because there are natural nonlinearities that limit the synaptic efficacy (chemical depletion, dynamic range, etc).

NEUROSOLUTIONS EXAMPLE 6.1

Training with the Hebbian rule

In this example, we introduce the Hebbian Synapse. The Hebbian Synapse implements the weight update of Eq. 6.2. The Hebbian network is built from an input Axon, the Hebbian Synapse, and an Axon, so it is a linear network. Since the Hebbian Synapse and all the other Unsupervised Synapses (which we will introduce soon) use an unsupervised weight update (no desired signal), they do not require a backpropagation layer. The weights are updated on a sample-by-sample basis.

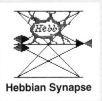

Hebbian Synapse

> This example shows the behavior of the Hebbian weight update. The weights with the Hebbian update will always increase, no matter how small the step size is. We have placed a scope at the output of the net and also opened a Matrix Viewer to observe the weights during learning. The only thing that the stepsize does is to control the rate of increase of the weights.
>
> Notice also that if the initial weight is positive, the weights become increasingly more positive, while if the initial weight is negative, the weights become increasingly more negative.

6.2.1 The Multiple-Input PE

Hebbian learning is normally applied to single-layer linear networks. Figure 6-2 shows a single linear PE with D inputs, which is called the Hebbian PE. The output is

$$y = \sum_{i=1}^{D} w_i x_i \tag{6.4}$$

According to Hebb's rule, the weight vector is adapted as

$$\Delta \mathbf{w} = \eta \begin{bmatrix} x_1 y \\ \ldots \\ x_D y \end{bmatrix} \tag{6.5}$$

It is important to get a solid understanding of the role of Hebbian learning, and we will start with a geometric interpretation. Equation 6.4 in vector notation is simply

$$y = \mathbf{w}^T \mathbf{x} = \mathbf{x}^T \mathbf{w} \tag{6.6}$$

that is, the transpose of the weight vector is multiplied with the input (which is called the inner product) to produce the scalar output y. We know that the inner product is computed as the product of the length of the vectors and the cosine of their angle θ,

$$y = |\mathbf{w}||\mathbf{x}| \cos \theta \tag{6.7}$$

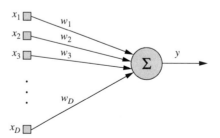

FIGURE 6-2 A D-input linear PE

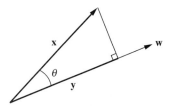

FIGURE 6-3 The output of
the linear PE in vector space

Thus, assuming normalized inputs and weights, a large y means that the input $\mathbf{x}$ is "close" to the direction of the weight vector (Figure 6-3), that is, that $\mathbf{x}$ is in the neighborhood of $\mathbf{w}$.

A small y means that the input is almost perpendicular to $\mathbf{w}$ (the cosine of 90 degrees is 0); that is, $\mathbf{x}$ and $\mathbf{w}$ are far apart. The magnitude of y therefore measures similarity between the input $\mathbf{x}$ and the weight $\mathbf{w}$ using the inner product as the similarity measure.

This is a very powerful interpretation. During learning the weights are exposed to the data and condense all this information in their value. This is the reason that the weights should be considered as the *long-term memory of the network*.

Long- and Short-Term Memory

Long-term memory refers to the storage of information from the past. Since the weights are adapted with the input information, their values are related to all the data that has been presented to the network. Hence they represent the long-term memory of the network.

It is also convenient to consider the activation in the PEs as short-term memory. The short-term memory we consider in this chapter is instantaneous, since the activations of the PEs discussed so far depend only on the current data sample. But later in Chapter 9 we consider other network topologies where the activations depend upon past samples.

The Hebbian PE is a very simple system that creates a similarity measure (the inner product, Eq. 6.7) in its input space according to the information contained in the weights. During operation, once the weights are fixed, a large output y signifies that the present input is "similar" to the inputs $\mathbf{x}$ that created the weights during training. We can say that the output of the PE responds high or low according to the *similarity* of the present input with what the PE "remembers" from training. The Hebbian PE thus implements a type of memory that is called an *associative memory*.

Associative Memory

We are very familiar with the concept of memory in digital computers, where a set of bits (0 and 1) are stored in a memory location in the address space of our computer. The computer memory is an organization of such locations that is accessed by the processor by an address and is therefore called *location addressable.* We can think of the computer memory as a filing cabinet, with each folder containing the data. The processor accesses the data by searching the tag of the folder. This is why computer memory is location addressable and local.

Associative memories are very different and in many ways resemble our own memory. They are *content addressable* and global. Content addressable means that the recall is not done through the address location, but through the content. During retrieval of information with an associative memory, no address is used, just the input data. When one of the inputs used in training is presented to the Hebbian PE, the output is the pattern created with the storage algorithm during training (we show this later). The memory is also global in the sense that all the weights contain the memory information in a distributed fashion, and the weights are shared by all the memories that eventually are stored in the system. This is unlike the computer memory, where the data is contained locally and independently in each location.

Associative memories are therefore more robust to destruction of information than computer memories. However, their capacity is limited by the number of inputs (as we will see in this chapter), unlike computer memories, where the size of the data path is independent of the number of memory locations.

NEUROSOLUTIONS EXAMPLE 6.2

Directions of the Hebbian update

This example shows how the Hebbian network projects the input onto the vector defined by its weights. We use an input composed of samples that fall on an ellipse in two dimensions and allow you to select the weights. When you run the network, a custom DLL displays both the input (blue) and the projection of the input onto the weight vector (black). The default is to set the weights to [1, 0], which defines a vector along the x axis. Thus you would be projecting the two-dimensional input onto the x axis. Changing the value of the weights rotates the vector. Notice that in any direction the output tracks the input along that direction; that is, the output is the projection of the input along that specified direction.

Notice also the Megascope display. When the input data circles the origin, the output produces a sinusoidal component in time, since the projection increases and decreases periodically with the rotation. The amplitude of the sinusoid is maximal when the weight vector is [1, 0], since this is the direction that produces a larger projection for this data set.

If we release the weights, that is, if they are trained with Hebbian learning, the weights seek the direction [1, 0]. It is very interesting to note the path of the evolution of the weights (it oscillates around this direction). Note also that the weights are becoming progressively larger.

6.2.2 The Hamming Network as a Primitive Associative Memory

The idea that a simple linear network embeds a similarity metric can be explored in many practical applications. Here we exemplify its use in signal detection, where noise normally corrupts messages. We assume that the messages are strings of bipolar binary values $(-1, 1)$ and that we know the strings of the alphabet (for instance, the ASCII code of the letters). A practical problem is to find the string sent from a given received string of five bits. We can think of an n-bit string as a vector in n-dimensional space. The ASCII code for each letter can also be thought of as a vector. The question of finding the value of the received string is the same as asking which ASCII vector is closest to the received string (Figure 6-4). Using the preceding argument, we should find the ASCII vector on which the bit string produces the largest projection.

A linear network can be constructed with as many inputs as bits in an ASCII code (here we use only five bits, although the ASCII code is eight bits long) and a number of outputs equal to the size of the alphabet (here 26 letters). The weights of the network are hard-coded as the bit patterns of all ASCII letters. More formally, the inputs are vectors $\mathbf{x} = [x_1, x_2, \ldots, x_5]^T$, the output is a scalar, and the weight matrix $\mathbf{S}$ is built from rows that are our ASCII codes, represented by $\mathbf{s}_i = [s_{i1}, s_{i2}, \ldots, s_{i5}]$, with $i = 1, \ldots, 26$. The output of the network is $\mathbf{y} = \mathbf{S}\mathbf{x}$.

The remaining question is how to measure the distance between the received vector and each of the ASCII characters. Since the patterns are binary, one possibility is to ask how many bit flips are present between the received string and all the ASCII characters. We should assign the received string to the ASCII character that has the fewest bit flips. This distance is called the Hamming distance (HD, also known as the Manhattan norm or L_1 norm).

When a character is received, each output i of the network is the dot product of the input with the corresponding row vector $\mathbf{s}_i$. Since the inputs and weights are bipolar binary values, this dot product can be expressed as the total number of positions in which the vectors agree minus the number of positions in which they differ, which is

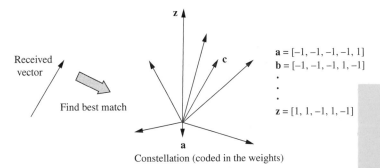

$$\mathbf{a} = [-1, -1, -1, -1, 1]$$
$$\mathbf{b} = [-1, -1, -1, 1, -1]$$
$$\mathbf{z} = [1, 1, -1, 1, -1]$$

Constellation (coded in the weights)

FIGURE 6-4 The problem of finding the best match to the received character in vector spaces

quantified as their HD. Since the number of positions in which they agree is $5 - HD$, we have

$$\mathbf{s}_i \mathbf{x} = 5 - HD(s_i, x)$$

This equation states that if we add a bias equal to 5 to each of the outputs of our net, we can directly interpret the network output as a Hamming distance (to be exact, the weights should be multiplied by 0.5, and the bias should be 0.5 to obtain the HD). A perfect match will provide an output of 5. We therefore just need to look for the highest output to know which character was sent.

NEUROSOLUTIONS EXAMPLE 6.3

Signal detection with Hamming networks

In this example we create the equivalent of a Hamming net that will recognize the binary ASCII of five letters (A, B, L, P, Z). The input to the network is the last five bits of each letter. For instance, A is $(-1, -1, -1, -1, 1)$, B is $(-1, -1, -1, 1, -1)$, and so on.

Because we know ahead of time what the letters will be, we set the weights to the expected ASCII code of each letter. Here we are not going to use the Hamming distance but the dot-product distance of Hebbian learning. According to the associative memory concept, when the input and the weight vector are the same, the output of the net will be the largest possible. For instance, if $(-1, -1, -1, -1, 1)$ is input to the network, the first PE will respond with the highest possible output. Single-step through the data to see that, in fact, the net gives the correct response. Notice also that the other outputs are not zero, since they depend on the Hamming distance between the input and each set of weights.

When noise corrupts the input, this network can be used to determine which letter the input was most likely to be. Noise will affect each component of the vector, but the net will assign the highest output to the weight vector that lies closest to the noisy input. When the noise is small, the Hamming network still provides a good assignment. Increase the noise power to see when the system breaks down. It is amazing that such a simple device still provides the correct output most of the time when the variance of the noise is as high as 2.

Note that in the example we utilized the inner-product metric intrinsic to the Hebbian network instead of the Hamming distance, but the result is very similar. In this example the weight matrix was constructed by hand, due to the knowledge we have about the problem. In general, the weight matrix has to be adapted, and this is where the Hebbian learning is important. Nevertheless, this example shows the power of association for signal detection.

6.2.3 Hebbian Rule as Correlation Learning

There is a strong reason to translate Hebb's principle as in Eq. 6.1. In fact, Eq. 6.1 prescribes a weight correction according to the product between the jth and the ith PE activations. Let us substitute Eq. 6.6 in Eq. 6.5 to obtain the vector equivalent

$$\Delta\mathbf{w}(n) = \eta y(n)\mathbf{x}(n) = \eta\mathbf{x}(n)\mathbf{x}^T(n)\mathbf{w}(n) \tag{6.8}$$

In on-line learning the weight vector is repeatedly changed according to this equation, using a different input sample for each n. However, in batch learning, after iterating over the input data of N patterns, the cumulative weight update is the sum of the products of the input with its transpose multiplied by the original weight vector $\mathbf{w}(0)$:

$$\Delta\mathbf{w} = \eta\left(\sum_{n=1}^{N}\mathbf{x}(n)\mathbf{x}^T(n)\right)\mathbf{w}(0) \tag{6.9}$$

The factor that multiplies the initial weight in Equation 6.9 can be thought of as a sample approximation to the autocorrelation of the input data (apart from the normalizing factor $1/N$), which is defined as $\mathbf{R}_x = E[\mathbf{x}\mathbf{x}^T]$, where $E[.]$ is the expectation operator (see the appendix). The Hebbian algorithm is effectively updating the weights with a sample estimate of the autocorrelation function:

$$\Delta\mathbf{w} = \eta\hat{\mathbf{R}}_x\mathbf{w}(0) \tag{6.10}$$

Correlation is a well-known operation in signal processing and in statistics, and it measures the *second-order statistics* of the random variable under study. First- and second-order statistics are sufficient to describe signals modeled as Gaussian distributions, as we saw in Chapter 2 (i.e., first- and second-order statistics are what is needed to completely describe the Gaussian data cluster). Second-order moments also describe many properties of linear systems, such as the adaptation of the linear regressor studied in Chapter 1.

6.2.4 Power, Quadratic Forms, and Hebbian Learning

As we saw, the output of a linear network is given by Eq. 6.6. We define the power at the output given the data set $\{\mathbf{x}(1), \mathbf{x}(2), \ldots, \mathbf{x}(N)\}$ as

$$V = \frac{1}{N}\sum_{n=1}^{N}y^2(n) = \mathbf{w}^T\mathbf{R}_x\mathbf{w} \qquad \text{where } \mathbf{R}_x \approx \mathbf{R} = \frac{1}{N}\sum_{n=1}^{N}\mathbf{x}(n)\mathbf{x}^T(n) \tag{6.11}$$

V in Eq. 6.11 is a quadratic form, and it can be interpreted as a field in the space of the weights. Since $\mathbf{R}$ is positive definite, we can further say that this field is a paraboloid facing upward passing through the origin of the weight space (Figure 6-5).

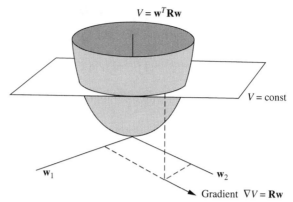

FIGURE 6-5 The power field as a performance surface

Energy, Power, and Variance

From the statistical point of view, the energy of a 1-D signal $x(n)$ is related to its variance. In fact, the energy of a stationary signal $x(n)$ with variance σ^2 and mean m is

$$E = E[x^2(n)] = \sigma^2 + m^2$$

where $E[.]$ is the expectation operator. If $m = 0$, the energy is equal to the variance, $E = \sigma^2$, so the energy is related to the second-order statistics of the signal.

The power V (or short-term energy) is defined as the energy in a finite window or for a finite number of samples. The power is also related to an estimation of the second-order statistics with finite data. The condition of zero mean is normally assumed in the discussion.

Let us take the gradient of V with respect to the weights:

$$\nabla V = \frac{\partial V}{\partial \mathbf{w}} = 2\mathbf{Rw}$$

We can immediately recognize that this equation provides the basic form for the Hebbian update of Eq. 6.10. If we recall the performance surface concept of Chapter 1, we conclude that the power field is the performance surface for Hebbian learning. Therefore when we train a network with the Hebbian rule, the algorithm is doing gradient *ascent* (seeking the maximum) in the power field of the input data. The sample-by-sample adaptation rule of Eq. 6.8 is merely a stochastic version and follows the same behavior. Since the power field is unbounded upward, we can also expect that Hebbian learning will diverge, unless some type of normalization is applied to the update rule. This is a shortcoming for our computer implementations, because the limited dynamic range causes overflow errors. But there are many ways to normalize the Hebbian update.

Hebbian as Gradient Search

To show that Hebbian acts as a gradient search, just differentiate Eq. 6.11 with respect to **W** to obtain

$$\frac{\partial J}{\partial \mathbf{W}} = \mathbf{W}^T \mathbf{R} + \mathbf{RW} = 2\mathbf{RW}$$

due to the Toeplitz properties of **R**. Gradient ascent changes the weights according to

$$\Delta \mathbf{W} = \eta \frac{\partial J}{\partial \mathbf{W}} = \eta \mathbf{RW}$$

which is exactly what we presented for the Hebbian rule (aside from the 2, which is included in the step size). Note that gradient ascent goes in the direction of the gradient, so there is no minus sign in the weight update, as in the LMS rule.

Is the Hebbian update ever stable? Let us write the Hebbian update as

$$\mathbf{W}(n+1) = \mathbf{W}(n) + \eta \mathbf{x}(n)\mathbf{y}^T(n) = \mathbf{W}(n) + \eta \mathbf{x}(n)\mathbf{x}^T(n)\mathbf{W}(n)$$

Applying the expectation operator, we get

$$\mathbf{W}(n+1) = (\mathbf{I} + \eta \mathbf{R}_x)\mathbf{W}(n)$$

where **R** is the autocorrelation function of the input and **I** is the identity matrix. The stability of this iterative equation is determined by the characteristic roots of the matrix $\mathbf{I} + \eta \mathbf{R}$. Since **R** is positive definite, all the roots will be positive, hence the iteration will diverge for any value of η.

NEUROSOLUTIONS EXAMPLE 6.4
Instability of the Hebbian update rule

This example shows that the Hebbian update rule is unstable since the weights grow without bound. We use a simple 2-D input example to show that the weight vector grows. We have opened a Matrix Viewer to see the weights, and we also plot the tip of the weight vector in the Scatter Plot as a blue dot (think of the weight vector as going from the origin to the blue dot). Notice, however, that the weight vector always diverges along the same direction. This is not by chance. Although unstable, the Hebbian network is finding the direction where the output is the largest. The more you train the network, the larger the weights get. Rerun the simulation several times to observe the behavior we describe.

6.2.5 Data Representations in Multidimensional Spaces

What does the direction of the gradient ascent represent? To understand the answer to this question, we have to talk about data representations in multidimensional spaces. We normally collect information about real-world events with sensors. Most of the time the data to model a real-world phenomenon is multidimensional; that is, we need several sensors (such as temperature, pressure, flow, etc.). This immediately says that the state of the real-world system is multidimensional. Each set of inputs is a point in a space where the axes are exactly our measurement variables. In Figure 6-6 we show a two-dimensional example. The system operation creates a cloud of points somewhere in this measurement space.

An alternative to describe the cloud of points is to define a new set of axes that are "attached" to the cloud of data instead of the measurement variables. This new coordinate system is called a *data-dependent* coordinate system. From Figure 6-6 we see that the data-dependent representation moves the origin to the center (the mean) of our cloud of samples. But we can do more. We can also try to align one of the axes with the direction where the data has the largest projection. This is called the principal coordinate system for the data. For simplicity we would also like the principal coordinate system to be orthogonal (more on this later). Notice that the original (measurement) coordinate system and the principal coordinate system are related by a translation and a rotation, which is called an affine transform in algebra. If we know the parameters of this transformation, we have captured a great deal of information about the structure of our cloud of data.

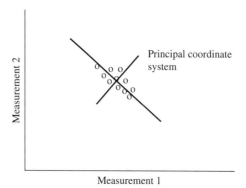

FIGURE 6-6   The principal coordinate system

The principal coordinate system gives us not only knowledge about the structure of the data but also versatility. We may want to represent our data in a smaller-dimensional space to simplify the analysis or to be able to visualize the data. Often times we are interested in preserving the variance of the cloud of points, since variance is loosely associated with information. To make the point clear, let us try to find only a *single direction* (i.e., a one-dimensional space) to represent most of the variance on our data. What direction should we use? If you think a bit, the principal coordinate system is the one that makes more sense, because we aligned one of the axes with the direction where the data has the largest variance. In this coordinate system we should choose the axis where the data has the largest projected variance.

Information and Variance

Extracting information from data is what learning is all about. Here we are using a layperson's concept of information, but we can also provide a technical definition. Shannon [1948] in a seminal paper proposed the following definition for entropy:

$$H(X) = -\sum_{k=1}^{N} p(x_k) \log(p(x_k)) = -E\{\log(p(x))\}$$

where p_k are the probabilities of a set of messages $\{x_1, \ldots, x_N\}$ occurring with probabilities $p_1, \ldots, p_N$. Entropy measures the amount of information in messages. The idea is the following: If we know what the message is ($p_k = 1$), the information carried is zero. On the other hand, if its content is unexpected (small p_k), the amount of information the message carries is rather large. This definition supports our intuition well, although Shannon utilized an axiomatic approach to derive the concept of information. Shannon's entropy definition has been the cornerstone for creating efficient and reliable communication systems (see Cover and Thomas [1991]), and it is also quite important in statistics and learning.

We may note that entropy uses all the information about the probability density function (pdf) of the data, but normally we do not know the pdf. It turns out that if the data is Gaussian distributed, that is, if

$$p(x) = \frac{1}{\sqrt{(2\pi)}\sigma} e^{-(1/2)[(x-m)/\sigma]^2}$$

then only two numbers, the mean m and the variance σ^2, are sufficient to describe the pdf of the data. This means that only the first- and second-order moments are nonzero. Therefore, for Gaussian-distributed data, the entropy can be written

$$H(x) = 0.5 \log(2\pi\sigma) + 0.5 \log E\left\{\left(\frac{x-m}{\sigma}\right)^2\right\}$$

and we conclude that it is proportional to the variance of the data. For Gaussian-distributed variables, information is a synonym of variance.

Now let us go back to the Hebbian network. The weights of the network that was trained with the Hebbian learning rule find the direction of the input power gradient. The output of the Hebbian network (the projection of the input onto the weight vector) will then be the largest variance projection. In other words, the Hebbian network finds the axis of the principal coordinate system where the projected output has the highest variance. What is amazing is that the simple Hebbian rule automatically finds this direction for us with a local learning rule.

Even though Hebbian learning was biologically motivated, it is a way of creating network weights that are tuned to the second-order statistics of the input data. Moreover, the network does this with a rule that is local to the weights. We can further say that Hebbian learning extracts the maximum amount of information about a Gaussian input, since from all possible linear projections it finds the one that maximizes the variance at the output (which is a synonym for information for Gaussian-distributed variables).

6.3   OJA'S RULE

To make Hebbian learning useful we must create a stable version by normalizing the weights. Perhaps the simplest normalization to Hebb's rule was proposed by Oja [1982]. Let us divide the new value of the weight in Eq. 6.2 by the norm of the new weight vector connected to the PE, that is,

$$w_i(n + 1) = \frac{w_i(n) + \eta y(n)x_i(n)}{\sqrt{\sum_i (w_i(n) + \eta y(n)x_i(n))^2}} \tag{6.12}$$

We see that this expression effectively normalizes the size of the weight vector to 1. If a given weight component increases, the others have to decrease to keep the weight vector at the same length, so weight normalization is in fact a constraint. Assuming a small step size, Oja [1982] approximated the update of Eq. 6.12 by

$$\begin{aligned} w_i(n + 1) &= w_i(n) + \eta y(n)[x_i(n) - y(n)w_i(n)] \\ &= w_i(n)[1 - \eta y^2(n)] + \eta x_i(n)y(n) \end{aligned} \tag{6.13}$$

producing Oja's rule. Note that this rule can be considered the Hebbian update with a normalized activity $x_i(n) = x_i(n) - y(n)w_i(n)$. The normalization is basically a "forgetting factor" proportional to the square of the output (see Eq. 6.13).

Oja's Rule and the Raleigh Quotient

Let $\mathbf{X} = [\mathbf{x}_1, \mathbf{x}_2, \ldots, \mathbf{x}_N]$ represent a set of data with N samples, where $\mathbf{x}_i \in R^D$. Without loss of generality we assume that the data is zero mean. To find the principal component we must find a vector $\mathbf{w} \in R^D$ that maximizes the Raleigh quotient

$$J = \frac{\mathbf{w}^T \mathbf{R} \mathbf{w}}{\mathbf{w}^T \mathbf{w}}$$

where $\mathbf{R} = \mathbf{X} \mathbf{X}^T$ is the data scattering matrix (N times the autocorrelation function). Analyzing the expression for J, we can conclude that the norm of $\mathbf{w}$ is irrelevant for the solution, so we can keep it constant at $\|\mathbf{w}\| = 1$. If we want to use the gradient-descent procedure to maximize J, we have to compute the gradient with respect to the weights, which gives

$$\nabla_w J = \frac{1}{\|\mathbf{w}\|^2} \sum_i y_i \left(\mathbf{x}_i - \frac{y_i}{\|\mathbf{w}\|^2} \mathbf{w} \right)$$

If we keep the norm equal to 1, this expression defaults to Oja's rule. Maximizing the output variance subject to the norm constraint produces Oja's rule.

Eq. 6.13 addresses the fundamental problem of Hebbian learning. To avoid unlimited growth in the weights, we applied a forgetting term. This solves the problem of weight growth but creates another problem. If the pattern is not presented frequently, it will be forgotten, since the network forgets old associations.

NEUROSOLUTIONS EXAMPLE 6.5

Oja's rule

This example introduces the Oja's Synapse (look at the Synapse with the label "Oja"). The network is still a linear network, but the Oja's Synapse implements Oja's weight update, described in Eq. 6.13. The overall network function is similar to the Hebbian network, except that now the weights stabilize, producing a vector in the direction of maximum change. The input data is the same as in the previous case. Notice that now the weights of the single-output network produce a vector oriented along the largest axis of the cloud of input samples (45 degrees). This is the direction that produces the largest possible output. Randomize the weights several times during learning to see that the network quickly finds this direction. Depending on the sign of the initial weights, the final weights will be both positive or both negative, but the direction does not change.

Oja's Synapse

> The step size now controls the speed of convergence. If the step size is too large, the learning will become unstable, as in the gradient-descent learning case. Large step sizes also produce rattling of the final weights (note that the weights form a linear segment), which should be avoided. If the step size is too small, the process will converge slowly. The best procedure is to start with the adaptation large and anneal its value to a small constant to fine-tune the final position of the weights. This can be accomplished with the scheduler.

6.3.1 Oja's Rule Implements the Maximum Eigenfilter

What is the meaning of the weight vector of a neural network trained with Oja's rule? To answer this question, let us study a single linear PE network with multiple inputs (Figure 6-2), using the ideas of vector spaces. The goal is to study the projection defined by the weights created with Oja's rule. We already saw that Hebbian learning finds the direction where the input data has the largest projection, but the weight vector grows without limit. With Oja's rule we found a way to normalize the weight vector to 1. We should expect that this normalization will not change the geometric picture we developed for the Hebbian network. In fact, it is possible to show that Oja's rule finds a weight vector $\mathbf{w} = \mathbf{e}_1$ that satisfies the relation

$$\mathbf{R}\mathbf{e}_1 = \lambda_1 \mathbf{e}_1 \qquad (6.14)$$

where $\mathbf{R}$ is the autocorrelation function of the input data and λ is a real-value scalar. This equation was already encountered in Chapter 1 and tells us that $\mathbf{e}_1$ is an *eigenvector* of the autocorrelation function, since rotating $\mathbf{e}_1$ by $\mathbf{R}$ (the left side) produces a vector colinear with itself. We can further show that in fact λ_1 is the largest eigenvalue of $\mathbf{R}$, so $\mathbf{e}_1$ is the eigenvector that corresponds to the largest eigenvalue. We conclude that training the linear PE with Oja's algorithm produces a weight vector that is the eigenvector of the input autocorreclation matrix, and produces at its output the largest eigenvalue. This linear network is called the maximum eigenfilter.

Proof of Eigenequation

To enhance the readability of the equations, we will use matrix notation and rewrite Oja's rule as

$$\frac{\mathbf{w}(n+1) - \mathbf{w}(n)}{\eta} = \mathbf{y}(n)\mathbf{x}(n) - \mathbf{y}^2(n)\mathbf{w}(n)$$

The differential equation that corresponds to this difference equation is

$$\frac{d\mathbf{w}(t)}{d(t)} = \mathbf{R}_x\mathbf{w}(t) - [\mathbf{w}(t)^T\mathbf{R}_x\mathbf{w}(t)]\mathbf{w}(t)$$

Any solution of this equation has to be an eigenvector e_i of **R** (see, for instance, Diamantaras and Kung [1996]). Now writing $w(t)$ as a linear combination of its basis vectors e_i,

$$w(t) = \sum_i \alpha_i(t)e_i$$

one can further show that the weights adapted with Oja's rule converge with probability 1 to either e_1 or $-e_1$ (i.e., to the eigenvector that corresponds to the largest eigenvalue of **R**). This is the reason a linear network adapted with Oja's rule is sometimes called the *maximum eigenfilter.*

Figure 6-7 shows a simple case in two dimensions. It shows a data cluster (black dots) spread along the 45-degree line. The *principal axis* of the data is the direction in 2-D space where the data has its largest power (projection variance). Imagine a line passing through the center of the cluster, and rotate it so that the data cluster produces the largest spread in the line. For this case the direction will be close to 45 degrees. The weight vector of the network of Figure 6-2 trained with Oja's rule coincides exactly with the principal axis, also called the principal component. The projection on the direction perpendicular to it (the *minor axis*) produces a much smaller spread. For zero-mean data the direction of maximum spread coincides with the direction where most of the information about the data resides. The analysis is the same when the data exists in a larger-dimensionality space D, but we cannot visualize it as well.

If you relate this figure with the NeuroSolutions example, the Oja's weight vector found the direction where the data produced the largest projection. This is a very important property, because the simple one-PE network trained with Oja's rule extracts the most information that it can from the input. In engineering applications where the input data is normally corrupted by noise, this system will provide a solution that maximizes the ratio of signal power (normally the sinusoidal component) to noise power.

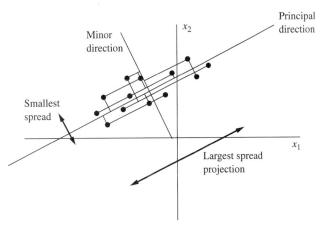

FIGURE 6-7 Projection of a data cluster onto the principal components

Definition of Eigenfilter

An eigenfilter is associated with the eigendecomposition we studied in Chapter 5. Recall that there we were looking for natural bases to decompose functions. Here we look at ways of naturally decomposing data clusters. The eigenfunctions are the bases from which the functions are exactly constructed by a finite weighted sum (the projection theorem), so they are the most efficient way to decompose any function.

Oja's rule when applied to the linear PE network implements a decomposition that finds the weights corresponding to the principal component direction. This direction maximizes the projection of the input data cluster. To find this direction, the input data has to be projected by a "filter" matched to the data, hence the name *maximum eigenfilter.* We should think of the weights of the network as the bases (as we did in Chapter 5) and the network output as the scalar in the projection theorem.

There is a very important concept hidden here. When we directly use data collected from sensors (measurements), the representation space is given by our measurements. This space may not best capture the relevant properties of the data. The principal directions tell us the bases that best represent the data.

6.4 PRINCIPAL COMPONENT ANALYSIS

We saw that Oja's rule found a normalized weight vector that is colinear with the principal component of the input data. But how can we find other directions where the data cluster has still-appreciable variance? We would like to create more axes of the principal coordinate system mentioned in Section 6.2.5. For simplicity we would like to create a data-dependent orthogonal coordinate system (i.e., all the vectors are orthogonal to each other) with unit length vectors (orthonormal coordinate system). How can we do this? Principal component analysis answers this question.

From linear algebra we know that if a D-dimensional vector $\mathbf{x}$ has zero mean and covariance matrix $\mathbf{C}$, then there exists an orthogonal transform $\mathbf{y} = \mathbf{Q}^T\mathbf{x}$ such that the covariance matrix of $\mathbf{y}$ is $\mathbf{\Lambda} = E\{\mathbf{yy}^T\}$ and

$$\mathbf{\Lambda} = \begin{bmatrix} \lambda_1 & \dots & 0 \\ \dots & \dots & \dots \\ 0 & \dots & \lambda_D \end{bmatrix},$$

where $\lambda_1 \geq \lambda_2 \geq \cdots \lambda_D$ are the eigenvalues of $\mathbf{C}$ and the columns of $\mathbf{Q}$ are the corresponding eigenvectors. $\mathbf{Q}$ is called the eigenvector matrix. The ith component of $\mathbf{y}$, $y_i = \mathbf{q}_i^T\mathbf{x}$ has the maximum variance among all normalized linear combinations uncorrelated with the other components. This vector $\mathbf{y}$ defines the vector of principal components of $\mathbf{x}$ and the procedure is called principal component analysis (PCA). For zero mean variables, the covariance matrix $\mathbf{C}$ defaults to the autocorrelation matrix $\mathbf{R}$ that we have been using in previous sections.

PCA is a very well known statistical procedure that has important properties. Suppose that we have input data of very large dimensionality (D dimensions). We would like to project this data onto a smaller-dimensionality space M ($M < D$), a step that is commonly called *feature extraction.* Projection always distorts our data somewhat (just think of a 3-D object and its 2-D shadow). Obviously, we would like to do this projection to M-dimensional space while *maximally preserving the dispersion* (variance from a representation point of view) about the input data. The linear projection that accomplishes this goal is the PCA.

PCA is therefore the best linear feature extractor for signal reconstruction. The error e in the approximation when we utilize M features is given by

$$e^2 = \sum_{i=M+1}^{D} \lambda_i \tag{6.15}$$

Equation 6.15 tells that the error power is equal to the sum of the eigenvalues that were discarded. For the case of Figure 6-7 the minimum error in representing the 2-D data set in a 1-D space is obtained when the principal direction is chosen as the projection axis. The error power is given by the projection on the minor direction. If we decided to keep the projection in the minor direction, the error incurred would have been much higher. This method of representing signals in successively larger spaces whose axes are determined from the data is called *subspace decomposition,* and it is widely applied in signal processing and statistics to find the best subspace of a given dimension that maximally preserves data information. There are well-known algorithms that analytically compute PCA, but they have to solve matrix equations (see the box on SVD below).

Can we build a neural network that implements PCA on-line with local learning rules? The answer is affirmative. We have to use a linear network with multiple outputs (equal to the dimension M of the projection space), as in Figure 6-8.

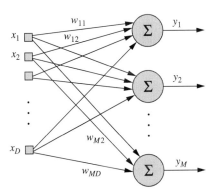

FIGURE 6-8 A PCA network to project the data from D to M dimensions.

The idea is very simple. First, we compute the largest eigenvector, as done earlier with Oja's rule. Then we project the data onto a space perpendicular to the largest eigenvector, and we apply the algorithm again to find the second largest principal component, and so on, until order $M \leq D$. The projection onto the orthogonal space is easily accomplished by subtracting the output of all previous output components (after convergence) from the input. This method is called the *deflation method* and mimics the Gram-Schmidt orthogonalization procedure.

Gram-Schmidt Orthogonalization

The question is very simple. Given a set of vectors $\{x_1, \ldots, x_m\}$ spanning a space S (i.e., the space of all their linear combinations), can we find a rotation that will orthogonalize all the vectors and preserve the span?

The solution was proposed many years ago by Gram-Schmidt in the form of a recursive procedure. Let us start with one of the vectors and make

$$\mathbf{v}_1 = \frac{\mathbf{x}_1}{\|\mathbf{x}_1\|^2}$$

Then find a direction orthogonal to the subspace defined by the k vectors already orthogonalized and normalize, which yields

$$\tilde{\mathbf{v}}_{k+1} = \left[\prod_{i=1}^{k}(\mathbf{I} - \mathbf{v}_i\mathbf{v}_i^T)\right]\mathbf{x}_{k+1}$$

which due to the previously orthogonalized vectors yields

$$\tilde{\mathbf{v}}_{k+1} = \mathbf{x}_{k+1} - \sum_{i=1}^{k}(\mathbf{v}_i^T\mathbf{x}_{k+1})\mathbf{v}_i \quad \text{and} \quad \mathbf{v}_{k+1} = \frac{\tilde{\mathbf{v}}_{k+1}}{\|\tilde{\mathbf{v}}_{k+1}\|^2}$$

It is interesting to look at this equation in a figure for the case of two vectors.

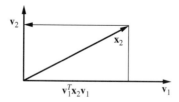

This method is in fact a deflation procedure, because it removes the contributions of the previous vectors to the current direction. To see this, we first have to define a projector as a matrix such that $\mathbf{Z}^2 = \mathbf{Z}$. We immediately see that $\mathbf{Z}\mathbf{Z}^T$ is a projector, so when applied to any vector, it will project it to the span of $\mathbf{Z}$. Now, the form $\mathbf{I} - \mathbf{Z}\mathbf{Z}^T$ is also a projector, and it will project any vector to the orthogonal space of $\mathbf{Z}$ (also called the null space of $\mathbf{Z}$). Gram-Schmidt thus uses an iterative projection to the orthogonal space of each vector, so it is a deflation procedure (see Diamantaras and Kung [1996]).

By slightly modifying Oja's learning rule we can implement the deflation method, as was first done by Sanger [1989]. We are assuming that the network has M outputs, each given by

$$y_i(n) = \sum_{i=1}^{D} w_{ij}(n)x_j(n) \qquad i = 1, \ldots, M \tag{6.16}$$

and D inputs ($M \le D$). To apply Sanger's rule the weights are updated according to

$$\Delta w_{ij}(n) = \eta y_i(n) \left[x_j(n) - \sum_{k=1}^{i} w_{kj}(n)y_k(n) \right] \tag{6.17}$$

This rule resembles the Oja's update, but now the input to each PE is modified by subtracting the product of the outputs from the preceding PEs and the respective weights. This implements the deflation method after the system converges. The weight update of Eq. 6.17 is not local, since we need all the previous network outputs to compute the weight update to weight w_{ij}. However, there are other rules that use local updates (such as the APEX algorithm [Diamantaras and Kung 1996]).

As we can expect from Eq. 6.17 and the explanation, the adaptation is coupled; that is, only after convergence of the first PE weights will the second PE weights converge completely to the eigenvector that corresponds to the second largest eigenvalue. A two-output PCA network has weight vectors that correspond to the principal and minor components of Figure 6-5. The power of the two outputs correspond to the largest and smallest eigenvalues, respectively. The interesting thing about subspace projections is that in many problems the data is already restricted to an (unknown) subspace, so PCA can effectively perform data compression while preserving the major features of the data.

NEUROSOLUTIONS EXAMPLE 6.6
Sanger's rule and PCA

This example introduces Sanger's rule (look at the synapse with the label "Sang" in the Breadboard). Sanger's rule implements PCA. The dimension M of the output determines the size of the output space, that is, the number of eigenvectors, and also the number of features used to represent the input data. PCA finds the M weight vectors that capture the most variance about the input data. For instance, a three-output Sanger's network will find three orthogonal vectors; the principal axis, which captures more variance than any other vector in the input space, and the two vectors that capture the second and third most. In this example we take a high-dimensional input (8×8 images of the 10 digits) and project them onto their M principal components. M is a variable that you can control by setting the number of outputs of the Sanger's network. The outputs of the PCA network are the features obtained by the projection.

Sanger's Synapse

We then use a custom DLL to recreate the digits using only the M features. This DLL takes the output of the Sanger's network and multiplies it by the transpose of **W**, so it recreates a 64-output image. This image shows us how much of the original information in the input we have captured in the M-dimensional subspace. When the two images are identical, we have preserved in the features the information contained in the input data.

The display of the eigenvectors (the PCA weights) is not easy, since they are vectors in a 64-dimensional space. After convergence they are orthogonal. We can use the Hinton probe to visualize their values, but it is difficult to find patterns. (In fact, the signs should alternate more frequently toward the higher order, meaning that finer details are being encoded.) Try different values for the subspace dimension M, and verify that PCA is very robust; that is, even with just a few dimensions the reconstructed digits can be recognized.

A word of caution is needed at this point. The PCA finds the subspace that best represents the ensemble of digits, so the best discrimination among the digits in the subspace is not guaranteed with PCA. If the goal is discrimination among the digits, a classifier should be designed for that purpose. PCA is a linear representation mechanism and only guarantees that the features contain the most information for reconstruction.

PCA decomposition is a very important operation in data processing because it provides knowledge about the hidden structure (latent variables) of the data. Thus there are many other possible formulations for the problem.

PCA, SVD, and KL Transforms

We have to briefly cover the mathematics of principal component analysis (PCA) to fully understand and apply the concept.

PCA and singular value decomposition (SVD) are intrinsically related. Let us start with the SVD because it is an algebraic operation applicable to any matrix. The goal of SVD is to diagonalize any matrix, that is, to find a rotation where only the diagonal elements are nonzero.

Consider the matrix $\mathbf{Z}$ with M rows and N columns ($M \times N$). For every such matrix there are two orthonormal matrices, $\mathbf{U}$ ($M \times M$) and $\mathbf{V}$ ($N \times N$) and a pseudodiagonal matrix $\mathbf{D} = diag\{\sigma_1, \ldots, \sigma_p\}$ ($M \times N$), where $P = \min\{M, N\}$ such that

$$\mathbf{Z} = \mathbf{UDV}^T \quad \text{or} \quad \mathbf{Z} = \sum_{i=1}^{P} \sigma_i \mathbf{u}_i \mathbf{v}_i^T$$

The vectors $\mathbf{u}$ and $\mathbf{v}$ are called the left and right singular vectors of $\mathbf{Z}$, while the σ are called the singular values of $\mathbf{Z}$.

SVD is intrinsically related to the eigendecomposition of a matrix. In fact, if we post-multiply by $\mathbf{Z}^T\mathbf{U}$, we obtain $\mathbf{ZZ}^T\mathbf{U} = \mathbf{UDV}^T\mathbf{Z}^T\mathbf{U} = \mathbf{UDD}^T$. We can likewise show that $\mathbf{Z}^T\mathbf{ZV} = \mathbf{VD}^T\mathbf{D}$. Now $\mathbf{DD}^T$ and $\mathbf{D}^T\mathbf{D}$ are square diagonal matrices, and so the vectors $\mathbf{u}$ and $\mathbf{v}$ are the eigenvectors of the matrices $\mathbf{ZZ}^T$ and $\mathbf{Z}^T\mathbf{Z}$, respectively:

$$\mathbf{ZZ}^T\mathbf{u}_i = \sigma_i^2 \mathbf{u}_i \qquad i = 1, \ldots, M$$
$$\mathbf{Z}^T\mathbf{Z}\mathbf{v}_i = \sigma_i^2 \mathbf{v}_i \qquad i = 1, \ldots, N$$

Now let us define PCA. Consider a vector $\mathbf{x} = [x_1, \ldots, x_D]^T$ with mean zero and co-variance $\mathbf{R} = E[\mathbf{xx}^T]$, which is a symmetric matrix ($D \times D$). PCA produces a linear transformation of the data $\mathbf{y} = \mathbf{Wx}$ where the columns of $\mathbf{W}$ form an orthonormal basis. PCA has a very nice property: It minimizes the mean square error between the projected data (to a subspace M) and the original data. The reconstructed data from the projections is a vector $\hat{\mathbf{x}} = \mathbf{W}^T\mathbf{y} = \mathbf{W}^T\mathbf{Wx}$. PCA thus minimizes

$$J = E\{\|\mathbf{x} - \hat{\mathbf{x}}\|^2\} = tr(\mathbf{R}) - tr(\mathbf{WRW}^T)$$

where $tr(.)$ means the trace of the matrix. The trace of $\mathbf{WRW}^T$ is effectively the variance of y, i.e.

$$tr(\mathbf{WRW}^T) = \sum_{i=1}^{M} y_i^2$$

Thus the minimization of J implies the maximization of the variance of y, which is also the variance of the estimated projection. This provides still another interpretation for PCA: PCA is the linear projection that maximizes the variance (power) of the projection to a subspace.

It is interesting to analyze the characteristics of the PCA projection, that is, the structure of $\mathbf{W}$. If the eigenvalues of $\mathbf{R}$ $\{e_1, \ldots, e_D\}$ are ordered in descending order of the eigenvalues $\{\lambda_1, \ldots, \lambda_D\}$, we can show that

$$\min J = \sum_{i=M+1}^{D} \lambda_i \qquad tr(\mathbf{WRW}^T) = \sum_{i=1}^{M} \lambda_i$$

These two equations basically state that if we project the data with PCA to a subspace of dimension M, we preserve the variance given by the sum of the first M (principal) eigenvalues. The error can also be easily obtained by adding the $D - M - 1$ (minor) eigenvalues.

The projections are called the principal components of x. They are statistically uncorrelated:

$$E\{y_i, y_j\} = \mathbf{e}_i^T \mathbf{R} \mathbf{e}_j = 0$$

and their variances are equal to the eigenvalues of $\mathbf{R}$:

$$E\{y\} = \mathbf{e}_i^T \mathbf{R} \mathbf{e}_i = \lambda_i$$

and are arranged by descending order of variance.

Since $\mathbf{R}$ is a symmetric matrix, we can say that it can always be decomposed as

$$\mathbf{R} = \mathbf{e} \Lambda \mathbf{e}^T = \sum_{i=1}^{D} \lambda_i \mathbf{e}_i \mathbf{e}_i^T$$

where Λ is a diagonal matrix with entries λ_i, the eigenvalues, and $\mathbf{e}_i$ are the eigenvectors. This equation shows the special function that eigenvectors represent for a matrix. They diagonalize it; that is, they represent the direction in space where we can compute the entries of the matrix using only scalar operations. Alternatively, once the eigenvectors and eigenvalues are known, we can construct $\mathbf{R}$ with scalar operations! This means we have found the structure of the data.

We see that the PCA is actually operating with the eigenstructure of $\mathbf{R}$, hence its importance. In general, only the data is known, not $\mathbf{R}$. Even when $\mathbf{R}$ is known, normally its eigenstructure is not quantified. But when we perform PCA, we discover the dependencies on the data, and we can even project it to a subspace to simplify the analysis and lose the least variance.

Now the equivalence between SVD and PCA should be clear. In fact, if $\mathbf{Z}$ is square and symmetric, the two orthogonal matrices $\mathbf{U}$ and $\mathbf{V}$ become the same, and SVD becomes equivalent to PCA.

Last, we would like to define the Karhunen-Loeve transform (KLT). This transform was originally developed to study decompositions of continuous time signals. But for finite duration (D), discrete signals, it can be formulated in the following way.

Consider the stationary random process $\mathbf{x}(n)$ with zero mean and autocorrelation matrix $\mathbf{R}$ with elements $\mathbf{R}(l, k) = E[x(n - k)x(n - l)]$. The KLT is defined as the set of bases $\mathbf{u}_i(n)$ that satisfy the relation

$$\sum_{k=0}^{D-1} \mathbf{R}(l, k) \mathbf{u}_i(k) = \lambda_i \mathbf{u}_i(l) \qquad i, l = 0, \ldots, D - 1$$

We can write this expression in matrix form to read $\mathbf{R} \mathbf{u}_i = \lambda_i \mathbf{u}_i$, and we immediately recognize the eigenvalue equation involving the (time) autocorrelation of the data. KLT and PCA therefore yield the same solution for the case of finite-duration, discrete signals.

6.4.1 PCA for Data Compression

PCA is the optimal linear feature extractor. This means that there is no other linear system that is able to provide better features for reconstruction. One of the obvious PCA applications is therefore data compression. In data compression the goal is to be able to transmit as few bits per second as possible while preserving as much of the source information as possible. This means that we must "squeeze" into each bit as much information as possible from the source. We can model data compression as a projection operation where the goal is to find a set of bases that produce a large concentration of signal power in only a few components.

In PCA compression the receiver must know the weight matrix containing the eigenvectors, since the estimation of the input from the eigenvalues is done by

$$\tilde{\mathbf{x}} = \mathbf{W}^T \mathbf{y} \tag{6.18}$$

The weight matrix is obtained after training with exemplars from the data to be transmitted. It has been shown that for special applications this step can be completed efficiently and is done only once, so the receiver can be constructed beforehand. The reconstruction step requires $M \times D$ operations, where D is the input vector dimension and M is the size of the subspace (number of features).

6.4.2 PCA Features and Classification

We may think that a system able to optimally preserve signal energy in a subspace should also be the optimal projector for classification. Unfortunately, this is not the case. The reason can be seen in Figure 6-9, where we have represented two classes. When the PCA is computed, no distinction is made between the samples of each class, so the optimal 1-D projection for reconstruction (the principal direction) is along the x_1

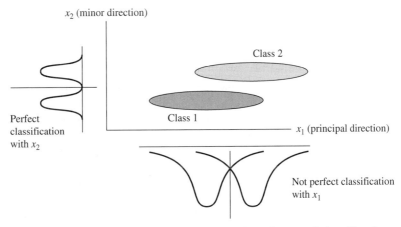

FIGURE 6-9 The relation between eigendirections and classification

axis. However, it is easy to see that the best discrimination between these two clusters is along the x_2 axis, which from the point of view of reconstruction is the minor direction.

PCA chooses the projections that best reconstruct the data in the chosen subspace. This may or may not coincide with the projection for best discrimination. A similar situation occurred when we addressed regression and classification (first example of Chapter 2). A linear regressor can be used as a classifier, but there is no guarantee that it produces the optimal classifier (which by definition minimizes the classification error).

However, PCA is appealing for classification, since it is a simple procedure and experience has shown that it normally provides good features for classification. But this depends on the problem, and there is no guarantee that classifiers based on PCA features will work well.

NEUROSOLUTIONS EXAMPLE 6.7

PCA for preprocessing

In this example we use PCA to find the best possible linear projection for reconstruction, and then we use an MLP to classify the data into one of 10 classes (the digits). Notice that this problem was already solved in Chapter 3 with the perceptron, and we obtained perfect classification using the input data directly.

The only way we can do a fair comparison is to limit the number of weights in the two systems to the same value and compare performances.

6.5 ANTI-HEBBIAN LEARNING

We have seen that Hebbian learning discovers the directions in space where the input data has the largest variance. Let us make a very simple modification to the algorithm by including a minus sign in the weight update rule of Eq. 6.1:

$$\Delta w_{ij} = -\eta x_j y_i \qquad (6.19)$$

This rule is called the *anti-Hebbian rule.* Let us assume that we train the system of Figure 6-2 with this rule. What do you expect this rule will do?

The easiest reasoning is to recall that the Hebbian network maximizes the output variance by doing gradient ascent in the power field. Now, with the negative sign in the weight update equation, the adaptation will seek the minimum of the performance surface; that is, the output variance will be minimized. Hence the output of the linear network trained with anti-Hebbian will always produce *zero output,* because the weights will seek the directions in the input space where the data clusters have a point projection. This is called the *null* (or *orthogonal*) *space of the data.* The network finds this direction by doing gradient descent in the power field.

If the data fills the input space, the only way to minimize the network output is to drive the weights to zero. On the other hand, if the data exists in a subspace, the weights will find the directions where the data projects to a point. For Figure 6-7 anti-Hebbian learning will provide zero weights. However, if the data was one dimensional, that is, along the 45-degree line, then the weights would be placed along the 135-degree line.

NEUROSOLUTIONS EXAMPLE 6.8

Anti-Hebbian learning

In this example we use the Hebbian synapse with a negative step size to implement an anti-Hebbian network. The anti-Hebbian rule minimizes the output variance; thus it will try to find a weight vector that is orthogonal to the input (the null space of the input) such that the projection of the data onto the weight vector is always zero.

There are two cases of importance. Either the data lies in a subspace of the input space, in which case the zero output can be achieved by adapting the weight vector perpendicular to the subspace where the input lies, or the input samples cover the full input space, so the only way to get a zero output is to drive the weights to zero.

Notice how fast the anti-Hebbian network trains. If the data moves in the input space, notice that the weights are always finding the direction orthogonal to the data cluster.

This behavior of anti-Hebbian learning can be considered *decorrelation;* that is, a linear PE trained with anti-Hebbian learning decorrelates the output from its input. We must realize that Hebbian and anti-Hebbian learning have complementary roles in projecting the input data, which are very important for signal processing. For instance, the new high-resolution spectral analysis techniques (such as MUSIC and ESPRIT [Kay 1988]) are based on ways of finding the null space of the data, so they can be implemented on-line using anti-Hebbian learning. We provide an example in Chapter 9.

6.5.1 Convergence of Anti-Hebbian Rule

Another interesting thing is that the convergence of the anti-Hebbian rule can be controlled by the step size, as in LMS or back-propagation. This means that if the step size is too large, the weights will get progressively larger (diverge), but if the step size is below a given value, the adaptation will converge. From the known paraboloid shape of the power field in weight space, we know it has a single minimum. Hence the situation is like gradient descent, which we studied in Chapter 1. What is the value under which the weights converge to finite values?

The anti-Hebbian update for one weight is

$$w(n + 1) = w(n)(1 - \eta x^2(n)) \tag{6.20}$$

If we take expectations and use induction, as we did in Section 1.6.3 to compute the largest step size for the LMS, we can conclude that

$$w(n + 1) = (1 - \eta\lambda)w(n) \qquad \textbf{(6.21)}$$

which is stable if

$$\eta < \frac{2}{\lambda} \qquad \textbf{(6.22)}$$

where λ is the eigenvalue of the autocorrelation function of the input. We can immediately see the similarity to the convergence of the LMS rule. For a system with multiple inputs the requirement for convergence has to be modified to

$$\eta < \frac{2}{\lambda_{\max}} \qquad \textbf{(6.23)}$$

where $\lambda_{\max}$ is the largest eigenvalue of the input autocorrelation function, as for the LMS case.

NEUROSOLUTIONS EXAMPLE 6.9

Stability of anti-Hebbian rule

This example shows that the anti-Hebbian rule is stable for the range of values given by Eq. 6.23 when random data is utilized. Change the step size to see the compromise between rattling and speed of convergence achieved with the anti-Hebbian rule. Since the weight update is done sample by sample, when the data has deterministic structure, divergence may occur at step sizes smaller than the ones predicted by Eq. 6.23. The same behavior was encountered in the LMS.

6.6   ESTIMATING CROSS-CORRELATION WITH HEBBIAN NETWORKS

Suppose that we have two data sets formed by N exemplars of D-dimensional data $x_1, \ldots, x_D$ and $d_1, \ldots, d_D$, and the goal is to estimate the cross correlation between them. Cross-correlation is a measure of similarity between the two sets of data that extends the idea of the correlation coefficient (see appendix and Chapter 1).

In practice we are often faced with the question of how similar are the $\{x\}$ and $\{d\}$ data sets. Cross-correlation answers this question. Let us assume that the data samples are ordered by their indices. The cross correlation for index i, j is

$$r_{xd}(i, j) = \frac{1}{N}\sum_{k=1}^{N} x_{ik}d_{jk} \qquad 0 < i < D, \ 0 < j < D \qquad \textbf{(6.24)}$$

where N is the number of patterns and D is the size of the input and desired response vectors. The fundamental operation of correlation is to cross multiply the data samples and add the contributions. We can define the average operator as

$$A[\mathbf{u}] = \frac{1}{N} \sum_{k=1}^{N} u_k \tag{6.25}$$

The cross-correlation can then be defined as

$$r_{xd}(i, j) = A[\mathbf{x}_i \mathbf{d}_j] \tag{6.26}$$

where the vector $\mathbf{x}_i = [x_{i1}, x_{i2}, \ldots, x_{iP}]^T$ is built from the ith sample of all the patterns in the input set (likewise for $\mathbf{d}$). The cross-correlation matrix $\mathbf{R}_{xy}$ is built from all possible shifts i, j,

$$\mathbf{R}_{xd} = A \begin{bmatrix} \mathbf{x}_1\mathbf{d}_1 & \mathbf{x}_1\mathbf{d}_2 & \mathbf{x}_1\mathbf{d}_D \\ \ldots & \ldots & \ldots \\ \mathbf{x}_D\mathbf{d}_1 & \mathbf{x}_D\mathbf{d}_2 & \mathbf{x}_D\mathbf{d}_D \end{bmatrix} \tag{6.27}$$

The cross-correlation vector used in regression (Chapter 1) is just the first column of this matrix. Now let us relate this formalism to the calculations of a linear network trained with Hebbian learning. Assume that we have a linear network with D inputs $\mathbf{x}$ and D outputs $\mathbf{y}$ (Figure 6-10).

To compute the cross-correlation between $\mathbf{x}$ and the data set $\mathbf{d}$, we substitute the network output $\mathbf{y}$ in the Hebbian rule by the data set $\mathbf{d}$,

$$\Delta w_{ij} = \eta x_j d_i \tag{6.28}$$

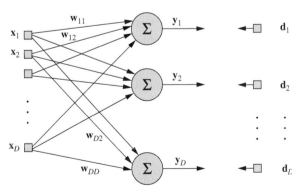

FIGURE 6-10   A multiple input, multiple output Hebbian network

which implements what we call *forced Hebbian learning*. We can write the output y_j as Eq. 6.4, but now with two indices i and j:

$$y_j = \sum_{i=1}^{D} w_{ij} x_i \tag{6.29}$$

The weight w_{ij}, when adapted with forced Hebbian learning, takes the form

$$w_{ij}(n+1) = w_{ij}(n) + \eta x_j(n) d_i(n) \tag{6.30}$$

If $w_{ij}(0) = 0$ after N iterations, we get

$$w_{ij}(N) = \eta \sum_{n=1}^{N} x_j(n) d_i(n) \tag{6.31}$$

By comparing Eq. 6.24 with Eq. 6.31, we conclude that the weight w_{ij} trained with forced Hebbian learning is proportional (after N iterations) to the cross-correlation element r_{ij}. If $\eta = 1/N$ and the initial conditions are zero, this is exactly r_{ij}. Notice also that the elements of the cross-correlation matrix are precisely the weights of the linear network (Eq. 6.27). For this reason the linear network trained with forced Hebbian learning is called a *correlator* or a *hetero-associator*. Hence forced Hebbian learning is an alternative, on-line way of computing the cross-correlation function between two data sets.

NEUROSOLUTIONS EXAMPLE 6.10

Forced Hebbian computes cross-correlation

In this example we show how forced Hebbian learning computes the cross-correlation of the input and desired output. We have a three-input network that we would like to train with a desired response of two outputs. We have created a data set with four patterns. The cross correlation computed according to Eq. 6.24 is

$r(0,0) = 0.5$; $r(0,1) = r(1,0) = 0$; $r(1,1) = 0.25$; $r(0,2) = 0.5$; $r(1,2) = 0.25$

Let us use the Hebbian network and take a look at the final weights. Notice that we started with weights at zero value and stopped the network after 10 iterations of each batch (four patterns) with a step size of 0.025 (1/40).

There are two important applications of this concept that we address in this chapter. One uses cross-correlation with anti-Hebbian learning to find what is different between two data sets and can be considered a novelty filter. The other, possibly even more important, is a memory device called an associative memory.

6.7 NOVELTY FILTERS AND LATERAL INHIBITION

Let us assume that we have two data sets x and d. Taking x as the input to our system, we want to create an output y as *dissimilar* as possible to the data set d (Figure 6-11). This function is very important in signal processing (decorrelation) and in information processing (uncorrelated features), and it seems to be at the core of biological information processing. We humans filter out with extreme ease what we know already from the sensor input (either visual or acoustic). This avoids information overload. It seems that what we do first is to equalize the incoming information with what is expected so that *unexpected things stand out*.

We can consider that the incoming data is represented by x and what the system already knows is represented by d, so novelty is the part of x that is not represented in d. From the point of view of vector operations, this is equivalent to finding a rotation of $\mathbf{x}$ such that $\mathbf{y}$ is orthogonal to $\mathbf{d}$ (i.e., in the null space of $\mathbf{d}$). The system of Figure 6-11 with the learning rule of Eq. 6.19 where $\mathbf{d}$ substitutes for $\mathbf{y}$ (i.e., $\Delta w_{ij} = -\eta x_j d_i$) does exactly this job.

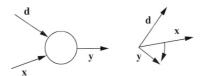

FIGURE 6-11 The function of a decorrelation PE

NEUROSOLUTIONS EXAMPLE 6.11

Novelty filter with anti-Hebbian learning

In this example we show a novelty filter. We have created a three-dimensional input signal that represents the output of a system under normal operating conditions. This system could be a car (outputs = velocity, acceleration, and turning angle), a power plant, or any other system. We train the novelty filter on this data, and anti-Hebbian learning will learn its null space—the vector where the input projection is always very close to zero. The weights are fixed at this point.

When the system changes slightly (abnormal system operation) and its output is fed to the trained novelty filter, the filter output is no longer close to zero because the new signal is no longer in the null space of the filter weights. This indicates that the system is no longer operating normally. We change the parameters of the system midway in the experiment. From the filter output you should be able to pinpoint where the change occurred. Notice that the network inputs (normal and abnormal operating conditions) look very similar throughout the segment, so it would be difficult to find the change in the system by hand.

6.7.1 Lateral Inhibition

Another very useful strategy to decorrelate signals is to create lateral connections between PEs adapted with anti-Hebbian learning (see Foldiak [1989]). Let's analyze the topology depicted in Figure 6-12. In the figure, c is the lateral inhibition connection from y_i to y_j. We use the $+$ superscript to mean the preactivity (input) of the PEs. Note that

$$y_i = y_i^+$$
$$y_j = cy_i^+ + y_j^+$$

The cross correlation between y_i and y_j is

$$R_{ij}(y_i, y_j) = c\sum_{n=1}^{N}[y_i^+(n)]^2 + \sum_{n=1}^{N}y_i^+(n)y_j^+(n)$$

If the power of y_i is greater than zero, there is always a value

$$c = -\frac{\sum_{n=1}^{N}y_i^+(n)y_j^+(n)}{\sum_{n=1}^{N}[y_i^+(n)]^2}$$

which will decorrelate y_i and y_j, that is, make $R(y_i, y_j) = 0$. Notice that this value is the negative of the cross correlation between the ith and jth PE activations, so if we use anti-Hebbian learning with a small step size, the outputs will be decorrelated. Notice that one of the characteristics of PCA is that the outputs are orthogonal, that is, the outputs are uncorrelated. Lateral inhibition basically achieves the same effect; however, the variance of the outputs is not constrained, nor are the weight vectors.

The interesting thing about lateral inhibition is that it can provide an alternative method to construct networks that find the principal component space with a local learning rule, or even provide whitening transforms (i.e., a transform that not only orthogonalizes the input data but also normalizes the eigenvalues).

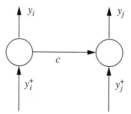

FIGURE 6-12 Lateral inhibition connections

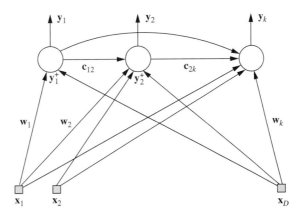

FIGURE 6-13   The APEX topology for PCA

6.7.2 APEX Model for PCA

Diamantaras [1996] has shown that the network of Figure 6-13 implements PCA when the weights are adapted according to

$$\begin{cases} \Delta w_i = \eta y_i(n)[x(n) - y_i(n)w_i] \\ \Delta c_{ji} = -\eta y_i(n)[y_j(n) + y_i(n)c_{ji}] \end{cases}$$

Note that the weights are adapted using Oja's rule, while a form of anti-Hebbian learning is used to adapt the lateral connections. Note that all the quantities are local to the weights, so the rule is actually local. The system learns the principal components in parallel, unlike Sanger's rule that is based on deflation.

6.7.3 Whitening Transform

A whitening transform is a very important linear transformation in adaptive systems, because it transforms any data described by an autocorrelation $\mathbf{R}$ with an arbitrary eigenvalue spread into an orthonormal matrix (i.e., a matrix with all the eigenvalues equal to a constant). For whitened data the LMS algorithm is as fast as Newton's method since the eigenvalue spread is 1. Whitening the input data drastically improves the speed of linear learning systems using first-order methods. We now present a topology and learning rule that will produce a whitening transform [Silva and Almeida 1991].

   The network that implements the whitening transform is like the one in Figure 6-13. The idea of the algorithm is very similar to the Gram-Schmidt procedure, but it adapts all the vectors at the same time, yielding a symmetric adaptation structure. The adaptation rule reads

$$w_{ij}(n+1) = (1+\eta)w_{ij}(n) - \eta \sum_{k=1}^{D} y_i(n)y_k(n)w_{kj}(n)$$

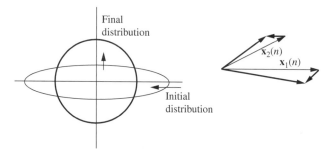

FIGURE 6-14 Whitening transform and the corresponding weight update

Notice that this formula specifies a weight update that is not local to the weights. However with lateral inhibition we can easily implement it in a single-layer network (Figure 6-13). Notice that the sum over k can be implemented by bringing a lateral inhibition connection from the kth PE to the ith PE with a weight copied from the forward connections and connecting the jth input with the kth PE. Silva discusses another implementation and also proves the convergence of the algorithm. The interesting thing about this transformation is that it creates an orthonormal space at the output by equalizing the eigenvalues instead of by rotating the axis, as done in PCA (Figure 6-14). This is reportedly much faster than PCA for a variety of problems.

6.8 LINEAR ASSOCIATIVE MEMORIES (LAMs)

Information processing requires memorization of information. In digital computers one memory location stores one bit of information, so the information is stored individually. An interesting task is to seek ways to store information in a more global way, that is, by having several PEs store many data patterns, and then to ask the question, What system is more efficient and robust to noise?

The linear associator, also called a linear associative memory (LAM), provides an alternative computer memory paradigm. The research has strong ties to psychology, since today it is fairly well accepted that the brain does not store each bit of information separately. Many neurons (cell assembly) store many patterns.

The system of Figure 6-10 trained with the forced Hebbian rule (Eq. 6.28) can be used as an associative memory, that is, a device that can be trained to associate an input **x** to a response **d**. Then, in the absence of **d**, **x** can produce an output **y** that resembles **d**. The question is, How can information be stored globally, and how can we retrieve it?

We use matrix notation for convenience. Let the input set of N elements be denoted as a vector **x**. Likewise, **y** is the corresponding N-component output vector. The output, being linear, can be obtained as $\mathbf{y} = \mathbf{W}\mathbf{x}$, where **W** is the weight matrix. Forced

Hebbian learning constructs each weight according to Eq. 6.28, which can be written in matrix notation as the outer product, $\mathbf{W} = \mathbf{d}\mathbf{x}^T$. When the input $\mathbf{x}$ is entered in the linear associator, the output created by the system is thus

$$\mathbf{y} = \mathbf{d}\mathbf{x}^T\mathbf{x} \propto \mathbf{d} \qquad (6.32)$$

which is proportional to the original output utilized in the training (remember that $\mathbf{x}^T\mathbf{x}$ is a constant equal to the length of the vector $\mathbf{x}$).

The interesting question is, What happens when more than one input vector is stored in the memory? Can we still recover each one of the inputs, or is the output contaminated by the other inputs?

NEUROSOLUTIONS EXAMPLE 6.12

LAM application

In this example we use a linear associative memory (LAM) to associate area codes (three digits) with prices for long-distance phone calls (two digits). When we input an area code, we would like the network to output the correct price for the corresponding long-distance phone call rate. During training we use heteroassociation to train the LAM. We have encoded the area codes and rates as binary digits (12 and 8 bits, respectively). Hence this LAM will have 12 inputs and 8 outputs.

We have created input files that contain a set of three binary-encoded area codes and prices. We have also added a custom DLL that allows us to display a sequence of binary digits as the equivalent number. Once the network is trained, we can present the area code, and the system will produce the corresponding long-distance call rate at the output.

It is interesting to ask where the information is stored. The answer is in the weights throughout the network. This is rather different from the storage we use in digital computers, where the memory is addressed. If we lose the address, the item stored can never be recovered. Here we recall the output by providing the input (i.e., the content of the memory, so they are called *content addressable memories* (CAMs)).

CAMs are very robust. Use a Matrix Editor to zero one or several weights, and observe that the output barely changes. (Notice that the numbers displayed are subject to an encoding, so they change only when there are drastic modifications in one of the bits.) If one bit was lost in the address or content of a computer memory, the original content would be impossible to retrieve (unless coding—which is redundancy—was used).

Another interesting thing is that these memories cover the input space with a similarity measure (the inner-product metric, as we have seen previously). For numeric inputs this is not often important, since numeric information is normally precise. But for names, words, concepts, and so on, similarity is very useful (Is his name Gary, Cary, Gerry, or Larry?). To see this property of LAMs, let us change just one of the input digits and verify that the output is basically unchanged. These are nice properties of LAMs that make them very good models for human memory in cognitive science.

6.8.1 Crosstalk in LAMs

Let us assume that we have K input-output vector pairs $\mathbf{x}_k \rightarrow \mathbf{d}_k$. The associative memory is trained by repeated presentation of each input, so using the principle of superposition, the final weight matrix is the sum of the individual weight matrices:

$$\mathbf{W} = \sum_{k=1}^{K} \mathbf{W}_k \tag{6.33}$$

where each $\mathbf{W}_k = \mathbf{x}_k \mathbf{x}_k^T$. When an input vector $\mathbf{x}_l$ is presented to the network, its output is

$$\mathbf{y} = \mathbf{W}\mathbf{x}_l = \mathbf{d}_l \mathbf{x}_l^T \mathbf{x}_l + \sum_{k=1, k \neq l}^{K} \mathbf{d}_k \mathbf{x}_k^T \mathbf{x}_l \tag{6.34}$$

The associative memory output is built up from two terms. The first, which is the true output for the input $\mathbf{x}_l$ is added with a term that is called the *crosstalk* because it measures how much the other outputs interfere with the true one. But if the crosstalk term is small, Eq. 6.34 tells us that in fact the associative memory is able to retrieve the pattern that corresponds to $\mathbf{x}$ during training (the association).

The crosstalk is a function of how similar the input $\mathbf{x}_l$ is to the other inputs $\mathbf{x}_k$. This can be better understood in a geometric setting. Assume that the input patterns are vectors in a D-dimensional vector space. The output of the linear associator, being a product of a matrix by a vector (Eq. 6.34), rotates the input $\mathbf{x}_l$ to obtain y. The goal is to obtain a rotation that produced the expected association to $\mathbf{d}_l$. What Eq. 6.34 is saying is that the actual output $\mathbf{y}$ is constructed by two terms. The first is the desired output $\mathbf{d}_l$ scaled by the length of $\mathbf{x}_l$, and the second is a sum of contributions that depend on the inner product of all the other input patterns $\mathbf{x}_k$ with $\mathbf{x}_l$. Figure 6-15 shows the construction for two vectors only.

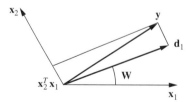

FIGURE 6-15 Output with crosstalk

If the inputs are all orthogonal, the inner product of $\mathbf{x}_l$ and $\mathbf{x}_k$ is zero (zero crosstalk), and the linear associator produces perfect recall. However, if the input patterns are not orthogonal, each one of the $\mathbf{y}_k$ in the sum is multiplied by the projection of the input vector k on l, which can add up to a large number, rotating and changing the length of the true output $\mathbf{d}$. If the crosstalk term is comparable to the first term, the linear associator produces an output that has nothing to do with the expected response $\mathbf{d}$.

This analysis brings us immediately to the concept of *storage capacity*, which is defined as the maximum number of patterns that can be stored and recalled without degradation. Associative memories, unlike computer memories, have finite storage capacity. We know that in a space of dimension D, there are only D possible orthogonal directions, so perfect recall is limited to a number of patterns equal to the size of the input space (length of the input vector). In practical conditions the inputs may not be orthogonal to each other, so if orthogonality is not enforced, the crosstalk term may be large even for a number of patterns less than D. But it is always possible (although computationally expensive) to project a set of D vectors onto a D-dimensional orthogonal basis (as we saw with PCA). In fact, we do not need to perform PCA, we just need to find a spanning orthogonal set of vectors, which is possible with simpler algorithms. Using such a preprocessor, we can thus say that perfect recall can be achieved for a number of patterns equal to the size of the input layer. Therefore the storage capacity of the linear associator equals D. When the number of patterns is larger than the space dimensionality, a severe degradation of performance can be expected.

NEUROSOLUTIONS EXAMPLE 6.13

LAM and crosstalk

This example is exactly the same as before, but now we have added more patterns that happen to be correlated (nonorthogonal). This will produce crosstalk. Run the network and observe that now the output values do not correspond to the desired response for two reasons. First, the outputs that were zero now have nonzero values (watch the size of the bars), and second, for some patterns the output does not match the desired values. The errors get worse when the number of 1s in the patterns increases and also when more patterns are included. This is the problem of crosstalk.

This analysis describes the theoretical basis for associative memories. When we train such a system with a set of input-output vectors using Hebbian learning, the network produces an output similar to the individual output, provided that the number of patterns is less than the input space dimensionality. Orthogonalization of the patterns may have to be performed to achieve perfect recall.

LAMs are very different from computer memories. They are content addressable and global, while computer memories are location addressable and local. Hence they have very different properties: Computer memory is precise (no crosstalk), has no limitation on size (just increase the width of the address bus), but is brittle. Once a bit is in error, the full memory system breaks down (which requires error correction). On the other hand, LAMs are very robust to errors in the weights, but they suffer from limited storage and crosstalk. They also have the wonderful property of association; that is, the pattern that is closest to the input is recalled. How often have you wished to have the property of association when retrieving information from a computer database?

In Chapter 11 we will see another type of associative memory with recurrent connections that is able to clean crosstalk to a certain extent, clean the noise from the input, or even complete partially occluded patterns by feeding back the output to the input several times. In each iteration a better approximation of the stored pattern is obtained, so the system can self-correct errors. The most famous of these recurrent memories is the Hopfield network.

6.9 LMS LEARNING AS A COMBINATION OF HEBBIAN RULES

The LMS rule studied in Chapter 1 can be created by a combination of Hebbian-type rules between the desired response and the learning system input. In fact, if we recall the LMS rule

$$\Delta w_{ij} = \eta \varepsilon_i x_j \tag{6.35}$$

and note that the error ε can be expressed by

$$\varepsilon_i = d_i - y_i \tag{6.36}$$

we get

$$\Delta w_{ij} = \eta(d_i x_j - y_i x_j) \tag{6.37}$$

that is, the LMS rule is a combination of a Hebbian term between the desired response and the input and an anti-Hebbian term between the PE output and its input. The first term substitutes the desired response for the system output, so it is the forced Hebbian term. LMS is thus a combination of forced Hebbian and anti-Hebbian rules.

We can interpret the LMS adaptation as a composition of two different Hebbian forces: the forced Hebbian term that makes the output similar to the desired response and the anti-Hebbian term that decorrelates the input and the system output. The forced Hebbian term does gradient ascent on the performance surface and is unstable, as we saw earlier. The anti-Hebbian term decorrelates the input from the output and drives the output to zero, allowing a range of step sizes to produce convergence to the minimum of the performance surface. The anti-Hebbian term controls the convergence of the LMS algorithm, since the product of desired and input responses is independent of the weights. It is understandable that the range of step sizes for convergence of the anti-Hebbian and LMS rules are the same.

An important conclusion is that the Hebbian principle of correlation is also present in supervised learning. This simple derivation calls our attention to the fact that the learning principles studied so far in neurocomputing (Hebbian, LMS, and back-propagation) are based on correlation learning (or compositions of correlation learning).

We can alternatively consider the LMS algorithm as a "smart" forced Hebbian learning rule because it correlates the system output with the desired response, as Hebbian learning does, but does so without being unstable (for a range of step sizes) due to the anti-Hebbian component. Hence we can expect that the LMS will improve forced Hebbian learning in the same way as Oja's rule improved Hebbian learning.

6.9.1 Improving the Performance of Linear Associative Memories (OLAMs)

An alternative to orthogonalization of the input patterns is to use different learning rules during training. We can interpret the individual output pattern as the desired response for the linear associator, and then train it with the error

$$\boldsymbol{\varepsilon} = \mathbf{d} - \mathbf{y} = \mathbf{d} - \mathbf{W}\mathbf{x} \tag{6.38}$$

instead of directly with $\mathbf{d}$ (Eq. 6.28). This equation should remind us of the supervised learning procedure used in regression (Chapter 1), which led to the design of the LMS algorithm. Supervised learning can thus be applied to train the linear associator for heteroassociation. Note that with LMS training the weights are being modified at each iteration by

$$\Delta\mathbf{W}(n) = \eta\boldsymbol{\varepsilon}(n)\mathbf{x}^T(n) = \eta\mathbf{d}(n)\mathbf{x}^T(n) - \eta\mathbf{y}(n)\mathbf{x}^T(n) \tag{6.39}$$

The first term is the desired forced Hebbian update, which is combined with a term that decorrelates the present output y from the input (the anti-Hebbian term). If we compare Eq. 6.39 with Eq. 6.28, we can conclude that the anti-Hebbian term reduces the crosstalk term at each iteration, so training the associative memory with LMS is an efficient way to improve its performance in terms of reduced crosstalk for correlated input patterns. A LAM trained with LMS is called an optimal linear associative memory (OLAM).

NEUROSOLUTIONS EXAMPLE 6.14

Optimal LAMs

This example uses the same basic network and files as the previous example, but now we train the LAM using LMS. Notice the difference in the breadboard (the backpropagation plane). Observe the network during training, and watch the response approximate the ideal response obtained with the orthogonal patterns. If we train enough and the number of patterns is less than the size of the space, the ideal response will be obtained.

One issue that is worth raising is why are we interested in using forced Hebbian learning to train associative memories when LMS works better. From an engineering point of view optimal LAMs should be used. It turns out that the Hebbian paradigm has been utilized by cognitive scientists to study models of human memory. The mistakes associative memories make have the same general character as human memory deficiencies.

Associative memories trained with forced Hebbian learning become rather bad when the density of 1s in the patterns is high; that is, they work reasonably well *only for sparse patterns*. We can understand this, since when the patterns have sparse nonzero values (e.g., only one in 50-bit-long patterns), they are approximately orthogonal, so there is little crosstalk. It turns out that the human brain has so many neurons that the encoding in human memory is probably also sparse, so Hebbian learning makes sense. Moreover, there is physiological evidence for Hebbian learning, while the biological implementation of LMS is unclear at this stage.

6.9.2 LAMs and Linear Regression

You may have noticed that the topologies are similar for the LAM of Figure 6-10 and the linear regression problem we studied in Chapter 1. The marked difference here is that we are interested in multiple-input, multiple-output linear topologies, while in Chapter 1 we studied only the multiple-input, single-output case. But the desired response in multiple regression can also be a vector, in which case the topology for regression becomes exactly that of Figure 6-10. The desired response is effectively the forced response in LAMs, so the difference has to be found in other aspects.

You may recall that in Chapter 1 we used the LMS algorithm to find the optimal regression coefficients, while in LAMs we utilized Hebbian learning. But now that we also propose to use the LMS to find the optimal LAM weights, even this difference is watered down. What is the difference, if any, between a LAM and a linear regressor, which provide least squares solutions?

The difference is very subtle. In linear regression we want to pass a single, optimal hyperplane by *all* the desired samples, while in the LAM we want to output a response that is as close as possible to *each* of the true forced responses. The answer lies in the number of exemplars. In LAMs we just saw that the number of exemplars must be less than the size of the input layer to guarantee small crosstalk. In linear regression the opposite is true. We normally want (and have) more patterns than the size of the input layer of the regressor, so the real difference between a LAM and a regressor is the amount of data, which provides two distinct solutions to the least squares problem. The solution to the LAM is the unconstrained case (more equations than data), while the regression solution is overconstrained (more data than equations). The solution obtained by the LMS for associative memories is in fact one of infinitely many solutions (R is not full rank because we have less data than dimensions). It is interesting that the storage capacity quantifies the dividing line between the unconstrained and the constrained least squares.

Optimal LAMs

The LMS is an iterated method to train a LAM optimally. One can show that the optimal LAM weights have to meet the solution.

$$\mathbf{W}^* = \mathbf{Y}\mathbf{X}^{-1}$$

which exists as long as the inverse of **X** exists (here **X** and **Y** are the matrices constructed from the full training set). This means that the patterns must be linearly independent (instead of orthogonal, as required for Hebbian training). If we have fewer patterns than inputs, the optimal solution is not unique. We can show [Kohonen 1984] that in this case

$$\mathbf{W}^* = \mathbf{Y}(\mathbf{X}^T\mathbf{X})^{-1}\mathbf{X}^T = \mathbf{Y}\mathbf{X}^+$$

which involves the computation of $\mathbf{X}^+$, the pseudo-inverse of **X**. There is a method to compute $\mathbf{W}^*$ recursively (Greville's theorem) using a nonlocal algorithm that resembles the LMS: The LMS with a small step size is a good approximation to this recursive algorithm. See also Hecht-Nielsen [1990].

This also gives a new insight into the terminology of *memorization* in our discussion of generalization in Chapters 4 and 5. The linear network can either memorize (working as a LAM) or generalize the statistical properties of the input-desired response pairs (working as a regressor). We see that the distinctive factor is the relation between the number of input samples versus the number of network weights. Remember that, if we want to create a regressor and the data is less than the number of input dimensions, LMS will provide an associative memory, not a regressor! This clearly shows the risk and the weakness of MSE learning and emphasizes the importance of capacity control (optimal hyperplanes) discussed in the support vector machine theory, Section 5.8. We also conclude that the existence of crosstalk is what makes the linear network generalize.

A similar phenomena occurs with a nonlinear system. If we train it for function approximation with a small number of samples (either for nonlinear regression or classification), we may end up with an associative memory, and it will never generalize well.

6.10 AUTOASSOCIATION

There are basically two types of associative memories: the heteroassociators and the autoassociators. As we have just seen, heteroassociation, or simply association, is the process of providing a link between two distinct sets of data (e.g., faces with names). Heteroassociation is the most widely used associative memory paradigm. Autoassociation links a data set with itself. You may wonder where autoassociation will be useful.

It turns out that autoassociation can be used for input reconstruction, noise removal, and data reduction.

In autoassociation the output pattern is equal to the input (substitute $\mathbf{x}$ for $\mathbf{d}$ in Figure 6-10), and the system is trained either with forced Hebbian learning or with LMS. If we substitute $\mathbf{x}$ for $\mathbf{d}$ in Eq. 6.24, we see that the cross-correlation function becomes the autocorrelation function, and so the weight matrix of Eq. 6.27 becomes the autocorrelation matrix of the input:

$$\mathbf{W} = \mathbf{x}\mathbf{x}^T \tag{6.40}$$

Thus when a pattern is presented to the input and no crosstalk is present, the autoassociator produces an output

$$\mathbf{W}\mathbf{x} = \mathbf{x}\mathbf{x}^T\mathbf{x} \rightarrow \mathbf{R}\mathbf{x} = \lambda\mathbf{x} \tag{6.41}$$

since $\mathbf{x}^T\mathbf{x}$ is a constant equal to the length of the input vector. Recall, that this is exactly the condition for a vector to be an eigenvector of a matrix, so we conclude that the *autoassociator performs an eigendecomposition* of the autocorrelation function; that is, the power of the outputs will be the eigenvalues of the autocorrelation function, and the weights are the associated eigenvectors.

Hebbian as the Minimization of the Reconstruction Error

Let us interpret Hebbian learning in a supervised learning context. In fact, if we have a performance criterion exterior to the network, it is equivalent to thinking of an error, hence of a desired response. What is the implicit desired response in Hebbian learning? It is the input signal itself, and the minimization is to reconstruct $\mathbf{x}$ from $\tilde{\mathbf{x}}$, which is the projection of $\mathbf{y}$ into $\mathbf{W}$, that is, $\tilde{\mathbf{x}} = \mathbf{W}^T\mathbf{y}$. A figure will clarify this procedure.

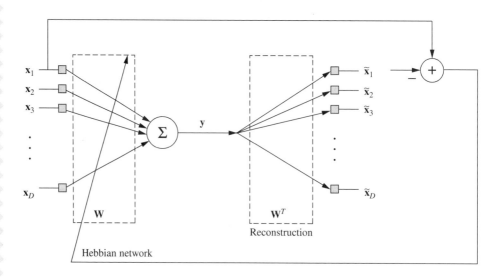

This means that the criterion is the mean square difference between the input and the projected output, that is,

$$J = E(\mathbf{d} - \mathbf{y})^2 = E(\mathbf{x} - \tilde{\mathbf{x}})^2$$

If we substitute the definition of $\mathbf{y} = \mathbf{Wx}$, we get

$$J = E(tr[(\mathbf{x} - \tilde{\mathbf{x}})(\mathbf{x} - \tilde{\mathbf{x}})^T]) = tr(\mathbf{R}_x) - tr(\mathbf{WR}_x\mathbf{W}^T)$$

since

$$tr(E[\mathbf{W}^T\mathbf{Wxx}^T\mathbf{W}^T\mathbf{W}]) = tr(\mathbf{WR}_x\mathbf{W}^T)$$

Now we have a more refined definition of what Hebbian learning is accomplishing from a vector-space point of view. In fact, Hebbian learning can be interpreted as either maximizing the variance of $\mathbf{y}$ (the projection variance, Eq. 6.11) or minimizing the reconstruction error between the input and its version obtained after projecting the output $\mathbf{y}$ on the weight vector (transposed).

The problem is that if we train the system with forced Hebbian learning and the inputs are not orthogonal, there will be crosstalk. However, if the learning rule is the LMS, the crosstalk will be decreased to virtually zero (one can show the solution exists, unlike the case of heteroassociation).

Notice that in the topology of Figure 6-10 there is no flexibility in the reconstruction. We can produce a more powerful network called an *autoencoder* (or *autoassociator*) if we include an extra layer of linear PEs, as in Figure 6-16. The network is normally trained with backpropagation (although the PEs are linear) since there is no desired signal at the hidden layer. We normally impose a constraint that the output matrix $\mathbf{W}_2 = \mathbf{W}_1^T$. Under this constraint we can show that the network will operate in the same way as the PCA network studied in Section 6.4. The square of the signals z_i are effectively the eigenvalues, and their number selects the size of the reconstruction space.

With this constraint we can alternatively train the network using LMS to determine the output-layer weights and then copy them to the transpose locations (reversal of the indices) in the input layer. For this case the weight update using the LMS rule

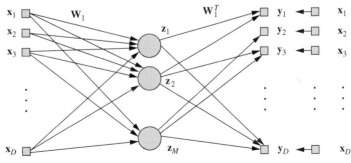

FIGURE 6-16 Autoassociator with $\mathbf{W}_2 = \mathbf{W}_1^T$

for the output-layer weights is

$$\Delta w_{ij}(n) = \eta(x_i(n) - w_{ij}(n)z_j(n))z_j(n) \tag{6.42}$$

which can be recognized as Oja's rule. The autoassociator is a linear system, so it has been analytically studied in depth [Baldi and Hornik 1989]. We now know that the performance surface of the autoassociator is nonconvex with saddle points but does not have local minima. This means that the convergence to the global minimum can be ensured by appropriately controlling the learning rates.

It is possible to lift the constraint of the transpose between the input and the output weight matrices and simply train the network with backpropagation (we cannot use straight LMS since we have a hidden layer). It can be shown that in this case the PCA solution is not always obtained, although the system still performs autoassociation, and the solution found by the hidden PEs always exists in the principal component space (but the outputs of the bottleneck layer are not necessarily eigenvalues [Baldi and Hornik 1989]). The interesting thing is that in some cases the autoassociator with no constraints on W_2 is able to find projections that seem to better preserve the individuality of each input class, which makes it better for classification. However, no linear solution will be able to provide a better reconstruction error than the PCA.

NEUROSOLUTIONS EXAMPLE 6.15

Autoassociator and PCA

This problem is a duplication of the reconstruction of digits using PCA, but now will use an autoassociator trained with backpropagation. Notice the architecture with a hidden layer (called the bottleneck layer). This network effectively computes the PCA when the second weight matrix is restricted to be the transpose of the first weight matrix. For the system to train well, we have added a minor amount of noise to the input. In this example there is no constraint on the weight matrices.

Experiment with the number of the PEs in the bottleneck layer and compare the accuracy of the digits obtained with this autoassociator and with the PCA with the same subspace. Notice that the reconstruction error is higher than PCA, but the digits seem to be better discriminated. Use an MLP with the confusion matrix to quantify this observation.

6.10.1 Pattern-Completion and Noise-Reduction Properties of the Autoassociator

Another interesting property of the autoassociator is the pattern-completion property, which is very useful for noise reduction and recovery of missing data. Suppose that a segment x^l of an input vector x is lost (for instance, during transmission). Let us see whether we can recover the full vector after passing it through the autoassociator. The part of x that is lost is orthogonal to what was kept x^k, so this is equivalent to decomposing $\mathbf{x}$ into two orthogonal components, $\mathbf{x} = \mathbf{x}^k + \mathbf{x}^l$, for instance,

$$\mathbf{x} = \begin{bmatrix} x_1 \\ x_2 \\ 0 \\ 0 \end{bmatrix} + \begin{bmatrix} 0 \\ 0 \\ x_3 \\ x_4 \end{bmatrix}$$

Now if we write the weight matrix $\mathbf{W}$ as a function of the lost and kept parts,

$$\mathbf{W} = (\mathbf{x}^k + \mathbf{x}^l)(\mathbf{x}^k + \mathbf{x}^l)^T \qquad \qquad \textbf{(6.43)}$$

the output becomes

$$\mathbf{y} = (\mathbf{x}^k + \mathbf{x}^l)(\mathbf{x}^k + \mathbf{x}^l)^T \mathbf{x}^k \qquad \qquad \textbf{(6.44)}$$

We can show using the orthogonality of $\mathbf{x}^k$ and $\mathbf{x}^l$ that the output is

$$\mathbf{y} = (\mathbf{x}^k + \mathbf{x}^l)\alpha \qquad \qquad \textbf{(6.45)}$$

where α is a scalar ($\alpha = (\mathbf{x}^k)^T \mathbf{x}^k$), that is, that the true output $\mathbf{x}$ is obtained. The same argument can be used to show that the autoassociator filters out noise. These are very important properties for data transmission.

NEUROSOLUTIONS EXAMPLE 6.16

Autoassociator and pattern completion

In this example we show how an autoassociator can be used for pattern completion. If the autoassociator is trained with noisy inputs, it will eventually learn the important parts of the input pattern. Then after training, if we input patterns that are noisy or incomplete (e.g., digits with missing segments), the autoassociator will reconstruct the correct image because it has enough information from the input pattern to correctly reconstruct the output pattern.

6.10.2 Supervised versus Unsupervised Training

An interesting observation from the autoassociator discussion is that we reached the same solution with very different learning paradigms: For the PCA we used unsupervised learning, but for the autoassociator we used a supervised procedure (the LMS rule) on a linear architecture with a transpose constraint ($\mathbf{W}_2 = \mathbf{W}_1^T$) and a desired response $d(n) = x(n)$. The conclusion is that supervised learning using the minimization of the L_2 criterion *defaults to unsupervised (Hebbian) learning when the desired signal is equal to the input.*

We should ask what the real difference is between supervised and unsupervised learning. Until now we stated that the existence of the desired response made the difference, but the example of the autoassociator proved us wrong, so we have to further qualify the differences.

A learning system adapts its coefficients from the environment using one or several sources of information. In unsupervised learning the only source of information from the environment is the input. In supervised learning there is more than one source of information: the input and the desired response. For the learning to be qualified supervised, however, the information contained in the desired response must be different from the input source. Otherwise, as we just saw, supervised learning defaults to an unsupervised solution.

A further question is the efficiency of both learning strategies. It may be that even if we want to conduct unsupervised learning, a supervised training rule is preferable for more efficient extraction of information from the input signal [provided that we appropriately choose the desired response, e.g., $d(n) = x(n)$]. We submit that in this context *supervised learning is more efficient than unsupervised learning*. This is reasonable, since the desired signal plays a specific goal in supervised learning, and we now know efficient algorithms to search the performance surface (the gradient-descent rule). We saw earlier that the autoassociator of Example 6.16 that was trained with backpropagation learned much faster than the PCA network of Example 6.6. The other practical condition for which supervised learning defaults to unsupervised is prediction, as we will encounter in Chapter 10. Others may exist.

6.11 NONLINEAR ASSOCIATIVE MEMORIES

Up to now we covered only linear associative memories, or LAMs. But there is no reason to limit ourselves to linear PEs. In fact, when the PEs are nonlinear, more robust performance is normally obtained. Some designs are even able to automatically provide a normalized output when the input is normalized, which simplifies learning. The topology of a nonlinear associative memory is shown in Figure 6-17.

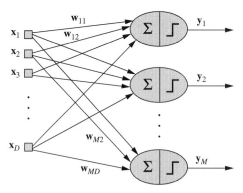

FIGURE 6-17 A nonlinear associative memory (NLAM)

Note that the nonlinear PE affects only the output of the memory, so the Hebbian learning of Eq. 6.1 has exactly the same form for nonlinear networks. One important advantage of bringing in the nonlinearity is to threshold the output of the LAM. For binary-encoded data the threshold can clean much of the crosstalk error from the output. We can see from Eq. 6.34 that mistakes occur only when the crosstalk term is larger in magnitude than the threshold used to make the binary assignment. The nonlinear LAM is more robust to noise. Equivalently, if the input is contaminated by noise, the output can be noise free, which is impossible with the LAM.

NEUROSOLUTIONS EXAMPLE 6.17

Nonlinear associative memories

Here we modify the breadboard of Example 6.12 with output nonlinear PEs. The big advantage of the nonlinearity is that it can threshold the errors (crosstalk) if it is below the level needed to make the decision (which is normally set at half of the dynamic range). This means that if the true output was a 0, but the crosstalk was 0.4 (between 0 and 1), the output is still 0, the correct response. Since this is done at the output, we can consider the nonlinearity either part of the network or simply an external readout.

When we implement this type of network in NeuroSolutions and train it with LMS, we have to make sure that the error is passed through a linear backpropagation component to mimic the effect of Hebbian learning, otherwise the final weights will differ from the linear solution. We can see that the system totally cleans its outputs, so it provides a better memory.

Example 6.17 shows some of the advantages of the nonlinearity. However, the vector space interpretation for the outputs is lost due to the nonlinearity. For instance, we can no longer talk about eigenfilters or PCA. However, the network may in fact perform better than the linear counterpart in some applications. In the autoassociator, when the bottleneck layer is built from nonlinear PEs, it has been shown that the result is still PCA; that is the linear solution is obtained. However, if the network becomes multilayer, the nonlinear network may perform better. These are presently active areas of research.

6.12 PROJECT: USE OF HEBBIAN NETWORKS FOR DATA COMPRESSION AND ASSOCIATIVE MEMORIES

6.12.1 Data Compression

In data compression we have a source of data, a communication channel, and a receiver (Figure 6-18). Communication channels have a usable bandwidth; that is, for a given error rate the number of bits per second—the *bit rate*—has an upper bound. The goal

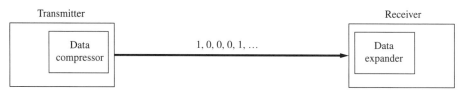

FIGURE 6-18 Data transmission with compression

is to be able to transmit as few bits per second as possible while preserving as much information as possible about the source. This means that we must squeeze into each bit as much information as possible from the source. We can immediately see the prominent role of PCA for data compression. Moreover, we can model data compression as a projection operation where the goal is to find a set of bases that produce a large concentration of signal power in only a few components.

In practical applications data compression has been based on simpler schemes, where the projection vectors are fixed functions instead of being signal dependent, as in the PCA. A good example is the cosine basis of JPEG, called the discrete cosine transform (DCT) [Rao and Huang 1996]. But notice that there is no need for such constraints, since the determination of the optimal projection is an off-line operation, so we can strive for optimal decompositions as long as the reconstruction can be done efficiently.

In PCA compression the receiver must know the weight matrix containing the eigenvectors, since the estimation of the input from the eigenvalues is done by Eq. 6.18. The weight matrix is obtained after training with exemplars from the data to be transmitted. It has been shown that for special applications this step can be completed efficiently and is done only once. But in general, a given set of coefficients for given signal types (e.g., in images a set of coefficients for people's faces, outdoor natural scenes, buildings, etc.) will provide better results. Notice, however, that new image coding schemes such as MPEG already provide this type of labeling, so the receiver can be constructed beforehand. The reconstruction step requires $M \times N$ operations, where N is the input vector dimension and M is the size of the subspace (number of features).

NEUROSOLUTIONS EXAMPLE 6.18

Data compression with PCA

We have already shown data compression with PCA but here we treat the breadboard in more realistic terms. We have included one extra Synapse and an extra Axon between the output of the bottleneck layer and the reconstruction layer to clearly show the transmitter at left and the receiver. The extra Synapse depicts the communication channel.

With the PCA the compressor first has to be trained and its weights transmitted to the receiver (which we have done with a DLL), but this is needed only once after the weights converge. Run the network and experiment with the number of features.

Next let us include a noise source at the receiver to mimic the noise in the communication channel. Notice that the PCA encoding is very immune to white, zero-mean noise. Effectively, the eigenvectors work as low-pass filters, so the noise is averaged out.

6.12.2 Associative Memory

Associative memories are one of the most widely used applications of Hebbian networks. In particular, in the cognitive sciences LAMs are used because of the analogies between associative memories and mammalian memory. In general, when the size of the input vectors are much larger than the number of patterns to be stored, this type of memory provides an effective way of associating input patterns with output patterns. The systems train fast, and there are no local minima, so they are practical.

Image processing is such an application due to the large input vector of a normal image. In fact, an $N \times N$ image is a point in an N^2-dimensional space, so we can store many image-to-image associations in a matrix of weights. In these cases we may not even need all the weights for perfect recall. This project explores the size of the weight matrix for association in image processing. Due to the size of the systems involved, you may need a fast computer for training.

NEUROSOLUTIONS EXAMPLE 6.19

OLAMs and arbitrary connections

In this example we use a LAM trained with the LMS rule (an OLAM) to associate facial images of three people with images of their names. To reduce network complexity, we use the Arbitrary Synapse to reduce the number of weights in the system. A fully connected weight matrix would contain over 400,000 weights (48×48 pixel input and 7×30 pixel output). The system uses roughly 20,000 weights, which gives more than enough power to solve the problem. Remember that we have only three images, which is much less than the capacity of the network.

6.13 CONCLUSIONS

This chapter presented linear networks adapted with Hebbian learning and similar rules (Oja's and Sanger's), which are in principle unsupervised learning types. We showed that such networks can be used for data representation, also called feature extraction, since they project high-dimensional data to smaller dimensional output spaces. Hence PCA networks can be used as data preprocessors for other connectionist topologies such as the MLP.

There are analytic procedures to compute PCA, so we might think that this class of networks can be easily substituted by mathematical operations, which is true but does not address the implementation issues that are important in practical cases. Here all the learning rules were implemented sample by sample and eventually with local algorithms, so they are well suited for on-line distributed implementations. When the matrices are ill conditioned, the numerical solutions fail, while the adaptive solutions provide one of the many possible solutions.

Another application of linear networks trained with forced Hebbian learning is as associative memories. We saw that associative memories work with principles similar to those of human memory, since the memory is contained in the interconnection weights (pattern of activity). They are content addressable (it is enough to input the data to get the recall), unlike computer memories, which require an address to retrieve the data. They are also robust to noise and to failure in the components. On the other hand, they have limited storage.

We also presented other interesting views, such as linking supervised and unsupervised learning. We pointed out the fact that LMS can be thought of as a composition of forced Hebbian and anti-Hebbian learning, which shows that the learning rules studied so far explore only correlation about the input patterns (or second-order statistics about the data clusters).

Hebbian networks are very useful in many engineering applications, and they train rather quickly, so they are well suited to on-line applications.

6.14 EXERCISES

6.1 Think of another way to limit the weight growth in Hebbian learning. Specify a network to implement your rule.

6.2 Formulate the Hamming network in terms of a Hebbian network (as implemented in the Example 6.3).

6.3 For example 6.5, go to the function generator and change the period to 1,000 samples. Also make the input sine waves 90 degrees out of phase. Now run the network and explain what you observe. How can you make the weights follow the input all the time? What does this tell you about forgetting?

There are two stable positions for the weights. Can you describe them? Now go to the second panel of the example and see the difference when you schedule the step size.

6.4 Compare the performance of the PCA-MLP combination with that of the perceptron in Chapter 3 when you add noise to the input. Explain why the system is now much more robust to noise and show that the more PCA components, the less robust the system is. (Note: You have to place the noise component directly over the input file for proper operation.)

6.5 In the anti-Hebbian Example 6.9, change the Hebbian component to an Oja component and observe the difference. Can you explain it? See Eq. 6.13.

6.6 Compare the adaptation rule of the whitening transform with Sanger's rule.

6.7   Consider the following names:

> HOPFIE
> WIDROW
> FREEMA
> HAYKIN
> VAPNIK
> DGHEBB
> WERBOS
> MCPITT
> RBLATT

Code each letter into the last five bits of the corresponding ASCII code and create an associative memory with the outputs 1 to 9. Evaluate the crosstalk experimentally in the following cases: Represent 1 by 1 and 0 by 0. Then represent 0 by -1. Compare the results.

What is the capacity of your LAM? Input the word WIENER and look at the result. Also try FISHER. What can you conclude?

6.8   Show in a vector diagram why Eq. 6.39 reduces crosstalk (compare also with Figure 6-15).

6.9   Relate the power field with the performance surface of the Adaline and then explain the relation of LMS with Hebbian learning.

6.10   What is the difference between the autoassociator trained with backpropagation and the PCA network? Which one provides the smallest MSE? Using the Breadboard of Example 6.7, place the L_2 criterion to help compute the error. Explain these results in view of the theory.

6.11   Compare the OLAM with a linear regressor with the same number of inputs and outputs.

6.12   Do you see any advantage of using a nonlinear associative memory?

6.15   NEUROSOLUTIONS EXAMPLES

6.1 Training with the Hebbian rule

6.2 Directions of the Hebbian update

6.3 Signal detection with Hamming networks

6.4 Instability of the Hebbian update rule

6.5 Oja's rule

6.6 Sanger's rule and PCA

6.7 PCA for preprocessing

6.8 Anti-Hebbian learning

6.9 Stability of anti-Hebbian rule

6.10 Forced Hebbian computes cross correlation

6.11 Novelty filter with anti-Hebbian learning

6.12 LAM application

6.16 CONCEPT MAP FOR CHAPTER 6

REFERENCES

Baldi, P., and Hornik, K., Neural networks and principal component analysis: Learning from examples without local minima, *Neural Networks*, 1:53–58, 1989.

Cover, T., and Thomas, J., Elements of Information Theory, Wiley, New York, 1991.

Diamantaras, K., and Kung, S., *Principal Component Analysis Networks: Theory and Applications*, Wiley, New York, 1996.

Foldiak, P., Adaptive network for optimal linear feature extraction, *Proc. Int. J. Conf. Neural Networks,* 1:401–405, 1989.

Hebb, D., *The Organization of Behavior: A Neurophysiological Theory,* Wiley, New York, 1949.

Hecht-Nielsen, R., *NeuroComputing,* Addison-Wesley, Reading, MA, 1990.

Kay, S., *Modern Spectral Analysis,* Prentice Hall, Englewood Cliffs, NJ, 1988.

Kohonen, T., *Self-Organization and Associative Memory,* Verlag, New York, 1984.

Oja, E., A simplified neuron model as a principal component analyzer, *Journal of Mathematical Biology,* 15:239–245, 1982.

Rao, K., and Huang, J., *Techniques and Standards for Image Video and Audio Compression,* Prentice Hall, Englewood Cliffs, NJ, 1996.

Sanger, T., Optimal unsupervised learning in a single layer linear feedforward neural network, *Neural Networks*, 12:459–473,1989.

Shannon, C., A mathematical theory of communication, *Bell Systems Technical Journal,* 27:379–423, 1948.

Silva, F., and Almeida, L., A distributed decorrelation algorithm, in Gelenbe (Ed.), *Neural Networks, Advances and Applications*, North Holland, 1991.

COMPETITIVE AND KOHONEN NETWORKS

The goal of this chapter is to introduce the following concepts:

- Competitive learning
- Clustering networks
- Data representations (vector quantization)
- Kohonen SOM networks
- Competitive networks and classification
- Modular networks

7.1 INTRODUCTION

Competition for resources is a way of diversifying and optimizing the function of the elements of a distributed system. We see it everywhere, from the way our society is organized to biology. The important aspect of competition is that it leads to optimization at a local level without the need for global control to assign system resources. This is of paramount importance in distributed systems, since for them global control cannot be implemented without enormous overhead.

The PEs of a competitive network receive identical information from the input, but they compete (either by lateral connections in the topology or by the formulation of the learning rule) for resources. The PEs specialize in a different area of the input space, and their outputs can be used to represent in some way the structure of the input space.

None of the networks or learning rules studied so far explicitly use the idea of competition. Backpropagation of errors in a nonlinear network leads to a specialization of PEs, but only indirectly and at a high cost (slow convergence). RBFs, due to their local nature, specialize in different areas of the input space, but this specialization is hard-coded. The PEs in associative memories also specialize, but by using correlation, which is a linear operation. This means that only global restrictions are placed on the solutions found.

In this chapter we introduce specific topologies and learning rules that are geared toward direct competition of resources. Competition is intrinsically a *nonlinear operation*, and as such, its mathematical treatment lags with respect to other areas of adaptive systems. However, its appeal as a fast method to self-organize the network resources is far reaching and has been used very effectively in practice.

Grossberg[1] introduced most of the ideas of competition in mathematically dense terms. His networks work in continuous time and are complex. Kohonen[2] took a more engineering-oriented approach to these ideas and introduced an enhanced set of principles that are easily implemented in digital systems. His approach is the one used in this text.

We divide competition into two basic types: hard and soft. Hard competition means that only one PE wins the resources. Soft competition means that there is a clear winner, but its neighbors also share a small percentage of the system resources. In neurobiology soft competition is widespread and was inspirational for the models developed so far.

---

[1] Stephen Grossberg is a very influential neural network researcher who has developed through the years a very sophisticated theory of biological information processing. In particular, he was one of the initiators of self-organizing networks. His adaptive resonant theory (ART) network is a good example of self-organization. However, his models are normally described in continuous time, using sophisticated mathematics, which are beyond the scope of this textbook. See *Neural Networks and Natural Intelligence*, MIT Press, 1988.

[2] Teuvo Kohonen can be credited as the developer of practical self-organization algorithms. See *Self-Organizing Maps*, Springer Verlag, 1995.

7.2 COMPETITION AND WINNER-TAKE-ALL NETWORKS

The typical competitive neural network consists of a layer of PEs, all receiving the same input. The PE with the best output (either maximum or minimum, depending on the criteria) will be declared the winner. The concept of choosing a winner is a fundamental issue in competitive learning. In digital computers, choosing the best PE is incredibly simple (just a search for the largest value). The concept of choosing a winner, however, often requires a global controller that compares each output with all the others. As discussed many times, global control is troublesome in distributed systems. For this and other reasons (e.g., biological plausibility) we wish to construct a network that will find the largest (or smallest) output without global control. We call this simple system a *winner-take-all network*. Let us assume that we have N inputs $x_1, x_2, \ldots, x_N$, and we want to create an N-output network that will provide only a single positive output in the PE that corresponds to the largest input, while all the outputs of all other PEs are set to zero:

$$y_k = \begin{cases} 1 & x_k \text{ largest} \\ 0 & \text{otherwise} \end{cases} \tag{7.1}$$

Figure 7-1 displays a topology we can use to implement this network. Each PE has a semilinear nonlinearity (clipped linear region) with a self-exciting connection with a fixed weight of $+1$, and it is laterally connected to all the other PEs by negative weights $-\varepsilon$ (lateral inhibition) where $0 < \varepsilon < 1/N$. We assume that all inputs are positive, the slope of the PE is 1, and the initial condition for no input is zero output. The input is presented as an initial condition to the network, that is, it is presented for one sample and then pulled back. The lateral inhibition drives all the outputs toward zero at an exponential rate. As all the smaller PEs approach zero, the largest PE (PE k) will be less and less affected by the lateral inhibition. At this time the self-excitation drives its output high, which enforces the zero values of the other PEs. Hence this solution is stable. Note that the PEs compete for the output activity, and only one wins it.

This network topology is unlike any of the ones we covered so far, because there is *feedback* among the PEs. We study feedback later, but here we point out that the output takes some time to stabilize, unlike the feedforward networks, which are instantaneous

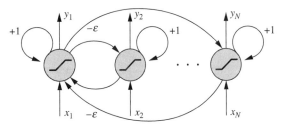

FIGURE 7-1 Winner-take-all network

(i.e., a pattern is presented, and a stable output is obtained). This architecture provides a glimpse of the difficulty found in the implementation of the competitive principles in continuous time. Another difference is that the weights are fixed a priori, so this topology does not need training.

The function of the winner-take-all network is unlike any of our previous networks. Only one output is active at a time, which means that one output is singled out from the others according to some principle (here, the largest value). The amplitude difference at the input could be small, but at the output it is very clear, so the network *amplified the differences,* creating a selector mechanism that can be applied to many different problems. A typical application of the winner-take-all network is at the output of another network (such as a LAM) to select the highest output. Thus the net makes a "decision" based on the most probable answer. For example, in the previous chapter we showed an example of the Hamming network. The winner-take-all network could be used to pick the winner based on the Hamming distance between the input and the stored patterns, thus selecting the symbol that was most likely to have been transmitted.

NEUROSOLUTIONS EXAMPLE 7.1

Winner-take-all networks

This example shows how minute differences in the input patterns can give rise to outputs that are easily separable. In a sense, this network magnifies differences. The idea is very simple: The input signal is fed to a network that implements the winner-take-all function. The input is then removed (i.e., the network input works as the initial condition for the winner-take-all layer).

Winner-Take-All Axon

Notice the special arrangement of the lateral connections and their weights. This arrangement ensures that the lateral inhibition decreases all outputs until only a single output is significantly different than 1. The self-feedback then makes that output grow until the PE saturates. Run the example and see how the convergence time depends on the value of the lateral inhibition. Observe also that these weights cannot be larger than $1/N$.

As mentioned before, the winner-take-all operation is trivial to implement in a digital computer and for efficiency reasons does not use this feedback architecture. The ease with which competition can be implemented and formulated in digital computers has led to a simpler understanding of the principles involved.

7.3 COMPETITIVE LEARNING

The LAM is an associator, while the winner-take-all network is a selector. Instead of using two networks in series, as discussed earlier, the goal of competitive learning is to devise a learning rule that can be applied to a *single-layer topology* and that *tunes the PEs to different areas of the input space*. Each PE works as a decoder for each area. The topology is a simple, one-layer, linear feedforward network (the nonlinearity is only at the final stage where the winner is selected). Hence the ideas of vector spaces can be applied.

Competitive learning is an *unsupervised* learning paradigm, so it extracts information from the input patterns alone, without the need for a desired response. As in association, we would like the information contained in the input patterns to be encoded in the weights. Correlation can do this for us, but associative memories are linear networks, so all the weights respond more or less to the full input space. An alternative way to represent the data is to let each PE specialize in a portion of the input space. The issue is, how do we keep the weights from responding to the full space?

7.3.1 The Instar Network

Grossberg proposed a PE that is able to recognize a single vector pattern based on a modified Hebbian rule that automatically accomplishes weight normalization for normalized inputs. The network is a single McCulloch-Pitts PE (Figure 7-2) but trained with the following in star rule:

$$w_{ij}(n + 1) = w_{ij}(n) + \eta y_i(n)(x_j(n) - w_{ij}(n)) \qquad (7.2)$$

where $y(n)$ is taken as the thresholded output that ranges from zero to one. Analyzing Eq. 7.2 we conclude that the weights are updated only if the PE is active, since the output multiplies (gates) the weight update. This rule is similar to Oja's (Eq. 6.13) but note that the weight is not multiplied by the output. Gating the update implies that the PE learns only when the output is active. When the PE is active the instar rule has the net effect of moving the weights toward the input in a straight line proportional to the size of η (Figure 7-3). Since the weights are attracted to the input position, if the input is normalized, the weights also become normalized.

A trained instar PE provides a response of 1 for data samples located near the training pattern (the bias controls the size of the neighborhood). Hence the instar rule is able to recognize one vector pattern or a class "similar" to the pattern stored in the weights. The instar is a many-input-to-a-single-output network that creates a 0/1 type of association.

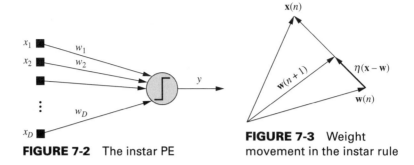

FIGURE 7-2 The instar PE

FIGURE 7-3 Weight movement in the instar rule

NEUROSOLUTIONS EXAMPLE 7.2

The instar network

We saw that one of the disturbing facts about Hebbian learning was the divergence of the weights. One alternative not yet explored is to compute the weight update with the output of a nonlinear PE. This brings two advantages: First, the update is going to be a fraction of the update for the linear case, because y is thresholded. Second, when the output is zero, the update will be zero. These simple facts cure the divergence of the Hebbian update. The simple instar network receives a vector input and produces a scalar output, which responds to the activation seen during training.

7.3.2 Competitive Rule with the Winner-Take-All Network

The instar rule is very similar to the principle we seek, since its weights are updated only when the PE is active (i.e., the data is close to the present weight value). It is interesting to note that this rule is similar to Hebb's rule and Oja's rule.

$$\text{Hebb's rule:} \quad \Delta w = \eta y x$$
$$\text{Oja's rule:} \quad \Delta w = \eta(yx - y^2 w)$$
$$\text{Instar rule:} \quad \Delta w = \eta(yx - yw)$$

As in Oja's rule, the second term helps take care of the instability in Hebb's rule. When we use the instar rule with a nonlinear PE, however, infrequent patterns are preserved as long as the PE is inactive. If we use the instar rule in a winner-take-all network, we do not need to gate the Hebbian update with the PE output, because the competition does this automatically; that is, $y(n)$ in Eq. 7.2 is

$$y_i(n) = \begin{cases} 1 & \text{for } i = i*, \text{ the winning PE} \\ 0 & \text{for all other PEs} \end{cases} \tag{7.3}$$

Hence the competitive rule defaults to

$$\mathbf{w}_{i*}(n + 1) = \mathbf{w}_{i*}(n) + \eta(\mathbf{x}(n) - \mathbf{w}_{i*}(n)) \tag{7.4}$$

where $i*$ is the PE that wins the competition. All the other PEs keep their previous weights. Note that this rule first assumes a competition step to find the PE that is closest to the input and then updates its weights by moving them toward the input (Figure 7-3) in a straight line from the previous weight location.

The step size η $(0 < \eta < 1)$ controls how large the update is at each step and requires the same considerations as other step sizes we have used previously. If the step size is close to 1, the network will converge quickly, but any new input can upset the clusters. On the other hand, small η makes the convergence slow. A compromise is to use a variable step size during learning. Start with a large η and then decrease it progressively.

NEUROSOLUTIONS EXAMPLE 7.3

Competitive learning

In this example we show the competitive learning rule applied to a single PE. The new component is called Standard Full Competitive, and it is implemented as a Synapse that changes its weights according to Eq. 7.4.

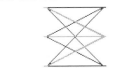

Standard Full Competitive Synapse

The weights of the PE move in a straight line between their current position and the current input, with the size of the movement dictated by the step size. Assuming that we have a cluster of input points, small step sizes result in slow convergence, but the trajectory will be smoothed so that the PE seems to move directly toward the center of the input cluster. Large step sizes create faster convergence, but each individual input has a larger influence on the weights of the PE. Thus larger step sizes result in a noisier trajectory, which is a problem at the end of training, since there will be significant rattling about the center of the cluster.

7.3.3 Criterion for Competition

Thus far we have not discussed which criterion is used to select the winner in a winner-take-all operation. Since we are interested in associating inputs with PEs, a proximity measure is in order; that is, the PE that is closest to the present input should win the competition. The inner product between the input and the present weights is an efficient choice, since it can be computed locally by $\mathbf{w}^T \mathbf{x}$. However, the inner product is sensitive not only to directions but also to the length of vectors; that is, it may provide the wrong metric in cases where the inputs and weights are not normalized. Such a case is illustrated in Figure 7-4. The PE that wins the competition is not PE_1, which is closest to the input $\mathbf{x}$, but PE_2, which has the largest inner product due to an unusually high weight value.

The inner product can still be used if the inputs are normalized to unit length (which will also make the weights normalized), but it may distort the data, affecting the clustering accuracy. An alternative is to implement the Euclidean distance as the metric to define the winner:

$$\|\mathbf{x} - \mathbf{w}\| = \sqrt{\sum_k (x_k - w_k)^2} \tag{7.5}$$

where the summation runs over the input dimensions. Since the square root is a computationally expensive function, this distance metric is less efficient than the inner product. Also, do not forget that while the winner is found with a maximization operator for inner products, a minimization operator is needed with the Euclidean distance:

$$\text{winner} = \max_i(\mathbf{W}_i^T \mathbf{x}) \quad \text{or} \quad \text{winner} = \min_i(|\mathbf{x} - \mathbf{w}_i|^2) \tag{7.6}$$

Sometimes the L_1 norm (or the Manhattan metric) is preferred, since it involves only subtractions and absolute values.

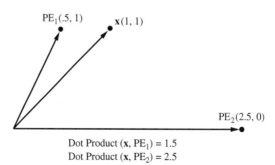

FIGURE 7-4   Wrong choice of winner for the inner (dot) product

NEUROSOLUTIONS EXAMPLE 7.4

Winner metric and performance

This example shows how the metric affects the competitive algorithm. Remember that the dot product must have its data normalized to unit length to work properly. At first this may not seem like a harsh restriction, but remember that in a two-dimensional space only points on the unit circle have unit length. This is a very small portion of the input space, and forcing each point to be on the unit circle may significantly warp the natural clustering of the data.

7.4 CLUSTERING

The competitive rule allows a single-layer linear network to group and represent data samples that lie in a neighborhood of the input space. Each neighborhood is represented by a single output PE. This operation is commonly called *clustering* in pattern recognition. From the point of view of the input space, clustering is dividing the space into local regions, each of which is associated with an output PE. The input space is divided as a honeycomb. The weights of each PE represent points in the input space called *prototype vectors.* If we join prototype vectors by a line, its perpendicular bisector will meet other bisectors, forming a division that resembles a honeycomb (Figure 7-5). Mathematically this division is called a *Voronoi tessellation,* or simply a tessellation. Data samples that fall inside the regions are assigned to the corresponding prototype vector. Clustering is therefore a continuous-to-discrete transformation.

The most important engineering application of competitive learning is *vector quantization.* In telecommunications, data reduction is needed for economic reasons (e.g., to carry as many telephone calls as possible over a single channel or to store audio signals as efficiently as possible). An algorithm that has achieved the role of a standard in communications is vector quantization. With vector quantization, instead of transmitting the values of each data sample, the data is first categorized in clusters for which the centers, called the *codebook entries,* are known to the transmitter and the

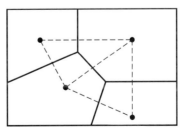

FIGURE 7-5 Example of a tessellation

receiver. Then just the cluster number is transmitted instead of the data samples. At the receiver the cluster number is replaced with the codebook entry to recreate the transmitted signal. We can see that if we have enough clusters, the error between a data sample in a neighborhood and its center is small, so the fidelity is high. We gain two things with this technique: First, we do not need to send the data samples in full precision; we just send an integer. Moreover, the more-frequent samples can be encoded with small numbers so that the overall data rate is decreased.

The ultimate requirement of a vector quantizer is to have a set of clusters that minimizes the distance between the centers of each cluster and the input that falls into each cluster. Thus, for good-quality output, the vector quantization must use a high-quality clustering algorithm to minimize the residuals for each input. We will see the requirements of vector quantization later.

From a theoretical viewpoint, clustering is a form of nonparametric density estimation. In the absence of a desired response, the best we can do for categorization is to use the information about the input data distribution to separate inputs into groups that share the same region in data space. The basic idea of clustering is to seek regions of high sample density—*data clusters*—and represent their centers in the network. Cluster centers thus represent the local means of the data distribution, where the definition of *local* is based on the number of centers we are willing to have.

The typical nonneural clustering algorithm is the K-means clustering algorithm [Duda and Hart 1973]. The idea is to find the best division of N samples by K clusters C_i such that the total distance between the clustered samples and their respective centers (that is, the total variance) is minimized. The criterion as an equation reads

$$J = \sum_{i=1}^{K} \sum_{n \in C_i} |x_n - \gamma_i|^2 \tag{7.7}$$

where γ_i is the center of class i. This is similar to regression, except that the residuals in linear regression are the distance from each point to the regression line. In clustering, the residuals are the distance between each point and its cluster center. Minimizing the residuals (total variance) provides the best clustering. The K-means algorithm starts by randomly assigning samples to the classes C_i, computes the centers according to

$$\gamma_i = \frac{1}{N_i} \sum_{n \in C_i} x_n \tag{7.8}$$

then reassigns the samples to the nearest cluster, and reiterates the computation. One can show that J decreases at each step until it reaches a minimum.

If we interpret J as a performance criterion, its minimum can be obtained by taking the gradient with respect to the unknowns (the centers). If we use the gradient estimate proposed by the LMS, an on-line version of the algorithm will modify the centers incrementally according to

$$\Delta\gamma_i(n) = \eta(x(n) - \gamma_i(n)) \tag{7.9}$$

Note from Eq. 7.4 that this is exactly the competitive update if we link the cluster center with the jth PE weight. Competitive networks thus implement an on-line version of K-means clustering instead of the required batch adaptation of K-means.

NEUROSOLUTIONS EXAMPLE 7.5

Clustering and Voronoi tessellation

In this example we demonstrate clustering and classification. The main data set we will use consists of data collected from a machine tool. The data is the X and Y displacement of the tool's spindle and can be clustered into three regions. These three regions roughly correspond to normal operation, chatter in the tool, and breakage. We also introduce a new display in this example. The Voronoi diagram is used to differentiate between clusters in the input space. It is created by scanning the input space and finding the assignment given by the winner-take-all network. Each PE corresponds to a cluster or region of input space (where it is the closest to all the points in that region). The Voronoi diagram shows the different regions of input space (or clusters) and is helpful in determining how the clustering will generalize to other data points. The output of such a system can be interpreted as classifying the samples, but notice that here only the information about the input data structure is used.

The Linear Scheduler is a component that schedules the step size of the competitive layer. Basically, it linearly ramps the parameter of the component that it is attached to (here the step size) between an initial and final epoch count. The initial value of the parameter is read from the component. The slope is given by the value of beta: If beta is negative, the component parameter is decreased; if beta is positive, the parameter is increased. Moreover, the user can select an upper and lower absolute bound for the parameter. This component should be used with all the unsupervised components.

7.4.1 Clustering and Classification

It is important to understand the difference between clustering and classification. Clustering is the process of grouping input samples that are spatial neighbors. Classification involves the labeling of input samples via some external criterion. Clustering is an unsupervised process of grouping, while classification is supervised. Figure 7-6 shows an example of clustering and classification. Notice that there are four different clusters of data and two classes of data. Since clustering is determined only by the natural grouping of the input data, there are many possible clustering combinations. For example, cluster 1 and 2 could be considered one cluster, which in this case would agree with the class 1 label, but it is obvious that many other cases are possible.

Since clustering is unsupervised, it cannot be used directly for classification. However, in many practical applications, data from each class tends to be dense, and

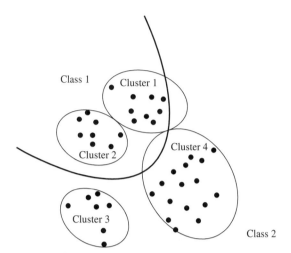

FIGURE 7-6 Clustering versus classification

there is a natural valley between classes. In such cases clustering can be a *preprocessor for classification.* For instance, if the clustering from Figure 7-6 were used as the input to a classifier, the task would be very simple: Simply classify anything in cluster 1 and cluster 2 as class 1. What we gain are simpler classification networks. Just think of an RBF network with one Gaussian per sample or one Gaussian per cluster.

7.5 IMPROVING COMPETITIVE LEARNING

Competitive networks have some limitations that need to be discussed. First, we must realize that competitive learning algorithms can be applied only to one-layer structures, which means that only simple (convex) partitions can be created in the input space. Second, the number of clusters (PEs) has to be decided in advance. Third, the learning rates must be properly set, as in any adaptation procedure. We recommend that scheduling be used, initially with a large step size that is progressively reduced during training.

There are other aspects of competitive learning that are not as easily controlled. One is related to the winner-take-all nature of the competition. If a PE weight vector is far away from any of the data clusters, it may never win the competition, so its weights are never adapted. This implies that the PE is not being utilized to solve the problem (a *dead* PE). These dead PEs are common when we apply the algorithm to large networks and data sets. There is a procedure called a *conscience term* to mitigate this problem.

The idea is that each PE should be penalized if it starts winning more than its fair share and should be helped to win otherwise (the PE's "conscience" makes it feel guilty for winning too often and will inhibit it from winning again). The fair share is estimated by the inverse of the number of PEs. Each PE keeps a count of the fraction

of time it wins by

$$c_i(n + 1) = c_i(n) + \beta \left(o_i(n) - c_i(n)\right) \qquad \textbf{(7.10)}$$

where $o(n)$ is the outcome of the present competition (1 if the PE wins, 0 if it loses), and β is a small positive constant (0.0001). This is an on-line method of estimating each PE's win percentage. Each time a PE wins, the estimate of its winning percentage is increased, and each time it loses, its estimate is decreased. Each PE updates its own bias as

$$b_i = \gamma(1/N - c_i) \qquad \textbf{(7.11)}$$

where γ is a positive constant (10 is a reasonable value). The bias is the penalty term for winning too often and is subtracted from the normal distance before a winner is selected:

$$D(w_i, x) - b_i \qquad \textbf{(7.12)}$$

where $D(.)$ is the Euclidean distance (if the inner product is used, change the sign of b_i). If the PE was winning less than its share, b_i is positive, so the chances of winning the competition increase. On the other hand, if the PE was winning more than its share, the bias is negative, and the distance is increased so that the PE will be less likely to win again. After determining the winner with this modified distance, the weights are updated the same as in conventional competitive learning.

NEUROSOLUTIONS EXAMPLE 7.6

Competition with conscience

In this example we introduce a new component called the Conscience Full and discuss its parameters β and γ.

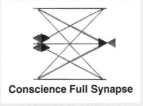

Conscience Full Synapse

The β parameter is used to determine how fast the win percentage is updated on-line. If β is too small, the win percentage is not updated fast enough, and PEs that are winning too often are not penalized enough. If it is too large, the win percentage rattles too much, and the conscience term has too much influence on the learning. The γ term is used to indicate how much penalty should be assigned. The larger γ is, the more evenly distributed the nodes should be over the input data. If γ is too large, however, the penalty is large for even small differences in win percentage. The setting of the β and γ parameters may sound difficult, but in general there is a wide range of workable values.

7.5.1 Determining the Number of Clusters

One aspect that tremendously affects the quality of the clustering is the number of centers, which is controlled by the number of output PEs. There is nothing in the algorithm that allows us to find the best number of clusters. When the number of PEs is smaller than the number of clusters, each PE represents more than one cluster, and the PE is actually placed at the center of mass of all the observations represented by the PE. This may be very different from the natural cluster centers. On the other hand, when the number of PEs is larger than the number of actual clusters, some PEs may stall (without conscience) or more than one may represent the same cluster, which means that clusters are artificially split. The designer must decide the number of clusters either by using a priori information about the problem or by trial and error. This is a common problem with this type of algorithm.

NEUROSOLUTIONS EXAMPLE 7.7

Performance and the number of clusters

In this example we study how the number of PEs affects the clustering performance of a competitive network. If too many PEs are selected, they split natural data modes, causing problems since the data is not divided by natural clusters. However, joining several PEs may still provide a reasonable division. If too few PEs are utilized, one PE is assigned to several data clusters, so the output of the competitive network will never represent the structure of the data well.

Conscience is always used to avoid dead PEs. To see how much the conscience term affects the results (especially with many PEs), you should also set $\gamma = 0$ during the simulations.

There is still another problem in competitive learning that does not have a quick fix. The problem is that there is no metric for how good the winner is, because the principle of competition is differential in nature. This means that the PE that wins the competition is the closest to the input, but we do not know if it is far away or close to the PE weights. To quantify the distance, we have to calibrate the output of the network, which is difficult and rarely done. Adaptive resonance theory (ART) takes care of these difficulties, as we will see later.

7.6　SOFT COMPETITION

Thus far we have discussed hard competition where there is only one winner: One PE is active, and all the others are inactive. Soft competition allows not only the winner but also its neighbors (which can be defined in multiple ways) to be active. Soft competition creates a "bubble" of activity in the output space where the closest PE is the most active (highest output) and its neighbors are less active. Soft competition is widespread in the nervous system, and it implements important functions, such as specialization of resources without global control, common forms of representation, and simplicity of access to information. Similar to the winner-take-all feedback network from earlier in this chapter, a softmax network can be created using lateral feedback. In this case, however, the lateral weights vary with distance from the PE. PEs that are close actually excite one another, whereas PEs that are distant inhibit one another. Since more than one PE is active for each input, more than one PE has its weights updated for each input, although the update is typically attenuated by the PE's distance from the winner.

NEUROSOLUTIONS EXAMPLE 7.8

Effect of the Mexican hat

In this example we briefly show how we can create a softmax network using lateral feedback, which will help in implementing soft competition. In this example we have set the lateral weights from every PE according to the distribution in the following figure:

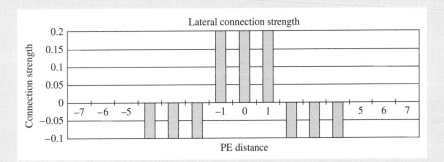

This is called a "Mexican hat" distribution, in which each PE reinforces its nearest neighbors, inhibits PEs that are a moderate distance away, and has no effect on very distant PEs.

Superficially, soft competition seems very similar to hard competition, but this similarity is misleading. Soft competition builds *neighborhood relationships* between the PEs, that is, they become tied by a similarity metric, unlike the PEs of the winner-take-all network. Topological mappings are therefore possible from the space of inputs to the space of PEs. None of the previous competitive networks have this ability.

One of the important applications of topological mappings is to perform data reduction and preserve local neighborhood information. There are other ways to project the input data onto a smaller space (e.g., PCA), but projections created with soft competition preserve the fine detail of the data clusters. Therefore, if two inputs are mapped to points in the output space that are close, then the two inputs will also be close in the input space. This type of mapping has important applications for classification and data visualization.

7.6.1 Softmax as Soft Competition

We saw in Chapter 3 that for multiple-class classification problems we should use the softmax at the output layer of multilayer perceptrons. The advantage was that we could interpret the outputs as probabilities (as long the network was trained with the MSE criterion). The softmax is effectively a competitive structure that forces the sum of the activity feeding the PE to be 1. It is important to realize that this normalization of activity can be interpreted as competition, because if one PE produces a larger output, the others are forced to be lower, since the sum is constrained. In fact, any normalization, such as the one imposed in statistics by the probability density function (the area under the curve has to be 1) enforces competition.

From another view, limited resources also impose competition. In biology the simple fact that a cell has access to finite energy (food) means that it has to establish a priority for what it needs to do, because any function utilizes energy. What we are saying is that the competition principle is implicitly used in many information processing systems and in statistics. What we did here was to make the principle more explicit and develop networks that learn based on competition. Competitive learning is the least studied of all the learning rules, and much more work is needed to obtain an understanding of competitive learning that equals that of gradient-descent or correlation learning.

7.7   KOHONEN SELF-ORGANIZING MAP

The Kohonen self-organizing map (SOM) network performs a mapping from a continuous input space to a discrete output space, preserving the topological properties of the input. This means that points close to each other in the input space are mapped to the same or neighboring PEs in the output space. The basis of the Kohonen SOM network is soft competition among the PEs in the output space.

The Kohonen SOM is a fully connected, single-layer linear network (Figure 7-7). The output generally is organized in a one- or two-dimensional arrangement of PEs, which are called neighborhoods. The one-dimensional neighborhood organizes the PEs in a line of elements, so each element only has two neighbors (the preceding and the following PE). A one-dimensional SOM can be thought of as a string of PEs, where each PE is restricted to be near its two neighbors. When the SOM adapts to an input of higher dimensions, it must stretch and curl itself to cover the input space. For example,

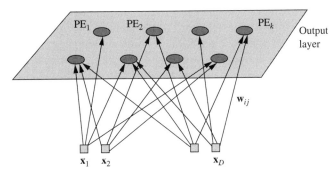

FIGURE 7-7   Architecture of the SOM with a
2-D output

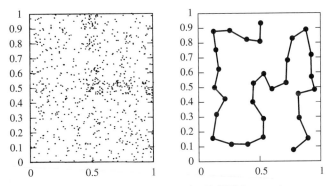

FIGURE 7-8   2-D input data and 1-D SOM mapping

Figure 7-8 shows a one-dimensional SOM mapping a two-dimensional input space. The
input is a set of random points in two dimensions. The PEs are represented by the solid
circles in the second plot (based on their weights), and the lines connect neighboring
PEs; this is the image of the string. The output PEs are arranged in this string, which is
stretched and curled so that it can cover the input space yet still maintain the required
neighborhood relationships—every PE is close to its neighbors.

On the other hand, a two-dimensional neighborhood creates more neighbors,
which has the effect of creating more flexible mappings. When we choose a two-
dimensional neighborhood in two-dimensional space, we see that the PEs spread toward the data samples more rapidly. In principle, Kohonen maps could be arranged in
higher-dimensional spaces, but this is hardly ever done.

7.7.1 The Learning Algorithm

The idea of soft competition is crucial to understanding the function of the Kohonen
SOM. The weights connecting the input to the output perform association between
weights and inputs. The PE whose weight vector is closest to the present input wins

the competition. This description also applies to the competitive rule discussed in Section 7-3, but SOM learning improves on this rule.

In the Kohonen SOM not only the winner of the competition but also its neighbors have their weights updated according to the competitive rule (Eq. 7.2). To simplify the computation of the algorithm, the lateral inhibition network is assumed to produce a Gaussian distribution centered at the winning PE. Thus, instead of recursively computing the activity of each PE, we simply find the winning PE and assume the other PEs have an activity proportional to the Gaussian function evaluated at each PE's distance from the winner. Since we are again applying the instar-type learning rule, which scales the competitive rule by the output activity of each PE, the Kohonen SOM competitive rule becomes

$$\mathbf{w}_i(n + 1) = \mathbf{w}_i(n) + \Lambda_{i,i*}(n)\eta(n)(\mathbf{x}(n) - \mathbf{w}_i(n)) \tag{7.13}$$

where the $\Lambda_{i,i*}$ function is a *neighborhood function* centered at the winning PE. Typically, both the neighborhood and the step size change with the iteration number (so they can be gradually decreased). The neighborhood function Λ is normally a Gaussian:

$$\Lambda_{i,i*}(n) = \exp\left(\frac{-d_{i,i*}^2}{2\sigma^2(n)}\right) \tag{7.14}$$

with a variance that decreases with iteration. It starts by covering almost the full map and then gets progressively reduced to a neighborhood of zero; that is, only the winning PE gets updated. Note that for the winning PE the adaptation rule defaults to the competitive update of Eq. 7.4. But for the neighbors of the winning PE, the updates are reduced exponentially by the distance to the winning PE. All other weights outside the effective range of Λ remain unchanged. As the size of the neighborhood shrinks, the network moves from "very soft" competition (nearly every PE is somewhat active) to hard competition (only the winning PE is active).

It is the spatial neighborhood that makes the Kohonen SOM so different from the other competitive neural networks. The spatial neighborhood brings the structure of the input space to the SOM output. There is evidence that the SOM creates a discrete output space where topological relations within input-space neighborhoods are preserved. What this means is that the distribution of data samples in the input space is approximately preserved. This makes the SOM useful for density function approximation. Moreover, points that are close in the input space are mapped to PEs that are also neighbors. This property is very interesting for some applications that require the preservation of an input-space metric. It is important to remember that all these properties come about just by using the information from the input. The SOM is created in an unsupervised manner.

How does the spatial neighborhood create this topological mapping? Remember that the competitive rule we are using drives the weight vectors toward the current input. Since the winning PE and its neighbors are updated at each step, the winner and all of its neighbors move toward the same position, although the neighbors move more slowly as their distance from the winning PE increases. Over time, this organizes the PEs so that neighboring PEs (in the SOM output space) share the representation of the same area in the input space (are neighbors in the input space), regardless of their initial locations.

The selection of parameters is crucial to achieve a topology-preserving map from the input space to the discrete output. Experience has shown that there are two phases in SOM learning. The first phase deals with the topological ordering of the weights; that is, where the neighborhoods are defined. Here we assume that it takes N_0 iterations. During this phase the neighborhood function should start large, covering the full output space to allow PEs that respond to similar inputs to be brought together. But the neighborhood needs to shrink to a single PE or a PE and its nearest neighbors. A linear decrease in neighborhood radius specified by

$$\sigma(n) = \sigma_0(1 - n/N_0) \qquad (7.15)$$

is normally used. During this period the learning rate should be high (above 0.1) to allow the network to self-organize (and eventually untangle the map). The scheduling of η is normally also linear:

$$\Delta\eta(n) = \eta_0(1 - n/(N + K)) \qquad (7.16)$$

where η_0 is the initial learning rate and K helps specify the final learning rate.

The second phase of learning is called the convergence phase, and it is usually much longer. In this phase the PEs fine-tune to the details of the input distribution, and the learning rate should be kept small (0.01) while using the smallest neighborhood (just the PE or its nearest neighbors).

The choice of the number of PEs is done experimentally. The number of output PEs affects the accuracy of the mapping and the training time. Increasing the number of PEs increases the resolution of the map but also dramatically increases the training time.

NEUROSOLUTIONS EXAMPLE 7.9

Kohonen linear neighborhood

In this example we demonstrate the operation of a one-dimensional SOM, which is implemented with a new component called Line Kohonen Synapse.

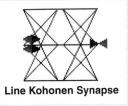

Line Kohonen Synapse

We demonstrate the importance of the neighborhood size and the topological mapping capabilities of the SOM. In this example the clusters are presented in sequence. We display the outputs of each PE in the Megascope, so the triangular types of responses (which mean that the PE wins for a given cluster) should be ordered if the map associates neighborhoods in the input space to the output PE. In the first panel we do not use neighborhood annealing, so the linear output map is ordered only by chance. Notice that once the neighborhood is properly annealed, the neighborhoods in the input are consistently mapped to the output space. Play with the annealing rate to see its effect on the proper construction of the Kohonen map.

NEUROSOLUTIONS EXAMPLE 7.10

Kohonen 2-D neighborhood

In this example we demonstrate the operation of a two-dimensional SOM.

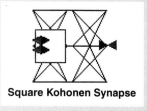

Square Kohonen Synapse

We show how 2-D SOM learning is like twisting and stretching a plane to cover the input space. We present several types of input space densities to show how well the SOM works. You should try several different learning rates (and annealing rates) to understand the SOM's sensitivity to training parameters.

7.7.2 SOM Properties

Input Space Approximation   The SOM is able to preserve the structure of the input space relatively well. This was a shortcoming of the competitive networks, in which the metric of the input space was lost and only the location of the clusters of the distribution were modeled. This application is very important for data reduction, and it is the goal of vector quantization.

Topology Ordering   The PEs in the SOM output are topologically ordered in the sense that neighboring PEs correspond to similar regions in the input space.

Density Matching The SOM preserves the data densities of the input space reasonably well; that is, regions with more data points are mapped to larger regions in the output space.

NEUROSOLUTIONS EXAMPLE 7.11

SOM Topological ordering

In this example we demonstrate the topological ordering, input space approximation, and density-matching capabilities of the SOM. This is done with different sample densities. You should run each example and modify the parameters so that you obtain the prescribed results. Note that we are training the SOM faster than normal, to save time. As a result, the desired properties are not always obtained.

7.7.3 SOM as a Vector Quantization Algorithm

There are well-established algorithms to perform vector quantization, such as the LBG algorithm [Linde, Buzo, and Gray 1980]. The LBG algorithm has been shown to be optimal in terms of minimizing the average distortion measure between the input sample x and the transmitted x' vector (the class center):

$$D = \frac{1}{2}\int_{-\infty}^{\infty} f(x)|x - x'|^2 dx \qquad (7.17)$$

where $f(x)$ is the pdf of the input. In the theory an internal encoding-decoding step is assumed (Figure 7-9), where the input is first coded, creating $c(x)$, which is eventually added with noise and finally decoded to obtain x'.

The interesting point is that in order to reach optimality, two conditions are required:

- For an input sample x the code $c(x)$ should be chosen to minimize the distortion between x and the reproducing vector x'.
- Given the code c, the reproduction vector x' should be the centroid of the input vectors that were coded by $c(x)$.

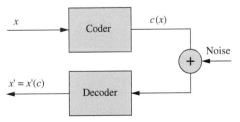

FIGURE 7-9 Vector quantization model

The LBG algorithm is a batch-mode version of the Kohonen algorithm with a neighborhood size of zero. The Kohonen SOM can thus be interpreted as an optimal vector quantization algorithm.

7.8 CREATING CLASSIFIERS FROM COMPETITIVE NETWORKS

All the unsupervised rules explained so far use only the information contained in the input samples. For instance, clustering is simply defined by the structure of the input data (and the number of PEs). In some cases a clustering algorithm can be used for classification, since it responds to a distance metric in the input space. Therefore, when one PE wins the competition, this says that the input data belongs to a certain region of the input space, which is the purpose of classification. But classification is more general: First, classes can be constructed by more than one cluster. Second, in classification we know the labels for some of the data (the training set), so the classifier can place the discriminant function not only as a function of the input data structure, but also as a function of the class label information. If the classes are unimodal and well separated, a clustering algorithm and a classifier will yield the same results. However, when the class structure is intertwined and the classes have a multimodal structure, classification and clustering produce very different results. Nevertheless, we get the feeling that we should be able to create a classifier from a clustering algorithm.

The RBF network is a neural topology that explores this concept. Since the Gaussians are local in space, when a Gaussian PE has a high response, it means that the particular input is located in a certain area of the input space, and the output weights can learn the mapping to one of the classes. This is what we will do next, but the Gaussian layer is going to be replaced by a competitive network.

7.8.1 Learning Vector Quantization (LVQ)

Kohonen proposed the learning vector quantization algorithm (LVQ) as a way to fine-tune the boundaries of the tessellation regions using information from class labels. The idea is very simple to state. If the competitive rule produces the correct class label, then no modification to competitive learning is necessary. However, if the clustering produces the wrong assignment, then the PE weights should be "repelled" from the present cluster. This is achieved by the following rule:

$$\Delta w_{i*j} = \begin{cases} \eta(x_j - w_{i*j}) & \text{correct class} \\ -\eta(x_j - w_{i*j}) & \text{wrong class} \end{cases} \tag{7.18}$$

This rule has some problems when the input data is multimodal, but the algorithm works well to fine-tune the boundaries of the clusters according to the classification labels. Kohonen proposed more sophisticated LVQ algorithms to deal with multimodal data [Kohonen, 1995].

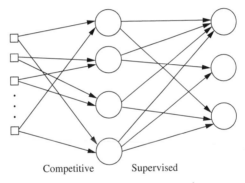

Competitive   Supervised

FIGURE 7-10   Counterpropagation network

7.8.2 Counterpropagation Networks

Hecht-Nielsen [1991] proposed a hierarchical feature classifier composed of a hidden competitive layer that feeds a layer of linear PEs (Figure 7-10). The competitive layer is trained first, and then the output weights are trained using the class labels (desired response) with the LMS rule, very much like the training of the RBF network.

> supervised learning. Notice that the back plane goes only until the WinnerTakeAll Axon, since the first layer is trained competitively.
>
> The problem we are solving is the machine tool data of Chapter 5. Here the solution is also very good and training very fast. After convergence, the output-layer weights of the counterpropagation network simply describe the average value of the class labels. This can be used to create a vector quantizer.
>
> You should experiment with the number of PEs and discover its importance in terms of classification accuracy.

An interesting aspect of the counterpropagation network is that since the hidden layer has digital activations (on/off), the LMS weight update can be written as

$$\Delta w_{ij} = \eta(d_i - y_i)x_j = \eta(d_i - w_{ij})x_j \qquad (7.19)$$

since the network output is simply the weight value connecting the active hidden PE and the output PE. This means that the output-layer weights are the average value of the class label for that particular tessellation region. In other words, the network learns to implement a table lookup function, where the key value is the output weight and the key encoding is implemented by the unsupervised portion of the network.

Counterpropagation networks can fully implement a vector quantizer. The unsupervised part provides the clustering, and the supervised part can implement the code to be sent to the receiver. These networks train very fast compared with the MLP (which can also learn how to implement a vector quantizer).

7.8.3 Grossberg's Instar-Outstar Network

At the beginning of this chapter we described the instar network. A very similar network, called the *outstar network,* can associate a scalar input to a vector output for pattern recall. The learning rule is obtained by switching the roles of inputs with outputs in Eq. 7.2; that is,

$$w_{ij}(n + 1) = w_{ij}(n) + \eta x_j(n)(y_i(n) - w_{ij}(n)) \qquad (7.20)$$

Note the similarity of Eq. 7.20 to Eq. 7.19, which trains the output of the counterpropagation network. If the output is substituted by the desired response, the result is exactly the same.

Grossberg proposed a three-layer network composed of an input layer that does normalization (using shunting activation), followed by a competitive layer linked to an outstar (Figure 7-11). The connection between the input and the competitive layer is a set of instar PEs; that is, the winner of the competitive layer is the PE that has the weights closest to the current input. The outstar then associates that PE with a predetermined output, which normally is done with supervised learning. Hence $y(n)$ in Eq. 7.20 is replaced with the desired response $d(n)$. Thus we have exactly the same func-

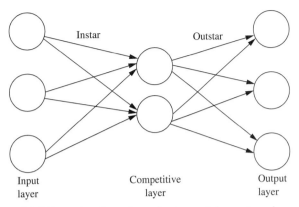

FIGURE 7-11   Grossberg instar-outstar network

tion as the counterpropagation network. The difference between the two networks is the normalization of the input layer. In addition, Grossberg did all the development in continuous time for real time operation, which is more involved.

7.9   ADAPTIVE RESONANCE THEORY (ART)

The instar-outstar maps input data to output patterns. But can the same basic architecture be used for cluster discovery? This is possible if the desired response becomes the input, $d(n) = x(n)$, and the output of the system becomes the competitive layer. The instar creates a winner, and the outstar maps it back to the input to check the similarity between the cluster and the data. In this way we can check whether the cluster is a good match to the input, which is impossible to do directly in competitive learning. In fact, competitive learning assigns the winner based on a min (or max) function; that is, the difference between the input and the cluster prototype (the mismatch) can be large in absolute terms. The winner can therefore be a very poor match for the input pattern. The instar-outstar described here solves this problem, but the network has some shortcomings for cluster discovery.

The big problem of the instar-outstar network is the instability produced by the instar learning and the limited resources. The special form of the instar rule (Eq. 7.2) imposes a decay on the associations. This means that old associations tend to be overridden by new data. We could decrease the learning rate to keep "old memories," but this would negatively affect the learning of new associations. This is the so-called *stability–plasticity dilemma.*

To solve this dilemma, we can use the outstar portion of the net and require that the present data must be within a prespecified distance to the cluster center. If not, the sample will not be used to update the cluster weights. The problem is that we would not use all the data for training. Grossberg implemented a facility to add new PEs to the competitive layer when there is no "resonance" between the present data and the existing clusters, that is, when the input data is outside a prespecified neighborhood of the current winner. The specification of the neighborhood is controlled by a vigilance parameter.

This network has been called adaptive resonance theory (ART) and is able to dimension itself for data clustering, unlike any of the other competitive networks. Moreover, it can also be used for detecting previously unseen patterns when it creates new clusters after the learning period. There are important engineering applications for novelty filters, such as failure detection. However, setting the vigilance parameter is a delicate operation.

7.10 MODULAR NETWORKS

In earlier chapters we described multiple-PE network topologies that were trained in *cooperation;* that is, all the PEs were trained at the same time for the common goal of solving the problem. Competition and its winner-take-all function changed this view, because now only part of the network is responsible for mapping a portion of the input data space. So far the competition has been limited to the learning rule, not to the network topology.

This view of competitive learning can be brought also to the level of network topology to create what have been called *modular networks.* Modular networks are built from expert networks, all of which work with the same input and are coordinated by a competitive gating network (Figure 7-12).

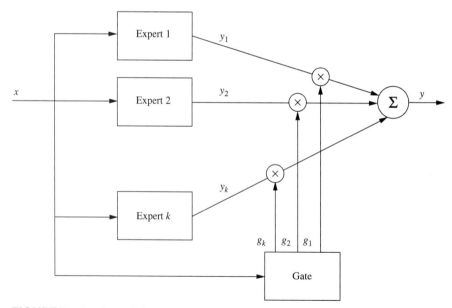

FIGURE 7-12 A modular network

The output of the modular network is

$$y = \sum_{i=1}^{K} g_i y_i \qquad (7.21)$$

where g_i is the the gate output. The gate can receive information either from the input or from the performance of each expert network. In the case shown in Figure 7-12, the role of the gate is to find out which weighting should be given to each expert contribution, in other words, what is the conditional probability that the present sample is produced by the model of expert k? Statistical reasoning therefore can be used to train such networks, as is done in the mixture of experts [Jacobs et. al. 1991].

Alternatively, if we use a hard partitioning (0/1) for the gate; we are in the realm of competitive learning. In this case it is easier to have the gate monitor the output of each network and adapt the one that has the best performance.

NEUROSOLUTIONS EXAMPLE 7.14

Modular network

This NeuroSolutions example implements hard competition in the output space by modifying the learning criterion. The problem is to create a network that will learn how to approximate a V-shaped function in the input space. But instead of using a single network, as we demonstrated in Chapter 5, here we use two linear networks (called expert networks, since they specialize in a piece of the input space). We know that an MLP can solve this problem, but now we are using multiple linear networks to do a piecewise linear approximation to the functional mapping.

At the input we have a ramp generator, and at the output we use the triangular wave as the desired response. We use two linear regressors, which can only scale and displace the ramp. However, we train the two networks in tandem by using a very clever rule. If network 1 provides a smaller error for the present sample, only the weights of network 1 will be adapted. Likewise, when network 2 produces the smallest error, only its weights get adapted. We have created this simple rule in the DLL of the error criterion. Train the network and see how quickly the network learns to assign each piece of the V to a single expert network.

The use of competitive learning to create expert networks should be contrasted with committees of networks. In committees we use several networks to cooperatively solve a problem, but here we are creating competition among the networks to force them to learn something different. This idea is very powerful and leads to practical solutions for many problems.

7.11   CONCLUSIONS

Both the Hebbian learning networks from Chapter 6 and the competitive networks from this chapter can be used for data representation. The major difference between these two unsupervised methods is that Hebbian learning tends to extract information globally from the input space, whereas competitive networks are used to cluster similar inputs. Hebbian networks are associators, while competitive networks compete for resources. The competition in these networks allows them to "divide and conquer" the problem without the need for global control. Each PE responds to the inputs that are nearest to it. With hard competition, only the closest PE is active (and thus has its weights updated). With soft competition, the closest PE is active, and its neighbors are also active, although somewhat less than the winning PE. This allows for a topological mapping of the input where neighbors in the input space are mapped to neighbors in the output space.

7.12   EXERCISES

7.1   Extend the Breadboard of the LAM in Example 6.14 with a winner-take-all network. First train the network and then test the combined network in a single-step mode (to make sure that the inputs are stable). This works well but limits how fast you send new inputs in; that is, it is not a static operation. Change the constants in the winner-take-all network to make it work as fast as possible.

7.2   Provide details to implement competition with an L_1 norm (see Eq. 7.6). Work with Example 7.3 (choose the boxcar metric in the competitive synapse).

7.3   What input space characteristics do you lose when you do clustering? For instance, can you determine distances among clusters precisely? What do you gain with clustering?

7.4   Draw three different data clouds to illustrate the following cases: (1) clustering is equivalent to classification; (2) clustering is harmful for classification. Elaborate on the second case. How would you minimize the chances of this happening in practice?

7.5   In your opinion, what is the worst limitation of the clustering algorithms described in Sections 7.4 and 7.5? Illustrate your point with the Voronoi diagram of Example 7.7.

7.6   Do you see any problem with the conscience term explained in Eq. 7.10?

7.7   Explain how you would use a Kohonen network in high-dimensional data visualization.

7.8   Example 7.11 uses too high a learning rate for demonstration purposes. Set these parameters without this constraint so that they always provide reliable topographic maps.

7.9   During Kohonen learning of the data in Example 7.9, the weights always converge toward the origin of the space in the initial stages of learning. Explain why.

7.10   Experiment with the Breadboard of Example 7.14 using other data sets.

7.13 NEUROSOLUTIONS EXAMPLES

7.14 CONCEPT MAP FOR CHAPTER 7

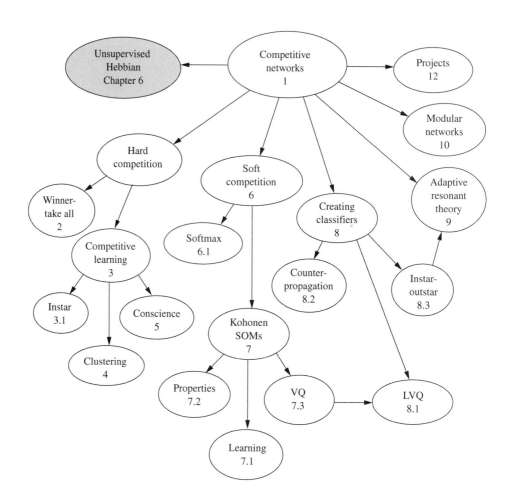

REFERENCES

Duda, R., and Hart, P., *Pattern Classification and Scene Analysis,* Wiley, New York, 1973.

Hecht-Nielsen, R., *NeuroComputing,* Addison-Wesley, Reading, MA, 1991.

Jacobs, R., Jordan, M., Nowlan, S., and Hinton, G., Adaptive mixtures of local experts, *Neural Computation,* 3:79–87, 1991.

Kohonen T., *Self Organizing Maps,* Springer Verlag, New York, 1995.

Linde, Y., Buzo, A., and Gray, R., An algorithm for vector quantization design, *IEEE Trans. on Communications,* COM-28:84–95, 1980.

PRINCIPLES OF DIGITAL SIGNAL PROCESSING

This chapter covers the following basic ideas:

- Digital representation of continuous signals
- Filtering as a projection
- Time and frequency analysis

- Fourier transforms
- Filter frequency response
- Digital filter design

This chapter is not meant to be an introduction to digital signal processing (DSP), but a survey of the field in terms of fundamental concepts and tools. Many excellent books have been written on the subject of DSP, and we strongly encourage the reader to consult them for a thorough treatment (see, for example, [Oppenheim and Schafer 1989] and [Haykin and VanVeen 1999]).

8.1   TIME SERIES AND COMPUTERS

This chapter studies linear systems that work with time signals. Thus far we worked with several types of multidimensional data sets, but we hardly ever referred to time. Problems that do not involve time (such as the classification of patterns) are called *static*. Time establishes an order in the input data; that is, the data samples can be indexed by a continuous variable t (Figure 8-1), and we will call them *time signals* or *time series*. As you may expect, time provides an extra structure to the input space that can be exploited with appropriate topologies such as the *delay line*. Time also brings the need for other data analysis tools. Engineers long ago discovered that the linear processing of time signals can be better understood in what is called the *frequency* or *spectral domain*. We will briefly study the frequency domain and show that we can easily quantify the effect of a linear system on a signal as a modification to its spectrum.

Most of the messages that we perceive from the external world with our sensory organs (such as hearing, vision, and smell) and man-made systems such as radio and TV transmissions are phenomena that exist in time. The messages are normally coupled with physical variables (pressure waves in hearing, light waves in vision, electromagnetic waves for TV) that can be modeled as real functions $x(.)$ of a real variable t. This means that for every value of t, $x(t)$ is a real-valued function. Time is a continuum, and the physical variables are also continuous, so these signals are called *analog signals*. We normally impose some simplifying constraints on $x(.)$ to make the mathematics easier, without affecting the applicability of the conclusions to the signal of interest. For

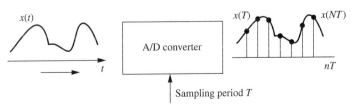

FIGURE 8-1 Analog-to-digital conversion

the discussion to follow it is sufficient to assume that $x(.)$ is smooth and has finite energy:

$$\int_{-\infty}^{\infty} x^2(t)\, dt < \infty \tag{8.1}$$

Digital computers cannot work directly with analog signals. We need to sample the analog signal. The process of *sampling* can be visualized as "stopping" time at instant $t = n_0$ and making a measurement $x(n_0)$ on $x(t)$, that is,

$$x(n_0) = x(t)\big|_{t=n_0} \tag{8.2}$$

Nature of Analog Signals

Analog signals exist in a continuum. This means that between any two values in the time line there exist an infinite number of intermediate values. This causes problems when we want to represent analog signals in digital machines. To understand why, just think how many memory locations the computer needs to represent a piece of an analog signal between [0,1]. If there are an infinite number of points on the real line between 0 and 1, we would need an infinite number of memory locations. This is the reason that we need to sample or discretize the time line.

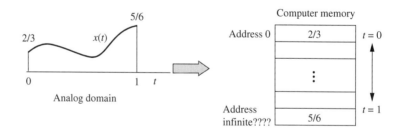

The physical device that implements sampling is called an analog-to-digital (A/D) converter. Normally the signal is sampled several times. For mathematical and implementation simplicity, sampling is done periodically. Every T seconds, called the *sampling period*, the analog signal $x(t)$ is measured, producing a signal $\{x(nT)\}$ called a *sequence*, or a *time series*. The time series $x(nT)$ is a discrete version of $x(t)$.

Notice that after the A/D converter we get a sequence of real numbers

$$\{x(nT)\} = x(T),\ x(2T),\ x(3T),\ \ldots,\ x(NT)$$

so the independent variable of the signal was transformed from a real number to an integer. Rigorously speaking, the A/D converter also *quantized* the amplitudes of $x(t)$ so that we can store the values of $x(nT)$ in a finite number of bits, but this is not important to this discussion.

Quantized Signal

A quantized signal is a signal whose amplitude is a multiple of a quantity called the *quantization step.* The quantization step is chosen according to the number of bits of the A/D converter utilized, and it is related to the precision of the voltage measurement performed in the converter. For instance, an 8-bit A/D converter has a quantization step of 2^{-8}. This gives exactly 256 different values to measure the amplitude of the analog signal. Normally there are 128 positive values and 128 negative values.

We can consider that the A/D converter creates a grid in the amplitude axis. When the A/D converter receives the command to convert, it measures the analog voltage and then assigns the voltage to the closest point in this amplitude grid.

We can see that there is an error in going from the analog voltage to the quantized voltage, but this error is always smaller than the quantization step.

A good rule of thumb is to consider that the signal-to-noise ratio (SNR) is 6 dB/bit. A b-bit A/D converter has a SNR of $6(b - 1)$ dB, since one bit is the sign bit. For instance, an 8-bit A/D converter has a 42-dB SNR. This means that the quantification noise floor of an 8-bit A/D is 100 times smaller than the largest signal.

Digital computers can work with a quantized $x(nT)$ directly. For instance, each sample can be stored in a computer memory location of b bits (where b is the number of bits of the A/D converter), and arithmetic can be directly performed with each sample in the computer ALU (arithmetic and logic unit).

Sampling changes the nature of $x(t)$, since the signal becomes a function of a discrete variable. The important question is: Do we lose any information when going from $x(t)$ to $x(nT)$?

If we are careful, we don't. It all depends on how fast we sample the signal $x(t)$ with respect to its fastest rate of change. Intuitively, we expect that if the analog signal $x(t)$ is sampled at a sufficiently high rate (i.e., with a high enough density of measurements), its sampled version $x(nT)$ should contain the same information as the original $x(t)$.

A central result in sampling theory says that if the signal $x(t)$ is sampled at a rate f_s more than twice the value of its largest frequency, that is,

$$f_s = \frac{1}{T_s} > 2f_{\max} \qquad (8.3)$$

then $x(t)$ can be recovered from $x(nT)$ precisely, and the samples $x(nT)$ contain all the information to reconstruct the analog signal. This is called the *Nyquist theorem,* and the smallest rate that meets this criterion for a given signal is called the *Nyquist sampling rate.*

It is very important to know what frequency means and how to measure the largest frequency of $x(t)$ to apply this theorem. The Nyquist theorem states that even when interested in analog signals $x(t)$, we can study their properties using their discrete versions $x(nT)$. This result revolutionized signal processing, because engineers could use computers to attenuate noise or otherwise modify signal properties instead of building analog hardware. It also gave rise to the exciting field of digital signal processing (DSP). Here we concentrate on digital signal processing concepts.

Nyquist Theorem

Let us take a sine wave of period T and sample it with a frequency $10/T$, that is, so that there are 10 samples per cycle. Frequency is defined as $f = 1/T$ and is measured in Hertz (or radians per second for $w = 2\pi/T$). The samples obviously preserve the information of the sine wave (amplitude and frequency) as shown in the following figure.

Now sample the same sine wave at $f = 2/T$ (i.e., two samples per cycle). We still get a sine wave of the same frequency, but notice that we have only one point per half cycle, so we are getting dangerously close to distorting the wave.

Now try $f = 1/T$. You see that we obtain a flat line, that is, the information in the samples does not match the original signal anymore. Now try $f = 1/2T$. We get back a sine wave, but now of a different frequency! We say that we are *aliasing* the sine wave.

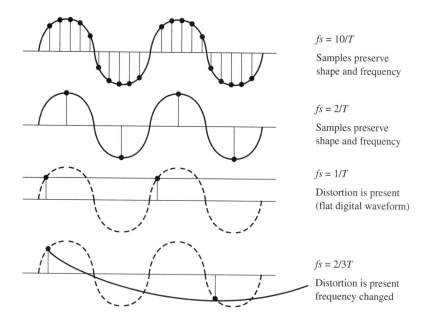

$fs = 10/T$

Samples preserve shape and frequency

$fs = 2/T$

Samples preserve shape and frequency

$fs = 1/T$

Distortion is present (flat digital waveform)

$fs = 2/3T$

Distortion is present frequency changed

This example shows that sampling has to be done according to the fastest variation contained in $x(t)$. We saw in Chapter 5 that any periodic signal could be decomposed into sine waves, so to preserve the information contained in $x(t)$, we have to find its maximum frequency and choose a sampling frequency at least twice this value. This is called the Nyquist theorem.

The Nyquist theorem makes a lot of sense if we think about it carefully. It basically says that if we want to represent fine detail in a waveform, we have to have sufficiently dense samples. Otherwise we end up with digital signals that do not resemble the original analog ones. This error is called the *aliasing error*, the error that distorts the analog signals when they are sampled because of too low a sampling frequency.

Given an analog signal $x(t)$ and a sampling frequency f_s, sampling preserves the information of $x(t)$ only up to $f_s/2$. All the other frequencies present in $x(t)$ are aliased back to the range 0–$f_s/2$. There are thus two potential types of errors when digitizing an analog signal:

- Information from frequencies above $f_s/2$ is lost.
- Higher frequencies in the analog signal can even add noise to the lower frequencies, since they appear aliased back in the interval 0–$f_s/2$.

This is why a golden rule of sampling is to *always prefilter the input signal with an analog filter with a cutoff at $f_s/2$* (more on filters later in the chapter). This practice avoids aliasing but cannot compensate for the missing frequencies above $f_s/2$.

8.2 VECTORS AND DISCRETE SIGNALS

Signals that have finite energy have a one-to-one correspondence with vectors. The correspondence is trivially explained for discrete signals of a *finite length NT*, such as the ones we are interested in here. Consider the finite duration signal $\{x(n)\}$ with N samples $x(n)$, $x(n-1)$, ..., $x(n-N-1)$ (we drop T from the notation when no confusion arises). One way to create a vector from $\{x(n)\}$ is to think of $\{x(n)\}$ as a point in an N-dimensional space, where every sample is the projection of $\{x(n)\}$ onto the N orthonormal axes ϕ_0, ϕ_1, ..., ϕ_{N-1} (Figure 8-2).

We can therefore represent the discrete signal $\{x(n)\}$ by a vector $\mathbf{x}$ of N components:

$$\mathbf{x} = [x(n), x(n-1), x(n-2), \ldots, x(n-N-1)]^T \tag{8.4}$$

where the superscript T means transpose. Its length (or its norm), assuming an orthonormal basis, is

$$\text{len}(\mathbf{x}) = \sqrt{x^2(n) + \cdots + x^2(n-N-1)} = \sqrt{\sum_{i=0}^{N-1} x^2(i)} \tag{8.5}$$

which can also be recognized as the square root of the energy of the discrete signal $\{x(n)\}$. Hence, for finite energy signals, the length of the vector is finite. A discrete signal of length N is thus a vector in an N-dimensional vector space.

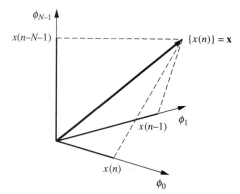

FIGURE 8-2 A discrete signal as a vector

8.2.1 The Delay Operator

One important question is to find the basis $\{\phi_i\}$ assumed in the decomposition of Eq. 8.4. When the signal $\mathbf{x}$ is written in terms of the projections in each basis, we get

$$\mathbf{x} = \sum_{i=0}^{N-1} x(i)\boldsymbol{\phi}_i \qquad (8.6)$$

Comparing Eq. 8.4 with Eq. 8.6, we see that $x(n - i) = x(i)\phi_i$, which means that

$$\boldsymbol{\phi}_i = \delta(n - i) \qquad (8.7)$$

where δ is the *Dirac delta function,* which we already encountered in Chapter 5. We conclude that delta functions are the bases to represent discrete signals in the time domain. We saw in Chapter 5 how important the projection theorem was to explain function approximation. We are also seeing how important the projection theorem is for understanding digital signals.

This reasoning leads to an equivalent way of expressing discrete time signals as combinations of delta functions, if we substitute Eq. 8.7 in Eq. 8.6:

$$x(n) = \mathbf{x} = \sum_{i=0}^{N-1} x(i)\delta(n - i) \qquad (8.8)$$

This means that in order to represent a discrete signal of length N as a vector, we need to have access to the current and the past $N - 1$ samples. In an on-line operation, each time tick generates another sample; therefore we have to store the past samples needed to construct the vector. A delay line is the natural topology to implement the decomposition of Eq. 8.8. The *ideal delay* element is a linear system, denoted by z^{-1} (*z notation*), that delays the input signal by one sample (Figure 8-3).

A *delay line* is a single-input, multiple-output system built from a cascade of these ideal delays. If we cascade $N - 1$ delays together, we will be able to work with the present sample n and access $N - 1$ samples into the past (i.e., back to time $n - N + 1$) (Figure 8-4).

FIGURE 8-3 The ideal delay element

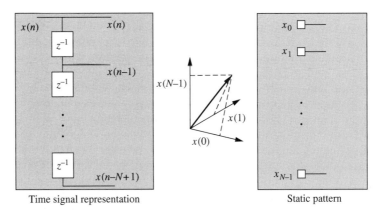

Time signal representation   Static pattern

FIGURE 8-4 Comparison of time signals with static patterns

8.2.2 Signal Space

The space whose axes are the signals at the taps of the delay line is called the *reconstruction* or *signal space*. With every time tick the signal vector slowly changes position in phase space, creating a trajectory that is called the *signal trajectory* (Figure 8-5).

If you recall from Chapter 5, data samples from static problems were also interpreted as vectors in a space of dimensionality equal to the size of the data components (Figure 8-4). Therefore, there seems to be no real difference between time series in signal space and data samples with no time tagging. In principle this is true, but there are some practical differences that are worth mentioning.

Let us construct a new pattern by adding a new sample. When a new sample $x(n + 1)$ of the time series comes into the delay line, all the elements of the delay line shift down one sample to make room for the arriving sample, and the last element $x(n - N + 1)$ is lost. All the intermediate values are still stored in the delay line, but in a different position (Figure 8-5). The vector constructed in this way for time $n + 1$ is different *but not radically different* from the vector at time n, which is unlike the static case where a new set of N numbers are brought from the database for each new input. Therefore a system that uses static data has a response that is totally unrelated from pattern to pattern.

On the other hand, the sequential flow of samples through the delay line produces a sequence of vectors in the reconstruction space that are related by the structure of the time series. In fact, the projection on the x axis at time n becomes the projection on the y axis at time $n + 1$, and so on, *producing a spiraling trajectory*. The points visited in the reconstruction space (the signal trajectory) obviously depend on the properties of

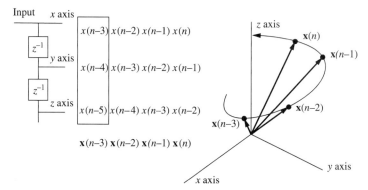

FIGURE 8-5 The tap delay line and the reconstruction of the signal trajectory in phase space

the time series and may allow a system connected to the delay-line output to extract and model the time structure of the time series.

Suppose that we are interested in analyzing a single, discrete, periodic signal with 1,000,000 samples. This signal is a vector in a million-dimensional space, which is an enormous space. From what we know of the *curse of dimensionality,* the problem seems hopeless. This is where the structure embedded in time signals comes to our rescue. The signal time structure will constrain the possible locations of the vectors in the input space, effectively limiting the position of the signal trajectory to a subspace of much lower dimensionality. The subspace where the vectors created from the time signal exist is called the *signal subspace.* This dimensionality reduction can be huge. For instance, the requirement to represent any periodic signal is a reconstruction space of at most the length of the period in samples. In our example, if the period is 50 samples, we need at most 50 dimensions to represent the time series, irrespective of the length of the overall signal. The signal trajectory of periodic signals becomes a closed curve with a length equal to the period, and the points visited in state space thereafter are the same.

It turns out that the actual number of dimensions to represent the signal subspace of periodic signals is normally much less than the size of the period in samples. It all depends on the complexity of the trajectory, that is, the structure of the time series. The constant signal is a point in state space. A sine wave creates the simplest signal trajectory, which is an ellipse with the principal axis aligned with the bisector of the first quadrant. *The ellipse always exists in a plane.* The number of points (and the eccentricity) of the ellipse changes with the number of points per period, but the shape remains the same. Therefore we only need two dimensions to represent any sinusoidal signal, irrespective of the number of samples. Notice also that the trajectory does not cross itself; that is, there is a one-to-one mapping from the time series to the trajectory and vice versa. This shows that choosing the dimension of the reconstruction space equal to the number of samples of the period may actually be inefficient. However, a very complex periodic signal (for example, a segment of white noise periodically repeated) may in fact require a reconstruction space as large as the period in samples. When the reconstruction space is not large enough, the signal trajectory may cross a previous branch. When this happens, we lose the one-to-one mapping between trajectories and time series. For example, when we reach a point where two branches cross in signal space, we do not know which exit branch to take.

NEUROSOLUTIONS EXAMPLE 8.1

Signal space

We will use the 3-D State Space Probe to show the reconstruction of a sine wave in 3-D space. The 3-D State Space Probe uses the current sample and two samples from the past of the signal to plot the current point in three dimensions. If the input is periodic, like a sine wave, then the reconstruction periodically visits the same points in space. The structure of the time signal limits the region of the 3-D reconstruction space where the trajectory lies. For the case of the sine wave, the trajectory is an ellipse, which always exists in a plane (two dimensions). Even if the reconstruction is done in a higher-dimensional space, the signal trajectory still resides in a subspace. Change the sliders of the 3-D display to see the full trajectory.

State Space Probe

In the case of the sine wave, the reconstruction space is a plane that is oriented along the first quadrant bisector. If you change the delay used in the reconstruction, the trajectory "opens up," and the ellipse approaches a circle. Notice that the delay selection does not drastically change the overall shape of the trajectory, but the relative position of the reconstruction space varies, and the trajectory covers a wider area in the reconstruction space, since the samples become less correlated.

One of the goals in digital signal processing is to find a reconstruction space dimension that appropriately quantifies the signal characteristics. The size of the reconstruction space determines the length N of a time window that slides over the full time series (Figure 8-6). The length of the time window may correspond to the size of the delay line and establishes the dimensionality of the reconstruction space.

For processing purposes, the dimensionality of the reconstruction space should be higher than the size of the signal subspace; otherwise there is information in the original time series that is difficult or impossible to capture. Unfortunately, the choice of the time window length is a nontrivial matter, because the dimensionality of the signal subspace is difficult to quantify and depends on the goal of the processing. This is an added difficulty both in temporal pattern recognition and in signal processing. For instance, if

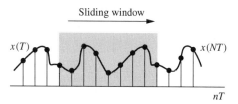

FIGURE 8-6 Sliding time window

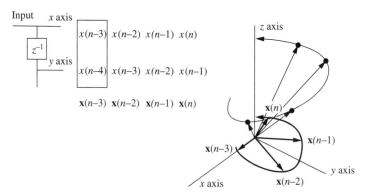

FIGURE 8-7 Reconstruction of the same signal in a 2-D space

we reconstruct the trajectory of Figure 8-5 in 2-D space, a different trajectory emerges, which may make the processing of the signal more difficult (Figure 8-7).

Dimension of Reconstruction Space

Signals with the same period may have different subspace dimensions. The more complicated the signal is in time, the larger the dimensionality of the corresponding subspace. Random noise has no time structure and fills the space of any dimension. Static pattern data is similar to random noise. We need a space of maximum dimensionality (i.e., equal to the number of the components of the data vector) to represent it, since we do not know a priori any relationships among the data components.

The dimension of the reconstruction space has been an object of intense studies. Takens[1] proved that for time series produced by dynamical systems, the size of the reconstruction space should be in the worst case equal to $2D + 1$, where D is the size of the attractor of the dynamics. The arguments are rooted in topological theory that an object of dimension D may need a space of size $2D + 1$ to be reconstructed without intersection of surfaces. See Kaplan and Glass [1995].

[1]Takens is a Dutch mathematician who formulated a very useful theorem showing that we can access the dynamic information of the system that produced the time series if the size of the reconstruction space is large enough.

NEUROSOLUTIONS EXAMPLE 8.2

Signal space and the delay line

This example introduces the delay line component, which is called TDNN Axon in NeuroSolutions because of the famous time delay neural network. The TDNN level of the Inspector selects the number of taps (the number of delays is the number of taps minus 1, since we always use the present input) and the number of delays between consecutive taps (normally set at one sample, i.e., z^{-1}). We can also select the number of inputs in the PE at the Axon level of the Inspector. In this example we construct a single-input delay line with two taps and create a reconstruction in a 2-D space with the Scatter Plot.

TDNN Axon

For the sine wave, the 3-D and 2-D reconstructions are very similar. Let us add a second sine wave component of a different frequency at the input. The trajectory for the sum of two sine waves is still clear in 3-D but does not make sense in the 2-D projection, since the signal trajectory folds. Play with the controls of the 3-D probe to visualize the 3-D trajectory. Notice that the 3-D trajectory has enough "space" to flow and never intersect a previous branch (except at the end of the period). This does not happen in the 2-D plot. A system connected to this two-tap delay line will have a harder time reconstructing one of the sine waves. Experiment with the period of the sine waves.

Experiment also with the reconstruction delay both in the 3-D plotter and in the 2-D reconstruction by changing the number of delays between the taps. The trajectories change shape when the delay is modified, but we can show that they are all topologically equivalent. In principle, all trajectories thus contain the same information. However, a smoother trajectory facilitates the extraction of time information by a system connected to the taps. The accuracy and speed of learning therefore depend on the delay.

8.2.3 Dynamics versus Statistics

We have seen that mapping a time signal to the signal space effectively created a time-to-space mapping. If we take a snapshot of the signal space, we see a cloud of points, just

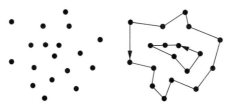

FIGURE 8-8 Static data cluster versus dynamic time sequence

as happened in pattern recognition. In such a case, we are obliged to resort to a statistical description of the data clusters to attain our goal (either regression or classification). But consider for a minute that you have access to the sequence that generates the samples, that is, that you are interested in the dynamics underlying the data. Data clusters that are indistinguishable from a statistical point of view suddenly become different if we can remember the sequence by which the data samples occur. In Figure 8-8, the left cluster of points seem to belong to the same class. However, if we have the two trajectories shown at right, we may conclude that they in fact belong to two different phenomena.

Time helps remove ambiguity from the data. But to do this, the system must have *short-term memory,* that is, it must remember the past values of the data, and of course our data models must take time into consideration. This is the goal of digital signal processing and more generally of dynamics. Short-term memory helps a learning system capture more information about the time-varying input data. As a rule of thumb, if the problem we are trying to solve has dynamics, we should always use a system topology with short-term memory. This chapter provides a review of the most important concepts about the analysis and design of linear dynamical systems.

8.3 THE CONCEPT OF FILTERING

8.3.1 The Linear Combiner

The simplest example of signal processing is a linear combination of the signals at the taps of the delay line (Figure 8-9). This structure is called the *linear combiner* or a linear finite impulse response (FIR) system. The linear combiner is a linear system.

Linear Systems

A system H is called linear if it obeys the following relation:

$$y_2(n) = H(x_2(n)), \qquad y_1(n) = H(x_1(n)) \Rightarrow \alpha y_1(n) + \beta y_2(n) = H(\alpha x_1(n) + \beta x_2(n))$$

which means that the principle of superposition applies (α and β are constants).

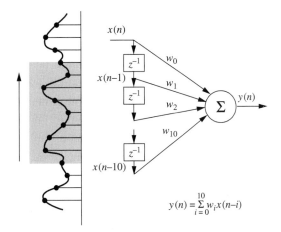

FIGURE 8-9   The windowing effect of the size of the delay line

The output of the linear combiner is calculated by

$$y(n) = \sum_{i=0}^{N} w_i x(n - i) \tag{8.9}$$

where N is the size of the delay line and w are parameters called *weights* or *filter coefficients*. With our interpretation of the output of the delay line as a vector of past samples, we can rewrite this expression in vector notation as the inner product:

$$y(n) = \mathbf{w}^T \mathbf{x}(n) = \mathbf{x}^T(n)\mathbf{w} \tag{8.10}$$

You may recall the same basic expression from the Hebbian networks in Chapter 6 or the linear regressor in Chapter 1. But remember, in Hebbian networks or linear regression $\mathbf{x}$ was a vector of values with no time tagging, while here $\mathbf{x}$ is a vector composed of the last N samples of the time series.

8.3.2 Filtering as a Projection

The interpretation of the input-output operation remains the same for the linear combiner, the Hebbian PE, or the linear regressor. The difference is the space utilized for the analysis. According to Eq. 8.10, a linear combiner produces a scalar output value. The past N inputs provide one vector in an N-dimensional space (with coordinates $x(n - i)$). Let us assume for simplicity that when time advances, this vector remains in a hyperplane in this N-dimensional space (the signal subspace; Figure 8-10). The output [interpreted as a vector from the origin to the output $y(n)$] is a linear combination of these past inputs and must exist in the same subspace. The actual value of $y(n)$ is the projection of $\mathbf{x}$ on the weight vector $\mathbf{w}$, which specifies the direction of the projection (Figure 8-10).

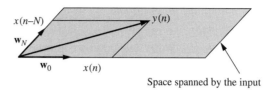

FIGURE 8-10 The projection in the space is controlled by the weights

We conclude that the linear combiner is a *linear projector in signal space.* If we modify the weight values **w**, the output of the system will change because the relative positions of the present input vector and the weight vector are not maintained, so the projection on **w** will change. This observation is crucial to understanding signal processing with the linear model; a linear system creates a projection of the input on a vector that is defined by the system parameters and that exists in a manifold created by the last signal samples.

Notice that even with a fixed weight vector, the projection varies in time because the signal subspace is changing with time. Depending on the relative position of the weight vector and the signal trajectory, this projection may preserve much of the information of the input signal, which exists in a much larger-dimensionality space, or may severely distort it. For instance, if the weight vector matches one of the signal-space axes, the output signal is always the same as the input (apart from a delay). If the signal trajectory is in a hyperplane with very different extents in each axis and we use a weight vector along the largest extent, we also recover the signal with small error. On the other hand, if the weight vector is placed along the smallest extent, we obtain a signal very different from the original. The role of the linear system designer is to choose the projection direction such that the desired information contained in the input signal is preserved. This is the fundamental idea of filtering. Remember that the linear combiner with $N + 1$ weights has a memory of only N samples. Any event that happens more than N samples in the past does not have any bearing on the present linear combiner output.

NEUROSOLUTIONS EXAMPLE 8.3

Linear combiner in signal space

Let us create a 3-tap delay line with the TDNN Axon to match the 3-D plot. Now let us implement a linear combiner with a Synapse and a Bias Axon. Let us set the weights by hand to $(1, 1, 1)$ to show the output of the linear combiner in the 3-D plot. Change the weights and justify why the signal is modified (the projection changes).

This requires some thinking. Notice that if the weights are 1, 0, 0 (or combinations with just one nonzero weight), the output is exactly the same as the input (except possibly delayed). This means that projections on any of the axes preserve the input wave shape. But if we start combining different weight values $(1, 1, 1)$, the projection is no longer along the axis, and the signal trajectory starts to be distorted (distortion may be good if we want to separate a signal from high-frequency noise). The weight vector (1, 1, 1) is along the first quadrant bisector of the reconstruction space, which coincides with the major axis of the ellipse (the sine wave trajectory), so it should preserve the sine wave shape.

Add a noise component at the input. Show that (1, 1, 1) preserves the sine wave and reduces the noise, while (0, −2, 1) produces predominantly the noise. This last vector is oriented in the orthogonal plane of the sine-wave trajectory. This is the principle of filtering: orienting the projection so that particular parts of the signal trajectory are emphasized, while others are attenuated.

8.3.3 Filtering Examples

Filtering is a selective and user-defined distortion of the input signal. Many applications in engineering require the selection of only partial information from the input signal. Let us study this operation in the signal space.

Filtering Operation

Filtering, as we have said, is the selective removal of frequency components. In many practical situations, signals are contaminated with noise, so it is often critical to remove this unwanted noise. For instance, the electric power we use in the home or office is modulated at 60 Hz for efficiency (to reduce the power loss in the wiring). As you might expect, 60-Hz components exist everywhere there is electricity (in Europe the electric power is 50 Hz). This can be very annoying when we try to measure electric signals of low amplitude. For instance, the human body functions as a great antenna for 60-Hz signals, so when we want to measure faint electrical signals created by our heart or brain, we have to deal with the 60-Hz interference. One way to handle this problem is to prefilter the physiological signals with a linear system that removes the 60-Hz power-line interference and lets the rest of the signal pass undistorted.

The issue, as we will see later in this chapter, is how to design such filters. Here we would like to point out that our discussion naturally was based on ideas from the frequency content of the signals. The time domain description was never mentioned in the discussion. This is normally the case, and it is the other motivating factor for defining signals in the frequency domain. More specifically, we can say that the steady-state behavior of linear systems calls for frequency domain representations. For transient response analysis, the advantage of the frequency domain is not as clear.

Probably the simplest example of filtering is the case of a signal created by the addition of two sinusoids of different frequencies, when we want to recover just one of them. We saw that a sinusoid always provides an ellipse as a signal trajectory. When another sinusoid of a different frequency is added to the original signal, the signal trajectory becomes more complex, effectively orbiting a torus. (For simplicity we assume that the amplitude of the higher-frequency sinusoid is smaller than the amplitude of

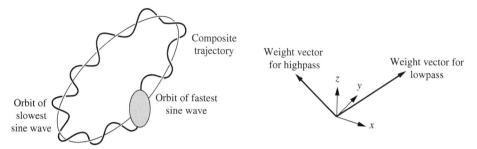

FIGURE 8-11   Illustration of the composite signal trajectory of two sine waves

the lower-frequency one and that the difference in frequency is large.) One of the fundamental differences is that the trajectory is no longer 2-D; that is, signals with more frequencies have more complex trajectories that do not exist in a 2-D space.

Let us assume that we want to recover the sinusoid of lowest frequency (or to filter out the high-frequency sinusoid). Just by imagining the signal trajectory (Figure 8-11), we can see that if the weight vector is chosen as the bisector of the first quadrant (corresponding to the principal axis of the torus), which is (1, 1, 1) for a 3-D space, we will recover the lowest-frequency sine wave. The highest-frequency sine wave will be attenuated, since the samples of the composite signal have zero projection on this weight vector, going up and down the plane of the orbit. There are many other weight vectors for the linear combiner that provide only the lowest-frequency sine wave. These filters are called *lowpass filters*. Can you think of another choice of **w** to implement a highpass filter?

Likewise, if we find a weight vector that is perpendicular to the midsection of the torus, we obtain an output that contains only the variation produced by the highest-frequency sine wave. Such a weight vector is, for instance, (1, −2, 1), and the linear combiner with these values is called a *highpass filter.* Can you find another choice for **w** to implement a highpass filter?

NEUROSOLUTIONS EXAMPLE 8.4

Filtering in signal space: the two-sine-wave case

In this example we use the previous NeuroSolutions Breadboard and show that orienting the weight vector emphasizes different parts of the signal trajectory. Let us use two sine waves of different frequencies as the input to our system. With a three-tap system the discrimination between the different components is not very large. However, if we use higher-dimensional spaces (i.e., tap delay lines with more taps), the discrimination can be as high as we want; we can completely remove one of the frequencies. A simple lowpass filter has all its weights equal to $1/N$, while a simple highpass filter with an even number of taps has alternating coefficients (e.g., 1, −1, 1, −1). These choices provide vectors along the first quadrant bisector and one of its orthogonal directions, respectively.

Filtering with the linear combiner can always be interpreted as in the previous example, but not all the signals are as easy as the addition of two sine waves. For instance, a triangular wave produces a signal trajectory that looks like a rectangle, but the small sides are effectively tilted at an angle, going up and down off the main plane of the orbit. Therefore, a lowpass filter distorts this orbit, rounding off the corners of the rectangle, since they will be projected to the main plane of the orbit. Likewise, the highpass filter accentuates the corners that go up and down from the planar orbit, creating a waveform that looks like a rectangular wave.

NEUROSOLUTIONS EXAMPLE 8.5

A triangular wave in 3-D space

Let us change the input to a triangular wave and analyze the trajectory. Change the filter weights to see the difference in the projection. If the dimension of the reconstruction space is increased, the projection results are more dramatic, but we lose the ability to visualize the resulting trajectories.

For a square wave you should now be able to determine what is going to happen. During the time that the wave is a positive constant, the signal trajectory collapses to the point $(1, 1, 1)$ in 3-D. However, when the signal changes from positive to negative, the trajectory goes through the points $(1, 1, -1)$, $(1, -1, -1)$, to $(-1, -1, -1)$. Likewise, when the wave goes from negative to positive, the points visited are $(-1, -1, 1)$, $(-1, 1, 1)$, and again $(1, 1, 1)$. Notice how different this is from the smooth trajectory produced by the sine wave. Using a linear combiner with a $(1, 1, 1)$ weight vector, we obtain a smoother signal, which resembles an ellipse of the same period as the square wave. If the projection uses the weight vector $(0, -2, 1)$, a trajectory with many discontinuities appears.

NEUROSOLUTIONS EXAMPLE 8.6

Square wave in 3-D space

Let us change the input to a square wave and analyze the trajectory. Change the filter weights to see the difference in the projection. If the dimension of the reconstruction space is increased, the projection results are more dramatic, but we lose the ability to visualize the resulting trajectories.

This signal space interpretation provides a qualitative explanation for the function of the linear combiner. We saw that the linear combiner projects the input signal onto a vector that exists in a linear space. The direction of this vector is controlled by the weights of the linear combiner. Depending on the relative direction of the weight vector and the signal trajectory, some of the features of the original signal are preserved, and some others are attenuated. This is the idea of filtering. The problem with this interpretation is that it is difficult to quantify exactly what is going to happen to the input signal, which motivates the need for other analysis tools.

8.4 TIME DOMAIN ANALYSIS OF LINEAR SYSTEMS

Although the vector space methodology leads to a conceptual understanding of a linear combiner, it is not very usable for the systematic quantification of how the linear system affects the input signal properties. The widespread use of linear systems in engineering is due to the existence of easy and systematic methods to quantify their properties. Signal processing developed two basic methodologies to study linear system properties: the *time domain approach* and the *frequency domain approach*. We start with the time domain methodology.

8.4.1 The Impulse Response

A very important quantity to describe a linear system is the *impulse response*. As the name indicates, the impulse response $h(n)$ is the output of the system when the input is a delta function (also called an impulse) applied at time zero, $\delta(n)$. In linear systems, the time that the response takes to stabilize for a constant input is called the *transient time,* and the system output during that time is called the *transient response*. The impulse response is sometimes also called the transient response.

The impulse response completely describes a linear system. Nonlinear systems do not have this property, so with a nonlinear system we have to either know the equation for the map or probe all the points of the input space to find the corresponding output (as we did in Chapter 3 with the discriminant probe). For the linear combiner the impulse response is, from Eq. 8.9,

$$h(n) = \sum_{i=0}^{N} w_i \delta(n - i) \tag{8.11}$$

which means that the impulse response of the linear combiner is simply a time function with sample values equal to the weights $h(i) = w_i$ (the first time sample is equal to the first weight, etc.). Hence, for an N-delay FIR filter, the impulse response will have at most $N + 1$ nonzero values; that is, it always will be of finite extent, hence the name finite impulse response (FIR) for this type of linear system. These properties are easily verified by considering that a single value of one will progressively move through the tap delay line of the linear combiner.

Impulse Response

The impulse response is by definition the response of the system when the input is an impulse at $n = 0$. This means that Eq. 8.9 can be written by substituting $h(n) = y(n)$ and

$x(n) = \delta(n)$, which yields

$$h(n) = \sum_{i=0}^{N} w_i \delta(n - i) = w_0 \delta(n) + w_1 \delta(n - 1) + w_2 \delta(n - 2) + \ldots$$

What this equation means is that the impulse response of a FIR is exactly the copy of its weights spread out in time. For instance, if the weights of the filter are $w_0 = 0.5$, $w_1 = 0.25$, $w_2 = 1$, the impulse response is $h(0) = 0.5$, $h(1) = 0.25$, $h(2) = 1$. By knowing the weights in a FIR, we know the impulse response (or vice versa).

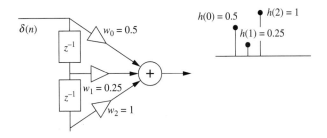

NEUROSOLUTIONS EXAMPLE 8.7

Impulse response of a FIR filter

The impulse response of a FIR filter is very easy to visualize. Just enter by hand some values for the weights of the linear combiner, and take note of them. Then choose the impulse function as the input to the filter and run the data sample by sample with the *step exemplar* button. Place a Matrix Viewer at the output. The output of the linear combiner matches the values you entered as the weights, producing a time response. This is easy to understand if we envisage the impulse being multiplied by the weights and being moved forward every time tick. Note that the time response is related to the weights by $h(i) = w_i$. This makes sense, since at time $n = 0$ the output reproduces the first weight w_0, at $n = 1$ the output reproduces the second weight w_1, and so on.

8.4.2 Convolution

The importance of the impulse response is the following fact: The response $y(n)$ of a linear system to an *arbitrary* input $x(n)$ can always be calculated by the *convolution* of the input $x(n)$ with the system impulse response $h(n)$:

$$y(n) = x(n) * h(n) = \sum_{i=-\infty}^{\infty} x(i)h(n - i) = \sum_{i=-\infty}^{\infty} x(n - i)h(i) \qquad (8.12)$$

where the $*$ indicates convolution. This is a very important property, because knowing the impulse response (for instance, after measuring the response of the system to an impulse *only once*), we can calculate beforehand how the system will respond to any other known input. We just need to program the operation of convolution in a computer to predict the response of the system to hypothetical inputs.

Notice that the impulse response in Eq. 8.12 appears reversed in time, since the summation index i has a negative sign (or equivalently, the input appears reversed in time). This time reversal is a mathematical necessity to translate the normal operation of the system when it receives a time signal. Let us look at Figure 8-8 to see what is happening.

Assume that all the taps of the filter are initialized to zero. The first sample of the input $x(0)$ multiplies the first filter coefficient, so the output at $n = 0$ is equal to $y(0) = w_0 x(0)$; for the next time tick ($n = 1$) the sample $x(0)$ is moved to the next tap and multiplies w_1, while $x(1)$ multiplies w_0. The output is $y(1) = w_0 x(1) + w_1 x(0)$. For the next time tick, $x(0)$ multiplies w_2, and the output becomes $y(2) = w_0 x(2) + w_1 x(1) + w_2 x(0)$. Notice how this sum of products coincides with Eq. 8.12 for the same points. The process continues on for every time tick.

Convolution Operation

Although very important, the convolution operation is tricky, since it cannot be computed in a point-by-point fashion as, for instance, a change in scale. If we are given an input and the impulse response, convolution is *not* a simple point-by-point multiplication of the two signals.

The equation specifies

$$y(n) = x(n) * h(n) = \sum_{i=-\infty}^{\infty} x(i)h(n - i) = \sum_{i=-\infty}^{\infty} x(n - i)h(i)$$

If the system is causal (i.e., if the system does not have an output before the input is applied), the response to an input applied at $n = 0$ can be simplified to

$$y(n) = x(n) * h(n) = \sum_{i=0}^{n} x(i)h(n - i)$$

Let us read this equation carefully. This construction is better visualized in the i domain. Notice that for *each* sample of y (a value of n), we have a *sum of terms* over the i variable (see the following figure). These terms are the multiplication of the input $x(i)$ with the impulse response reversed in time $h(n - i)$. One of the two waveforms is therefore flipped in time. The value of the output is the sum of products, that is, the area under the intersection of the two waves. When time progresses (the index n increases), the relative positions of the input and the impulse response change, since the impulse response is affected by the index n. Hence the total length of the response is the sum of the lengths of each wave (minus 1).

Notice also that the convolution can be computed alternatively by switching the roles of $x(.)$ and $h(.)$. The following figure exemplifies the graphic construction of the convolution.

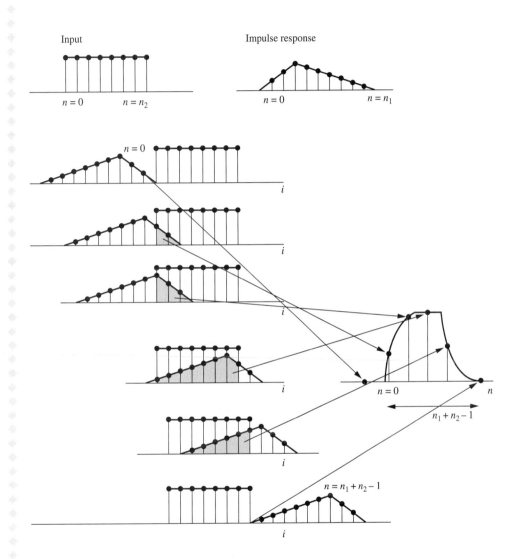

Remember that the convolution transforms the product of the overlapped samples (between the input and impulse response) at time n into an amplitude value at the output of the filter. This is strange, but effectively it is what *any* linear system does!

The convolution for FIR filters can still be computed easily by hand, and it is an excellent opportunity to understand the concept fully. For FIRs the limits in Eq. 8.12

are finite (0 and N) when the input is applied at time $n = 0$. The convolution of a signal segment of length M with a FIR of length N is at most $M + N - 1$ samples long.

NEUROSOLUTIONS EXAMPLE 8.8
More on the impulse response of a FIR filter

The same process explained in the previous example works for any input, but since the input normally has more than one nonzero sample, we have to multiply and add the contributions from each tap. This is formulated as the convolution sum shown in Eq. 8.12 and explained in Appendix A.

We now do the convolution in NeuroSolutions. Notice that the Breadboard has two parts: The left part helps us create arbitrary waveforms by using the impulse function and letting the FIR filter create the wave shape (by choosing the weights). Note that we are using this left FIR as an arbitrary signal generator. The right part of the Breadboard implements our FIR system, for which we want to compute the output using convolution.

Use sample-by-sample execution and copy the values produced by Neuro-Solutions to a piece of paper. Now compare this with the "Convolution Operation" box on pages 384–385, which explains the convolution, to understand the process. Knowing the input wave shape and the FIR impulse response, you should be able to derive the output of the system by hand. The output of NeuroSolutions is your gold standard; your results should match the ones obtained in the simulator.

In particular, you should understand why you have to reverse in time one of the waveforms (either the input or the impulse response) and find out why the output is of length equal to the sum of the lengths minus 1. Just picture in your mind the FIR filter receiving the samples and computing the output with the block diagram.

Some of the important properties of linear systems, such as that the output appears only after the input is applied (causality), should be clear from this example. In addition, the output peaks after a few samples (i.e., there is always a delay in the response of the system). If the FIR impulse response is symmetric (called *linear phase*), it should peak at $(N - 1)/2$ (if N is odd).

A problem with convolution is that it is not a simple, sample-by-sample operation like the addition or multiplication of samples. We see from Eq. 8.12 that to compute the response $y(n)$ for each time tick n, a very large (eventually infinite) number of products have to be added together (as many as the length of the impulse response). We need very fast digital computers or alternative descriptions.

8.4.3 Matched Filters

An important engineering problem is the search for transients of a given shape in a noisy background, which is called *detection*. Areas where detection is important are radar, sonar, and biomedical applications. One way to create a linear system that can be used for detection is to include the a priori knowledge (the transient wave shape) as the weights of a FIR filter. As you may expect from the convolution, the procedure calls for the reversal in time of the transient shape to specify the filter weights. This filter is called the *matched filter* precisely because its impulse response is the transient shape reversed in time. If we look at the convolution equation (Eq. 8.12) we can see that the output of the matched filter is the sum of the squares of the waveform samples when the impulse response is the waveform reversed in time. This happens to be the autocorrelation function evaluated at lag zero.

The matched filter is an optimal filter in the sense that it maximizes the output signal energy to the noise power at one point in time:

$$\max y(N) = \frac{R(0)}{\sigma^2}$$

where N is the length of the transient and the denominator is the variance of the noise, which is assumed white in this formulation. The point in time where the output peaks is the last sample of the transient, since at that time the output is $R(0)$, which represents the power in the transient and is the largest value of the autocorrelation function.

The matched filter output can be thresholded and used as a detector when the transients appear in background noise. The amplitude of the transient may be buried in noise, but the matched filter is able to find the correlation in time and transform it into an amplitude value that peaks above the noise floor. Therefore, by observing the matched filter output and finding the peaks, we can obtain the location where the transients occur. This is the best possible linear system for this application, and it resembles the eigenfilter and the Hamming net discussed in Chapter 6, except that now the patterns exist in time. Matched filters are used frequently in communications for optimal receivers.

NEUROSOLUTIONS EXAMPLE 8.9
Matched filtering

Consider the case of a transmitter that creates a pulse of energy of a known shape, but we do not know when the pulse arrives. To make matters worse, the transmission is noisy, so we receive not only the transient but a great deal of noise. How can we reliably find when the pulse is received?

To solve this problem, let us first create the matched filter. This is easy, since we just need to encode the weights of the linear combiner as the samples of the transient (reversed in time). Now we can simply observe the output of the matched filter with a threshold to find where the transients occurred. Note that the setting of the threshold depends on the noise power. If it is set too low, we get too many detections (the ones that do not correspond to the transient are called false alarms, or false positives), while if the threshold is set too high, we may miss some pulse occurrences (called missed detections, or false negatives). The figure of merit for such a system is the plot of the detection probability against the number of false alarms as a function of the threshold (which is called the *receiver operating characteristics (ROC) curve*). The ROC is the best way to evaluate a detector.

8.5   RECURRENT SYSTEMS AND STABILITY

Thus far, we have focused on the linear combiner as a finite impulse response (FIR) filter. A second class of systems is composed of infinite impulse response (IIR) filters, and they contain recurrent/feedback connections. An important aspect of IIR systems is that they are not inherently stable like the FIR systems. This section will discuss recurrent systems and their stability.

8.5.1 First-Order Recurrent Systems

Let us study the following discrete recurrent system:

$$y(n) = (1 - \mu)y(n - 1) + x(n) \tag{8.13}$$

where $1 - \mu$ is a coefficient called the *feedback coefficient,* $y(.)$ is the output, and $x(.)$ is the input. This system is called recurrent because the output at time n depends on the output at a previous time (in this case the last output). Equation 8.13 is called a *difference equation,* and it is related to differential equations in continuous time.

Continuous and Digital Filters

This equation corresponds to the simplest analog lowpass filter, which is described by the first-order differential equation

$$\frac{d}{dt}y(t) = \mu y(t) + x(t) \tag{8B.1}$$

and can be built with a capacitor and a resistor with time constant μ. If we approximate the differential by the forward difference,

$$\frac{d}{dt}y(t) \approx y(n + 1) - y(n) \tag{8B.2}$$

Eq. 8.13 is obtained. This equation is called a difference equation because the difference operator is used to approximate the differential.

There are important relationships between continuous time systems described by differential equations and the discrete systems we are studying with difference equations.

In fact, the forward difference operator and the substitution of t by nT allow us to go from continuous time to discrete time (but there are other more rigorous ways of linking the two domains). T, the sampling period, must be very small to preserve the goodness of the approximation.

Another important characteristic of both the linear combiner and the recurrent system is that they have responses only after the input is applied. Such systems are called causal, or nonanticipatory, and they are the only ones that can be built in analog hardware. Any physically realizable system is causal. With computers we can play tricks and implement noncausal FIR systems. The idea is to use memory and delay the output of the system with respect to real time so that it responds to events that happen in the near future.

The block diagram of this system is shown in Figure 8-12, and it clearly shows the *feedback connection* from the output to the input adder. Note how easy it is to write the difference equation from the block diagram (or vice versa). The initial condition $y(0)$ needs to be specified to compute Eq. 8.13 [normally $y(0) = 0$]. Let us evaluate the impulse response of this system [$x(n) = \delta(n)$]. Just by following the block diagram we can immediately see that

$$h(0) = 0 + 1$$
$$h(1) = (1 - \mu) + 0$$
$$h(2) = (1 - \mu)^2 + 0$$
$$\cdots$$
$$h(n) = (1 - \mu)^n + 0 \tag{8.14}$$

The first remark is to note that the impulse response is of infinite extent. This system therefore does not belong to the same class as the linear combiner. Linear systems that have infinite impulse response are called IIR (infinite impulse response). They must have some type of internal feedback mechanism. Another important observation is that the impulse response shape is controlled by the feedback parameter. If $0 < \mu < 1$, the impulse response will decay exponentially toward zero, with a decay rate given by the feedback coefficient. It is exactly zero only when $n = \infty$, but for all practical purposes it becomes zero after a finite time n_0. The closer μ is to 1, the slower will be the decay

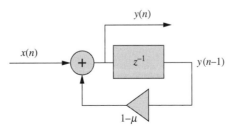

FIGURE 8-12 First-order recurrent system

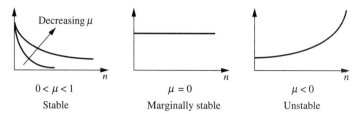

$0 < \mu < 1$ $\mu = 0$ $\mu < 0$

Stable   Marginally stable   Unstable

FIGURE 8-13 Impulse response of the first-order recurrent system

of the impulse response (Figure 8-13). For $\mu < 0$ or $\mu > 2$, the response will diverge (for zero initial conditions); that is, it will become larger and larger. Note that this case is impossible to obtain with FIR systems.

NEUROSOLUTIONS EXAMPLE 8.10

IIR filters

We introduce one more NeuroSolutions component that creates the first-order recurrent system of Figure 8-11. This system has the one-sample delay in the feedback loop, and the feedback parameter can be set in the Inspector.

Integrator Axon

We use an impulse at the input and display the response in a MegaScope. The goal is to show that the response is controlled by the feedback parameter. By making the parameter close to 1, the response slowly decays to 0. For values above 2 or less than 0, the response explodes. Let us also use the 3-D probe to see that the response linearly approaches the point (0, 0, 0) in state space when the feedback parameter is between 0 and 1. Finally, input a sine wave to see that the response takes some time to stabilize. The time that the response takes to approximately reach the final value is still called the transient response.

The behavior of the first and third cases of Figure 8-13 is qualitatively different. In the first case the response to the delta function decays to zero, and the system follows any input applied thereafter to it, while in the third case the response to the transient never disappears. The goal in signal processing is to have the system respond to inputs (eventually taking away unwanted portions such as noise or amplifying the signal, as when we listen to music), so we would like the system to always have a *finite-duration transient response*. Hence we have to guarantee that the response to transients will die away, which can be done by the control of the feedback parameter.

8.5.2 Definition of Stability

There are many definitions of stability, but the bounded-input bounded-output (BIBO) definition is the most commonly used for linear systems. Let us define BIBO stability. A system is BIBO stable if it responds with a finite-amplitude signal to any input that is also of finite amplitude. From Eq. 8.12 this means that *the sum of the impulse response values has to be finite*. Hence the linear combiner with N taps is intrinsically stable.

If the definition of stability is applied to the recurrent system, we see that the system will be stable for $0 < \mu < 1$ and unstable for $\mu < 0$ and $\mu > 2$. A stable linear system has an impulse response that approaches zero such that its sum is finite. For $\mu = 0$ the stability depends on the initial condition, and it is called *marginally stable* for this reason. Hence we see that recurrence brings new properties to linear systems (and also new worries, such as stability).

In the FIR the impulse response of an Nth-order FIR is the filter weight values (it takes at most N samples to reach zero). In recurrent systems the impulse response is of infinite extent, and the relationship between successive values is controlled by just a few parameters (the feedback parameters). In the system of Figure 8-12, the stability is captured by the value of the feedback parameter $(1 - \mu)$. The absolute value of the feedback parameter must be less than 1 for stability, that is, $|1 - \mu| < 1$.

NEUROSOLUTIONS EXAMPLE 8.11

Second-order recurrent system

Let us build a second-order linear recurrent system in NeuroSolutions. We have to use a TDNNAxon with two taps and a Full Synapse that feeds the taps back to the input of the Axon. When the interconnection is established, the system complains that an infinite loop is created, and we have to include an extra delay in the feedback. Hence a two-tap TDNN connected in this way creates a recurrent system described by the following difference equation:

$$y(n) = ay(n - 1) + by(n - 2) + x(n)$$

The first weight in the Full Synapse is a, and the second is b. You can verify that the system is stable only for a subset of the values a, b. There are several possible regimes of the impulse response. A decaying exponential is obtained for $b > 0$ and $a + \sqrt{a^2 + 4b} < 2$. A decaying, oscillating response is obtained for $b < 0$, $|4b| > |a^2|$, and $a^2 + 2b < 2$. For $a^2 + 2b = 2$ a sine wave is obtained (the system is marginally stable). For all the other values the response is unstable. We will see later how these values come about.

It is instructive to visualize in state space the stable oscillating regime. The system output spirals down to the origin of state space and stays there.

8.6 FREQUENCY DOMAIN ANALYSIS

8.6.1 Signal Spectrum

The impulse response is a very powerful method to describe linear systems, but it is not very practical for the following reasons:

- When the linear system is described by its impulse response, the system output cannot be computed with sample-by-sample evaluations (because it requires a convolution between the input and the impulse response).

- The response of a linear system (with an N-sample-length impulse response) to an N-sample-length input signal using convolution requires $O(N^2)$ multiplications.

- The time domain description is not very appropriate to quantify the effect of linear systems in terms of filtering, which is at the core of linear signal processing.

An important goal is to seek methods that preserve the descriptive power of the impulse response but can be directly used to describe filtering and to compute the output of the system as a point-by-point operation more efficiently than $O(N^2)$.

Such an alternative technique exists and is based on the idea of Fourier analysis, also called *spectrum*. The description of a signal by means of its spectrum is called *spectral analysis*. Without knowing it, we already covered the fundamental theory that leads to the definition of the spectrum when we studied function approximation in Chapter 5.

Our goal is to seek a new representation for time signals that will make the processing by linear systems easy to understand and apply. Since we are interested in linear systems that are linear operators, we know that their eigenfunctions are complex exponentials.

Eigendecomposition Explained

A linear shift invariant operator H, when applied to a complex exponential e^{sT}, changes only its magnitude and phase:

$$y = He^{st} = \lambda e^{st} \tag{8B.3}$$

where λ is a complex number. Thus, if an arbitrary time function $u(t)$ is decomposed into exponentials

$$u(t) = \sum_i \alpha_i e^{s_i t} \tag{8B.4}$$

then the response of H to $u(t)$ can always be evaluated as a sum of weighted responses to exponentials:

$$Hu(t) = H\left[\sum_i \alpha_i e^{s_i t}\right] = \sum_i \alpha_i H\left[e^{s_i t}\right] = \sum_i \alpha_i \lambda_i e^{s_i t} \tag{8B.5}$$

where the λ_i do not depend on $u(t)$. Fourier analysis is a special case of this decomposition where the complex exponentials have zero real part. For continuous time operators this decomposition gives rise to the Laplace domain analysis of linear systems, where the system is represented by the operator H. In a nutshell, the Laplace analysis is the study of the linear system in the complex plane $s = \sigma + j\omega$.

In the case of discrete time operators it is convenient to change the variable for the analysis from s to $z = e^{sT}$, called the Z transform. The Laplace and Z transforms achieve the same goal, but one is applicable to continuous systems, while the other is for discrete systems. Notice that we already saw the z notation when we defined the ideal delay operator.

Let us reiterate the advantage of eigendecompositions. They are very efficient, since they provide an orthonormal basis, and they naturally decompose the signals, that is, they achieve perfect reconstruction with just a few bases.

8.6.2 Decomposition in Phasors: Fourier Analysis

It is interesting to decompose discrete signals into complex exponentials of the form

$$e^{snT} = e^{anT + j\Delta\omega nT} \tag{8.15}$$

where s is a complex variable, n is an integer, a and $\Delta\omega$ are real quantities, and T is the sampling period. The quantity w is inversely proportional to time, and it is called the *frequency*. Frequency is measured in radians per second (or alternatively, in Hertz). The quantity $\Delta\omega$ is called the *frequency resolution* and can be defined as the smallest frequency increment that can be represented in NT seconds, that is, $\Delta\omega = 2\pi/NT$. What this means is that if we observe a signal for a long time (large NT), we can discriminate minor frequency changes. If the window of observation is short, our frequency resolution is coarse. The resolution $\Delta\omega$ is also the slowest frequency that can be reliably measured in a window of NT seconds.

The spectrum is by definition the decomposition of the signal $\{x(n)\}$ onto the basis set formed by the complex exponentials $e^{j\omega nT}$ with zero real part ($a = 0$), which are called phasors. Basically, a phasor is a single-frequency component that describes an ellipse in signal space, as we saw in the first example of this chapter. Decomposition in phasors is called Fourier or harmonic analysis.

Concept of Phasor

A phasor is a unit-length vector rotating at a constant speed, as originally proposed by Steinmetz. It can be represented by $u(t) = e^{j\omega t}$, where the rotation frequency is ω. Euler's relation states that $e^{j\omega t} = \cos \omega t + j \sin \omega t$, which means that a phasor is a "complex" waveform that gives rise to our well-known sinusoidal waveforms (see the following figure).

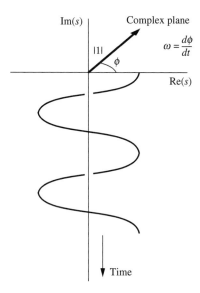

We can imagine Euler's relation and the relation between phasors and real sinusoids if we observe this figure. The goal is to have the phasor rotating and plot its projection on the real line as a function of time.

When the vector is aligned with the real axis at time zero, the amplitude is 1. When it starts rotating, the amplitude decreases monotonically on the real axis (and increases on the imaginary axis), until it is zero for $\phi = \pi/2$ (it is 1 on the imaginary axis). Then it starts to be negative and is maximally negative for $\phi = \pi$ (at this point it is zero on the imaginary axis). At $\phi = 3\pi/2$, its amplitude decreases until zero and then increases again until $\phi = 2\pi$. It repeats this behavior for larger values of the angle ϕ, so we see that in time it gives rise to a periodic wave with period 2π.

We can also show that if the rotating speed is constant, the projections must be sinusoidal with a constant frequency. Thus we can think of our well-known sinusoid as the projection on the real line of the complex phasor. Notice also that when the rotating speed is faster, the frequency of the sinusoidal projection increases.

The complex vector $\mathbf{u}(t)$ can be represented by its modulus (length) and phase as

$$\mathbf{u}(t) = \begin{cases} \left| e^{j\omega t} \right| \\ \tan^{-1}(e^{j\omega t}) \end{cases}$$

For the phasor we see that the modulus is 1, and the arctangent is simply ωt. If we want to plot each one of these functions (now real) independently over time, we obtain what are called respectively the *magnitude* and the *phase representation* for the phasor. Being a complex quantity, the phasor requires two plots to be represented over time.

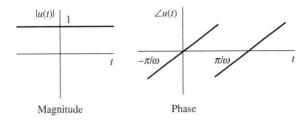

Magnitude   Phase

Notice that the phase plot is discontinuous, due to the arctan function, but can be made continuous by adding 2π at the jumps (phase unwrapping).

Alternatively, we could plot the real and the imaginary parts of the phasor to obtain a cosine for the real part and a sine for the imaginary part, as Euler's relation shows.

We see that the phasor is the elementary function in the complex domain, exactly as the sine wave is the elementary function for time representations. Every time we encounter a phasor, we should think of a vector of unit length rotating at a constant speed ω. Since we started this study in vector spaces, the phasor seems the best way to introduce harmonic or spectral analysis. However, an equivalent explanation can be given in terms of sine waves. The phasor's rotating speed actually corresponds to the frequency of the sine wave.

We saw that a signal $x(n)$ with a finite length NT can be considered as a vector in N-dimensional space. Therefore we need exactly N phasors (each rotating at a different frequency), given by

$$e^{jn\Delta\omega T} = e^{j2\pi\frac{n}{N}} \qquad n = 0, 1, \ldots, N - 1 \tag{8.16}$$

to span the same space. It is easy to show that the complex exponentials are orthonormal (i.e., they are an orthogonal set of vectors with unit magnitude).

We now have two alternative discrete representations for the signal $x(n)$, one using delta functions, yielding the time domain representation, and the other using phasors or single-frequency vectors. Do we lose any information when $x(n)$ is represented in this new orthogonal basis of the same size as the time domain basis? *The length of a vector is independent of the orthonormal basis, so we do not lose any information.* The signal is simply decomposed into different elemental components; in other words, the bases are no longer $\{\delta(n - i)\}$ but become phasors, as shown in Eq. 8.13, which lead to easier interpretation in many cases.

Parseval's Theorem

Parseval's theorem is well known in linear system theory and is a consequence of the property that vectors do not change length when the orthonormal basis is changed. The theorem states that

$$\sum_{n=-\infty}^{\infty} x^2(n) = \frac{1}{2\pi j} \oint_C X(v)X(v^{-1})v^{-1} \, dv$$

where C is a closed contour that belongs to the region of convergence of $X(z)$. In practical terms what this theorem says is that the energy of the sequence $x(n)$ can be computed either in the time domain (left side) or through the spectrum (right side). For the discrete Fourier transform (DFT) this expression reduces to

$$\sum_{n=0}^{N-1} x^2(n) = \frac{1}{N} \sum_{k=0}^{N-1} X^2(k)$$

The projection of $\{x(n)\}$ on each of the phasors is represented by $X(k)$, where k indicates the phasor used ($1 < k < N$); that is, k is the *frequency index* (Figure 8-14). $X(k)$ is called the kth Fourier coefficient, and the set of all $X(k)$ is called the discrete Fourier series (DFS) of $x(n)$, or the spectrum of $x(n)$.

Unlike $x(n)$, $X(k)$ is a complex function, which can be decomposed into its magnitude, called the *magnitude spectrum* $|X(k)|$, and its phase, called the *phase spectrum* $\underline{/X(k)}$. We can represent $x(n)$ in the time domain or equivalently by the two plots, the magnitude spectrum and the phase spectrum (Figure 8-15). Notice that the magnitude spectrum is symmetric with respect to $N/2$, while the phase spectrum is antisymmetric as long as $x(n)$ is a real signal.

8.6.3 The Discrete Fourier Series

One of the relevant aspects of Fourier or harmonic analysis is that there are analytic expressions to compute $X(k)$ from $x(n)$, and vice versa. These are called the *discrete*

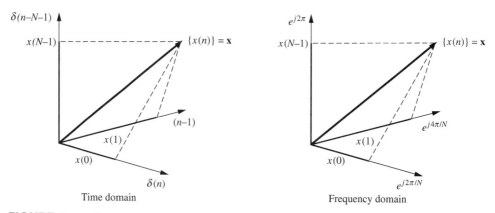

FIGURE 8-14   Decomposition of a time sequence in delays and in complex exponentials

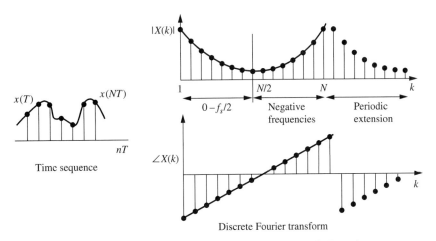

FIGURE 8-15   Time series and its DFT (magnitude and phase)

Fourier series (DFS) pair:

$$X(k) = \sum_{n=1}^{N} x(n)e^{-j2\pi k \frac{n}{N}}$$

$$x(n) = \frac{1}{N}\sum_{k=1}^{N} X(k)e^{j2\pi k \frac{n}{N}} \tag{8.17}$$

We already saw these expressions in Chapter 5 when we discussed function approximation, without knowing these implications. There we computed the Fourier coefficients $X(k)$ as the inner product of the signal with the bases. Let us interpret the meaning of the spectrum $X(k)$ by looking at the second equation in the pair. Each basis is a phasor (which really corresponds to a sinusoid) with different frequencies $n\Delta\omega$, multiples of the smallest frequency $\Delta\omega$ ($\omega = 2\pi/NT$) that can be represented in the time window. According to Eq. 8.17 we get back $x(n)$ by adding all the phasors multiplied by the projections on each phasor, which are the Fourier coefficients $X(k)$.

Therefore the spectrum is telling us how much of the energy of the windowed input signal $x(n)$ exists at each phasor frequency. For instance, a sine wave of normalized frequency k_1 (k_1 corresponds to the frequency $w = 2\pi k_1/NT$) has a spectrum with just one nonzero coefficient $X(k_1)$ exactly at the frequency k_1 of the sine wave (with a value equal to the amplitude of the sine wave). If the signal is composed of two sine waves, the spectrum contains two lines at the respective sine-wave frequencies. We can see that, at least for sinusoidal signals, the DFS gives a much more compact representation than the time representation (the signal amplitude changes according to a complicated relation over the period). However, a square wave, which is such an easy signal to describe in time (only two amplitudes), requires an infinite number of amplitudes when decomposed in phasors.

Properties of DFS

The discrete Fourier series is so important in signal processing that we have to provide a synopsis of its properties here. Moreover, we will see that knowing these properties for the DFS is enough to know and understand the properties of the other Fourier analysis transforms.

1. The DFS is a linear operator:

if
$$x_3(n) = ax_1(n) + bx_2(n)$$
then
$$X_3(k) = aX_1(k) + bX_2(k)$$

2. Parseval's theorem: The energy of a signal can be computed either in the time or in the frequency domain.

$$\sum_{n=0}^{N-1} |x(n)|^2 = \frac{1}{N} \sum_{k=0}^{N-1} |X(k)|^2$$

3. Delaying a time signal multiplies the transform by the equally delayed basis:

$$x(n - \tau) \leftrightarrow X(k)e^{-j\frac{2\pi}{N}\tau}$$

4. The convolution in time is equivalent to a multiplication of the transforms (and vice versa).

Some important remarks are in order. Notice that the DFS is *periodic with N* (the number of samples in the time window). Its magnitude is symmetric with respect to sample $N/2$, while the phase spectrum is antisymmetric. The value $k = N/2$ corresponds to the highest frequency that can be represented with the chosen sampling frequency $(\frac{1}{2}f_s)$. Values of k above $N/2$ correspond to the negative frequencies and can be ignored from the interpretation of real signals (since the magnitude spectrum is symmetric). The separation between consecutive values of k is called the *frequency resolution* and is given by

$$\Delta f = \frac{1}{NT} \tag{8.18}$$

in Hertz (or $2\pi/NT$ in radians per second). We can see that the higher the number of points used in the time signal (longer windows), the better is the spectral resolution.

Computers can easily compute the DFS through a fast algorithm called the fast Fourier transform (FFT).

How to use the FFT

The fast Fourier transform (FFT) is an algorithm that computes the DFT very efficiently. To use the FFT appropriately, we have to choose its parameters wisely. What we are really interested in is estimating the spectrum from a finite data set, so we have to worry about the resolution and the variance of the estimator.

The resolution is controlled by the number of data samples used in the window, which is normally called the length of the FFT. This length has to be a multiple of 2 for the fast algorithm to work. Once the length is selected, the resolving power of the method (the frequency resolution) is set by $\Delta f = 1/NT$, so we have to select N appropriately.

Another issue is the variance of the estimator. Experience shows that the estimator has a large variance; that is, the shape of the FFT is highly dependent on the data in the window. To decrease the variance, we normally divide the data set in several windows, take individual FFTs, and average the FFTs together. The variance decreases with the number of individual FFTs being averaged, so the larger the better.

Unfortunately, this means that there are conflicting requirements when we have a finite number of samples. Either we use a long window to get better resolution but sacrifice on the variance (i.e., the variance is high), or we use smaller windows and average the individual FFTs, which reduces the variance but sacrifices resolution because the window size is reduced. We have to get the best compromise for the problem at hand. Sometimes we overlap the windows to get more individual estimates for the same resolution. NeuroSolutions allows the user to set all of these parameters.

NEUROSOLUTIONS EXAMPLE 8.12

The fast Fourier transform (FFT)

NeuroSolutions has a probe that computes and displays the magnitude of the FFT of a segment of data. We choose the variable we want to graph, place a data buffer on the access point, and place the FFT Probe on top of it. In the Inspector you must select the size of the window (if smaller than the data buffer), the size of the FFT (which must be a power of 2, i.e., 32, 64, 128, 256, etc.), the number of independent FFTs that will be averaged together to decrease the variance of the estimation, and finally the percentage overlap between the successive windows. This probe is more than a simple FFT; it is a consistent spectrum estimator (called the Welch spectrum estimator). But if we select 1 as the number of FFTs, this will give us just the spectrum. The probe displays only the spectral magnitude.

If we input a sine wave (30 samples/period) and compute the 64-point FFT, it will show two lines symmetric with respect to the midpoint of the display. Note that the horizontal axis of the FFT display is frequency, in a linear scale, from 0 to f_s. The middle of the display is $f_s/2$. The right half of the display corresponds to the negative frequencies and should be the same as the left side (for real functions). This is the reason we sometimes just display the first half of the spectrum. The left peak of the spectrum should correspond to the frequency of the input sine wave (the right peak is just its negative frequency counterpart). If you create a two-samples-per-cycle sine wave (the highest possible frequency), you should see just one spectral line at $f_s/2$.

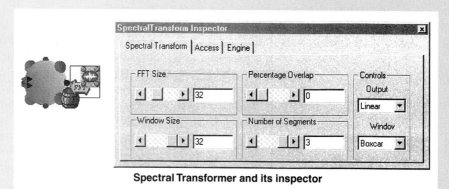

Spectral Transformer and its inspector

Input two sine waves of different frequencies (6 and 30 samples/period). The display shows four lines representing two frequencies. Notice that it is much simpler to interpret the FFT plot than the time signal. Let us now select two frequencies that have contiguous periods (16 and 17 samples/period). The 64-point FFT displays just two peaks instead of four, because it does not have enough resolution to discriminate the two peaks (use Eq. 8.17). You have to increase the FFT length to 512 to be able to resolve the two peaks (use Eq. 8.17 again).

There is a one-to-one relationship between signals in time and their spectra; that is, representations of signals in one domain or in the other are perfectly equivalent. A nice property of the signal spectrum is that the signal components along each one of the bases are orthogonal to each other, while in the time domain the signal components along each axis are not orthogonal (when the bases are the delays). For many problems we do not even need to compute the phase spectrum; we simply work with the magnitude. The importance of spectral analysis can be better appreciated if we blend it with the analysis of linear systems.

Relationship between DFS, FT, DFT, LT, and Z

We recommend that a digital signal processing book [Oppenheim and Schafer 1989] be consulted for a more in-depth comparison of the transforms. Here we would just like to relate all the signal processing transforms, because this is hardly ever done, and when looked at from the point of view of projection, they can all be integrated in the same framework.

Let us first enumerate all the transforms with their applications:

- Laplace transforms (LT), utilized in the study of linear systems in continuous time
- *Z* transforms, utilized in the study of discrete time linear systems
- Fourier transforms (FT), applied in the study of continuous time signals
- Fourier series (FS), applied in the study of continuous time-periodic signals
- Discrete Fourier transforms (DFT), applied in the study of discrete time signals
- Discrete Fourier series (DFS), applied in the study of discrete time-periodic signals
- Fast Fourier transform (FFT), just an efficient algorithm to compute the DFS and the other Fourier transforms in an interval

These transforms are normally taught in different courses, so they are interpreted as being different, but in fact they are all related to each other, as shown in the following figure.

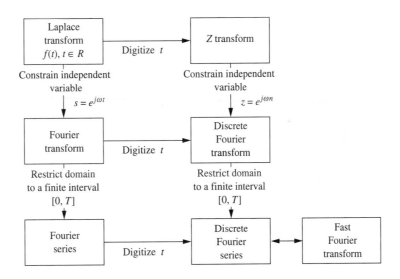

Here we start with the Laplace transform $F(s)$, which is defined as

$$
\begin{cases}
F(s) = \displaystyle\int_{-\infty}^{\infty} f(t)e^{-st}\,dt \\[2ex]
f(t) = \dfrac{1}{2\pi j} \displaystyle\oint_{C} F(s)e^{st}\,ds
\end{cases}
$$

where s is the complex variable $s = \sigma + j\omega$ and C is a contour in the region of convergence of the function. Hence $F(s)$ is a complex function of a complex variable.

If we digitize the time variable ($t = nT$) to obtain a discrete signal, we obtain the Z transform $F(z)$:

$$
\begin{cases}
F(z) = \displaystyle\sum_{n=-\infty}^{\infty} f(nT)z^{-n} \\[4mm]
f(nT) = \dfrac{1}{2\pi j} \displaystyle\oint_C F(z)z^{n-1}\,dz
\end{cases}
$$

where z is the complex variable $z = e^{sT}$ and C is a contour in the region of convergence of the function. Hence $F(z)$ is also a complex function of a continuous complex variable. Due to the relationship between s and z, we can consider that the $j\omega$ axis in the s domain is mapped onto the unit circle in the z plane.

The Laplace and Z transforms are used in the study of linear systems, both the transient and the steady-state responses. But the Laplace transform is applicable to continuous systems, while the Z transform is applicable only to discrete systems.

Now let us talk about Fourier analysis, which includes all the other transforms. The Fourier transform $F(\omega)$ of $f(t)$, $t \in R$, is defined as

$$
\begin{cases}
F(\omega) = \displaystyle\int_{-\infty}^{\infty} f(t)e^{-j\omega t}\,dt \\[4mm]
f(t) = \dfrac{1}{2\pi} \displaystyle\int_{-\infty}^{\infty} F(w)e^{j\omega t}\,dw
\end{cases}
$$

and it is also a complex function of a complex variable. If we restrict $s = j\omega$, the Laplace transform becomes the Fourier transform; that is, the Fourier transform is the intersection of the Laplace transform with the plane $s = j\omega$, so the Fourier transform only partially analyzes linear systems: their steady-state response.

The Fourier series $F(k)$ of $f(t)$, $t \in [0, T]$, is defined as

$$
\begin{cases}
F(k) = \displaystyle\int_0^T f(t)e^{-j\frac{2\pi}{T} kt}\,dt \\[4mm]
f(t) = \dfrac{1}{2\pi} \displaystyle\sum_{k=-\infty}^{\infty} F(k)e^{j\frac{2\pi}{T} kt}
\end{cases}
$$

so it is also a complex function of a complex variable. But notice now that the function $f(t)$ is restricted to the interval $[0, T]$ and the transform is discrete, $F(k)$, but with an infinite number of coefficients. The Fourier series can be used to study periodic signals, since for these signals it is sufficient to know their properties during one period.

Now we digitize our signal $f(t)$ to obtain the discrete transforms. The discrete Fourier transform $F(\omega)$ of $f(nT)$ is defined as

$$
\begin{cases}
F(\omega) = \displaystyle\sum_{k=-\infty}^{\infty} f(nT) e^{-j\omega k} \\[2em]
f(nT) = \dfrac{1}{2\pi} \displaystyle\int_{0}^{2\pi} F(w) e^{j\omega k}\, dw
\end{cases}
$$

This is also a complex function of a complex variable. Notice that since the time variable was discretized, $F(\omega)$ is computed through a sum. The discrete Fourier transform is related to the Z transform by a restriction on the independent variable. In fact, the DFT is the intersection of the Z transform with a cylinder of radius 1, so it is also only applicable for studying the steady-state response of linear systems.

Finally, we define the discrete Fourier series of $f(nT) \in [0, N-1]$ as

$$
\begin{cases}
F(k) = \displaystyle\sum_{i=0}^{N-1} f(iT) e^{-j\frac{2\pi}{N}ki} \\[2em]
f(nT) = \displaystyle\sum_{i=0}^{N-1} F(i) e^{-j\frac{2\pi}{N}ni}
\end{cases}
$$

Note that this transform can be thought of as a sampling of the discrete Fourier transform at N equally spaced points on the unit circle. It is also equivalent to the Fourier series if we sample the time variable. The DFS assumes both periodic time and frequency signals.

The fast Fourier transform is simply a fast algorithm to compute the DFS, but since the DFS is a sampling of the DFT, the FFT can also be used to estimate the DFT. Moreover, it can also estimate the FT (and the FS) of the continuous signal provided that we sample it according to the Nyquist theorem, so the FFT is a general tool in Fourier analysis.

From this presentation it is obvious that all these transforms are related. Knowing the property of any one of them is sufficient if the appropriate modifications to the domains are observed. Another important observation is that all these transforms are specific instances of the projection theorem on a different, but related, set of bases:

LT bases are the continuous variable e^{-st}.

ZT bases are the continuous variable e^{-snT}.

FT bases are the continuous variable $e^{-j\omega t}$.

These three continuous transforms must be studied in Hilbert spaces, since the variables are continuous (infinite-dimension spaces).

The FS bases are the variables $e^{-j\frac{2\pi}{T}it}$.

The DFT bases are the variables $e^{-j\omega k}$.

The DFS bases are the variables $e^{-j\frac{2\pi}{N}ki}$.

These three transforms can be studied in vector spaces, as we present in this book. As we can immediately see, all these bases belong to the complex exponential family, either discrete or continuous and also purely complex or with real or complex parts. These different bases provide the specific properties of each of the decompositions.

8.7 THE Z TRANSFORM AND THE SYSTEM TRANSFER FUNCTION

We just presented the basic concepts of spectral analysis applied to signals. Can we apply the same principles to systems, and are there any advantages? A system is described by its impulse response, which can also be interpreted as a signal, so we can apply the ideas of the transform domain to the impulse response, but this route is neither elegant nor efficient (it requires a priori knowledge of the impulse response).

In linear system theory the important aspect is to quantify the output signal given the input and a description of the system. The linear system output can be computed by either

- The *convolution* of the impulse response with the input, or
- Generating the output sample by sample by means of the *difference equation*

The difference equation (Eq. 8.9 or 8.13) immediately gives an algorithm to compute the system output, but it is not very good at quantifying what is happening to the input signal characteristics, due to the fact that both the system and the input are mixed in the same equation. It would be wonderful if we could enhance our understanding of the difference equation by decoupling the system function from the input. This is exactly what the Z transform does.

The Z transform simplifies the study of discrete time linear systems because it transforms difference equations into algebraic ones, providing a theoretical framework for working with delay operators. The definition of the Z transform of a discrete sequence $x(n)$ is

$$X(z) = \sum_{n=-\infty}^{\infty} x(n)z^{-n} \tag{8.19}$$

where z is a complex variable. To exemplify the power of the method, let us take the Z transform of the one-sample delay $\delta(n-1)$:

$$D(z) = \sum_{n=-\infty}^{\infty} \delta(n-1)z^{-n} = z^{-1} \tag{8.20}$$

Eq. 8.20 states that the Z transform of the delay operator is the infinite sum of terms of the time function multiplied by z^{-n}. It turns out that $\delta(n-1)$ has a nonzero value of 1 only when $n = 1$, so all the terms of the sum are zero except the term $n = 1$, which is evaluated as z^{-1}. The delay operator we defined previously as the fundamental building block for the memory element is the Z transform of the one-sample delay. Now we understand why we used the label z^{-1} for the block of Figure 8-3.

If we apply the definition of the Z transform (Eq. 8.19) to the linear combiner (Eq. 8.9), we get

$$Y(z) = \sum_{n=-\infty}^{\infty} \sum_{i=0}^{N} w_i x(n-i) z^{-n} = \sum_{i=0}^{N} w_i \left(\sum_{n=-\infty}^{-\infty} x(n-i) z^{-n} \right)$$

$$= \sum_{i=0}^{N} w_i \left(\sum_{n=-\infty}^{\infty} x(n) z^{-n-i} \right) = X(z) \left(\sum_{i=0}^{N} w_i z^{-i} \right) = X(z)H(z) \qquad \textbf{(8.21)}$$

where $Y(z)$ and $X(z)$ are the Z transforms of the output $y(n)$ and of the input $x(n)$, respectively. This expression clearly shows that the effect of the linear combiner on the input $x(n)$ can be *individually* studied in the Z domain by the properties of the polynomial in z of order N (a purely algebraic form).

$$H(z) = \sum_{i=0}^{N} w_i z^{-i} \qquad \textbf{(8.22)}$$

The quantity $H(z)$ is called the *system transfer function,* and it is the Z transform of the impulse response (Eq. 8.22 shows this for the FIR case). Note that the Z transform also naturally *decoupled* the effect of the system from its input, since the Z transform of the output is a product of the two (Eq. 8.21).

Similar to the impulse response, the system transfer function completely describes the behavior of the linear system, but with some advantages. Notice that Eq. 8.21 computes the Z transform of the output of the linear combiner, but now we obtain the Z transform of the output by a *point-by-point multiplication* of the Z transform of the input with the system transfer function. Taking the inverse Z transform, we get back $y(n)$.

A comparison of Eq. 8.21 with Eq. 8.11 shows that convolution in the time domain was mapped to multiplication in the Z domain. This is one of the reasons that the transform domain representation of linear systems is so widely used. The transfer function was derived for the linear combiner but can be extended to any linear system.

Types of Discrete Time Linear Systems

An interesting property of the most common discrete linear systems (shift-invariant) is that their output can be expressed as a difference equation involving the present input and the past input and output values:

$$y(n) = \sum_{p=1}^{P} b_p y(n-p) + \sum_{q=0}^{Q} a_q x(n-q) \qquad \textbf{(8B.6)}$$

where P is the number of previous outputs used, Q is the number of previous inputs, and b_p and a_q are the free parameters of the system that combine the previous outputs and inputs, respectively. This equation is the most general difference equation that will be studied here and corresponds to a system called an *autoregressive moving-average system (ARMA)*, which is shown in the following figure.

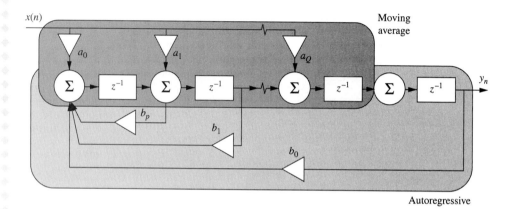

If all the b_p are zero, the system output is a weighted combination of past inputs only, and it is called a *moving-average (MA) system,* finite impulse response (FIR), or linear combiner. If all the a_q ($q > 0$) are zero (except the first), the system is called an *autoregressive system (AR).* Both the ARMA and the AR belong to the class of infinite impulse response (IIR) systems. Here we study mostly the linear combiners, although most of the theory developed also applies to the IIR case.

There is an important way of rewriting these equations using the delay operator. If we apply the Z transforms to Eq. 8B.6, we get

$$Y(z)\left(1 - \sum_{p=1}^{P} b_p z^{-p}\right) = X(z)\left(\sum_{q=0}^{Q} a_q z^{-q}\right) \qquad \textbf{(8B.7)}$$

where $X(z)$ and $Y(z)$ are the Z transforms of the input and the output, respectively. The transfer function H is by definition the ratio of $Y(z)$ over $X(z)$:

$$H(z) = \frac{Y(z)}{X(z)} = \frac{\sum_{q=0}^{Q} a_q z^{-q}}{1 - \sum_{p=1}^{P} b_p z^{-p}} \qquad \textbf{(8B.8)}$$

From this equation we see that the *zeros* of the transfer function are controlled by the location of the zeros of the numerator polynomial, while the *poles* of $H(z)$ are the zeros of the denominator polynomial. Therefore MA systems have only zeros, AR systems have only poles, and ARMA systems have both zeros and poles. When we compute the transfer function along the unit circle, we obtain the frequency response of the system:

$$H(e^{j\omega T}) = H\left(z|_{z=e^{j\omega T}}\right) \tag{8B.9}$$

The frequency response is useful for studying the steady state of the system, while the transfer function is required to study the transient response and stability of the discrete system.

8.8   THE FREQUENCY RESPONSE

We already saw in Chapter 5 that a linear system accepts the complex exponentials as eigenfunctions. The implications of this fact are far reaching, because we can construct the output of *any* linear system H by independently computing the system response to each complex exponential of the input and summing the result. Here we are interested in making this decomposition for phasors, which are complex exponentials with unit modulus ($a = 0$). As we saw in the box "Eigendecomposition Explained" (pp. 392–393),

$$y(n) = Hx(n) = H\left(\sum_i \alpha_i e^{j\omega_i n}\right) = \sum_i \alpha_i H(e^{j\omega_i n}) = \sum_i \alpha_i \lambda_i e^{j\omega_i n} \tag{8.23}$$

where the λ_i (complex numbers) represent the effect of the linear system at each frequency. We call the system effect at each frequency, $H(e^{j\omega_i}) = \lambda_i$, the *system frequency response*. The system frequency response is complex, so it is described by its magnitude frequency response and the phase response.

Equation 8.23 means that *any* linear system H affects the phase and the amplitude of each frequency of the input signal and that the effect can be computed independently at each frequency. Thus, if the input is expanded in phasors (the DFS), a simple frequency-by-frequency multiplication by the frequency response provides the DFS of the output:

$$Y(e^{j\omega_i}) = H(e^{j\omega_i})X(e^{j\omega_i}) \tag{8.24}$$

This is a very important relation, because it lets us predict what is going to happen to our input signal when it goes through a linear system, provided that we know $H(e^{j\omega})$ and the spectrum of our input signal beforehand.

Circular Convolution

It is important to note here that Eq. 8.24 implies that both time functions, $x(n)$ and $h(n)$, are extended with a number of zeros equal to the extent of the other function (let us say that both functions have extent N, so their total length is $2N - 1$). If we take the inverse DFS, we see that

$$y(n) = \sum_{i=0}^{2N-1} x(i)h(n-i)$$

We know that the extent of the convolution is equal to the sum of extents of each signal minus 1, so this expression makes sense. If we did not extend the sequences with zeros, Eq. 8.24 would have failed to provide the right answer. The reason can be found in a fundamental fact of discrete sequences and DFS: They are both periodic with the number of samples in the window (N).

The effect of a discrete linear system is still defined as the convolution of the input and the impulse response, but it is a circular convolution. For two sequences of length N the circular convolution also has length N, but we see that the "linear convolution" that we defined produces $2N-1$ samples, so the linear convolution and the circular convolution do not provide the same results unless we extend the original time sequences with a number of zeros equal to the other sequence. In this case, the circular convolution is equal to the linear convolution. See Oppenheim and Schafer [1989] for a full discussion.

Notice how clear Eq. 8.24 is for the analysis of the effect of the linear system (just a point-by-point multiplication in the magnitude and an addition in the phase responses). Alternatively, it allows us to specify through design the frequency response of the system to achieve our processing goal. To obtain the steady-state time response $y(n)$, we just need to take the inverse DFS (Eq. 8.17).

Transfer Function versus Frequency Response

We now have two transform domain representations for a linear system: the transfer function and the frequency response. How do they differ? In fact, they are intrinsically related to each other. The frequency response is the transfer function computed for a specific locus (set of points) in the z domain. This locus is the unit circle. If we take a look at the definition of the z variable and make $a = 0$, we obtain the curve $z = e^{j\omega T}$, which defines the unit circle. Along this locus we are finding how the transfer function of the system changes when only the variable ω changes.

This is such an important case, however, that people decided to give it a name: the frequency response. The frequency response tells us how the system is responding to phasors of different frequencies (the different ω values). This is called the steady-state response. However, the knowledge of the frequency response only *partially* describes the system, since we still do not know the response of the system to points that do not belong to the unit circle.

An important case for which the frequency response does not provide sufficient information is the response to transients, such as when the input is turned on or off or changes very rapidly. This response is sometimes called the *transient response.* In such cases we need to study the transfer function, because it is not enough to know the frequency response. There may be many different linear systems with the same frequency response (the same steady-state response to phasors) but with markedly different transient responses.

NEUROSOLUTIONS EXAMPLE 8.13

Analysis of the output in the frequency domain

Let us experimentally verify Eq. 8.24 using the filters we worked with previously, the linear combiner and the first-order recurrent system. We input a square wave and compare the spectrum of the output with the spectrum of the input and the frequency response of the system. We should be able to see that the spectrum of the output is a sample-by-sample multiplication of the spectrum of the input with the system frequency response.

Since the spectrum of the impulse is flat, we should be able to see why the impulse response is so important: We only need to compute the spectrum of the output to obtain the system frequency response.

The big advantage of the frequency response is that it can be computed with the FFT, while the system transfer function requires the computation of the Z transform, which is much more difficult. But remember that the frequency response provides only partial information about the system in the form of its steady-state behavior (e.g., no information about the transient response is obtained from the frequency response). In many applications, the steady-state response is enough for the design.

NEUROSOLUTIONS EXAMPLE 8.14

Minimum phase systems

Although the frequency response is very important, we should realize that it provides only partial information about the system response. For instance, the frequency response is insensitive to a change in the phase of the system response. We show this by moving the zero of a linear combiner from inside the unit circle to outside, but in such a way as to preserve the distance to the unit circle (which is called the mirror location). We see that the frequency response does not change, but the impulse response is different. One system is called minimum phase (the one with the zero inside the unit circle), and the corresponding filter with the zero outside (in the mirror location) is called the maximum phase.

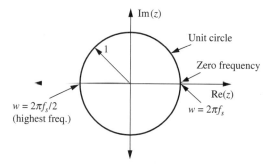

FIGURE 8-16 The *Z* plane and the unit circle

8.9 FREQUENCY RESPONSE AND POLES AND ZEROS

We saw the intrinsic relationship between frequency response and the system transfer function. One aspect that engineers use frequently in practice is to sketch the frequency response from the knowledge of the *poles* and *zeros* of the transfer function. This is important, because from the difference equation one can easily obtain the system transfer function and from there the location of the poles and zeros. For instance, from Eq. 8.13, we obtain

$$y(n) - (1 - \mu)y(n - 1) = x(n)$$
$$Y(z)[1 - (1 - \mu)z^{-1}] = X(z)$$
$$H(z) = \frac{1}{1 - (1 - \mu)z^{-1}} = \frac{z}{z - (1 - \mu)}$$

which immediately tell us that the transfer function has a zero at $z = 0$ and a pole at $z = (1 - \mu)$ (remember that the pole is the zero of the denominator polynomial). With this knowledge, can we sketch the approximate frequency response without taking the FFT of $h(n)$?

The shape of the frequency response $H(e^{j\omega T})$ is *uniquely specified by the location of the poles and zeros of the transfer function* $H(z)$. When ω varies from 0 to 2π, the analog frequencies are scanned from 0 to f_s (Figure 8-16); that is, we have all the knowledge of how the system responds to each frequency.

Scales in the Unit Circle

The *unit circle* is the locus of the points $z = e^{j\omega T}$. The frequency response is computed when z varies along the unit circle from 0 to 2π. But there is another scale imposed on the unit circle, the frequencies that correspond to the analog-world frequencies.

If the analog frequencies f are normalized by the sampling frequency f_s (called the *normalized frequency*), they also map from 0 to 2π. The highest analog frequency corresponds to $\frac{1}{2}$ the sampling frequency, and it appears midway between 0 and 2π, that is, at π or $z = -1$. Zero analog frequency appears at $z = 1$, and the analog frequencies for the negative part of the spectrum appear between π and 2π. The index k of the DFS is measured in normalized frequency. The following table shows some key frequencies and z values.

Normalized frequency	Angles	z values
0	0	$1 + 0j$
$f_s/4$	90	$0 + j$
$f_s/2$	180	$-1 + 0j$
$3f_s/4$	270	$0 - j$
f_s	360	$1 + 0j$

We can also conclude that $H(e^{j\omega T})$ is periodic with $2\pi/T$, as we would expect. The linear combiner transfer function (in fact, the transfer function of any FIR filter) has only zeros (the poles at $z = 0$ are not counted, since they represent delays and do not affect the frequency response; i.e., $z = 0$ is a symmetry point for the unit circle). The transfer function of IIR filters in general has poles and zeros that affect the frequency response.

It should be clear from the study of the first-order recurrent system that a stable system has poles inside the unit circle. Poles outside the unit circle have a modulus greater than 1, which correspond in the time domain to growing exponentials that violate our definition of stability.

The frequency response can be graphically obtained by considering the response of the system as the height of a "tent" that is placed around the unit circle. A system pole is like a stick that supports the tent from the inside, while a zero is like a stake for the tent. The height of the stick is the inverse of the difference from the pole to the unit circle, while the length of the stake "rope" is proportional to the distance from the zero to the unit circle.

Depending on the location of the poles and the zeros, different "tent" configurations are obtained. The height of the tent at a given frequency location is the amplitude of the system frequency response; a high value at a given frequency means that this frequency will appear enhanced at the output, while a value close to zero means that the frequency will be attenuated.

Second-Order Systems

The system of equations

$$y(n) = ay(n-1) + by(n-2) + x(n)$$

which we encountered before, is a second-order system. The following figure shows the block diagram.

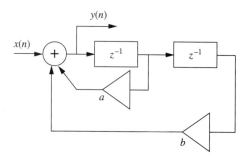

Its transfer function is

$$Y(z) = az^{-1}Y(z) + bz^{-2}Y(z) + X(z) \rightarrow$$

$$H(z) = \frac{1}{1 - az^{-1} - bz^{-2}} = \frac{z^2}{z^2 - az^1 - b}$$

which shows that the system has a double zero at $z = 0$ and a pair of poles at

$$z_{1,2} = \frac{a \pm \sqrt{a^2 + 4b}}{2}$$

We see that if the square root is positive, both poles are on the real axis. However, for b negative and $|4b| > |a^2|$, the poles have a nonzero imaginary part. In this case they have to appear in complex conjugate pairs if the coefficients a and b are restricted to be real. When the poles are real and positive, the impulse response of this system decays monotonically to zero, and it implements a lowpass filter. When the poles are real and negative, we have a highpass filter (the impulse response alternates exponentially to zero). When the poles are complex, this system implements a *bandpass filter,* also called a *resonator.*

Previously, we gave the stability conditions in terms of the impulse response. A much more convenient (and equivalent) formulation is to limit the location of the poles of the system. We can show that the poles of stable causal systems have to be inside the unit circle. Zeros can be placed anywhere.

There is an alternative way to write the resonator equation that is very convenient for finding the location of the poles when they are complex conjugates. We can show that if the poles of the resonator are $z_{1,2} = re^{\pm j\theta}$,

$$H(z) = \frac{z^2}{z^2 - 2r \cos \theta z + r^2}$$

By equating a and b to these values, we thus can immediately find where the poles are, since r is the magnitude of the poles and θ the angle from the positive real axis.

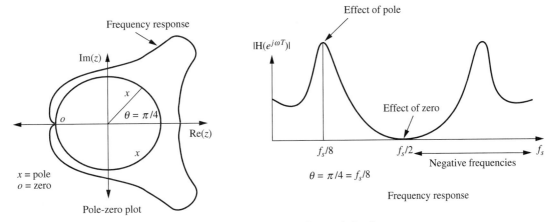

FIGURE 8-17   Relationship between the pole–zero plot and the frequency response

In DSP language, the singularities of the transfer function (poles and zeros) sculpt the system frequency response. When $H(z)$ has a zero at a certain angular frequency, the frequency response $H(e^{j\omega T})$ has a valley (attenuation) at that frequency, since the numerator of the frequency response $H(e^{j\omega T})$ is small. On the other hand, when $H(z)$ has a pole at a given radial frequency, the frequency response $H(e^{j\omega T})$ has a peak (gain) around that frequency (Figure 8-17), since its denominator has a small value, which corresponds to a large value of the inverse.

The closer the singularities (poles or zeros) are to the unit circle, the more noticeable are their effects (sharp peaks and narrow troughs, respectively) on the frequency response. The relationship between singularities and their effect on the frequency response is very important, because after knowing the pole–zero plot, we can immediately qualitatively predict the modifications that will occur to the input signal after processing, as we discuss next.

Dominant Pole Approximation

The dominant pole approximation is very handy when we want to find the approximate center frequency and the bandwidth of a filter with many poles. First, we should rank the poles by their absolute value. We should focus on the pole pair (complex poles appear in conjugate pairs) that has the largest absolute value and discard the other poles. Let us assume that the largest pole is $z_0 = \alpha + j\beta$. The magnitude of the pole is $|z_0|$.

The gain of the filter is approximately

$$H_{max}(z) \approx \frac{1}{2}\frac{1}{1 - |z_0|}$$

The normalized −3-dB frequency of the maximum is approximately

$$k_{max} = \tan^{-1}\left(\frac{\beta}{\alpha}\right)$$

The normalized bandwidth is approximately

$$\omega_{band} = 2(1 - |z_0|)$$

These formulas come from geometric considerations in the Z plane. Remember, they are approximations that depend on how appropriate the approximation of the dominant pole really is.

A similar approximation can be done for zeros, except that the peak is substituted by its inverse, which provides the magnitude of the trough. The effects of the dominant pole can be added to the effect of the dominant zero.

NEUROSOLUTIONS EXAMPLE 8.15

Frequency response of the second-order system

This example is aimed at enhancing our understanding of poles and zeros and their effect on the frequency response. We use for this illustration the second-order resonator and the second-order anti-resonator. The former, as you recall, has a pair of poles, and the latter has a pair of zeros. We can then expect that the resonator will control the peaks of the frequency response, while the anti-resonator will control the placement of the zeros. It is important that you understand the difference between these two types of effects to the frequency response.

We start with the anti-resonator. A simple three-tap FIR does the job and implements the simple equation

$$y(n) = x(n) + ax(n - 1) + bx(n - 2)$$

which has roots (zeros of the transfer function) in the Z domain at

$$z_{1,2} = \frac{-a \pm \sqrt{a^2 - 4b}}{2}$$

When the zeros are complex (conjugate), it is preferable to consider that $b = r^2$ and $a = 2r\cos\theta$.

Change the values of a and b and see the effect on the transfer function. Note in particular that when the zero is at the unit circle, the response at that frequency is exactly zero. Keep the angular direction the same and change the modulus of the zero to observe the trough in the frequency response become more and more pronounced. Finally, place zeros in the positive real axis and also in the negative real axis to see the shape of the frequency response.

Next let us work with the resonator with the same parameters a and b. A simple two-delay system with feedback is sufficient to implement the resonator, with equation

$$y(n) = ay(n-1) - by(n-2) + x(n)$$

which has roots (poles of the transfer function) in the Z domain at

$$z_{1,2} = \frac{a \pm \sqrt{a^2 + 4b}}{2}$$

When the poles are complex (conjugate), it is preferable to consider $-b = r^2$ and $-a = 2r \cos \theta$.

Change the values of a and b and see the effect on the transfer function. In this case you have to be much more careful, since for many values of a and b the system will be unstable, so you will not be able to compute the FFT. But you should also find out the effect of the poles in controlling the height and location of the peaks of the frequency response. You should use the approximate formulas given in Appendix A on resonators to estimate the magnitude of the response and see whether it matches the NeuroSolutions result.

The effects of poles and zeros are *additive* in the frequency response, so just by studying these two simple cases, you can generate *any* frequency-response shape by implementing the required number of poles and zeros. (There are different ways of doing this, but probably the easiest here is to cascade the resonators, the anti-resonators, or both. You can do this in NeuroSolutions.)

8.10 TYPES OF LINEAR FILTERS

We can design $H(e^{j\omega})$ to perform a desired operation on the input signal instead of simply finding out what the linear system did to the input. This is the basic idea of *filtering*. For instance, let us assume that our signal is contaminated by high-frequency noise. High-frequency noise can be recognized as a small, fast-changing ripple on top of the waveform. One way to remove the noise is to design a linear system that will let our signal go through undisturbed yet attenuate the noise. Linear systems with prespecified frequency responses are called filters.

Filter-Shape Factors

The frequency response of a realizable lowpass filter is shown in the following figure. We can define the *passband* as the set of frequencies that pass through the filter without being appreciably attenuated. There is always a certain "ripple," deviation from perfect unity gain, primarily for frequencies close to the edges of the passband. This ripple is a design factor that can be controlled.

The edges of the passband are called the *cutoff frequencies* and are also a design specification. The edge is smooth, so there is always a problem of defining it. Normally the −3-dB attenuation from the passband is considered the cutoff frequency.

The gain goes from practically 1 in the passband to very low values in what is called the *stopband* of the filter. The filter attenuates the input frequencies that fall in the stopband. It is this frequency selectivity that makes filters so useful. The edges of the stopband, as well as the stopband attenuation (in decibels), are normally specified.

The edges of the passband and the stopband do not coincide in a practical filter (i.e., a filter with finite orders). The difference in frequency from the passband edge to the stopband edge is called the *transition band.* Good filters have low ripple in the passband, short transition bands, and high attenuation in the stopband (called the filter-shape factor). Ideal filters have zero ripple, zero transition band, and infinite attenuation in the stopband.

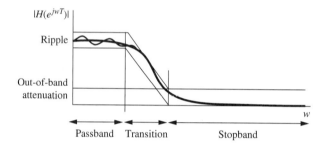

As an example, let us use the input and filter as shown in Figure 8-18. A filter that attenuates high-frequency noise is called a *lowpass filter* (because it multiplies low frequencies by numbers close to 1 and high frequencies by very small numbers), and the magnitude of its frequency response should ideally be like the bottom middle graph

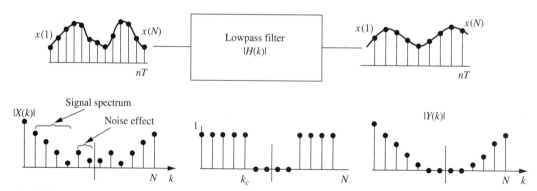

FIGURE 8-18 The effect of a lowpass filter on a noisy time series

of Figure 8-18:

$$H(k) = \begin{cases} 1 & k < k_c \\ 0 & k > k_c \end{cases}$$

Observing the magnitude spectrum of $X(k)$ we see that the energy falls off with k (toward the high frequencies) but that there is an increase of energy close to $f_s/2$, which is produced by high-frequency noise.

The lowpass filter frequency response is flat (magnitude 1) until the sample k_c, which corresponds to the cutoff frequency. This is an ideal filter that multiplies frequencies above k_c by zero. The spectrum of the output signal, $|Y(k)|$, is easy to construct since it is a product of the input spectrum $|X(k)|$ and the frequency response $|H(k)|$. Notice that for frequencies below k_c, $|Y(k)|$ is identical to $|X(k)|$, but for frequencies above k_c it is zero. The corresponding time signal $y(n)$ is smoother but identical to $x(n)$. Unfortunately, this ideal lowpass filter (called the boxcar filter for obvious reasons) is not realizable in practice, but we can approximate its response fairly well.

We can also conclude from this discussion that linear filtering works *only* if the signal spectrum and the noise spectrum do not overlap; otherwise, to attenuate the noise, we also attenuate the signal. This is where other, more sophisticated filtering procedures or nonlinear systems are necessary.

NEUROSOLUTIONS EXAMPLE 8.16

Lowpass FIR filter

Let us implement a lowpass FIR filter and show that the signal in the passband is transmitted without attenuation, while in the stopband it is attenuated. Add high-frequency noise to show that it can be separated, whereas if the noise is white, there will always be noise at the output.

The traditional types of filters (highpass, lowpass, bandpass, and bandstop) are shown in Figure 8-19. As the names indicate, lowpass and highpass filters accentuate the low and high frequencies, respectively; a bandpass filter lets a narrow band of frequencies pass and attenuates all the other frequencies; and the bandstop filter (also called a notch filter) attenuates only a narrow band of frequencies.

These transfer functions can be achieved by appropriately choosing the order and the filter coefficients in Eq. 8.9. There are well-accepted procedures to design digital filters to meet attenuation and frequency requirements (any book on digital signal processing addresses filter synthesis), but we will not pursue these issues here. We will design filters through optimization, that is, by providing the desired response and letting the linear combiner find the best set of weights to meet the requirements.

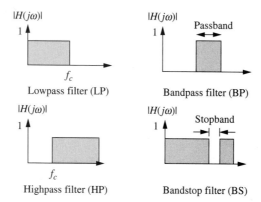

FIGURE 8-19   The four most common filter types

8.11   PROJECT: DESIGN OF DIGITAL FILTERS

Linear filters are very useful as a preconditioning stage. Data collected from the real world is almost always corrupted by noise of various kinds, so the ability to disregard parts of the signal spectrum is very important for good results. We present a very simple design for FIR filters that can be easily accomplished by hand, without the need for filter design programs. Filter design packages provide excellent filter characteristics through optimization, but they are recipes that do not provide insight. By going through the frequency-sampling design, you can develop a better understanding of filters.

The idea is to work with the equation

$$y(n) = x(n) + x(n - N) \tag{8.25}$$

which can be written in the Z domain as

$$G(z) = \frac{Y(z)}{X(z)} = 1 + z^{-N} \tag{8.26}$$

The zeros of this equation can be recognized as the Nth roots of unity, which means that the zeros of the linear system are equally spaced along the unit circle. The frequency response is obtained as

$$G(z)\big|_{z = e^{j\omega T}} = \left| 1 + e^{-N\omega T} \right| = 2 \left| e^{-jN\omega T/2} \right| \left| \cos \frac{N\omega T}{2} \right| \tag{8.27}$$

that is, the modulus of a cosine function (also called a comb filter).

This is very interesting, since with just one addition and the use of memory we created N zeros. Potentially, any of the lobes of the cosine function can be used as a passband for a bandpass filter. The first lobe (which peaks at $w = 0$) can be used for a lowpass filter.

NEUROSOLUTIONS EXAMPLE 8.17

Creating the base function for filtering

The first step in this filter design is to create the function $G(z)$, which provides many possible passbands. In this example we experiment with the function $G(z) = z^{-3} + 1$. We always provide the impulse response and the corresponding magnitude of the frequency response. Two things to look for are the frequency where the function has its peak and the -3-dB bandwidth. The peak is always obtained midway between the zeros, so the trick is to find the zeros of the equation $G(z)$. The -3-dB points are roughly half the distance between zeros. Verify these guidelines in the Breadboard. You should change the number of taps in the memory element. You can also change the values of the weights. In particular, implement Eq. 8.26 with a subtraction instead of an addition.

This transfer function is still not a usable filter, except as a periodic notch filter, because all the frequencies $\omega = k\omega_s/2N$ are eliminated.

To create low-, high-, or bandpass filters, we have to select a region of frequency as the passband, and all the other frequencies should be the stopband, so we have to eliminate some of the multiple lobes created by Eq. 8.25.

This can be done if we place zeros at exactly the locations where the unwanted peaks of Eq. 8.27 exist, since this will make the overall gain at these frequencies equal to zero. We can accomplish this simple idea by cascading other FIRs to the network that creates Eq. 8.27. The simplest case is to cascade a single zero at $z = 1$, that is,

$$H(z) = G(z)(1 - z^{-1}) \tag{8.28}$$

The frequency response of $(1 - z^{-1})$ is as shown in NeuroSolutions, so we can expect that a bandpass filter is obtained around $\omega_s/3$.

NEUROSOLUTIONS EXAMPLE 8.18

Cascading stages to create different filters

Here we implement the new transfer function $G_1(z) = (1 - z^{-1})$ and then cascade it with the original $G(z)$. $G_1(z)$ peaks at $f_s/2$ (or π), since it has a zero at the zero frequency. It is therefore a highpass filter. When we cascade the two functions together, we multiply their frequency responses, so $G_1(z)$ selects the peaks of $G(z)$ that are going to have a larger value.

This example provides the basic concept for the design of the frequency-sampling class of filters. First, we create a base function with many lobes, one at the frequency where we want to place the passband of our filter. Then we eliminate the unwanted lobes by placing zeros at the locations where the unwanted lobes have maximum amplitude. These zeros are implemented by networks that will be cascaded over the original filter. It is simpler to work with second- or first-order FIRs, which create a pair of complex zeros or simply a real zero. They knock out pairs of peaks or a peak at *dc* or $\omega_s/2$. We are ready now to learn how to choose N and the coefficients of cancellation networks.

8.11.1 Bandpass Filter Design

It is easy to show that the peak frequencies of Eq. 8.27 occur at

$$\omega_p = \frac{k\omega_s}{N} \qquad k = 0, 1, 2, \ldots, N - 1 \tag{8.29}$$

The bandwidth of a lobe is

$$B = \frac{\omega_s}{2N} \tag{8.30}$$

Notice that the center frequency and the bandwidth are interrelated by these two equations ($\omega_p = 2kB$), so narrowband filters require high orders.

Knowing ω_p and the bandwidth B of the desired filter, we have to select k, ω_s (above the Nyquist rate to avoid aliasing), and N. Since these filters have smooth transition bands, we should not try to find an exact fit. First find a good compromise of an integer ratio between the bandwidth and center frequency, and then the design is easy.

The bandwidth is the ratio of ω_s/N, so we select the smallest ω_s above the Nyquist rate that satisfies $\omega_s = 2NB$. From this we can easily choose k in Eq. 8.29.

Now we have to eliminate the lobes that do not correspond to the passband of the filter. To do this, we have to design second-order (and eventually first-order) FIR filters to eliminate the remaining lobes of Eq. 8.26.

The equation for a system with a pair of zeros on the unit circle is given by

$$H_i(z) = z^{-2} - 2\cos\phi_i z^{-1} + 1 \tag{8.31}$$

which is called an anti-resonator. The angle should coincide with the unwanted peak lobes,

$$\phi_i = \frac{2K}{N}\pi \qquad \begin{cases} k = 1, 2, \ldots, \mathrm{int}\left(N - \dfrac{1}{2}\right) \\[2mm] k \neq \dfrac{N\omega_p}{\omega_s} \end{cases} \tag{8.32}$$

The total filter order is $2N - 2$. The bandpass filters generated by Eq. 8.26 require a first-order system with a zero at $z = 1$, and, for N even, a pair of zeros at -1 and 1.

There is a function very similar to Eq. 8.26 that also generates bandpass filters: Just substitute the plus sign by a minus sign.

$$G(z) = 1 - z^{-N} \qquad (8.33)$$

This effectively rotates the zeros in the unit circle by π/N, so everything we said before is applicable with minor modifications to the formulas. The formula for the bandwidth is the same, but the center frequency is now given by

$$\omega_p = \frac{(2K + 1)\omega_s}{2N} \qquad (8.34)$$

and the anti-resonators should be placed at

$$\phi_i = \frac{2K + 1}{N}\pi \qquad \begin{cases} k = 0, 1, 2, \dots, \text{int}\left(\dfrac{N}{2}\right) - 1 \\[2mm] k \neq \dfrac{N\omega_p}{\omega_s} - \dfrac{1}{2} \end{cases} \qquad (8.35)$$

For N odd, an extra first-order FIR with a zero at $z = -1$ must be added. To choose which of these two families we need to use, just substitute the center frequency and bandwidth in the equation $\omega_p = 2B(K + \alpha/2)$. If $\alpha = 0$, choose Eq. 8.26; otherwise, choose Eq. 8.33.

Note that this design is linear phase, that is, the phase response continuously increases (after unwrapping). We can continue the addition of zeros midway between the stopband zeros to improve the filter-shape factor.

As a design example, suppose that we want to design a bandpass filter with a center frequency of 150 Hz and a bandwidth of 120 Hz when the minimal sampling frequency (Nyquist rate) is 500 Hz.

First let's ask the question whether we can live with a bandwidth of 150 Hz for this application. If the response is affirmative, $\omega_s = B$ and $N = 4$, which gives a sampling rate of 600 Hz. Since $K = 0$ and $\alpha = 1$,

$$G(z) = 1 - z^{-4} \qquad (8.36)$$

The anti-resonator has to cancel the second lobe of the frequency response, so $\phi = 135$, $2\cos 135 = -1.414$, which can be approximated by

$$H_i(z) = z^{-2} + 1.5z^{-1} + 1 \qquad (8.37)$$

The final filter is

$$H(z) = (1 - z^{-4})(z^{-2} + 1.5z^{-1} + 1) \qquad (8.38)$$

NEUROSOLUTIONS EXAMPLE 8.19

Bandpass filter design

In this example we perform the calculations outlined in the text. Note that each of the individual filters is very simple. We can easily enter by hand the coefficients of the filters in the linear combiner. First we create the second-order anti-resonator of Eq. 8.37 just to visualize its frequency response. Then we create the base function of Eq. 8.36 and cascade the two together. Notice that the combined frequency response is the product of the individual frequency responses. We recommend thinking in terms of the zero plot.

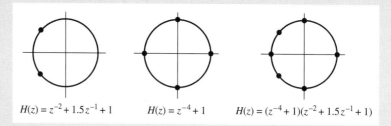

$$H(z) = z^{-2} + 1.5z^{-1} + 1 \qquad H(z) = z^{-4} + 1 \qquad H(z) = (z^{-4} + 1)(z^{-2} + 1.5z^{-1} + 1)$$

We have created a more complex filter by creating more individual filters. Alternatively, we could have cascaded more filters (the preferred method). You should develop the zero plot and figure out why the frequency response looks the way it does. Note also that the stopband attenuation is improved but that the passband is still very much like a lobe of a sine wave, so flatness in the passband was not improved.

8.11.2 Design of Lowpass and Highpass Filters

A lowpass filter is a bandpass filter centered at zero frequency, so only Eq. 8.26 can be used. In the case of the lowpass filter the only design parameter is the bandwidth, so N and w_s should be chosen to meet Eq. 8.29. The other lobes of $G(z)$ can be canceled by anti-resonators as done before.

A highpass filter in the digital domain is a filter centered at $\omega_s/2$ (since this is the largest frequency that can be represented in the digital domain), so only Eq. 8.33 can be used to create $G(z)$.

We can design this type of FIR filter using very simple concepts. We can even avoid multiplications altogether if we approximate the scalar in the anti-resonator by descending powers of two. This will affect the ripple in the stopband because we will not exactly cancel the peak of $G(z)$.

One other aspect that we would like to demonstrate is the opposite forces of poles and zeros to shape the frequency response. We saw that poles provide gain, while zeros provide attenuation. For instance, if in the filter $G(z) = 1 - z^{-4}$ we cascade a first-order IIR filter with a pole at $z = 1$, what frequency response are we going to get?

The pole at $z = 1$ will cancel the zero at $z = 1$, so basically the filter will end up with a larger gain at $\omega = 0$, effectively creating a lowpass filter. The problem is that the pole–zero cancellation is dangerous, since if the cancellation is not perfect, the system may become unstable.

NEUROSOLUTIONS EXAMPLE 8.20

Pole–zero cancellation

This example exemplifies pole–zero cancellation. Instead of creating FIR filters by adding many first- and second-order filter sections, we may want to exploit pole–zero cancellation. For instance, if we create the base filter section with many zeros (80), we end up with 80 zeros uniformly spaced along the unit circle. If we want to create a lowpass filter, we need to place second-order anti-resonators at all the 39 peaks of the function. This is hard work. Instead, we may decide to cancel the zero at $z = 1$ with a pole at $z = 1$. Such a function has a transfer function $H(z) = 1/(z-1)$. The combined system has a very large gain at $z = 1$, that is, a lowpass filter. We demonstrate this simple design on a piece of music.

8.12 CONCLUSIONS

In this chapter we covered many new concepts that are the foundations of digital signal processing. As we said in the beginning, this chapter is not intended to substitute for an in-depth study of DSP, but simply to present some of the most fundamental concepts of the field to appreciate the differences between static and time signals. More important, the discussion presents the tools of the trade. We hope that the reader is able to understand why DSP uses the tools that it does. Unfortunately, to become an expert in them, the reader will have to consult the many excellent books written on the subject [Oppenheim and Schafer 1989; Haykin and VanVeen 1998].

We started with the important observation that discrete signals of finite length can be put into a one-to-one relationship with vectors. This is rather important because it allows us to think of filters as projection operators. Although interesting, this perspective does not offer an easy quantitative analysis of what happens to the signal characteristic when it passes through filters. But time domain or frequency domain analysis permits a precise quantification of the effects of filtering. We developed both approaches. We showed that frequency domain analysis has advantages when dealing with filters. It provides easy interpretation (pointwise operations) of the effect of filtering, but it requires the introduction of more concepts, such as the spectrum. Once we get over the daunting name, however, we find that the spectrum is just another decomposition of a time signal, now using phasors. A phasor is a rotating unit vector of a given frequency. The spectrum shows how the energy in the signal is divided in frequency bins.

With these concepts we can design filters that achieve a predefined distortion of the input signal. One might wonder why we want to distort a signal, but when we think of additive noise, we can see the need for filtering as a spectral shaping tool. We showed how to design FIR filters with a very simple approach.

8.13 EXERCISES

8.1 Explain in your own words the differences between analog and digital signals.

8.2 If a continuous sine-wave signal has frequency $f_0 = 100$ Hz, what is the minimum sampling frequency to avoid aliasing? If you sample at $f_s = 170$ Hz, can you tell how the digital signal looks, and what is its analog frequency after sampling?

8.3 If you have the signal

$$x(n) = \begin{cases} 1 & n = 0, 1, \ldots, 9 \\ 0 & \text{otherwise} \end{cases}$$

and you pass it through the system $\delta(n - 3)$, what do you obtain at the output?

8.4 Construct the delay line with three taps followed by a PCA network suggested in Example 8.1. Put a scope at the output of the first PE output to see what happens to the noise. Explain the result.

8.5 In Example 8.3, find other weight vectors that attenuate either the noise or the sine wave at the output. You should present a geometric explanation for your choices.

8.6 For Example 8.4 with the two sine waves, why can we not attenuate the high frequencies better? Go to a higher-order filter ($N = 10$) and design a lowpass filter. Compare and explain the two results.

8.7 In Example 8.8, convolve the square wave with the triangular wave. Do the calculations by hand and compare with the NeuroSolutions result. Repeat with waveforms of your choice.

8.8 Example 8.9 is very useful. You should study it thoroughly. Here we study the performance in terms of the threshold. Start with a low threshold and create a plot of the number of correct detections (hits) versus the number of wrong detections (false positives). Then raise the threshold until no event is missed. This curve is the receiver operating characteristics (ROC) curve. Plot the ROC for the matched filter.

8.9 Compute the impulse response of the second-order system:

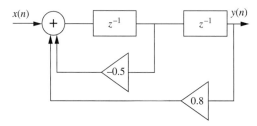

Is the system stable? Go to Example 8.11 and check your answer.

8.10 Show that the phasors $\{1, e^{j\Delta\omega T}, e^{j2\Delta\omega T}, \ldots, e^{j(N-1)\Delta\omega T}\}$ form an orthonormal set. Use the definition of the inner product.

8.11 Compute the N-point DFS of the following signals:

$$x(n) = \sin\frac{5n\pi}{N}$$

$$x(n) = \cos\left(\frac{2n\pi}{N}\right)^2$$

$$x(n) = \begin{cases} 1 & n \leq 10 \\ 0 & N > n > 10 \end{cases}$$

8.12 For the signals of Problem 11, set a value for N and use Example 8.12 to check your answers.

8.13 Using Example 8.12, show that the highest frequency you can represent is $N/2$, which is placed right in the middle of the display. Do the same for the lowest frequency that you can reliably determine from a DFS with N samples.

8.14 This problem explores spectral representations. Go to the first panel of the Breadboard of Example 8.12 and do the following: In the Signal Generator Inspector, keep the period at 32 and change the Signal Generator to a sine wave, a triangular wave, and a square wave. Then observe the spectra. How is the smoothness of the time signal related to spectral components?

8.15 Repeat Problem 14, but now use $T = 128$ samples, and compare with the previous spectra. How does the number of points per period affect the DFS?

8.16 The impulse response of a FIR is $h(n) = 1,1,1$. What is the transfer function? For the FIR $h(n) = 1, -2, 1$ what is the transfer function? We found both of these systems early in this chapter. Can you now quantify their filtering properties better?

8.17 Evaluate the frequency response of the two filters in Problem 16. Go to Example 8.13 and verify your answer.

8.18 Determine the poles and zeros for the two systems of Problem 16.

8.19 Run the filter of Example 8.15 of order 3 with weights [0.3, 0.3, 0.3]. Now change the order of the filter to 10 with weights [0.1, ..., 0.1]. Explain the results in terms of filtering and frequency response.

8.20 Filter the music file with a 16th-order highpass filter implemented with the sampling method described in the project of Example 8.20.

8.14 NEUROSOLUTIONS EXAMPLES

8.1 Signal space

8.2 Signal space and the delay line

8.3 Linear combiner in signal space

8.4 Filtering in signal space: the two-sine-wave case

8.5 A triangular wave in 3-D space

8.6 Square wave in 3-D space

8.15   CONCEPT MAP FOR CHAPTER 8

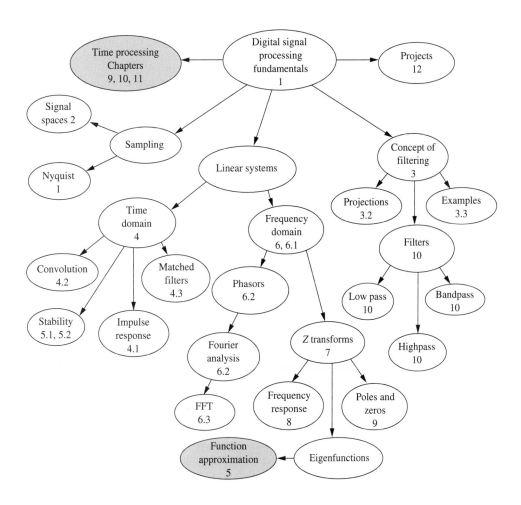

REFERENCES

Haykin, S., and VanVeen, B., *Signals and Systems,* Wiley, New York, 1999.

Kaplan, D., and Glass, L., *Understanding Nonlinear Dynamics,* Springer Verlag, New York, 1995.

Oppenheim, A., and Schafer, R., *Discrete Time Signal Processing,* Prentice Hall, Englewood Cliffs, NJ, 1989.

Principe, J., and Smith, J., Design and implementation of linear phase FIR filters for biological signal processing, *IEEE Trans. Biomed. Eng.,* vol. BME-33:550–559, 1986.

ADAPTIVE FILTERS

The goal of this chapter is to introduce the following concepts:

- Adaptive linear filtering
- The adaptive linear combiner
- Temporal PCA networks
- Many useful applications of adaptive filters

9.1 INTRODUCTION

In this chapter we study a different way of designing filters. Instead of synthesizing filters according to user specifications, as we did in Chapter 8, we assume that the desired response is available. Hence we can use the ideas of adaptation to automatically produce the required functions without ever synthesizing the filter transfer function. For obvious reasons this methodology is called *adaptive filtering*.

An adaptive filter is a special type of neural network that is linear, which means that it can be studied in linear vector spaces. Our present knowledge of linear adaptive systems can be framed in relatively simple mathematics, when compared with that required for general (nonlinear) neural networks. Excellent textbooks on adaptive filters are Widrow and Stearns [1985] and Haykin [1986]. We will see that adaptive filters are nothing but regressors in the signal space. The output of each tap of the delay line is considered a component of the input signal, and the goal is to regress it onto the desired signal. Normally, we do not use a bias in linear filters to preserve the properties of linearity, as discussed in Chapter 8.

We also extend to time the theory of Hebbian networks covered in Chapter 6. This is hardly ever done, but we will see that very interesting functions can be created with temporal PCA networks.

Although much of the theory in this chapter is a restatement of the theory from Chapter 1, this chapter shows how adaptive filters (the linear combiner and temporal PCA) can be applied to various signal-processing functions. Applications that we cover are prediction, model-based spectral analysis, system identification, inverse modeling, interference cancellation, echo cancellation, adaptive inverse control, maximum eigenfilters, PCA in time, spectral analysis by eigendecomposition, noise cancellation, and blind source separation. As you can see, adaptive filters can be applied to solve many different problems using adaptive concepts.

9.2 THE ADAPTIVE LINEAR COMBINER AND LINEAR REGRESSION

The linear combiner was discussed in Section 8.3. It is built from a delay line of $D - 1$ delays (D taps) and an adder, represented by the equation

$$y(n) = \sum_{i=0}^{D-1} w_i x(n - i) \tag{9.1}$$

The impulse response of this system is specified by the weights w_i, and its region of support is D samples long. Hence this system has a finite impulse response (FIR). The output of the linear combiner is a linear combination of the present and past $D - 1$ inputs. Depending on the filter weights, we can create any of the filter types discussed in Chapter 8 (lowpass, highpass, bandpass, or bandstop). If the filter order is large enough, any transfer function can be constructed with the linear combiner. Filter design by spec-

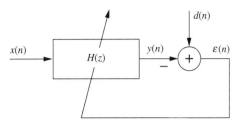

FIGURE 9-1 Paradigm to adapt the weights of the linear combiner

ification is applicable when the signal and the noise are very well characterized and the signal and noise spectra do not overlap. In such cases the design procedure is very well suited to solve the filtering problem.

Unfortunately, not all problems of interest fall in this category. Sometimes the signal and the noise spectra overlap, or the signal has characteristics that change slowly over time. In such cases, predefining the filter coefficients is not appropriate. More generally, filtering involves removing or accentuating certain frequencies, but we may have different goals, such as signal modeling, prediction, and so on. This is the reason alternatives to designing filters by specification have been developed. Here we study methods to adaptively determine the filter coefficients from the data.

The *adaptive linear combiner* is a linear system with adaptive weights. Instead of fixing its weights according to some design criterion (i.e., filter synthesis) we are back to the framework of adaptive theory. A desired response is presented, and the filter weights are modified so that a minimum of a cost function is achieved (Figure 9-1).

This block diagram is identical to the one presented for regression or classification, but it is more similar to regression than to classification because normally the desired response is also a discrete signal with many amplitude values instead of $\{1, -1$ (or $0)\}$ as in classification. We can therefore interpret the function of the adaptive linear combiner as *a linear regressor (without bias) from the input time series to the desired time series*. Note that the order of the regressor is established by the number of taps in the delay line. In spite of the similarity with regression, which warrants a review of Chapter 1, we will formulate the problem of finding the optimal filter coefficients as done in adaptive filter theory to enhance our understanding and specifically address time series analysis.

9.3 OPTIMAL FILTER WEIGHTS

The pioneering work in optimal filtering theory was done concurrently by Wiener [1949] and Kolmogorov [1977]. They solved the following problem in continuous time (i.e., in infinite vector spaces, called *Hilbert spaces*): Given a signal $x(t)$ contaminated by noise $n(t)$, find the best linear system that is able to approximate another signal $d(t)$. $d(t)$ could be any signal, including the signal $x(t)$ advanced by τ seconds. In this most general case, the linear system would work as a predictor and filter. Here we cover only the discrete time case (finite vector spaces).

The problem is set up exactly like the regression problem. Let us define the error signal as the difference between the desired response $d(n)$ and the system output $y(n)$:

$$\varepsilon(n) = d(n) - y(n) \tag{9.2}$$

when the input to the linear combiner with D weights is the signal $x(n)$. We assume that all these signals are statistically stationary; that is, they are random vectors, but their statistical properties do not change over time. We define the mean square error (MSE) as the expected value of the error square:

$$\text{MSE} = J = \tfrac{1}{2} E\{\varepsilon^2(n)\} \tag{9.3}$$

This means that the optimization criterion is the power of the error, or the L_2 norm of the error. We want to choose the filter weights to minimize J. To find the optimal weight values, we derive the cost with respect to the unknowns (the filter weights) and set it to zero:

$$\frac{\partial J}{\partial w_k} = 0 \qquad k = 0, \dots, D - 1 \tag{9.4}$$

Substituting Eq. 9.2 into Eq. 9.3 with y given by Eq. 9.1, we obtain a set of D equations in D unknowns called the *Wiener-Hopf equations:*

$$\frac{\partial J}{\partial w_k} = -E\left(x(n)d(n) - \sum_{i=0}^{D-1} w_i x(n-k)x(n-i)\right) = 0 \tag{9.5}$$

The solution, using vector notation, is the well-known equation

$$\mathbf{p} = \mathbf{R}\mathbf{w}^* \tag{9.6}$$

which has the same form as the solution of the regression problem. The structure of the solution is the same; however, $\mathbf{R}$ and $\mathbf{p}$ have a slightly different meaning here when compared with the regression case. They represent the *time autocorrelation* of the input and *time cross-correlation* functions between the input and the desired response.

We define the autocorrelation function in time as

$$\mathbf{R} = E\left[\mathbf{x}_n \mathbf{x}_n^T\right]$$

$$= E \begin{bmatrix} x^2(n) & x(n)x(n-1) & \dots & x(n)x(n-D+1) \\ x(n-1)x(n) & x^2(n-1) & \dots & x(n-1)x(n-D+1) \\ \dots & \dots & \dots & \dots \\ x(n-D+1)x(n) & x(n-D+1)x(n-1) & \dots & x^2(n-D+1) \end{bmatrix} \tag{9.7}$$

and the cross-correlation function as

$$\mathbf{p} = E[\mathbf{d}_n \mathbf{x}_n] = E[d(n)x(n) \quad \ldots \quad d(n)x(n - D + 1)]^T \tag{9.8}$$

These definitions use the statistical operator $E[.]$. In practice, the statistical operator is substituted by the temporal operator $A[.]$:

$$A = \lim_{N \to \infty} \frac{1}{N} \sum_{i=1}^{N} x(i) \tag{9.9}$$

If *ergodicity* holds, the autocorrelation and cross-correlation functions computed with temporal operators approach their statistical counterparts. Commonly, the limiting operation is also dropped, which means that the estimation is done within a window of M samples. The autocorrelation matrix becomes

$$\mathbf{R} = A[\mathbf{x}_n \mathbf{x}_n^T] = \begin{bmatrix} r_n(0, 0) & \ldots & r_n(0, D - 1) \\ \ldots & \ldots & \ldots \\ r_n(D - 1, 0) & \ldots & r_n(D - 1, D - 1) \end{bmatrix} \tag{9.10}$$

The autocorrelation function for lags k_1, k_2 is obtained by cross multiplying the time series $x(n - k_1)$ with a shifted version of itself $x(n - k_2)$:

$$r_n(k_1, k_2) = \sum_{i=0}^{M-1} x_n(n - k_1 - i)x_n(n - k_2 - i) \qquad k_1, k_2 = 0, \ldots, D - 1 \tag{9.11a}$$

This is repeated for each lag up to $D - 1$ to obtain all the entries of Eq. 9.10. The subindex n means that the computation is done for the time series around sample n. The cross-correlation vector $\mathbf{p}$ is obtained in basically the same way, but now by cross multiplying the desired signal with shifted versions of the input:

$$p_n(k) = \sum_{i=0}^{M-1} d(n + i)x(n - k + i) \qquad k = 0, \ldots, D - 1 \tag{9.11b}$$

M should be at least 10 times larger than the lag D of the autocorrelation function to obtain a reasonable estimate for the longest lag.

We can show [Widrow and Stearns 1985] that with the optimal weights given by Eq. 9.6, the error $\varepsilon(n)$ becomes decorrelated with the system output; hence it is also decorrelated with respect to the inputs, that is,

$$E[\varepsilon(n)x(n - i)] = 0 \qquad i = 0, \ldots, D - 1 \tag{9.12}$$

This gives a very powerful interpretation of the Wiener solution: The Wiener filter finds the weights such that the system output (which has to exist in the space spanned by the

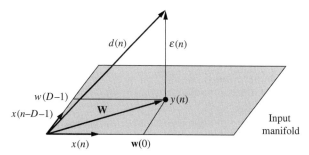

FIGURE 9-2   The Wiener solution in vector spaces

input, since it is an inner product with $x(n - i)$) is the orthogonal projection of the desired signal onto the input space (Figure 9-2). The orthogonal projection minimizes the error (the distance) between the desired response and the system output. Kolmogorov developed Eq. 9.12 independently to solve the minimization of MSE and its geometric interpretation.

Instead of analytically computing the optimal solution, we can search for the optimal set of weights, as discussed in Chapter 1. It turns out that the cost in the space of the weights is a paraboloid of equation

$$J = \tfrac{1}{2} \sum_i d^2(i) + \tfrac{1}{2} \mathbf{w}^T \mathbf{R} \mathbf{w} - \mathbf{p}^T \mathbf{w} \tag{9.13}$$

where $\mathbf{R}$ and $\mathbf{p}$ are the estimates of the autocorrelation and cross-correlation function respectively, $\mathbf{w}$ is the weight vector, and $d(n)$ is the desired time signal. An efficient search procedure to find the single minimum cost is to use gradient information. Under this paradigm the weights are modified proportionally to the negative of the gradient estimated at each point:

$$\mathbf{w}(n + 1) = \mathbf{w}(n) - \eta \nabla \mathbf{J}(n) \tag{9.14}$$

where η is a step-size parameter and n is the iteration index. The most useful estimator of the gradient was proposed by Widrow and Stearns [1985]. Instead of estimating the gradient through a statistical average, Widrow proposed the direct use of the instantaneous value of the gradient at each sample, that is,

$$\nabla \tilde{\mathbf{J}}(n) = -\varepsilon(n) \mathbf{x}(n) \tag{9.15}$$

This gives rise to the famous LMS algorithm to adapt the weights:

$$\mathbf{w}(n + 1) = \mathbf{w}(n) + \eta \varepsilon(n) \mathbf{x}(n) \tag{9.16}$$

where $\mathbf{w}(n + 1)$ is the vector of weights at iteration $n + 1$, $\varepsilon(n)$ is the error at iteration n, and $\mathbf{x}(n)$ is the input vector at iteration n. There are better algorithms to adapt the linear combiner, but the LMS is still widely used due to its excellent compromise of simplicity and robustness versus computational complexity.

RLS Algorithm

The recursive least squares (RLS) algorithm is an on-line implementation of Newton's method that we discussed in Chapter 1. The RLS algorithm utilizes a set of weights that is always the optimum given the data, unlike the LMS algorithm. If we use the analytic approach to solve the Wiener-Hopf equation, the RLS algorithm—although iterative— provides exactly the same coefficient values at the end of the data sequence as the analytic solution (for the same initial conditions). The RLS algorithm is also appealing because there is no step size. The problem with the RLS algorithm is that it is computationally more demanding than the LMS [with a complexity of $O(D^2)$]. See Haykin [1986]. Here we provide only a very brief explanation of the algorithm.

Let us assume that the input of the linear combiner is $\mathbf{x}(n)$ and the weights are $\mathbf{w}(n)$. The estimation of the autocorrelation function at time n is denoted by $\mathbf{R}(n)$. The RLS algorithm specifies that the weights should be adapted according to

$$\mathbf{w}(n) = \mathbf{w}(n-1) + \mathbf{k}(n)[d(n) - \mathbf{x}^T(n)\mathbf{w}(n-1)]$$

where

$$\mathbf{k}(n) = \frac{\mathbf{P}(n-1)\mathbf{x}(n)}{1 + \mathbf{x}^T(n)\mathbf{P}(n-1)\mathbf{x}(n)}$$

and

$$\mathbf{P}(n) = \mathbf{P}(n-1) - \mathbf{k}(n)\mathbf{x}^T(n)\mathbf{P}(n-1)$$

where $\mathbf{P}(n) = \mathbf{R}^{-1}(n)$.

We start computing the gain vector $\mathbf{k}(n)$ by using the previous estimate of the inverse of $\mathbf{R}$ [i.e., $\mathbf{P}(n-1)$] and the present input vector $\mathbf{x}(n)$. Once we have $\mathbf{k}(n)$, we can update the weights with the present input $\mathbf{x}(n)$ and also reestimate the new $\mathbf{P}(n)$. Notice that these formulas are recursive, always using the previous available values for the estimates. The initialization is normally done with $\mathbf{w}(0) = 0$ and $\mathbf{P}(0) = \alpha\mathbf{I}$, where $\alpha = 1/\sigma^2$ (σ^2 is the power of the input).

The computational cost of the algorithm is proportional to $O(D^2)$, but notice that we are using second-order information (correlation function information) to update the weights, so the convergence is much faster and the final values more precise. The RLS is an on-line implementation of Newton's method.

The RLS has problems in nonstationary environments, since the gain $\mathbf{k}(n)$ tends to zero when the algorithm converges. If the properties of the data change, the algorithm cannot update the weights, since $\mathbf{k}(n)$ is zero (or very small). This is why we normally apply RLS with an exponentially decaying window on the estimate of $\mathbf{R}(n)$. See Haykin [1986].

NEUROSOLUTIONS EXAMPLE 9.1

Design of filters using adaptation

In this example we explore the power of adaptive filters. A very good example is to create filters that pick the harmonics of a square wave. As we know, the square wave has a Fourier spectrum characterized by spectral lines at the odd harmonics of the period of the wave. We can see this easily by placing an FFT probe on top of the Axon being fed with a square wave.

The goal of the adaptive filter is to individually pick the harmonics. The desired response is a sine wave of the particular harmonic. The adaptive filter is in fact implementing a bandpass function, but instead of using one of the filter synthesis programs to come up with the coefficients, we use the desired response and the LMS algorithm to automatically design the filter for us. This is a good alternative in some cases.

Change the frequency of the desired signal to see how fast the weights adapt to the change. We can stop the simulation at any time and freeze the weights to compute the frequency response.

With adaptive filters, we are not confined to creating the conventional filters we have studied in Chapter 8. We can smoothly design the frequency response. For instance, we can transform a square wave to a triangular wave of the same period. Find the frequency response of such a system using NeuroSolutions.

9.3.1. Wiener Filter as a Predictor

One interesting application of the Wiener filter is when the desired response $d(n)$ is the input advanced in time, that is, $x(n + n_0)$. This special case is something magical, because its goal is to "predict the future" of a time series. But the filter is simply computing the best approximation for a future value of the time series, given the past samples. Since time signals have a time structure, that is, they do not change radically from sample to sample, it is possible to locally extrapolate what the next sample is from the past N samples. Wiener was able to formulate prediction mathematically, which was a landmark result.

NEUROSOLUTIONS EXAMPLE 9.2

Adaptive filters for prediction

Prediction is just a special type of filtering. In fact, prediction implements a type of lowpass filter that depends on the short-term time structure of the time series. The desired response in prediction is the signal advanced by a number or samples (let us start with one). The predictor has to look into the past of the signal and linearly combine the samples to obtain a good approximation to the position of the next sample. In a sense, we are linearizing the trajectory around the present sample (the tangent space) and extrapolating to find the next value.

Let us use a smooth signal first (the sum of two sine waves). If you let the system run, you quickly find that the error becomes very small if the FIR has at least eight taps and a delay of 2 between taps. Alternatively, you will need 16 taps and a delay of 1 to get comparable results, but notice that the system has twice as many coefficients. Notice that the frequency response is in fact a lowpass type of filter and that prediction is in fact a kind of extrapolation.

If you now use a square wave with period 32, you find that the system does not work well at all. Can you discover why? The square wave is discontinuous, so there is no way the predictor can anticipate the abrupt change in amplitude by just looking at eight samples of the recent past of the signal. To predict the waveform, a full cycle must be present in the delay line (at least 32 taps with a unity delay). With this choice, the predictor works very well. Note once again that it is sufficient to increase the delay between taps to 4 and keep the number of coefficients at 8 (there is no need to have 32 weights).

Another case where the predictor performs poorly is when there is white noise in the data. Since the samples of white noise are uncorrelated from sample to sample, there is no information in the past of the signal to help predict the future values. In general, signals that have a very complex time structure are difficult to predict with small models. We can get an idea of the predictability of the signal if we visualize it in state space and find abrupt jumps in the plot.

You are now ready to bring in your pet data set to predict it. (We do not take responsibility if you try to predict the stock market!)

9.3.2 The Wiener Filter as a Function Approximator

Chapter 5 was devoted to presenting a unified view of regression and classification as special cases of a broader problem called function approximation. But remember that, at the time, only static problems were being addressed. Now we know how to handle time functions with filters, and in particular we know how to optimally set the linear combiner's parameters to approximate the desired time series. Can we extend the views of function approximation to the Wiener filter?

The answer is affirmative, and it is rather important for framing the application domain of linear combiners. If we compare Figure 9-1 with Figure 5-1, we can see the similarity immediately. Here we assume that the desired signal $d(n)$ is a fixed but unknown function of the input $x(n)$, that is, $d(n) = f(x(n))$. The role of the Wiener filter is precisely to discover a linear approximation to the unknown function $f(.)$.

The noticeable difference here is the use of time functions, while in Chapter 5 the data was multidimensional but static. However, in Section 8.2 we provided a mapping from time to a vector space called the signal space, which essentially showed that a segment of a time series can always be mapped to a point of a vector space of appropriate dimensionality. The difference between time functions and static data therefore washes away if we consider that the approximation is being performed in the signal space. Another minor difference is that we do not use a bias in the linear combiner (to comply with the definition of a linear system).

We can thus conclude that the linear combiner is doing *regression in the signal space*. Looking at the Wiener filter operation from the point of view of function approximation, we see that it is a linear function approximator. The bases of the signal space are the input signal and its delayed versions (i.e., they are time varying) so the linear combiner is finding the best projection of the desired signal onto the input signal space. The best projection must lie in the input signal space, since it is a linear combination of the bases.

This function approximation property can be put to good use in engineering. We already saw the application of Wiener filters to prediction. In Section 9.6 we discuss system identification and noise cancellation.

Linear System Identification Fundamentals

Linear system identification is such an important problem that we have to spend some time analyzing it. Perhaps it is best to look at system identification from the point of view of function approximation. As a form of function approximation, the three important problems in system identification are

- Defining the bases
- Computing the parameters
- Selecting the order of the approximation

As we have seen with the linear combiner, we want to work with a linear model and adapt its parameters. Hence the topology utilized in the model system dictates the type of bases we will be using. The parameters of the model have to be adapted, and we have to make decisions regarding the order of the model.

When a linear combiner is selected, the bases are the signal and its past samples, as clearly seen from Eq. 9.1. Since the model is a weighted sum of the input alone, this type of model is called a moving average (MA). Once the topology is set, the only differences among MA models are their parameters and their order. The order can be determined as we did in Chapter 5 by the Akaike or Rissanen (MDL) criteria. The parameters can be adapted with least squares or, if we prefer, with LMS or RLS.

Experience has shown that if the plant belongs to the same family implemented by the model system, results can be very good with very small orders. This can be understood if we think in terms of eigendecompositions. If the plant is MA, then our MA model performs an eigendecomposition, which is guaranteed to be very efficient. Unfortunately, not all linear systems are MA models. When the order is very large, we can show that MA models can still approximate any other linear system at the expense of a large number of coefficients.

The most general linear system is given by

$$y(n) = \sum_{p=1}^{P} b_p y(n-p) + \sum_{q=0}^{Q} a_q x(n-q)$$

which has an output given by a weighted sum of previous (and present) inputs with previous outputs. Such a system is called an autoregressive moving average (ARMA) model. ARMA models are very powerful but very difficult to work with in practice, because of three major reasons: they may become unstable during adaptation; the algorithms to update their parameters are more computationally demanding; and a search can be caught in local minima (the performance surface is no longer convex as in the MA). They are therefore less often utilized than the MA models, but the appeal is that ARMA modeling is an eigendecomposition for linear systems. Note that the ARMA model is decomposing the output in a space created by the previous inputs and its own past states.

When we discussed linear systems, we presented systems which have a response dependent only on the system output

$$y(n) = \sum_{i=1}^{D} y(n-i) + x(n)$$

which is called an autoregressive (AR) model. Note that the AR model is an extension of the first-order recurrent system that we studied in section 8.5.1. AR models have very nice characteristics: First, they are very flexible because they can approximate any other linear system well. Second, they correspond to many physical processes, so they have a large chance of providing eigendecompositions. Third, we can often use a trick to adapt an AR model that avoids the problem of possible instability: We use the prediction framework and adapt an MA model. Once this MA model is adapted, we simply work with its inverse. Therefore, we can find the optimal parameters using the normal equations (Eq. 9.5). Fourth, the AR model is linked to a fundamental theorem on the decomposition of time series (Wold decomposition; see Haykin [1986]). The workhorse of linear system identification is the AR model.

9.4 PROPERTIES OF THE ITERATIVE SOLUTION

The properties of the iterative solution to find the minimum of J have been extensively studied in Chapter 1, and they also apply to the adaptation of the linear combiner. The fundamental difference is the nature of the autocorrelation and cross-correlation functions, which now are related to time information. Here we summarize only the most important ideas.

9.4.1 Largest Step Size

The largest step size η_{max} to guarantee convergence to the optimal value is

$$\eta_{max} < \frac{2}{\lambda_{max}} \tag{9.17}$$

where λ_{max} is the largest eigenvalue of the input time autocorrelation function **R**. In practice we choose

$$\eta = \frac{\eta_0}{1 + tr[\mathbf{R}]} \tag{9.18}$$

where η_0 has to be set according to the problem (0.01–0.1) and the trace of **R** can be estimated by the signal power at the taps

$$\sum_{i=0}^{N} x^2(n - i)$$

The trace of **R** is the sum of the eigenvalues, so $tr[\mathbf{R}]$ is an upper bound for λ_{max}. Notice that if the input power changes, the step size changes automatically. This is called the *normalized step size,* and it is the preferred way to adapt the linear combiner.

NEUROSOLUTIONS EXAMPLE 9.3

Choosing the step size

Please check the convergence/divergence of the linear combiner as a function of the step size. We provide the Breadboard for the linear combiner for your convenience, but since Examples 9.3 through 9.5 are duplications of the ones in Chapter 1, we will not elaborate the details.

9.4.2 Speed of Adaptation

In steepest descent, each weight converges to the minimum with a different time constant given by the inverse of the respective eigenvalue. The mode with the longest time constant is

$$\tau_{max} = \frac{1}{\eta \lambda_{min}} \tag{9.19}$$

so the search time is limited by the adaptation of the slowest mode. The existence of many time constants is readily apparent in the learning curve. This means that the largest step size is limited by the largest eigenvalue (Eq. 9.17), and the speed of adaptation is limited by the smallest eigenvalue (Eq. 9.19). Hence the eigenvalue spread of the input autocorrelation function defines the performance of the steepest-descent algorithms (LMS in particular).

For time signals the speed of adaptation is coupled with the actual time it takes to adapt the linear combiner, because when we multiply the number of samples by the sampling period, we obtain time in seconds. A good estimate is $4\tau_{max}$.

NEUROSOLUTIONS EXAMPLE 9.4

Speed of convergence

Please check the speed of convergence of the linear combiner as a function of the step size.

9.4.3 Rattling

The choice of the step size in LMS is a compromise between the speed of adaptation and misadjustment. The faster the algorithm converges, the higher is the misadjustment, that is, the excess error with respect to the theoretical minimum error. The misadjustment can be approximated by

$$M = 0.5\eta tr[\mathbf{R}] \tag{9.20}$$

If we assume that the eigenvalue spread of $\mathbf{R}$ is small, we can say that the algorithm converges in

$$\text{Settling time} = 4\tau = \frac{D}{M} \tag{9.21}$$

This gives the following rule of thumb: For a misadjustment of 10 percent, the algorithm converges in a number of samples equal to approximately 10 times the number of weights. We can therefore think of translating speed of adaptation to actual external time (in seconds) by multiplying the number of samples by the sampling period. In many applications, the adaptation time of the linear combiner is reasonable, yielding systems that can track changes in the signal dynamics.

NEUROSOLUTIONS EXAMPLE 9.5

Misadjustment

Please check the rattling of the linear combiner as a function of the step size.

9.4.4 Neural versus Adaptive Systems

There is a major difference between the neural network models covered so far and the adaptation of the linear combiner. In ANNs we always work with a training set and test the performance on an independent test set. We may have to reuse the training set samples many times until the ANN converges. But notice that once the ANN is trained, its weights are fixed for the test set. Thus, although the ANN has trainable weights, they are frozen during the testing. Therefore, the *ANN is no longer adaptable after training.*

Adaptive filters are utilized in a different way. They are *continuously adapted;* that is, the weights are always being modified according to the LMS rule. There is no training set/test set division when working with adaptive filters. When the data is first sent through an adaptive filter, the performance of the system is far from optimal, but the system parameters quickly find reasonable values (convergence in about $10D$ samples). The essence of this feature is the use of the input signal and its delayed versions as the bases for the approximation.

An advantage of this procedure is that the system is able to *track changes* in the structure of the time series, which does not occur with the training procedure applied to ANNs. However, the system forgets old data and can be driven from its optimal parameter setting if outliers (noise spikes) occur. It will recover rather quickly, however, due to the good tracking properties of LMS in a linear topology.

There is clearly a trade-off between trainable versus adaptive weights, or between neural and adaptive systems. A neural system seeks to model the data as long-term memory in its weights, while the linear combiner is basically a tracker, that is, it has only short-term memory. For general use, an intelligent system needs both. This is not easy to do. Within the linear model, the Kalman filter[1] solves this problem by using the state information. The state is estimated from the data, and it corresponds to the long-term memory of the system. When the system cannot predict the input, it decides to update the output for tracking. Unfortunately, we still do not have a general framework to accomplish a similar decomposition for the nonlinear model.

NEUROSOLUTIONS EXAMPLE 9.6

Tracking ability

This example shows the tracking ability of the linear combiner. Tracking is a new concept that makes sense only in time series. The goal is to be able to change the filter weights so that a change in the desired response or the relationship of input to desired signal is followed. This is a very important characteristic in real-world problems where the data may slowly change (and sometimes not that slowly).

Tracking is intrinsically a compromise. On one hand, we would like the linear combiner to reach the bottom of the bowl with low misadjustment, which means a small step size. On the other hand, if the location of the minimum changes with time, we would like to have a sufficiently large step size to follow it to the new location. The trade-off can only be solved experimentally.

9.5 HEBBIAN NETWORKS FOR TIME PROCESSING

The Hebbian networks discussed in Chapter 6 can be extended to time processing if a delay line is incorporated at their input (Figure 9-3). The input signal $x(n)$ flows

---

[1]Rudolf Kalman, who invented the Kalman filter, is one of the most influentcial electrical engineers alive. The Kalman filter is an optimal filter that solves the optimization in space state using the recursive minimum mean square estimation. See Haykin [1986] for a signal processing view of Kalman filters.

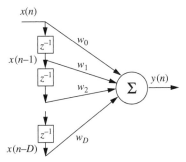

FIGURE 9-3 Hebbian PE
extended to time

into the delay line, and the Hebbian PE receives not only the present input but also $D - 1$ past samples. As in its static counterpart, the PE estimates the eigenvectors and eigenvalues of the autocorrelation of the input, but now the input is a signal in time. Karhunen and Loeve did the original work in this area, and temporal PCA is called the Karhunen-Loeve transform (KLT) in their honor[2]. The mathematics are very difficult for continuous time signals (the original formulation), but we already know all the mathematics needed to treat the case of discrete signals of finite length.

We will call the discrete version of the KLT *temporal PCA*. The solution of the temporal PCA is also an eigendecomposition given by

$$\sum_{k=0}^{D-1} \mathbf{r}(l, k)\mathbf{e}_i(k) = \lambda_i\mathbf{e}_i(l) \qquad i, l = 0, \ldots, D - 1 \tag{9.22}$$

or in matrix form

$$\mathbf{Re}_i = \lambda_i\mathbf{e_i} \qquad i = 0, \ldots, D - 1 \tag{9.23}$$

where λ_i and $\mathbf{e}_i$ are the eigenvalues and eigenvectors, respectively, of the autocorrelation matrix $\mathbf{R}$ given by Eq. 9.10.

The temporal PCA equations proceed analogously to the static PCA case. Since the eigenvectors are orthonormal,

$$\mathbf{e}_i^T\mathbf{e}_j = \delta_{ij} \tag{9.24}$$

they form a complete basis in the D-dimensional space. Thus the vector $\mathbf{x}(n)$ can be synthesized without error by an expansion over the D eigenvectors:

$$\mathbf{x}(n) = \sum_{i=0}^{D-1} u_i(n)\mathbf{e}_i = \mathbf{Eu}(n) \tag{9.25}$$

---

[2]Karhunen and Loeve were two European mathematicians who independently discovered the eigendecomposition in Hilbert spaces. See Loeve [1963].

with $\mathbf{E} = [\mathbf{e}_0, \mathbf{e}_1, \ldots, \mathbf{e}_{D-1}]$. The matrix $\mathbf{E}$ is deterministic and full rank. The coefficients $u_i(n)$ of the expansion can be found from

$$\mathbf{u}_i(n) = \mathbf{e}_i^T \mathbf{x}(n) \rightarrow \mathbf{u}(n) = \mathbf{E}^T \mathbf{x}(n) \qquad (9.26)$$

The $u_i(n)$ are called the *principal components*. We have seen in Chapter 6 that Sanger's rule is an on-line algorithm to compute this decomposition, so we can adapt the parameters of the network of Figure 9-3 with Sanger's rule to compute the temporal PCA. In this network the eigenvectors $\mathbf{e}_i$ are the weight vectors $\mathbf{w}_i$. The power of the outputs are the principal components $u_i(n)$. We can recover the input $\mathbf{x}(n)$ from the weight vectors if we use Eq. 9.25.

9.5.1 Properties of Temporal PCA

When viewed as a set of eigenfilters, the eigenvectors of the autocorrelation matrix have very interesting properties. In the limit of long windows, the KLT expansion reduces to a Fourier basis, and the eigenvalues become the power spectrum (see Van Trees [1968]). For a finite number of delays, the relationship between eigenvalues and the power spectrum is not exact but is a good starting point. Temporal PCA becomes a set of FIR bandpass filters with center frequencies attracted to the peaks of the spectrum.

Less well known is the relationship between the ordered eigenvalues and spectral peaks. Assume that the eigenvalues of $\mathbf{R}$ are ordered from largest to smallest, $\lambda_0 \geq \lambda_1 \geq \ldots \geq \lambda_{D-1}$. As the number of delays approaches infinity, the maximum eigenvalue of $\mathbf{R}$ approaches the maximum value of the power spectrum of $x(n)$, and the power spectrum of the corresponding maximum eigenfilter becomes an impulse centered at the corresponding maximum frequency of the power spectrum, that is,

$$\lambda_0 = \underset{w}{\text{Max}}[X(w)]$$

where $X(w)$ is the power spectrum of $x(n)$. In fact, the second eigenvalue and eigenvector also exhibit the same properties. This can best be explained in terms of the orthogonality of sine and cosine waves. For any pure sinusoidal basis, a second orthogonal basis of the same frequency can be found through a 90-degree phase shift of the original basis. For finite but sufficiently large D, the first two eigenvectors act as bandpass filters around the peak in the signal spectrum. The passband becomes increasingly narrow as the number of taps is increased. Generalizing for the other components, we can say that eigenfilters can be approximately regarded as filters matched to peaks in the signal spectrum.

A multiple-output Hebbian network trained with Sanger's rule computes the PCA components on-line, on a sample-by-sample basis. If instead of Hebbian learning we use anti-Hebbian learning, a new set of functions (novelty filters) are possible, as we briefly mentioned in Chapter 6.

9.6 APPLICATIONS OF THE ADAPTIVE LINEAR COMBINER

It is very instructive to address the applications of the adaptive linear combiner. Here we present simulations that use the adaptive linear combiner for prediction (time series identification), interference canceling, echo cancellation, line enhancement, system identification, and adaptive controls. How can the same system be used for so many applications? We will see that the principle involved—exploiting correlation between the desired response and the filter output—is always the same, but the adaptive filter is used in different arrangements, producing very different results.

9.6.1 Prediction

In prediction the desired signal is the input advanced by n_0 samples. Normally $n_0 = 1$, which is called *single-step prediction*. We study single-step prediction here, but multi-step prediction ($n_0 > 1$) is the same, except that the task becomes increasingly more difficult for larger n_0.

Prediction is widely applied in forecasting and modeling. Forecasting is more easily understood, and it is the task we explain first. In forecasting problems, we know a time series up to the present time n. We wish to know what the next sample, $x(n + 1)$, of the time series is going to be. The idea is that if we can train a system to predict the former values of the time series (i.e., if the time series for sample $k < n$ is fed to the system and the request is to predict sample $k + 1$), then the system will also accurately predict sample $n + 1$.

It is obvious that we have to assume that the structure of the time series *does not change over time* (i.e., the signal is *stationary*); otherwise, the goal is illusory. In many applications this model is reasonable, and even if the signal time structure changes, we assume that it changes slowly, so that the system can continuously track the changes.

Figure 9-4 shows the block diagram to implement single-step prediction. The input signal is delayed by one sample before it is fed to the linear combiner. The desired

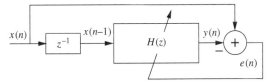

FIGURE 9-4 Block diagram to implement single-step prediction

signal is the current value of the input $x(n)$. The input of the linear combiner is therefore delayed one sample with respect to the desired response.

NEUROSOLUTIONS EXAMPLE 9.7

Prediction of time series

This Breadboard shows the prediction of a complicated time series, the sunspot data. Sunspot activity is an example of a phenomenon that we cannot control but that affects us greatly (loss of radio communications, weather, etc.), so the only option is to look ahead and see what is going to happen. The sunspot data is very complex (possibly chaotic), but short-term prediction with the linear combiner is possible.

Let us select the size of the tap delay line as 16. This is the variable that controls the size of the model, so it has to be experimentally determined. As we saw, larger models normally work better, but this depends on the type of data. Here, for instance, larger models do not improve performance because the data is chaotic. Larger models simply utilize more information from the past to establish the value of the next sample. But if the time series changes rapidly and it is aperiodic, this is of no help (remember the square wave?). You should experiment with this variable in the Breadboard.

The accuracy of the prediction is not uniform along the training set. To see this, modify the learning from *batch* (which uses the full data) to *custom* with 500 *samples per update* in the Back Controller. You also have to modify the reporting on the L2 Criterion from *batch* to *weight update*. The accuracy drops rapidly for multistep prediction. You can create multistep prediction by going to the desired response file and customizing it (create a segment starting at samples 2, 3, etc.). Watch the MSE for the different cases.

The prediction of the future of the time series seems an impossible problem due to the causality inherent in any physical system. However, if we look at it from the point of view of signal space, prediction is really a simple problem of locally fitting the best hyperplane to the signal trajectory. The source of the error can be due to the fact that the hyperplane is not a good fit to the trajectory or that the characteristics of the signal have changed from the present to the future.

9.6.2 Prediction for Modeling

We can interpret prediction as the identification of the linear system that produced the time series $x(n)$. Let us analyze the block diagram of Figure 9-5. Here we assume that there exists a hidden linear model $M(z)$ that generates the time series $x(n)$ when its input is white noise. (White noise is a random signal that contains equal amounts of every possible frequency, i.e., its FFT has a flat spectrum.)

When we use the linear adaptive filter $H(z)$ to predict the next sample and the prediction is successful, the output error is also white noise, that is, $E(z) = k$.

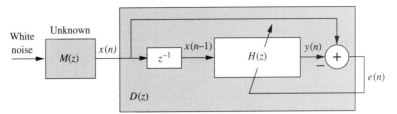

FIGURE 9-5 Prediction as modeling the system that produced the time series

Under this condition, it is easy to show that the block $D(z)$ has to be equal to $k/M(z)$, since

$$M(z)D(z) = k \rightarrow M(z) = \frac{k}{1 - z^{-1}H(z)} \qquad (9.27)$$

which means that the zeros of $H(z)$ correspond to the poles of the unknown system $M(z)$. By using the adaptive linear combiner (which is a moving-average (MA) model) we are modeling $M(z)$ as an autoregressive (AR) model. This inversion of models is rather important and should be remembered. Hence this scheme produces very good results when the time series has spectra with sharp peaks and broad valleys, which is indicative of an all-pole model. When the time series spectrum has narrow valleys, a linear combiner of small order is not very effective.

The coefficients of the linear combiner store the extracted information from the time series, in the sense that different time series normally yield different AR coefficients (note, however, that two time series can yield the same AR coefficients, as long as they have the same autocorrelation function). Therefore the AR coefficients can be used to characterize the time series. For example, in speech recognition, the model parameters are used as input to a classifier.

The order of the linear combiner is related to the complexity of the time series. Each spectral peak requires a pair of poles, so it will require two weights in the linear combiner. The spectral "tilt," that is, how the energy decays across frequency, must also be modeled and requires several other (real) poles, which also imply extra weights. By counting the number of peaks in the spectrum (and increasing this number somewhat to model spectrum tilt), we can estimate the order of the linear combiner. If more accurate estimation is required, then the Akaike or Rissanen criteria explained in Chapter 5 should be utilized.

NEUROSOLUTIONS EXAMPLE 9.8

Prediction for modeling

One application of prediction is to derive the signal generation model. We can apply this approach to extract parameters of real-world data and use them to quantify the system that produced the data (called signal modeling) or as features for pattern classification.

For signal modeling, we use the same Breadboard as in Example 9.7. We let the system train and look at the frequency response of the system, which is obtained by sending an impulse through the model and taking the FFT. After training, the filter weights and the parameters of the system that generated our input signal should be very similar.

Next we illustrate the use of the linear combiner for feature extraction. We start with a six-tap delay line, and the data to be used is the sustained sound "a." We let the system train and look at the coefficients. Then we modify the file to the sustained sound "i" to see the difference in the coefficients. Notice also how different the two frequency responses are, but since they are FIR, we can see broad peaks. If you look closely at the spectra of the input and the frequency response, they seem to be inverted.

Train the system several times, and see that the weights are similar. Now change the training to batch, and see how much smoother the overall spectrum gets. Increase the size of the delay line and observe as the frequency response becomes more wavy, with more detail. The weights of the linear combiner can be used to classify the speech segment. They are, in fact, used in speech recognition, and they are called the linear predictive coding (LPC) coefficients.

Let us point out the ingenuity of the prediction formulation for system identification. Notice that we are using a supervised framework, but we have just a single time series, which is exactly what characterizes unsupervised (self-organizing) frameworks. Prediction is one of the cases (the other being autoassociation, studied in Chapter 6) where a supervised framework is used to model the input data.

9.6.3 Model-Based Spectral Analysis

The prediction framework also provides a very powerful method of doing spectral analysis, by computing the spectrum of a time series using an implicit model. Equation. 9.27 basically explains it all. Note that if the input to $M(z)$ is white (and normalized power), then the spectrum of the time series is $X(z) = M(z)$, so we can also say that the Z transform of the time series is

$$X(z) = \frac{k}{1 - z^{-1}H(z)} = \frac{k}{1 - \sum_{i=0}^{D-1} w_i z^{-i-1}} \tag{9.28}$$

when a linear combiner with D delays is used for the model. Notice that the spectrum of the time series can be computed by making $z = e^{j\frac{2\pi}{L}}$ where L is the number of frequency samples we want to obtain in our spectral representation. This spectrum estimator assumes an AR model for the time series and produces very peaky spectra (in fact, distorting the spectrum for signals that have a different generation mechanism). It is frequently used in spectral analysis when one wants to quantify the presence of closely packed sine waves and the data segments are of short duration.

When LMS is the learning algorithm to obtain the weights of the model, the precision of the technique is poor due to the difficulties of gradient-descent learning (rattling and coupled modes). Note that the weights define the position of the poles of the inverse system, so even if all but one of the coefficients are at their optimal values, all the poles will be misplaced. This high sensitivity to the placement of the zeros in inverse modeling is well known. Therefore in AR-based spectral analysis we normally prefer the RLS algorithm or the analytic solution (called the Levinson-Durbin algorithm; see Haykin [1986]).

NEUROSOLUTIONS EXAMPLE 9.9

Prediction for spectral analysis

In the previous example we were a step away from doing model-based spectral estimation. Conceptually, what we need to do is to invert the MA model obtained during training to create a system given by Eq. 9.28. Note that this can be achieved easily if we create a TDNNAxon of order N in cascade with a Full Synapse and feedback its output to the TDNNAxon. All the weights determined during training should be copied (entered by hand) into the Full Synapse.

The difficulty comes in the quality of the model obtained during LMS training. Notice that for model-based spectral analysis we are creating a recurrent system, that is, a system with poles that may be unstable, so any minor discrepancy in the linear combiner weights may lead to unstable spectral models. Particularly for speech, where the signal has a peaky spectrum, this is almost always the case, unless the step size of the LMS is well controlled (also try batch learning, which tends to be more accurate). Try to display the spectrum obtained during the training of the "a" and "i" sounds in the previous example.

Model-based spectral analysis is one application that is much more demanding than prediction. In fact, there are many similar sets of coefficients that provide a small prediction error. However, only one of these will be the actual model for the system that generated the signal. Prediction uses an input-output model, while in model-based spectral analysis we are also interested in finding the parameters of the system.

9.6.4 System Identification

In system identification the goal is to model the input-output transfer function of an unknown plant by injecting a common signal to both the plant and the adaptive linear combiner. The output of the plant becomes the desired response for the linear combiner (Figure 9-6).

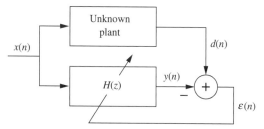

FIGURE 9-6 Adaptive filters for system identification

The goal of the task is to minimize the output error, and since the error is $e(n) = d(n) - y(n)$ or the difference between the plant output and the model, minimizing the error makes the model output as close as possible to the plant output. The importance of input-output modeling is that it completely describes the external behavior of the unknown plant.

When the output of the adaptive linear combiner approximates the desired response, it produces an equivalent input-output model for the plant. The error can go to zero only if the plant is exactly modeled by the linear combiner. In this case, this means that only moving-average plants can be modeled exactly (if the order of the linear combiner is large enough). In all other cases, the modeling is approximate. Normally, the injected signal to the plant is white noise or a signal of broad spectrum to excite all the modes of the plant.

NEUROSOLUTIONS EXAMPLE 9.10

System identification

The data for this example was created in the following way. In a different Breadboard we stored both the input white noise and the output of a plant that is a very simple and known system (all weights equal to $1/N$ with $N = 6$). The input is assigned to the input of our linear combiner, and the desired response file contains the output of the plant. We are effectively using the block diagram of Figure 9-5.

Now the idea is to train the system, having as a variable the size of the model. We place both MegaScopes and FFTs at the inputs, outputs, and desired responses so that we can have an idea of the system behavior during adaptation. We also have a probe that shows the frequency response of the model. We see that after adaptation the weights are very similar to the plant parameters, which proves that the identification was successful.

We have done this assuming that we knew the order of the unknown system. Now we should change the number of taps to a smaller and a larger value and see the effect in the error and in the values of the weights. We should also try a more difficult plant with poles and zeros to see that, in fact, the error is higher. Increasing the order of our model, however, is able to decrease the modeling error.

Note that the linear combiner and its parameters are simply an input-output model of the unknown system. This is the reason it is called black-box modeling. When little is known about the plant, the procedure is reasonable. Alternatively, physical modeling can yield better results by providing the functional form of the plant, but it requires much more knowledge about the real-world system, which may not be available.

Remember that system identification involves the choice of a family of models. The family is defined by the topology of the model. In this case, the family is the moving average (MA) models. But we will see other choices later (and in the next chapter). The choice of the element within the family is defined by the parameterization, that is, the model order and the actual value of the coefficients. As you can expect from the description, this is not a unique procedure; there are many possible models for a given unknown plant. We should use Occam's razor argument to pick the smallest model that meets our performance criterion. In Chapter 5 we presented several methods to find the best model order, but in linear systems Akaike's criterion is probably the most widely used.

9.6.5 Inverse Modeling

The idea of inverse modeling is very important in many applications and complements the direct modeling approach that we just discussed. In inverse adaptive modeling the model system is in series with the unknown plant, and the input to the plant is also the desired response of the model (Figure 9-7).

Assuming that the output error is small, we can see that $y(n)$ is quite similar to the input $s(n)$, in other words, that the combination of the unknown plant and the model cancel each other. In terms of transfer functions this means

$$Y(z) \approx S(z) = H(z)P(z)S(z) \;\rightarrow\; H(z) = \frac{1}{P(z)} \tag{9.29}$$

Inverse modeling with a linear combiner produces an autoregressive model (AR) of the plant. The modeling is perfect only if the plant is an all-pole system and the model has the same size as the plant. Otherwise, the overall plant input-output can only be approximated with the inverse model and may require large model orders for reasonable results. Another concern is the type of input. In practice we would like to have an input that is able to excite all the important modes of the plant; otherwise, they will not show up at the output, which means that they will not be modeled. A practical approach is to add small amounts of white noise, called dither noise, to the plant input.

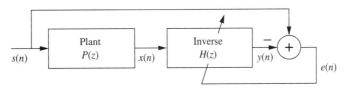

FIGURE 9-7 Inverse modeling

NEUROSOLUTIONS EXAMPLE 9.11

Inverse modeling

Let us start with a very simple case of a first-order recurrent system as our plant. This case can be perfectly identified by a two-tap FIR filter. Take note of the value of the recurrent parameter.

Use a square wave at the input to produce a reasonable excitation of the plant. Let the system adapt and notice that the error goes to zero, meaning we obtained perfect modeling. Read back the coefficients and observe that they exactly match the recurrent system parameters.

Now let us use a more complex signal-generation model. We will use a system that has poles and zeros (ARMA), here one pole and one zero. The pole can be exactly matched with the linear combiner; however, the zero of the model can be modeled only by a system with poles, so the linear combiner can only approximate the plant model. We know that in principle an infinite linear combiner order is needed, but in practice the error here is very small after an order of 7 or so (it depends on the value of the feedback coefficient—try several and observe the dependency).

Now change the input (and desired signal) to a sine wave and verify that the error goes quickly to zero; however, the coefficients are different from the previous values. Disable learning in the Controller to fix the weights, and modify the input back to a square wave. The waveform is distorted; that is, the identification was not successful.

The reason can be found in the inappropriate excitation of the plant (the output contains only the response to a single frequency), which makes the inverse problem very difficult to solve. (It is easy to find weights to match the amplitude and phase of the sine wave, but this does not mean that the full plant response has been identified.) Add noise and observe that the coefficients approach those of the plant.

You might think that the impulse is a good input signal, since it has all the frequencies. But effectively this is not so when a sample-by-sample adaptation is used to modify the system parameters, since in the time domain the waveform is impulsive. This means that the weights will jump up and down, which does not lead to a smooth convergence toward the optimal values. White noise also has a flat spectrum, and it is a much better choice for adaptive systems, since the time waveform is a blend of all frequencies at all times. Try these two choices with this Breadboard.

In practical cases we have to handle two conditions: The plant, being a physical system, may include delays, and there may be plant noise (Figure 9-8). Nevertheless, the same basic scheme can be utilized, except that we include a delay in the forward path, by delaying the desired signal k samples. A good rule of thumb is to set k as one half of the model order. The inclusion of plant noise may seriously affect the determination of the inverse, but when the noise is white, reasonable results can still be obtained.

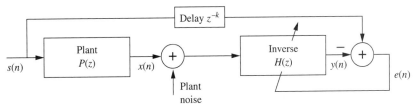

FIGURE 9-8 Practical inverse modeling for plants with noise and delays

NEUROSOLUTIONS EXAMPLE 9.12

Inverse modeling of nonminimum phase plants

This is basically the same Breadboard as in the previous example, but now the system is a little more complex. It is now an autoregressive moving average system (ARMA) with a transfer function

$$H(z) = \frac{a + bz^{-1}}{1 - cz^{-1}}$$

First, make $a = 1$, $b = 0.5$, and $c = 0.5$, as before. Let us input a square wave and create a model with two taps. As you can see, the MSE is quite high, and the output waveform is far from the square wave. Now let us increase the order of the model to 5. Run the example again, and see that the error decreased quite a bit and that the output is much closer to the square wave, even with the white noise added to the input. We can increase the model even further (to order 10), but notice that the improvement is not as drastic. The output of the linear combiner has many ripples, so although the MSE is slightly better in terms of waveform fitting, the improvement is questionable.

Turn off the noise. Go back to five taps, and change the FIR coefficients to $b = 1.5$. Note that the pole is the same and that the zero is in the mirror location with respect to the unit circle (i.e., the frequency responses of the previous system and this system are the same). Run the example and observe that the response is much worse than before. What happened? Looking closely at the input scopes, you will notice that now there is an appreciable delay between the output and the input waveforms, much larger than before. We have effectively created, with $b = 1.5$, a nonminimum phase plant. The linear combiner is faced with a much harder problem, since its desired response rises earlier than the signal applied to its input. We are thus asking the system to be anticipatory, which is impossible for any causal system.

This is where incorporating a delay between the input to the cascade and the desired response makes sense. Let us delay the desired response by creating a phase of $-18°$ (two samples). Run the example and verify that the MSE is again low and that the output looks much closer to a square wave. Put the noise back on and experiment with the order of the model.

Notice how much harder inverse modeling is than the direct modeling of Example 9.10.

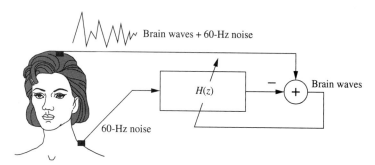

FIGURE 9-9 Removal of 60-Hz interference from brain waves

Important applications of inverse modeling are adaptive equalization of communication channels and adaptive inverse control.

9.6.6 Interference Canceling

Interference canceling is very useful when the time series of interest is disturbed with an additive narrowband interference, such as the power-line 60-Hz frequency (50 Hz in Europe). In the modern world we are surrounded by power lines, and so the 60-Hz interference is pervasive. Biological signals are very weak (from microvolts to millivolts), and the body works as an antenna at these frequencies, so data collection in medicine is very vulnerable to the 60-Hz noise contamination. The goal is to find a way to filter out the 60-Hz noise from the collected signal. Traditional filtering ideas would develop a filter with a single input that would allow the signal through and attenuate the noise (notch filter). Interference canceling requires an extra collecting probe that only receives the 60-Hz signal from the subject. The idea is to use an adaptive filter to subtract the 60-Hz signal from the collected physiological signal (Figure 9-9).

For narrowband interference the adaptive filter $H(z)$ requires only two weights, because its job is to find the best amplitude and phase of the 60-Hz sinusoidal noise reference input to match the 60-Hz noise collected with the brain wave probe. Assuming that the brain waves are uncorrelated with the noise, the MSE will be minimized when the noise is removed from the brain waves.

Sometimes no other probe is available to collect the 60-Hz signal, but we can artificially generate a 60-Hz signal and assume that the line frequency is sufficiently close to 60 Hz (the line frequency varies with the load on the power system). It can be shown that in this case the adaptive filter (after adaptation) is simply a constant-coefficient notch filter, but here we have not designed the filter explicitly; we used the power of adaptation to automatically find the weights.

NEUROSOLUTIONS EXAMPLE 9.13

Interference canceling

We start with an example with synthetic data to explain the methodology. Let us assume that we have a square-wave signal that was added to a sine wave of a known frequency, but we do not know the phase nor the amplitude of the sine wave. How can we subtract it from the square wave?

One idea is to create a two-tap adaptive filter that receives as the input a sine wave of the same frequency as the interference. This filter receives as its desired response the mixed square-wave + sine-wave signal. What do you expect the adaptive filter will do? It will try to modify its weights so that it will produce at its output a sine wave of the same phase and amplitude as the interference. This is the best the adaptive filter can do to decrease the difference between its output and the desired response. But notice that when the filter adapts to this solution, the error becomes very close to the square wave that we would like to recover. This is the principle of noise canceling with adaptive filters.

Let us create a simple Breadboard with a two-tap linear combiner that receives as input the sine wave and that gets as the desired response the square wave with the sine interference. We place a MegaScope on the Breadboard so that we can see the error, the desired response (mixed signal), the input, and the output of the adaptive filter (the signals are displayed in this order). We also place an FFT probe to show the spectrum of the error and the output. Notice the system adapting. The error begins very close to the desired response, but when the system adapts, the error approaches the square wave because the system output approaches the sine wave that was added to the square wave. This can also be seen in the spectrum of the error, which starts with a low-frequency double peak and approaches the spectrum of the square wave toward the end of adaptation.

This example illustrates the power of adaptive filters for noise canceling, but notice that this only works well when the interferences are narrowband signals that we hope do not overlap with the signal spectrum. To see how crucial this is, just modify the frequency of the sine wave to coincide with the fundamental frequency of the square wave (you also have to change the frequency of the input of the filter to match the expected new frequency). The filter now removes all the energy at the fundamental frequency of the square wave, as can be seen in the spectrum of the error. Hence the error is no longer the expected square wave.

The electroencephalogram (EEG) is a signal collected with electrodes from the scalp that monitors brain activity. The signal is rather tiny (in the range of a few to hundreds of microvolts) and has a spectrum between 0.5 to 50 Hz. Very high quality (low noise and high common-mode rejection ratio) amplifiers are required to amplify the EEG, but even the best amplifiers are unable to successfully remove 60-Hz interference. Either we must collect the EEG in shielded rooms (which are very expensive), or we have to find a signal-processing technique to cancel the 60-Hz interference. This is where adaptive filters can be used, as explained in the text.

Here we have a segment of the EEG with 60-Hz interference. The signal is sampled at 500 Hz, so a 60-Hz wave has approximately eight samples per cycle. Since we did not collect any other channel, we artificially generate a sine wave of eight samples per cycle to input to the adaptive filter. Run the system and observe how the EEG, which is very irregular, becomes cleaner. Observe the output of the system, which contains only a sine wave.

The same basic idea can be used, for instance, to filter DC (zero frequency) from a data set, by creating a highpass filter. For this case the input to the adaptive filter (a simple adaptive constant is sufficient) is a DC value such as 1. The value of the step size controls the cutoff filter of the highpass filter.

NEUROSOLUTIONS EXAMPLE 9.14

Adaptive DC removal

This example is just another application of the cancellation idea that may be very useful for preprocessing. Many times the data we collect from the outside world has a DC bias due to instrumentation problems, and we would like to use just the AC component. This is particularly true for filtering, since a lot of signal-processing algorithms (such as PCA) assume zero DC data.

If we use a single-tap adaptive filter with a constant value at the input, and our data is presented as the desired response, we effectively create a DC remover, or highpass filter.

Notice that the selection of the step size also defines the cutoff frequency of the filter. This is clear from the visualization of the spectrum of the filter output. Let us modify the step size to see the effect on the operation. If we increase the step size, the output of the filter becomes more and more like the EEG. This is because the step size effectively controls the bandwidth of the adaptive filter. We can understand this if we consider that with a larger step size the system can change the weights faster, so it will be able to subtract more energy from the desired response. On the other hand, if we decrease the step size, the filter takes a little longer to converge but gets only the DC value. We can see this easily in the spectrum of the filter output.

In neural networks the step size just controls how fast the system adapts, but in adaptive filtering the step size also controls the bandwidth of the system (since the adaptation of the adaptive filter happens in time, so there is a physical meaning to what signal feature the weights adapt).

Another interesting application of interference canceling is the removal of noise from speech in high-noise environments such as factories, plane cabins, and so on. The idea is basically the same. The noisy speech is collected with a microphone, providing the primary signal source, and an extra microphone captures only the noise.

In these more general cases the adaptive filter has to be of larger size, since the noise source is normally far from a narrowband signal. For each two taps, the filter is able to suppress a single harmonic of the interference. The method is effective when the noise conditions are regular (stationary) or vary slowly and have marked harmonic content (such as noise produced by rotating machinery). In cases of broadband noise, only the low frequencies are reasonably canceled.

NEUROSOLUTIONS EXAMPLE 9.15

Real example of noise canceling

This example shows the power of interference canceling applied to more complex signals: speech and a washing machine noise. Our speaker is Homer Simpson, and his voice mixed with noise from a washing machine is presented to the reference input of the system $(s + n)$. At the primary input of the linear combiner we present just the noise (n). The linear combiner is specified as size 5, since the washing machine noise has a broader spectrum but still has a salient peak. The linear combiner will try to cancel the noise in the desired response, leaving only Homer's voice. We present the signals and their spectra on scopes for visualization of the progression of learning.

After presenting the speech segment, we listen to the error, which contains Homer's voice. We attached a DLL to the error output of the criterion, which calls the Windows 95 routine that plays sound files. Notice that in the beginning Homer's voice is mixed with lots of noise, but after a few iterations it becomes intelligible. Can you understand what he is saying?

The same principle of noise cancellation can be applied to different problems, for instance, to the enhancement of low-level sine waves in high-noise backgrounds. Only one signal source is utilized (Figure 9-10). The signal is split into the primary input and the reference input, which is delayed to decorrelate the noise but preserve the signal correlation, since we assume it is periodic.

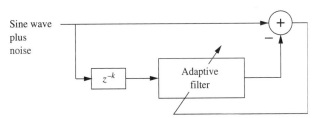

FIGURE 9-10   Line enhancer with the LMS

NEUROSOLUTIONS EXAMPLE 9.16

Finding periodic signals in noise

This example explores the same basic principles of noise cancellation, but the application is different. Here we would like to find weak sine waves in high-noise backgrounds. We delay the input from the desired response to decorrelate the noise. However, this will not decorrelate the signal, since the sine is still correlated from period to period (it is periodic). The adaptive filter tries to correlate the desired response with its input. Although we are searching for a sine wave (two weights should suffice), we recommend using a slightly larger model (four to six weights), since the samples will be very noisy. Experiment with the delay, the learning rate, and the filter size, and observe the differences in the spectra.

9.6.7 Echo Cancellation

Echo cancellation and adaptive equalization are probably two of the most widely applied interference canceling schemes due to their importance in communications. Here we will explain echo cancellation. It turns out that our telephone channels are not ideally terminated; when signals travel from the source to the destination they are reflected back to the source. This is the familiar echo that we can hear in long-distance phone calls. The echo is annoying and decreases the intelligibility of speech, so phone companies built special devices called echo cancelers to attenuate the echo.

The culprit of this problem is a transformer (called the hybrid) that receives a two-wire input from the phone and creates a four-wire output (the long-distance trunk) to send our conversation multiplexed with others. The net effect is that when caller A speaks, caller B receives the voice, but there is a return path between the hybrids of callers A and B that injects caller A's voice in the outgoing port, and bounces it back to caller A's phone, appearing delayed in time (Figure 9-11). For satellite communications this delay for the long echo path reaches 400 ms and is very annoying. (The local echo is not disturbing because our ear filters it automatically, by means of the precedence effect.) When caller B talks, the same thing occurs in the reverse direction.

A possible implementation of an echo canceler is to use an adaptive linear combiner in parallel with each hybrid, as shown in Figure 9-12, to subtract the echo from the incoming signal. The adaptive filter at the left filters the echo for caller A, and it effectively identifies the system composed by the channels and the hybrid of caller B. For a sampling rate of 8 KHz a linear combiner with at least 128 taps is required.

More recently, with the widespread use of modems for data transmission in our homes and offices, a similar problem occurs, but now the disturbing echo is from reflections in the local subscriber loop (the short-path echo). The echo is much more troublesome in data transmission because the data rates are very high, which means

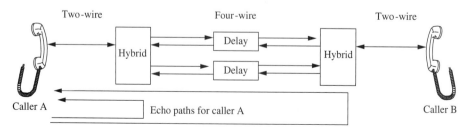

FIGURE 9-11 The source of echo in phone lines

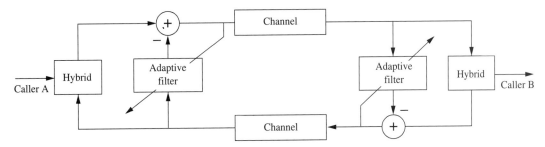

FIGURE 9-12 Echo cancelers using adaptive filters

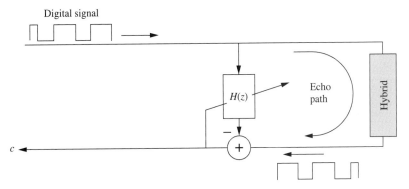

FIGURE 9-13 Echo cancellation with adaptive filter

that any modification of the shape of the waveforms (as produced by adding a 0 with a 1) can be interpreted as the wrong symbol, so the message must be repeated.

Adaptive filters can also be used to attenuate the digital echo quite effectively and all modems operating above 4800 baud have a built-in adaptive filter (Figure 9-13). The idea is to have the filter subtract the echo by learning the echo-path transfer function. The signal that goes back to the modem is basically echo free. The efficiency of the echo canceler is measured in ERLE (echo return loss enhancement), defined as

$$\text{ERLE} = 10 \log \frac{E\{d^2(n)\}}{E\{e^2(n)\}}$$

which computes how much the echo was attenuated.

NEUROSOLUTIONS EXAMPLE 9.17

Echo cancellation

The data used in this example is fabricated but represents conditions found in the real world. We generated a pulse train to model a bit stream created by a modem.

This signal is then passed through a transfer function that models the lossy path of a 2-4 wire transformer as

$$H(z) = \frac{0.1(1 + z^{-1})(-1 + z^{-1})^2}{(1 + 0.3z^{-1})^3}$$

The output signal is then added to the incoming signal to the modem, which here is modeled by a simple square wave. Instead of receiving just the square wave, the modem sees the square wave plus the echo of the outgoing bit stream.

The role of the adaptive filter is to subtract the echo from the square wave. To do this, the adaptive filter receives as the input the bit stream sent out by the modem and tries to figure out the echo (by identifying the hybrid lossy transfer function). We have placed MegaScopes and FFT probes to observe the adaptation process.

Notice that the advantage of this technique is that it will always adapt to changes in the echo transfer function, which are known to change from line to line and with the load in the lines.

9.6.8 Adaptive Inverse Control

Another important application of adaptive filters is in control engineering. The idea of controlling an unknown plant is to design a system (controller) that will produce a prespecified plant output.

Probably the most widely used method of plant control is feedback. The controller receives the command input and provides an input to the plant. The plant output is measured and fed back to the controller so that it can relate changes in the plant input with the changes produced at the plant output. Feedback control is useful, but the application of the method is not always straightforward due to physical constraints. Other methods exist, such as inverse modeling (Figure 9-14).

In inverse modeling the adaptive filter $H(z)$ is placed in cascade with the unknown plant, and the output of the combination seeks to match the input signal (or its delayed version). This block diagram is basically the inverse modeling that we described in Section 9.6.5. When the error is small, we see that the adaptive-filter transfer function is the inverse of the plant (Eq. 9.29). The delay is necessary because the plant may either have delays or be nonminimum phase, that is, have zeros outside the unit circle,

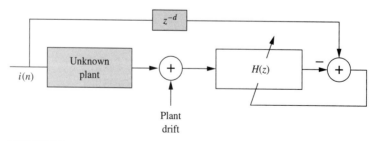

FIGURE 9-14 Inverse modeling with plant drift and a delay

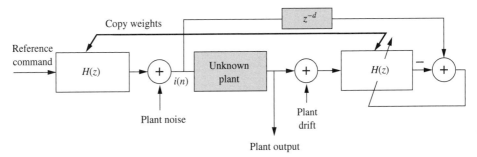

FIGURE 9-15   Adaptive inverse model control

which may cause the system model to be poor or unstable (although not in this case, since we are using a linear combiner). The inclusion of the delay improves the inverse model.

With the inverse model available, we can now construct a controller between the command input and the plant just by duplicating the adaptive filter used in the inverse modeling and copying its weights, as shown in Figure 9-15.

With this arrangement the plant output will closely follow the command input applied to the controller, since we "predistort" the command to the plant by the controller. This predistortion is exactly what the plant needs to follow the command input. This theoretical picture is complicated by two primary factors: nonminimum phase plants and plant drift, which can be handled but are not discussed here.

NEUROSOLUTIONS EXAMPLE 9.18

Adaptive inverse control

Here we will try to control a model of a patient's lung while under anesthesia. The controller will determine the internal settings of a mechanical ventilator that helps the patient breathe. We will use adaptive inverse control for this task.

Humans breathe with negative pressure by exerting their diaphragm and chest muscles to inhale air. Mechanical ventilation is positive pressure, actually blowing air into the lungs, and it is almost exclusively controlled with a proportional flow control valve (PFCV), which controls the flow rate of the ventilator.

The model of the lung implemented here is a simple, first-order dynamic system modeling lung compliance and resistance. When the left and right compliances and resistances are equal, the system can be modeled as its electrical equivalent, as shown on page 462. The goal is to control the pressure at the patient's airway (at the end of the ventilator tubing). There is resistive pressure which is a function of the flow (when flow ceases the resistive pressure goes to zero), and compliant pressure, which is based on the amount of air in the lung and the compliance ("stretchiness") of

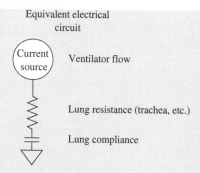

Equivalent electrical circuit

Current source — Ventilator flow

Lung resistance (trachea, etc.)

Lung compliance

the lung, which yields

$$V = \frac{1}{C} \int I\,dt + IR$$

The purpose of the ventilator is to apply a square wave of pressure to the lungs. However, due to the lung compliance and resistance, what actual flow waveform should the ventilator produce to create a square wave of pressure in the lung? This is exactly what our implementation will figure out. The input to the controller is the square wave of pressure (we just model the rising slope here). Connected to the output of the controller is the "lung," here modeled as an Axon. The output of the lung is then fed to the adaptive part of the controller, which identifies the inverse lung model. Its parameters are copied to the controller, which predistorts the command input so that the desired behavior is obtained.

This scheme can even be refined to include a reference model that will relax the condition that the plant input and the desired response of the inverse model be the same (eventually delayed).

Now let us see how we can implement such a complex scheme in Neuro-Solutions. First, there are the controller and its function. We use a linear combiner followed by a logistic nonlinearity. The need for the nonlinearity arises because the real controller (the ventilator) can produce only positive signals (positive ventilator pressure). The weights of the controller are copied from the inverse model that follows the plant. A DLL transmits the coefficients. The input to the controller is a square wave added with white noise. We use white noise so that we always provide a driving force for the adaptation (the square wave is featureless except during the jumps and, just like the sine wave of our previous example, is not sufficient to drive all the modes of the plant).

The lung dynamics given by the preceding equation are modeled in the Axon. The Axon is an input-output device, so through DLLs we can create arbitrary, complex programs in C language that model real systems. For each input to the Axon the C program creates the corresponding model output.

The inverse model is created by a linear combiner followed by the same logistic nonlinearity. The desired response to the inverse model is received from the input to the lung through a DLL. Let us see how this works.

9.7 APPLICATIONS OF TEMPORAL PCA NETWORKS

The ideas and learning algorithms covered in Chapter 6 for Hebbian networks can also be extended to time signals with minor modifications in the topology. We present here an example of an eigenfilter, the decomposition into principal components of a discrete signal, a subspace method for sinusoid detection in broadband noise, and blind source separation of speech signals.

9.7.1 Maximum Eigenfilter

Suppose that we have a signal that is generated by a subtractive process where some frequencies are eliminated, which happens, for instance, in the force signal collected from the cutting head of rotating machinery. Such signals have spectra with a large concentration of energy in several ranges of frequencies but have nulls, which show their moving-average (MA) generation. Instead of applying the previously discussed spectral analysis method using prediction, which implies an AR model, we use temporal PCA here. PCA in time produces MA models that seek the peaks of the spectrum. The single-output system, called the maximum eigenfilter, seeks the largest peak in the spectrum but assumes at the same time an MA model. Basically, the maximum eigenfilter finds a projection vector in the input space where the output power is maximized (see discussion in Chapter 6). It maximizes the Rayleigh quotient.

We can train a temporal PCA network with a single output using Oja's algorithm to solve this problem. The output power will be the largest eigenvalue over time, while the filter weights correspond to the eigenvector. The larger the delay line, the more coefficients the filter will have, and hence the sharper the eigenfilter main lobe will be. The matched filter is an eigenfilter for transients.

NEUROSOLUTIONS EXAMPLE 9.19

Maximum eigenfilter

Let us create a synthetic signal to exemplify the largest eigenfilter model and then apply it to real-world data. We create a signal through a subtraction process. Consider a pulse of four nonzero samples $(-0.2, 1, -0.5, -0.3)$ that repeats itself every 15 samples. Let us now add four versions of the same signal but delayed in time by equal amounts, and add noise. We can consider this signal as a model for the force pulse produced by a rotating machine with five teeth, and what we measure with a force sensor is the overall waveform.

The spectrum of this signal has many peaks, and the goal is to find the fundamental component. We can use the maximum eigenfilter to solve this problem. Let us create a delay line with 15 taps and use Oja's rule to train the system (just one output). We see that the output grabs the largest peak. Now we freeze the weights (by setting the learning rate to zero) and send an impulse through to compute the system frequency response. Since this is a FIR filter (implementing an MA model), we expect to see a frequency response with a large lobe and many side lobes sculpted by zeros. We can increase the number of taps in the delay line and see that the output spectrum gets sharper, as we would expect from the theory.

The second example is to extract the fundamental component of the sunspot time series. As we have seen, the time series is very noisy, but it has a quasi-periodic oscillation. Let us use a tap delay line of 20 and train the eigenfilter with Oja's rule. We see the waveform progressively becoming cleaner, showing that the high-frequency information is being removed. If we freeze the weights and send a pulse through, we see the frequency response of the lowpass filter, which was automatically obtained to preserve the most information about the largest mode in the spectrum. This type of processing can be considered preprocessing for the subsequent analysis, and it is one of the attributes of eigenfilters.

9.7.2 Optimal Filter Banks

If the network of the previous example is extended with more outputs (Figure 9-16) and Sanger's rule is utilized in the training, an optimal filter bank is achieved. The size of the time window determines the accuracy and the size of the autocorrelation function estimator. The number of output PEs establishes the number of principal components extracted. The optimal filter bank maximizes the projected power to a subspace.

When the input signal has the maximum power concentrated at low frequencies (low pass spectrum), and there is a monotonic decay of power across frequency, the temporal PCA defaults to a bank of optimally designed bandpass filters, which for very large windows approximate the spectral decomposition achieved with the FFT. In temporal PCA, pairs of neighboring PEs tune to the same basic band, since a given frequency band can be covered by two orthogonal components of the same basic frequency (as the sine and cosine waveforms). As we can expect, the bandpass filters are FIR; that is, PCA in time implements an MA model.

We can easily observe the frequency response of each eigenfilter if we stop training and input a delta function to the system. The analysis of the decomposition is not

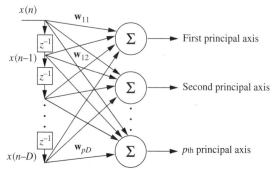

FIGURE 9-16 Optimal filter bank

straightforward, except for the limit of long windows or for signals that have a line spectra, such as the square wave. Closely analyzing the solution for this case, we see that the zeros of lower-order eigenfilters are placed over the top of the peaks of higher-order eigenfilters, which can be expected from the orthogonality condition of the PCA components.

When the input signal spectrum is not lowpass or the limit of long windows is not verified, this simple analysis no longer holds. The principal component still captures the largest spectral mode (which is broad and may be anywhere in the spectrum). The lower-order eigenfilters have to compete for the other spectral modes, but now there is no guarantee that the eigenfilters will be unimodal and ordered. Nevertheless, the system still finds the best (ordered by variance) orthogonal projection of the input.

NEUROSOLUTIONS EXAMPLE 9.20

Optimal filter bank

Let us use a square wave as the example of a signal that has a lowpass, monotonically decreasing spectrum. If the PCA decomposition in time is implemented with Sanger's rule, we see that the system self-organizes in such a fashion that pairs of eigenfilters grab one harmonic of the square wave. If we stop the training and estimate the frequency response, we see that the eigenfilters are effectively organized in pairs of increasing frequency. Note also that the zeros of the higher-order eigenfilters are placed on top of the preceding eigenfilter's bandpass frequencies.

Now let us change the input to a speech segment of the sound "ah" as in "hot." The first three formants should appear at $f_1 = 730$ Hz, $f_2 = 1,090$ Hz, and $f_3 = 2,440$ Hz. We use a PCA network with 20 input taps and 6 outputs. After training you will see the first two eigenfilters peak at the first formant, the second two at the second formant, and the last two picking up some low-frequency activity but also some higher-frequency activity. If we change the FFT display to log, we can see this feature more clearly. Notice that this decomposition produces very interesting features in the time domain.

9.7.3 Spectral Analysis by Eigendecomposition

Spectral estimation based on autoregressive models loses accuracy rapidly when the noise in the data increases. Alternatively, the eigenvectors of the autocorrelation function can be used to find sine waves in white noise. The idea is that in the eigendecomposition of the autocorrelation function, the input signal energy is divided into orthogonal components. Since sine waves are the natural modes of PCA decomposition for long observation windows, one of the eigenvectors is associated with the sine wave, while the noise projects everywhere.

NEUROSOLUTIONS EXAMPLE 9.21

Noise removal by PCA

Let us utilize the previous Breadboard but now change the input source to a single sine wave with a large amount of additive noise. We decrease the number of outputs to 3 to show exactly what we described in the text. We chose the number 3 because a sine wave will appear in two eigenfilters, while the third eigenfilter will simply show the noise.

We start with the sine-wave amplitude of 1, 10 samples per cycle, and add uniform noise of variance 2. The sine wave is only faintly visible in the time signal, but the spectrum still shows a very clear peak. The network has no problem with providing a nice sine wave in the first two eigenfilters. If we now decrease the amplitude of the sine to 0.3, we do not see the sine wave even in the spectrum, but the system still trains to produce the sine wave. For an amplitude of 0.1 the system is unable to find the sine wave; thus there is a limit to this technique. We can increase the window to 50 samples and decrease the learning rate. Most of the time we can see a spectral line that can be traced to the sine wave in the spectrum of the first eigenfilter.

This same idea can be extended to multiple sine waves in noise or other signals. The directions that contain only the white noise components generally correspond to smaller eigenvalues. If we truncate the eigendecomposition when there is a large drop in the magnitude of eigenvalues, we thus retain the signal components (signal subspace) and attenuate the noise.

An alternative uses only the noise subspace (normally represented by the last PCA component) to find the sinusoidal components. The noise subspace is orthogonal to the signal subspace. If we use the minor component of the PCA as a filter, we guarantee that it will have zeros in the unit circle where the signal components are located. We can copy the weights of the minor component to a recurrent system implementing the inverse system, whose frequency response has peaks where the sinusoids are located (since the zeros give rise to poles of the inverse model). We already did this when we discussed model-based spectral analysis, except that here we are using the eigenfilter that corresponds to the noise subspace as the model. It has been shown that this method is highly accurate for determining the frequency of sinusoids (the MUSIC algorithm [Kay 1988]). One of the problems of this method is that it requires knowledge of the number of sinusoids included in the signal to appropriately set the size of the PCA space to at least one larger than twice the number of sinusoids.

NEUROSOLUTIONS EXAMPLE 9.22

Spectral analysis by eigendecomposition

We can use the previous Breadboard to train the PCA in the case of sine wave plus noise. We will use the anti-Oja rule, which is simply anti-Hebbian normalized to unit norm weights. Hence the network has a single output, and we select a five-tap network. In principle, we only need a three-tap filter, but the lack of resolution will be noticeable. We train the system using the Scheduler for the step size. Once the PCA has converged, we copy the weights of the weight matrix and call it $H(z)$. These weights represent the eigenfilter that represents the noise subspace, and its frequency response is guaranteed to have zeros at the frequency of the sinusoid embedded in noise. According to the theory of noise subspaces, the spectral estimator should be $1/H(z)$.

To create this transfer function, we create a recurrent system in Neuro-Solutions by feeding back the output of a linear combiner to itself. The recurrent system transfer function is $1/[1 - z^{-1}G(z)]$ where $G(z)$ is the feedforward transfer function. To obtain the spectral estimator with this Breadboard, we have to make $G(z) = 1 - H(z)$. This can be accomplished easily if we exchange the signs of all the coefficients of $H(z)$ and add 1 to the leading term (i.e., the coefficient for lag zero). Run the network and observe that the spectrum peaks at the desired frequency. With this method the frequency can be estimated very accurately.

9.7.4 Blind Source Separation

Blind source separation is an important problem in science and in engineering. It can be formulated in the following way: Suppose that we have M sources $s_1(n)$, $s_2(n), \ldots, s_M(n)$ assumed statistically independent, which are unknown, and mixed by a linear but unknown system $\mathbf{A}$ (i.e., $\mathbf{X} = \mathbf{AS}$). Here we deal only with the case that the mixing is instantaneous; that is, the system is an unknown scalar mixing matrix $\mathbf{A}$. We do not know the sources nor the mixing matrix, but we collect M signals $x_1(n)$, $x_2(n), \ldots, x_M(n)$ from the output of the mixing system (i.e., we have as many mixed signals as sources). The goal is to find a system $\mathbf{W}$ that is able to demix the signals (i.e., $\mathbf{Y} = \mathbf{WX}$ with $y_1(n) \approx s_i(n)$; see Figure 9-17). This is a difficult problem, since we do not know the sources nor the mixing matrix.

To illustrate this problem, let us assume that we are in a room with many people talking at the same time (called the cocktail party effect). Our auditory cortex is able to focus on a given speaker and distinguish his or her voice from the others. Our senses are basically doing blind source separation because we do not know the source (the speech is unknown to us) and because the room acoustics and the placement of the subject with respect to the others and to us is unknown. Humans can do this separation

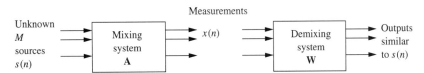

FIGURE 9-17   The problem of blind source separation

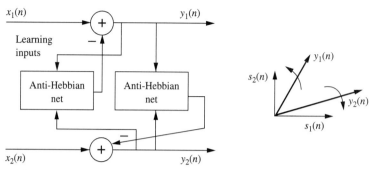

FIGURE 9-18 The solution based on novelty filters

with just two ears, but here we assume that we have as many measurements $x(n)$ as sources $s(n)$.

We use the ideas of anti-Hebbian learning coupled with a tap delay line to create a system that will be able to demix the signals. How can this simple idea be used to perform blind source separation? For the sake of simplicity let us use just two sources. We will use a recurrent system built from two anti-Hebbian networks, like the ones in Figure 9-18 [Principe et al. 1996].

By assumption, $s_1(n)$ and $s_2(n)$ are orthogonal (since we assumed that they are independent). When we start the adaptation using anti-Hebbian learning, $y_2(n)$ will push $y_1(n)$ away from it, while $y_1(n)$ will make $y_2(n)$ rotate away from its direction. As the figure shows, they will stop the rotation when $y_1(n)$ is orthogonal to $y_2(n)$, which coincides (apart from a permutation and scaling) with the directions of $s_1(n)$ and $s_2(n)$. This is the principle that we will use to do blind source separation.

NEUROSOLUTIONS EXAMPLE 9.23

Blind source separation with anti-Hebbian learning

This Breadboard is complex, not because of the task, but because of the implementation in NeuroSolutions. There are two identical parallel channels, that are interconnected, as shown in Figure 9-18. Each is a tap delay line followed by a set of weights, which are adapted using anti-Hebbian learning with weight normalization. The normalization of the weight vector to unit length is necessary to avoid convergence to the trivial solution (zero weights). This is accomplished by writing a DLL for the adaptation.

The first two Axons in each channel are there just for synchronization purposes. The two mixed signals are applied to the input of the network, and the output is plotted in scopes. We also create a sound file from the top channel so that we can appreciate the evolution of the demixing while the system is training. In the beginning it is impossible to understand the sentence. After 15 iterations over the data set this system is able to demix the two speech signals.

> Notice that filtering would be impossible, since the two speech waveforms share the same frequency band. The demixing uses the statistical properties of the two waveforms to achieve the separation, without knowing the sources nor the mixing matrix.

9.8 CONCLUSIONS

In this chapter we covered adaptive filters. We showed that an adaptive filter is a linear regressor in signal space because it tries to fit a line to a signal trajectory. We showed that we can adapt linear filters with our well-known LMS procedure.

Another class of linear systems that we covered is the temporal PCA network. Borrowing the ideas of PCA from Chapter 6, we can extend them to time by including a tap delay line in the PCA architecture. Temporal PCA computes eigendecompositions in time. We can therefore design maximum eigenfilters, novelty filters, and KLTs.

Probably the most important part of Chapter 9 is the application section. Here we tried to show many possible uses of adaptive filters and their advantages in digital signal processing. We cover a wide range of applications, from prediction, system identification, and noise cancellation to inverse adaptive controls. We also showed how temporal PCA networks can be used in spectral analysis, in blind source separation, and for eigenfilters.

9.9 EXERCISES

9.1 Use the Breadboard of Example 9.7 to predict the signal stored in the file prob9.1 contained in folder chapter9 of the data directory (CD-ROM).

9.2 Use the Breadboard of Example 9.8. to create the model of the data for Problem 1.

9.3 Use the Breadboard of Example 9.9 to estimate the power spectrum of the signal stored in the file prob9.1 contained in folder chapter9 of the data directory (CD-ROM).

9.4 Use the Breadboard of Example 9.10 to identify the system where the output is stored in the file prob9.1 contained in folder chapter9 of the data directory (CD-ROM).

9.5 Use the Breadboard of Example 9.12 to create an inverse model of the plant whose output is stored in the file prob9.1 contained in folder chapter9 of the data directory (CD-ROM).

9.6 Use the Breadboard of Example 9.13 to attenuate the noise in the sound file prob9.6 contained in folder chapter9 of the data directory (CD-ROM).

9.7 Use the Breadboard of Example 9.16 to find a periodic component in the signal stored in the file prob9.7 contained in folder chapter9 of the data directory (CD-ROM).

9.8 Use the Breadboard of Example 9.17 to cancel the echo in the signal stored in the file prob9.8 contained in folder chapter9 of the data directory (CD-ROM).

9.9   Use the Breadboard of Example 9.19 to create the maximum eigenfilter for the signal in the file prob9.9 contained in folder chapter9 of the data directory (CD-ROM).

9.10   Use the Breadboard of Example 9.20 to create a PCA decomposition of the signal stored in the file prob9.10 contained in folder chapter9 of the data directory (CD-ROM).

9.11   Use the Breadboard of Example 9.21 to remove the noise from the signal in the file prob9.11 contained in folder chapter9 of the data directory (CD-ROM).

9.12   Use the Breadboard of Example 9.22 to estimate the power spectrum of the signal in the file prob9.12 contained in folder chapter9 of the data directory (CD-ROM).

9.13   Use the Breadboard of Example 9.23 to separate the speech signals in the file prob9.13 contained in folder chapter9 of the data directory (CD-ROM).

9.10   NEUROSOLUTIONS EXAMPLES

9.1   Design of filters using adaptation

9.2   Adaptive filters for prediction

9.3   Choosing the step size

9.4   Speed of convergence

9.5   Misadjustment

9.6   Tracking ability

9.7   Prediction of time series

9.8   Prediction for modeling

9.9   Prediction for spectral analysis

9.10   System identification

9.11   Inverse modeling

9.12   Inverse modeling of nonminimum phase plants

9.13   Interference canceling

9.14   Adaptive DC removal

9.15   Real example of noise canceling

9.16   Finding periodic signals in noise

9.17   Echo cancellation

9.18   Adaptive inverse control

9.19   Maximum eigenfilter

9.20   Optimal filter bank

9.21   Noise removal by PCA

9.22   Spectral analysis by eigendecomposition

9.23   Blind source separation with anti-Hebbian learning

9.11   CONCEPT MAP FOR CHAPTER 9

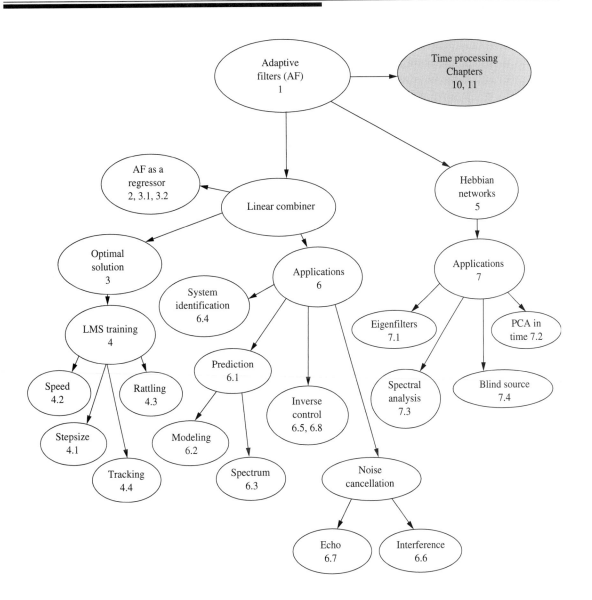

REFERENCES

Haykin, S., *Adaptive Filter Theory*, Prentice-Hall, Englewood Cliffs, NJ, 1986.

Kay, S., *Modern Spectral Estimation,* Prentice-Hall, Englewood Cliffs, NJ, 1988.

Kolmogorov, A., English translation in Kailath, *Linear Least-Square Estimation,* Stroudsburg, PA, Dowden, Hutchinson and Ross, 1977.

Loeve, *Probability Theory,* Van Nostrand, New York, 1963.

Principe, J., Wang, C., and Wu, H., Temporal decorrelation using teacher forcing anti-Hebbian learning and its application to blind source separation, *Proc. IEEE Workshop on Neural Networks for Signal Processing*, 413–422, 1996.

Van Trees, H., *Detection, Estimation, and Modulation Theory*, Wiley, New York, 1968.

Widrow, B., and Stearns, S., *Adaptive Signal Processing,* Prentice-Hall, Englewood Cliffs, NJ, 1985.

Wiener, N., *Extrapolation, Interpolation and Smoothing of Stationary Time Series,* MIT Press, Cambridge, MA, 1949.

TEMPORAL PROCESSING WITH NEURAL NETWORKS

The goal of this chapter is to introduce the concepts of:

- Time processing with neural networks
- Time-lagged feedforward networks (TLFNs)
- The focused topology

- Memory PEs
- Generalized feedforward memories

10.1 STATIC VERSUS DYNAMIC SYSTEMS

Chapter 9 was the first chapter to cover systems that process time information. Before that chapter, all the learning systems we studied implemented static input-output transformations (static mappers). The system response was computed instantaneously from the available input pattern and did not change if the input was kept constant. This is an important subset of learning systems, but, as we saw in Chapters 8 and 9, there are systems that do not have instantaneous responses to inputs. They need some time to stabilize their outputs for a given input excitation.

A linear combiner has memory, that is, it preserves the past values of the input internally in the tap delay line. When an input is applied, the input samples need to propagate through the filter topology. The response of the FIR for a constant input stabilizes only after a time equal to the number of delay line taps (the transient response). Static mappers have zero transient time, while the linear combiner has a finite transient response.

Another important class of systems with nonzero transient response is the recurrent topology that we discussed in Chapter 8. Recurrent topologies have feedback, where the system output or the output of an intermediate PE is fed back to the input or internal PEs. The feedback brings the influence of the past input (or past output) to the response at the present time, so it is also a form of memory. If the system has feedback, the response in general takes time to stabilize. For some values of the system parameters the response may never stabilize, so we see that new system properties (stability) emerge for recurrent systems. Both these systems (memory based or recurrent) are called *dynamic networks*. All analog systems are dynamic because their responses take a finite time to reach a steady value (if at all). This naturally creates the concept of time scale and introduces new properties when compared with static mappers. In Chapters 8 and 9 we restricted the study to linear dynamic networks, but here we will expand the scope to include nonlinear dynamic networks.

The weights in a static mapper, such as the multilayer perceptron, also represent memory about the data it has been trained with. This type of memory should not be confused with the memory we discussed for the linear combiner. Therefore we call long-term memory the information contained in the weights, and short-term memory the past information available as data within the neural network topology.

Short-Term versus Long-Term Memory

What is the computational difference between short- and long-term memory? This is a critical and difficult question that has not been properly studied. Static mappers, such as the MLP, have long-term memory, since the information utilized during system training is converted into weight values using the learning rules. Static mappers contain a repository of past information that we associate with memory. However, they are unable to differentiate time relationships, because the information collected through time is collapsed in the weight values.

Dynamic systems are different. Because they have short-term memory structures or recurrent connections, they are sensitive to the sequence of presentation of information. They also have weights, so they also have long-term memory. But unlike static mappers, these weights code differences within the time window of observation.

In digital simulations we have the power to artificially control time. The sampling frequency links the samples to time, but we can, for most practical applications, think of the data as a sequence of numbers and ignore the underlying time scale. Moreover, the availability of short-term memory structures used at the system input allows the system to work with many samples at a time, as if the input was static. In this sense short-term memory structures have the power to transform dynamic phenomena into multidimensional static patterns. We saw this in Chapter 8 where the output of a delay line of D taps was shown to be equivalent to a point (a static pattern) in a space of size D. An important question is: Are dynamic models preferable to static models? This is a difficult question to answer. Conventional statistics requires static data, or at least properties that do not change over time (stationary signals). A signal in time is a function, so functional analysis is required for their study, which complicates matters. It is fair to say that our mathematical tools are much more developed for static than for dynamic models, which may explain the generalized use of static modeling in neurocomputing.

On the other hand, we see that the processing power of biological systems is still more accurate and robust than most man-made systems, and we have to pause and wonder why. If there is any advantage in time processing, biological systems, which evolved embedded in time signals, must have learned how to use time for information processing. It is therefore important to look at time processing as a promising, albeit more complicated, alternative to the more conventional theory of static machines. When compared with static systems, the weights of dynamic systems are capable of codifying enhanced information about the input (through filtering in the short-term memory window). In fact, we can consider a static mapper as a special case of a dynamic system with a window length of one sample.

Static versus Dynamic Modeling

It is important to understand the source of the difference between the two types of systems. As an example, suppose that we have two clusters of points with the same mean and variance but that belong to two different classes. Training an MLP to distinguish these two classes is virtually impossible. However, let us assume that the two classes have different time histories, as were created by two sinusoidal signal sources of different frequencies. It is obvious that we may separate the two classes with a linear combiner, but we will never be able to separate them with an MLP. This is an extreme case to illustrate the difference between static versus dynamic modeling. In static modeling we are using statistical properties of the data clusters to distinguish them. In time phenomena, time imposes a structure in the input space (see Chapter 9) that may be used to separate data clusters with overlapping statistics, in other words, the sequence in which the points are visited is different, and this difference can be used for separation.

In many practical cases we do not know whether there is a time structure underlying our data, and so it is not clear whether dynamic modeling will help to improve performance. The trouble (as we will see in Example 10.1) is that the window in time where we seek the information is crucial for good performance.

NEUROSOLUTIONS EXAMPLE 10.1

Time disambiguates data clusters

Let us create the problem we discussed above: a single-input data file containing the amplitudes of two alternating sine waves of different frequencies and equal amplitudes. Let us assume that one frequency is one class and the other frequency belongs to another class. If we try to separate the two segments with a single-input, one-hidden-layer MLP, the class separation must be based on the amplitude of each sample. It is easy to convince ourselves that the task is impossible, since the two classes have exactly the same amplitude mean and range. We show this with the Scatter Plot.

Now let us substitute the Input Axon by the simple, first-order, recurrent low-pass filter we introduced in Chapter 8. Notice that the number of inputs and system topology are the same; however, when we run the system, the separation becomes possible, with some error. Notice that the errors are near the DC value.

What is the new information that the recurrent PE brings to the processing? The recurrent PE adds its past value to the present input bringing information from the past samples to the present processing task. This shows that the recurrent system is exploring information from the signal time structure and that this information is crucial to solve the problem.

If we change the value of the time constant to 0.5, the MLP is unable to differentiate the two classes. How much information we use from the past (given by the value of the feedback parameter) is therefore crucial to separate the classes.

Note that if we knew that the signals were sine waves, other simpler methods could be used to make the separation (a simple zero-crossing detector could do the classification). But here we are using the black-box approach, assuming no knowledge about the patterns to solve the problem.

Dynamic neural networks are topologies designed to explicitly include time relationships in the input-output mappings. Time-lagged feedforward networks (TLFNs) are a special type of dynamic network that integrate linear filter structures inside a feedforward neural network to extend the nonlinear mapping capabilities of the network with a representation of time. In this context, the delay line of the linear filter is called a *short-term memory mechanism*. In TLFNs a representation of time is created inside the learning machine, as opposed to windowing the input signal. We start by studying several linear short-term memory mechanisms and combine them with nonlinear PEs in restricted topologies called *focused*. Focused TLFNs have memory only at the input layer and can still be adapted with static backpropagation, so we can use our existing tools and knowledge to apply focused TLFNs for time processing. Then we study the function of memory PEs and show that they define the basis for the local projection space. The delay line is compared with the context PE, and then a unifying memory PE called the gamma PE is introduced.

10.2 EXTRACTING INFORMATION IN TIME

As we saw in earlier chapters, the static classification problem is well understood. It can be formulated as a special case of an arbitrary mapping between two vector spaces (function approximation) with indicator functions. In static pattern recognition the dimension of the input data vector defines the size of the pattern space (e.g., if the experiment has two independent variables, the size of the input space is two dimensions). In static pattern recognition the data clusters are described statistically (mean and variance or more rigorously with the probability mass function). The classification problem remains the same when we shuffle the presentation of the data to the learning machine, because we assume that there is no ordering in the data clusters (i.e., we assume no internal sequencing in the data). In static pattern recognition the way the data is drawn from the input space is irrelevant.

Let us now assume that, instead of static inputs, we seek to recognize *time patterns* from an M-dimensional, locally stationary signal $x(n)$. Locally stationary means that we assume that the signal is stationary for the length of observation, as in Figure 10-1.

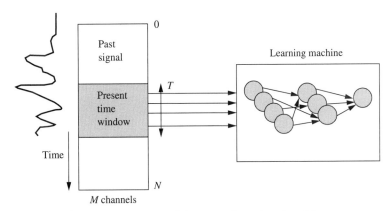

FIGURE 10-1 Processing of time-varying signals with an external window

In temporal problems the measurements from the world are no longer an independent set of input samples but *functions of time*. A single sensor produces a sequence of measurements that are linked by an ordered relation, the signal time structure. If we change the order of the samples, we are distorting the time signal $x(n)$ and changing its frequency content, so sample order must be preserved in temporal processing.

An important question is how to select the *length of time* (called the window length) to represent the properties of $x(n)$. As we saw in Chapter 8, the signal time structure limits the dimensionality of the manifold where the signal trajectory exists. We can normally work with small-dimensional spaces without loss of information. The problem is that we have to find the appropriate *reconstruction space size* by selecting the length T of the time window. Moreover, we can use this projection to enhance the difference between the signal we are interested in and all the others (i.e., by adapting the network coefficients). This is the basic idea of filtering.

NEUROSOLUTIONS EXAMPLE 10.2

Disambiguating data with the tap delay line

For the same problem of Example 10.1, let us change the input PE to a tap delay line. Enter the values of the filter weights (all 1s, which corresponds to a lowpass filter). Start with three taps and find out that the system never learns. Then go to five taps and verify that the system learns fairly well. Then go to 15 and see that the number of errors decreases. Reduce the number of taps but proportionally increase the delay between taps to find that what matters is not the number of weights in the system, but the length of the time window.

Next let the weights of the FIR adapt automatically. Now find out whether the system found the same solution. . . . It did not. This means that there are other solutions that minimize the error, which points out the importance of filtering.

To exploit the signal's time structure, the learning machine must have access to the time dimension. Since physical systems are causal, the search is restricted to the *past* of the signal. Physical structures that store the past of a signal are called short-term memories, or simply memory structures. Basically, a short-term memory structure transforms a sequence of samples into a point in the reconstruction space.

In Chapter 9 the tap delay line was introduced and was used in conjunction with a simple adder to build the linear combiner. In this case we can either consider the memory as a window over the data or part of the learning machine. With the former view the linear combiner is just a regressor, which does not offer the right perspective for understanding filtering. Moreover, the first-order recurrent system also has memory, but this memory cannot naturally be described in terms of a windowing operation. Therefore a more rigorous approach must be taken.

In this chapter we incorporate memory structures *inside* the learning machine. This means that instead of using a window over the input data, we will create PEs

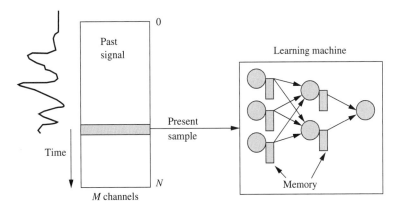

FIGURE 10-2   The new paradigm for processing time signals

dedicated to storing either the history of the input signal or the PE activations (Figure 10-2).

By bringing the memory inside the learning machine, we expect to improve the efficiency of the representation of time because the learning machine can:

- Choose the size of the time window that best suits the processing task.
- Choose the weighting of the data samples in the window to decrease the output error.
- Receive only the present sample from the external world, just like the biological archetype.

The added advantage of temporal processing is that the learning system can utilize filtering (frequency domain information) to reach the processing goal. It is also obvious that the learning machine is now required to perform a more complex function, because it has to codify time information. Fully recurrent networks have this ability, but they are complex. In this chapter we study topologies of intermediate complexity, between that of static networks and fully recurrent networks.

10.3 THE FOCUSED TIME-DELAY NEURAL NETWORK (TDNN)

We already have the knowledge to create, train, and understand our first dynamic neural network by joining the linear combiner and the multilayer perceptron. More specifically, we replace the adder from the linear combiner with several nonlinear PEs in a feedforward arrangement. Alternatively, we replace the input PEs of an MLP with a tap delay line. This topology is called the *focused time-delay neural network (TDNN)*. It is called focused because the memory is only at the input layers (Figure 10-3). TDNNs with

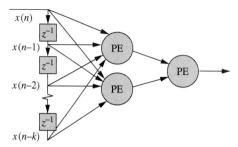

FIGURE 10-3 A focused TDNN with one hidden layer and a tap delay line with $k + 1$ taps

short-term memory distributed across the network were first applied by Waibel [1989] for speech recognition.

The delay line of the focused TDNN stores the past samples of the input. The combination of the tap delay line and the weights that connect the taps to the PEs of the first hidden layer are simply linear combiners followed by a static nonlinearity. The first layer of the focused TDNN is therefore a filtering layer, with as many adaptive filters as PEs in the first hidden layer. The outputs of the linear combiners are passed through a nonlinearity (of the hidden-layer PE) and are then further processed by the subsequent layers of the MLP to achieve one of the following tasks:

- In classification the goal is to find weights that separate the signal trajectories, which correspond to different time patterns.

- In system identification the goal is to find the weights that produce a network output that best matches the present output of the system by combining the information of the present and a predefined number of past samples (given by the size of the tap delay line).

- In prediction the goal is to approximate the next sample as a nonlinear combination of past input samples (given, once again, by the size of the tap delay line).

For all practical purposes we can think of the focused TDNN as an MLP that uses not only the current sample of the time series, but also a certain number of past samples. We can design an MLP equivalent to the focused TDNN if we use multiple samples from the time series instead of a single input and the tap delay line. Effectively, we place a rectangular window over the time series and choose an MLP with as many inputs as samples in the window. Note, however, that in this interpretation the memory becomes external to the network.

The problems of designing TDNN topologies are the same as for the MLP, with the addition of choosing the size of the tap delay line (also called the memory layer). We will discuss later a more rigorous way to address this issue. Here it suffices to say that the size of the memory layer depends on the number of past samples that are needed to describe the input characteristics in time. This number depends on the characteristics of the input and the task, so it has to be determined on a case-by-case basis. Before we are able to apply focused TDNNs to solve problems, we have to address how to train them.

10.3.1 Training the Focused TDNN

One of the appeals of the focused TDNN of Figure 10-3 is that it can still be trained with static backpropagation, provided that a desired signal is available at each time step. The reason is that the tap delay line at the input does not have any free parameters, so the only adaptive parameters are in the static feedforward path. To train these weights we simply use the backpropagation algorithm of Chapter 3 without any modifications. We have already successfully used static backpropagation to train the network weights for Examples 10.1 and 10.2. We further discuss the training of dynamic neural networks in the next chapter.

10.3.2 Applications of the Focused TDNN

The focused TDNN topology has been successfully used in nonlinear system identification, time series prediction, and temporal pattern recognition. We have demonstrated this topology with temporal pattern recognition for the simple case of discriminating between two sine-wave segments. We now create a more challenging task of phoneme classification.

NEUROSOLUTIONS EXAMPLE 10.3

Temporal pattern recognition with the focused TDNN

In this example we exemplify the power of the focused TDNN to classify phonemes. A phoneme is the fundamental building block for the sounds that make up our spoken language. The phoneme is the sound equivalent of a letter in our written alphabet. The problem with phonemes is that they exist in time. The phonemes are produced by puffs of air coming out of the lungs that make our vocal cords vibrate (sometimes) and are shaped by the resonances of our vocal tract. When we collect sounds with a microphone, we translate the sound into electrical voltages, and we can see them on an oscilloscope. Each phoneme corresponds to a different waveform, so if we want a TDNN to differentiate among phonemes, we have to do time processing.

Speech researchers found that a good way to characterize phonemes is to model the time series with an AR model. In Chapter 9 we saw that through prediction we can adapt the linear combiner to predict the next time series sample. The coefficients of the predictor are called linear predictive coding (LPC) coefficients and are used here to characterize each segment of the speech waveform. Every 10 ms (roughly 128 samples) we read the coefficients of the linear combiner, obtaining a set of 11 LPC coefficients. Thus the speech time series is translated into a sequence of LPC vectors (of size 11), which will be input to the focused TDNN.

Now the problem of training the TDNN is relatively easy to explain. When the sound we want to classify appears in the time series, we give a desired response of 1 to the TDNN. When the phoneme is absent, the desired response should be 0. We therefore have to create different desired signals in time to train the TDNN to recognize phonemes. Here the desired response will be a square wave of 0 (phoneme absent) and 1 (phoneme present). This is one of the differences between temporal and static pattern recognition: The desired response is also a time signal.

The other big difference between static and temporal pattern recognition is that here the pattern has an unknown and variable duration. We therefore have to set the size of the tap delay line so that it looks back in time to recognize the time structure of the phoneme, which is translated here into a sequence of LPC vectors. This is not a trivial problem. If the window is too small, there may not be enough data from the past and performance will suffer. On the other hand, if the window is too long, there will be many more weights in the network which will result in slower training. The size of the window is thus a design parameter. In the TDNN we have to physically modify the network topology to adjust the length of the window in time. In this example the LPC coefficients contain some of the temporal information, thus we only need three taps for our tap delay line.

In the TDNN we can still use static backpropagation to train the system. There are no recurrent connections—the memory simply creates a larger static set of inputs to the standard MLP. This is one of the advantages of this topology; the weight gradients are instantaneous because the net is static. Let us train the system and see how it works.

As with the examples of previous chapters, you should modify the parameters of the system to see how well it works and when it fails. Understanding why a system fails is normally much more enlightening than when everything goes right. In particular, you should observe the difference between dynamic and static pattern recognition. Just set the tap delay line to have a single tap, so that the classification is done with only one LPC vector. Try to train the system. You will see that the performance drops; by including time information, the classifier is improved.

Next, the focused TDNN is applied to nonlinear system identification, extending the linear combiner to nonlinear models.

NEUROSOLUTIONS EXAMPLE 10.4
Nonlinear system identification with the focused TDNN

This example studies system identification. To illustrate the power of the TDNN, we are going to model a nonlinear plant and compare the results of the TDNN with those of the linear combiner with the same number of delays. The plant is given by the following equations:

$$x_1(k+1) = \left(\frac{x_1(k)}{1 + x_1^2(k)} + 1\right)\sin(x_2(k))$$

$$x_2(k+1) = x_2(k)\cos\{x_2(k)\} + x_1(k)\exp\left(-\frac{x_1^2(k) + x_2^2(k)}{8}\right)$$

$$+ \frac{u^3(k)}{1 + u^2(k) + 0.5\cos\{x_1(k) + x_2(k)\}}$$

$$y(k) = \frac{x_1(k)}{1 + 0.5\sin(x_2(k))} + \frac{x_2(k)}{1 + 0.5\sin(x_1(k))}$$

The input is

$$u(k) = \sin\frac{2\pi k}{10} + \sin\frac{2\pi k}{25}$$

The block diagram for system identification is still the same as in the linear case. A common input is given to the TDNN and the plant, and the desired response for the TDNN is obtained from the plant output. We have stored both the input and the plant response in files to make them compatible with NeuroSolutions. In this case the input is a sum of two sinusoids. We put Megascopes at the input and at both the model and plant outputs to see how the learning progresses.

We start with the linear combiner of order 10. Run the simulator and observe that the error immediately stalls at a very large value. Increasing the size of the linear combiner does not help because of the nonlinear nature of the plant. Put a FFT at the input and output and observe that new frequencies are created by the plant; hence a linear system is hopeless in this case.

Let us now see how the focused TDNN does. It is amazing that a TDNN with seven PEs in the hidden layer does an almost perfect job, and the training is very fast. Modify the size of the hidden layer and of the input layer to better understand their role in the solution. For instance, is there a size of the tap delay line below which the system does not train, irrespective of how many PEs we use in the hidden layer? Conversely, is there a minimum number of hidden PEs below which, no matter how large the time window, the system never trains?

Finally, we apply the focused TDNN to chaotic time series prediction.

NEUROSOLUTIONS EXAMPLE 10.5

Nonlinear prediction with the focused TDNN

This example deals with nonlinear prediction. As explained in Chapter 9, prediction is a form of system identification in which both the input and desired signal come from the same source but at different time intervals (the input is delayed, normally by one sample). With this introduction we can see that if the system that created our time series is not linear, the linear combiner will not be able to perform as well as the TDNN.

The example that we prepared is a time series that is produced by a nonlinear dynamic system, the Mackey-Glass system, given by

$$\frac{dx}{dt} = -0.1x(t) + \frac{0.2x(t-\tau)}{1 + x^{10}(t-\tau)}$$

As we can immediately see, the system is nonlinear (notice the power of 10 in the denominator), with a delayed feedback (the delay τ), so we can expect a very complex oscillation. Notice that the equations are written in continuous time, so we have to discretize the system. Here we use a fourth-order Runge-Kutta integration, downsample it by 6, normalize to $[-1, 1]$, and use a delay of 30 (this is called the MG30 time series). MG30 is a chaotic time series, because the waveform is always different and unpredictable in the long run.

Once we have the time series, we just need to delay the input to the TDNN by 1 and run the Breadboard. We compare the performance of the TDNN with that of the linear combiner of the same memory size. As we can see, the TDNN is superior in capturing the fine detail of the waveform, but the linear combiner does an excellent job in approximating the major features of the waveform, which clearly shows why linear systems have been in use for so long and still satisfy most of the requirements.

You should experiment with the size of the delay line and the size of the hidden layer to better understand the Breadboard. You can also delay the input by more than one sample and see how much more difficult the task becomes. The linear system breaks down quickly, while the TDNN still works reasonably well.

If the waveform is chaotic, that is, unpredictable in the long run, does it make sense to try to predict it? As we can see, there is a deterministic equation that relates the samples, so locally there is a structure that can be captured by the predictor. One of the interests in chaotic time series prediction is related to the difficulty of the task, which provides an excellent ground for testing predictors. Moreover, many signals from the real world that we usually model as noise may in fact be chaotic, and we may be able to model them.

The focused TDNN is a great compromise between simplicity and processing power, but it is not the only dynamic neural network topology, as we saw in Example 10.1 with the first-order lowpass filter. We are interested in formulating a theory for the processing of time signals with neural networks, so we will develop a new neural component explicitly designed to remember the past, which we call the *memory PE*. We will see that the ideas of filtering explained in Chapter 8 are crucial to understanding the memory PEs.

10.4   THE MEMORY PE

Figure 10-4 shows a block diagram of the new memory PE, where $g(.)$ is a delay function. The memory PE receives in general many inputs $x_i(n)$, and produces multiple outputs $\mathbf{y} = [y_0(n), \ldots, y_D(n)]^T$, which are delayed versions of $y_0(n)$, the combined input:

$$y_k(n) = g(y_{k-1}(n)) \qquad y_0(n) = \sum_{j=1}^{p} x_j(n) \qquad \textbf{(10.1)}$$

Analyzing Eq. 10.1, we conclude that these short-term memory structures can be studied by linear adaptive filter theory if $g(.)$ is a linear operator. It is important to emphasize that the memory PE is a *short-term* memory mechanism, to make clear the distinction from the network weights, which represent the *long-term* memory of the network.

The memory PE has a biological interpretation (Figure 10-5). When the biological neuron receives multiple connections from the same axon at different levels of its dendritic tree, the signal propagation toward the soma produces different time delays. The cell responds to the average field, so the output is a weighted sum of delayed versions of the original excitation. Although these aspects are not fully understood, the

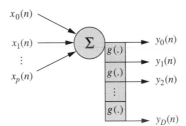

FIGURE 10-4   The memory PE

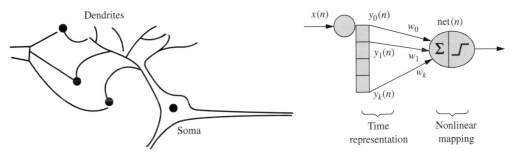

FIGURE 10-5   Similarity between biological neuron and the memory PE feeding an M-P PE

dendritic tree works as a signal representation stage. If we represent the cell with a McCulloch-Pitts PE and the dendritic tree with a single-input memory PE, the combination of the two PEs by means of a set of weights creates a processing block that incorporates the same basic principles of signal representation and nonlinear response. Figure 10-5 shows the similarity of the biological neuron with the memory PE feeding an M-P PE.

10.4.1 The Delay-Line PE

When the memory PE is built from a delay line, we call it a *delay-line PE,* and it implements memory by delay, that is, by simply holding past samples of the input signal. The delay-line PE is the memory structure used in the TDNN.

The delay-line PE is a multidimensional single-input, multiple-output linear system where the tap outputs are delayed by one sample from the previous tap (Figure 10-6). The delay-line PE with D outputs can be represented by

$$\mathbf{y}(n) = [y(n), \ldots, y(n - D + 1)]^T \quad y(n) = \sum_{j=1}^{p} x_j(n) \tag{10.2}$$

where $y(n)$ is the combined input to the PE. Comparing Eq. 10.2 with Eq. 10.1, we verify that $g(.)$ is the delta function operator $\delta(n - 1)$. Note that a delay-line PE with D outputs has $D - 1$ delays. At sample time n, the output of the delay-line PE of size D stores only samples that occurred after (and including) time $n - D$, that is, $D - 1$ samples into the past. Any input event occurring before time $n - D$ is not represented at the output. The delay-line PE with $D - 1$ delays implements a time window of length D samples positioned at the current sample.

10.4.2 The Context PE

The first-order recurrent system of Figure 8-12 and (Eq. 8.13) can be used to implement a linear context PE for general use in neural networks. This type of memory is called *memory by feedback,* and the memory PE is called a *context PE.* It is only necessary to

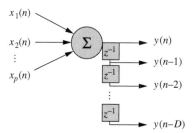

FIGURE 10-6 The delay line PE

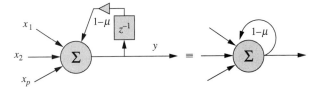

FIGURE 10-7   A linear context PE and its representation

equip it with multiple inputs and eventually a bias

$$y(n) = (1 - \mu)y(n - 1) + \mu\left(\sum_{i=1}^{p} x_i(n)\right) + b \quad i \neq j \tag{10.3}$$

which is depicted in Figure 10-7. Note that the combined input is multiplied by μ for normalization purposes.

We normally represent this PE as in the right diagram of Figure 10-7, where the delay is not apparent, but remember that context PEs always have a delay of one sample in the feedback loop.

NEUROSOLUTIONS EXAMPLE 10.6

Context PEs revisited

Let us revisit the first example of this chapter and analyze why the system with a context PE at the input was able to solve the discrimination task reasonably well. Note that from now on we will replace the Context PE with the Integrator PE (they differ only in a normalization factor).

Integrator Axon

Attach a Megascope to the output of the recurrent PE to see why the network is capable of classifying the two signals. Although the two sine waves at the input have the same amplitude, at the output of the recurrent PE they have *different* amplitudes because the recurrent PE is a lowpass filter and it filters (attenuates the amplitude of) the high-frequency sine wave more. These two different amplitudes are enough for the MLP to create a decision surface between the two amplitudes and distinguish the two regimes. Notice that with this explanation we also understand the errors clearly: When the low-frequency sine wave passes close to zero, the MLP is fooled and assigns those samples to the high-frequency sine wave.

10.4.3 Memory Depth and the Length of the Impulse Response

The signal-processing function of these two types of memory is to hold information from the past. The question that we have to ask is how long and how accurate is the information kept in the memory structure, which naturally leads to the concepts of *memory depth* and *resolution*. In the case of linear memories, the memory properties are related to the characteristics of the impulse response of the memory PE. Memory by feedback and memory by delays hold the information from the past differently.

The delay line PE represents the past of the signal $y(n)$ in a discontinuous way. For delays within the memory size D the past is represented exactly, but beyond this limit it is totally forgotten. The only way to represent events further back in time is to extend the size of the delay line, which requires a modification of the topology of the PE. Figure 10-8 shows an impulse at $n = 0$ and the progression of time by the position of the window advancing along the time line. Abruptly at $n = D + 1$ the response of the memory PE loses all its information from the impulse. Note that D is the length of the impulse response, which is also called the *region of support* of the response.

D is exactly the number of samples for which the output of the delay-line PE "remembers" the impulse at $n = 0$. Let us explain this terminology. When the output of the PE is different from zero, there is evidence at the output that an event (in this case an impulse) occurred somewhere within D samples. So a D-tap delay-line PE remembers D samples in the past, or has a memory depth of $D - 1$ samples.

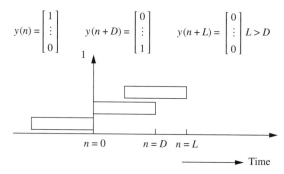

FIGURE 10-8   Response of the delay line PE

NEUROSOLUTIONS EXAMPLE 10.7

Memory depth of the tap-delay line

Let us construct a delay-line PE in NeuroSolutions and show that the effect of an impulse disappears after a number of samples given by the number of taps. This explains why in previous examples the TDNN "starts" to work abruptly when the size of the memory reaches a critical value. The tap delay line has an "all-or-nothing" type of memory.

Let us now study the context PE. Again, suppose that an impulse is applied at time $n = 0$ to two context PEs, H_1 and H_2, given by Eq. 10.3, with $\mu_2 < \mu_1$ ($0 < \mu_2, \mu_1 < 1$). In Figure 10-9 the impulse response appears *reversed in time,* as dictated by the convolution operation. We measure the system response $y(n)$ at time $n_t > 0$ by multiplying the input by the reversed impulse response sample-by-sample and summing the result. The response is practically zero for H_1 and nonzero for H_2. You can visualize how this system responds at n_t to a delta function at $n = 0$ by measuring the value of the impulse response at $n = 0$. By means of the impulse response, the information of the event occurring at $n = 0$ *was brought forward in time* to $n = n_t$. In the first case there is a trace of a response (a memory trace), while in the second case the system simply "forgot" what happened at $n = 0$.

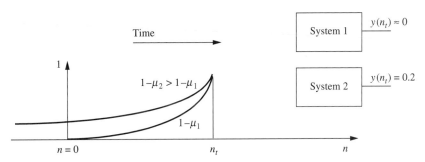

FIGURE 10-9 Response of two different lowpass filters to an impulse

---

NEUROSOLUTIONS EXAMPLE 10.8

Memory depth of the context PE

Let us show the memory trace in NeuroSolutions. When an impulse is presented to the memory, the output decays exponentially in time. Note that the region of support of the impulse response is infinite, but for all practical purposes it is finite, since the amplitude becomes negligible after a finite time. Also note that when you change

> the feedback parameter, the region of support of the memory changes. This is the beauty of these memories for neurocomputing: If the system can adapt the feedback parameter, it can choose the value that minimizes the output mean square error and work with the best possible memory depth without changing the topology. In the TDNN, to change the region of support, a change in the topology is required.

In the context PE the memory depth can be increased without any topological modifications by decreasing the feedback parameter μ. This is unlike the case of the delay-line PE.

The recurrent system of Figure 10-7, with a single delay unit, displays an impulse response that decays toward zero with a time constant τ:

$$e^{-1/\tau} = 1 - \mu \rightarrow \tau \approx \frac{1}{\mu} \tag{10.4}$$

In reality the region of support of the impulse response is infinite. But after some time (taken normally as four time constants) the response becomes so small that any noise can corrupt the system output. The equivalent power under this decaying exponential and the rectangular window of N samples is obtained with a number of samples equal to half of the time constant, $N = \frac{2}{\mu}$.

Notice that the past samples are not preserved exactly, as in the case of the delay-line PE. In the context PE, the output is an addition of the present input to a weighted version of the past output (see Eq. 10.3), so the information from the past is progressively distorted. This is the reason that we sometimes talk about a memory trace, a modified version of the input.

The memory trace in a context PE gracefully degrades in time, unlike the response of the delay-line PE, where the transition from memory to forgetting is abrupt. Moreover, the memory depth of the context PE is controlled by the system parameter μ. In an adaptive system framework, recurrent systems are advantageous, since the system can control its own memory depth by changing the parameter instead of the topology. But notice that the flexibility of this memory PE is very limited, since the system can control only the rate of decay of the memory trace.

10.4.4 Memory PE Properties

With this explanation we are ready to distill two definitions that characterize linear memory PEs. We define a *linear memory PE* as an (eventually multidimensional) single-input multiple-output system whose transformation kernel $g(n)$ is a causal and normalized impulse response:

$$\sum_{n=0}^{\infty} |g(n)| = 1 \quad g(n) = 0 \text{ for } n < 0 \tag{10.5}$$

We define *memory depth M* as the center of mass (first moment in time) of the impulse response $g_D(n)$ of the last memory tap D:

$$M = \sum_{n=0}^{\infty} n g_D(n) \tag{10.6}$$

where $g_k(n) = g(n) * g_{k-1}(n)$ and $*$ is the convolution operation.

Similarly, we define the *memory resolution R* as the number of taps per sample (or unit time). With this definition the memory depth and the resolution are coupled:

$$RM = D$$

This has interesting implications, since for a given number of taps D, an increase in R (resolution) implies a decrease in M (depth). In other words, the only way to increase depth and resolution at the same time is to increase D, the number of taps of the memory.

Applying these definitions to the tap delay line shows that $M = D$ and that $R = 1$. For the context PE the memory depth is $1/\mu$, and the resolution is μ.

Memory Depth of the Context PE

The impulse response of the context PE is

$$h(n) = \mu(1 - \mu)^n$$

Its Z transform, as we saw in Chapter 8, is

$$H(z) = \frac{\mu}{z - (1 - \mu)}$$

Now the definition of the memory depth in the time domain can be converted to the frequency domain as the derivative with respect to z of the system transfer function evaluated at $z = 1$:

$$M = \sum nh(n) = -z \frac{dH(z)}{dz}\Big|_{z=1} = \frac{1}{\mu}$$

10.5 THE MEMORY FILTER

Let us examine the signal-processing operation produced by attaching a single-input memory PE to a sigmoidal PE through a set of weights (Figure 10-10). If we restrict our analysis to the subsystem created by the memory PE and the output of the linear

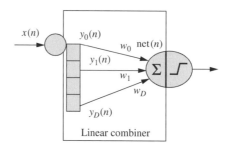

FIGURE 10-10 Block combining the memory PE with the next sigmoidal PE

part [$net(n)$] of the nonlinear PE, we can recognize a topology similar to the linear combiner. The delayed versions of the input signal $x(n)$ created by the memory PE are then multiplied by weights w_k and summed to obtain $net(n)$. Hence we will call this arrangement a *memory filter,* and its function is to project the input signal $x(n)$ into a linear manifold defined by the memory traces $y_i(n)$. The signal $net(n)$ is the result of the projection of the input vector $x(n)$ on the weight vector **w**. Wan [1994] called this special configuration of the memory filter a *FIR synapse.*

The fundamental conclusion from this observation is that, besides the qualitative properties of memory depth and resolution, we can use the theory and tools of filtering explained in Chapter 8 to study the effects of the memory PE on the mappings.

NEUROSOLUTIONS EXAMPLE 10.9

Interpretation of focused TDNNs as nonlinear memory filters

Let us go back to the topology of Example 10.2 and interpret what is happening in the input layer. Start with a three-tap delay line and two hidden PEs. We place a 3-D probe at one of the channels of the input so that we can see the two signals in signal space. We also place a Megascope and a Scatter Plot at the preactivity of the hidden layer so that we can see the outputs of the two memory filters. The Megascope shows the projections produced by the memory filters. We start with fixed coefficients: One of the filters will be lowpass (all 1s), and the other highpass $(1, -2, 1)$.

The Scatter Plot shows us exactly the set of points that the MLP is trying to separate, so this Scatter Plot shows the pattern space. We have configured the display so that it first shows one class and then the other class. The goal of the MLP training is to place discriminant functions for classification in the space created by the output of the memory filters.

Let us experiment with the number of delays between consecutive taps, Δ. Start with $\Delta = 1$. The two signal trajectories are narrow ellipses, which makes them difficult to separate visually in 3-D space. The projections in the decision space are on top of each other, so the MLP has difficulty in placing the two discriminant functions on this space. The classification results are poor.

Now increase Δ to 3. Notice that the signal trajectories open up in 3-D space (now the ellipses use more of the signal space, making the differences in trajectories clearer). Notice now that the projections with the lowpass and highpass filters that form the decision space are further apart, so it should be easier for the MLP to do the placement of its discriminant functions. The errors are exactly at the point that the two projections cross each other. Notice that the linear projections (implemented with the linear memory filters) do not have the power to move these trajectories to different parts of the decision space. They are both anchored at the origin.

Finally, we can let the system learn all of the parameters, including the weights of the memory filters. Do this with the same three tap memory and triple delay. The system found a good solution, as shown by the MSE and the output. Let us now look at the weights of the memory filters. Amazingly enough, the optimal weights do not correspond to our solution of lowpass and highpass filters.

We can see clearly from the output of the filters in the Scope that the solution found is to zero one of the waveforms while letting the other through. (If you want to visualize the frequency response of each filter, just copy the weights to a piece of paper and go to Example 7.16 to plot the frequency response.) This can be achieved if the filters are such that they place one of the zeros at the frequency of one the sine waves. This particular solution works for this case of a single-frequency input, so the solution found is actually pretty smart and minimal. We need one filter, that is, one hidden-layer PE, to do this, which means that a perceptron can solve this problem. Adaptive systems tend to find the most obvious solution.

Substitute the input sine waves by triangular waves of the same frequencies, and redo the problem to see what solution is found.

10.5.1 Memory Traces as a Projection of the Input Signal

The linear context PE is a projection operator in many ways similar to a constrained memory filter. In fact, the output of the context PE is the inner product (convolution) of the input with the impulse response of the PE, as shown in Figure 10-11.

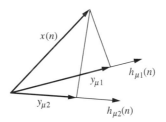

FIGURE 10-11 Dependence of the output on the parameter μ

The projection is onto the impulse response vector, which is equivalent to the projection onto the FIR weight vector (since the weight vector is effectively the impulse response). But unlike the linear combiner, the impulse response of the context PE is restricted to a decaying exponential. The value of the PE output $y(n)$ becomes a function of the feedback parameter μ. When μ varies, the relative position between the impulse response vector and the input vector changes. We conclude that the feedback parameter has the ability to control how much of the past is retained at the context PE output. But note that the context PE is restricted to a lowpass filter, while the delay-line PE with the weights to the next layer may implement a FIR filter of arbitrary type. There are some more subtle differences. Selecting μ effectively changes the size of the projection space and orientation of the projection.

Projection with the Context PE

The projection implemented by the context PE cannot be analyzed in finite-dimension vector spaces, since the impulse response is infinite. However, we can approximately study it, taking into consideration that there is a finite effective memory depth given by $1/\mu$. Using this approximation the context PE can be interpreted as a projection on a linear manifold of size int$(1/\mu)$.

The number of degrees of freedom of this projection is nevertheless very different from the delay line. In the delay line the bases are the past values of the input. The output is constructed by weighting the values of each basis with the filter coefficients to obtain a direction. We have as many coefficients as bases to choose the direction of the projection.

In the case of the context PE a similar model can be used to analyze the projection operated by the system, but the details are different. The bases can still be considered the previous samples, but now the weighting is not independent from axis to axis; it is fixed by the value of the feedback coefficient. The most recent past sample is weighted by $1 - \mu$, two samples in the past by $(1 - \mu)^2$, and so on. There is no flexibility to choose the values of the filter coefficients independently. This means that the projection vector is always biased toward the first basis, where the weights are larger. Obviously, this limits the projection directions that can be created with the context PE. The context PE is able to create projections that are only lowpass filters of the input.

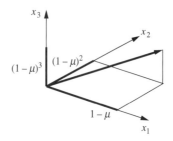

The projection vector always exists in the first quadrant. The direction approaches the bisector of the first quadrant when μ approaches 0, and the projection space dimension is very large (since the effective dimension is $1/\mu$). The context PE is therefore practically equivalent to the linear combiner with all weights equal to one, which we identified before as a lowpass filter.

In the other extreme of μ close to 1, the projection approaches the first projection axis (since the largest weight is associated with the sample $n - 1$, and the geometric ratio is close to zero), which is able to represent the input without error in large-dimensional spaces, but the size of the projection space is very small, since it is 1-D (just the present sample). Hence there is a clear trade-off between the size of the projection space and the resolution of the representation.

The conclusion of this analysis is the following. With the context PE we do not need to consider the projection space, since we control the location of the projection vector directly (i.e., this system is single-input, single-output). However, we can still analyze the projection as in the case of the linear combiner, but now there is only one free parameter that controls the direction of the projection and the effective size of the memory space at the same time. The context PE is only able to create lowpass projections. Another important characteristic is that the size of the projection space is controlled by the free parameter.

10.6   DESIGN OF THE MEMORY SPACE

As we have seen in the section on memory PEs, there are basically two types of memory mechanisms: memory by delay and memory by feedback. We seek to find the most general linear delay operator (special case of the ARMA model) where the memory traces $y_k(n)$ would be recursively computed from the previous memory trace $y_{k-1}(n)$. This memory PE is the generalized feedforward memory PE (Figure 10-12). We can show that the defining relationship for the generalized feedforward memory PE is [Principe et al, 1993]

$$g_k(n) = g(n) * g_{k-1}(n) \qquad k \geq 1 \qquad \textbf{(10.7)}$$

where $*$ is the convolution operation, $g(n)$ is a causal time function, and k is the tap index. Since this is a recursive equation, we have to provide a value for $g_0(n)$

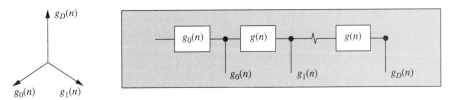

FIGURE 10-12   The generalized feedforward structure

independently. In the Z-domain Eq. 10.7 reads

$$G_k(z) = G(z)G_{k-1}(z) = G_0(z)G^k(z) \tag{10.8}$$

where k is the stage in the cascade and we are denoting transforms by capital letters. This relationship means that the next memory trace is constructed from the previous memory trace by convolution with the same function $g(n)$, the memory kernel yet unspecified. Different choices of $g(n)$ provide different choices for the projection space axes.

When we apply the input $x(n)$ to the generalized feedforward memory PE, the tap signals $y_k(n)$ become

$$y_k(n) = g(n) * y_{k-1}(n) \qquad k \geq 1 \tag{10.9}$$

the convolution of $y_{k-1}(n)$ with the memory kernel. For $k = 0$ we have

$$y_0(n) = g_0(n) * x(n) \tag{10.10}$$

where $g_0(n)$ may be specified separately. The projection $\hat{x}(n)$ of the input signal is obtained by linearly weighting the tap signals according to

$$\hat{x}(n) = \sum_{k=0}^{D} w_k y_k(n) \tag{10.11}$$

as shown in Figure 10-13.

The most obvious choice for the basis is to use the past samples of the input signal $x(n)$ directly, that is, the kth tap signal becomes $y_k(n) = x(n - k)$. From Eq. 10.9 it is easy to show that this choice corresponds to

$$g(n) = \delta(n - 1) \tag{10.12}$$

and we are back to the delta function operator used in the tap delay line [in this case $g_0(n)$ is also a delta function $\delta(n)$]. The memory depth is strictly controlled by D; that is,

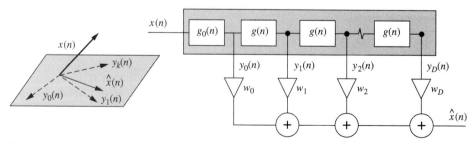

FIGURE 10-13 The memory filter created by the generalized feedforward memory PE

the memory traces store the past D samples of the input. The TDNN uses exactly this choice of basis.

The context PE equation in our notation is

$$y_0(n) = (1 - \mu)y_0(n - 1) + \mu x(n) \tag{10.13}$$

where $1 - \mu$ is the feedback parameter. It is easy to show that we can write

$$y_0(n) = \mu(1 - \mu)^n * x(n) \tag{10.14}$$

When compared with Eq. 10.10, the context PE becomes a special case of a single-tap ($D = 1$) generalized feedforward structure with

$$g_0(n) = \mu(1 - \mu)^n \tag{10.15}$$

and $y_0(n)$, the memory trace, becomes a processed version through convolution of the input samples.

10.7 THE GAMMA MEMORY PE

The gamma memory PE is a special case of the generalized feedforward memory PE where

$$g(n) = \mu(1 - \mu)^n \qquad n \geq 1 \tag{10.16}$$

and $g_0(n) = \delta(n)$. Figure 10-14 shows the block diagram for the gamma memory PE. The gamma memory is basically a cascade of lowpass filters with the same time constant $1 - \mu$. As can be seen from Figure 10-14, when the number of stages $D = 1$, the gamma memory defaults to the context unit, and when the feedback parameter $\mu = 1$, the gamma memory becomes the tap delay line [de Vries and Principe 1992]. As a result, the gamma memory contains as special cases the context PE unit and the delay

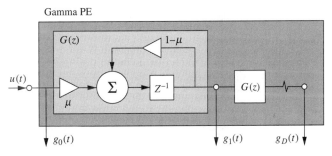

FIGURE 10-14 The gamma memory PE

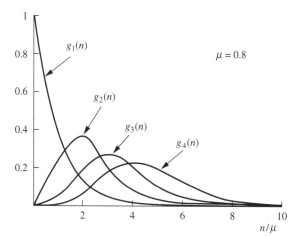

FIGURE 10-15   Impulse response of the gamma kernel from $k = 1$ to $k = 4$ for $\mu = 0.7$

line PE used in TDNN or in the FIR synapses. Hence the gamma memory appears as a unifying structure for the most common connectionist memories.

Figure 10-15 shows the family of impulse responses from the input to tap k in the gamma memory PE, which is mathematically given by

$$g_k(n) = \binom{n-1}{k-1}\mu^k(1-\mu)^{n-k} \qquad n \geq k, k \geq 1 \tag{10.17}$$

These functions are discrete versions of the integrands of the gamma function, hence the name given to the memory PE. They form a complete basis in L_2 space (i.e., we can approximate a finite energy signal arbitrarily closely as a weighted sum of these functions). In the context of memory structures, they can be interpreted as impulse responses of the memory PE from the input to the different taps. These impulse responses peak at k/μ when $k > 0$.

In the frequency domain Eq. 10.17 can be written as

$$G_k(z, \mu) = \prod_{i=1}^{k}\left(\frac{\mu z^{-1}}{1 - (1-\mu)z^{-1}}\right)i \tag{10.18}$$

Alternatively, the tap signals of the gamma memory can be interpreted as lowpass filtered versions (memory traces) of the input. The filters are all equal, with a pole at $z_p = 1 - \mu$. The transfer function from the input to the kth tap thus has a pole of multiplicity k. This means that the memory traces for deeper taps correspond to progressively filtered versions of the input. Signals are therefore progressively more delayed but also more filtered.

An important property of this family is that the time axis is scaled by the parameter μ, which means that there is a change in time scale from the input to the memory traces (uniform time warping). When this parameter is adapted with the information of the output mean square error, the neural system can choose the best time scale to represent the input signal information. The memory depth and resolution for the gamma memory are respectively

$$M = \frac{D}{\mu} \quad \text{and} \quad R = \mu \tag{10.19}$$

The gamma memory has the powerful property of decoupling the memory depth M from the order of the memory D. This is a very important property that is not shared by the delay line. Just consider that a given application requires a memory of 100 samples, but three free parameters are sufficient to model the memory traces. A tap delay line will need 100 taps and equivalently 100 parameters. This is inefficient, because we know only three are sufficient. During adaptation in a perfect world, the system must discover this and set 97 weights to zero. In reality, noise may make all the parameters different from zero, which will produce poor performance.

The context PE is able to decouple the memory depth from the free parameters of the system, but it can only model one of the modes of the input since it has a single parameter (projection to a one-dimensional space). The gamma PE produces a D-dimensional space to represent the input, which is much more powerful. The gamma PE is more versatile than the tap delay line PE because there is an extra parameter in the representation that controls the time axis scale. This means that the memory PE can represent in D taps N samples into the past ($N > D$); that is, the dimensionality of the input space is reduced when the gamma kernel is used to build the memory filter. Hence the gamma PE normally leads to a much more parsimonious representation of time information.

It is important to remember that recursive memories may become unstable. The stability of the gamma memory PE is guaranteed by limiting the value of the feedback parameter μ to values $0 < \mu < 2$.

10.7.1 The Gamma Filter

The linear topology weighting the taps of the gamma memory creates a very interesting filter called the *gamma filter* (Figure 10-16) [Principe et al. 1993]. The gamma filter has a feedforward topology, but it is an IIR filter with a multiple pole at $z = 1 - \mu$. The gamma filter is very similar to the linear combiner in the sense that it creates a projection space of size equal to the dimensionality of the filter and whose output is the linear projection onto the weight vector (which exists in the projection space). However, the gamma filter has several important advantages.

The bases are no longer the input signal and its delayed versions, but are the convolution of the input with the gamma bases. These bases decouple the memory depth from the memory resolution, unlike the linear combiner. This has potential importance in system identification for real-world systems, which tend to have very long (exponentially decaying) impulse responses. In such cases the gamma filter is able to provide a smaller fitting error than the linear combiner for a given filter size.

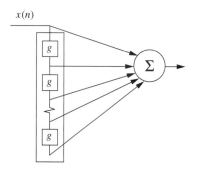

FIGURE 10-16 The gamma filter

Moreover, with the gamma filter the output MSE becomes a function of the μ parameter; that is, under the framework of adaptation the gamma filter has the ability to choose the best compromise between depth and resolution for the task at hand. It does this without any topological modification (as would be required with the tap delay line) simply by changing the feedback parameter. Unfortunately, the performance surface is nonconvex, so the search can be caught in local minima. The adaptation of the gamma-filter feedback parameter will be explained in the next chapter.

Gamma Filters as an Extension of Wiener Filters

The gamma filter can be considered as an extension to the famous Wiener filter. Let us define the cost as $J = E\{e^2(n)\}$, where $E\{.\}$ is the expectation operator. Let us call the D-tap vector $x(n) = [x_0(n), \ldots, x_{D-1}(n)]^T$ and the weight vector $\mathbf{w} = [w_0, \ldots, w_{D-1}]^T$. Therefore

$$J = E\{d^2(n)\} + \mathbf{w}^T \mathbf{R} \mathbf{w} - 2\mathbf{p}^T \mathbf{w}$$

where $\mathbf{R}$ and $\mathbf{p}$ are, respectively, the autocorrelation function of the tap signals and the cross-correlation vector between the tap signals and the desired response. Note that the input in the linear combiner is effectively replaced by the tap signals. The goal of adaptation is to find the minimum of J in the space of the D weights and μ. Taking the partial derivatives with respect to the weights and μ, we obtain the optimal filter weights as

$$\begin{cases} \mathbf{R}\mathbf{w} = \mathbf{P} \\ \mathbf{w}^T[\mathbf{R}_\mu \mathbf{w} - 2\mathbf{p}_\mu] = 0 \end{cases} \tag{10B.1}$$

where

$$\mathbf{R}_\mu = \frac{\partial \mathbf{R}}{\partial \mu} = 2E\left\{ \mathbf{x}(n) \frac{\partial \mathbf{x}^T(n)}{\partial \mu} \right\}$$

and

$$\mathbf{P}_\mu = \frac{\partial \mathbf{P}}{\partial \mu} = E\left\{ d(n)\frac{\partial \mathbf{x}(n)}{\partial \mu} \right\}$$

Note that the first equation in Eq. 10B.1 is the same as the Wiener-Hopf equation for the linear combiner. The difference once again is that the autocorrelation is not of the input but of the tap signals. The extra scalar condition is a result of the extra parameter in the gamma filter, and as we discussed, it represents the optimal memory depth for the application. Although the gamma kernels have infinite extent, they can be computed exactly in the frequency domain (provided that $x(n)$ has a computable Fourier transform). Equation 10B.1 has a form that applies to all the generalized feedforward filters described by Eq. 10.7.

NEUROSOLUTIONS EXAMPLE 10.10

Gamma filter for system identification

This example presents the system identification problem solved in Chapter 9 with the linear combiner. As we have shown, the delay line is a special case of the gamma filter when $\mu = 1$, so if we start with $\mu = 1$, we are mimicking the linear combiner. This is an important case, because we can see what we gain by using the gamma memory instead of the more conventional delay line. The gamma memory PE is shown in the figure; remember that now it has one parameter, which is the feedback parameter (μ).

Gamma Axon

Run the example with $\mu = 1$ and write down the error. Now enter different values, $\mu = 0.8, 0.6, 0.4, 0.2$, and see how the MSE changes. You will see that for this problem $\mu = 0.4$ provides the smallest error. The beauty of the gamma memory is that it allows the same topology to provide different projection spans, which is impossible to do with the tap delay line. For gamma memory the bases are a convolution of the input with the kernel $g(n)$, while for the tap delay line they are simply the delayed versions of the input. Notice that for this problem the difference in terms of MSE is appreciable.

> How can we decrease the error with the linear combiner? The solution is to increase the size of the tap delay line (the filter order). For this problem the required memory depth is $3/0.4 \approx 7$ samples (Eq. 10-18), so let us try a seventh-order FIR and see the results. As we can expect, this linear combiner works better, since it has longer memory depth (and more coefficients, which is not always better under noisy conditions). But the issue is that we have to guess a priori the size of the memory. Try a sixth-order FIR and see that the results are much worse than the seventh-order FIR.

10.8 TIME-LAGGED FEEDFORWARD NETWORKS

A time-lagged feedforward network (TLFN) is a feedforward arrangement of memory PEs and nonlinear PEs (the TDNN is an example of a TLFN). The short-term memory in TLFNs can be of any type and distributed in any layer. The advantage of TLFNs is that they share some of the nice properties of feedforward neural networks (such as trivial stability), but they can capture the information present in the input time signals. In this section we study a special case of TLFNs called *focused TLFNs*.

10.8.1 Focused TLFNs

In the focused TLFN the memory PEs are restricted to the input layer (Figure 10-17). The overall input-output mapping created by a focused TLFN is decomposed in two stages: the memory PE layer, that is, a linear time-representation stage, and a nonlinear mapper between the representation layer and the decision (output) space, which is *static but nonlinear*. Let us analyze the function of this network when all the elements are trained to minimize the output (Figure 10-18).

The representation stage finds the best projection of the input signal onto an intermediate projection space. This search is directed by the backpropagated error, which is equivalent to an implicit desired signal at the output of the representation stage. We can therefore use the Kolmogorov interpretation to say that, with the optimal weights, the

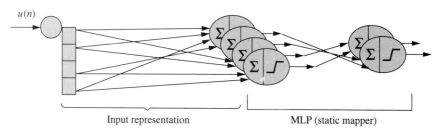

FIGURE 10-17 Single-input focused TLFN

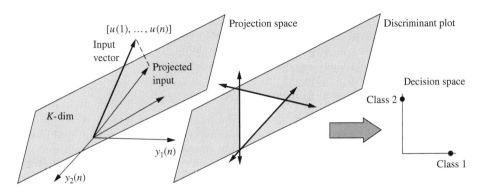

FIGURE 10-18 Projection of the input $u(n)$ and the nonlinear mapping produced by the MLP

output of the representation stage is the orthogonal projection of the input signal onto the projection space. The representation stage is exploring in an optimal way (through linear filtering) the spectral differences embedded in the time series patterns.

In TLFN architectures the mapping stage is a feedforward neural network, such as the MLP (or RBF). The MLP inputs are the outputs of the memory filters. Hence the space where the nonlinear mapping takes place has bases created by the hidden PE outputs that can be interpreted as the outputs of the memory filters. The number of bases is given by the number of memory filters.

The MLP places its discriminant functions in the projection space to achieve the desired processing goal. Normally, the goal is the minimization of an error in the decision (output) space. Note, however, that the weights of both the representation and mapping layers are trained together, so the user has no direct control on the projection space.

In this topology the dimension of the projection space (the number of memory filters) and the number of input PEs of the MLP are normally coupled together. There is no reason to couple the size of the space to the number of hidden PEs, as we saw in Chapter 3. We can decouple the number of axes from the number of hidden PEs by explicitly including in the topology the output of the memory filters as an extra layer of linear PEs, as we show in the following example.

NEUROSOLUTIONS EXAMPLE 10.11

Increasing versatility for TLFN architectures

We can separate the number of FIRs from the number of hidden PEs by explicitly including a layer of linear Axons and connecting them to the MLP with a Synapse (with fixed weights of 1).

With this arrangement we can show and control the effect of each part (representation or decision) in the mapping. The size of the decision space is controlled by the number of memory filters, while the number of discriminant functions is controlled by the number of PEs in the hidden layer.

Remember that the Scatter Plot shows us the pattern space. This is where the MLP is going to draw its decision surface. But the difficulty of the task is that the projections are also changing, since the weights of the memory filters are being adapted. Overall, the system tries to minimize the number of errors in the classification and moves the projections so that they are easy to classify with linear discriminant functions. Notice, however, that all the action occurs around the origin, so the order of the filter counts, as well as the number of PEs.

10.8.2 Focused TLFNs as Function Approximators

In Chapter 5 we developed the idea that neural networks are function approximators. At that time we mentioned only the special cases of the linear regressor and the classifier. In Chapter 9 we presented this same interpretation for the adaptive linear combiner. By separating the function of the delay line and the regressor, we showed that the linear combiner does *function approximation in the signal space,* and in this regard it is equivalent to the linear regressor.

Here we revisit the same topic for TLFNs. We submit that the previous perspective of dividing the function of focused TLFNs into signal representation and nonlinear mapping is very general and very productive. Applying this interpretation to the focused TDNN, we can immediately conclude that the focused TDNN is *a universal function approximator in the signal space.* In fact, the delay line produces a representation-preserving mapping onto the signal space (an embedding provided that the size of the delay line is large enough; see the following box on Takens' Embedding Theorem), and the MLP is able to approximate arbitrarily complex functions in the newly created signal space. Sandberg [1997a] proved this statement mathematically. The demonstration basically states that the focused TDNN can approximate arbitrary time-invariant mappings that have a finite region of support. Other TLFNs share the same property of the TDNN, as we discuss later.

Takens' Embedding Theorem

Takens proved that some properties (dynamic invariants) of the dynamic system that produced the time series can be preserved if we transform the time series into a sufficiently large reconstruction space; N, the size of the space, should be at least $2M + 1$, where M is the number of degrees of freedom of the dynamic system. He proposed that the point coordinates of the reconstructed trajectory be read as N-tuples of the time series. For instance, for a reconstruction in a 3-D space, consecutive triples of the time series should be read at a time, with the first time series sample being the x coordinate of the first point in the reconstruction space, the second sample the y coordinate, the 3rd sample the z coordinate, the fourth sample the x coordinate of the second point, and so on (see the following figure). When the points of the reconstructed space are connected, a trajectory is found from which properties of the original dynamic system can be estimated (such as dimension and Lyapunov exponents). This means that some of the important dynamic properties of the original signal are preserved in this reconstruction.

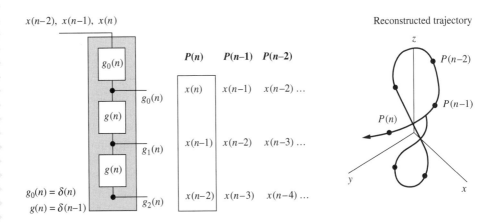

A powerful aspect of this theory is that the Takens embedding is naturally implemented by generalized feedforward structures. In fact, a delay line with three taps provides $x(n)$, $x(n-1)$, and $x(n-2)$, which are exactly the coordinates needed to reconstruct the points of the trajectory in the reconstruction space.

This alternative view of memory structures is very enlightening, because we can see that the PE that receives the output of the memory filter is effectively working with the trajectory in state space, that is, it is accessing the dynamic information. At least as a first approximation, this methodology helps us set the size N of the memory filter as twice the size of the dimension of the dynamical system that produced the time series.

The dimension of the dynamic system can be estimated from the time series using, for instance, the *correlation dimension algorithm* [Abarbanel 1996]. But unfortunately, there is still a free delay parameter Δ in Takens' embedding theorem that is unspecified. Its function is basically to uncorrelate the samples in time as much as possible. If Δ is not set right, the training can be very slow. We can experiment with the selection of Δ by changing the number of delays between the tap outputs.

Note that Takens' embedding theorem is a mathematical formulation of the ideas of signal space and reconstruction space that were presented in Chapter 9. It shows that the signal trajectory can preserve information about the dynamics of the system that produced the time series.

The arbitrary mapping capability of the focused TDNN is very important because it makes this neural topology highly suited for function approximation involving time signals, extending to time the universal approximation results of the MLP and RBFs in vector spaces. As we discussed in Chapter 9, function approximation in time is what engineers call system identification. Therefore we can understand the reason why the focused TDNN outperformed the linear combiner for system identification and time series prediction.

Nonlinear System Identification with Neural Networks

System identification is a very important application in engineering. Very often we are interested in modeling the input-output relationship of an unknown plant. We saw in Chapter 9 that this problem is a practical application of function approximation. In fact, we can consider the output of the system $d(n)$ as a fixed but unknown function of $x(n)$, that is, $d(n) = f(x(n))$. The role of the model is to approximate the function $f(.)$ by using a set of bases that are defined by the topology of the model system.

The linear combiner implements a set of linear bases, so we are effectively doing function approximation with a (moving-average) linear system. We covered other possibilities in Chapter 9, but we restricted our attention to linear bases. In this chapter we relax this constraint and work with nonlinear systems of the TLFN class. With TLFNs we can use the same block diagram (Figure 9.24 is copied here for reference) but develop nonlinear models of the unknown plant.

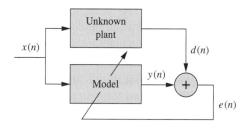

In nonlinear moving-average (NMA) modeling, the output of the model is a nonlinear function of its input:

$$y(n + 1) = f[x(n), x(n - 1), \ldots, x(n - k + 1)] \tag{10B.2}$$

This equation states that the model is fundamentally feedforward. A TDNN is effectively an NMA model of the plant when it is used as the model. The TDNN is a nonlinear version of the linear combiner and an alternative to Volterra models (which are also NMA).

In nonlinear autoregressive NAR (models) the output of the model is given by

$$y(n + 1) = f[y(n), y(n - 1), \ldots, y(n - k + 1)] \tag{10B.3}$$

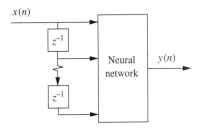

In this equation the next output is a function of the past values of the output. This type of model is used in prediction, where we train an NMA model, but due to the block-diagram form of prediction, we are fitting an NAR model to the data.

In general we use a nonlinear autoregressive with external input (NARX) model for system identification:

$$y(n + 1) = f[y(n), y(n - 1), \ldots, y(n - k + 1), x(n)]$$ **(10B.4)**

In other words, we drive our TLFN with a signal (also fed to the plant) and the past outputs of the TLFN.

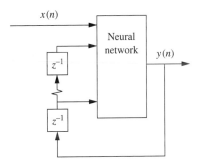

The nonlinear autoregressive moving-average (NARMA) is the most general class of nonlinear models, and it is a blend of the two previous types:

$$y(n + 1) = f[y(n), \ldots, y(n - 1), y(n - k + 1), x(n), x(n - 1), \ldots, x(n - j)]$$ **(10B.5)**

That is, we drive the TLFN with its past outputs (global feedback) and with the input and its delayed versions.

A fundamental aspect of system identification is to understand when a given model should be used, given the knowledge that we have about the plant. In terms of the function approximation paradigm, this means that we have to choose the basis appropriately. A

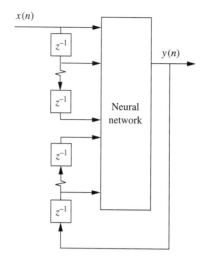

related problem is how we are going to parameterize our nonlinear models. Once again, the NARMA (Eq. 10B.5) seems to be a very general parameterization, but in some cases simpler and easier to train parameterizations may exist.

10.8.3 Focused TLFNs Built from Context PEs

When the memory of a focused TLFN is a delay line, we obtain the focused TDNN. We already discussed the focused TDNN, and we have seen the power of such networks. But we saw that the tap delay line was not the only type of memory PE. Let us examine the topology of Figure 10-19.

The topology has an input layer of context PEs followed by an MLP. The first layer of input PEs can be also thought of as a representational layer for time information. The context PEs remember the past values of the input indirectly because their output is

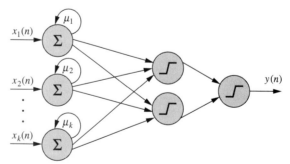

FIGURE 10-19 MLP with an input layer of context PEs (focused architecture)

a weighted average of the present and past inputs. The hidden-layer PEs nonlinearly combine this information to produce the desired output. This topology is also a *focused topology* and implements a *static nonlinear function* of the present and past of the input. The focused topology of Figure 10-19 is a recurrent neural network, but notice that the recurrency is *local to the PE*. One of the advantages of locally recurrent neural networks is that we can judge the stability of the system by constraining the value of the local feedback parameters so that the local PE is stable. If local stability is enforced, the global system will be stable.

The goal of the following examples is to solve the same three classes of problems that were presented for the focused TDNN with the focused TLFN built from context PEs. We will show that the TLFN produces acceptable results, although the context memory structure is less versatile than the linear combiner.

NEUROSOLUTIONS EXAMPLE 10.12

Phoneme classification with focused TLFNs (context PEs)

This example solves the phoneme classification problem of Example 10.3 with a focused TLFN built from context PEs. Run the network and verify the performance. Change the context PE parameter and observe its effect on performance.

NEUROSOLUTIONS EXAMPLE 10.13

Nonlinear system identification with focused TLFNs (context PEs)

This example is the system identification problem solved in Example 10.4 with the TDNN. Here we apply the focused TLFN to solve the problem. If we try the straight architecture with the default time constant of 0.9, we find that it fails. The reason is that for this system identification case we have a single input, and so the context PE is limited to lowpass-filtering this input with a single time constant. The MLP is unable to extract the necessary information to find the mapping.

We can help the system if we provide several views of the input with different time constants, which can be easily done with a layer of context PEs with different feedback parameters. To implement this modification, go to the Matrix Editor on top of the context PE and enter values between 0 and 1 for each PE. Observe that, in fact, the focused TLFN now works as well as the TDNN does. The lesson is that creating a space where signals differ in their frequency content is very useful for function approximation. We saw in Chapter 5 that having more bases helps the reconstruction. The same is true here. A single context PE gives you a single view of the trajectory. Many context PEs provide a multispectral view of the same trajectory, which captures much more information. This reasoning will be expanded later for designing the memory space.

NEUROSOLUTIONS EXAMPLE 10.14

Nonlinear prediction with focused TLFNs (context PEs)

This example is the prediction of the Mackey-Glass signal using a focused TLFN built from context PEs. As in the previous example, we have a single input, so we need to create a projection space to represent signals in time. We can do this by creating a layer of context PEs with different time constants.

Run the example and verify that for this problem the TDNN works slightly better. The context PEs are lowpass filters, so they smooth out the sharp discontinuities of the input signal. The approximation therefore suffers near the sharp transitions (peaks and troughs). We can expect this from the discussion on memory depth and memory resolution. The context PE increases one at the expense of the other. This compromise is nevertheless better than the delay line PE, where there is no compromise (the delay line always uses the highest resolution).

10.8.4 Focused TLFNs with Gamma Memories

The gamma memory can be used as the first layer of the focused architecture, yielding another type of focused TLFN that has been called the *focused gamma neural network*. Sandberg [1997b] also showed that the focused gamma network is a universal function approximator. Just as the gamma filter has advantages over the linear combiner, the gamma network has several advantages over the focused TDNN. Experience has shown that the gamma network is able to provide a smaller output error than a focused TDNN with the same number of parameters in identification of plants with a long region of support (as is the case for most real plants). Another interesting characteristic of the gamma neural network is that it has the capability to produce a uniform warping of the time axis.

The following examples yield a one-to-one comparison of the TDNN with the gamma TLFN. Since the gamma memory for $\mu = 1$ defaults to a tap delay line, we can immediately see in the same Breadboard the change in performance between the two types of memory.

NEUROSOLUTIONS EXAMPLE 10.15

Phoneme classification with a focused TLFN (gamma memory)

This example deals with the phoneme classification. We have replaced the tap delay line with a gamma memory. Remember that $\mu = 1$ defaults to the tap delay line, so we can obtain the performance of the TDNN. Run the network, which is set with $\mu = 0.5$ for the value of the gamma memory. Notice that it performs very well. This is a great example to see how the network is assigning internal resources, and when one output is correct, the others modify themselves to grab their own desired response.

Modify the gamma parameter to 1, and see that now the system has more difficulty solving the task and trains to a larger error. This tells us that longer memory depth is important for classifying phonemes, more important than high resolution (which is provided by $\mu = 1$).

Just to see how well the network can solve this problem when optimized, let us substitute the output PE by a softmax nonlinearity. You have to decrease the step size to 0.05 and the momentum to 0.5. Run the network and see how perfect the classification is (remember that this is the training set, so this fact tells little about the overall accuracy in the task). The Softmax cleans the outputs because it guarantees that the sum of outputs has to be 1 (competition).

In classification applications, the Softmax should be the component of choice.

NEUROSOLUTIONS EXAMPLE 10.16

Nonlinear system identification with a focused TLFN (gamma memory)

The system identification example is also a good test of the gamma TLFN. Most real-world plants have long impulse responses, since they are typically IIR. We know that the TDNN has a memory that is FIR (the tap delay line), so for adequate modeling, long memories are necessary. But long tap delay lines mean many parameters, which make the TDNN overparameterized and reduces generalization. The answer is to use generalized feedforward memories such as the gamma. The gamma memory, because it is globally FIR but has an IIR kernel, can choose the appropriate memory depth with the selection of a single parameter. For the gamma, $D = K/\mu$, so for a fixed number of taps (K) we can increase D, the memory depth, by decreasing μ. Let us see how this helps for the nonlinear plant.

Start with $\mu = 1$ and write down the final MSE. Then enter $\mu = 0.7$ and let the system adapt. Note that the error now is smaller and the waveform is smoother. Experiment with more taps and find that the improvement as a function of μ is not as apparent.

NEUROSOLUTIONS EXAMPLE 10.17

Nonlinear prediction with a focused TLFN (gamma memory)

Finally, we show an example where the gamma memory does perform better than the TDNN. Let us do nonlinear prediction on the Mackey-Glass time series. The waveform, if you recall, has a great deal of detail (high frequencies), mainly at the extremes (peaks and troughs). The gamma basis with small μ emphasizes depth at the expense of resolution. The MG30 does not require a long depth, but it needs the detail to follow the high frequencies in the waveform.

Let us start with a tap delay line of 5 and $\mu = 0.7$. Write down the error, and repeat the experiment with $\mu = 1$. You can see that the error is smaller for the TDNN.

This does not necessarily mean that the gamma memory is worse for predicting the MG30. Suppose that we reduce the memory to $K = 3$ taps. Now, with $\mu = 1$, the prediction is poor, since there is not enough depth. Now if we select $\mu = 0.5$, the error improves. Even for this application, depth is important for discovering the correct mapping.

One of the issues that you may have noticed is that we have to manually enter the value of μ, and there is no guarantee that it is the best value for minimizing the MSE. In the next chapter we present a method to adapt μ based on gradient descent using the output MSE. In such cases the gamma memory always provides the best compromise between depth and resolution.

There are several other delay operators that can be defined to create TLFNs, each exploring differently the information contained in the input signal spectrum. Effectively, each delay operator establishes a different basis to project the time signal.

More Versatile Memories

There are several linear operators fitting our definition of a generalized feedforward memory PE that can be used as short-term memory mechanisms for neural networks. We review here two useful cases, but the choice of the most appropriate memory PE for a given application remains an open question.

A set of bases intimately related to the gamma functions is built with the Laguerre functions. The Laguerre functions are an orthogonal span of the gamma space, which means that the information provided by both memories is the same. The Z-transform of the Laguerre functions is given by

$$L_i(z, \mu) = \sqrt{1 - (1 - \mu)^2} \frac{(z^{-1} - (1 - \mu))^{i-1}}{(1 - (1 - \mu)z^{-1})^i} \qquad i = 1, 2, \ldots \qquad \textbf{(10B.6)}$$

It can be shown that the Laguerre functions can be recursively computed, following the definition of the generalized feedforward structures given in Eq. 10.7. In fact, the Laguerre PE is a cascade of a lowpass filter with impulse response

$$g_0(n) = \sqrt{1 - (1 - \mu)^2}(1 - \mu)^n \qquad \textbf{(10B.7)}$$

followed by a cascade of all-pass functions with a kernel given by

$$g(n) = (1 - \mu)^n + (1 - \mu)^{n+2} \qquad \textbf{(10B.8)}$$

It is easier to write the equations in the Z domain, as

$$L_i(z, \mu) = G_{i-1}(z) \frac{\sqrt{1 - (1 - \mu)^2}}{1 - (1 - \mu)z^{-1}} \qquad G_{i-1}(z) = \prod_{j=1}^{i-1} \left(\frac{z^{-1} - (1 - \mu)}{1 - (1 - \mu)z^{-1}} \right) i \qquad \textbf{(10B.9)}$$

It is interesting to analyze the difference between the Laguerre and gamma memory traces: the gamma memory PE attenuates the signals at each tap because it is a cascade of leaky integrators with the same time constant. The Laguerre memory PE has a front-end lowpass filter, but the next stages are all-pass filters, each all-pass filter places a zero in the mirror location (with respect to the unit circle) of the pole of the previous stage and includes a pole of their own at the same pole location. This topology effectively creates a basis using a Gram-Schmidt orthogonalization of the tap signals after the lowpass filter, which we know produces an orthogonal basis when the input is an impulse (or white noise). The Laguerre PE thus does not attenuate the tap signals in amplitude but still delays the signal components. This leads to a set of oscillating basis functions. The following figure compares the response of the Laguerre and the Gamma PE to an impulse, which produces the set of Laguerre and gamma bases, respectively.

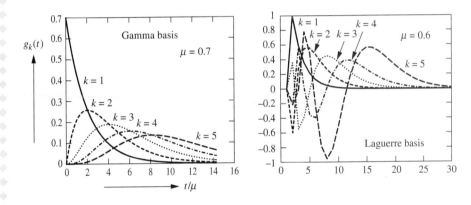

The advantage of the Laguerre PE is that the tap signals (the bases) are obtained by convolving the lowpass-filtered input with an orthogonal set of functions (the all-pass functions), so the basis is less correlated and the adaptation speed becomes faster, especially when μ is close to 0 or 2. The Laguerre memory is still very easy to compute and has only one free parameter, μ. The all-pass function is the closest realizable analog-circuit implementation to the ideal delay operator.

The gamma memory PE has a multiple pole that can be adaptively moved along the real Z-domain axis; that is, the gamma memory can implement only lowpass ($0 < \mu < 1$) or highpass ($1 < \mu < 2$) transfer functions. The highpass transfer function creates an extra ability to model fast-moving signals by alternating the signs of the samples in the gamma PE (the impulse response for $1 < \mu < 2$ has alternating signs). But with a single, real

Laguerre PE

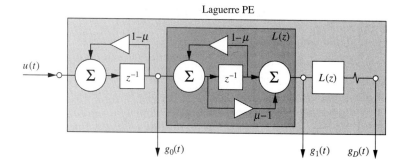

parameter the adaptation is unable to move the poles to complex locations is the z domain values. Two conditions may require a memory structure with complex poles: first, when the information relevant for the signal-processing task appears in periodic bursts, and second, when the input signal is corrupted by periodic noise. A memory structure with adaptive complex poles can successfully cope with these two conditions by selecting the time intervals where the information is concentrated (or the time intervals where the noise is concentrated).

The following figure shows the gamma II kernel, implementation.

Gamma II PE

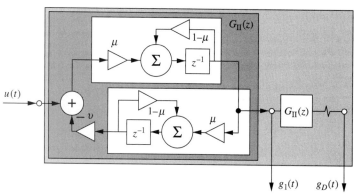

In the Z domain the transfer function of the gamma II kernel is

$$G_{II}(z) = \frac{\mu(1 - v)[z - (1 - \mu)]}{[z - (1 - \mu)]^2 + v\mu^2}$$

(10B.10)

which corresponds in the time domain to a kernel given by

$$g(n) = r^n \cos(w_0 n)$$

where $\quad r = \sqrt{(1 - \mu)^2 + v\mu^2} \quad$ and $\quad w_0 = \tan^{-1} \frac{\mu \sqrt{v}}{1 - \mu}$

(10B.11)

Notice that for stability, the parameters μ and ν must obey the condition $0 < \mu(1 + \nu) < 2$ and $\mu > 0$. Complex poles are obtained for $\nu > 0$.

In terms of versatility, the gamma II has a pair of free complex poles, the gamma has a pole restricted to the real line in the Z domain, and the tap delay line has the pole set at the origin of the Z domain ($z = 0$). A multilayer perceptron equipped with an input memory layer with the gamma II memory structure implements a nonlinear mapping on an ARMA model of the input signal. The following table shows a comparison of the characteristics of the memory PEs.

	Tap delay	Gamma	Laguerre	Gamma II
Depth (k taps)	k	k/μ	no closed form	no closed form
Resolution	1	μ	no closed form	no closed form
Stability	Always	$0 < \mu < 2$	$0 < \mu < 2$	$0 < \mu(1 + \nu) < 2$
Filter	All-pass	Lowpass	Low/all-pass	Bandpass
Pole	0	$1 - \mu$	$1 - \mu$	r, w_0

10.8.5 How to Adapt the Focused TLFN

How can focused TLFNs be trained? We saw that focused TDNNs can be trained with static backpropagation, provided that a desired signal exists at each time step. But notice that the TDNN does not have adjustable parameters in the delay line, while other focused TLFNs, such as the one in Figure 10-14, have one parameter in the memory structures. If we preselect the value of the feedback parameter μ, static backpropagation can still be used because the adaptive part of the network is static. Even if the feedback parameter is changed manually or automatically during operation, this effect is equivalent to a change at the input, so the gradient computation for the feedforward network weights is still static. This is one of the advantages of the focused topologies and the reason for their name.

A word of caution is in order at this moment. The feedback parameter of these memories cannot be adapted correctly by the backpropagation algorithm discussed in Chapter 3. Moreover, if the recurrent connections occurred in the hidden layers, even if the recurrent parameter was kept constant, static backpropagation could not be used to train the weights between the input and the location of the recurrent PEs. The gradients would become time dependent, and the backpropagation algorithm covered in Chapter 3 would not be prepared to handle them. We will address these issues in the next chapter. For all these reasons, you can see the special niche occupied by the focused TLFN.

10.9   FOCUSED TLFNs BUILT FROM RBFs

Radial basis functions (RBFs) are the other alternative for creating universal mapping networks. RBFs were explained in Chapter 5, and they can substitute for the MLPs in

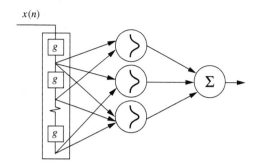

FIGURE 10-20 A focused TLFN built from a memory layer and an RBF network

the focused TLFNs. This type of focused TLFN is built from a memory-representation layer followed by an RBF, as shown in Figure 10-20.

The idea of the topology is the same as that of the TLFNs built with MLPs. The representation layer produces the embedding from the time series to the signal space. In the signal space the RBFs find the mapping to the desired response. Note, however, that the RBFs work directly in the signal space when the tap-delay line is used as the memory layer (there are no weights between the input and the RBF PEs). The gamma memory has an advantage here because it still provides a projection on the gamma basis. The RBF centers and variances should be adapted as discussed in Chapter 5.

One potential advantage of the RBFs is that once the centers and variances are established, the adaptation is linear in the parameters, so RBFs normally train much faster than MLPs. However, one potential disadvantage is that we may need many RBFs when the signal space is large. The gamma memory is particularly well suited as the memory for RBFs because it tends to decrease the size of the reconstruction space. For system identification many researchers do not adapt the centers and variances. Since the signal trajectory in general visits the full space (if the embedding dimension is correctly specified), placing the centers randomly or in a grid is commonly preferred. We are going to exemplify the performance of TLFNs built from RBFs in the same three problems we encountered before.

NEUROSOLUTIONS EXAMPLE 10.18

Phoneme recognition with a focused RBF-TLFN (gamma memory)

The first problem is temporal pattern recognition. We now have the memory structure feeding an RBF layer. Notice that the weights of this layer are used solely to establish the centers of the RBF network. Hence they are going to be trained in the unsupervised mode using competitive learning. Once the centers are established and the variances estimated, the second phase of training is to find the weights that best meet the class specifications.

Train the network and see that it does a good job of classifying the three phonemes. Modify the number of RBFs and the number of delays to see the impact on accuracy. RBFs must cover the representation space well, otherwise performance will be poor. Unlike the sigmoids, the RBF Gaussians are local, so they just "see" a small portion of the signal space. Hence we need many centers (here 100), and it is important to place them in areas that have data. Notice that with a delay line of 5 taps for 11 LPC coefficients we have a 55-dimensional space, which is very large. This is why the gamma memory is very useful for these networks; it can cover a given memory depth with many fewer taps, decreasing the size of the signal space. Include a gamma memory instead of the delay line and see that the performance is normally better.

NEUROSOLUTIONS EXAMPLE 10.19

Nonlinear system identification with a focused RBF-TLFN (gamma memory)

In this example we solve the system identification problem for the nonlinear system of Example 10.4. We start with the gamma memory instead of the tap delay line to decrease the size of the signal space.

The network is basically the same as before, except that now it is a single-input, single-output system. We again have the two phases of learning; first, unsupervised to place the centers of the RBFs and to estimate the variances, followed by the adaptation of the output weights. Run the network and observe that it works as well as or better than the TDNN case, with much faster training. Now you understand why this topology is attractive for real-time applications. You can compare the performance of the memory kernel (gamma versus tap delay line) by selecting $\mu = 1$ (tap delay line).

NEUROSOLUTIONS EXAMPLE 10.20

Nonlinear prediction with a focused RBF-TLFN (gamma memory)

This example implements a nonlinear predictor for the MG30 chaotic time series. The network is basically the same, here with 25 RBFs. Notice that the time series is well modeled even with a few RBFs, but notice that the extremes of the waves lack detail. This is the price we pay for using the gamma memory, since we are trading detail (resolution) for depth. In this case the fine detail of the time series requires more resolution than depth.

10.10 PROJECT: ITERATIVE PREDICTION OF CHAOTIC TIME SERIES

Neural networks are well suited for the prediction of time series produced by nonlinear models, which we call here *nonlinear time series.* The idea is to extend the prediction model discussed in Chapter 9. The block diagram of the linear combiner is replaced with a focused TLFN trained with backpropagation in a single-step prediction framework. One important consideration is to choose the size of the projection space appropriately. For predicting nonlinear time series produced by deterministic systems, Takens' embedding theorem can be used to help in this definition. Basically, the theorem states that we have to find the size of a reconstruction space where the trajectories do not cross. We can estimate the dimension of this space, but the algorithms are difficult to work with; see [Abarbanel 1997].

As an alternative, we can experiment with the size of the delay line and the value of the delay (i.e., multiple delays) using the simulator, as we experimented with the size of the MLP topology in Chapter 3. The results of nonlinear predictors frequently outperform the prediction with linear models, but both yield reasonable approximations.

Prediction can also be thought of as the first step toward *dynamic modeling,* where the overall goal is to identify the dynamic system that created the time series. Once the predictor is trained, a dynamic model can be obtained by feeding back the output into the input (delayed by one sample). This creates an autonomous system, as Figure 10-21 shows. Can the preceeding prediction methodology create a good dynamic model? Our model is considered good if it can create in autonomous mode a time series with the same characteristics as the original time series (see [Haykin and Principe 1998]).

When we attempt to use the linear system in autonomous mode, the results are disappointing, since the output quickly approaches zero (or oscillates). With the focused TDNN the response does not normally decay to zero but hardly ever resembles the original time series. How can we design improved dynamic models?

An important modification to the overall methodology of signal prediction is to introduce the concept of iterative prediction. Notice that until now we always used the time series as the input to the neural network. However, when we want to generate the time series from our trained model, we are using the most current output of the model as input (Figure 10-21). This arrangement is called *iterative prediction.* We first seed the predictor with one or more points in state space, compute the output, and feed it back to the input for a number of samples. Try this in NeuroSolutions, and experiment with

FIGURE 10-21 Iterative prediction for dynamic modeling

the parameters to see the effect in the training MSE and in the quality of the generated time series.

NEUROSOLUTIONS EXAMPLE 10.21

Iterative prediction with focused TLFNs with feedback

In this example we provide a little more detail to the problem of modeling a chaotic time series. This is important because neural networks are posed to play an important role in this area. We are going to demonstrate that not only can TLFNs predict the chaotic signal, as we saw in the previous examples, they can also learn the dynamics from the time series and produce a system that can generate the *same* signal. In a sense, they have identified the parameters of the system that produced the time series, and they can be used in place of the original dynamic system.

Signal generators are important, and those most widely used in engineering are the oscillators. But a linear system with constant parameters cannot autonomously generate waveforms more complex than a sinusoid. This is because the transient dynamics of a linear system go to either a point attractor or a limit cycle. The limit cycle produces the sinusoid.

Let us now consider the MG30. This is a very complex waveform. How can we build a system that produces such a waveform? There is a trivial way: Input white noise into a linear system and keep on adapting the parameters. This will provide a waveform very similar to the MG30, but notice that the source of complexity is in the white noise input. White noise potentially contains all waveforms, so by filtering, we can obtain the one we want.

The second more difficult way to generate the MG30 is to use a system *without* an external input. Such a system is called autonomous. Feeding the output of the system to itself creates a signal generator. Can we design an autonomous system that produces the MG30? We can immediately rule out linear systems. Hence we must have a nonlinear dynamic system. It turns out that dynamic neural networks can be taught to generate complex (even chaotic) time series such as the MG30. This is what we demonstrate in this example.

We start with the linear combiner. We can train it to a very small prediction error, but when we fix the weights and feed back the output to the input, the output decays to zero (or to a limit cycle). The autonomous dynamic regimes of a linear system are not very exciting.

Now let us do the same thing with the TDNN. We train it to a very small prediction error. Then we fix the weights and feed the output back to the input. Now the output resembles the MG30. In fact, the error (compared with the signal it has been trained with) is very small up to sample 50, and then the error increases (and depending on the training may go back down). But the two waveforms are visually very similar. Let us take an FFT of each to see that their spectra match almost exactly. We have created a system that behaves just like the MG30.

> The appeal of this method is that we never use the information about the equation. We just picked a time series and used it to train the TDNN. In principle, this technique can therefore be used to create synthetic models from real-world signals. This application is called *dynamic modeling*.
>
> Experiment with the size of the TDNN to discover when it fails to produce a waveform similar to the MG30.

10.11   CONCLUSIONS

This chapter brought together the two fundamental concepts of nonlinear topologies and time which were independently developed in Chapters 3 and 9, respectively. The MLP is a powerful mapper, but it works only with static patterns. On the other hand, the linear combiner can work with time signals, but its mapping ability is reduced since it can perform only linear approximations. Combining a memory structure with the MLP gave rise to the class of dynamic networks known as time-lagged feedforward networks (TLFNs).

TLFNs are powerful mappers and have the advantage that they can be trained with static backpropagation, provided that the memory layer is placed at the input, a topology called *focused*. However, static backpropagation cannot train the feedback connections that may be present in some TLFNs, so they have to be manually selected. The next chapter deals with the training of TLFNs and fully recurrent systems.

This chapter introduced the concept of the memory PE as a special PE configured to process time signals. In a sense, the memory PE brings the representation of time to the inside of the neural topology, with the advantage of internal (and hopefully better) control of time representations. We quantified the properties of memory PEs and gave the interpretation of the memory PE and its connection weights to the other network PEs as a filter.

We also presented the two fundamental connectionist memory mechanisms, memory by delay and memory by feedback, and showed that the gamma memory is a unifying principle in this perspective. However, the gamma memory can still be extended to other memory mechanisms that extract other information from the time series (the gamma II memories). This important chapter opens up the possibility of using nonlinear systems for time processing. The major hurdle that we still need to conquer is how to train arbitrary topologies built from memory PEs and nonlinear PEs.

10.12   EXERCISES

10.1   Can you see any advantage in bringing memory into the neural network topology?

10.2   Is there any difference between using the focused TDNN and applying a time window of the same size to the input data?

10.3 Experiment with Example 10.4. Increase the size of the linear system and see how it affects performance. You can also implement one of the preprocessors of Chapter 6 or 7 to see whether it helps the performance of the neural network.

10.4 Use Example 10.5 with the Lorenz time series. Experiment with the size of the delay line and the size of the MLP for better results. Present the learning curve. How can you decide whether the MSE is acceptable or not? Does the MSE normalized by the power of the input make sense to you?

10.5 From the point of view of digital signal processing, analyze the advantage of using a memory structure at the input of the M-P PE in Figure 10-5.

10.6 Compute the memory depth and resolution for a $D = 20$ tap delay line PE and for a context PE with $\mu = 0.01$. Provide two examples where you would prefer one over the other.

10.7 What do you gain over the tap delay line when you use a gamma memory? Make your point clear by analyzing a time series where the information is mixed over 25 samples, but only four parameters are sufficient to represent the system that created the time series.

10.8 State at least one disadvantage of the gamma memory by analyzing Figure 10-18. How could you compensate for it?

10.9 You should study Example 10.9 well because it provides an inside look at how a TLFN works. In particular, you should try to answer this question: In principle, the memory filters that separate the two regimes should be lowpass and highpass filters, but the solution found through adaptation is neither one. Can you explain why?

10.10 Provide an example for which the TLFNs are not a good mapping model. Explain your reasons.

10.11 State one advantage of the combination gamma-RBF over tap delay line–RBF, and of the combination tap delay line–RBF over tap delay line–MLP. Also provide a disadvantage for each combination.

10.12 Explain in your own words the difference between static networks and dynamic networks. Write a small essay about the difference for speech recognition.

10.13 NEUROSOLUTIONS EXAMPLES

10.14   CONCEPT MAP FOR CHAPTER 10

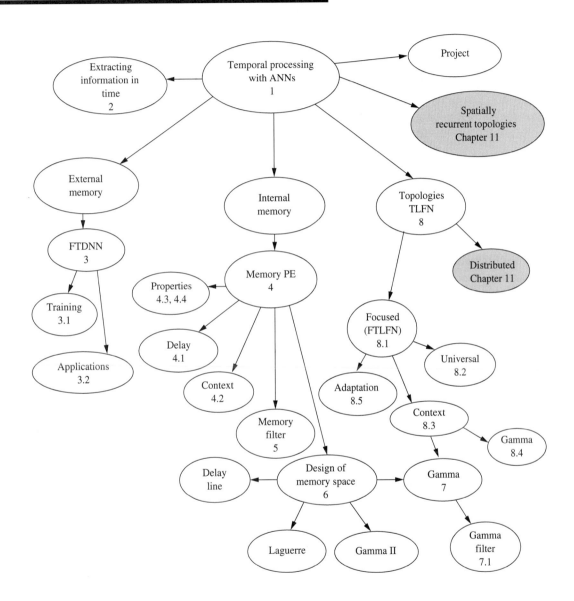

REFERENCES

Abarbanel, H., *Analysis of Observed Chaotic Data,* Springer, New York, 1996.

de Vries, B., and Principe, J., The gamma model: A new neural network model for temporal processing, *Neural Networks,* 5:565–576, 1992.

Haykin S., and Principe J., Dynamic modeling with neural networks, *IEEE Signal Processing Magazine,* 15 (3):66, 1998.

Principe, J., de Vries, B., and Olivieira, P., The gamma filter: A new class of adaptive IIR filters with restricted feedback, 41:649–656, 1993.

Sandberg, I. and Xu, L., Uniform approximation of multidimensional myopic maps, *IEEE Trans. on Circuits and Systems*, 44:477–485, 1997*a*.

Sandberg, I. and Xu, L. Uniform approximation and gamma neural networks, *Neural Networks,* 10:781–784, 1997*b*.

Waibel, A., Phoneme recognition using time delay neural networks, *IEEE Proc.*, ASSP-37:328–339, 1989.

Wan, E., Time series prediction using a network with internal delay lines. In *Time Series Prediction: Forecasting the future and understanding the past,* 195–217, Addison-Wesley, 1994.

TRAINING AND USING RECURRENT NETWORKS

The goal of this chapter is to introduce the following concepts:

- Why backpropagation cannot train recurrent systems
- Algorithm for backpropagation through time
- Distributed TLFNs
- Recurrent networks
- Hopfield's computational energy
- Grossberg's additive neural model
- Applications of recurrent neural networks

11.1 INTRODUCTION

In the previous chapter we were able to create time-lagged feedforward networks (TLFNs) that processed information over time and were easy to train. Basically, they could implement static (but arbitrary) mappings from the present input and its memory traces to the desired response. There is often a need to extend the network capabilities to time-dependent nonlinear mappings. This means that short-term memory mechanisms have to be brought inside the feedforward network topologies (TLFNs) or that the networks have to be made spatially recurrent, that is, recurrent connections must be created among some or all PEs. We call these spatially recurrent networks simply *recurrent networks.*

The complexities of these two solutions are very different. TLFNs have locally recurrent connections and can be made stable by enforcing the stability of the short-term memory mechanisms, while it is much more difficult to guarantee stability of recurrent networks. Moreover, TLFNs are easier to train than recurrent systems, so they are more practical. Lastly, we can still interpret how a TLFN is processing the information by combining our knowledge of MLPs with adaptive filters, while the complex interconnectivity of the recurrent system usually inhibits our ability to study the system.

You should have noticed how carefully we picked the focused TLFN topology so that we could still use the static backpropagation algorithm. This is no longer possible for distributed TLFNs nor for recurrent networks. One of the central issues that we have to address in this chapter is how to train recurrent networks. We start by extending static backpropagation to adapt systems with delays, that is, systems where the ordered list depends not only on the topology, as in Chapter 3, but also on the time order. This concept gives rise to the backpropagation-through-time (BPTT) algorithm, which trains recurrent networks with a segment of a time series. Learning a segment of a time series is called *trajectory learning.* This is the most general case for learning in time. BPTT is applied to train gamma networks, distributed TLFNs, and fully recurrent networks. We also study how recurrent systems are trained to memorize static patterns by extending static backpropagation to what has been called *fixed point learning.*

We also superficially study dynamic systems in terms of their fundamental definitions and topologies. An example of the insight gained with dynamics is Hopfield's interpretation of the computational energy of a recurrent neural system. We cover this view and see how it can be used to interpret a recurrent system with attractors as a pattern associator. We end the chapter (and the book) with a description of Freeman's model, which is a new class of information-processing system that is locally stable but globally chaotic.

Throughout the chapter we provide applications of time-lagged feedforward networks ranging among nonlinear system identification, nonlinear prediction, temporal pattern recognition, sequence recognition, and controls.

11.2 SIMPLE RECURRENT TOPOLOGIES

All the focused TLFNs studied in Chapter 10 implement static nonlinear mappings. Although focused TLFNs have been shown to be universal mappers, there are cases where the desired function is beyond the power of a reasonably sized, focused TLFN. We can easily imagine a sequence of input values that gives rise to two different outputs depending on the context. Either we have enough memory to span the full context, or the network will be unable to discover the mapping. Jordan and Elman proposed simple networks based on context PEs and network recurrency that are easy to train (because the feedback parameters are fixed) and accomplish the mapping with small topologies (Figure 11-1).

Note that both the Jordan and Elman nets have fixed feedback parameters and there is no recurrency in the input-output path. They can be approximately trained with straight backpropagation. Elman's context layer receives input from the hidden layer, while Jordan's context layer receives input from the output.

These systems are in principle more efficient than the focused architectures for encoding temporal information, since the "memory" is created by recurrent connections that span several layers; that is, memory is inside the network, so the input-output nonlinear mapping is *no longer static*. However, the Jordan and Elman networks are still

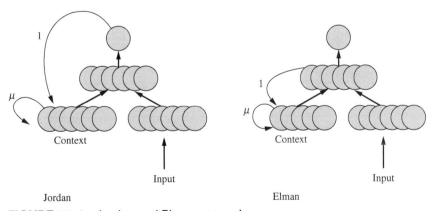

FIGURE 11-1 Jordan and Elman networks

special architectures that were derived to simplify their training. Notice that the outputs of the context layer can be thought of as external inputs (which are controlled by the network instead of by world events) so that there is no recurrency in the input-output path. Both systems have been utilized for sequence recognition and are sometimes called *sequential networks*. Jordan networks can even associate the same (fixed) input with several output sequences, depending on the context.

NEUROSOLUTIONS EXAMPLE 11.1

Jordan's network

We are going to use a data set with time dependencies. Suppose that we have nine items coded as amplitude levels $0.1, 0.2, \ldots, 0.9$, which appear randomly in a sequence. However, when each item appears, we know that it will appear for a predetermined number of time steps. For instance, 0.1 appears for one time step, 0.2 for two time steps, and 0.9 for nine time steps. Elman associated the random values with consonants that are followed by a predetermined number of vowel sounds.

Can a network learn the time series? The answer must be no, because each subsequence appears randomly. However, the error should not be uniformly high over time, since there is a predictable part in the time series structure, namely, the length associated with each level. A network that can capture the time structure should yield a low error once a given level appears at the network input.

Our first architecture is the Jordan network, which feeds back the output of the system to a layer of context PEs. The network has a single input and a single output. The desired response is the same as the input but advanced one time step (i.e., the network is trained as a predictor). We use backpropagation to train the system, although this is an approximation, as we will see shortly. We start with five hidden PEs and five context PEs with fixed feedback, but feel free to experiment with these parameters. Running the network, we observe the expected behavior in the error. The error tends to be high at the transitions between levels.

In Chapter 10 we worked with a time series built from two sine waves of different frequencies. Since this is a problem of time structure, let us see whether the Jordan network can also learn it. The answer is negative, since the feedback is from the output; if the output is always wrong, the feedback does not provide valuable information.

NEUROSOLUTIONS EXAMPLE 11.2

Elman's network

We repeat the previous problem, but now with an architecture that feeds back the state to the context PEs; that is, the hidden-layer activations are providing the input to the context PEs.

The Elman network works as well as the Jordan network for the multilevel data set and is able to solve the two-sine-wave problem of Chapter 10. Working with the past system state seems more appealing than working with the past output. Again, notice that we are using static backpropagation to train the weights of the system.

We saw that one of the difficult problems in the processing of time signals is to decide the length of the time window. Normally we do not know the length of time where the information relevant to processing the current signal sample resides. If the window is too short, only part of the information is available, and the learning system is working with only partial information. If we increase the size of the window too much, we may bring in information that is not relevant (i.e., noise), which negatively affects learning. We saw in Chapter 10 that the value of the feedback parameter controls the memory depth in the context PE, so in principle, its adaptation from the data may solve our problem.

In this chapter we lift the restriction of working with constant feedback coefficients and special architectures, so we first have to understand the problem created by feedback when training neural networks.

11.3 ADAPTING THE FEEDBACK PARAMETER

Let us consider the simple context PE. An appealing idea for time processing is to let the system find the memory depth that it needs to represent the past of the input signal. If we utilize the information of the output error to adapt the feedback parameter $1 - \mu$ (which we will call μ_1), then the system will work with the memory depth that provides the smallest MSE. This is possible in principle since the feedback parameter μ_1 is related in a continuous way (a decaying exponential) to the PE output. To adapt the feedback parameter we will need to compute the sensitivity of the output to a change in μ_1.

Can static backpropagation be used to adapt μ_1? The answer is a resounding no. The reason can be found in the *time-delay operator* (z^{-1}) and in the recurrent topology. The time-delay operator creates an *intrinsic ordering* in the computations, since the output at time $n + 1$ becomes dependent on the output value at time n (Figure 11-2).

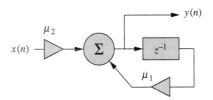

FIGURE 11-2   A first-order recurrent system

When we derived the backpropagation algorithm in Chapter 3, we mentioned that the algorithm would compute gradients for any ordered topology, that is, any topology that obeys a dependency list (see Eq. 3.34). This dependency list was static; it addressed only the dependencies created by the network topology. However, the delay also imposes a *time dependency* on the variables, so it will interfere with the dependency list created by the topology, which does not consider time. In practical terms, the recurrent connection makes a tremendous difference.

Let us compute the sensitivity of the output with respect to the weights μ_1 and μ_2 for the network depicted in Figure 11-2. The input-output relationship is

$$y(n) = \mu_1 y(n-1) + \mu_2 x(n) \tag{11.1}$$

The partial derivative of $y(n)$ with respect to μ_2 is simply

$$\frac{\partial}{\partial \mu_2} y(n) = x(n) \tag{11.2}$$

The derivative of $y(n)$ with respect to the feedback parameter μ_1 contains two terms (derivative of the product):

$$\frac{\partial}{\partial \mu_1} y(n) = y(n-1) \frac{\partial}{\partial \mu_1} \mu_1 + \mu_1 \frac{\partial}{\partial \mu_1} \big(y(n-1) \big) \tag{11.3}$$

The first term in Eq. 11.3 is similar to Eq. 11.2, but notice that $y(n-1)$ also depends on μ_1 because of the recursive nature of Eq. 11.1. This is a major difference between the static case and the recurrent system. Notice that Eq. 11.3 basically says that the effect of any change in the parameter μ_1 (the recurrent parameter) lasts forever, while the effect of a change in the feedforward parameter μ_2 matters only in the current sample.

As you may recall, the backpropagation algorithm covered in Chapter 3 did not include this effect, since there were no feedback connections. The algorithm in Chapter 3 was called static backpropagation exactly for this reason. This also means that for recurrent topologies the equations need to be rederived to cope with time dependencies.

11.3.1 Error Criteria for Training Dynamic Networks

The fundamental difference between the adaptation of the weights in static and recurrent networks is that, in the latter, the local gradients depend on the time index. Moreover, the types of optimization problems are also different, because we are generally interested in quantifying the performance of adaptation within a time interval instead of instantaneously.

The most common error criterion for dynamic neural networks is *trajectory learning* where the cost is summed over time from an initial time $n = 0$ until the final time

$n = T$:

$$J = \sum_{n=0}^{T} J_n = \sum_{n} \sum_{m} \varepsilon_m^2(n) \qquad (11.4)$$

where J_n is the *instantaneous error* and m is the index over the output PEs (we omitted the summation on the patterns for simplicity). The time T is the length of the trajectory and is related to the length of the time pattern or of the interval of interest. The cost function is therefore obtained *over a time interval,* and the goal is to adapt the adaptive system weights to minimize J_n over the time interval. Equation 11.4 resembles the batch mode cost function if we relate the index n with the batch index. But here n is a time index, so we are using different samples of the time series to compute the cost.

For dynamic systems trained with *fixed-point learning* the static error criterion can still be used:

$$J = \sum_{m} e_m^2 \qquad (11.5)$$

This cost measures the performance, assuming that the output and desired signals do not vary over time (after the system relaxes to a steady state). Since the states $y(n)$ in a dynamic network are time dependent, the sensitivity of the cost with respect to the states also becomes time dependent. The only way to implement fixed-point learning is to let the system response stabilize (arrive at a steady state) and then apply the criterion.

11.4 UNFOLDING RECURRENT NETWORKS IN TIME

To apply the backpropagation procedure for recurrent networks, we need to adapt the ordered list of dependencies for recurrent topologies. As we saw in Eq. 11.1, the present value of the activation $y(n)$ (also called the *state*) depends on the previous value $y(n-1)$. The sensitivity of the present state also depends on the previous sensitivity in Eq. 11.3. There is a procedure called *unfolding in time* that produces a time-to-space mapping, replacing a recurrent network by a much larger feedforward network with repeated coefficients. As long as the network is feedforward, we can apply the ordered list. As an example, let us take the case of the network at the top of Figure 11-3, which shows a linear dynamic PE (PE #1) followed by a static, nonlinear PE (PE #2). The goal is to adapt μ and w_1.

The forward equation for this system is

$$\begin{aligned}
y_2(n) &= f(w_1 \cdot y_1(n)) \\
y_1(n) &= \mu y_1(n-1) + x(n)
\end{aligned} \qquad (11.6)$$

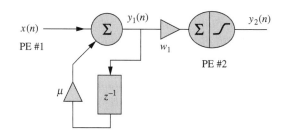

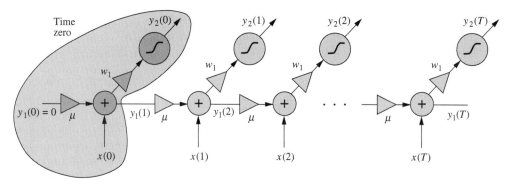

FIGURE 11-3 Unfolding in time of a simple recurrent network

Each time tick n produces an output $y_2(n)$ that is a function of the previous value of $y_1(n-1)$ combined with the present input $x(n)$. Notice the dependence on the initial condition, normally set to zero ($y_1(0) = 0$). Each time tick creates a stage of the unfolded network. Each additional time tick will be a similar network cascaded on the previous one (Figure 11-3). Provided that the recurrent network is in operation for a finite time, we can replace it with a static, feedforward net with $T + 2$ inputs and $T + 1$ outputs. This operation is called unfolding the network in time. From this unfolded network we can generate an ordered *dependency list* for the recurrent network, as we did in Chapter 3:

$$L = \{\{\mu, w_1\}, y_0, \dots, y_{2T+1}\} \tag{11.7}$$

since the unfolded network has $2T + 2$ state variables. However, in this particular case we know that there are only two state variables, at different time steps, so we can rename the state variables, invoking the implicit time order:

$$L = \{\mu, w_1, y_1(0), y_2(0), y_1(1), y_2(1), \dots, y_1(T), y_2(T)\} \tag{11.8}$$

Note that the weights appear first in the list, since all the state variables depend on them. Next the states are ordered by their index on the topology (as we did for the MLP), but the same state variables are repeated, indexed by time from time zero to T. For the unfolded network of Figure 11-3 the even states correspond to the values that $y_1(n)$ takes over time.

A procedure to establish the dependency list is to first label, from left to right, all the state variables (output of adders in the topology) along with the output to create the dependency list at $n = 0$. Feedback loops are simply not considered. Next we replicate the variables in the same order for all other time ticks until $n = T$. Therefore, in simple cases, just by looking at the network structure, we can infer the dependency list quite easily; that is, we can skip the network unfolding once we understand the procedure. Now we just need to apply the backpropagation algorithm to the dependency list of Eq. 11.8.

11.4.1 Extending Static Backpropagation to Time: BPTT

We can apply the ordered derivative procedure explained in Chapter 3 to the dependency list of Eq. 11.7, which yields Eq. 3.35. We can instead apply the ordered derivative procedure to Eq. 11.8, which is equivalent because we just count the states differently. In this case we have a double sum going over the original network state variables (in our case y_1 and y_2) and also the variables created by the time unfolding (indexed by time $n = 0, \ldots, T$):

$$\frac{\partial J}{\partial y_i(n)} = \frac{\partial^d J}{\partial y_i(n)} + \sum_{\tau > n} \sum_{j > i} \frac{\partial J}{\partial y_j(\tau)} \frac{\partial^d}{\partial y_i(n)} y_j(\tau) \qquad (11.9)$$

Note that we use time $\tau > n$ to enforce the rule that we can compute dependencies only of variables that are to the right of the present variable in the list. With this new labeling of variables, time as well as topology information appears in the ordered derivative equation. We could still use the numbering of states in the unfolded network, but we would lose the power of interpreting the solution.

Likewise, the sensitivity with respect to all the weights (μ and w are treated equally) can be written

$$\frac{\partial J}{\partial w_{ij}} = \sum_n \sum_k \frac{\partial J}{\partial y_k(n)} \frac{\partial^d}{\partial w_{ij}} y_k(n) \qquad (11.10)$$

where we use the fact that the weights are first in the ordered list (sum over all times and states), the weights are internal, and the cost is computed over time as in Eq. 11.4.

The first important observation is that the time index τ in Eq. 11.9 is greater than the present time n, so the gradient computation in recurrent networks using the backpropagation procedure is *anticipatory*. We saw that there are no physically realizable systems that are anticipatory (i.e., that respond before the input is applied). However, in digital implementations we can implement anticipatory systems during finite periods by using memory. We simply wait until the last sample of the interval of interest and then clock the samples backward in time, starting from the final time.

The second observation relates to the number of terms necessary to compute gradients over time. It is known that a recurrent system propagates any present change in one of its state variables to all future time (due to the recurrency). This indicates that, in principle, the sensitivity of one of the state variables at the present time also needs all its future time sensitivities to be computed accurately. However, notice that in Eq. 11.9 the summation term blends only the *explicit or direct dependence* of $y_j(\tau)$ on $y_i(n)$ in time and on the topology, so we are computing dependencies over time with explicit dependencies on the topology. For example, if we closely examine the feedforward equation Eq. 11.6 (or Figure 11-3), we see that the present value of $y_1(n)$ depends explicitly only on the previous value $y_1(n-1)$. However, the topology produces a link to $y_2(n)$. In the ordered list (Eq. 11.8) only $y_1(n+1)$ and $y_2(n)$ depend explicitly on $y_1(n)$. This shows the advantage of the ordered list in computing sensitivity information.

With this prologue we are ready to apply Eq. 11.9 to the two state variables $y_2(n)$ and $y_1(n)$ and to the weights μ and w_1. For $y_2(n)$ we see that all the terms in the sums are zero, since PE #2 is a nonrecurrent output PE. Therefore

$$\frac{\partial J}{\partial y_2(n)} = -\varepsilon(n) \tag{11.11}$$

where $\varepsilon(n)$ is the injected error at time n. For $y_1(n)$ we get

$$\frac{\partial J}{\partial y_1(n)} = 0 + \mu \frac{\partial J}{\partial y_1(n+1)} + w_1 f'(net_2(n)) \frac{\partial J}{\partial y_2(n)} \tag{11.12}$$

Let us analyze Eq. 11.12. We have no injected error, since PE #1 is internal. The double sum of Eq. 11.9 has two terms different from zero, since $y_1(n)$ has two direct dependencies, one from the time variable $y_1(n+1)$ and the other from the topology (PE #2), $y_2(n)$. The direct dependence over time gives the first nonzero term, while the dependence over the topology gives the second term.

Now for the weight gradients we get immediately from Eq. 11.6

$$\frac{\partial J}{\partial w_1} = \sum_n \frac{\partial J}{\partial y_2(n)} f'(net_2(n)) y_1(n) \tag{11.13}$$

and for the feedback parameter

$$\frac{\partial J}{\partial \mu} = \sum_n \frac{\partial J}{\partial y_1(n)} y_1(n-1) \tag{11.14}$$

There are many implications of this derivation. Probably the most important is that by unfolding the network in time, we are still able to apply the backpropagation procedure to train the recurrent network. This new form of backpropagation is called *backprop-*

agation through time (BPTT) because the ordered list is now reversed not only in the topology (from the output to the input), but also in time (from the terminal time $n = T$ to $n = 0$).

The second important observation is that BPTT is *not* local in time. This may come as a surprise, but the beautiful locality of the backpropagation algorithm on the topology does not extend to time. We can see this easily by noting that both the state gradient (Eq. 11.12) and the weight gradient (Eq. 11.14) are a function of more than one time index.

The third implication is the interpretation of the sensitivity equations as activities flowing in the dual network. Let us see the form of the dual PE for the linear context PE of Eq. 11.1. We rewrite Eq. 11.12 with our previous convention of error signals, $e(n)$ and $\delta(n)$ (since the PE is an internal PE in the topology, the error that reaches it is internal):

$$e(n) = \mu_1 e(n + 1) + \delta(n) \tag{11.15}$$

If we interpret the error that is backpropagated from the output as the input to the dual network, the dual of the linear recurrent PE is as shown in Figure 11-4.

Notice that the dual network is constructed from the original network with the same rules presented in Chapter 3, with the addition that the delay has been substituted by an advance of one sample; that is, *the dual of the delay is the advance in time.* If we start by running the dual system from $n = T$, the sign of the advance operator is reversed, so the transfer functions of the original and dual systems can be implemented with the delay operator.

In Chapter 3, Section 3.6.3, we showed how to implement static backpropagation as a data-flow machine, that is, without explicitly deriving the equations for adaptation, but simply constructing the dual network and specifying the forward and the backward maps of each component. The maps for the static components are shown in Section 3.6.4. *We are now in a position to extend the data-flow procedure to dynamic neural networks, since we discovered the dual of the delay operator, the only operator we have not encountered before.* We will be using the same notation, so the equations to include the *i*th linear context PE of Eq. 10.3 (no bias) in our data-flow machine

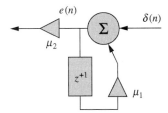

FIGURE 11-4 Dual of the linear recurrent PE

are

Forward (activation) map $y_i(n) = (1 - \mu)y_i(n - 1) + \mu \left[\sum_j w_{ij} x_j(n) \right]$

Backward (error) map $e_i(n) = (1 - \mu)e_i(n + 1) + \sum_j w_{ij} \delta_j(n)$ **(11.16)**

and the weight update is given by

$$\frac{\partial J}{\partial \mu} = \sum_n \left[-y(n - 1) + \sum_j w_{ij} x_j(n) \right] e_i(n)$$

You should compare these equations with Eq. 3.40 and 3.41, respectively, to see the effect of the dynamics. Note that the sum over the trajectory (n) can be computed sample by sample from the maps in Eq. 11.16. The sums over j are available at the PE since they represent the input activation and the injected error, respectively.

The data-flow algorithm of static backpropagation must be adapted to cope with the time-varying gradients, but the modifications are minor.

- First, the data for the full trajectory (T samples) is sent through the network (one sample at a time), and the activations are stored locally at each PE.
- Next, the set of outputs is compared with the desired trajectory, using our criterion of choice to build the error sequence.
- This error sequence is reversed in time according to the BPTT procedure to compensate for the required advances in time, which are the dual of the delay.
- The reordered error sequence is sent through the dual network, and the local errors are stored locally. NeuroSolutions implements this procedure using the Dynamic Controller.
- Once the sequence of local errors and local activations exist at each PE, the weight update can take place using any of the first-order search methods described in Chapter 4.

Due to the fact that BPTT is not local in time, we have to compute the gradients of all the weights and states over a time interval, even if only part of the system is recurrent, as in the TLFN topologies found in Chapter 10. We have to prespecify the initial time and the final time. This affects the storage and computational requirements of the algorithm. Even for the case of the focused TLFN topology that has a single recurrent connection at the input, if BPTT is selected to adapt μ, *all* gradients need to be computed over time.

Backpropagation versus BPTT

If the network is static or dynamic but feedforward, such as the TDNN, and the desired signal is known for all time, there is no point in using BPTT even for the case of trajectory learning. We can use straight backpropagation and add up the gradients over the specified time interval, as we did in batch learning. This can be easily proved by analyzing Eq. 11.4. However, there are cases where the dynamic network is feedforward (TDNN) but the desired signal is known only at the terminal time. In this case we have to use BPTT, since we do not have an explicit error at each time step.

As specified in the text, once BPTT is applied to one portion of the network (for instance, the feedback parameter in the gamma network), the easiest way is to adapt *all* the weights with BPTT, although strictly speaking, only the weights that lie in the topology to the left of the recurrent connection need to be updated with BPTT. However, it is easier to implement the learning algorithm uniformly.

NEUROSOLUTIONS EXAMPLE 11.3

Training the feedback parameter of Elman's network

This is our first example using BPTT. The first thing to notice is that the Controllers are different; now they have three dials.

**Dynamic Controller
and Back Dynamic controller**

Their functionality is also different, since now they have to orchestrate the firing of the data through a trajectory and command the PEs (and the duals) to store their activities (and errors). The errors also have to be reversed in time (starting from the error at the last time step toward the beginning).

The user has one extra level of variables for BPTT, which is related to the size of the trajectory and the initial conditions. Open the Dynamic Controller Inspector and look at the *dynamic* page. Notice that you have three choices: static (the same as the Static Controller), fixed point, and trajectory learning. We are interested in trajectory for this example. The size of the trajectory is called the *number of exemplars,* so when we set the *number of samples per exemplar,* we are specifying the length of the trajectory. In the same panel we can further specify the initial conditions. If we click the box *"zero state between exemplars,"* for each new trajectory the state of the network (i.e., the values of activations and errors) will be reset. Normally we do *not* want this, since it creates discontinuities between adjacent trajectories. Once we specify the parameters in this panel, the simulations work in exactly the same way as before.

We are now ready to use BPTT to train the feedback parameters of the Elman network of Example 11.2. We choose the size of the trajectory as 15 samples. This

DynamicControl Inspector ✕

| Dynamic | Static | Weights | Auto Macros | Code | Display | Engine |

Temporal Activation

Static ○ Fixed Point ○ Trajectory ⦿

Samples / Exemplar [15]

☐ Zero state between exemplars

means the Controller will fire 15 samples at a time from the input file, each PE will store 15 activations, the network output will be compared with 15 samples of the desired response, and a 15-long error vector will be created. This error vector will be reversed in time and fired through the dual network, one error at a time. At the end of the trajectory each PE and its dual will have 15-sample-long activation and error vectors, and momentum learning can then be used to update the weights. Notice that the weights are updated with the cumulative error along the trajectory. The process is then repeated for the next 15 samples of the input file, and so on.

Running the network, we see that it learns very fast. The initial values of the feedback parameters are set to 1 (no memory), and they slowly change to the appropriate value that minimizes the output MSE. This is the beauty of the context PE. It automatically configures its memory to minimize the output MSE. Notice that the time constants spread out to cover all the time scales well. The final error is normally smaller than when the network is trained with static backpropagation using an arbitrarily chosen feedback parameter.

11.4.2 Computing the Gradient Directly

As we saw in Chapter 3 for the MLP, the gradients can also be computed by applying the chain rule directly to the cost (Eq. 11.4) to obtain

$$\frac{\partial J}{\partial w_{ij}} = -\sum_n \sum_m \varepsilon_m(n) \frac{\partial}{\partial w_{ij}} y_m(n) \qquad i, j = 1, \dots, N \tag{11.17}$$

We denote the gradient variables (sensitivity of the states) with respect to the weights as

$$\alpha_{ij}^m(n) = \frac{\partial}{\partial w_{ij}} y_m(n) \tag{11.18}$$

To compute the state sensitivities, we use the forward equation for the neural network to yield

$$\alpha_{ij}^m(n) = f'(net_m(n))\left[\Delta_{im}y_j(n) + \sum_l w_{ml}\alpha_{ij}^i(n)\right]$$

(11.19)

where f' is the derivative of the nonlinearity and Δ_{im} is the Kronecker delta function, which is 1 only when $m = i$. It is important to compare this equation with the one given in Chapter 3 (Eq. 3.39) to see the differences brought in by the recurrency (the sum in the parentheses).

If the weights change *slowly* compared with the forward dynamics, we can compute these equations for each time sample instead of waiting for the end of the trajectory:

$$\frac{\partial J}{\partial w_{ij}} = -\sum_m \varepsilon_m(n)\alpha_{ij}^m(n)$$

(11.20)

This is why this procedure is called real-time recurrent learning (RTRL). It is interesting that the RTRL algorithm is *local in time but not local in space,* so in some sense it is the dual of BPTT. In fact, Eq. 11.17 shows that we are computing all the sensitivities with respect to every weight w_{ij}, so the computation is not local in the topology (in space), but it also clearly shows that the method is local in time. The time locality makes it appealing for on-line applications and VLSI implementations. The direct method was computationally unattractive for static networks when compared with backpropagation. It is even more so for dynamic networks and small trajectories, as we will discuss later.

Let us apply RTRL to the topology of Figure 11-3. Since there are only two weights, it is easy to see that the procedure gives

$$\frac{\partial J}{\partial \mu} = \frac{\partial J}{\partial y_2(n)}f'(net_2(n))w_1\left[y_1(n-1) + \mu\frac{\partial}{\partial \mu}y_1(n-1)\right]$$

(11.21)

and

$$\frac{\partial J}{\partial w_1} = \frac{\partial J}{\partial y_2(n)}f'(net_2(n))y_1(n)$$

(11.22)

Notice that the formulas to compute μ and w with RTRL are different from the ones obtained for BPTT (Eqs. 11.13 and 11.14). However, we can show that for the same initial conditions, at the end of the interval the two sets of equations provide the same updates, so they are equivalent [Haykin, 1994]. For small networks RTRL provides very compact equations, which may be beneficial for understanding dynamic training.

For instance, it is clear from Eqs. 11.21 and 11.22 that the local gradients are a function of $f'(.)$, so to ensure stability the largest slope of the recurrent PE nonlinearity should be less than 1; otherwise, we may be amplifying the errors. If we use an α of 1 in the PE nonlinearity, as is normally the case, we are in the marginally stable case. This is often forgotten and produces instability in training over time.

NEUROSOLUTIONS EXAMPLE 11.4

The effect of the slope of the nonlinearity in recurrent networks

Let us go back to the Elman network and set the slope of the hidden PEs to a large value. The training becomes very difficult, producing unusable results most of the time. Try a large value and decrease the step size to see whether you can control the learning. You will see that it is very difficult.

Another important thing to notice is that the system output seems quite normal (just flat), but the internal PEs are all pegged, that is, stuck at one extreme value or the other. Here the system is unstable, but it does not behave like an unstable linear system (the output goes to infinity) due to the nonlinearity. Recurrent systems behave very differently from static systems, so you have to be much more careful while training them.

We recommend that the slope of the nonlinearity be set at 0.8. We also recommend that you place a Megascope over the hidden PEs to see whether they are pegged all the time. If they are, the PE is simply not responding, and the network effectively has fewer degrees of freedom.

Training the Gamma Filter

The gamma filter was presented in Chapter 10 as an alternative to the Wiener filter. It is basically a gamma memory followed by an adder. Since the gamma memory is locally recurrent, the gamma filter cannot be trained with static backpropagation.

The gamma filter is defined as

$$y(n) = \sum_{k=0}^{D} w_k x_k(n)$$

$$x_k(n) = (1 - \mu)x_k(n-1) + \mu x_{k-1}(n-1) \qquad k = 1,\ldots,D \tag{11B.1}$$

where $x_0(n) = x(n)$ is the input signal and $y(n)$ is the output. The weights and the gamma parameter μ are adapted using the gradients of the cost function given by Eq. 11.4. We can use RTRL and immediately get

$$\Delta w_k = -\eta \frac{\partial J}{\partial w_k} = \eta \sum_{n=0}^{T} e(n)x_k(n)$$

$$\Delta \mu = -\eta \frac{\partial J}{\partial \mu} = \eta \sum_{n=0}^{T} e(n) \sum_{k=0}^{D} w_k \alpha_k(n) \tag{11B.2}$$

where $\alpha_k(n) = \partial x_k(n)/\partial \mu$. This gradient can be computed on-line by differentiating the gamma filter equation (Eq. 11B.1), yielding

$$\alpha_0(n) = 0$$

$$\alpha_k(n) = (1 - \mu)\alpha_k(n-1) + \mu\alpha_{k-1}(n-1) + [x_{k-1}(n-1) - x_k(n-1)] \tag{11B.3}$$

Using the ideas of RTRL, for small step size η we can drop the summation over time in Eq. 11B.2. Notice that these equations are local in time, and the complexity to adapt a filter of order k is O(K). NeuroSolutions does not implement this procedure directly; BPTT must be used to adapt the gamma filter.

11.4.3 Comparing RTRL and BPTT

Computational Complexity of RTRL   RTRL computes the sensitivity of every system state with respect to all the weights. However, for trajectory learning it has the important characteristic of being local in time. When the weights change slowly with respect to the forward dynamics, the quantities in Eq. 11.17 can be computed on-line, that is, for every new time sample. This means that the state gradients ($\alpha_{ij}^m(n)$) are computed forward in time with every sample. If the desired signal is available for every sample of the trajectory, the errors $\varepsilon_m(n)$ are obtained, and the weight gradients $\partial J/\partial w_{ij}$ can also be computed for every new sample. If the desired signal is available only at the end of the trajectory, the state gradients have to be stored for the length of the trajectory, and then at the final time the weight gradients can be computed.

With this explanation we can compute the number of computational operations required and the storage requirements of the algorithm. For a fully connected N-PE system there are N^2 weights, N^3 gradients, and O(N^4) operations required for the gradient computation per sample. If the length of the trajectory is T, this means O(N^4T) overall computations. However, the number of items that need to be stored (assuming that the desired signal is available) is independent of time and is O(N^3), which is the number of instantaneous state gradients.

The disproportionately large number of computations means that the method is realistic only for small networks. An interesting aspect is that RTRL can be applied in conjunction with static backpropagation, in networks where the feedforward path is static, but the input is recurrent (as in the focused architectures). The recursive memory is trained dynamically and the feedforward network is trained statically. When implemented, this combination is the most efficient way to train focused TLFNs, since all the computations become local in time.

Training Focused TLFNs

The goal is to be able to adapt the feedback parameter μ of a locally recurrent memory (memory at the input layer) in a focused TLFN with an algorithm that can be integrated with static backpropagation. Let us treat the case of the gamma memory. The gamma memory forward equation for tap k is

$$y_k(n + 1) = (1 - \mu)y_k(n) + \mu y_{k-1}(n) \tag{11B.4}$$

Let us take the derivative of y with respect to μ using the direct differentiation method:

$$\frac{\partial}{\partial \mu} y_k(n + 1) = (1 - \mu)\frac{\partial}{\partial \mu} y_k(n) + \mu \frac{\partial}{\partial \mu} y_{k-1}(n) + y_{k-1}(n) - y_k(n) \tag{11B.5}$$

The direct differentiation method thus provides an on-line approximation (for small step sizes) to adapt the μ parameter. It is necessary to integrate this equation with the information available in a backpropagation environment.

The goal is to adapt μ using static backpropagation. Let us assume that the gamma memory PE is connected to several (p) hidden PEs of the MLP in the focused TLFN. Then we can write

$$\frac{\partial J}{\partial \mu} = \sum_{i=1}^{p} \frac{\partial J}{\partial y_i(n)} \frac{\partial}{\partial \mu} y_i(n) \qquad \textbf{(11B.6)}$$

where $y_i(n)$ are the outputs of the gamma memory PE, the sum is extended to p, and J is the output criterion. During a backpropagation sweep the errors that are propagated from the output through the dual system up to the gamma memory PE are exactly $\partial J / \partial y_i(n)$. Thus μ can be adapted using a mix of static backpropagation and RTRL. According to Eq. 11B.6, the dual system provides $\partial J / \partial y_i(n)$, which is multiplied by Eq. 11B.5 and then summed across the gamma PEs. Equation 11B.5 can be thought of as a new "dual" of the gamma memory PE in the static backpropagation framework, since it instantaneously computes the sensitivities.

Notice that the implementation of Eq. 11B.5 (the instantaneous dual gamma PE) must have memory to store each of the previous values of the sensitivities ($\partial y_i(n)/\partial \mu$). What we gain is a sample-by-sample update algorithm that does not require the storage of the states of the feedforward components since it is using static backpropagation. Since we have a single adaptive parameter, the implementation of the RTRL part (Eq. 11B.5) is still efficient. The following figure shows a block diagram of the steps involved in the adaptation of μ. Notice that these equations are valid only when the gamma PE is at the input; when it is connected to a hidden layer all the gradients to the left of the gamma memory PE become time dependent.

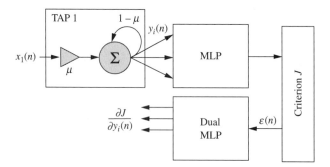

Computational Complexity of BPTT The basic observation for applying the backpropagation formalism in the training of recurrent networks is to change the activations of a network evolving through time into activations of an equivalent static network in which each time step corresponds to a new layer (unfolding the network in time). Static backpropagation can then be applied to this unfolded network, as we have seen (Eq. 11.9). These equations can be put in a one-to-one correspondence with the data-flow algorithm. As in the static case, there is also an intrinsic order in the computations:

1. An input is presented and an output computed. The process is repeated for the trajectory length T, and the local activations are stored locally.

2. Once the network output is known for the full trajectory, a sample-by-sample difference with the desired signal is computed for the full trajectory such that the error signal $\varepsilon(n)$ is generated. This error must be backpropagated from the end of the trajectory ($n = T$) to its beginning ($n = 0$) through the dual topology. Local errors are also stored.

3. Once the local errors and local activations for each time sample are available, the weight update for the trajectory can be computed using the specified search methodology.

4. The process is repeated for the next trajectory. Normally, trajectories are stacked to better teach the time relationships.

As we can see, the computational complexity of BPTT (number of operations and storage) is much larger than that of static backpropagation. The number of operations to compute one time step of BPTT in an N-PE fully connected network is $O(N^2)$, so for the trajectory of size T it becomes $O(N^2 T)$. This is much better than for RTRL. The problem is the storage requirements. As we can see, the activations need to be saved forward, which gives $O(NT)$. This means that for long trajectories, compared with the size of the net, the BPTT algorithm uses more storage than RTRL. The following table shows a comparison of the two algorithms.

	RTRL	BPTT
Space complexity	$O(N^3)$	$O(NT)$
Time complexity	$O(N^4 T)$	$O(N^2 T)$
Space locality	No	Yes
Time locality	Yes	No

It is interesting that BPTT is local in space but not in time, while RTRL is local in time but not local across the network. NeuroSolutions implements BPTT to train recurrent neural networks for trajectory learning. The data-flow algorithm explained in Chapter 3 for static backpropagation can also implement BPTT and fixed-point learning with the appropriate control of the data flow. The local maps for the neural components are associated with the PE and are independent of the type of training strategy. This attests to the importance of the data-flow implementation of backpropagation mentioned in Chapter 3.

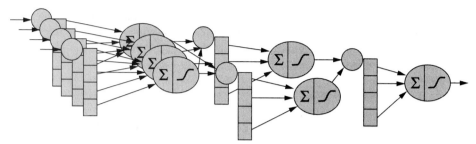

FIGURE 11-5   A time-lagged feedforward network

11.5   THE DISTRIBUTED TLFN TOPOLOGY

The learning machines created as a feedforward connection of memory PEs and nonlinear sigmoidal PEs are called time-lagged feedforward networks (TLFNs). Figure 11-5 shows the general topology of TLFNs.

The focused architectures can produce only a static nonlinear mapping of the projected representation, but there is no need to restrict ourselves to this simple case. As shown in Figure 11-5, we can also populate the hidden layers with memory structures and then produce time-varying nonlinear maps from the projected space to the output. These TLFNs with memory throughout the topology are called *distributed TLFNs.* Each memory PE in the TLFN is effectively *processing information over time* by working with the projections of the PE activations of the previous layer on its local linear memory space. The size of each memory space (i.e., the number of bases) is determined by the number of memory taps.

TLFNs use memory PEs that are ideal delays or locally recurrent, such as the tap delay line PE, the gamma memory PE, or the Laguerre memory PE. When the bases are created by local IIR filters, the span of the memory space (i.e., the amount of past information that is retained in the memory-space bases) is not uniquely determined by the number of delays, but also becomes a function of the feedback parameters that the learning system can control through adaptation.

When the memory filters have feedback, distributed TLFNs are recurrent networks. However, the global signal flow is feedforward; the networks are always stable, provided that the locally recurrent memory PEs are stable, and train better than fully recurrent networks. The most important characteristic of distributed TLFN topologies is that when they are recurrent, the feedback is restricted to be local. Moreover, the recursive part is linear, so we can utilize the well-developed linear adaptive filter theory to partially study these networks.

Vector-Space Interpretation of TLFNs

The vector-space interpretation of a memory PE explains the adaptation of the TLFN weights as a local approximation of the desired response by a weighted sum of memory traces $y_k(n)$.

These signals are the bases of the local projection space. Let us study the case of a gamma memory PE inside the neural network (see the following figure).

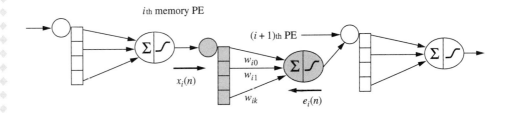

The gamma delay line of size D produces a basis that represents a memory space of size D, but the bases are no longer a direct use of the past values of the input, as in the ideal delay line. The bases are already a linear projection of the input trajectory (convolution with the gamma kernel). When the parameter μ adapts to minimize the output MSE, the projections rotate, and the span of the projection space changes as a consequence of the different time constants (the effective length of the impulse response also changes). The relative angle between the gamma basis vectors does not change with μ. Hence a decrease in the error must be associated with a decrease in the relative position between the desired signal and the projection space (see the following figure).

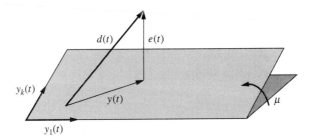

The recursive parameter in the gamma structure changes the span of the memory space with respect to the input signal (which can be visualized as a relative rotation and change in dimensionality between the input signal and the projection space). In terms of time domain analysis, the recursive parameter is finding the length of the time window (the memory depth) containing the relevant information to decrease the output MSE.

The gamma PE is more powerful than the tap-delay-line PE, but the search for the best orientation of the projection space is not trivial. We can show [deVries and Principe, 1992] that the performance surface has many local minima. Most of the time any of the local minima provides a better solution than the linear combiner of the same order, so there is still a net gain in using the gamma memory.

NEUROSOLUTIONS EXAMPLE 11.5

The issue of memory depth in the bus driver problem

This is a benchmark problem to find the memory depth of TLFNs. It is called the bus driver problem, because it can be enunciated as the decision made by a bus driver who is going down a route with many bus stops. The driver will stop at the next bus stop if the bell rings before the stop. However, the driver does not have control of how far in advance the passenger rings the bell.

A simple flip-flop in the bell line will solve this problem using an AND function (if there is a bus stop and the bell flip-flop is high, then stop the bus). However, here we would like to use a TLFN, so the issue is one of learning and memory. The network has two inputs, one for the bus stops along the way and the other for the bell. The system is trained with a signal that contains the information about where the bus should stop.

From the point of view of complexity, this is a trivial problem as long as the TLFN has sufficient memory (the AND can solve it). But learning the relation in time is not easy, since the TLFN will be bombarded with time signals and has to find the relationship between the two inputs that makes the output follow the desired response. The input file is constructed from 1s and 0s (1 means a possible stop or a ring) asynchronously spread in time. The system is trained with static backpropagation to clearly show the effect of the memory depth.

The purpose of the example is to show that a TLFN with memory in the hidden layer can complement the memory at the input layer, eventually saving weights (the number of weights in the first layer tends to be the largest).

We use a gamma memory in the first layer and a tap delay line in the second layer. First we set the hidden layer memory to 1 (just the current sample, i.e., no memory) and the number of taps in the gamma to 5. The largest time distance between a ring and a stop is 10 and occurs in the second and the fifth stops. Run the network and see that it does not learn these two stops.

Now change μ to 0.5. As shown in the memory depth formula, this should provide enough depth to learn all the stops. This is indeed the case.

An alternative is to increase the memory in the hidden layer. Let us divide the number of taps between the input and the hidden layer (five at the input and seven at the hidden layer) and set μ to 1 for the gamma. This solves the problem. We can even use 2 taps and 10 taps and still get a good solution. This means that putting memory in the hidden layer "adds" to the memory in the input layer (in fact, in a nonlinear way due to the nonlinearity of the PE).

11.5.1 How to Train Distributed TLFNs

The supervised training of TLFNs follows the gradient-descent procedure on a cost function defined by the output mean square error (MSE) over time (Eq. 11.4). Since distributed TLFNs are systems with internal or recursive memory, either real-time recurrent learning (RTRL) or backpropagation though time (BPTT) must be used.

As we discussed extensively in Chapter 3, to train neural networks using the data-flow framework, two pieces of information are required:

- The implementation of the data-flow algorithm
- The local maps for the PEs

We saw in Section 11.4.1 how the data-flow algorithm of backpropagation is extended to BPTT and how it is implemented in the dynamic controller of NeuroSolutions. The local maps depend exclusively on the form of the PE. The local maps for the sigmoid PEs, the softmax, the linear PE, and the Synapse are exactly the same as those covered in Chapters 1 and 3. The local maps for the context PE are given in Eq. 11.16, hence we just need to address the maps for the new memory PEs (gamma, Laguerre, gamma II) to complete the training of distributed TLFNs.

11.5.2 Training Gamma TLFNs with BPTT

The data-flow implementation is intrinsic to BPTT and it is implemented by the dynamic controller, but the local maps depend on the PEs chosen. In Section 11.4.1 we presented the local maps for the context PE, which are going to be the basis to develop the equations written below. But note that the gamma memory is a single-input, multiple-output component, so its dual is a multiple-input, single-output component. The equations will be written for the kth tap of the ith gamma PE. For simplicity we will omit the ith index when no confusion arises.

Activation map $y_k(n) = (1 - \mu)y_k(n - 1) + \mu y_{k-1}(n - 1)$

Error map $e_k(n) = (1 - \mu)e_k(n + 1) + \mu e_{k+1}(n + 1) + \sum_j w_{jk}\delta_j$ **(11.23)**

The activation map is used by the gamma memory component while the error map is used by the dual gamma memory PE. We should remember that for $k = 1$ (the first tap) the activation map has to take into consideration the spatial connections to the ith gamma PE, that is,

$$y_{i1}(n) = (1 - \mu)y_{i1}(n - 1) + \mu \sum_j w_{ij}x_j(n - 1)$$

The second equation in Eq. 11.23 is just the application of Eq. 11.9 to the gamma memory. In fact, the gamma memory is a cascade of first-order recursive elements in which the stage is indexed by k. The last sum comes from the fact that each tap of the gamma memory dual also receives inputs from the spatial topology. It represents the errors being fed to the kth tap of the ith dual PE. To update the feedback parameter using straight gradient descent, the weight update is

Weight update $\dfrac{\partial J}{\partial \mu} = \sum_{n,k}[y_{k-1}(n - 1) - y_k(n - 1)]e_k(n)$ **(11.24)**

These equations are all that is necessary to update the recursive coefficient with BPTT in systems using the gamma memory, regardless of the topology.

Note that in Eq. 11.23 the activation is equivalent to Eq. 11B.1, but the error in Eq. 11.23 is different from the formula obtained in Eq. 11B.3, since they have been developed under two different methods (RTRL for Eq. 11B.3 versus BPTT for Eq. 11.23). However, as was said previously, the gradient obtained over the same interval will be identical.

Training Alternative Memories

To train TLFNs with Laguerre PEs, we need to specify two maps, the state equations, the state gradients (i.e., the backpropagated errors), and the formula to update the weights of the Laguerre PE. Since the Laguerre PE is just a minor modification to the gamma PE, we present only the results

Activation $\quad\quad y_k(n) = (1 - \mu)y_k(n - 1) + y_{k-1}(n - 1) - (1 - \mu)y_{k-1}(n - 1)$

Error $\quad\quad\quad \varepsilon_k(n) = (1 - \mu)\varepsilon_k(n + 1) + \varepsilon_{k-1}(n + 1) - (1 - \mu)\varepsilon_{k-1}(n + 1)$

for all taps after the first ($k > 1$). For the first tap the equations read

Activation $\quad\quad\quad\quad y_1(n) = (1 - \mu)y_1(n - 1) + \alpha x(n - 1)$

Error $\quad\quad\quad\quad\quad \varepsilon_1(n) = (1 - \mu)\varepsilon_1(n + 1) + \alpha\varepsilon(n + 1) + \delta(n)$

where $\alpha = \sqrt{1 - (1 - \mu^2)}$ and it is the implementation of the front-end lowpass filter. $x(n)$ and $\delta(n)$ represent the joint input to the PE and its dual, respectively. The weight update using straight gradient descent is

Weight update $\quad\quad \dfrac{\partial J}{\partial \mu} = \sum_{n,k}[y_{k-1}(n - 1)\varepsilon_k(n) - \varepsilon_k(n)y_k(n - 1)]$

This is what is needed to train networks with a Laguerre memory PE.

To adapt the gamma II PE in a TLFN, the following two local maps are needed:

$$y_k(n) = 2(1 - \mu)y_k(n - 1) - [(1 - \mu)^2 + v\mu^2]y_k(n - 2) + \mu y_{k-1}(n) - (1 - \mu)y_{k-1}(n - 1)$$
$$\varepsilon_k(n) = 2(1 - \mu)\varepsilon_k(n + 1) - [(1 - \mu)^2 + v\mu^2]\varepsilon_k(n + 2) + \mu\varepsilon_{k-1}(n) - (1 - \mu)\varepsilon_{k-1}(n + 1)$$

The weight update equations are

$$\frac{\partial J}{\partial \mu} = \sum_{n,k}[-2y_k(n - 1) - (2v\mu - 2(1 - \mu))y_k(n - 2) + y_k(n) + y_{k-1}(n - 1)]e_k(n)$$

$$\frac{\partial J}{\partial v} = \sum_{n,k}[\mu^2 y_k(n - 2)]e_k(n)$$

With these maps we can train *any* topology that includes these memory PEs with BPTT.

Next we present examples of two different topologies that use the gamma memory. The simplest is the gamma filter, which is a linear system. The second topology is a nonlinear TLFN with gamma memory.

NEUROSOLUTIONS EXAMPLE 11.6
Output MSE and the gamma memory depth

This example illustrates the importance of the memory depth for system identification. We use the nonlinear system first presented in Chapter 10 and the topology is a gamma filter with five taps. There are two parts to this example. First, we would like to show that the MSE changes with the value of μ, so we still step the values of μ from 1 to 0.1 by hand and record the final MSE. As you can see, the curve is bowl shaped; that is, there is an intermediate value of μ that produces the smallest output MSE (in fact, if we have enough resolution, we will see that the curve is *not* convex, with five minima). Notice that the Wiener filter provides the MSE of $\mu = 1$, which is not the smallest for this example (and hardly ever is).

   The second step is to find out whether we can train the μ parameter with BPTT to reach the minimum of the performance curve. A good rule of thumb is to use a step size for the feedback parameter at least 10 times smaller than for the feedforward weights. Notice that the system quickly found the best value of the μ parameter in this case.

NEUROSOLUTIONS EXAMPLE 11.7
Frequency doubling with a focused TLFN

To get a better intuition of how different a recurrent memory is from a tap delay line, we present the following problem. We wish to construct a dynamic neural network that will double the frequency of an input sinusoid. Anyone familiar with digital signal processing knows that a nonlinear system is required for this task.

   First let us build a one-hidden-layer focused gamma net with two PEs, tanh nonlinearity, a linear output PE, and an input layer built from a gamma memory with five taps. The period of the input sine wave is set at 40 samples per period, and the output at 20 samples per period. BPTT with an 80-sample trajectory is utilized to adapt all the weights, including the recursive parameter μ of the gamma memory.

   Notice that the μ parameter starts at 1 (the default value, which corresponds to the tap delay line). The value decreases to 0.6 in 150 iterations, yielding a memory depth of 8.3 samples. This means that with five taps the system is actually processing information corresponding to eight samples. This memory depth was found through adaptation, so it should be the best value to solve this problem.

   Now let us reduce the size of the gamma memory from five taps to three taps, keeping the MLP architecture and the task the same. This time μ converges to

0.3, giving an equivalent depth of 10 samples (K/μ). This makes sense, since the memory depth to solve the problem is determined by the input-output map (frequency doubling), and it is the same in both cases. The second system had fewer taps, so the parameter μ that controls the memory depth adapted to a lower value. As expected, the dynamic neural net was thus able to compensate for the fewer taps by decreasing the value of the recursive parameter and achieving the same overall memory depth. The memory resolution in the latter case is worse than in the previous case. The tap delay line with three taps will never solve this problem.

It is interesting to place a Megascope at the hidden layer to visualize how the network is able to solve the frequency doubling. The solution is very natural. The PE activations are 90 degrees apart. One is saturated to the most positive value, and the other to the most negative value, yielding half sinusoids. Then the top layer can add them up easily.

With the trained system, let us fix the weights and see how it generalizes. Modify the input frequency and find the range for which the output is still a reasonable sinusoid of twice the frequency of the input.

We conclude that when the data-flow implementation of BPTT is used to train TLFNs, only the topology of the network and the local maps need to be specified; hence there is no need to rewrite the learning equations for each new topology. This brings flexibility and great savings to the simulations because TLFNs have highly complex topologies. This data-flow approach to train TLFNs was implemented in NeuroSolutions in 1992, but the methodology was only published by Wan in 1996.

11.6 DYNAMIC SYSTEMS

TLFNs encapsulate the recurrencies into the processing elements, (i.e., in the memory PE), and all the other connections are feedforward and instantaneous. There is no reason why a PE output cannot be fed to some other PE that is already connected to the original one, producing a feedback loop across the topology, as we did in a restricted fashion in the Elman and Jordan networks. In spatially recurrent systems, assuming an instantaneous map at the PE, an instantaneous connection between the PEs (a product by a weight) leads to infinite loop, which is unrealistic and cannot be modeled. Delays therefore have to be incorporated either at the PE or at the interconnection level to create time dependencies. We need a rigorous way to treat this type of system, and the best strategy is again to use the ideas from dynamics and mathematical system theory, where these issues were addressed a long time ago.

In Figure 11-6, $y(n)$ is the system output, and it is a time function. Such a system is called a *dynamic system,* a system whose state changes with time. A first-order dynamic system can be described by a relationship (a function) that links the next value

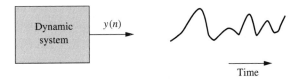

FIGURE 11-6   A dynamical system producing a
time series

$y(n + 1)$ to the present $y(n)$:

$$y(n + 1) = f(y(n)) \tag{11.25}$$

This is one of the simplest dynamic systems we can think of, since it is governed by *first-order dynamics;* that is, the (next) value at time $n + 1$ depends only on the (previous) value at time n. As we saw in Chapter 8, Eq. 11.25 is called a *first-order difference equation.* If the function $f(.)$ is a constant μ, we obtain a first-order *linear* dynamic system. We already studied such a system in Chapter 10 in the form of the context PE. But $f(.)$ may also be a nonlinear function, and in this case the system is a first-order *nonlinear* dynamic system.

In neural networks we are interested in first-order nonlinear dynamic systems. In fact, each PE of all the networks studied so far can be modeled in a very general way by a first-order nonlinear difference equation:

$$y(n + 1) = f(x(n) + wy(n)) \tag{11.26}$$

where $x(n)$ is the input to the PE, f is one of the nonlinearities studied, and w is a constant.

11.6.1 The State-Space Model

A productive (and rigorous) way to think jointly about static and dynamic PEs is to introduce the concept of the *state-space model* [Haykin, 1994]. Let us assume that there is an internal variable in the PE that describes its state at sample n. We call this variable the *state variable, net(n)*. We can rewrite Eq. 11.26 using the state variable as a set of equations:

$$net(n + 1) = wnet(n) + x(n)$$
$$y(n + 1) = f\left(net(n + 1)\right) \tag{11.27}$$

where w is a constant that may depend on the iteration. Having a set of two equations enhances our understanding. The first equation is *dynamic* and shows the evolution of the state through time; in neural networks it is a linear first-order difference equation. $x(n)$ is the combined input to the PE. The second equation is *static* (both $y(.)$ and $net(.)$

depend on the same instant of time), and it shows the nonlinear relationship between the output of the PE and the state. A dynamic neural network is a distributed interconnection of these PEs.

11.6.2 Static versus Dynamic PEs

Now we can better understand the relationship between the static PE covered in Chapters 1 through 7 and the dynamic PEs we have discussed for temporal processing. Basically, the static PE represents only the second equation in Eq. 11.27. The function $f(.)$ is the nonlinear map that we found in the McCulloch-Pitts PE or the sigmoid PE. For all practical purposes, the static PE receives the input *through the state*.

The dynamic PE is different. The next state is a function of the previous state (dynamics) and of the combined input to the PE. The state is then nonlinearly modified to provide an output.

The memory PE that we studied conforms with this principle, except that $f(.)$ is the identity; that is, we were using the states as the outputs. It is instructive to analyze the equation of a nonlinear context PE, which is obtained by including the nonlinearity in Eq. 10.3 of Chapter 10:

$$y_i(n) = f\left(\sum_j w_{ij} x_j(n) + b_i + (1 - \mu)y_i(n - 1) \right) \qquad j \neq i \qquad \textbf{(11.28)}$$

where f is one of the sigmoid nonlinearities found in Chapter 3. The recurrent nonlinear PE is depicted in Figure 11-7. In Eq. 11.28 the quantity in parentheses is the state equation that represents a dynamic system, since it depends on two different time indices.

Eq. 11.28 should be contrasted with the equation that defines the McCulloch-Pitts PE indexed by sample n, which we copy here for convenience:

$$y_i(n) = f\left(\sum_j w_{ij} x_j(n) + b_i \right) \qquad j \neq i \qquad \textbf{(11.29)}$$

Note that the M-P PE is static, because the output depends only on its current input (or equivalently, on the current outputs of the other PEs when connected in a network),

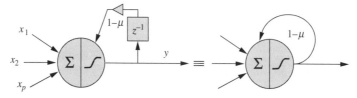

FIGURE 11-7 Nonlinear context PE

while in Eq. 11.28 the output at time n depends on the previous output at time $n - 1$. This is the big difference between a static and a context PE.

11.7 RECURRENT NEURAL NETWORKS

How can we construct recurrent neural networks? There are probably many different ways, but here we describe one that allows us to construct recurrent neural networks directly from the previous static components. Let us implement the static map of Eq. 11.27 with the PE to achieve total compatibility with all the PEs studied so far. Moreover, let us assign the dynamics to the connectivity among PEs in the following way: If the connection is feedforward, we use the present value of the activation, but if the connection is a feedback connection, we include a delay of one time step in the activation. This can be written as

$$net_i(n + 1) = \sum_{j<i} w_{ij}y_j(n + 1) + \sum_{j\geq i} w_{ij}y_j(n) + I_i(n + 1)$$

$$y_i(n + 1) = f(net_i(n + 1)) \tag{11.30}$$

where $I(n)$ is an external input connected to the PE. Note that we divided the computation of the state into *two sums:* The first is the feedforward connections, for which the first index of the weight is always larger than the second index with our notation. The second sum is the feedback connections, for which the first index is always smaller than the second. Such a system is called a *(fully) recurrent neural network* (Figure 11-8).

Once again we have to remember that there are *no instantaneous loops* in this network; that is, all the feedback loops include a delay of one sample. Unfortunately, this is never represented in the diagrams of recurrent networks. When a dynamic system is built, it is a good practice to include a z^{-1} symbol in the feedback connections to avoid any confusion.

The recurrent networks include the feedforward systems (MLPs and linear combiners) as well as the TLFNs as special cases. In fact, let us write the interconnection

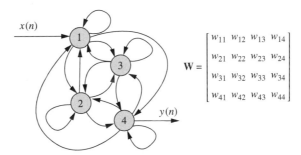

$$\mathbf{W} = \begin{bmatrix} w_{11} & w_{12} & w_{13} & w_{14} \\ w_{21} & w_{22} & w_{23} & w_{24} \\ w_{31} & w_{32} & w_{33} & w_{34} \\ w_{41} & w_{42} & w_{43} & w_{44} \end{bmatrix}$$

FIGURE 11-8 Fully recurrent network

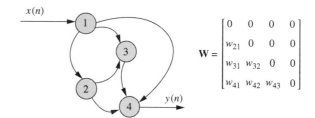

FIGURE 11-9 The corresponding feedforward network

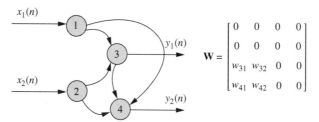

FIGURE 11-10 The corresponding layered network (perceptron)

matrix for a fully recurrent system with N PEs (Figure 11-8). In such cases the weight matrix is fully populated with nonzero values.

A fully recurrent network with N PEs has N^2 weights. Note that the diagonal terms in **W** are the self-recurrent loops to each PE. The upper triangular weights represent feedback connections, while the lower triangular weights represent feedforward connections.

In order for the system to be feedforward, the main diagonal weights, as well as the upper triangular weights (with the numbering as in Figure 11-8), are zero. The feedforward network is depicted in Figure 11-9. Note that this system is static. A layered system has even fewer nonzero connections (Figure 11-10).

In feedforward systems the first weight index is always larger than the second (with our notation). For the layered system of Figure 11-10, which includes the MLP, we added another input and another output; otherwise there would be PEs that would not have input or for which the output would not be connected to the external world.

The TLFNs can also be derived from the fully recurrent system when some of the PEs are made linear and their connectivity restricted to cascades, as in the memory PE. This arrangement indicates a specialization (prewiring) for temporal processing.

Distributed TLFN Architectures

In neurocomputing it is known that a general linear delay mechanism can be represented by temporal convolutions instead of multiplicative instantaneous interactions such as those found in MLPs. This model has been called the *convolution model* [Cohen and Grossberg, 1983], and in discrete time the activation of the *i*th PE reads

$$y_i(n + 1) = f\left(\sum_{\substack{j=0 \\ i>j}}^{N} \sum_{k=0}^{D} w_{ijk} y_{jk}(n)\right) + I_i(n) \tag{11B.7}$$

where $I_i(n)$ is a network input (if the PE is not an input, $I_i(n) = 0$), $y_i(n)$ is the activation at the *i*th PE at time *n*, *N* is the total number of PEs, and *K* is the number of states (taps) of the delay subsystem that implements the short-term memory mechanism. The index *k* is associated with the states of the memory filter. The activation of the *k*th tap of the *j*th PE is written $y_{jk}(n)$. The weight w_{ijk} connects the *k*th tap of the *j*th PE to the *i*th PE. Since the topology is required to be feedforward, the condition $i > j$ must be imposed.

The activation of each PE depends explicitly on the past value of either the input or other states, so that the time history can be captured more easily during training. We can think of the convolution model as a combination of a nonlinear function $f(.)$ with a short-term linear memory mechanism represented by $net(.)$, where

$$net_{ij}(n) = \sum_{k=0}^{D} w_{ijk} x_{jk}(n) \tag{11B.8}$$

As written, the memory mechanism can be globally recurrent. The memories in TLFNs are a special case of Eq. 11B.8, when $net_i(n)$ is a locally recurrent linear filter, created by cascading delay operators. We can recognize this arrangement as a generalized feedforward filter. The memory filter is no longer restricted to be finite impulse response (FIR) as in the TDNN; it can also be an infinite impulse response (IIR) adaptive filter with local feedback. The processing function of TLFNs can be described as a combination of nonlinear PEs and time-space mappings built from local linear projections. The delay operators have been addressed in Chapter 10.

Let us write the TLFN equations in matrix form. Define the signal vectors

$$\mathbf{x}_k = [x_{1k}, \dots, x_{Nk}]^T$$
$$\mathbf{I} = [I_1, \dots, I_N]^T$$

and parameter matrices $\mathbf{p} = \text{diag}_N(p_i)$ and

$$\mathbf{W} = \begin{bmatrix} w_{11k} & \cdots & w_{1Nk} \\ \cdots & \cdots & \cdots \\ w_{N1k} & \cdots & w_{NNk} \end{bmatrix}$$

where $\mathbf{p}$ is the matrix with the parameters of the generalized feedforward memory (GFM). Here *k* is the index of the state variables associated with the GFM. We can eliminate *k* if we define the GFM state vector

$$\mathbf{X} = [\mathbf{x}_0, \mathbf{x}_1, \dots, \mathbf{x}_D]^T$$
$$\mathbf{\Pi} = [\mathbf{I}, \mathbf{0}, \dots, \mathbf{0}]^T$$

the nonlinearity and the matrix of decay parameters

$$\mathbf{F}(net) = \begin{bmatrix} f(net) & 0 & 0 \\ 0 & net & 0 \\ 0 & 0 & net \end{bmatrix} \qquad \mathbf{P} = \begin{bmatrix} p_1 & \dots & 0 \\ \dots & \dots & \dots \\ 0 & \dots & p_K \end{bmatrix}$$

and the matrix of weights

$$\mathbf{\Omega} = \begin{bmatrix} \mathbf{w}_0 & \mathbf{w} & \dots & \mathbf{w}_k \\ p_1 & 0 & \dots & 0 \\ 0 & \dots & \dots & 0 \\ 0 & \dots & p_k & 0 \end{bmatrix}$$

Then any TLFN can be written as

$$\frac{d\mathbf{Y}}{dt} = -\mathbf{PX} + \mathbf{\Omega Y} + \mathbf{\Pi}$$

which is an $N(D + 1)$-dimensional convolution model. As we see later, if we analyze the structure of the matrix **W**, we see that the matrix is not fully populated, meaning that the neural topology is prewired when compared to the most general convolution model.

11.8 LEARNING PARADIGMS FOR RECURRENT SYSTEMS

11.8.1 Fixed-Point Learning

How can we train recurrent systems to associate a static input with a static desired response? Here we present an extension of backpropagation to train recurrent systems, which has been called *fixed-point learning*. The cost function is given by Eq. 11.5. Our goal is to use the paradigm of static learning, that is, to present a static input pattern, clamp it, compare the (steady-state) response with the desired static response, and back-propagate an error. With a local activation and a local error, any gradient-descent update can be used to adapt the weights. Can backpropagation still be used for this task? Notice that now the system is not instantaneous, as the MLP is. When an input is presented to a stable recurrent system, the output "relaxes" (i.e., slowly evolves) to a final value. We say that the recurrent system has an *attractor,* or a *fixed point.* After relaxing to a fixed point the system response does not change; hence, the system becomes static.

We are not going to provide a demonstration here (see Almeida [1987]), but backpropagation can be extended to train a recurrent system with fixed points if the following procedure is followed:

1. Present the static input pattern for a number of samples (clamp it) until the output stabilizes.
2. Compare the output with the static desired pattern, form the error, and backpropagate the error through the dual system, just as was done in the static case.
3. Apply the error in the dual system (clamp it) until the propagated error stabilizes.
4. Then utilize the search procedure of your choice to update the weights. Repeat the procedure for the next pattern.

There are three important remarks to be made. The input pattern and the error have to be clamped (held at a constant value) until the response stabilizes. This process converges as long as the forward system is stable; that is, the system outputs must stabilize. If the forward system is stable, the dual system is also stable, so the local errors will also stabilize. However, the relaxation time constants of the two systems can be different from each other and change from iteration to iteration. In fact, experience shows that the relaxation time constants often decrease (i.e., activations and errors take longer to stabilize) when the system approaches the solution.

The other aspect is that the learning rates have to be slow. Unlike the static case, here we have two dynamic processes at play: the dynamics of learning that change the system weights and the dynamics of the recurrent system. The dynamics of learning have to be much slower than the dynamics of the system (adiabatic condition); otherwise we are not training one system but a family of systems, and no guarantee of convergence exists.

As a result of these four steps, we can see that standard backpropagation is a special case of the fixed-point learning procedure (no relaxation). To implement fixed-point learning, we just need to control the relaxation across iterations appropriately. Any of the recurrent topologies can thus be trained with fixed-point learning if the goal is to create a mapping between two static patterns (the input and the desired response). An important question that does not have a clear answer is the advantage of using a recurrent topology versus an MLP to learn static mappings. Due to the fine tuning required to successfully train a recurrent system with fixed-point learning, we suggest that the MLP be tried first.

NEUROSOLUTIONS EXAMPLE 11.8

Learning the XOR with a recurrent neural network

In this example we will solve the old XOR problem, but now using a recurrent topology and fixed-point learning. The topology is a fully connected set of PEs that receive input from the file and produce an output through one of the PEs. We use an

ArbitrarySynapse with a weight of 1 at the output. All the other weights are adaptive. We can solve this problem with just two PEs, and this is how many we will use.

We use fixed-point learning to train this system. If we go to the dynamic level of the Dynamic Controller Inspector, we can select fixed-point learning. The difference between fixed-point and trajectory learning is that the same sample is always sent to the network during the specified number of samples per exemplar. The goal is to let the system relax to a stable output so that we can compute a meaningful error, send it to the dual network, let the dual network stabilize, and then compute the weight updates. The time the system takes to relax depends on the current weights, so this is a difficult variable to set, but as an initial guess we can use a long relaxation time of 100 samples (enter 100 in the "exemplar per sample" window). We should monitor the appropriateness of the relaxation time by putting a Megascope on the hidden-layer PEs.

We are ready to train the system. There is a local minimum at 0.5 (input weights go to zero and the system stalls), so we may have to randomize the weights. The selection of the step size and momentum are very important for this problem. Notice that the system trains better for long relaxation times. We have two PEs but many weights, so this topology is not as efficient as the MLP. It may, however, be more resistant to noise than the MLP.

11.8.2 Learning Trajectories

One of the unique applications of recurrent networks is to learn time trajectories. A trajectory is a sequence of samples over time. Trajectory learning is required when we want to specify the system output at every time sample, such as in temporal pattern recognition, some forms of prediction (called multistep prediction), and control applications. The cost function is given by Eq. 11.4. We dare to say that a recurrent system is naturally trained in time since it is a dynamic system, so trajectory learning is rather important in many dynamic applications of neural networks. Static networks cannot learn time trajectories, since they do not possess dynamics of their own.

Unlike the previous case of fixed-point learning, here we seek to train a network so that its output follows a prespecified sequence of samples over time. In a sense, we not only enforce the final position, as in fixed-point learning, but we are also interested in defining the intermediate system outputs (i.e., a trajectory). Another case of interest is when the desired response is known at each time step but sometimes later in the near future. The learning system has to be run forward until the desired response is available, and then the weights updated with all the information from the time interval.

There are two basic principles to implement trajectory learning: real-time recurrent learning (RTRL) and backpropagation through time (BPTT). We already covered these two training paradigms in Section 11.4. With the same boundary conditions they compute the same gradients; hence they are equivalent. However, the computation and memory requirements of the two procedures are very different, as we discussed in Section 11.4.3.

NEUROSOLUTIONS EXAMPLE 11.9

Trajectory learning: The figure 8

This example shows that a recurrent system can follow trajectories in time. We start with a simple case of learning a figure-8 trajectory in 2-D space using an MLP. We start by using prediction to train the system.

It is more interesting to actually see whether the trained system can be used to generate the trajectory autonomously. Toward this goal we feed the output back to the network input and disconnect the signal input. Can the neural network trained as a predictor still generate the figure 8? Try to verify that it is almost impossible.

We then train the recurrent system with the global feedback loop, but we have to face a problem. Which system input will we use: the waveform generators or the feedback? Since we want the neural network to ultimately create the trajectory without an external input (just the feedback), we should disconnect the input, but notice that the training becomes very difficult.

It will be very difficult to move the weights to the right values using the error computed over the trajectory. You may want to do this, but it takes a long time to train, and the learning rates have to be small. Also, you have to avoid the local minima problem (e.g., if the trajectory length is equal to the length of the figure 8, zero is a local minimum).

An alternative is to use *both* the input and the feedback, but in a scheduled way. In the beginning of training most of the information should come from the input to help put the weights at approximately the correct positions. But toward the end of training only the feedback should be active. We can do this either by segmenting the trajectory into a portion that comes from the signal generator and another portion that comes from the feedback or simply by creating a weighted average between the two signals. In the beginning of training a large segment should be given to the signal generator, and toward the end of training most of the data should come from the feedback.

Observe the system train (it takes a while). Once it is trained, you can fix the weights, and you can see that it keeps producing the trajectory 8; that is, we have created an oscillator with a very strange waveform. This is a powerful methodology for dynamically modeling complex time series (e.g., we can replace the simple figure 8 by arbitrarily complex trajectories created by real-world time series).

A word of caution is in order here. In the literature we sometimes see training of recurrent networks with static backpropagation. This is *not* correct, since, as we have seen, the gradients in recurrent systems are time dependent. When we use static backpropagation, we are effectively *truncating the gradient* at the current sample; that is, we are basically saying that the dual system is static, which is at best an approximation and can lead to very poor results. On the other hand, this does not mean that we need the full length of the trajectory to effectively compute the gradient over time. An interesting approach is to find a reasonable number of samples to propagate back the gradients, which leads to what has been called *truncated backpropagation* (see Puskorius et al. [1996]). Truncated backpropagation is more efficient, since we are no longer storing the activations and sensitivities during the full length of the trajectory.

11.8.3 Difficulties in Adapting Dynamic Neural Networks

It is fair to say that enough knowledge exists to train MLP topologies with backpropagation. However, it is not easy to adapt dynamic neural networks, whether TLFNs or fully recurrent topologies. The difficulty stems not only from the sheer computational complexity that produces slow training, but also from their complex performance surfaces, the possibility of instability (in fully recurrent systems), and the natural decay of gradients through the topology and through time. Training recurrent neural networks with BPTT (or with RTRL) is still today more of an art than a science, so extreme care should be exercised when training dynamic neural networks. We would like to add that TLFNs are easier to train than fully recurrent networks and should be the starting point for any solution.

The performance surface of dynamic neural networks tends to have very narrow valleys, so the step size must be carefully controlled to train them. Adaptive step-size algorithms are preferred here. In NeuroSolutions we can schedule the step size by hand when automatic algorithms do not perform well.

During training the recurrent network can become unstable. The nonlinearity in the PEs will not allow the system to blow up, but the PEs become pegged and may oscillate widely between the extreme values. Monitoring for this situation and resetting learning is normally the only way out. In effect, such PEs are not being used for processing functions, and the effective number of degrees of freedom of the system is much smaller than the number of available PEs would suggest. There are definitions of stability more appropriate than BIBO stability for nonlinear systems, but they are difficult to apply.

Another problem is the decay of the gradient information through the nonlinearities, which has been called the *long-term dependency problem* (see Bengio et al. [1994]). A dynamic neural network in a classification task tends to have its hidden PEs saturated, so that it can operate like a finite-state machine. In such cases the gradients are attenuated greatly when the system is trained with BPTT, which makes training difficult and very slow. There is no known mathematical solution to this problem, but engineering solutions have been proposed. This characteristic of dynamic networks implies that using memory PEs inside the network topology, as we did in the distributed TLFN network, may simplify training and make the networks more accurate.

Advantage of Linear Memory PEs

One of the problems of fully recurrent systems is that they tend to work as finite-state machines; that is, their PEs tend to saturate on and off during operation. If we think of Markov models [Rabiner and Juang, 1986]—the other technology for dealing with extracting information in time—this seems reasonable, in fact, essential for capturing the complex structure of time signals.

The problem is that recurrent systems take a long time to train, if they can be trained at all. The difficulty has been called the long-term dependency problem. It simply means that when we train a recurrent net with PEs that are saturated, the gradients are going to be heavily attenuated, so the relationships are either poorly learned or impossible to learn.

This is where the linear memory structures come to our rescue. The advantage of linear memories is that the gradients are not attenuated when backpropagated through them. The disadvantage is that they are unable to create nonlinear relationships (states). However, a clever mix of memory PEs and nonlinear PEs, as done in TLFNs, has been shown to provide better results than fully recurrent topologies. See Giles et al. [1997].

All these aspects raise the question of the applicability of gradient-descent learning to training dynamic neural networks. Recently, alternative training procedures using decoupled Kalman filter training (dKft) have been proposed with very promising results [Feldkamp and Puskorius, 1998].

11.9 APPLICATIONS OF DYNAMIC NETWORKS TO SYSTEM IDENTIFICATION AND CONTROL

System identification and control is probably the area that benefits most from the power of dynamic neural networks and BPTT. We already presented a few applications of ANNs to system identification in Chapter 10. The advantage of ANNs is that they are *adaptive universal mappers*. However, in Chapter 10 we did not know how to adapt the feedback parameters, so we had to restrict ourselves to only a few topologies.

Now with the introduction of BPTT we can lift this restriction and apply *any* ANN topology (static or dynamic) to identify or control plants. There are many different ways to establish a successful strategy to do this. See Narendra and Parthasarathy [1990] for a complete discussion. Here we address some preliminary issues that are important for the understanding and application of the material covered in this book.

11.9.1 Adapting ANN Parameters in Larger Dynamic Systems

In Chapter 3 we showed how to optimally design a system built from an adaptive subsystem (a neural network) with other static subsystems that were differentiable with fixed parameters. Enhancing this view when the subsystems are dynamic is critical for system identification and control. In practical applications we may be faced with the task of including neural networks in larger systems built from unknown plants or other engineering systems (such as controllers), and of course we would still like to be able to optimally set the network parameters.

If you recall, the reason we could easily adapt an ANN inside a larger system is that backpropagation is local in space. This means that the ANN only cares about the signals that were transmitted from the input (through an unknown subsystem) and back-propagated from the output (also through another unknown subsystem). Since back-propagation was generalized to BPTT, we can still fully apply the same principle, but now extended to a dynamic neural network. Since BPTT is not local in time, how-ever, we have to work with gradients from a segment of data. To preserve the on-line learning ability, we have to advance the trajectory one sample at a time. However, for some applications the use of trajectory chunking is still practical and leads to more ef-ficient implementations than RTRL. The length of the trajectory is important, because it should be long enough to capture the dynamics of the overall system; however, this is not known a priori, so the trajectory length is subject to experimentation. Notice also that to avoid discontinuities at the end of the trajectories, the system state at the fi-nal trajectory time must be stored and used as the initial condition for the following trajectory.

Dynamic backpropagation is probably the most widely used method in the neural control literature (see Narendra and Parthasarathy [1990]). Dynamic backpropagation combines RTRL and backpropagation. It adapts the static neural networks using back-propagation but uses RTRL to propagate forward the sensitivities. Each representation of Figure 11-11 requires a different analysis. For example, dynamic backpropagation for the block diagram of Representation 1 can be written as

$$\frac{\partial e(n)}{\partial w_i} = P(v, \alpha)\frac{\partial v(n)}{\partial w_i} \tag{11.31}$$

where the sensitivity in the ANN is computed with backpropagation, while the propa-gation of the parameter change is done with RTRL on a copy of $P(v, \alpha)$.

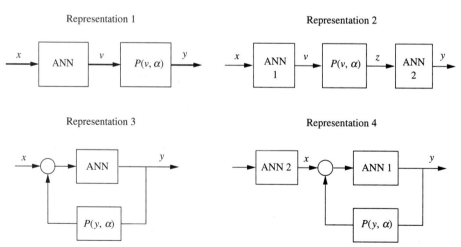

FIGURE 11-11 The four most common configurations involving ANNs and fixed dynamic systems

Dynamic Backpropagation

In the control literature we see that, instead of BPTT, the preferred method to adapt a mixture of neural networks and dynamic systems is dynamic backpropagation. Dynamic backpropagation is a blend of RTRL with static backpropagation. The parameters of the ANN are adapted with backpropagation, but the sensitivities are passed forward among submodules using the old idea of RTRL.

The advantage of this technique is that it provides adaptation sample by sample, being intrinsically on-line. The disadvantages are that it is computationally demanding and it depends on the particular arrangement of subsystems. As we will see later, a proliferation of blocks, basically one per parameter, is needed to pass the sensitivity forward. During BPTT the gradients are all local to the topology, so it can be applied irrespective of the topological configuration of the system. However, BPTT is not local in time, which means that the adaptation must be done for a trajectory.

Let us present the ideas of dynamic backpropagation as applied to representation 1 of Figure 11-11. For this representation we need to find the parameter set of the ANN, here represented by w_i, but since the output of the net $v(n)$ is not directly accessible, we have to include the system $P(v, \alpha)$ in the computation of the error. Assume that the error at the output is $e(n) = d(n) - y(n)$. Since y is the output of the cascade, and $P(v, \alpha)$ is independent of w,

$$\frac{\partial e(n)}{\partial w_i} = P(v, \alpha)\frac{\partial v(n)}{\partial w_i}$$

We already know how to compute $\partial v(n)/\partial w_i$ for every time tick using backpropagation, but every time we change one of the parameters, there is a corresponding change in the output error (for the present time and for future time, since $P(v, \alpha)$ is dynamic). This change can be computed if the sensitivity of the ANN is passed forward through a copy of $P(v, \alpha)$ as in the following figure.

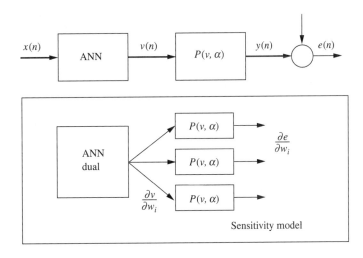

Notice that in general we need as many copies of $P(v, \alpha)$ as outputs in the ANN (one system generates a partial derivative $\partial e(n)/\partial w_i$). This is where the computational complexity gets out of hand quickly. But notice that we can update the parameters of the ANN for *each* time step, which is an advantage.

If we want to work with any of the other representations, this simple sensitivity model has to be appropriately modified, but it is possible in all cases to update the weights at each step.

Hence learning can be implemented on a sample-by-sample basis (in real time). The problem is that the forward propagation of sensitivities is very expensive computationally, and the method must be adapted to the particular system interconnectivity (block diagram).

NEUROSOLUTIONS EXAMPLE 11.10

Training an embedded neural network in a dynamic system

To show that we can use BPTT in a system built from ANNs and other dynamic components, let us solve the following problem. Consider a feedback system (representation 3 in Figure 11-11) where the forward transfer function is $g(v) = v/(1 + 4v^2)$ and the feedback $P(v, \alpha)$ is linear and given by $H(z) = (-1.12z + 0.33)/(z^2 - 0.8z + 0.15)$. The input is $x(n) = 2\sin(\pi n/25)$. The goal is to identify this feedback system, assuming that we know the feedback transfer function; in other words, we want to identify the forward path only. We cannot disconnect the two components, so training must be done in the integrated system, since we only know the combined output. We use BPTT for this task.

The Breadboard has two basic networks: one called the modeled plant and the other called the ANN model. The modeled plant has an unknown subsystem implemented by the top Axon with a DLL and a feedback subsystem, which is known and also modeled by an Axon with a DLL. The feedback block, called the known feedback model, is copied to the ANN model at the bottom of the Breadboard. The desired response for the ANN model comes from the modeled plant, also through the DLL on the L2 component, while the input is fed to both the plant and the ANN model. This arrangement is pure system identification.

The ANN model identifies only the feedforward part of the plant, which is easier than identifying the full plant with feedback. As a rule of thumb, our ANN models should include as much information as available from the external world. This Breadboard shows how you can do it.

11.9.2 Indirect Adaptive Control

Probably the most general control problem is one in which we do not have an equation for the plant, but we have access to the plant input and output. How can we derive a

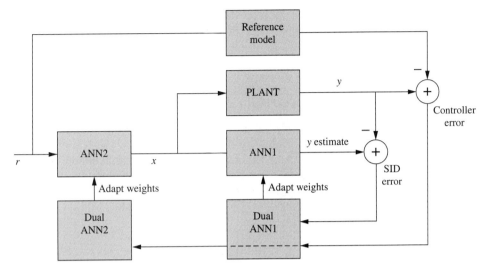

FIGURE 11-12   Indirect adaptive control

model to control such a plant? This question can be answered with the system identification concepts covered in Chapter 9, extended now to TLFNs. The block diagram we will use, shown in Figure 11-12, is called *indirect adaptive control.*

The main idea is to use two neural networks, one to *identify* the plant and the other to *control* the plant. The identification model is then used to pass the errors back to adapt the controller. If the plant is dynamic, BPTT (or dynamic backpropagation) must be used to train the models. The figure also shows an extra input-output loop that includes the *reference model.* The reference model dictates the required plant behavior when the input is $r(t)$. It allows us to compensate for known plant characteristics such as delays, thus simplifying the training process.

Let us explain the figure. Since we do not have an equation for the unknown plant, it would be impossible to adapt the controller (ANN2), which requires sensitivities generated by comparing the reference input (desired behavior) to the plant output. Hence we create a neural network identifier (ANN1), which will learn to produce an output that is similar to that of the plant. A typical topology for ANN1 is the NARX model (Chapter 10), in which the output is a nonlinear function of both the plant input (and its past values) and the plant output (and its past values), but other choices are possible.

Once the system identification (SID) neural network ANN1 is adapted, it behaves like the plant in terms of input and output, but most important, we created a known system description for which the dual network can be obtained. Therefore the controller ANN2 can be adapted by simply backpropagating the errors through the dual of ANN1.

This scheme requires us to adapt ANN1 first (possibly off-line), fix its parameters, and then adapt the controller ANN2. When both the controller and the system identifier are trained at the same time, the step size for ANN2 (the controller) has to be much smaller than that of ANN1 (the system identifier). Once again, the rule of thumb of 10 times slower is a good starting point.

NEUROSOLUTIONS EXAMPLE 11.11

Training a neural controller

We solve the following problem with NeuroSolutions. Suppose that we want to control a plant with unknown characteristics using Figure 11-12. We have the ability to only excite the plant and measure the output. A fundamental problem is how to adapt the weights of the controller, since we need the dual of the plant. So we have to use the black-box approach of indirect adaptive control. We will use a reference input $r(n) = \sin(2\pi n/25)$. The unknown nonlinear plant is described by the second-order differential equation

$$y(n + 1) = f[y(n), y(n - 1)] + x(n)$$

where

$$f[y(n), y(n - 1)] = \frac{y(n)y(n - 1)[y(n) + 2.5]}{1 + y^2(n) + y^2(n - 1)}$$

This function is implemented in the top Axon through a DLL and labeled "model plant."

There are two parts to the solution. The first step is to identify the plant; the second is to train the controller. In the first step we create ANN1, labeled "ANN for system ID," which is a one-hidden-layer focused TDNN. Filtered white noise is input to both ANN1 and the plant. The desired response is transmitted from the plant output through the DLL placed on the L2 Criterion. This is the pure system-identification configuration, and static backpropagation is used to adapt the plant model. In the second panel we simply check the result of the system-identification step. Notice that the backpropagation plane was discarded, since ANN1 (the plant model) will keep its weights fixed after the identification.

In the third panel we implement ANN2 (the controller) of Figure 11-12. We also use a focused TDNN with one hidden layer to create the controller and adapt it with BPTT. Even though we can train a focused TDNN with static backpropagation, we are backpropagating through ANN1, which has memory, thus we must use BPTT. Notice the interconnections. ANN2 receives as input the reference input (delayed by one sample), and its desired response is obtained from the difference of the plant output and the reference input. However, the error signal is propagated through the dual of ANN1 (the plant model). We have to assume that the system identification is sufficiently accurate, since we are passing the forward signal through the unknown plant and the errors through the dual of the plant model. If the plant model and the plant are different, this backpropagation strategy has catastrophic consequences.

11.10   HOPFIELD NETWORKS

Hopfield[1] networks are a special case of recurrent systems that use threshold PEs, do not have hidden PEs, and where the interconnection matrix is symmetric. The original Hopfield model did not have self-recurrent connections (Figure 11-13).

We can describe the discrete Hopfield network in discrete time as

$$y_i(n+1) = \text{sgn}\left(\sum_{j=1}^{N} w_{ij} y_j(n) - b_i + x_i(n)\right) \qquad i = 1, \ldots, N \qquad \textbf{(11.32)}$$

where sgn represents the threshold nonlinearity $(-1, 1)$ and b is a bias. We assume that the update is done sequentially by PE number. The input is a binary pattern $\mathbf{x} = [x_1, x_2, \ldots, x_N]^T$ and works as an initial condition; it is presented to the network and then taken away to let the network relax, so it disappears from Eq. 11.32. Due to the sign function we can see that the points visited during relaxation are the vertices of a hypercube in N dimensions. For simplicity the bias terms are set to zero in the following discussion.

Let us analyze the function of such a network for pattern association. Suppose that we have a binary input pattern $\mathbf{x}^p$, and we want this input pattern to be stable at the output; that is, we want the system to be an autoassociator and produce a stable output pattern $\mathbf{y} = \mathbf{x}^p$. The condition for a fixed point implies

$$y_i = \text{sgn}\left(\sum_{j=1}^{N} w_{ij} y_j\right) \qquad \textbf{(11.33)}$$

because at this point the forward equation (Eq. 11.32) has become stable and produces no change, that is, the system is at the fixed point, also called the attractor. It can be

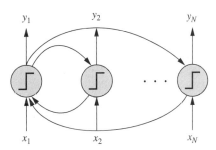

FIGURE 11-13   The Hopfield network

[1] John Hopfield is a theoretical biologist who studied the properties of a fully recurrent neural network using the ideas of dynamics, which led to the powerful concept of computational energy. See Hopfield [1982].

shown [Hopfield 1982] that to meet this condition, the weight matrix becomes

$$w_{ij} \propto x_i^p x_j^p \qquad (11.34)$$

or in words, the outer product of the patterns automatically computes the weights of the Hopfield network without the need for any learning laws. Alternatively, we can use Hebbian learning to create the weight matrix, just as with the static associative memory.

The weight matrix $\mathbf{W}$ is a symmetric matrix. But notice that this associative memory is *dynamic;* when we present the input $\mathbf{x}$ to the network as an initial condition, the system dynamics produce an output sequence $\mathbf{y}(n)$ that takes some time to stabilize but will approximate the stored pattern.

NEUROSOLUTIONS EXAMPLE 11.12

Hopfield network dynamics

This first example with Hopfield networks shows the dynamics of the system. We have created a three-input, three-output Hopfield network with two point attractors at vertices of the unit cube, $(1, -1, 1)$ and $(-1, 1, -1)$. Examine the weight matrix to see that they comply with Eq. 11.34.

Each of these attractors creates a basin of attraction. The input sets the initial condition for the system state. Hence the system state evolves toward the closest attractor under the "force" of the computational energy. This force is rather strong, as we can see by the "acceleration" of the system state.

Try inputs that will put the system state close to the boundary of the two bases (here the boundary is the plane $x - y + z = 0$). At exactly these locations the final value is zero. However, all the other values produce a convergence toward one of the two point attractors.

The attractive feature of Hopfield networks is that even when the input is partially deleted or corrupted by noise, the system dynamics still take the output sequence $\mathbf{y}(n)$ to $\mathbf{x}^p$. Since the system dynamics are converging to $\mathbf{x}^p$, we call this solution a point attractor for the dynamics. This system can also store multiple patterns P with a weight matrix given by

$$w_{ij} = \sum_{p=1}^{P} x_i^p x_j^p \qquad (11.35)$$

Just as we saw in the feedforward associative memory, there is crosstalk between the memory patterns, and the recall is possible only if the number of (random) input patterns is smaller than $0.15N$, where N is the number of inputs. For the case of very large N the probability of recall (99 percent of the memories recalled with an asymptotic probability of 1) of m patterns is guaranteed only if

$$\frac{m}{N} < \frac{1}{4 \ln N} \qquad \textbf{(11.36)}$$

which is rather disappointing, since it approaches zero even for large N. The intriguing property of the Hopfield network is pattern completion and noise removal, which is obtained by the convergence of the system state to the attractor.

NEUROSOLUTIONS EXAMPLE 11.13

Pattern completion in Hopfield networks

This example shows the convergence of the Hopfield network in a more realistic situation. We have created a 64-input Hopfield network to present the characters developed in Chapter 6, where we also treated the case of associative memories. We would like to show that the same behavior of association is also present in the Hopfield case.

We created a weight matrix by hand using Eq. 11.34. We can present the pattern at the input (just once) and watch the output pattern appear. This Hopfield network converges very quickly.

A more interesting observation is that even when the patterns are noisy or fragmented, the end result is still the full pattern. We can understand this in terms of basins of attraction. If the input places the system state within the appropriate basin of attraction, the final output will be the stored pattern, which is the complete (or noise-free) character. Try adding more noise (larger noise variance) to the characters to see how much the system can handle.

11.10.1 The Energy Function

We presented the practical aspects of Hopfield networks, but we assumed that the dynamics do in fact converge to a point attractor. Under what conditions can this convergence be guaranteed? This is a nontrivial question due to the recurrent and nonlinear nature of the network.

The importance of the Hopfield network comes from a very inspiring interpretation of its function provided by Hopfield [1982]. Due to the extensive interconnectivity, it may seem hopeless to try to understand what the network is doing when an input is applied. We can write the dynamic equations for each PE as in Eq. 11.32, but due to the fact that these difference equations are highly coupled and nonlinear, their solution seems to be beyond our reach. In practice this is not so. When the weight matrix is symmetric, the PEs are threshold nonlinearities, and the biases are zero, we can show that the network accepts an *energy function H*

$$H(y) = -\frac{1}{2}\sum_i \sum_j w_{ij}y_i y_j \tag{11.37}$$

Derivation of Energy Function

For the discrete-time Hopfield network considered here, it was shown that the function

$$H(y) = -\frac{1}{2}\sum_{i=1}^{N}\sum_{j=1}^{N} w_{ij} y_i y_j - \sum_{j=1}^{N} b_j x_j + \sum_{j=1}^{N} G(y_j)$$

$$G(y_i) = \int_0^{y_j} f(y)dy$$

is a Lyapunov function for the network, provided that the weight matrix is symmetric and the nonlinearity is sufficiently steep. Notice that if the biases are zero, the second term disappears, and if the nonlinearity approaches the step function, the last term approaches a constant.

The existence of a Lyapunov function for a given dynamic system guarantees stability (in the sense of Lyapunov). A Lyapunov function is a scalar function of the state with the following properties:

- It is continuous and has a continuous first partial derivative over the domain.
- It is strictly positive except at the equilibrium point.
- It is zero at the equilibrium point.
- It approaches infinity at infinity.
- It has a first difference that is strictly negative in the domain except at the equilibrium point.

A quadratic function of the state is a Lyapunov function for linear systems. For nonlinear systems the form of the Lyapunov function is unknown and is normally difficult to find. Hence the importance of Hopfield's work.

$H(y)$ trivially obeys all the conditions except for the last one. The proof shows that when the Hopfield network evolves according to its dynamics, H either stays the same or decreases, proving the strictly negative condition. See Hopfield [1982] for the complete proof.

The energy function is a function of the configuration of the states $\{y_i\}$ that is *nonincreasing* when the network responds to *any* input. We can show this by proving that every time one PE changes state, H decreases. When the PE does not change, H

remains the same. This means that the global network dynamics pull the system state to a minimum (along the gradient of H) that corresponds to one of the stored patterns. The location of the minimum in the input space is specified by the weights chosen for the network. Once the system reaches the minimum (the memory), it will stay there, so this minimum is a fixed point, or an attractor.

When the Hopfield network receives an input, the system state is placed somewhere in weight space. The system dynamics then relax to the memory that is closest to the input pattern. Around each fixed point there is thus a *basin of attraction* that leads the dynamics to the minimum. This explains why the Hopfield network is so robust to imprecisions (added noise or partial input) of the input patterns. Once the system state is in the basin of attraction for a stored pattern, the system relaxes to the undistorted pattern. (There are some practical problems, however, since when we load the system with patterns, spurious memories are created that may attract the system to unknown positions.)

An energy surface with minima and a basin of attraction creates the mental picture of a *computational energy* landscape, which is similar to a particle in a gravitational field. This metaphor is very powerful, because suddenly we are talking about global properties of a tremendously complex network in very simple terms. We have ways to specify each connection locally, but we also have this powerful picture of the computational energy of the system. This is pictorially depicted in Figure 11-14.

Hopfield provided one of the strongest links between information processing and dynamics. The existence of the computational energy function makes the convergence of the state of the Hopfield network to the stored pattern the same dynamic problem as a ball rolling down a hill in a gravitational field (which also accepts a potential function). We can then say that a dynamic system with point attractors implements an associative memory, whether the "hardware" is VLSI, a computer running these algorithms, biological neurons, or a solar system. Hopfield's view was crucial for the revival of neural networks in 1987.

Note that the Hopfield network, although a dynamic system, becomes "static" after convergence. Therefore other paradigms must be examined to understand the

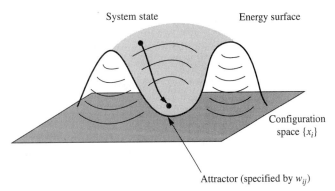

FIGURE 11-14 Computational energy over the configuration space

temporal processing that constantly occurs in our brains. Notice that dynamic systems may have singularities higher than the zero order (point attractor), such as limit cycles and chaotic attractors.

The Hopfield network is normally used with prespecified weights. They can be computed easily for the case of associative memories. We can also apply the fixed-point learning algorithm to train a single-layer network as an associative memory. However, there is no guarantee that the network is a Hopfield network, unless the weight matrix symmetry is externally enforced.

NEUROSOLUTIONS EXAMPLE 11.14

Training a recurrent network as an associative memory

Up to now we have created the weights of the Hopfield network by hand, by loading them without training. However, we can also use fixed-point learning as the training rule to find the weights.

In general, we can no longer say that we have a Hopfield network, since the weights may not be symmetric, but this should not discourage us from using such a training procedure. On rare occasions the system may become unstable, but we have workable solutions that are obtained without actually entering the weights by hand.

In this example, we use the association between long-distance phone calls and their prices (from Chapter 6) to show that the Hopfield-like network can be used as a heteroassociative memory.

Hopfield networks have also been used in optimization, because we can link the energy surface to problem constraints. The optimal solution is found by relaxing the system with the present input to find the closest solution (the attractor). Mapping the problem solution to the network is the difficult part and has to be done on a case-by-case basis [Hopfield and Tank, 1986].

NEUROSOLUTIONS EXAMPLE 11.15

Hopfield networks for optimization

The convergence of the Hopfield network to point attractors can also be explored for optimization problems. Just imagine that the solution of an optimization problem is coded in the energy function of the network. When an input is given to the network, the system state evolves, providing the optimal answer to that particular instance, since the Hopfield network minimizes the energy. The difficulty is in encoding the optimization problem in the energy function, but once this is done, the simple application of an example to the network provides an output that is the desired answer.

Here we treat a simple problem: analog-to-digital conversion. Hopfield and Tank [1986] showed that we can see the problem of converting an analog signal into bits as an optimization, which can then be solved by a Hopfield network.

We restrict our example to two-digit conversions; that is, we approximate the integer input X by

$$X \approx x_1 + 2x_2$$

where x_1 and x_2 will be 0 or 1. Hence the range for X is the set of integers [0, 3]. Hopfield proposed the performance index

$$J(\mathbf{x}) = 0.5 \left[X - \sum_{i=1}^{2} x_i 2^{i-1} \right]^2 - 0.5 \left[\sum_{i=1}^{2} 2^{2i-2} x_i (x_i - 1) \right]$$

where the first term computes the error and the second is a constraint that is minimized when the values of x_i are 0 or 1. This leads to a Lyapunov function of the type of Eq. 11.35 (but extended with the bias term), which can be implemented with

$$\mathbf{W} = \begin{bmatrix} 0 & -2 \\ -2 & 0 \end{bmatrix} \qquad \mathbf{b} = \begin{bmatrix} X - 0.5 \\ 2X - 2 \end{bmatrix}$$

The user-supplied value X is applied directly to the bias of the two PEs instead of the conventional input (as in the associative memory example). We have created a very simple Breadboard and two input fields in NeuroSolutions. Enter 0, 1, 2, or 3 in the box labeled X and the double of the first digit in the box $2X$. Try several inputs and watch the network provide the result.

Although very important from a conceptual point of view, Hopfield networks have met with limited success in real-world applications, mainly due to the spurious memories that limit their capacity to store patterns.

11.10.2 Brain-State-in-a-Box Model

Another interesting dynamic system that can be used as a clustering algorithm is Anderson's brain-state-in-a-box (BSB) model [Anderson, 1977]. BSB is a discrete-time neural network with continuous state (such as the Hopfield network with sigmoid nonlinearities). However, the equation of motion is

$$y_i(n + 1) = f\left(x_i(n) + \alpha \sum_{j=1}^{N} w_{ij} x_j(n) \right)$$

$$f(u) = \begin{cases} 1 & \text{if } u \geq 1 \\ u & \text{if } -1 \leq u \leq 1 \\ -1 & \text{if } u \leq -1 \end{cases} \qquad\qquad \textbf{(11.38)}$$

The nonlinearity is a threshold with a linear transition region. We assume here that there is no external bias and that α is a parameter that controls the convergence to the fixed points. The model is called "brain state in a box" because such a network has stable attractors at the vertices of the hypercube $[-1, +1]^n$, provided that $\mathbf{W}$ is symmetric and positive semidefinite or $\alpha \leq 2/|\lambda_{\min}|$. We can show that the BSB behaves as a gradient system that minimizes the energy of Eq. 11.38. The weight matrix to create the memories at the vertices of the hypercube follows the Hebbian rule of Eq. 11.35, where the values of x_i are restricted to be ± 1. We can show that the asymptotic capacity of the BSB model is identical to that of the Hopfield network.

The BSB model, however, is normally used as a clustering algorithm instead of an associative memory. Both systems create a basin of attractions and have point attractors, but the BSB has faster convergence dynamics, and its basins of attraction are more regular than in the Hopfield network. Hence it is possible to divide the input space into regions that are attracted to the corners of the hypercube, creating the clustering function.

NEUROSOLUTIONS EXAMPLE 11.16

Brain-state-in-a-box model

The BSB model is basically a positive-feedback nonlinear system. Due to the shape of the nonlinearities, the system has to converge to one of the corners of the hypercube; that is, the system amplifies the present input until all the PEs saturate. Hence the BSB is very sensitive to the initial pattern position in the input space, which has yielded its application in decision feedback. For the corners of the hypercube to behave as point attractors, all that is required is that the diagonal elements of the weight matrix be larger than the off-diagonal elements.

Here we have a simple 2-D example of the BSB. Enter a value in the boxes, and you will see the system relax to the closest corner. The system is similar in function to the Hopfield network, but here the location of the attractors is predefined at the vertices of the hypercube. Hence it can be used for clustering.

11.11   GROSSBERG'S ADDITIVE MODEL

If we abstract what we know about the interconnectivity of PEs, we realize that all the neural networks presented so far have much in common. Each PE has simple first-order dynamics. It receives activations from other PEs multiplied by the network weights, adds them, feeds the result to a static nonlinearity, and possibly adds a weighted version of the previous value. This sequence of operations can be encapsulated in continuous time for each PE by a first-order differential equation as follows:

$$\frac{d}{dt}y_i(t) = -\mu y_i(t) + f\left(\sum_j w_{ij}y_j(t) + b_i\right) + I_i(t) \qquad i = 1, \ldots, N, j \neq i \quad \textbf{(11.39)}$$

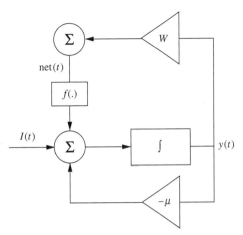

FIGURE 11-15 Grossberg's additive model

where $I(t)$ represents the forcing function, $y_i(t)$ represents the state of the dynamic system, and N is the number of PEs in the system. This is called *Grossberg's additive model* [Grossberg, 1982], and it is one of the most widely used neural models. In the additive model the weights are not a function of the state nor of time (after adaptation). Equation 11.39 implements a computationally interesting model if the three dynamic variables, $I(t)$, $y(t)$, and w, span three different time scales. The parameters w contain the long-term system memory, and $y(t)$ the short-term system memory. When $I(t)$ is presented to the neural system, $y(t)$ reflects the degree of matching with the long-term memory of the system contained in the weights. Figure 11-15 shows the block diagram of Grossberg's model.

Notice that all the connections are vectorized (multidimensional pieces), and they represent the computation, not the actual topology. A neural model is an *abstraction* of the neural network because it characterizes the dynamics and does not consider the interconnection matrix (i.e., the topology that we normally call the neural network). In the additive model the interaction among the PEs is additive, and the PEs have first-order dynamics. It is interesting to note that the additive model without the nonlinearity $f(.)$ defaults to the ARMA model, the most general linear system model.

In discrete time the equation becomes a difference equation of the form

$$y_i(n+1) = (1 - \mu)y_i(n) + f\left(\sum_j w_{ij}y_j(n) + b_i\right) + I_i(n)i = 1, \ldots, N, j \neq i \quad \textbf{(11.40)}$$

Grossberg's additive model gives rise to all the neural networks studied in this book. A dynamic neural network is obtained when the *external patterns are attached to $I(n)$* and the *initial states* of the dynamic system are *held constant* (normally zero) in Eq. 11.40.

Fully recurrent neural networks are the most general implementation of dynamic neural networks, but some other special cases are also possible. For instance, when the first term of Eq. 11.40 is zero, it means that there are no self-connections. When the first term is zero and the sum index j is kept smaller than i ($i > j$), the topology is feedforward but dynamic. TLFNs are also a special case of this topology where some of the PEs are linear and prewired for time processing.

The static mappers (MLPs) are obtained when the connections are restricted to be feedforward, the external inputs are applied to the initial states, and the forcing functions [$I(n)$] are zero in Eq. 11.40. When the initial states of the dynamic system are clamped by the inputs, there is no time evolution of the states that characterize the relaxation, and $y(n + 1)$ can be computed in zero steps.

Recurrent neural networks are regarded as more powerful and versatile than feedforward systems. They are able to create dynamic states. They have a wealth of dynamic regimes (fixed points, limit cycles, chaotic attractors) that can be changed by controlling the system parameters. They are thus very versatile and useful for modeling signals that vary in time, such as in time series analysis, control applications, and neurobiological modeling.

Gamma Model Equations

We have seen that changing the memory PE produces a different type of TLFN. The gamma model is built from combining a feedforward topology with memory PEs of the gamma type. The purpose of showing the equations here is to provide an introduction to the mathematical treatment of the gamma model [deVries and Principe, 1992]. At the same time, the complexity of the equations highlights the advantages of using the data-flow implementation of back-propagation when compared with normal equation-based learning. Using the convolution model of Eq. 11B.7, we can easily obtain the dynamic equations that describe the gamma model as

$$y_i(n + 1) = f\left(\sum_{\substack{j=0 \\ i>j}}^{N} \sum_{k=0}^{D} w_{ijk} y_{jk}(n)\right) + I_i(n)$$

$$y_{i,k}(n) = (1 - \mu_i)y_{i,k}(n - 1) + \mu_i y_{i,k-1}(n - 1) \tag{11B.9}$$

The following figure represents the block diagram of the gamma model.

Note that the second equation relates the signals at the gamma PE taps, while the first equation simply combines the temporal signals into a feedforward topology of nonlinear PEs. The equation that is specific to the gamma memory PE is therefore the second one.

To train the gamma model with BPTT, the gradients with respect to both the system states and the weights w_{ij} and μ_i are necessary, as given by Eq. 11B.10. We present just the results here [deVries and Principe 1992].

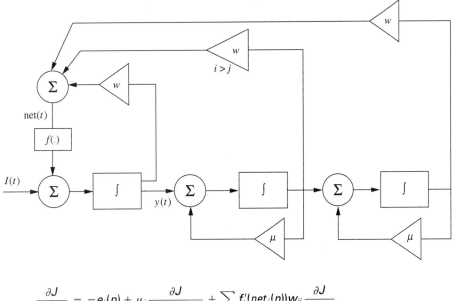

$$\frac{\partial J}{\partial y_i(n)} = -e_i(n) + \mu_i \frac{\partial J}{\partial y_{i1}(n+1)} + \sum_{j>1} f'_j(net_j(n))w_{ji}\frac{\partial J}{\partial y_j(n)}$$

$$\frac{\partial J}{\partial y_{ik}(n)} = (1-\mu_i)\frac{\partial J}{\partial y_{ik}(n+1)} + \mu_i \frac{\partial J}{\partial y_{i,k+1}(n+1)} + \sum_{j>i} f'_i(net_j(n))w_{jik}\frac{\partial J}{\partial y_j(n)} \quad \text{(11B.10)}$$

$$\frac{\partial J}{\partial w_{ijk}} = \sum_n f'_i(net_i(n))x_{jk}\frac{\partial J}{\partial y_{ik}(n)}$$

$$\frac{\partial J}{\partial \mu_i} = \sum_k \sum_n [x_{i,k-1}(n-1) - x_{ik}(n-1)]\frac{\partial J}{\partial y_{ik}(n)}$$

After analyzing the complexity of these equations, you can imagine the difficulty of making sure the equations are right and the training algorithms translate such procedures without errors. As we have been saying all along, however, the data-flow method avoids explicitly writing these equations. We just need to graphically specify the topology, have available the local maps for the nonlinear and gamma memory PEs, and specify the size of the trajectory in the dynamic controller.

11.12 BEYOND FIRST-ORDER DYNAMICS: FREEMAN'S MODEL

Neurocomputing has been centered on Grossberg's neural model for many years, but alternate models exist. Here we briefly describe a biologically realistic model of the cortex that was proposed by Walter Freeman [1975, 1992] following his studies of the rabbit olfactory system. The interesting thing about Freeman's model is that it is a computational model built from locally stable, coupled, nonlinear oscillators, and it produces chaotic activity. Information is processed by the global chaotic dynamics, unlike any of the previous models, where information processing requires stable dynamic regimes (remember the fixed points of Hopfield's associative memory).

The simplest biological system we model is the cell assembly, an aggregate of thousands of neurons. Freeman models the cell assembly (K0 model) as a second-order nonlinear dynamic system, described by

$$\frac{1}{ab}\left[\frac{d^2x(t)}{dt^2} + (a+b)\frac{dx(t)}{dt} + abx(t)\right] = Q(x(t)) \tag{11.41}$$

where a and b are constants, $x(t)$ represents the system state, and $Q(x(t))$ is a forcing function. This forcing function brings the contributions of other PEs through a nonlinearity $Q(x)$ where

$$Q(x) = \begin{cases} Q_m\left[1 - \exp\left(-\frac{e^x - 1}{Q_m}\right)\right] & \text{if} \quad V > -\mu_0 \\ -1 & \text{if} \quad V \le -u_0 \end{cases} \tag{11.42}$$

The nonlinearity belongs to the sigmoid class, but it is *asymmetric*. As we can see, this neuron model is divided into two parts: one is a linear, time-dependent operator defined as a second-order differential equation followed by a static nonlinearity. This division is in tune with the models used in neurocomputing. The nonlinearity models the synaptic transmission, while the dynamic equation models the transmission through axons and integration though dendrites.

To create a discrete network (a neural network) to approximate the continuous time behavior of Eq. 11.41, the impulse response of the linear subsystem is digitized and approximated by a three-tap gamma filter. This provides the implementation for the K0 model shown in Figure 11-16.

The next level in the hierarchy is the modeling of interactions between cell assemblies. Freeman proposes that the individual cell assemblies modeled by the K0s are effectively connected by excitatory and inhibitory interactions with constant coupling coefficients, which represent mitral–granular cell interactions. He proposes the development of tetrads of K0 models, interconnected as shown in Figure 11-17, where the negative and the positive signs mean inhibitory and excitatory connections, respectively. The tetrad of K0 models is called a KI model. Each group is described by a set of eight differential equations with fixed connections. Since all the elements so far are fixed, they represent the building block for the model of the olfactory system and are called *Freeman's PE*. Freeman's PE models the processing in the cortical column. Each column is therefore a neural oscillator. Table 11-1 shows the coefficients of Freeman's PE that have been derived from neurophysiologic measurements. The same table also shows the patterns stored in the model for the simulations given later in this chapter.

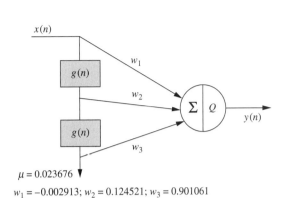

FIGURE 11-16 Gamma implementation of the K0 model

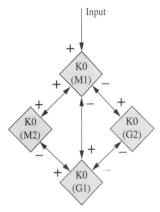

FIGURE 11-17 KII set, called here Freeman's PE

TABLE 11.1   Freeman's PE Parameter Set

KII	[**WMM_H; WMM_L; WGG**] = [0.3; 1.5; 0.25]
	[**WMM; WMG; WGM; WGG**] = [0.3; 5; 0.2; 0.25]

Patterns stored

$$\begin{bmatrix} 1 & 0 & 0 & 0 & 0 & 1 & 0 & 0 & 0 & 0 & 1 & 0 & 0 & 0 & 0 & 1 & 0 & 0 & 0 & 0 \\ 0 & 0 & 1 & 1 & 0 & 0 & 0 & 1 & 0 & 0 & 0 & 1 & 0 & 0 & 0 & 0 & 0 & 0 & 1 & 0 \\ 0 & 1 & 0 & 0 & 1 & 0 & 0 & 0 & 0 & 0 & 0 & 0 & 1 & 0 & 0 & 0 & 0 & 0 & 0 & 0 \\ 0 & 0 & 0 & 0 & 0 & 0 & 1 & 0 & 0 & 0 & 0 & 0 & 0 & 0 & 0 & 1 & 0 & 0 & 0 \\ 0 & 0 & 0 & 0 & 0 & 0 & 0 & 0 & 1 & 1 & 0 & 0 & 0 & 1 & 0 & 0 & 0 & 1 & 0 & 1 \end{bmatrix}$$

KIII	[**WPP; WMM_H; WMM_L; WGG**] = [0.2; 4; 0.5; 1.5]
	[**WMP; WEM; WAM_L; WCB; WBC**] = [0.5; 1.0; 1.0; 1.5; 1.0]
Internal	[**WMM; WMG; WGM; WGG**] = [0.25; 1.5; 1.5, 1.8]
	[**WEE; WEI; WIE; WII**] = [1.5; 1.5; 1.5; 1.8]
	[**WAA; WAB; WBA; WBB**] = [0.25; 1.4; 1.4; 1.8]
	[**W1; W2; W3; W4**] = [1.6; 0.5; 2; 1.5]
	[**Te1; Te2; Te3; Te4**] = [11; 15; 12; 24]
	[**Ts1; Ts2; Ts3; Ts4**] = [20; 26; 25; 39]

Patterns stored

$$\begin{bmatrix} 1 & 0 & 0 & 1 & 0 & 0 & 1 & 0 \\ 0 & 1 & 0 & 0 & 1 & 0 & 0 & 1 \end{bmatrix}$$

WMG, for example, means gain from element **G** to element **M**. **W1–W4** are gains associated with $f1(.)–f4(.)$.

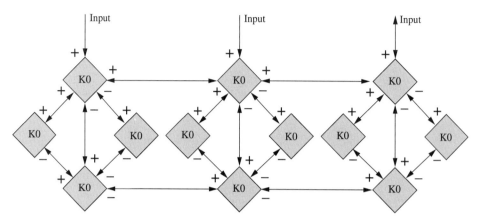

FIGURE 11-18   The connections of several Freeman's PEs

The KII model is a connected arrangement of Freeman's PEs (each K0 is connected to all other K0s in the same topological position) as shown in Figure 11-18. The
KII system models the olfactory cortex as a dynamic system with two basins of attraction. When no forcing input is applied, the KII model has a fixed point at the origin, but
when an input is applied, the system changes state to an oscillatory regime with large
amplitude. The following simulation exemplifies the dynamics.

NEUROSOLUTIONS EXAMPLE 11.17

Simulating Freeman's KII model

This example shows the NeuroSolutions implementation of the KII model. The KII
model is an arrangement of KI sets, which we called Freeman's PE. Freeman's PE is
an arrangement of four K0 sets, each of which is approximated by a gamma network
of Figure 11-16. The connections to form the Freeman's PE (internal unit feedback)
and KII model (global feedback among channels) have been separated for readability. Notice that a DLL implements the asymmetric sigmoidal nonlinearity.

We would like to show the response of the KII model to a step input. The
model is a 20-PE system that receives 1 or 0 from the input. When we plot the response of one of the PEs that receive an input, we see that the amplitude of the PE
oscillation increases. When the input is set to zero, the system state slowly decreases
to zero. We depict time plots of the input and outputs of an active and an inactive
PE. We also show the phase plot of one of the active Freeman's PEs (output of the
excitatory input versus the inhibitory input). This example shows that the local PEs
are stable oscillators with an amplitude modulated by the input. Hence the codifica-
tion of information is contained as a spatiotemporal pattern of amplitudes over the
model.

According to Freeman, the central olfactory system consists of two layers of coupled oscillators, the olfactory bulb (OB) and the prepiriform cortex (PC), mediated by lumped control of the anterior olfactory nucleus (AON). The receptor input connects to periglomerular cells (PG) and mitral cells (M). The mitral cells transmit to granular cells (G) and to the AON and PC. From the PC the final output is sent to other parts of the brain by deep pyramidal cells (P) and back to the OB and AON.

The central olfactory system is implemented by the KIII model, which is a hierarchical arrangement of KII models (Figure 11-19). The input is a fixed-weight, fully connected layer of excitatory K0 models (the periglomerular cells, PG). The second layer is the KII model described earlier (which models the olfactory bulb, OB). This is where learning takes place by changing the excitatory-to-excitatory connections

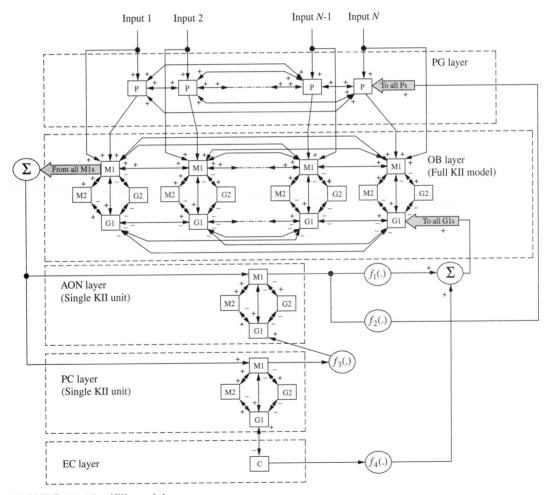

FIGURE 11-19 KIII model

using modified Hebbian learning. The next layer is a single Freeman's PE (modeling the anterior olfactory nucleus, AON), followed by another Freeman PE (modeling the prepiriform cortex, PC), which finally connects to a K0 set (modeling the pyramidal cells, P). There are extensive (but not full) connections in the topology: The output of the OB layer is fed to the AON and the PC layers with diffuse connections (modeling the medial olfactory tract). Feedback transmission is implemented from the PG and PC layers through long dispersive delays (also modeling the medial olfactory tract), which are represented in Figure 11-19 as $f(.)$. The parameters of the Freeman's PE in layers AON and PC are different from the OB layer (in fact, creating incommensurate oscillating frequencies); see Table 11-1.

The KIII model is a chaotic dynamic system. With no input the system at the OB layer produces chaotic time series with small amplitude and no spatial structure (the basal state). When a previously stored pattern is presented to the system, the OB layer still produces chaotic time series but "resonates" in a stable spatial amplitude distribution. This spatial distribution is what codifies the stored pattern. Hence the system works as an associative memory. However, the interesting thing is that the dynamics are no longer toward a point attractor, as in the Hopfield network, but to a spatiotemporal chaotic attractor. Freeman states that this system is capable of very fast switching among patterns and is robust to noise in the patterns.

NEUROSOLUTIONS EXAMPLE 11.18

Simulating Freeman's KIII model

This example demonstrates the oscillation produced by an eight-PE OB layer. The Breadboard is rather large. We have labeled each block according to Figure 11-17. Notice that the Breadboard is a replication of basically two pieces: the KII model and the gamma filter implementing the dispersive delay operator. Each has different parameters according to biological measurements.

The input is a rounded pulse. When there is no input, the system lies in a chaotic basal state in which each PE time series has the same basic amplitude but is very complex, as shown in the Megascope. When the pulse is applied, the system jumps to a new state, and the phase space plot (excitatory versus inhibitory PEs) shows a phase transition to one of the wings of the chaotic attractor. When the input disappears, the system goes back to its initial chaotic basal state. The system transitions are repeatable and fast. Notice that we do not need any extra mechanism to take the system from the pattern created by the excitation (as we did for the fixed point of the Hopfield network). The information is still coded in the amplitude of the chaotic oscillation across the PEs. Notice that all the parameters of the simulation were fixed (i.e., no learning is taking place).

The exciting thing about Freeman's model is that it extends the known paradigms of information processing that have low-order dynamics (Hopfield networks have dynamics of order zero, i.e., fixed points) to higher-order spatiotemporal dynamics. Moreover, the model was derived with neurophysiological realism. It is too early to predict its impact on artificial neural networks research and information-processing paradigms, but it embodies an intriguing dynamic system approach for information processing.

11.13 CONCLUSIONS

This chapter presented the development of learning rules for time processing with distributed TLFNs and fully recurrent networks. We showed the difficulty of training networks with delays, and we presented an extension to static backpropagation that was able to train topologies with delays. Backpropagation through time (BPTT) shares some of the nice properties of static backpropagation (such as locality in space and efficiency, since it uses the topology to compute the errors) but it is nonlocal in time. This creates difficulties that require the use of memory and backpropagating the error from the final time to the initial time (hence the name). With BPTT we harness the power to train arbitrary neural topologies to learn trajectories, which is necessary to solve problems in controls, system identification, prediction, and temporal pattern recognition. In a sense, this chapter closes the circle started with static nonlinear neural networks and time processing. Now we have the tools to train nonlinear dynamic systems.

In this chapter we also presented a view of dynamic neural networks as nonlinear dynamic systems. We tried to make the difference between static and dynamic neural networks more apparent. We could not discuss recurrent neural networks without presenting Hopfield networks, because of the perspective on computational energy. This analogy provides a "physical" view of computation in distributed systems that gives us insight into the nature of computation and the tools to quantify and design computational distributed systems.

We also introduced the idea of neural models. Neural models sit at the top of the systematized hierarchy of neural computation. Although we covered many neural networks throughout this book (linear regressors, MLPs, Hebbian, RBFs, Kohonen, linear combiners, TLFNs, recurrent networks), they all belong to the same neural model. This clearly leaves the search for other neural models open.

We finished the chapter by providing a glimpse of other computational paradigms that may become important in the future due to their biological realism and information principles based on higher-order (chaotic) dynamic regimes. Freeman's model points to the ultimate paradox: The quest for systematization (understanding) and organization that characterizes humans and their society emanates from brains that may be based on chaotic dynamics.

11.14 EXERCISES

11.1 State the differences between a Jordan and an Elman network and present two cases where each would be preferable.

11.2 If you disturb one weight of a TDNN with a memory size of $N = 10$ at $t = 0$, for how many samples in the future will you be able to measure the perturbation? What about the recurrent system of Figure 11-2 when μ is changed at $t = 0$?

11.3 Unfold the following network in time and present the ordered list in time. Compute the BPTT equation for a and b.

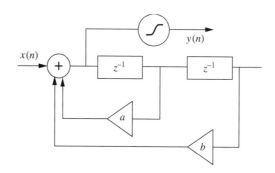

11.4 Present in a table the equation and its dual for the following components: sigmoid axon, synapse, delay, softmax.

11.5 Show how you would implement BPTT for the following network ($T = 10$ steps) using the duals and the data-flow method. (Each arrow shows a weight.)

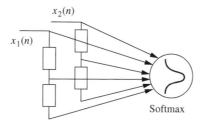

11.6 You have a fully connected network with 100 PEs to be trained by trajectory learning for $T = 1,000$ steps. Which method, BPTT or RTRL, provides the best computational solution (number of computations)? Which provides the best solution in terms of storage?

11.7 Create one state-space model for the problem of Example 11.3. We recommend that you define the state as the output of the adder.

11.8 Confirm the limit of Eq. 11.36 using the Breadboard of Example 11.14.

11.9 Modify Eq. 11.40 (and Fig 11-15) to obtain

- A one-hidden-layer MLP
- A focused TLFN (two taps)
- A Hopfield network
- An ARMA model

11.10 Study the effect of the relaxation on the training of the XOR problem of Example 11.8.

11.11 Fully train the system of Example 11.9 for the figure 8. Run the example several times and see how the system output follows the input signal. Now go to the test mode. In this mode the output of the net is fed back to the input, so there is no input. Change the bottom signal generators at both input and desired signal to a triangular wave. Include a phase shift of 90 degrees at the input and 101.25 degrees at the output. This creates a harder problem to train.

11.12 Study Examples 11.10 and 11.11 well. In particular, let the system train longer and change the inputs to observe differences in training.

11.15 NEUROSOLUTIONS EXAMPLES

11.16   CONCEPT MAP FOR CHAPTER 11

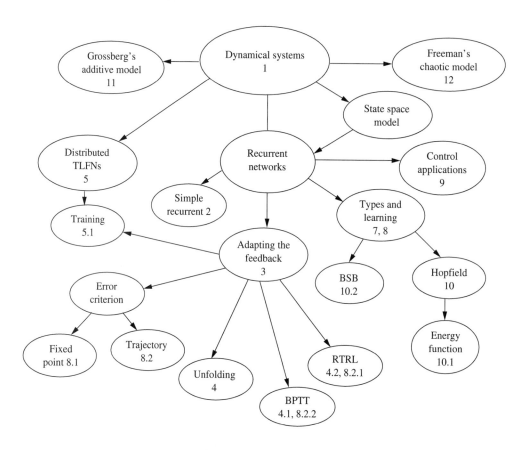

REFERENCES

Almeida, L., A learning rule for asynchronous perceptrons with feedback in a combinatorial environment, *First IEEE Int. Conf. Neural Networks,* 2:609–618, 1987.

Anderson, J., J. Silverstein, S. Ritz, and R. Jones, Distinctive features, categorical perception, and probability learning: Some applications of a neural model, *Psychol. Review,* 84:413–451, 1977.

Bengio, Y., Simard, P., and Frasconi, P., Learning long term dependencies with gradient descent is difficult, *IEEE Trans. Neural Networks,* 5:157–166, 1994.

Cohen, M., and S. Grossberg, Absolute stability of global patterns formation and parallel memory storage by competitive neural networks, *IEEE Trans. Syst. Man Cybernetics,* SMC-13, 99:815–826, 1983.

deVries, A., and Principe, J., The gamma model: A new model for temporal processing, *Neural Networks,* 5:565–576, 1992.

Elman, J., Finding structure in time, *Cognitive Science,* 14:179–211, 1990.

Feldkamp, L., and Puskorius, G., A signal processing framework based on dynamic neural networks with applications to problems in adaptation, filtering and classification, *Proc. IEEE,* 86:2259–2277, 1998.

Freeman, W., Tutorial on neurobiology: From single neurons to brain chaos, *Int. J. Bifurcation Chaos,* 2:451–482, 1992.

Freeman, W., *Mass Activation of the Nervous System,* Academic Press, 1975.

Giles, L., Liu, T., and Horne, B., Remembering the past: The role of embedded memory in recurrent neural architectures, in *Proceedings of the IEEE Workshop on Neural Networks for Signal Processing VII,* pp. 34–43, IEEE Press, 1997.

Grossberg, S., *Studies of Mind and Brain,* Reisel, 1982.

Haykin, S., *Neural Networks: A Comprehensive Foundation,* Macmillan, 1994.

Hopfield, J., Neural networks and physical systems with emergent collective computational abilities, *Proc. Natl. Acad. Sc. (USA),* 79:2554–2558, 1982.

Hopfield, J., and Tank, D., Computing with neural circuits: A model, *Science,* 233:625–633, 1986.

Jordan, M., Attractor dynamics and parallelism in a connectionist sequential machine, in *Proceedings of the Eighth Annual Conference on Cognitive Science Society,* pp. 532–546, 1986.

Narendra, K., and Parthasarathy, K., Identification and control of dynamical systems, *IEEE Trans. Neural Networks,* 1(1):4–27, 1990.

Puskorius, G., Feldkamp, L., and Davis, L., Dynamic neural networks methods applied to on-vehicle idle speed control, *Proc. IEEE,* 84:1407–1420, 1996.

Rabiner, L., and Juang, B., An introduction to hidden Markov models, *IEEE ASSP Magazine,* 3:4–16, 1986.

Wan, E., Diagramatic derivation of gradient algorithms for neural networks, *Neural Computation,* 8:182–201, 1996.

ELEMENTS OF LINEAR ALGEBRA AND PATTERN RECOGNITION

The goal of this appendix is to present the fundamental concepts of signals as vectors and to present the tools to analyze and transform vectors. This is followed by a brief introduction to random vectors and pattern recognition based on Bayes' theory.

A.1 INTRODUCTION

We are much more familiar with the typical operations we perform on real numbers than with the set theory concepts of the real numbers. However, the set properties are the ones that describe the structure of the space that provides the rules of the operations and ensures the correctness of the results.

Here we extend our reasoning and computational skills to ordered lists of real numbers called *vectors*. The branch of mathematics that studies vector operations is called *linear algebra*. Once we understand the fundamental principles of vector operations, we can simply operate with vectors and disregard the principles underlying these operations, exactly as we do with the operations with real numbers.

Neural networks receive many inputs (usually real numbers) and produce multiple outputs at a time, so they operate with vectors. One goal is to quantify the operation of the learning machine in some mathematical sense. While the mechanics of vector operations may not require knowledge of the fundamentals of linear algebra, this knowledge becomes very important when we try to analyze and understand the function of neural networks, so a brief introduction to linear algebra is worthwhile.

In neural networks we need efficient methods to deal with quantities that are multivalued. For instance, as inputs to a neural network to predict the stock market, we may use the present value of the S&P 500, its values a week ago and two weeks ago, the value of industrial production, the short-term interest rate, and so on (Figure A-1).

Each one of these variables can be treated separately as a number, but they can also be thought of as elements of a list that is sent in parallel to the neural net. The idea of treating several variables as a list can be mathematically formulated as a vector. A vector **x** is an ordered collection of numbers

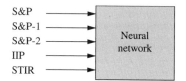

FIGURE A-1   A neural network with multiple inputs

$$\mathbf{x} = \begin{bmatrix} x_1 \\ \dots \\ x_N \end{bmatrix}$$

This is called a column vector of N elements. We have to specify whether the elements are integers, real numbers, or complex numbers. Normally we will work with vectors of real numbers, that is, a vector belongs to $\mathbf{R}^N$, the space of all the N-tuples of real numbers.

How do we operate with vectors? What are the properties of the operations? What is their meaning? The answer to these questions is the goal of this appendix.

A.2   VECTORS: CONCEPTS AND DEFINITIONS

We present here the most widely used operations with vectors and their meaning.

A.2.1 Definition of Linear Vector Space

The idea of a vector space is fundamental to operations with vectors, because it provides the structure of the space and the operations that are defined for vectors.

> **Definition:**   A vector space $\mathbf{X}$ is a set of vectors defined over a scalar field (here the real numbers) $\mathbf{R}$ that satisfy the following properties:

1. Vector addition: If arbitrary $\mathbf{x}_1$ and $\mathbf{x}_2$ belong to $\mathbf{X}$, then $\mathbf{x}_1 + \mathbf{x}_2$ also belongs to $\mathbf{X}$.
2. Vector addition is commutative; $\mathbf{x}_1 + \mathbf{x}_2 = \mathbf{x}_2 + \mathbf{x}_1$.
3. Vector addition is associative; $(\mathbf{x}_1 + \mathbf{x}_2) + \mathbf{x}_3 = \mathbf{x}_1 + (\mathbf{x}_2 + \mathbf{x}_3)$.
4. There is a unique neutral element for addition, the zero vector, such that $\mathbf{x}_1 + \mathbf{0} = \mathbf{x}_1$ for all $\mathbf{x}_1$.
5. For every $\mathbf{x}_1$ there is a unique vector $-\mathbf{x}_1$ such that $\mathbf{x}_1 + (-\mathbf{x}_1) = \mathbf{0}$.

6. For all scalars a belonging to **R** and vectors **x** belonging to **X**, we can define the multiplication $a\mathbf{x}$ that also belongs to **X**.

7. There is a unique neutral element for multiplication, such that $1\mathbf{x}_1 = \mathbf{x}_1$ for all $\mathbf{x}_1$.

8. Multiplication by a scalar is commutative; $a(b\mathbf{x}_1) = (ab)\mathbf{x}_1$.

9. Multiplication by a scalar is associative; $(a + b)\mathbf{x}_1 = a\mathbf{x}_1 + b\mathbf{x}_1$.

10. Multiplication by a scalar is distributive with respect to the addition of vectors; $a(\mathbf{x}_1 + \mathbf{x}_2) = a\mathbf{x}_1 + a\mathbf{x}_2$.

As we can see, these properties define a set of operations that can be done with vectors and show that the result is still a vector.

A.2.2 Notation and Construction

A vector is denoted by a bold letter. The elements of vectors are subscripted to show the ordering of the element in the list; for example, x_i is the ith entry in the list. Here a vector is a column of numbers. The size of a vector is equal to the number of its elements.

We can put vectors of size N into a one-to-one correspondence with points in $\mathbf{R}^N$. A vector **x** can be represented by a directed line segment that has the origin of the space as its initial point and the point with coordinates $(x_1, x_2, \ldots, x_N)$ as its end point (see Figure A-2). Thus we assign the ith element of the vector to the projection of x onto the ith axis.

A.2.3 Transpose of a Column Vector

The transpose of a column vector **x** is denoted by $\mathbf{x}^T$, and it is a row vector with the same elements:

$$\mathbf{x} = \begin{bmatrix} x_1 \\ \ldots \\ x_N \end{bmatrix} \qquad \mathbf{x}^T = [x_1 \quad \ldots \quad x_N]$$

The transpose of a row vector produces a column vector.

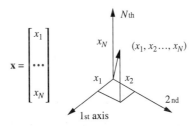

FIGURE A-2 Vectors and points in $\mathbf{R}^N$

A.2.4 Vector Addition and Subtraction

We can add or subtract only vectors of the same size, that is, with the same number of elements. To add two vectors of the same size, we add or subtract the elements of the same index $z_i = x_i + y_i$:

$$\mathbf{z} = \begin{bmatrix} z_1 \\ z_2 \\ \ldots \\ z_N \end{bmatrix} = \mathbf{x} + \mathbf{y} = \begin{bmatrix} x_1 + y_1 \\ x_2 + y_2 \\ \ldots \\ x_N + y_N \end{bmatrix} \tag{A.1}$$

There is an intuitive, geometric picture for the vector addition operation. Vector addition corresponds to the geometric addition of the corresponding directed line segments, so it is easy to visualize. The vector subtraction operation is similar, but instead of adding the components we subtract them. Vector subtraction corresponds also to the geometric subtraction of the corresponding directed line segments (reverse the direction of the vector that is being subtracted; see Figure A-3).

A.2.5 Length (or Norm) of a Vector

A norm of a vector is a function that produces a scalar. The best-known norm is the L_2 norm. The L_2 norm of a vector is a scalar that is equal to its length. The norm is denoted by $\| \ \|$ and is computed as

$$\|\mathbf{x}\| = \sqrt{x_1^2 + \cdots + x_N^2} \tag{A.2}$$

The length of a vector in an N-dimensional space is simply the extension of the Pythagorean theorem to N dimensions, so the L_2 norm corresponds to the Euclidean distance.

A.2.6 Multiplication by a Scalar

A real constant a times a vector is the multiplication of a by every element x_i:

$$a\mathbf{x} = \begin{bmatrix} ax_1 \\ \ldots \\ ax_N \end{bmatrix} \tag{A.3}$$

This operation scales the vector length by the same constant a.

A.2.7 Inner or Dot Product

The inner product is the vector operation equivalent to the multiplication of real numbers. The inner product of two vectors $\mathbf{x} = [x_1, \ldots, x_N]^T$ and $\mathbf{y} = [y_1, \ldots, y_N]^T$ is the

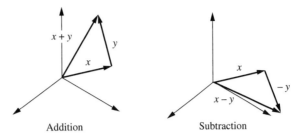

FIGURE A-3 Addition and subtraction of vectors

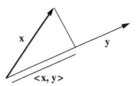

FIGURE A-4 Inner product of two vectors

scalar

$$\langle \mathbf{x}, \mathbf{y} \rangle = \sum_{i=1}^{N} x_i y_i \tag{A.4}$$

The inner product can be visualized as the projection of one vector onto the other (Figure A-4). The inner product is a very common operation with vectors. Note that the inner product of a vector with itself gives the square of its length. Another notation for the inner product $\langle \mathbf{x}, \mathbf{y} \rangle$ is $\mathbf{x} \cdot \mathbf{y}$, so the inner product is also called the dot product.

A.2.8 Cauchy-Schwartz Inequality

The absolute value of $\langle \mathbf{x}, \mathbf{y} \rangle$ is

$$|\langle \mathbf{x}, \mathbf{y} \rangle| \leq \|\mathbf{x}\| \|\mathbf{y}\| \tag{A.5}$$

A.2.9 Angle between Vectors

The angle θ between two vectors is defined by

$$\cos \theta = \frac{\langle \mathbf{x}, \mathbf{y} \rangle}{\|\mathbf{x}\| \|\mathbf{y}\|} \tag{A.6}$$

A.2.10 Orthogonal Vectors

Two vectors are orthogonal when the angle between them is 90 degrees, which implies that their inner product is zero (Eq. A.6). The concept of orthogonality can also be

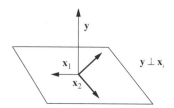

FIGURE A-5 Vector normal to a space

extended to spaces. A vector is orthogonal to a space when it is orthogonal to all vectors in the space; that is, the vector must lie along the normal to the space (Figure A-5).

The vectors that lie along the axes of $\mathbf{R}^N$ are orthogonal. It is easy to write the coordinates of orthogonal vectors by thinking about the axes of the space:

$$\mathbf{x} = \begin{bmatrix} 1 \\ 0 \\ 0 \end{bmatrix} \qquad \mathbf{y} = \begin{bmatrix} 0 \\ 1 \\ 0 \end{bmatrix} \qquad \mathbf{z} = \begin{bmatrix} 0 \\ 0 \\ 1 \end{bmatrix}$$

However, there are other, less obvious combinations that make vectors orthogonal (use the inner-product definition). When the norm of the orthogonal vectors in a set is 1, the set is called orthonormal. Dividing each orthogonal vector by its length creates the orthonormal set. We can then conclude that in an N-dimensional space, we can have at most N orthogonal vectors.

A.2.11 Linearly Independent Vectors

A set of vectors $\{\mathbf{x}_i\}$ is called linearly independent if the equation

$$a_1\mathbf{x}_1 + a_2\mathbf{x}_2 + \cdots + a_N\mathbf{x}_N = 0$$

is true if and only if all the constants a_i are zero. In a linearly dependent set of vectors at least one vector can be represented by a linear combination of the others, so some are superfluous because they can be composed from other elements in the set. A linearly independent set of vectors is minimal; we need them all since we cannot represent any as a sum of the others.

A.2.12 Span of a Space and the Concept of a Basis

The span of a collection of vectors $\{\mathbf{x}_i\}$ is the space of all their linear combinations. What this means is that if we have three linearly independent vectors, we can span the 3-D space, because we can create any vector as a linear combination of these three linearly independent ones. For this reason a set of linearly independent vectors is also called a basis. The dimension of a vector space is the size of the maximum number of linearly independent vectors.

Note that a basis does not mean that the vectors are orthogonal, but simply linearly independent. However, orthogonal bases have convenient properties, and we should try to work with them. One such property is that in an orthogonal basis the projection in each direction can be computed independently of the others.

A.2.13 Gram-Schmidt Orthogonalization Procedure

Gram-Schmidt orthogonalization is a procedure to obtain orthogonal vectors $\{\mathbf{o}_i\}$ from any linearly independent set $\{\mathbf{x}_i\}$. Start with the first vector of the $\mathbf{x}$ basis and make $\mathbf{o}_1 = \mathbf{x}_1$. Then take the second vector $\mathbf{x}_2$, and subtract from it the part that lies along the direction $\mathbf{x}_1$, that is, $\mathbf{o}_2 = \mathbf{x}_2 - a\mathbf{o}_1$, where a is the inner product of the two vectors $\mathbf{o}_1$ and $\mathbf{x}_2$:

$$a = \frac{\langle \mathbf{x}_2, \mathbf{o}_1 \rangle}{\langle \mathbf{o}_1, \mathbf{o}_1 \rangle} \tag{A.7}$$

Continue the process to obtain all the other vectors:

$$\mathbf{o}_k = \mathbf{x}_k - \sum_{i=1}^{k-1} \frac{\langle \mathbf{x}_k, \mathbf{o}_i \rangle}{\langle \mathbf{o}_i, \mathbf{o}_i \rangle} \mathbf{o}_i \tag{A.8}$$

A.2.14 Vector Expansion

In a vector space we can always represent any vector as a sequence of numbers that are the projections of the arbitrary vector on each basis. Take an arbitrary vector $\mathbf{x}$ in a vector space with basis $\mathbf{u} = [\mathbf{u}_1, \mathbf{u}_2, \ldots, \mathbf{u}_N]^T$. The vector can be written as

$$\mathbf{x} = \sum_{i=1}^{N} x_i \mathbf{u}_i \tag{A.9}$$

so we can always represent $\mathbf{x}$ by the column of numbers

$$\mathbf{x} = \begin{bmatrix} x_1 \\ \ldots \\ x_N \end{bmatrix} \tag{A.10}$$

This was our first definition of a vector, but now we relate it to a basis, as we should. We can appreciate the tremendous advantage of an orthogonal basis if we compute the components of vectors in a nonorthogonal basis. The component of the vector $\mathbf{x}$ over the jth basis is simply the inner product of the vector with that basis. From Eq. A.4 this gives

$$\langle \mathbf{x}, \mathbf{u}_j \rangle = \left\langle \sum_{i=1}^{N} x_i \mathbf{u}_i, \mathbf{u}_j \right\rangle \tag{A.11}$$

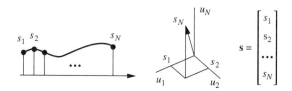

FIGURE A-6   Signals as vectors

which will be a function of every x_i. If the basis is orthogonal, we have a much simpler expression, since the inner product is zero for i different than j, yielding simply

$$x_j = \frac{\langle \mathbf{x}, \mathbf{u}_j \rangle}{\langle \mathbf{u}_j, \mathbf{u}_j \rangle} \tag{A.12}$$

A.2.15 Signals as Vectors

A discrete signal with N samples can be put in a one-to-one correspondence with vectors by using the vector expansion explained earlier. First, we count the number of samples and choose a space of the same dimensionality, N. Then we map the signal onto a point in this space by the following procedure: Assign the first signal sample to the value of the first coordinate in the N-dimensional space, the second sample as the value of the second coordinate, and so on. A discrete signal of length N thus becomes a point in an N-dimensional space. We have seen that vectors can also be put into a one-to-one correspondence with points in $\mathbf{R}^N$, so we can represent the signal as a vector with elements given by the time samples (Figure A-6).

Remember, however, that there is an implicit basis chosen when we go from a signal to a vector. If a different orthonormal basis to represent the vector is selected, the vector representation of the signal will probably be modified. But not everything changes. Since the length of a vector is independent of the orthonormal basis that is used to represent it, the length in the two representations will be the same.

A.3 MATRICES: CONCEPTS AND DEFINITIONS

In the following sections we present definitions and operations common with matrices.

A.3.1 Definition of a Matrix

Matrices are ordered arrangements of elements w_{ij}, like vectors but with two indices, a row index i and a column index j, as in

$$\mathbf{W} = \begin{bmatrix} w_{11} & \cdots & w_{1M} \\ w_{21} & \cdots & w_{2M} \\ \cdots & \cdots & \cdots \\ w_{N1} & \cdots & w_{NM} \end{bmatrix} \tag{A.13}$$

We can think of a matrix as a column vector of elements that are row vectors or vice versa. Alternatively, we can think of a row vector **x** as a matrix with one row and a number of columns equal to the dimension of the vector. A matrix is square when the number of columns is equal to the number of rows ($M = N$).

A.3.2 Addition and Subtraction of Matrices

Just as in vectors, the addition (or subtraction) of two matrices of the same size produces a third matrix of the same size with elements that are the addition (or subtraction) of the elements with the same index.

A.3.3 Multiplication of a Matrix by a Constant

The multiplication of a matrix by a constant equals the multiplication of each element of the matrix by the constant.

A.3.4 Toeplitz Matrix

A matrix is a Toeplitz matrix if it is a square matrix with identical elements in the main diagonal and the rest of the elements are symmetric with respect to the main diagonal. Toeplitz matrices are highly symmetric, so many simplified results are known for this class of matrices.

A.3.5 Vector-Matrix Multiplication

Vector-matrix multiplication is a very important operation. We define the multiplication of the row vector **x** by the matrix **W** as a new row vector **y** with a number of columns equal to the number of columns of **W** and elements given by

$$
[\longrightarrow] \begin{bmatrix} | & | & | \\ | & | & | \\ \downarrow & \downarrow & \downarrow \end{bmatrix} \qquad \mathbf{y} = \mathbf{Wx} = \begin{bmatrix} \sum_{i=1}^{N} x_i w_{i,1} & \sum_{i=1}^{N} x_i w_{i,2} & \ldots & \sum_{i=1}^{N} x_i w_{i,M} \end{bmatrix} \quad \textbf{(A.14)}
$$

We cannot always multiply a vector by a matrix. To execute the operation, the number of columns of **x** has to be equal to the number of rows of **W**. Vector-matrix multiplication is not commutative:

$$ \mathbf{xW} \neq \mathbf{Wx} \qquad \textbf{(A.15)} $$

As we will see, multiplying a vector by a matrix rotates the vector. If **x** is a column vector, we can only post multiply **W** by **x**; that is, $\mathbf{y} = \mathbf{Wx}$ is a column vector in which each element is the product of the corresponding row of **W** with **x**.

When we multiply a row matrix by a column matrix, we get a single element. Hence the multiplication of a row vector by a column vector is simply the inner product of the two vectors:

$$\mathbf{x}^T\mathbf{y} = [x_1 \quad \ldots \quad x_N]\begin{bmatrix} y_1 \\ \ldots \\ y_N \end{bmatrix} = \sum_{i=1}^{N} x_i y_i \tag{A.16}$$

A.3.6 Range and Null Space of a Matrix

The range of an $N \times M$ matrix $\mathbf{W}$ is a subspace defined by all possible nonzero vectors $\mathbf{y}$ of size M (the column vectors of $\mathbf{W}$) such that $\mathbf{y} = \mathbf{W}\mathbf{x}$, where $\mathbf{x}$ is an arbitrary N-dimensional vector. The null space is also a subspace where $\mathbf{A}\mathbf{x} = 0$ for an arbitrary N-dimensional $\mathbf{x}$.

A.3.7 Definition of the Matrix Transpose

The transpose of a matrix is another matrix in which the rows are exchanged with the columns. We denote transpose by a superscript T. The transpose of a column vector of size N becomes a row vector of the same size N. When we transpose a matrix, the diagonal elements remain unchanged. A square matrix that is equal to its transpose is called symmetric.

The transpose of a product is the product of the transposed matrices with the order reversed:

$$(\mathbf{W}\mathbf{Q})^T = \mathbf{Q}^T\mathbf{W}^T \tag{A.17}$$

A.3.8 Definition of Outer Product

The outer product is the "mirror image operation" of the inner product. It is the multiplication of a column vector by a row vector, which produces a matrix of row size equal to the size of the column vector and column size equal to the size of the row vector.

$$\mathbf{x}\mathbf{y}^T = \begin{bmatrix} x_1 \\ \ldots \\ x_N \end{bmatrix}[y_1 \quad \ldots \quad y_N] = \begin{bmatrix} x_1 y_1 & \ldots & x_1 y_N \\ \ldots & \ldots & \ldots \\ x_N y_1 & \ldots & x_N y_N \end{bmatrix} \tag{A.18}$$

A.3.9 Determinant of a Matrix

The determinant of a square matrix is a scalar given by

$$\det(\mathbf{W}) = \sum_{i=1}^{N} (-1)^{j+1} w_{1j} \det\left(\mathbf{W}_{1j}\right) \tag{A.19}$$

where $\mathbf{W}_{1j}$ is an $(N - 1)$ by $(N - 1)$ matrix obtained by deleting the first row and the jth column of $\mathbf{W}$. When the determinant is nonzero, the matrix is called *nonsingular,* or *full rank*. When the determinant is zero, the matrix is called *singular.* A diagonal matrix has a determinant that is the product of the diagonal elements.

A.3.10 Trace of a Square Matrix

The trace of a square matrix $\mathbf{W}$ is the sum of all the diagonal elements of $\mathbf{W}$:

$$tr(\mathbf{W}) = \sum_{i=1}^{N} w_{ii} \tag{A.20}$$

A.3.11 Inverse of a Matrix

The inverse of a square matrix $\mathbf{W}$ is another matrix $\mathbf{W}^{-1}$ that obeys the relation

$$\mathbf{W}\mathbf{W}^{-1} = \mathbf{I} \qquad \mathbf{I} = \begin{bmatrix} 1 & 0 & \dots & 0 \\ 0 & 1 & \dots & 0 \\ \dots & \dots & \dots & \dots \\ 0 & 0 & \dots & 1 \end{bmatrix} \tag{A.21}$$

The matrix $\mathbf{I}$ is called an identity matrix. The inverse of a product of matrices is

$$(\mathbf{W}\mathbf{Q})^{-1} = \mathbf{Q}^{-1}\mathbf{W}^{-1} \tag{A.22}$$

Only nonsingular matrices have inverses. If the matrix is diagonal, its inverse is simply the inverse of the diagonal elements.

A.3.12 Computation of the Inverse

The inverse of a square matrix $\mathbf{W}$ is

$$\mathbf{W}^{-1} = \frac{adj\mathbf{W}}{|\mathbf{W}|} \tag{A.23}$$

where $adj\mathbf{W}$ is the adjoint of $\mathbf{W}$ and $|\mathbf{W}|$ is the determinant of $\mathbf{W}$. The adjoint of $\mathbf{W}$ is

$$adj\mathbf{W} = \mathbf{C}^T \tag{A.24}$$

that is, the transpose of the matrix of cofactors of $\mathbf{W}$. To compute the cofactors, we first have to create the minors of $\mathbf{W}$. The minor M_{ij} of $\mathbf{W}$ is the determinant of $\mathbf{W}$ after the ith row and the jth column have been removed. The cofactor c_{ij} is the signed minor of $\mathbf{W}$:

$$c_{ij} = (-1)^{i+j} M_{ij} \tag{A.25}$$

The matrix of cofactors $\mathbf{C}$ is the matrix formed by c_{ij}. As an example, let us compute the inverse of

$$\mathbf{W} = \begin{bmatrix} 1 & 2 \\ 3 & 4 \end{bmatrix} \qquad \mathbf{C} = \begin{bmatrix} 4 & -3 \\ -2 & 1 \end{bmatrix} \qquad adj\mathbf{W} = \begin{bmatrix} 4 & -2 \\ -3 & 1 \end{bmatrix}$$

$$|\mathbf{W}| = 4 - 6 = -2 \qquad \mathbf{W}^{-1} = \begin{bmatrix} -2 & 1 \\ \frac{3}{2} & -\frac{1}{2} \end{bmatrix}$$

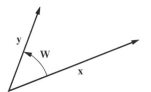

FIGURE A-7 Multiplication of a matrix by a vector

A.3.13 Rank of a Matrix

The rank of $\mathbf{W}$ is the dimension of the range of $\mathbf{W}$, that is, the number of linearly independent columns of $\mathbf{W}$. A full-rank matrix has a nonzero determinant and accepts an inverse.

A.3.14 Linear Transformation

A linear transformation is simply the multiplication of a vector by a matrix. A linear transformation of $\mathbf{x}$ produces a vector $\mathbf{y} = \mathbf{W}\mathbf{x}$ that is a rotation and a scaling of $\mathbf{x}$, as in Figure A-7.

If $\mathbf{W}$ is full rank, then $\mathbf{y}$ has the same dimension as $\mathbf{x}$, and it belongs to the range of $\mathbf{W}$. This corresponds to a change of direction and length. However, when $\mathbf{W}$ is singular (i.e., not full rank), the transformation is called a subspace projection, because the vector $\mathbf{y}$ exists in the null space of $\mathbf{W}$.

A.3.15 Linear Transformations Revisited

The linear transformation described in the previous section can be described in more general terms. It effectively corresponds to a transformation or mapping between two finite-dimensional vector spaces. Let $\mathbf{X}$ be a vector space called the domain; let $\mathbf{Y}$ be another vector space called the range. The transformation is a mapping relating each $\mathbf{x} \in \mathbf{X}$ to $\mathbf{y} \in \mathbf{Y}$. A mapping $\mathbf{A}$ is linear if these two conditions are met:

1. For all $\mathbf{x}_1$ and $\mathbf{x}_2 \in \mathbf{X}$, $\mathbf{A}(\mathbf{x}_1 + \mathbf{x}_2) = \mathbf{A}(\mathbf{x}_1) + \mathbf{A}(\mathbf{x}_2)$.
2. For all $\mathbf{x} \in \mathbf{X}$ and $w \in \mathbf{R}$, $\mathbf{A}(w\mathbf{x}) = w\mathbf{A}(\mathbf{x})$.

In this context it is important to relate an orthogonal basis of $\mathbf{x}$ to an orthogonal basis of $\mathbf{y}$. We can show that this relation is given by

$$\begin{bmatrix} a_{11} & \cdots & a_{1N} \\ \cdots & \cdots & \cdots \\ a_{M1} & \cdots & a_{MN} \end{bmatrix} \begin{bmatrix} x_1 \\ \cdots \\ x_N \end{bmatrix} = \begin{bmatrix} y_1 \\ \cdots \\ y_N \end{bmatrix} \tag{A.26}$$

There is thus always a matrix representation for the linear transformation between $\mathbf{x}$ and $\mathbf{y}$. However, the matrix representation is not unique. We can, for instance, change the orthogonal basis of $\mathbf{y}$ (there are many possible orthogonal bases of a vector space), which implies that $\mathbf{A}$ must be different.

A.3.16 Change of Basis

Suppose we have a basis of $\mathbf{X}$ called $\{\mathbf{x}_1\}$, a basis of $\mathbf{Y}$ called $\{\mathbf{y}_1\}$, and a linear transformation $\mathbf{A}$ between $\mathbf{X}$ and $\mathbf{Y}$, $\mathbf{Y} = \mathbf{AX}$. Now let us change the basis of $\mathbf{X}$ to $\{\mathbf{x}_2\}$ and the basis of $\mathbf{Y}$ to $\{\mathbf{y}_2\}$. For these new bases, the linear transformation is different, that is, $\mathbf{Y} = \mathbf{BX}$. How can we relate $\mathbf{A}$ and $\mathbf{B}$? The obvious answer is to relate the two basis sets.

Let $\mathbf{U}$ be a matrix that represents the new basis $\{\mathbf{x}_2\}$ in the original basis $\{\mathbf{x}_1\}$, that is,

$$\mathbf{x}_2 = \mathbf{U}\mathbf{x}_1 \qquad \mathbf{U} = \begin{bmatrix} u_{11} & \dots & u_{1N} \\ \dots & \dots & \dots \\ u_{N1} & \dots & u_{NN} \end{bmatrix} \tag{A.27}$$

Likewise, let $\mathbf{S}$ be another matrix that represents $\{\mathbf{y}_2\}$ in the original span $\{\mathbf{y}_1\}$. Then

$$\mathbf{B} = \mathbf{S}^{-1}\mathbf{A}\mathbf{U} \tag{A.28}$$

This is called a *similarity transformation* and represents the relationship between two matrices under a linear transformation. If we are careful in choosing the basis, the linear transformation becomes obvious.

A.3.17 Eigenvectors and Eigenvalues

This formulation applies only to square matrices. We saw that when we multiply a vector by a matrix, the vector generally changes direction. However, there are special vectors $\mathbf{e}$ for a given matrix $\mathbf{W}$ that do not change directions when multiplied by $\mathbf{W}$. These are called *eigenvectors* of $\mathbf{W}$, and they obey the relationship

$$\mathbf{W}\mathbf{e} = \lambda\mathbf{e} \tag{A.29}$$

The scalars λ are called the *eigenvalues* of $\mathbf{W}$. The advantage of operating with the eigenvectors is that matrix multiplication becomes a set of scalar operations, since we only need to multiply each vector component by the corresponding eigenvalue. If $\mathbf{W}$ is $N \times N$, the product of any vector by $\mathbf{W}$ requires N^2 multiplications. However, if $\mathbf{y}$ is in the eigenspace of $\mathbf{W}$, we need only N multiplications to obtain the result.

When $\mathbf{W}$ is $N \times N$, there are at most N distinct eigenvalues. When $\mathbf{W}$ is symmetric, the eigenvectors are orthogonal, so they become an orthogonal basis of the space. This has important implications, because we can rewrite $\mathbf{W}$ as

$$\mathbf{W} = \mathbf{\Phi}\mathbf{\Lambda}\mathbf{\Phi}^T \qquad \mathbf{\Phi} = [\phi_1 \quad \dots \quad \phi_N] = \begin{bmatrix} e_{11} & \dots & e_{1N} \\ \dots & \dots & \dots \\ e_{N1} & \dots & e_{NN} \end{bmatrix} \qquad \mathbf{\Lambda} = \begin{bmatrix} \lambda_{11} & \dots & 0 \\ \dots & \dots & \dots \\ 0 & \dots & \lambda_N \end{bmatrix}$$

$$\tag{A.30}$$

where $\mathbf{\Lambda}$ is a diagonal matrix of the eigenvalues of $\mathbf{W}$, and $\mathbf{\Phi}$ is the matrix with columns given by the eigenvectors of $\mathbf{W}$. We can always write any symmetric matrix $\mathbf{W}$ in this way. Notice that we effectively found a way to diagonalize the symmetric matrix $\mathbf{W}$.

In terms of a linear transformation of a vector $\mathbf{x}$, if the linear transformation is the eigenvector matrix $\mathbf{\Phi}$ and $\mathbf{y} = \mathbf{\Phi}^T \mathbf{x}$, then we found a way to represent $\mathbf{x}$ in a new coordinate system formed by the eigenvectors of $\mathbf{W}$. In this new coordinate system each projection can be computed independently of the others, that is,

$$y_i = \mathbf{\Phi}^T{}_i \mathbf{x} \qquad \text{for } i = 1, \ldots, N \tag{A.31}$$

In the new coordinate system we can write the matrix $\mathbf{W}$ as a diagonal matrix, so the transformation by $\mathbf{\Phi}$ diagonalizes $\mathbf{W}$, and it is called an *orthogonal transformation*. Under orthogonal transformations, Euclidean distances are preserved.

These results can be extended to nonsquare matrices and are called *singular value decomposition*.

A.3.18 Whitening Transformation

After applying an orthogonal transformation as done in the previous section, we can still make the diagonal matrix $\mathbf{L}$ an identity matrix (i.e., a diagonal matrix with all entries equal to 1) by including a new transformation to $\mathbf{\Phi}$ equal to $\mathbf{\Lambda}^{-1/2}$:

$$\mathbf{y} = \mathbf{\Phi}\mathbf{\Lambda}^{-1/2}\mathbf{x} \tag{A.32}$$

The transformation $\mathbf{\Phi}\mathbf{\Lambda}^{-1/2}$ is called a *whitening transformation*.

All the eigenvalues after a whitening transformation become identical. This is important for gradient-descent learning since the eigenvalue spread is one.

A.3.19 Derivative of a Matrix

We define the derivative of a matrix $\mathbf{W}$ with respect to a parameter α, as

$$\frac{\partial \mathbf{W}}{\partial \alpha} = \left[\frac{\partial w_{ij}}{\partial \alpha} \right] \tag{A.33}$$

A.4   RANDOM VECTORS

Up to now we have assumed that the input vector $\mathbf{x} = [x_1, \ldots, x_N]^T$ was a deterministic quantity, that is, a set of fixed real numbers obtained from the external world through measurements. In many important, practical applications related to classification and signal processing, it is important to reinterpret these numbers as random quantities.

Definition: A random variable is a set of real numbers whose values are controlled by a probability law.

Suppose that we create a vector of three components for an experiment. The values of the components are 1s and 0s. However, we are going to decide whether the element x_i is a 1 or a 0 by flipping a coin. If the coin lands heads up, x_i is a 1; otherwise, it is a 0. We immediately see that there is an underlying structure to the values of these vectors, dictated by the probability of having heads or tails. A vector created in this way is a random vector.

In practice, there are many unobservable variables affecting a given experiment. Although we are not sure whether the phenomenon is random or deterministic, sometimes it is more efficient to model it as random. A good example that is important for our study is the classification of patterns. Let us take handwritten digits. Each of us writes in a different way. If we want to develop a machine that automatically recognizes digits, a productive way is to model a given observation of a digit as a random vector. Suppose that we have 10 classes characterized statistically in pattern space (one for each digit). Then we ask the question: Which class is more probable, given our observation? The class that is more probable is the one to which we assign the observation. Thus we have to perform a statistical characterization of each class and make a statistical decision. The principles involved are briefly reviewed in the following sections.

Definition: Probability of an event A is the relative frequency n_A with which the event appears in a set of N measurements:

$$P = \frac{n_A}{N}$$

Probability of an event is always between $[0, 1]$. The sum of the probabilities of all the outcomes of an experiment has to add up to 1; that is, if the possible outcomes are A, B, and C, then

$$n_A + n_B + n_C = 1$$

A.4.1 Distribution Function

A random vector is characterized by a probability distribution function, defined as

$$P(x_1, \ldots, x_N) = \Pr\{x_1 \leq p_1, \ldots, x_N \leq p_N\} \tag{A.34}$$

where $\Pr\{x\}$ means the probability of an event x and $p_1, \ldots, p_N$ are simply numbers between 0 and 1. A shorthand notation for Eq. A.34 is

$$P(\mathbf{x}) = \Pr\{\mathbf{x} \leq \mathbf{p}\} \tag{A.35}$$

where $\mathbf{x}$ is a random vector. Basically, the distribution function measures the probability that an event is smaller than a given value $\mathbf{p}$. The distribution function is a monotonically increasing function (always larger than or equal to zero).

A.4.2 Density Function

The probability density function (pdf) is the derivative of the probability distribution function:

$$p(\mathbf{x}) = \frac{\partial^N}{\partial x_1 \cdots \partial x_N} P(\mathbf{x}) \tag{A.36}$$

We can alternatively define the pdf as

$$P(\mathbf{x}) = \int_{-\infty}^{x} p(\mathbf{y}) d\mathbf{y} \tag{A.37}$$

where $\mathbf{y}$ is a vector with N components, so in fact this is an N-dimensional integral. The pdf is always positive and sums up to 1 for all $\mathbf{x}$.

In practice we can visualize the shape of the pdf if we plot the *histogram*. The histogram is the relative frequency of events over the domain $\mathbf{x}$. We start by dividing the range of $\mathbf{x}$ into equal intervals Δx, and then we ask how many events occur in each interval. The pdf is the limit of the histogram for infinitely small Δx and infinitely many events. If the variable is discrete, the pdf is called the probability mass function.

A.4.3 The Mixture Density

We often work with random vectors obtained from different classes, each one having a specific pdf. These class pdfs are called *class-conditional* pdfs and are denoted $p(\mathbf{x}|C_i)$ or simply $p_i(\mathbf{x})$. We call these conditional pdf's *likelihoods,* since in practice we seek to model them as parametric forms, and in such cases they work as likelihood functions for the observed values. The mixture density of x is defined as

$$p(\mathbf{x}) = \sum_{i=1}^{L} P_i p(\mathbf{x}|C_i) \tag{A.38}$$

where P_i is the a priori probability of class i. We assume that there are L classes.

A.4.4 A Posteriori Probability and Bayes' Theorem

The probability of $\mathbf{x}$ belonging to one of the classes C_i is called the a posteriori probability of $\mathbf{x}$, $P(C_i|\mathbf{x})$.

Given the a priori probability, we can obtain the a posteriori probability by using the famous Bayes' theorem:

$$P(C_i|\mathbf{x}) = \frac{P_i p(\mathbf{x}|C_i)}{p(\mathbf{x})} \tag{A.39}$$

where P_i are the a priori probabilities, $p(\mathbf{x}|C_i)$ are the class conditionals or likelihoods, and $p(\mathbf{x})$ is the probability of $\mathbf{x}$.

A.4.5 The Central Problem of Pattern Recognition

When we have observations drawn from a mixture density, we want to find a rule that will associate the present observation with one of the classes. This is the central problem we face in real life. If you think a bit, you see that the probability of **x** belonging to one of the classes (the probability of class i, given **x**) is exactly the a posteriori probability of **x**. However, we normally cannot compute the a posteriori probability directly. This is where Bayes' theorem becomes important; if we know the a priori probability and the likelihood for each class, we can compute the a posteriori probability by Eq. A.39. For most cases the denominator is simply a normalizing constant that can be omitted. Pattern recognition thus deals with the estimation of conditional probabilities, that is, with the estimation of class pdfs, the only unknown in Eq. A.39.

A.4.6 Decision Surfaces

The a posteriori probability $P(C_i|\mathbf{x})$ is the probability of the class being i, given the present observation vector **x**. Bayesian decision making evaluates the a posteriori probability for each class and assigns the observation vector to the class j that has the highest a posteriori probability:

$$P(C_j|\mathbf{x}) > P(C_i|\mathbf{x}) \qquad \text{for all } i \neq j \tag{A.40}$$

This rule minimizes the number of errors. The pattern space is effectively divided into regions that are associated with each class. When a pattern vector falls into one of these decision regions, it is assigned (classified) to that class. This assignment rule may produce errors, but it is a strategy to minimize errors, given the information existing in the training set and the assumption of Gaussian statistics.

We can say that the goal of pattern-recognition machines is to find these decision regions in pattern space to provide good classification accuracy.

A.4.7 Discriminant Functions

According to Bayes' decision making, we only need to compare the a posteriori probabilities to make decisions about class partnership. This greatly simplifies things, and we can define functions $y_i(\mathbf{x})$, one for each class, that compute a partnership value over the full space. These functions are called *discriminant* functions. The classification is done by comparing discriminant functions; that is, we choose class j when

$$y_j(\mathbf{x}) > y_i(\mathbf{x}) \qquad \text{for all } i \neq j \tag{A.41}$$

In Bayes' formalism the discriminant functions are the a posteriori probabilities, but other ways to construct discriminant functions exist that do not require the estimation of probability density functions.

A.4.8 Moments of Distributions

Most of the time it is impractical to find the pdfs for each class analytically, so we resort to a description using moments. The most widely used moments are the first- and second-order moments, called respectively the *mean* and the *variance*. For Gaussian distributions they completely define the distribution.

A.4.9 Mean of a Random Vector

The mean of a random vector is defined as

$$M = E\{\mathbf{x}\} = \int \mathbf{x}p(\mathbf{x})d\mathbf{x} \tag{A.42}$$

where the integration (or summation for discrete spaces) is taken over the full space. The mean of a distribution gives the location of the center of mass of the distribution. E is the expected value operator, which is widely used in statistics.

The ith component of M is

$$m_i = \int_{-\infty}^{\infty} x_i p(x_i)dx_i \tag{A.43}$$

where $p(x_i)$ is the one-dimensional marginal density obtained by integrating $p(\mathbf{x})$ over all other components. The conditional expected value is defined as

$$M_i = E\{\mathbf{x}|C_i\} = \int \mathbf{x}p_i(\mathbf{x})d\mathbf{x} \tag{A.44}$$

where $p_i(\mathbf{x})$ is the class likelihood.

A.4.10 Variance of a Random Variable

The variance of a random variable x_i is defined as

$$\sigma_i^2 = E[(x_i - m_i)^2] \tag{A.45}$$

and it measures the dispersion around the mean. Its square root is called the *standard deviation*. The variance measures the power in a zero mean random variable.

A.4.11 Covariance Matrix

This is the important characterization of a distribution since it characterizes the dispersion around the mean. The covariance matrix of $\mathbf{x}$ is

$$\mathbf{\Sigma} = E[(\mathbf{x} - \mathbf{m})(\mathbf{x} - \mathbf{m})^T] = \begin{bmatrix} E[(x_1 - m_1)(x_1 - m_1] & \ldots & E[(x_1 - m_1)(x_N - m_N)] \\ \ldots & \ldots & \ldots \\ E[(x_N - m_N)(x_1 - m_1] & \ldots & E[(x_N - m_N)(x_N - m_N)] \end{bmatrix}$$

$$\text{(A.46)}$$

The components of the covariance matrix diagonal are the individual random-variable variances, and the off-diagonal terms are the covariances of pairs of random variables.

There are two important observations regarding covariance matrices. First, the elements of covariance matrices are all positive or zero, so the covariance matrix is semipositive definite. Second, the covariance matrix is square and symmetric, so it is a Toeplitz matrix. The covariance matrix can be written as

$$\mathbf{\Sigma} = E[\mathbf{x}\mathbf{x}^T] - \mathbf{m}\mathbf{m}^T \tag{A.47}$$

where $\mathbf{R} = E[\mathbf{x}\mathbf{x}^T]$ is the autocorrelation matrix of the random variable. The elements of the autocorrelation matrix are

$$\mathbf{R} = \begin{bmatrix} E[(x_1)(x_1)] & \ldots & E[(x_1)(x_N)] \\ \ldots & \ldots & \ldots \\ E[(x_N)(x_1)] & \ldots & E[(x_N)(x_N)] \end{bmatrix} \tag{A.48}$$

that is, the expected values of the cross products of random variables with different indices. This matrix is a Toeplitz matrix.

A.4.12 Cross-Correlation Matrix

The cross-correlation matrix is very much like the autocorrelation matrix, except two different random variables x and y are involved:

$$\mathbf{C} = \begin{bmatrix} E[(x_1)(y_1)] & \ldots & E[(x_1)(y_N)] \\ \ldots & \ldots & \ldots \\ E[(x_N)(y_1)] & \ldots & E[(x_N)(y_N)] \end{bmatrix} \tag{A.49}$$

This matrix is no longer a Toeplitz matrix.

A.4.13 Orthogonalization of the Covariance Matrix

Notice that the covariance matrix is a symmetric, semipositive definite matrix. Hence it can be orthogonalized, as discussed earlier,

$$\mathbf{\Sigma} = \mathbf{\Phi}\mathbf{\Lambda}\mathbf{\Phi}^T \tag{A.50}$$

where $\mathbf{\Phi}$ is the matrix built from the eigenvectors of $\mathbf{\Sigma}$ and $\mathbf{\Lambda}$ is the eigenvalue matrix of $\mathbf{\Sigma}$, which is diagonal. We can then apply a linear transformation to the space of

$\mathbf{x}$ and work on a new space $\mathbf{y} = \mathbf{\Phi}^T \mathbf{x}$ with axes given by the eigenvectors of $\mathbf{\Sigma}$. In this new space we can work with each eigenvector independently; the random vectors become uncorrelated. The eigenvalues become simply the variances of the transformed variables y_i.

A.4.14 Normal Distribution

Gaussian distributions are pervasive in the analytical study of random phenomena for several reasons. First, because of the law of large numbers, they are a reasonable assumption for large collections of experimental data (the law of large numbers says that the distribution of a sum of arbitrary distributions approaches a Gaussian when the number of terms tends to infinity). Second, the Gaussian function is analytically simple to work with, because it is totally defined by the first- and second-order moments (i.e., all the moments of higher order are zero). Third, if two Gaussian-distributed random variables are uncorrelated, they are also independent. The Gaussian distribution of a random variable x_i is defined as

$$p(x_i) = \frac{1}{\sqrt{2\pi}\,\sigma_i} \exp\left[-\frac{1}{2}\left(\frac{x_i - m_i}{\sigma_i}\right)^2\right] \tag{A.51}$$

For the random vector we have to define a multivariate normal distribution,

$$P(\mathbf{m}, \mathbf{\Sigma}) = \frac{1}{(2\pi)^{N/2}|\mathbf{\Sigma}|^{1/2}} \exp\left(\frac{-(\mathbf{x} - \mathbf{m})^T \mathbf{\Sigma}^{-1}(\mathbf{x} - \mathbf{m})}{2}\right) \tag{A.52}$$

where $\mathbf{m}$ is the mean vector and $\mathbf{\Sigma}$ is the covariance matrix. The exponent can be interpreted as a quadratic distance function of pairs of observations $x_i j_i$ to their respective means, normalized by the covariance. It is called the Mahalanobis distance from $\mathbf{x}$ to $\mathbf{m}$.

These definitions give us some more interesting properties of the multivariate normal distribution: The marginal densities are also Gaussian, and a (nonsingular) linear transformation of a Gaussian is still Gaussian. It is easy to find a projection that makes multivariate Gaussian variables independent if we apply the diagonalization procedure mentioned earlier. In this case the pdf is simply

$$p(\mathbf{x}) = \prod_{i=1}^{N} p(x_i) \tag{A.53}$$

A.4.15 Discriminant Functions for Gaussian Distributions

If the class clusters can be modeled as Gaussians, we can construct discriminant functions easily. First, we do not work directly with the discriminants defined earlier, but with their natural logarithms. Nothing changes, since the log is a monotonically increasing function, but the new discriminants

$$y_i(\mathbf{x}) = \ln p(\mathbf{x}|C_i) + \ln P(C_i) \tag{A.54}$$

become easier to apply. In fact, if we assume that the likelihoods are independent and Gaussian, the decision boundary becomes

$$y_i(\mathbf{x}) = \frac{(\mathbf{x} - \mathbf{m}_i)^T \boldsymbol{\Sigma}_i^{-1}(\mathbf{x} - \mathbf{m}_i)}{2} - \frac{1}{2} \ln |\boldsymbol{\Sigma}_i| + \ln P(C_i) \tag{A.55}$$

which are quadratic functions. If the class covariances are all the same ($\boldsymbol{\Sigma}_i = \boldsymbol{\Sigma}$), the decision surface becomes the intersection of the linear discriminants

$$y_i(\mathbf{x}) = \mathbf{W}_i^T \mathbf{x} + w_{i0} \tag{A.56}$$

where

$$\mathbf{W}_i^T = \mathbf{m}_i^T \boldsymbol{\Sigma}_i \qquad w_{i0} = -\frac{\mathbf{m}_i^T \boldsymbol{\Sigma}^{-1} \mathbf{m}_i}{2} + \ln P(C_i) \tag{A.57}$$

The decision boundaries correspond to hyperplanes perpendicular to the lines joining the class centers and crossing at a point w_{i0}.

A.4.16 Sample Estimates

Unfortunately, we still need an extra step to work with the data we collect from the external world. Even if we can make the assumption of Gaussianity for our data sets, we still do not know the mean vector and covariance matrix. We have to estimate these quantities from a finite number of observations. In general, when we cannot access or compute the true quantity, we have to settle for an approximation, called an *estimator* of the true quantity. Obviously, we would like to work with estimators that do a good job in the approximation. The biggest issue is that we are interested in estimating random quantities, so the estimators are themselves random variables, and it is not easy to compute upper bounds as we do when handling deterministic variables.

A.4.17 Maximum Likelihood

We explain here the maximum likelihood method. The idea behind maximum likelihood is very simple. It seeks to estimate the statistical quantity of the data that is more likely, given the observations. Here the statistical quantities of interest are the mean vector and the covariance matrix.

    Let us assume that the density function $p(\mathbf{x})$ that created our data set is a function of an unknown, but fixed, set of parameters $\theta = \{\theta_1, \ldots, \theta_M\}$. The data set of N vectors $\mathbf{x} = \{x_1, \ldots, x_N\}$ is assumed to be drawn independently from the distribution $p(\mathbf{x})$. The joint probability density function of the data set $\mathbf{x}$ is

$$p(\mathbf{x}|\theta) = \prod_{i=1}^{N} p(\mathbf{x}_i|\theta) \equiv L(\theta) \tag{A.58}$$

where $L(\theta)$ is a function of θ only for fixed $\mathbf{x}$, and it is called the likelihood of θ for the given $\mathbf{x}$. Maximum likelihood picks the θ that maximizes the likelihood or, equivalently, that minimizes the negative likelihood of the log of $L(\theta)$:

$$E = -\ln L(\theta) = -\sum_{i=1}^{N} \ln p(\mathbf{x}_i|\theta) \tag{A.59}$$

The optimization can be done analytically only for a handful of cases, including the case when $p(\mathbf{x})$ is Gaussian. When the parameter to be sought is the mean and $p(\mathbf{x})$ is assumed Gaussian, the maximum likelihood procedure gives

$$\mathbf{m} = \frac{1}{N} \sum_{i=1}^{N} \mathbf{x}_i \tag{A.60}$$

that is, the sample mean is the maximum likelihood estimate of the mean for Gaussian pdfs. If the parameter is the covariance matrix, under the Gaussian assumption the maximum likelihood estimate becomes

$$\Sigma = \frac{1}{N} \sum_{i=1}^{N} (\mathbf{x}_i - \mathbf{m})(\mathbf{x}_i - \mathbf{m})^T \tag{A.61}$$

which is the sample average of the outer product of $(\mathbf{x}_i - \mathbf{m})(\mathbf{x}_i - \mathbf{m})^T$.

A.4.18 Bias and Variance of Estimators

The bias of an estimator $\hat{\theta}$ is defined as the difference between the mean of the estimator and the true quantity θ:

$$\text{bias}(\hat{\theta}) = E[\hat{\theta}] - \theta \tag{A.62}$$

When the mean of the estimator is equal to the true mean, the estimator is called *unbiased*. The variance of the estimator is defined as the expected value of the square difference between the estimator and its mean:

$$\text{var}(\hat{\theta}) = E[E[\hat{\theta}] - \hat{\theta}]^2 \tag{A.63}$$

When the variance of the estimator decreases to zero and the estimator is unbiased, the estimator is called *consistent*. Hence the maximum likelihood estimate of the mean is consistent, since it is unbiased and the variance decreases to zero with the number of samples.

The mean square error of an estimator is defined as the expected value of the square difference between an estimator and the true quantity,

$$E[\hat{\theta} - \theta]^2 = \text{var}(\hat{\theta}) + \text{bias}(\hat{\theta})^2 \qquad \textbf{(A.64)}$$

The mean square error is the most widely used criterion to compare estimators.

A.4.19 Unbiased Estimator of the Covariance Matrix

The maximum likelihood estimator of the covariance matrix is biased. To obtain an unbiased estimate of the covariance, we have to replace N with $N - 1$ in Eq. A.61. This covariance matrix estimator is consistent.

A.5   CONCLUSIONS

In this appendix we attempted to provide an overview of the most important definitions and operations in linear algebra and applied probability to pattern recognition. If you need further information please consult the following sources.

Golub, G. and Van Loan, C., *Matrix Computation,* John Hopkins University Press, 1989.

Papoulis, A., *Probability, Random Variables and Stochastic Processes,* McGraw Hill, 1985.

NEUROSOLUTIONS TUTORIAL

This appendix is designed to describe the operation of NeuroSolutions without assuming any previous knowledge of neural networks. We do, however, assume a familiarity with PC software and windows. Although we don't assume previous knowledge of neural networks, the operation of NeuroSolutions will make more sense as you learn more about them. We recommend that you read through the tutorial quickly the first time through without focusing on the details. You should then periodically revisit the tutorial as you progress through the text.

The outline of this tutorial is as follows:

- Introduction to NeuroSolutions
- Introduction to the Interactive Examples
- The Fundamentals of NeuroSolutions
- Using Probes in NeuroSolutions
- Providing Input to Your Networks
- Training a Network
- Summary

B.1   INTRODUCTION TO NEUROSOLUTIONS

NeuroSolutions is based on an object-oriented approach to adaptive system design. The networks are broken down into a fundamental set of components that are individually simple but can be combined to create powerful systems capable of solving very complex problems. The NeuroSolutions user interface was inspired by the process of designing an electronic circuit. Different components are placed onto a "Breadboard" and are then wired together to form a circuit. The circuit is then tested by injecting signals and "probing" responses. This user interface provides much more flexibility than a typical "black box" simulator. NeuroSolutions includes a comprehensive collection of probes that allows the user/designer to monitor every aspect of the neural network during training and testing. The unique attributes of NeuroSolutions make it ideal for interactive training. This textbook ships with a restricted version of NeuroSolutions.

613

Because of its simplicity and power, NeuroSolutions is also ideal for neural network development.

B.1.1 Overview of This Tutorial

Section B.2 of this tutorial provides an overview of how to use the demonstrations/ examples in the textbook. It presents only the mechanics necessary to run the examples. The rest of the tutorial presents the methods to modify the breadboards used in the examples.

To reap the full benefits of this interactive teaching methodology, it is critical that you feel comfortable modifying and probing the examples—this is where the real learning begins. When you start modifying the parameters yourself and seeing how the modification affects the operation of the system, you will be learning important aspects of neural networks that are not easily taught in a textbook. We are firm believers in the "learning through experimentation" technique, and we feel that you will not only achieve a better understanding of the topics, but your retention will also be improved.

B.2   INTRODUCTION TO THE INTERACTIVE EXAMPLES

Throughout the hypertext you will come across interactive examples that consist of text describing the example and then a button that will execute the example. After reading the text, just click on the icon, and the NeuroSolutions example will start. Below is a figure of an example.

NeuroSolutions   2

In order to create a simulation that displays the MSE, we have to add a new component to the breadboard, the L2 Criterion. The L2 Criterion implements the mean square error Eq. 4 . The L2 Criterion requires two inputs to compute the MSE – the system output and the desired response. We will attach the L2 Criterion to the output of the linear PE (system output) and attach a file input component to the L2 Criterion to load in the value of the desired response from Table 1. In order to visualize the MSE, we will place a MatrixViewer probe over the L2 criterion (cost access point). This MatrixViewer simply displays the data from the component that it resides over – in this case, the mean square error.

New Components

L2 Criterion   **Matrix Viewer**

Run the demonstration and try to set the slope and bias to minimize the mean square error. Compute by hand the error according to Eq. 4 and see if it matches the value displayed.

NeuroSolutions Example

The examples have a common feel. A *Breadboard* is a NeuroSolutions "document window" that may have components, text, and buttons placed on it. The example

Breadboards consist of three subsections. The top section contains the text describing the example, the middle section contains the components that make up the example neural network, and the bottom section contains the various displays or graphs that "probe" the network.

The examples typically occupy multiple pages. To move to the next page you simply press the » button in the top right-hand corner. To exit the example immediately, press the X button. The examples in this tutorial and in the textbook are created on-the-fly using interactive macros in NeuroSolutions. Because of this, there is no way to return to the previous page of an example. Most examples are short, however, so you can exit the example and use the textbook to restart the example.

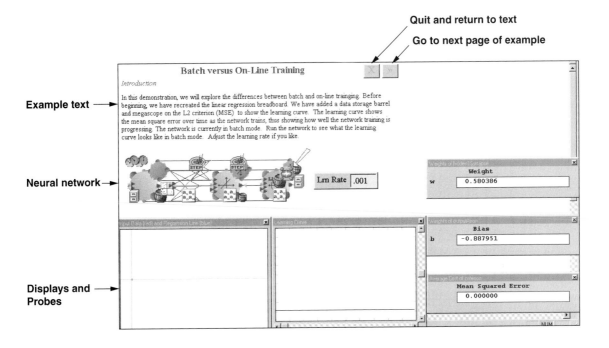

All the examples in the book are "live." The displays are created while you watch, and you can modify the parameters of the network at any time. All the network controls are grouped on one toolbar called the "control toolbar." Like other toolbars, the control toolbar can be moved virtually anywhere, but it is typically found just under the menu bar.

A completed network can be "run" by pressing the green "start" button. Running the network consists of presenting the input data to the network, allowing the data to move through and be operated on by the network, and creating the displays that show the parameters and outputs of the network. At the end of each run, the start button is deactivated to indicate that the network has completed its operation. To rerun the network, press the reset button and then press the start button. The following commands are most commonly used to control a simulation:

Control	Name	Action
▶	Start	Starts the simulation
‖	Pause	Pauses the simulation
✕	Reset	Resets the system counters and randomizes the network's initial conditions
0	Zero Counters	Resets the system counters without randomizing the network's initial conditions
▤	Step Epoch	Runs the simulation until the end of the next epoch of data
▤	Step Exemplar	Runs the simulation for one sample of data

You have just learned the fundamentals necessary to run the interactive examples. Let's try out a very simple example to reinforce these concepts.

TUTORIAL EXAMPLE 1

The goal of this example is to allow you to get used to the "look" and "feel" of Neuro-Solutions examples. Just click on the ⊕ icon and NeuroSolutions will launch the example. Once inside the example, follow the directions in the text. After the example has completed, you will return to this point.

B.3 BASIC OPERATION OF NEUROSOLUTIONS

NeuroSolutions' object-oriented user interface organizes its components into palettes. Each palette of components contains a family of components with similar function.

For example, all the output displays or probes are contained in a single palette. All the palettes can be found under the palette menu item.

If a palette is open, it will have a checkmark next to it. An opened palette looks and acts like a toolbar with a set of icons. The palettes can be moved and docked just like a standard windows toolbar. Below is an example of the Axon palette.

Components can be selected from a palette and stamped onto the Breadboard.

B.3.1 Stamping Components

If you put the cursor over the palette and wait a few seconds, you should see a small window pop up with the name of the component in it. This is called a "tool tip," and you can use it to determine which component you are selecting from the palette. When you click on a component, the cursor becomes a stamp when you place it over the Breadboard. If you click again anywhere in the Breadboard, the component will be copied to that location on the Breadboard. This operation is called *component stamping*. If you select a component from a palette and place the cursor over an existing compo-

nent from the same family on the Breadboard, the cursor will switch to a ![icon], which indicates the current selection will *replace* the component on the Breadboard.

TUTORIAL EXAMPLE 2

This simple example opens up a new Breadboard and allows you to stamp components on it. You should practice opening, closing, and moving palettes. Use tool tips to determine the name of the different components and then stamp a few on the Breadboard. Since some families cannot be stamped directly on the Breadboard, we suggest you start with the axon palette.

   If you select a component that cannot be stamped down, you may need to click the "selection cursor" button ![icon] to return to "selection mode."

B.3.2 On-Line Help

A complete description of every component is contained within the on-line help. The easiest way to access the help for a given component is to click on that component with

the Help cursor ![icon]. The Help cursor is located on the toolbar. Just click on it and then move the mouse over the component you want help for, clicking on the component's icon.

TUTORIAL EXAMPLE 3

This simple example allows you to experiment with using the help cursor to describe each component. This handy feature allows you to quickly and easily determine the function of each component. For now, don't worry too much about the contents of the help files; just practice using the Help cursor.

B.3.3 Connecting Components

Notice that on the axon family components (as well as those of some other families), there is a double-diamond contact point on the left ![icon] (the FemaleConnector) and a single-diamond contact on the right ![icon] (the MaleConnector). The data flow in Neuro-Solutions is designed to move from left to right on the Breadboard. To connect two components, simply drag the MaleConnector on the right of one component to the FemaleConnector on the left of the other component. The connection is visually indicated by three lines drawn between the components.

You will notice that while you are dragging the connector, the mouse arrow changes to a move cursor ✛, meaning that you can drop the MaleConnector ▶ onto any unoccupied portion of the Breadboard. If you place the cursor over a location that is an invalid connection, the cursor becomes a crossed circle ⊘, meaning that you cannot drop the MaleConnector in that place.

An alternative way to connect components is to select the first component (by clicking the left mouse button), then click the right mouse button on the second component, and select "Connect To" from the menu. The three connection lines will be automatically established.

TUTORIAL EXAMPLE 4

This example allows you practice connecting components.

B.3.4 Axons and Synapses

The building-block approach can easily be applied to build adaptive or neural systems. These networks primarily consist of processing elements (PEs) tied together with "weighted" connections. The Axon family (much of the terminology in NeuroSolutions is based on neurobiology) implements the PEs in the network, and the Synapse family implements the weighted connections.

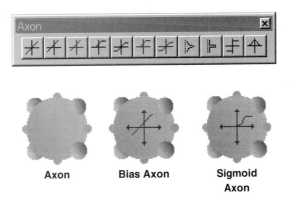

Axon   Bias Axon   Sigmoid Axon

The Axon family has two functions. The components sum all of their inputs and then apply a function to that sum. The different components in the Axon family apply different functions to the summation of their inputs. Each of the different images on the Axon family icons represents the function that is applied. The Linear Axon (called simply an Axon) just passes the sum of the inputs directly to the output. The Bias Axon sums the input and adds an offset. The Sigmoid Axon applies a thresholding function to the data. A single component of the Axon family can represent any number of PEs.

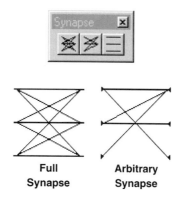

Full
Synapse

Arbitrary
Synapse

The Synapse family is used to connect Axons together. In general, each connection in a Synapse is assigned a weight that scales the data passing through it. Adjusting these weights is how a neural network or adaptive system is *trained* to perform the desired task. The member of the Synapse family most commonly used is the *Full Synapse*, and it connects every PE in one Axon component to every PE in the other Axon component. Thus, the Full Synapse component contains nm connections (and weights) if there are n input PEs and m output PEs. The *Arbitrary Synapse* allows you to select which of the nm possible connections to make between the axons.

B.3.5 Component Properties

Every NeuroSolutions component has a set of parameters that you can adjust. For instance, the Axon family components contain a parameter that sets the number of PEs represented by that component. You access a component's parameter set through a dialog box called the Inspector.

- You invoke the Inspector for any component on the breadboard by right-clicking its icon and choosing "Properties":

Invoking the Inspector

- You can also invoke the Inspector by left-click-selecting an icon and then pressing "Alt+Enter." The Inspector below shows some of the properties of the Linear

Axon. Notice that number of PEs in an Axon component can be defined via rows and/or columns, allowing you to create a matrix of PEs.

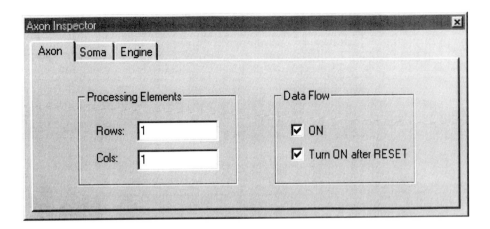

Once the Inspector is open, you can view or modify the parameters of other components by simply clicking on other icons on the breadboard.

A component's parameter set is organized according to property pages. The property pages are labeled on the tabs across the top of the Inspector. You access the various property pages by clicking on these tabs. The leftmost tab typically contains the most commonly used parameters for each component. Many of the other tabs are useful only to advanced users.

If multiple components have the same parameters, you can simultaneously edit the parameters of all the components using the following procedure:

- Invoke the Inspector for the first component.
- Click on the tab of the desired property page.
- Hold down the Shift key while left-clicking to select the remaining components.
- Edit any parameter(s) within the Inspector. Any changes you make in the Inspector will be reflected in all selected components, so long as they all have the same parameter.

For example, you can simultaneously change the number of PEs for a group of Axons, even if they have different transfer functions (linear, sigmoid, etc.).

TUTORIAL EXAMPLE 5

This example starts with a small network of connected components and allows you to manipulate the properties of those components with the Inspector.

B.3.6 The Data-Flow Controller and Running the Network

The last family we will discuss in this section is the Control family. The *Control family* is different from the *Control toolbar*, but they are related in operation. The control family contains components that control how the data flows through the network. The

simplest member of the Control family is the Static Controller . Its properties include parameters such as the amount of data in the input file, how many times to run the data through the network, whether and how the network should learn, and so forth. Thus, pressing the *Start* button on the Control toolbar tells the Static Controller to begin sending data through the network. The Control toolbar and Controller component work together to control the network.

The Control Toolbar

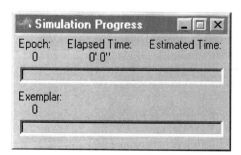

The Control Palette

To explain the properties of the Static Controller, we must define a few terms. An *exemplar* of data is one complete sample of the input for one time-step. If the network has multiple inputs, then an exemplar corresponds to one piece of data from each input. An *epoch* is a complete set of data presented to the network. Normally, an epoch is the number of data samples in the training set file. If there are 30 samples in a data file, then there are 30 exemplars in an epoch. Many times you may want to present the same data to the network multiple times; this is represented as the number of *epochs* per *run*.

If you double-click on the Static Controller, you will see a real-time view of the simulation's progress:

Simulation Progress		
Epoch:	Elapsed Time:	Estimated Time:
0	0' 0"	
Exemplar:		
0		

TUTORIAL EXAMPLE 6

This example starts with a small network of connected components and a Static Controller, and allows you to run the network using the Control toolbar.

We have now covered the fundamental techniques used in NeuroSolutions. The next two sections discuss the two most important families of components for use in the interactive book. These two families are the *Probe* family, which allows you to view the parameters or data in the network, and the *Input* family, which allows you to modify the inputs to the examples.

B.4   PROBING THE SYSTEM

The *Probe* family is the most powerful feature in NeuroSolutions. Obtaining a good grasp of the use of the Probe family will greatly increase your ability to interact with the examples.

Probe Family Palette

Each Probe provides a unique way of visualizing the data available throughout the network. Since the probes need data to display, they cannot be placed directly on the Breadboard; they must be placed on a network component with a *data access point*. For instance, the Axon and Synapse families all have multiple access points. The *activity* access point contains the output data from the component (after operation by the component), the *weight* access point contains the weights of the component, and so on. Let's assume we want to place a *Matrix Viewer* probe on an Axon to demonstrate some of the key probing concepts. The Matrix Viewer probe simply shows the data in numeric format.

Matrix Viewer

When you place a Matrix Viewer on an Axon, one of its page tabs will be the *Access* property page. This lists all the possible access points of the Axon. Selecting the access point in the Inspector determines what data the matrix viewer will show. The Matrix Viewer will move its position on the Axon slightly depending on which access point you select. The last thing we need to do is *double-click* on the Matrix Viewer to open its display window.

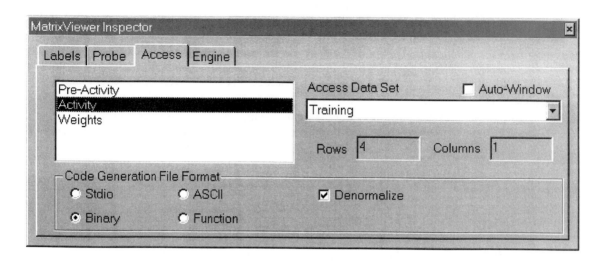

TUTORIAL EXAMPLE 7

This example loads a small network of connected components and a Static Controller, and allows you to place Matrix Viewers on the network and view the results.

B.4.1 Static Probes

There are two major types of probes in NeuroSolutions: *static probes* and *temporal probes*. Static probes such as the Matrix Viewer simply display the data at a specific instance in time. Temporal probes display data over time, like an oscilloscope or a graph of an output over time. Some of the more common static probes are the following:

Icon	Name	Description
	Matrix Viewer	Displays instantaneous data as a numerical matrix
	Matrix Editor	Similar to the Matrix Viewer, except that it also allows you to edit the data you are probing
	Bar Chart	Displays the data in a bar chart form
	Image Viewer	Displays the data as a gray-scale image

There are times where you might want to display a specific piece of data in two different ways—for instance, you may want both the numerical value (Matrix Editor) and a Bar Chart. To do this, you simply stamp the second probe *on top of* the first probe; this is called *stacking*, and the access point in the Inspector of the second component will simply say *Stacked Access*.

TUTORIAL EXAMPLE 8

This example loads a small network of connected components and allows you to place static probes at various locations on the network.

B.4.2 Temporal Probes

Temporal probes display data from multiple iterations of the network. For instance, some of the previous examples used a *MegaScope* to display the sine wave. The sine wave was presented to the network one sample at a time, but the MegaScope and its cohort, the *Data Storage* component, displayed the time history of the sine wave.

Icon	Name	Description
	MegaScope	Displays a line graph of the data similar to an oscilloscope
	Data Storage	Stores data from multiple iterations of the network for display by the temporal probes
	Scatter Plot	Displays the data as a set of points on an *X, Y* set of coordinates

The Data Storage component stores data over time as the network runs so that the temporal probe can display the data. Some of the properties of the Data Storage component are shown below.

Notice that the Data Storage component allows you to select the amount of data to store (buffer size) and how often it should send the data to the temporal probe (message every). The message every property determines how often the display is updated.

To create a new temporal probe, first stamp a Data Storage component and make sure it is at the correct access point. Then stack a temporal probe on top of it and adjust its parameters if necessary. For instance, the MegaScope allows you to display multiple signals, change the color of each signal's trace, and change the scale of both axes as well.

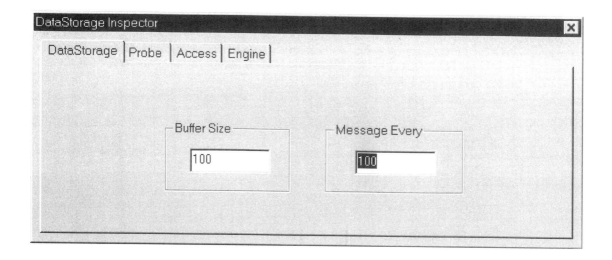

TUTORIAL EXAMPLE 9

This example allows you to create and experiment with temporal probes and the Data Storage component.

B.4.3 Data Transmitters

The probes display the data that they receive from the component they are stamped on. What if you want to display data from two different components on the same probe? The *Data Storage Transmitter* is the answer. You place a temporal probe on one component, and then place a Data Transmitter on the second component and tell it to transmit its data to the probe. The Data Storage Transmitter is on the *Transmitters* palette, and it

looks like a miniature barrel when placed on the Breadboard. It is the rightmost component on the palette.

      To set up the Data Storage Transmitter, you must do two things. First, make sure that it is located at the correct access point (e.g., will be sending the correct data). Second, you must tell it which Data Storage component to send the data to.

      On the Transmitter page of the Inspector you will see a list of possible receivers (Data Storage components). The *Receivers List* shows the name of each Data Storage

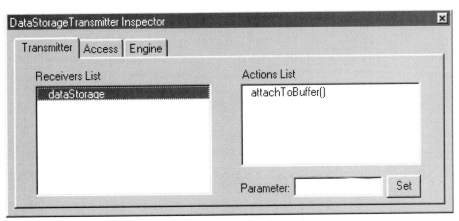

Data Storage Transmitter Inspector

component on the Breadboard (the name is taken from the *Component Name* property on the Engine page of each component). When you click on one of the receivers, a list of possible actions shows up in the Actions List. Double-click on the action of choice to make the connection (indicated by a "C"). In this case, we want the *attachToBuffer()* action, which sends the data from the Transmitter to the Data Storage component.

TUTORIAL EXAMPLE 10

This example uses a Data Storage Transmitter to create a single plot showing the input and the output of the network.

Were you were wondering what the other transmitters on the Transmitters pallette do? They can be used to signal events to other components. For instance, the *Threshold* transmitter can be used to tell the Static Controller to stop training when the error has reached a certain point.

This section has covered all you need to know to create probes in NeuroSolutions. Remember that probing a neural network may be the only way to fully understand how it is working. The next section covers the *Input* family, which allows you to use your own data in the neural networks.

B.5   THE INPUT FAMILY

The *Input family* of components provides data to the neural network. In a few of the previous examples, we have used a signal generator to input a sine wave into the network.

Input Family Palette

The three most common Input components are

Icon	Name	Description
![sine]	Function Generator	Generates sinusoids, square waves, ramps, or user-defined functions for input to the network
![file]	File	Reads a variety of file types and provides the data as input to the network
![noise]	Noise	Generates uniform or Gaussian noise; often stacked on top of other components to add dither

Like the Probe family, the Input family components are stamped onto access points of components in the network. You must select the correct access point to ensure that the data is entering the network at the correct place. The most common location for an Input family component is at the *preactivity* access point of the first (input) Axon in the network.

The Function Generator is very simple to use. Simply stamp the Function Generator on the appropriate component, check to ensure it is on the proper access point (the access page of the Signal Generator Inspector), and select the desired waveform. You can select both the shape of the waveform (sinusoid, square wave, etc.) and the number of samples per cycle.

TUTORIAL EXAMPLE 11

This example uses the previous networks but allows you to experiment with the Function Generator.

B.5.1 The File Component

The File component is probably the most commonly used Input component. It reads data from the file system (e.g., your computer disk) and provides that data as input to the network.

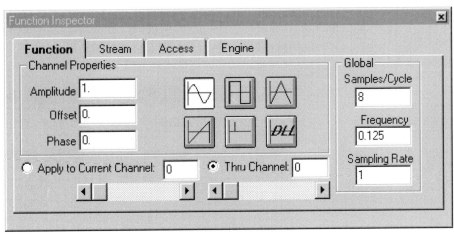

Function Generator Inspector

The File Component

Using the File component is rather easy, but there are quite a few options. First add a File component to the Axon and ensure that it is at the proper access point. Next, open the *File List* page in the Inspector of the File component.

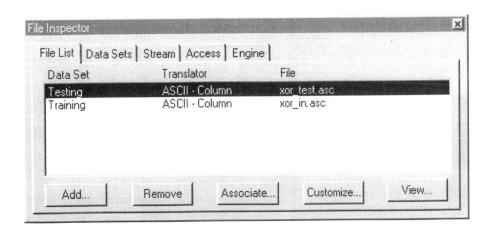

If there are files present that you would like to remove, click on the file and hit the *Remove* button. If you would like to add a new file to be read into the network, follow these steps:

- Click the *Add* button, find the data file you want to add by navigating through the file system, and then double-click the filename. The *Associate File* panel will appear, where you specify the file type and how it is to be used:

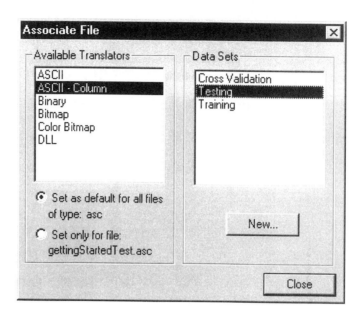

- Choose a translator from the list. NeuroSolutions offers translators to cover the vast majority of file types:

Translator	Format Description
ASCII	ASCII file format with no column headings
ASCII-Column	ASCII file format with descriptive column headings
Binary	32-bit floating-point
Bitmap	Series of black-and-white bitmap pictures
Color Bitmap	Series of color bitmap pictures
DLL	For loading custom-formatted files
Interactive Book	Special format designed for use with this book

NeuroSolutions provides three predefined data sets. The *Training* data set is the default data set and is used to train the network. Even though we haven't started training networks yet, you should always use the training set unless otherwise instructed. The *Testing* and *Cross Validation* data sets are used to test or verify that the network is learning appropriately. Since the Testing and Cross Validation sets are not used to train the network, they can be used to determine how

isn't valid; use id.

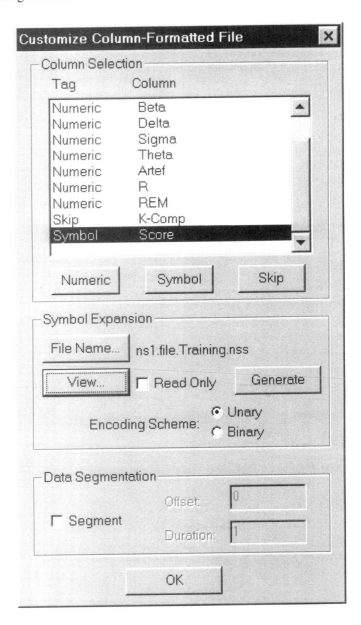

the network will perform on data it has not seen yet. For now, always use the Training data set.

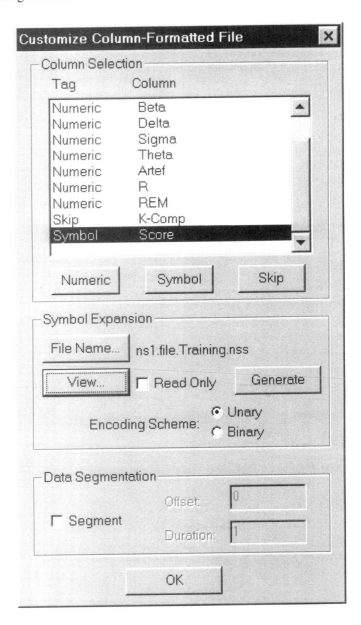

- Next, Click the *Close* button.
- If you have a data file with multiple columns, the Customize Column panel will be displayed next and allow you to select which columns you want to use as input.

The default is to use every column of data in the file. If there are columns you would like to skip, select each column and hit the *Skip* button.

- Click the *Close* button on this panel when you are done.
- If the data file has more columns than there are PEs in the Input Axon, Neuro-Solutions will ask you if you'd like to modify the number of PEs in the Input Axon—usually you can just click "Yes."

That's all. There are quite a few steps, but it is relatively straightforward. If you add multiple files to the same File component and data set, then the data will be added together before entry into the network.

One other thing that will come in handy is the ability to normalize your files. If you open the Inspector on the File component and go to the *stream* page, there is a checkbox labeled "Normalize." When this is checked, the data file will be normalized between the two values shown in the edit boxes left of the Normalize checkbox. This feature is used quite frequently in neural networks.

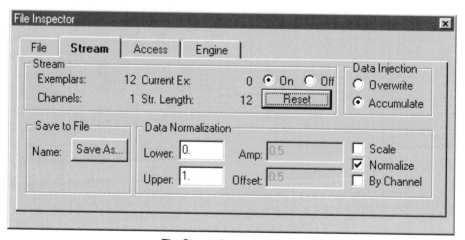

The Stream Inspector Page

TUTORIAL EXAMPLE 12

This example allows the user to manipulate the File component and load data files into the network.

B.6 TRAINING A NETWORK

This section discusses the extra components necessary to train an adaptive system using gradient descent. Don't worry if you don't understand the concepts; just focus on the mechanics. The textbook explains the concepts in detail.

Adaptive learning using gradient descent focuses on using the error between the system output and the desired system output to train the system. The learning algorithm adapts the weights of the system based on the error until the system produces the desired output. The *Error Criteria* family in NeuroSolutions computes different error measures that can be used to train the network.

The Error Criteria Palette

The Error Criteria components are typically connected to the output of the network. They have a *Desired* access point that requires a member of the Input family to provide it data (e.g., a File component or Function Generator). By far the most common criterion is the L_2 or Mean Squared Error (MSE) criterion. It simply computes the difference between the system output and the desired signal and squares it.

Icon	Name	Description
	L_1 Norm or Absolute Value	The absolute value of the error between the system output and the desired output
	L_2 Norm or Mean Squared Error	The squared difference between the system output and the desired output
	L_p Norm	The difference between the system output and the desired output raised to the pth power

---

TUTORIAL EXAMPLE 13

This example studies the Error Criteria component. In this example, we will use the *StepExemplar* button on the Control toolbar to single-step the network so we can analyze the error computation.

B.6.1 Learning and Backpropagation

Now that we know how to compute the error, we can use the error to modify the weights of the system, allowing it to learn. The goal of the system is for the system output to be the same as the desired output, so we want to minimize the mean squared error. The method used to do this is called *error backpropagation.* Essentially, it is a three-step process. First, the input data is propagated *forward* through the network to compute the system output. Next the error is computed, and propagated *backward* (thus the name *backpropagation)* through the network, and then it is used to modify the weights.

NeuroSolutions implements backpropagation of the error in a secondary "plane" that sits on top of the Axons and Synapses. This is called the backpropagation plane.

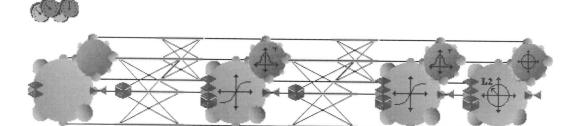

NeuroSolutions shows the backpropagation plane using smaller versions of the Axons and Synapses stacked on top of them. The backpropagation plane passes the errors backward from the Error Criteria component to the beginning of the network (and manipulates the errors along the way). NeuroSolutions adds a third plane that actually uses the errors in the backpropagation plane to change the weights in the network—this is where the learning actually happens. This plane is called the *gradient descent* plane and sits on top of the backpropagation plane. A typical gradient descent compo-nent is the Momentum component . Notice in the following figure that only the components with weights use the gradient descent components.

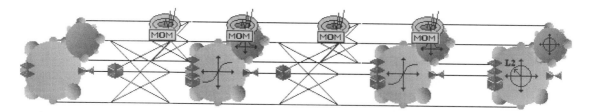

The last thing we need to discuss is the *Back Static Controller* . This controller sits on top of the Static Controller and controls the backpropagation and the gradient descent planes.

The details of all these components are not necessary at this point, so we will summarize what we have learned in an example.

TUTORIAL EXAMPLE 14

This example uses the Breadboard from the previous example, sets up the backpropagation plane and the gradient descent plane, and allows the system to learn.

B.7 SUMMARY

This concludes the tutorial for NeuroSolutions. Remember that the on-line help for NeuroSolutions is quite extensive. Also remember that the help cursor can be used to quickly bring up details on each of the NeuroSolutions components.

We'd like to make one additional comment. We have tried to convey in this tutorial the basics necessary to use the examples in the book—which focus mainly on adapting the example Breadboards. NeuroSolutions has a number of features we have not discussed here, such as the Neural Wizard. The Neural Wizard asks you questions through a series of dialog boxes and creates an entire neural network for you, including input files, probes, backpropagation planes, and so on.

As we mentioned at the beginning, don't worry if you don't understand everything in this tutorial. Many of the concepts in NeuroSolutions will make more sense after you understand more about neural networks. As you read through the book, you may want to revisit this tutorial to go through it in more detail or just refresh your memory.

DATA DIRECTORY

This appendix provides a description of the structure of the data directory and of the data available on the CD-ROM. The data is made available to illustrate different aspects of neurocomputing with the simulator and can be used for projects or further understanding of the material.

Each data set is contained in a different folder with a readme file. The name of the data folder is illustrative of the data it contains (e.g., data folder "spiral" contains the data set *spiral,* used for classification). The readme file provides a brief description of the data, how it can be used, and its source.

The data directory is structured into five categories: data for classification, data for regression, data for signal processing, data for the exercises, and data from the Neuro-Solutions examples:

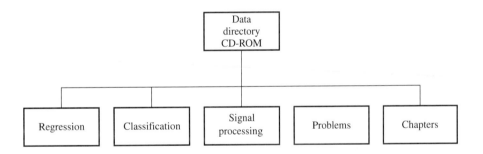

All the data files are organized in columns, and can be readily utilized in the simulator. Desired response files were created to facilitate running the examples. More data will be made available on the Wiley and NeuroDimension Web sites.

For each data set, two types of data files are included. The interactive book edition (IBE) of NeuroSolutions allows the user full access to the functionality of Neuro-Solutions when the file components read only IBE data files (dataset.ibe). When a file component reads an ASCII file, NeuroSolutions will still be fully functional but the Breadboards cannot be saved and data cannot be exported from NeuroSolutions. The IBE format allows the user to save Breadboards, weights, outputs, etc., but these files cannot be modified. The ASCII version is easily modified (e.g., columns can be skipped, etc.), but the data exporting restrictions are enforced.

The following table presents by category the data sets included on the CD-ROM.

Classification	Regression	Signal processing	Problems	Chapters
Blood testing	Abalone	Bugs	Ch2	Ch1
Breast cancer	Atmospheric	EMG	Ch3	Ch2
Credit screening	Body fat	Noise reduction	Ch4	Ch3
Echocardio	Lynx	Sunspots	Ch9	Ch4
Glass	MPH	SystemID1		Ch5
Images		SystemID2		Ch6
Iris		Yalefaces		Ch7
Mushroom		echo		Ch8
Music				Ch9
OCR				Ch10
Parity				Ch11
Sleepdata				
Sonar				
Spiral				
Synthetic1				
Synthetic2				
Vowel				
Wine				
WNBA				

GLOSSARY

AC Alternating current. In practice, the components of a signal that vary over time.

activation The output of a PE in an ANN topology.

Adaline Adaptive linear element, the processing element proposed by Widrow that implements a weighted sum of inputs.

adaptive systems Systems that change their parameters (through algorithms) in order to meet a prespecified goal, which is either an input-output map or an internal constraint.

adaptive filter theory A branch of signal processing that analyzes and designs filters that learn from the data. Instead of having coefficients that are set by designer specifications, adaptive filters have a learning algorithm that modifies their coefficients so that the desired response is approximated.

affine transformation Any linear transformation of the space coordinates. An affine transformation can be considered as a rotation and a translation of the space.

aliasing The error that is created when analog signals are sampled below the Nyquist frequency. It is called aliasing because high frequencies in the analog waveform are represented as lower frequencies in the digital signal.

analog signals Signals for which both the independent variable (time) and the values of the signal are real numbers.

a posteriori probability The probability of an event after some measurements are made.

artificial neural networks (ANNs) Adaptive, most often nonlinear distributed systems.

ASCII American Standard Code for Information Interchange, a standard for coding characters into binary strings.

attractor The trajectory (or point) that defines the limit set of the dynamics.

autocorrelation A measure of similarity of the samples' distribution, which is computed by the sum of the cross products between the data set and its shifted versions. The autocorrelation is a function of the shift.

backpropagation A training algorithm for multilayer perceptrons that extends the delta rule to hidden-layer networks. It uses the methodology of gradient-descent learning and solves the credit assignment problem by using the weight values in the topology.

batch training The adaptation of the weight based on an epoch update.

big O notation An approximate way to express the complexity of a computer algorithm, where only the most rapidly increasing factor is shown. Normally we are interested in multiplications, since they are the most time-consuming to execute in general-purpose computers.

bounded input, bounded output (BIBO) The most widely used criterion of stability for linear systems. It simply says that a system is stable if, for a bounded input, the response is also bounded.

bump A function that has large values over a limited space extent, that is, basically a local function. A multidimensional Gaussian is an example of a bump. This loose terminology indicates the nature of the region being created. Important theorems about function approximation with local functions exist.

causal system A system that produces a response only after an input is applied. Hence it is strictly nonanticipatory.

classes The natural divisions of the input data produced by the phenomenon under study (e.g., sick and healthy).

classification error The number of samples that were incorrectly classified (misclassifications) normalized by the total number of samples.

639

classifier   A machine that automatically divides input data into classes.

clustering   An unsupervised technique that groups data according to similarity (which also implies considering what is dissimilar).

code   A systematic translation of the data into bits.

committees   Ensembles of ANNs trained with the same data, often with different topologies, whose output is interpreted as a vote for the classification. Committees are appealing because they decrease the variance of the final decision, which is considered one of the most severe problems in semiparametric classifiers.

complex number   A number z that can be written as $z = Re(z) + jIm(z)$, where $j = \sqrt{-1}$.

confusion matrix   A matrix in which the man-made (rows) and the machine-made (columns) classifications per class are entered. A perfect classifier has only the diagonal populated. Errors appear in nondiagonal positions. The confusion matrix is an efficient way to observe the separability between classes.

connectionist   Normally taken as a synonym of neural networks. The name comes from the fact that neural networks are highly distributed systems where the computation is done in the links (connections between PEs).

context PE   A memory PE formed by a single, first-order recurrent system.

contour   A curve linking all the points with the same value of J (J = a constant). The contour plot for J is formed by concentric ellipsoids (ellipses for the 2-D case).

convex   A surface is convex when any point in a line joining two points in the surface belongs to the surface.

correlation coefficient   The ratio of the covariance between the input and desired data over the product of their standard deviations.

covariance   The sum of the cross products of the two variables with the means removed.

Cover's theorem   A linear classifier to asymptotically separate arbitrary data sets if the data is nonlinearly mapped to a sufficiently large feature space.

cross-correlation   A measure of the similarity between two different data sets, computed by the sum of the cross products between the two data sets at different lags (it is a function of the lag).

curse of dimensionality   An often-used expression that relates to the fact that classification problems become exponentially more difficult with the size of the space.

data-flow machine   The chaining of algorithmic operations that are necessary to implement the neural network function and its training. Since a neural network is distributed, data is sent into its input and transformed when it goes through the machine, as are the errors that are used during training.

DC   Direct current. In practice, the long-term average of a signal. Its spectrum is a delta function at zero frequency, with amplitude equal to the signal average.

decibel (dB)   The log of the ratio of two quantities, $20 \log_{10}(V1/V2)$. Negative values mean that the ratio is less than 1.

decision surface   The boundary (normally multidimensional) between the input data classes.

deflation   A method of computing the principal components that is similar to the Gram-Schmidt orthogonalization procedure: first compute the principal direction and subtract it from the decomposition before computing the next principal direction.

delay   An operator (linear system) that delays the input by one sample without distorting it; also, a type of memory in which the memory mechanism is a pure delay operator.

delay line   A single-input, multiple-output system created by a cascade of delay elements.

delta function   A function that is zero everywhere except when the argument is zero, where it has unit area.

The delta function that can be thought of as the limit of a rectangular pulse of height $1/\varepsilon$ and width ε when ε goes to zero. Mathematically, it is a function $\Delta(t)$ that obeys the relation

$$f(t) = \int_{-\infty}^{\infty} f(t - \tau)\Delta(\tau)d\tau$$

In discrete time it is defined as

$$\Delta(n) = \begin{cases} 1 & n = 0 \\ 0 & n \neq 0 \end{cases}$$

Practically, it yields the value of any function it is multiplied by at the sample number where the impulse occurs; that is, $f(n)\Delta(n - n_0) = f(n_0)$.

difference equation   An equation involving two or more variables at different time steps. Of importance for our study are the difference equations that have constant coefficients.

digital signal processing (DSP)   An expanding field in electrical engineering that modifies signal properties according to user specifications using computer algorithms (instead of analog hardware, as done in the past).

Dirac delta   (see delta function)

discrete Fourier series (DFS)   A decomposition of a time signal in terms of a sum of sine waves of different frequencies (or more generally, sum of phasors).

discriminant function   A function $g(x)$ that evaluates every position in pattern space and produces a large value for one class and low values for all the others.

dual or transpose network   The network obtained from the original network by reversing the signal flow and changing summing junctions with splitting nodes, and vice versa.

dynamic networks   Neural networks with short-term memory or with feedback connections that have outputs that depend on more than one time instant.

dynamic systems   Systems with outputs that depend on more than one time instant.

eigenfunctions   The natural modes of a system. A signal is an eigenfunction of a system (transformation) when the system output is a signal of the same shape but possibly of a different amplitude and phase. Eigenfunctions are related to the concept of eigenvectors in linear algebra.

eigenvalues   The scaling constants in the eigenvalue equation of a matrix. Eigenvalues can be considered as the projections of the data along the eigenvectors.

eigenvalue spread   The ratio of the largest over the smallest eigenvalue.

eigenvectors   Vectors **e** for a matrix **R** that yield $\mathbf{Re} = \lambda\mathbf{e}$, where λ are the eigenvalues.

epoch   One complete presentation of the input data to the network being trained.

ergodic   A condition of some stationary random processes in which the statistical moments obtained by statistical operators equal the moments obtained with time operators. A nonstationary random process *cannot* be ergodic.

fan-in   The number of inputs that feed a given PE.

fast Fourier transform (FFT)   A computational algorithm that computes the Fourier transform in $O(N \log(N))$ time, where N is the number of samples of the input signal. The discrete Fourier transform takes $O(N^2)$. Savings are enormous for large N.

feedback   A mechanism that is based on a recurrent connection from an output to an input.

feedforward   Having no recurrent connections.

fiducial point   The point where the function is being approximated.

filter   A linear system designed with a prespecified frequency response.

filter attenuation   The decrease in amplitude from the input to the output of a system at a given frequency, normally measured in negative decibels.

filtering   A selective removal of frequencies in the input signal to achieve a desired goal.

finite impulse response (FIR)   A type of linear system for which the impulse response is of finite extent. The response of FIR systems is constructed from linear combinations of past values of the input only.

first order search method   Gradient descent is called a first-order method because it uses only information about the performance surface tangent space. The Newton is a second-order method because it uses information about the curvature.

fixed-point learning   A training regime for dynamic systems where the input–desired response pair is specified for all time, which means using a dynamic system as a static system (i.e., as an MLP).

focused networks   Networks with memory PEs in the input layer whose gradients are time invariant.

Fourier series   Joseph Fourier, in the late 18th century, showed that any periodic signal, no matter how complex, could be decomposed into sums (possibly infinite) of simple sine waves of different frequencies. These decompositions are called the Fourier series. If $y(t)$ is real,

$$y(t) = Y_0 + \sum_{i=1}^{\infty} |Y_i| \cos\left(\frac{2\pi it}{T} + \theta_i\right)$$

frequency   The inverse of the period of a waveform. It is measured in cycles per second (Hertz or radians per second).

frequency domain approach   A set of methods that use frequency domain techniques to analyze and quantify linear systems. Examples are the idea of phasors, Fourier transforms, frequency response, and the system transfer function.

frequency resolution   The difference between two consecutive discrete frequencies. It is equal to the inverse of the window length times the sampling period.

frequency response   The Fourier transform of the impulse response, or the transfer function evaluated in the unit circle.

fully recurrent network   A network that has arbitrary feedback connections from input to hidden to output PEs.

functional analysis   The branch of analysis in which the functions do not depend on single numbers but on collections of components (eventually an entire range of a numerical function). An example is a function of a vector.

generalization   The ability to correctly classify samples that were not used to train the learning machine.

generalize   A machine generalizes when it produces the correct output for inputs that belong to the same class but were not used for training.

genetic algorithms   Global search procedures, proposed by John Holland, that search the performance surface, concentrating on the areas that provide better solutions. They use "generations" of search points computed from the previous search points using the operators of crossover and mutation (hence the name). See Goldberg, *Genetic Algorithms in Search, Optimization, and Machine Learning,* Addison-Wesley, Reading, MA, 1989.

geometric ratio   The ratio of two consecutive terms in a geometric progression.

global minimum   The minimum that achieves the smallest value of a function (normally MSE).

gradient   A vector that always points in the direction of maximum change, with a magnitude equal to the slope of the tangent to the curve at the point.

greedy   A greedy method is one that uses resources proportional to the size of the input.

Hessian   The matrix of the second derivative of the cost with respect to the weights.

highpass filter   A filter that attenuates the low frequencies and lets the higher frequencies pass without attenuation.

hyperplane   A planar surface in four or more dimensions. A hyperplane is still defined by any three points in four or more dimensions. To visualize a hyperplane in four dimensions, use the "flat land" approach, that is, try to visualize a plane when in a 2-D world.

ill conditioned matrix   A matrix whose determinant is almost zero. When the eigenvalue spread becomes very large, the matrix becomes more and more ill conditioned. See Appendix A.

ill posed problem   A problem is ill posed when small modifications of the input produce a large change in the outcome. Ill-posed problems very often arise when one tries to reverse a cause-effect relation.

impulse response   The response of a linear system to an impulse occurring at $n = 0$.

indicator function   A function that takes only two values, 1 and 0 (or -1).

infinite impulse response (IIR)   A linear system for which the impulse response is infinite and that has some type of internal feedback mechanism.

inverse Z transform   The inverse mapping from the z domain back to time, given by

$$x(n) = \frac{1}{2\pi j} \oint_C X(z) z^{n-1} dz$$

where C is a counterclockwise closed contour encircling the origin and belonging to the region of convergence of $X(z)$.

kernel   A function that implements the delay mechanism (also called operator).

learning curve   A plot of the MSE across iterations.

learning rate annealing   The progressive decrease of the learning rate across iterations.

learning rate scheduling   The choice of a variable step size, which starts large in the beginning of training and decreases progressively toward the end of adaptation.

least mean square (LMS)   A steepest-descent search algorithm that uses a very efficient estimate of the gradient (the product of the error and the input):

$$w(n + 1) = w(n) + \eta x(n)\varepsilon(n)$$

least squares   An analytic procedure that minimizes the MSE in linear optimization problems (i.e., problems that are linear in the unknowns).

likelihood   The probability density function of each event class.

linear combiner   A linear system that produces an output that is a weighted sum of past input samples.

linearly separable patterns   Patterns that can be perfectly classified by linear machines.

linear machine   A parametric classifier in which the discriminant functions are hyperplanes.

linear regression   The process of fitting (minimizing the sum of the square of the deviations) a cloud of samples by a linear model.

linear systems theory   A highly mathematical branch of electrical engineering that studies linear functions, their properties, and their implementations.

local error   The product of the error that reaches the PE times the derivative of the nonlinearity at the operating point. It is really the "effective error" that is used to correct the weights.

local maps   The definitions of the PE function and its dual network, which specify how the activations are modified when they go through the topology, and the errors when they flow across the dual topology.

long-term memory   Information contained in the network weights.

lowpass filter   A linear system that has unity gain for low frequencies (i.e., it lets low frequencies pass unattenuated up to a frequency called the cutoff frequency) and attenuates high frequencies.

manifold   A space in which the local geometry of each point looks like a little piece of Euclidean space.

mean square error (MSE)   The average of the square of the difference between the desired response and the actual system output (the error).

memory depth   The temporal extent of the system response after the application of an impulse at $n = 0$, that is, the number of time units at which the response of the system is nonzero.

memory filter   A linear structure used to store the past of the input.

memory resolution   The number of taps per sample.

memory structure   A multidimensional single-input, multiple-output device that takes an ordered sequence of points and produces a static pattern (i.e., a point in the multidimensional space).

memory trace   The signal at the output of a memory PE, which is a processed version of the past of the input.

misadjustment   The normalized excess MSE produced by rattling.

multilayer perceptrons   Feedforward neural networks with one or more hidden layers, that is, layers with nonlinear PEs that are not directly connected to the outside world.

nonconvex   A surface is nonconvex when it displays more than one minimum.

normalized LMS   The LMS algorithm with a step size normalized by an estimate of the input data variance.

on-line training   A learning procedure that modifies the weights after the presentation of every sample.

optimal classifier   The classifier that minimizes the classification error given the observations.

optimal discriminant function   The discriminant that produces the classification with the fewest errors.

ordered derivative   The partial sensitivity in an ordered network, which is made up of the explicit and implicit (through the network) dependencies.

ordered list   The list that summarizes the dependencies of the network topology. Each variable in the ordered list depends only on the variables to its left in the list. The weights appear first in the list.

outlier   A point that, because of observation noise, does not follow the characteristics of the input (or desired response) data.

pattern recognition   The creation of categories from input data using implicit or explicit data relationships. Similarities among some data exemplars are contrasted with dissimilarities across the data ensemble, and the concept of data class emerges. Due to the imprecise nature of the process, it is no surprise that statistics has played a major role in the basic principles of pattern recognition.

pattern space   The space of the input data. Each multivariate (N variables) data sample can be thought of as a point in a multidimensional (N-dimensional) space.

perceptron   A multiple-input, multiple-output pattern recognition machine made from one layer of McCulloch-Pitts PEs. The perceptron has adaptive weights.

performance surface   The total error surface plotted in the space of the system coefficients (weights).

plant   In control theory, the system to be modeled or controlled.

poles of $H(z)$ The values of z that make $H(z)$ infinite (i.e., the zeros of the denominator polynomial).

polynomial   A rational function that can be put in the form $y = \sum_{i=0}^{N} a_i x^i$, where both x and a are real numbers.

power spectrum   The Fourier transform of the autocorrelation function.

probability density function   Intuitively, the function that specifies the probability of a given event in an experiment. It is the limit of the histogram for an arbitrarily large number of trials. See the appendix for a more formal definition.

processing element (PE)   The fundamental computational block in the system. In neural networks PEs are also called neurons or units.

rattling   The perturbation around the optimal weight value produced by a nonzero learning rate.

recurrent system   A system in which the output depends on a previous value of the output. Hence it must have a recurrent loop where the output of an element feeds back into the system.

RLS   An on-line algorithm to compute the optimal weights (as opposed to the batch process to solve the least squares). Unfortunately, it is also much more computationally intensive than the LMS. See Haykin, S., *Adaptive Filter Theory,* Prentice Hall, Englewood Cliffs, NJ, 1996.

robust   A method is robust if it is not very sensitive to outliers. The term was coined in statistics and control theory to represent methods that have low sensitivity to perturbations.

saddle point   A point of zero curvature along at least one direction, but not all directions.

saliency   The importance of a weight for the overall input-output map.

sampling   An operation that creates a sequence of numbers from an analog signal in which each number is the value of the analog signal at the measurement

time. Sampling is physically done by an analog-to-digital (A/D) converter.

sampling theorem   We can uniquely reconstruct a time signal from its sampled representation if we sample at no less than twice the highest frequency present in the signal. (Also called the Nyquist theorem.)

scientific method   The methodology for discovery utilized in science. See Popper, K., *The Logic of Scientific Discovery,* Harper Torch, 1968.

second-order statistics   Measured by the covariance function. We saw that a Gaussian is fully described by the mean and variance for one dimension data and by the mean vector and the covariance matrix for multiple dimensions.

sensitivity   The partial derivative of a function with respect to one of its independent variables. It measures how much a small change in one of the independent variables affects the functional value.

series   An iterated sum of terms produced by a general rule with an eventually infinite number of terms. An example is

$$1 + \frac{1}{10} + \frac{1}{100} + \frac{1}{1000} + \cdots$$

shallow network   A network with few layers, that is, typically one or two hidden layers.

shift-invariant system   A system that produces the same output whether the signal appears at $t = t_0$ or any other time.

short-term memory   Past information available as variables (signals) within the topology.

sigmoid   Any smooth nonlinear function that is monotonically increasing and has an S shape.

signal subspace   A space of lower dimensionality in the reconstruction space that contains the signal vectors.

signal-to-noise ratio (SNR)   The ratio of the signal power to the noise power.

simulated annealing   A global search criterion by which the space is searched with a random rule. In the beginning the variance of the random jumps is very large. Every so often the variance is decreased, and a more local search is undertaken. It has been shown that if the decrease of the variance is set appropriately, the global optimum can be found with probability 1. The method is called simulated annealing because it is similar to the annealing process of creating crystals from a hot liquid. See van Laarhoven and Aarts, *Simulated Annealing: Theory and Applications,* Kluwer, Dordrecht, 1988.

sinc *(t)*   A time signal given by $\sin(at)/at$. It is the noncausal response of the ideal reconstruction filter.

singular value decomposition (SVD)   An analytical procedure that computes the orthogonal decomposition of data. See Golub and Van Loan, *Matrix Computations,* Johns Hopkins University Press, Baltimore, 1989.

spectral analysis   The analysis of the properties of signals using frequency domain information.

spectrum (or Fourier spectrum)   The ordered set of coefficients of the decomposition of the signal in phasors.

spline   The kth normalized B spline of degree $r - 1$ is given by the Cox-deBoor formula:

$$B_{k,r}(t) = \frac{t - t_k}{t_{k+r-1} - t_k} B_{k,r-1}(t) + \frac{t_{k+r} - t}{t_{k+r} - t_{k+1}} B_{k+1,r-1}(t)$$

with

$$B(t) = \begin{cases} 1 & t_k \leq t \leq t_{k+1} \\ 0 & \text{otherwise} \end{cases}$$

square-integrable function   Any function for which the integral of the square of the function over the domain is finite (here the real numbers).

standard deviation   The square root of the variance. The variance is the second moment of the data with respect to the mean.

state variable   An internal quantity in the system that changes during operation. It may be either the output of the PE or the weight. We use it to represent the output of the PE.

static mapper   A system whose output is dependent upon a single time instant (instantaneous response).

stationary signal   A signal whose statistical properties do not change over time.

statistical independence   Statistical independence between two variables x_1 and x_2 occurs when the joint pdf ($f(x_1, x_2)$) is equal to the dot product of the marginal pdfs ($f(x_1) \cdot f(x_2)$).

statistical learning theory   A new branch of statistics that analyzes the learning process mathematically (in functional spaces).

steepest descent   A search procedure that seeks the next operating point in the direction opposite to the gradient.

step size or learning rate   The constant that scales the gradient to correct the old weights.

supervised learning   Learning or adaptation in which a desired response can be used by the system to guide the learning.

support   The length of the impulse response, or the number of samples of the input that the output of the delay line "remembers." Memory depth quantifies this concept mathematically for recurrent memories.

support vectors   The samples that are close to the optimal hyperplane.

tessellation   A division of a space into convex regions that totally fill the space.

test set   The ensemble of input–desired response data used to verify the performance of a trained system. This data is *not* used for training.

time constant of adaptation   The exponent of the exponentially fitted envelope of the weight's geometric progression.

time-delay neural network (TDNN)   A dynamic neural network in which the memory structure is a tap delay line, the same memory used in the linear combiner of Chapter 9.

time domain approach   A set of analysis methods that use time domain information to analyze and quantify the response of linear systems. Examples are the impulse response and convolution.

time-lagged feedforward network (TLFN)   A network that has short-term memory structures anywhere in the network (i.e., either input, hidden, or output PEs) but still has a general feedforward topology. A TLFN has intermediate complexity, between a fully recurrent network and a static network, and is built from feedforward combinations of nonlinear PEs and linear filters.

topological mapping   A mapping that preserves a metric. In Chapter 7 this term means that local distances (neighborhoods) are preserved.

topology   The way the PEs are connected together in a neural network.

training set   The ensemble of input–desired response pairs used to train the system.

training the classifier   The task of defining the parameters of the discriminant function from the input data (the training set).

trajectory   The locus of points created by the time series in the reconstruction space.

trajectory learning   The most general case of training a dynamic system, which specifies the desired response during a time segment.

transfer function   The ratio of the transforms of the output and the input signals when the initial conditions are zero.

uncorrelated variables   Variables whose correlation is zero. Practically, this means that changing one variable has no effect on the value of the other.

unfolding   A method to create from a recurrent network an equivalent feedforward network. This is possible only for a finite time span.

unsupervised learning   Learning in which the system parameters are adapted using only the information of the input and are constrained by prespecified internal rules.

validation set   The ensemble of samples that will be used to validate the parameters used in the training (not to be confused with the test set, which assesses the performance of the classifier).

V-C dimension   Vapnik-Chervonenkis dimension, a measure of the capacity of a learning machine. See

Vapnik, V., *The Nature of Statistical Learning Theory*, Springer, New York, 1995.

Volterra expansions   Volterra expansions of a discrete system (y the output, u the input) have the form

$$y(n) = \alpha + \sum_{i=0}^{\infty} \beta_i u(n - i)$$

$$+ \sum_{i=0}^{\infty} \sum_{j=0}^{\infty} \gamma_{ij} u(n - i) u(n - j) + \cdots$$

weight track   A weight-space plot of the weight locations during adaptation.

white noise   A stochastic signal that contains all frequencies in equal amounts.

zeros of $H(z)$ The values of z that make $H(z) = 0$.

z notation   The delay operator in the complex domain. The Z domain is the transform domain notation for discrete signals. z is effectively an independent (complex) variable given by $z = e^{sT}$, where $s = \sigma + jw$, T is the sampling period, and j is the square root of -1.

Z scores   Variables that have been normalized to zero mean and unit standard deviation.

Z transform of $x(n)$ A complex function $X(z)$ given by

$$X(z) = \sum_{n=-\infty}^{n=\infty} x(n) z^{-n}$$

INDEX

NeuroSolutions™
The Neural Network Simulation Environment

- Intuitive icon-based graphical user interface
- Wide variety of pre-designed network architectures
- Allows the creation of custom network architectures
- Supports advanced learning paradigms such as back-propagation through time and recurrent backprop
- C++ code generation for both recall and learning
- Customized components through user-defined DLLs
- Extensive probing/visualization capabilities
- Recordable macro and OLE automation support

Why Upgrade?

- Utilize the full capabilities of NeuroSolutions
  - Use your own data (the Interactive Book Edition only allows you to use data included with the book)
  - Use the advanced features of NeuroSolutions such as code generation and customizable components
  - Use NeuroSolutions add-on programs such as Neuro-Solutions for Excel and the Custom Solution Wizard
- Access the new features available only in NeuroSolutions version 4.0
  - Genetic optimization of parameters and inputs
  - Fuzzy logic components
  - New improved user interface and probes
  - New wizards for simplifying common tasks
- Take advantage of educational and multi-seat discounts
- Outfit a research or teaching laboratory with Neuro-Solutions by purchasing a University Site License

Typical Applications of NeuroSolutions:

- Quality Control
- Financial Forecasting
- Economic Forecasting
- Fraud Detection
- Speech Recognition
- Targeted Marketing
- Bankruptcy Prediction
- Cancer Diagnosis
- Character Recognition
- Target Recognition
- Sales Forecasting
- Cost Reduction
- Process Modeling
- Process Control
- Machine Diagnostics

NeuroDimension, Inc.
1800 N. Main St., Suite D4 • Gainesville, FL 32609

1-800-ND-IDEAS (1-800-634-3327)
Outside U.S.: 352-377-5144
Fax: 352-377-9009
Email: info@nd.com
URL: http://www.nd.com

Online Resources for this Book

NeuroDimension has created a web site specifically for *Neural and Adaptive Systems: Fundamentals through Simulation* that provides invaluable material available free of charge, including:

- Additional data files in *interactive book* format for projects or experimentation
- Sample projects with solutions built in NeuroSolutions
- Users' *forum* and *data exchange*, allowing engineers, instructors, students, and researchers to exchange information, techniques, and data files
- Published and unpublished discussions of teaching with this new material

Please visit *www.nd.com/interactive_book*

Other NeuroDimension Products

 NeuroSolutions for Excel is a Microsoft Excel add-in that allows you to use NeuroSolutions directly from Microsoft Excel. It provides visual data selection, one-step training and testing, automated report generation, and much more.

 The Custom Solution Wizard is a tool that can generate a Dynamic Link Library (DLL) from a NeuroSolutions' network, allowing you to easily incorporate the neural model into your own applications. An ActiveX component allows you to easily use the neural network DLL from Visual Basic.

 TradingSolutions is a full-featured financial product that incorporates the power of neural networks to help you to track and predict financial market data. Features include: neural and data preprocessing wizards, built-in charts and spreadsheets, prediction analysis, and trading signal profitability analysis.

 Genetic Server and Genetic Library are tools that allow programmers to embed genetic algorithms into their own applications. Genetic Server is an ActiveX component designed to be used within Visual Basic (or VBA) and Genetic Library is a C++ library designed to be used within Visual C++.

 **NeuroDimension, Inc.**
1800 N. Main St., Suite D4 • Gainesville, FL 32609

1-800-ND-IDEAS (1-800-634-3327)
Outside U.S.: 352-377-5144
Fax: 352-377-9009
Email: info@nd.com
URL: http://www.nd.com